ERRATA

P. 26, fig. 13: nos. 2, 3 and 5 belong on the opposite side of the street

P. 27, l. 25: for ''Valdadon'' read ''Valadon''

P. 31, 2nd l. from bottom: following ''1886'' insert ''and began''

P. 38, last l.: for ''1887-88'' read ''1886-87 (?)''

P. 46, fig. 30: for ''c. 1888'' read ''c. 1889''

P. 47, l. 9: following *La* insert *Revue*

Pp. 48-49: This and subsequent discussions of the interrelating art theories of Vincent and Gauguin were written without knowledge of the important articles by Evert van Uitert, ''Vincent van Gogh and Paul Gauguin: a creative competition,'' *Simiolus*, IX: 3 (1977), pp. 149-68, and ''Vincent van Gogh in Anticipation of Paul Gauguin,'' *Simiolus*, X: 3-4 (1978-79), pp. 182-99.

P. 51, 4th l. from bottom: for ''Laval'' read ''Filiger (later)''

P. 52, l. 9: for ''1891'' read ''1889''

P. 121, n. 2, l. 2: for ''see note'' read ''F 1480''

P. 134, n. 3, l. 1: for ''repeated'' read ''reputed''

P. 168, SOURCES, l. 9: for ''of'' read ''for''

P. 177, 3rd col., l. 1: following ''earlier'' insert ''(W 272; misdated there to 1888)''

P. 180, ls. 7-8: enclose within parentheses ''*Japanese Prints*, cat. no. 532''

P. 180, l. 18: for ''precipice[1]'' read ''precipice''
        l. 27: for ''*Precipice*.'' read *Precipice*[1].''

P. 184, 2nd col., l. 17: delete ''which''

P. 228, 2nd. col., l. 33: following ''twenty-four'' insert ''year''

P. 240, n. 15: delete here and add to p. 237, n. 3

P. 254, n. 2F, l. 6: for ''fig. 96'' read ''fig. 17''

P. 265, SEPTEMBER, last. l.: add ''(He may have begun them in August.)''

P. 266, 2nd. col., AUGUST, l. 4: for ''reproduces'' read ''reproduce''

P. 328, n. 3: add ''See p. 101, n. 5, above.''

P. 341, 1st col., l. 18: for ''dance.[3]'' read ''dance.''

P. 376, 1891, l. 18: following ''winter'' insert ''1890-91''

Colour Plates

pl. 1   for correct dimension see cat. 60

pl. 2   for correct dimension see cat. 76

pl. 8   for correct title see cat. 106

pl. 16   for correct title see cat. 126

pl. 17   for correct title see cat. 63

pl. 22   for correct dimension see cat. 61

pl. 24   for correct title see cat. 55

pl. 25   for correct dimension see cat. 93

pl. 26   for correct title see cat. 96

pl. 28   for correct title see cat. 119

pl. 29   for correct dimension see cat. 121

pl. 30   for correct dimension see cat. 86

pl. 32   for correct title see cat. 135

Vincent van Gogh
and the Birth of
Cloisonism

Vincent van Gogh and the Birth of Cloisonism

Bogomila Welsh-Ovcharov

ART GALLERY OF ONTARIO, TORONTO / 24 JANUARY - 22 MARCH 1981

RIJKSMUSEUM VINCENT VAN GOGH, AMSTERDAM / 9 APRIL - 14 JUNE 1981

ART GALLERY OF ONTARIO / MUSÉE DES BEAUX-ARTS DE L'ONTARIO

TORONTO / CANADA

ISBN 0-919876-66-8

Canadian Cataloguing in Publication Data

Welsh-Ovcharov, Bogomila,
    Vincent van Gogh and the birth of cloisonism
Catalogue of an exhibition held at the Art
Gallery of Ontario, Toronto, 24 Jan.-22 Mar.,
1981, and Rijksmuseum Vincent van Gogh, Amsterdam,
9 Apr.-14 June, 1981.

ISBN 0-919876-66-8

1. Gogh, Vincent van, 1853-1890 -
   Exhibitions.
2. Post-impressionism (Art) - Exhibitions.
3. Painting, Modern - 19th century -
   Exhibitions.
I. Art Gallery of Ontario.   II. Rijksmuseum
   Vincent van Gogh.   III. Title.

ND653.G7A4 1981   759.492'074
C81-094264-X

THE COVER:

Vincent van Gogh (Dutch, 1853-1890)
*Still Life: Vase with Irises against
a Yellow Background*, 1890
oil on canvas: 50 x 52 cm
Loaned by the Rijksmuseum Vincent van Gogh
See catalogue no. 40

FRONTISPIECE:

Fernand Cormon's atelier, Paris (*circa* 1883-85).
Louis Anquetin on far left, in profile;
near him Toulouse-Lautrec in bowler hat;
Cormon seated facing the easel;
Emile Bernard, back row, far right.

PRINTED AND BOUND IN CANADA

Lenders to the Exhibition

Aargauer Kunsthaus, *Aarau, Switzerland*

Albright-Knox Gallery, *Buffalo*

Art Institute of Chicago

Boston Museum of Fine Arts, *Boston*

Boymans van Beuningen Museum, *Rotterdam*

Chrysler Museum at Norfolk

Cleveland Museum of Art

Galleria Civica d'Arte Moderna, *Milan*

Indianapolis Museum of Art

Hamburger Kunsthalle

Kunsthalle, *Bremen*

Kunstmuseum Basel, *Basel*

The McNay Art Institute, *San Antonio*

Metropolitan Museum of Art, *New York*

Musée des Arts Décoratifs, *Paris*

Musée des Beaux Arts, Nantes, *France*

Musée des Beaux Arts, Quimper, *France*

Musée d'Orsay, *Paris*

Musée National du Louvre, *Paris*

Musée Petit Palais, *Geneva*

Musée Rodin, *Paris*

Musées Royaux des Beaux-Arts de Belgique, *Brussels*

Musée Toulouse-Lautrec, Albi, *France*

Museum of Fine Arts, *Houston*

Museum of Modern Art, *New York*

Norton Gallery and School of Art, *West Palm Beach*

Ordrupgaardsamlingen, *Copenhagen*

Philadelphia Museum of Art

Rijksmuseum Kröller-Müller, *Otterlo, The Netherlands*

Rijksmuseum Vincent van Gogh, *Amsterdam*

Stedelijk Museum, *Amsterdam*

Sterling and Francine Clark Art Institute, *Williamstown*

Trustees of the Tate Gallery, *London*

Wadsworth Atheneum, *Hartford*

Durand-Ruel & Cie, *Paris*

Clément Altarriba, *Paris*

Mr. & Mrs. Arthur G. Altschul, *New York*

The family of Maurice Denis, *Alençon*

Lenoir M. Josey, Inc., *Houston*

LeGlouannec, *Paris*

Mrs. Catherine B. Taylor, Mrs. Camilla B. Royall and Mrs. B. Hrdy, *Houston*

Prof. and Madame Léon Velluz, *Paris*

C.L.E.H. van der Waals-Königs

and anonymous and private collection lenders

The Art Gallery of Ontario

gratefully acknowledges the support of

Ontario Ministry of Culture and Recreation

The Weston Group

and Several Members of the Gallery

Contents

5   LENDERS TO THE EXHIBITION

9   PREFACE
Simon H. Levie, William J. Withrow

12   ACKNOWLEDGEMENTS
Bogomila Welsh-Ovcharov

17   INTRODUCTION:
From Cloisonism to Symbolism
19   The Birth of Cloisonism
41   The Cloisonist-Synthetist Phase
51   Cloisonism and Symbolism

62   BIBLIOGRAPHIC REFERENCES

65   COLOUR PLATES

89   Vincent van Gogh (Dutch, 1853-1890)
96   WORKS

167   Paul Gauguin (French, 1848-1903)
172   WORKS

227   Louis Anquetin (French, 1861-1932)
232   WORKS

259   Emile Bernard (French, 1868-1941)
268   WORKS

317   Henri de Toulouse-Lautrec (French, 1864-1901)
323   WORKS

345   Jakob Meyer de Haan (Dutch, 1852-1895)
350   WORKS

359   Charles Laval (French, 1862-1894)
361   WORKS

369   Paul Sérusier (French, 1864-1927)
371   WORKS

375   Maurice Denis (French, 1870-1943)
377   WORKS

381   INDEX

384   THE OPERATIONS COMMITTEE

384   COLOPHON

Vincent van Gogh and the Birth of Cloisonism

Vincent van Gogh and the Birth of Cloisonism explores the relationship of a great Dutch artist to a tendency within French painting during the late 1880s which emphasized, at the expense of traditional perspective and modelling in the round, a structure of strong contour lines filled in by flattened areas of bright colour. The term "cloisonism," derived from a popular form of medieval enamel work, was first applied to the art of Louis Anquetin, who had developed his personal style in close association with such colleagues as Henri de Toulouse-Lautrec, Vincent van Gogh and especially Emile Bernard, who apparently inspired the adoption of Cloisonism by Paul Gauguin. The exhibition also investigates the importance of Neo-Impressionism to the development of Cloisonism and its repercussions within the Nabi and Art Nouveau movements.

The exhibition includes approximately forty-five works by van Gogh, half that number by each of Bernard and Gauguin and proportionately lesser representations of Anquetin and Toulouse-Lautrec. Due to their status on the periphery of the Cloisonist development, such artists as Charles Laval, Jakob Meyer de Haan, Paul Sérusier and Maurice Denis are represented by only a few examples each. Whereas the majority of items selected are paintings, an accompanying body of watercolours, drawings and graphics has been included to the extent that these media were relevant to individual artists. Inevitably some of the examples most significant to the exhibition context were unavailable for loan or else were available to one of the participating museums only. Every possible effort was made to secure appropriate substitutes for these full or half omissions, although several were of such unique importance that illustration and discussion in the catalogue must suffice. In compensation, a number of little-known or never before exhibited works of art, especially from within the *oeuvres* of Anquetin and Bernard, are here presented in public and catalogued for the first time. In addition many intended companion pieces have been re-united for the first time in recent decades.

The exhibition was proposed early in 1976 by Dr. Richard Wattenmaker, at that time Chief Curator of the Art Gallery of Ontario, as a result of his interest in the research being undertaken by Dr. Bogomila Welsh. Dr. Welsh, a Canadian art historian, studied at the University of Toronto, where she earned a PhilM degree with a thesis embodying her initial investigations of the career of Vincent van Gogh and his relationships to Bernard and Anquetin. Her PhD was subsequently earned under Professor J.G. van Gelder at Utrecht University with a dissertation on *Vincent van Gogh: His Paris Period, 1886-88*.

From the beginning it was recognized that in order to realize the exhibition, full co-operation between the Rijksmuseum Vincent van Gogh and the Art Gallery of Ontario was essential. The collaboration of our two institutions demonstrates once again the close ties which exist between Canada and the Netherlands, and between our two cities, Amsterdam and Toronto. The Rijksmuseum Vincent van Gogh under the Directorship of Dr. Johannes van der Wolk has made an extraordinary and essential loan of major Vincent van Gogh paintings and drawings and works by other artists which form the core of the show. To the Vincent van Gogh Foundation as well as to the Ministry of Cultural Affairs, Recreation and Social Welfare, we are most grateful for having given their consent to lend such a great number of works of art, many of which are key works from the collection of the Rijksmuseum Vincent van Gogh.

The Museum has played a vital role in negotiating several key loans and in its Curator Dr. Han van Crimpen's coordination of their movements. In addition to making a financial contribution toward the costs of the exhibition, the Rijksmuseum Vincent van Gogh has framed its loans especially for this show, a project with important scholarly and aesthetic implications.

The Art Gallery of Ontario, for its part, acted as principal organizer under the leadership of its Chief Curator, Dr. Roald Nasgaard. The Curatorial Department of the Gallery has been responsible for the administration of all the loans, the production of the catalogue and the installation of the exhibition in Toronto. The Gallery's Registrar, Mrs. Eva Robinson, facing the almost impossible task of tying down escalating insurance and shipping costs, has through her diligence and creativity made all the arrangements in these two vital areas. Mr. Barry Simpson, Exhibition Coordinator, has supervised the mechanics of the installation and has contributed to all aspects of planning. Dr. Bogomila Welsh, as Guest Curator, went far beyond the usual responsibilities of such an appointment which include the selection of the works to be shown and the writing of the catalogue. Dr. Welsh orchestrated the negotiations for many of the loans, many of which involved face-to-face meetings with the lenders in various parts of the world.

The non-Curatorial aspects of the show were coordinated by Mr. Alex MacDonald, Manager of Public Affairs, Chairman of an Operations Committee representing Trustees and Volunteers as well as the various supporting departments of the Gallery such as Administration, Communications, Coordination, Development, Education, Finance, Membership, Plant and Publications, all of which made important contributions. Miss Elizabeth Murray, non-Curatorial Coordinator who competently handled a multiplicity of detailed arrangements, deserves special mention.

While planning for the exhibition began some four years ago, it was only during the six or seven months prior to the Toronto opening that the impact of extraordinary prices for major works on the world art market was felt. Costs that had not been budgeted presented exceptional financial problems that could not possibly have been foreseen. We are therefore most grateful for the timely support of the Government of Ontario through the

Ministry of Culture and Recreation. In addition we are deeply indebted to The Weston Group and to several Members of the Gallery, who wish to remain anonymous, for their generous sponsorship.

No loan exhibition can be successfully realized without the good faith and generosity of the lenders. We therefore offer our heartfelt thanks to the more than forty lenders, both private and institutional, from eight countries, who have graciously entrusted their treasures to us. We hope the exhibition, along with Dr. Welsh's catalogue, will justify their faith in our two institutions.

Simon H. Levie
GENERAL DIRECTOR
RIJKSMUSEUM VINCENT VAN GOGH

William J. Withrow
DIRECTOR
ART GALLERY OF ONTARIO

Acknowledgements

When in 1976 Dr. Richard Wattenmaker suggested that I undertake an exhibition in an area of van Gogh's *oeuvre* which I had been researching during the past ten years, I hesitated because of the vast and complex problems which inevitably surface when assembling well-known works within this area of nineteenth century painting. I owe him my gratitude for allowing me to realize, in exhibition form, this little-known yet important preface to modern art.

An exhibition always depends on the generosity and cooperative efforts of a great number of individuals.

In particular I should like to first express my gratitude to both participating museums, the Art Gallery of Ontario and the Rijksmuseum Vincent van Gogh, for supplying all possible physical and moral guidance. I am especially indebted to the generosity of the Van Gogh Foundation and the General Director of the Rijksmuseum Vincent van Gogh, Dr. Simon H. Levie, who have consented to the loan of thirty-seven major works from the museum's collection, without which the representation of van Gogh's *oeuvre* would have been virtually an impossibility. William Withrow, Director of the Art Gallery of Ontario, should be credited for his continual faith when moments of great financial bleakness threatened cancellation of the exhibition; he continued to "hold the fort" and managed to make this project a reality.

My sincere appreciation to Dr. Johannes van der Wolk, Director of the Rijksmuseum Vincent van Gogh, for many organizational details in respect to his museum's collection.

Drs. Roald Nasgaard, Chief Curator of the Art Gallery of Ontario and Han van Crimpen, Chief Curator of the Rijksmuseum Vincent van Gogh, were instrumental in the negotiation of several important transatlantic loans, and I thank them both for their continual supportive cooperation and good faith.

Special thanks to the many curators from lending institutions, especially Susan Wise, Alexandra Murphy, John Walsh Jr., Charlotta Kotik, and Joop Joosten who met my requests with such enthusiasm and professionalism.

The generosity of the many lenders to this exhibition has made this exhibition a reality. To Rudi Oxenaar, Director of the Rijksmuseum Kröller-Müller I wish to express my special gratitude for allowing six major van Gogh paintings to be reunited with other works by the Dutch artist. The following museums also deserve special mention for consenting to loan more than one work of art: the Musée d'Orsay, Paris, the Musée Toulouse-Lautrec, Albi and the Wadsworth Atheneum, Hartford. Gunther Busch, Director of the Bremen Kunsthalle, James Wood, Director of the Art Institute of Chicago and Robert Buck, Director of the Albright-Knox Gallery and Dr. Sherman Lee, Director of the Cleveland Museum of Art have generously lent several major works from their museums' notable collections. I wish to thank especially the many private lenders who believed in the thesis of the show and who made their paintings available for public showing especially Mr. and Mrs. Clément Altarriba, Mr. and Mrs. Arthur Altschul, the family of Maurice Denis and Professor and Mrs. Léon Velluz.

I wish to thank the following people for their tireless efforts in their respective duties: Eva Robinson, Registrar, Barry Simpson, Exhibition Coordinator, Eduard Zukowski, Conservator, and Olive Koyama, Head of Publications for her patient editing and direction of the production of the catalogue. Denise Bukowski deserves credit for coordinating all aspects of publication. Alex MacDonald, Manager of Public Affairs, deserves credit for the energetic orchestration of what at times seemed insurmountable publication problems. Special thanks to Irene Buck for her meticulous and rapid typing of several manuscripts. I am particularly indebted to Frank Newfeld for the catalogue design and production.

To my husband, Professor Robert P. Welsh, my deepest gratitude for his helpful advice, editorial assistance and moral support throughout the three years of exhibition planning.

As this publication went to press I sadly learned of the death of my PhD dissertation advisor and distinguished van Gogh scholar, Professor J.G. van Gelder, whose personal support of my own research over the years must be considered an essential prerequisite for the final realization of the present exhibition.

My final note of gratitude is extended to my mother, Slavka Ovcharov, for three years of endurance beyond the call of maternal duty and to my son, Christopher Edward, for sharing his mother with *Vincent van Gogh and the Birth of Cloisonism*.

B.W.-O.

to the memory of

Ir. Dr. Vincent Willem van Gogh

1890-1978

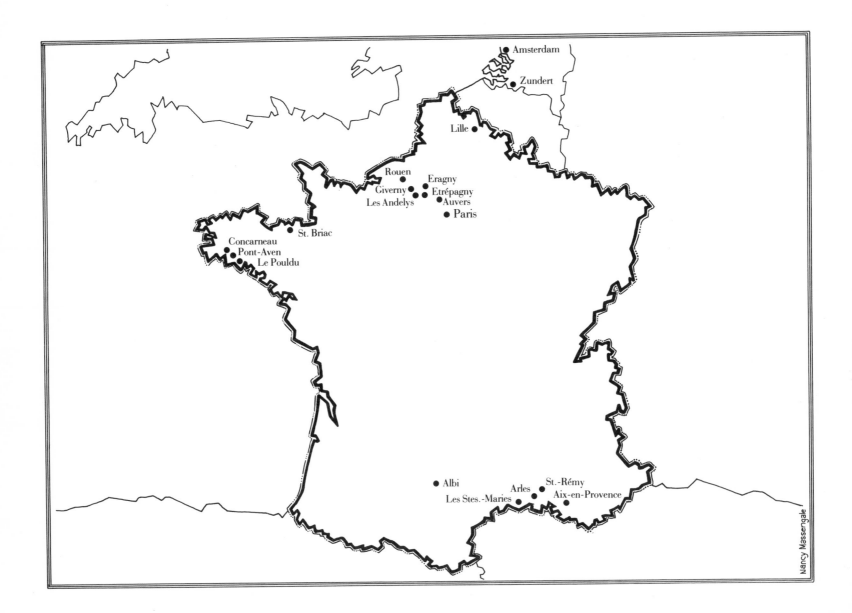

Amsterdam

Zundert

Lille

Rouen
Eragny
Giverny
Etrépagny
Les Andelys
Auvers
Paris

St. Briac

Concarneau
Pont-Aven
Le Pouldu

Albi
St.-Rémy
Arles
Les Stes.-Maries
Aix-en-Provence

Nancy Massengale

From Cloisonism to Symbolism

For France the decade of the 1880s was a period of territorial expansion: Tahiti (1880), Tunis (1881), Tonkin—now northern Viet-Nam (1884) and during the following three years several islands in Oceania. As with French foreign policy so too in French art. By mid-decade a certain movement away from Paris, the traditional artistic centre, was observable within the ranks of the French Impressionists. In 1886, for example, Claude Monet went as far afield as Belle Ile off the coast of Brittany in order to paint its ruggedly hostile shoreline, and Paul Cézanne was in his native Provence. Two years within the Parisian artistic milieu so fatigued the expatriate Dutchman Vincent van Gogh that he too sought solace in southern France at Arles, not far from Cézanne's residence at Aix. Paul Gauguin was the most extreme advocate of escape from debilitating civilization, choosing first the far reaches of the Brittany peninsula, then Martinique in the French Antilles and eventually, after seriously considering both Tonkin and Madagascar, Tahiti as exotic environments where the survival of primitive culture was expected to provide nourishment for his art. Brittany in particular became a foster home to a whole group of *avant-garde* artists in the circle of Gauguin, and both the so-called Pont-Aven and Nabi schools of painting were in origin deeply linked to this special region with its fabled Celtic past.

This diversity in centres of artistic activity was matched by a comparable diversity in the personal and group styles spawned in the mid-1880s as the Post-Impressionist period commenced. Georges Seurat and his Neo-Impressionist followers, popularly know as Pointillists because of the stipple technique which was their stylistic hallmark, surely wished the prefix ''neo'' to imply both continuity with and departure from the older Impressionists. Accordingly, they generally remained loyal to the working areas of Paris, the Seine River and the Norman coast which had been favoured by their Impressionist predecessors. As a first-generation Impressionist himself, Cézanne probably would have questioned the addition of the prefix ''post'' for his own work, had the label existed in his own lifetime, although few writers since have questioned its applicability to his production from the late 1880s and thereafter. Neither is its use questioned for the mature styles of van Gogh, Gauguin and Henri de Toulouse-Lautrec despite the appreciable idiosyncrasy of each. Individual peculiarities of style are to be found even within the Pont-Aven and Nabi groups, and one need only mention the names of Odilon Redon, Gustave Moreau and Eugène Carrière in order to suggest the wide range of personal styles which went to make up what increasingly is being called the Symbolist movement in French painting and sculpture.[1]

Because the question of defining French Symbolist painting within the broader context of European Post-Impressionism so necessarily depends upon a sound understanding of how the term originated and was defined, this question will be addressed in the present catalogue introduction. In contrast, the discussions accompanying specific works of art are intended, in their cumulative effect, to trace the development during the late 1880s of both individual artists and the group as an interacting whole.

The focus of the present study and the exhibition it serves is the role played by Vincent van Gogh within French *avant-garde* painting during the late 1880s. In particular the development of an art style which leading Parisian critics successively termed "Cloisonism," then "Synthetism" and finally "Symbolism" will be examined according to the relative contributions of the most early participants. Apart from Vincent himself the principal artists who participated in this development were Louis Anquetin, Emile Bernard, Paul Gauguin and Henri de Toulouse-Lautrec, while Charles Laval, Jakob Meyer de Haan, Paul Sérusier and Maurice Denis produced minor but significant individual variations of the Cloisonist-Synthetist style.

Vincent's contacts with French Impressionism, Neo-Impressionism and the so-called Pont-Aven painters Emile Bernard and Paul Gauguin have long been known. Yet a feeling persists that the instinctual expressionistic character of Van Gogh's art was so great that such contacts functioned merely as stepping stones (some would say stumbling blocks) to a mature and unique personal style. Not only are his own Impressionist, Pointillist and Gauguin-related paintings typically held to be weaker versions of styles created by others, but the possibility that he exerted any immediate influence within contemporary French painting has, until recently, been largely ignored. Hence the ill-fated sojourn made by Gauguin with Vincent in Arles during autumn 1888 has usually been viewed as involving a virtual master-pupil relationship, not least of all due to Gauguin's insistence and Vincent's seeming acquiescence on the point.[2] This presumption depends in turn upon the widely held belief that the Pont-Aven style, as exemplified in Bernard's *Breton Women in the Meadow* (cat. no. 104; pl. 9) and Gauguin's *Vision after the Sermon* (pl. 7), constituted a spontaneous collaborative innovation created in the Brittany hinterland during summer 1888, which proliferated in the tightly cohesive development of a Pont-Aven and Nabi stylistic movement. This simplistic, unitarian interpretation of events in France during the late 1880s can and should be challenged, if a fuller and better balanced understanding of the relevant artistic interrelationships is to be gained.

The following essay is organized according to a chronological sequence in which biographical events, phases of artistic development and critical reaction often remarkably coincide. Its three sections reflect both the changing personal alignments among the artists selected for exhibition and the successive stages in the development of Cloisonist style: first, The Birth of Cloisonism, 1886-87, when Vincent was in Paris and helped to bring

Fig. 1
Enamelled roundel from the religious chest of Abbot Boniface, 1108/18,
(Conques Abbey Treasure: illustrated in *Gazette des beaux arts* 1878: Exhibition of Medieval and Renaissance Treasures at the Trocadéro, Paris, 1878).

Fig. 3
Madonna and Child
twelfth century central
stained-glass window, west façade,
Chartres Cathedral.

Fig. 2
Attributed to the Master of the Grandmont Altar,
Processional Cross,
champlevé enamel and gilt copper,
French,
c. 1190,
(The Cleveland Museum).

together a group he called "Impressionists of the Petit Boulevard;" second, Cloisonism and Synthetism, 1888-early 1889, during which period Gauguin worked together with Bernard in Pont-Aven and then with Vincent in Arles; third, Cloisonism and Symbolism, summer 1889-early 1891, which includes Vincent's final year of activity and the public emergence of Gauguin as the leader of the Symbolist movement in painting. All three periods culminated in one or more important exhibitions and the first and third in major critical accounts of the precepts on art which were manifest herein. While certainly representing only one schema for an analysis of these artists within their period, it has the virtue of concentrating upon the concrete activities in which they were involved.

The Birth of Cloisonism: 1886-87

The name Vincent van Gogh is surely one of the best known in the history of art, but the same hardly can be said of "Cloisonism." The term is less well-known in this substantive form than in the French participle "cloisonné." Its usual reference is to the various forms of enamel work popular within religious art of the Byzantine tradition and such Western offshoots as the work produced in the late Middle Ages in Limoges, France. As explained by Philip Burty in his 1868 text, *Les Emaux cloisonnées anciens et modernes*, the history of the art form leads back to ancient times in the West and Near East.[3] "Cloison" literally means "partition" and in this strict definition refers to the thin metal strips or wires attached to a flat metal surface to form self-contained compartments, which are then filled with powdered glass mixed with metallic oxide colour agents and baked. After polishing, the surface appears as decorative outlines containing planes of evenly distributed colour (*see fig. 1*).[4] The expressive result of this and its sister technique of *champlevé* enamel work is analogous to the art of stained-glass windows (*figs. 2 and 3*) and related forms of late Medieval painting.

During the Renaissance and subsequent periods the popularity of this art medium had dwindled in Western Europe until it survived chiefly in liturgical instruments imitative of traditional forms. But in the mid-nineteenth century the art enjoyed a considerable revival, first in jewellery and goldsmith work and then in the fields of ceramics and decorative prints. Indeed, in both East and West brightly coloured enamel work was similarly employed for the decoration of so-called *cloisonné* vases. As Burty and other writers began to claim, the *cloisonné* aesthetic was also to be found by analogy in the art of popular

1   For a recent excellent general introduction to this issue, see R. Goldwater, *Symbolism* (New York: Harper and Row, 1979).

2   Gauguin's claim of having "enlightened" Vincent by freeing him from Neo-Impressionism was made in *Avant et Après*, a text dated 1903 (Eng. trans. by Van Wyck Brooks, *Paul Gauguin's Intimate Journals*, Bloomington: Indiana University Press, 1958, pp. 32-33). Vincent's acknowledgment of Gauguin as teacher is found in several letters (e.g. *CL*544a to Gauguin and *CL*626a to A. Aurier).

3   P. Burty, *Les Emaux cloisonnés anciens et modernes* (Paris: Martz, Joaillier, 1868).

4   This round plaque was exhibited 1878 in the Trocadéro Museum and reproduced in A. Darcel, "Le Moyen Age et la Renaissance au Trocadéro," *GBA*, 1878, p. 565.

Fig. 4   *Fig. 5*   *Fig. 6*

woodcut forms such as the inexpensive albums of Japanese prints then awakening interest in Parisian artistic circles (*figs. 4 and 5*) and even supplying motifs for contemporary French enamel *objets d'art* and jewellery (*fig. 6*). This identification of *cloisonné* decoration with Japanese modes of style has seemed so compelling to both nineteenth century and recent writers that there is a danger that the terms *Japonisme* and *Cloisonisme* might easily be confused. Yet, while they surely overlapped in reference to much late nineteenth century art, this frequent stylistic coincidence should not be allowed to obscure the broader range of historical art forms associated with the term *cloisonné*. In effect, the *cloisonné* aesthetic was gradually emerging as a distinct, if multiform, mode of art, which could be appreciated as an alternative tradition to the naturalism which had dominated Western art from the Renaissance through Realism. More important, it can be demonstrated that during the late 1880s within the circle of Vincent van Gogh and his French *avant-garde* colleagues, Cloisonism was implanted in French painting as one of the most preferred and influential forms of *l'art moderne*.

Not that this style of painting was based on sources hitherto unexplained in recent French painting: Japanese wood block prints and comparable Western forms of folk art functioned within the Realist and Impressionist movements as fairly common, if rarely overtly stated, sources of influence. James Whistler, Félix Bracquemond, Edouard Manet,

Fig. 4
Hiroshige
"The Nihonbashi Bridge at Daybreak"
1855,
colour print
(Rijksmuseum Vincent van Gogh, Amsterdam).

Fig. 5
Kuniyoshi: A Kabuki Actor,
full-length portrait of a Kabuki actor in a lion dance performance.
The title reads "Examples of Valour."
1847-50,
colour prints
(Rijksmuseum Vincent van Gogh, Amsterdam).

Fig. 6
nineteenth century cloisonné enamel jewelry:
bracelet, earrings, pin;
illustrated in *Les Emaux cloisonnés anciens et modernes*, Philipe Burty, Paris, 1868,
(collection: Gallery Martz, Paris).

Fig. 7
Edgar Degas
Dancer with a Bouquet,
1878,
pastel
(Museum of Art, Rhode Island School of Design,
Providence; Gift of Mrs. Murray S. Danforth).

James Tissot, Monet, Camille Pissarro and Edgar Degas are among those artists most frequently cited for having appropriated one or more aspects of the richly varied expressive and compositional devices of the Japanese print for transformation into a personal idiom.[5] Indebtedness assumed many forms, including the use of Japanese art objects as motifs *per se* (so-called *Japonaiserie*); "distortion" according to Western Renaissance traditions of perspective, foreshortening and viewpoint of the spectator; a general sharpening of contour outline and figural background relationships (especially in Manet); and compositional devices favouring asymmetry and truncation of subject motifs (especially in Degas; *see fig.* 7). This "snapshot" approach, as found in many Impressionist paintings, has sometimes been attributed to the influence of contemporary photography; this assumption has recently been convincingly challenged, and the art of Japan is now generally thought the more important causative factor.[6]

A tradition of popular woodcut prints traceable back to the late Middle Ages and generally classified by the nineteenth century as *Les Images d'Epinal* in reference to one of

[5]   See *Japonisme*.

[6]   K. Varnedoe, "The Artifice of Candor: Impressionism and Photography," *Art in America*, January, 1980, pp. 66-78.

several major centres of production could also be incorporated into modern French painting in a variety of ways ranging from the overt to the surreptitious. Thus Gustave Courbet's *Bonjour Monsieur Courbet* (*fig. 8*) at the Montpellier Museum involved a covert reference to a popular image of "the wandering Jew," (*fig. 9*) providing an instance where iconography (namely self-identification of the Realist artist as outcast, yet potential reformer, of society) overshadows style.[7] By way of contrast, in his *Fifer* (*see fig. 10*) Manet would seem to have been concerned chiefly with formal elements of style. Thus his poster-like image may be said to combine with playing-card simplicity of *métier* types featured in French *imagerie populaire* (*see fig. 11*), the starkness of outline and colour contrasts typified in *cloisonné* work, and nonetheless a veneration of Western portrait tradition in the manner of Velásquez and Goya as well.[8]

It must also be recognized that none of these Realist-Impressionist artists considered himself a Cloisonist or Japanist pure and simple. Each was influenced by a variety of other artists and art forms. Each thought that his personal achievement within the group movement provided the ultimate yardstick by which he should be judged. Most important, neither *Japonisme*, popular imagery nor *cloisonné* enamel work, alone or in combination, provided an underlying set of principles which might be used to explain the basis of Realist or Impressionist style. And if van Gogh, possibly following the critic Théodore Duret,[9] repeatedly identified the Impressionists as "the Japanese of France" (*CL*510-11, *CL*515) it was he, not they, who chose to offer this all-embracing categorization.

Fig. 8
Gustave Courbet
The Meeting, or Bonjour, Monsieur Courbet,
1854,
oil on canvas
(Musée Fabre, Montpellier).

Fig. 9
Le Juif errant,
French popular print of the eighteenth century,
from the frontispiece of E. Champfleury, *Imagerie populaire*, Paris, 1869.

Fig. 10
Edouard Manet
The Fifer,
1866
(Musée du Louvre, Paris).

Fig. 11
His Royal Highness the Prince Imperial, Sergeant of the First Regiment of the Grenadier Guards,
coloured lithograph,
second half of nineteenth century,
Pellerin of Epinal.

Fig. 10

Fig. 11

The designation "Le Cloisonisme" as applying to late nineteenth century French painting was first used as the sub-title of an essay by Edouard Dujardin devoted to the painter Louis Anquetin. This appeared in the March 1, 1888, issue of *La Revue indépendante*, of which the author was then managing editor. After admitting to a long-time acquaintance with the painter Louis Anquetin and a wish to describe the latter's "rather novel and special manner," Dujardin quickly mentions his twenty-seven-year-old subject's apprenticeship at the Bonnat and Cormon studios and enumerates the paintings and drawings with which he was then making his public debut at both the exhibition at *Les Vingt* in Brussels and at the *Société des artistes indépendants* in Paris. Anquetin is characterized initially as having given up his flirtation with Impressionism and Pointillism for painting "in flat tones" (*à tons plats*) and then as having embodied in such canvases as *The Mower at Noon: Summer* (cat. no. 74; pl. 4) and *Avenue de Clichy: Five O'Clock in the Evening* (cat. no. 76; pl. 2) the following pictorial system:

> At first sight, his works proclaim the idea of decorative painting: traced outlines along with strong and fixed colouration, which inevitably recall [primitative or popular] images and Japanism. Then, according to the generally hieratic character of the drawing and colour, one perceives an astounding veracity which is divorced from the impetuosity of romanticism. Above all, little by little, it is the deliberate, the reasoned, the intellectual and systematic construction, which require analysis.[10]

In this initial linking of Japanese art with popular imagery, both traditions are subsumed under the broader category of decorative painting. This essay is also notable for Dujardin's striking identification of the term "symbolism" with his own concept of Cloisonism. Accordingly Dujardin's analysis of Anquetin's art continues:

> The point of departure is a symbolic conception of art. In painting, as well as in literature, the representation of nature is a chimera. The ideal in the representation of nature (whether or not viewed via a temperament) is *trompe-l'oeil*. And, in a *trompe-l'oeil* picture, why do not the figures move about, hear sounds, etc? . . . [since] the system of representing nature leads logically to considering theater the supreme form of art. On the contrary, the aim of painting and literature is to give the *sense* of objects, according to the special means of painting and literature. That which [the artist] properly expresses is not the image but the *character* [of things.] Hence what good [is served] in retracing a thousand insignificant details observed by the eye? It is

---

7   See L. Nochlin, "Gustave Courbet's *Meeting*: A Portrait of the Artist as a Wandering Jew," *The Art Bulletin*, XLIX, Spring 1967, pp. 209-22.

8   For a fuller discussion, see A.C. Hanson, "Popular Imagery and the Work of Edouard Manet," in *French 19th Century Painting and Literature*, ed. U. Finke (Manchester: Manchester University Press, 1972), pp. 133-63.

9   Roskill, pp. 209-10.

10 Dujardin, p. 489. *P-I*, p. 166, n. 27, points out that parts of the Dujardin article mistakenly had been attributed to F. Fénéon but itself errs in giving the date of publication as May 19, 1888. Roskill, p. 258, n. 28, is correct in listing it as March 1888, and a notice by Gustave Kahn in the April issue of the periodical (pp. 163-64) tells us that the March issue had appeared on the first of that month. Although the term is sometimes transliterated into English with a double "n," the present writer prefers to honour Dujardin's original "Le cloisonisme."

necessary to grasp and reproduce—or, better said, to produce—the essential trait. A silhouette suffices to express a physiognomy. The painter, completely neglecting photography . . . seeks only to establish, with the least possible number of characteristic lines and colours, an intimate reality, the essence of the object which is imposed[11].

The anti-naturalist bias of this succinct statement of art theory is as manifest as the proto-abstract canon of design which it advocates. Indeed, both for the clarity of its verbal presentation and as the initial printed attempt to define the new Cloisonist-Symbolist phenomenon in painting, Dujardin's analysis is deserving of more than the passing homage it has received to date in serious texts on late nineteenth century French painting.

Apart from his repeated emphasis upon primitive and Japanese art as providing the historical model for a revitalized modern style freed from the visual ambiguities of the *trompe-l'oeil* tradition, Dujardin in fact accepts the well established academic distinction between line and colour as the basic components of the plastic arts.

First, an artist must [maintain] the very rigorous distinction between drawing and colouration. Do not invoke the vain pretext that lines do not exist in nature, [since] to confound outline and colour is not to have comprehended the special means of expression which they constitute. Outline expresses that which is permanent, colour that which is momentary. Outline, is quasi-abstract sign, gives the character of an object; unity of colour determines the atmosphere, fixes the sensation. From this [derives] the circumscription of outline and colour as conceived by popular imagery and Japanese art. The artists of the "image d'Epinal" and Japanese [woodcut] albums first trace lines within which are placed colours according to the "colour pattern" process. Likewise, the painter [Anquetin] traces his design with enclosing lines, within which he places his various [colour] tones juxtaposed in order to produce the desired sensation of general colouration. Drawing predicates colour and colour predicates drawing. And the work of the painter will be something like painting *by compartments*, analogous to *cloisonné* [works of art], and his technique consists in a sort of *cloisonisme*.[12]

It remains uncertain whether Dujardin's transformation of the technical term *cloisonné* into the label for an emerging tendency in French painting was invented solely by himself or primarily reflected the thinking of his friend Anquetin. Doubtless both men were cognizant of the widespread taste for Japanism within French *avant-garde* circles and of some of the publications pertaining to *cloisonné* techniques which had been appearing for over two decades. Given their close personal relationship, this consideration strongly implies that creation of the term *cloisonisme* in reference to the art of Anquetin had his full approval and understanding, if it was not possibly even employed at his own suggestion.

During the several years which followed, *cloisonisme* remained current as one of several designations for the style of art practised by not only Anquetin but also by Bernard and Gauguin. This continuing usage was as often a source of dismay as of satisfaction to the artists involved. Whereas in April 1888 another writer explained Dujardin's term as limited to the work of Anquetin and intended as a barb at the Pointillists, who hereafter might not be considered the sole leaders of *avant-garde* painting in France.[13] Bernard would seem to have written in some indignation to Vincent in Arles about the exclusive crediting of Anquetin as the creator of a new tendency in art based on Japanese principles. In a June 1888 letter to his brother Théo, (*CL* 500) Vincent, not having read Dujardin's article and thus possibly unaware of its use of the term *cloisonisme*, maintained with unintended irony that Seurat was the leader of this new tendency in art, while acknowledging that "in the Japanese style young Bernard has perhaps gone further than Anquetin." In later comment Bernard claimed that he and Anquetin together had developed Cloisonism through a study of Japanese prints and at a time (1886) which predated the possibility of any participation by Gauguin in this evolution.[14] Gauguin himself was resentful (*M* XCI) when the critic Félix Fénéon, in his review of the 1889 Volpini exhibition of the "Groupe Impressioniste et Synthétiste" cited the painter's indebtedness to his co-exhibitor Anquetin, whose work Gauguin claimed—almost certainly incorrectly—not to have known previous to this event.[15] Although demonstrably familiar with it,[16] Gauguin himself seems never to have employed the term Cloisonism in reference to his own style in his letters and writings on art, and it is quite possible that he selected the label *Synthétiste* for use at the Volpini exhibition partly in order to disassociate himself, as leader of the new anti-Pointillist *avant-garde*, from a label employed the previous year solely in reference to Anquetin. If so, presumably he was also irked to read Fénéon's opinion that *circa* 1886 the Neo-Impressionists had been the first to seek an "art of synthesis" and that Gauguin's aim, despite the difference of style, was analogous to theirs.[17]

These various reactions to critical jargon might easily be interpreted as a sign of discord and diagreement, but in truth they reflect a profound correspondence of interests and shared activities. Most readers of Dujardin's brief article would not realize that Anquetin's style, as embodied in his contributions to the Brussels *Les Vingt* and Paris *Indépendants* exhibitions of early 1888, was a product, however personally attained, of experiments in pictorial form evolved in close collaboration with such fellow artists as Bernard, Vincent and Lautrec.

Let us consider these facts. At one time or another during the years 1884-1886 all the above mentioned artists excluding Gauguin had been students at the Cormon studio located on the boulevard de Clichy. This *atelier libre* was first attended by close friends Lautrec and Anquetin, who, *circa* 1885, adopted the younger Bernard as a pro-Impressionist fellow renegade against academic canons of art. When the unpredictable Dutchman, Vincent van Gogh, arrived, he proved himself equally intractable to standard

[11]   *Ibid.*

[12]   *Ibid.*, p. 490.

[13]   G. Geffroy, "Chronique: Pointillé—Cloisonisme," *La Justice*, April 11, 1888.

[14]   *Notes*, p. 676.

[15]   Fénéon, I, p. 158 (originally "Autre groupe impressioniste," *La Cravache*, July 6, 1889).

[16]   See "The Cloisonné Vases," from *Gauguin's Intimate Journals*, pp. 63-67.

[17]   Fénéon, I, p. 157.

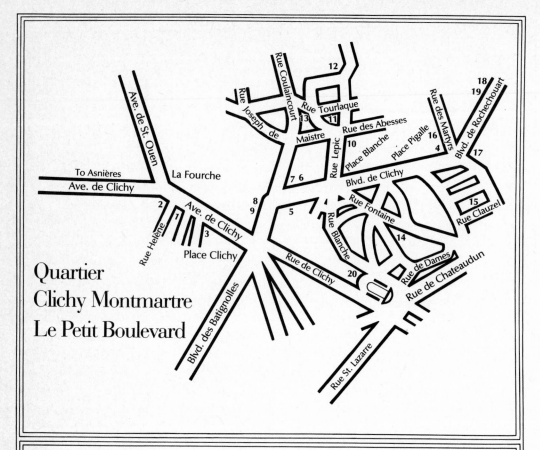

**Quartier
Clichy Montmartre
Le Petit Boulevard**

Rue Coulaincourt

Rue Tourlaque

12

Rue Joseph de Maistre

Ave. de St. Ouen

13

11

Rue des Abesses

Place Blanche

Rue Lepic

10

18

19

Rue des Martyrs

Place Pigalle

16

Blvd. de Rochechouart

4

17

To Asnières

La Fourche

Ave. de Clichy

7 6

Blvd. de Clichy

2

Ave. de Clichy

8

Rue Hélène

9

Rue Fontaine

15

Rue Clauzel

3

5

Rue Blanche

Place Clichy

Rue de Clichy

14

Blvd. des Batignolles

20

Rue de Dames

Rue de Chateaudun

Rue St. Lazarre

**Les Grands
Boulevards**

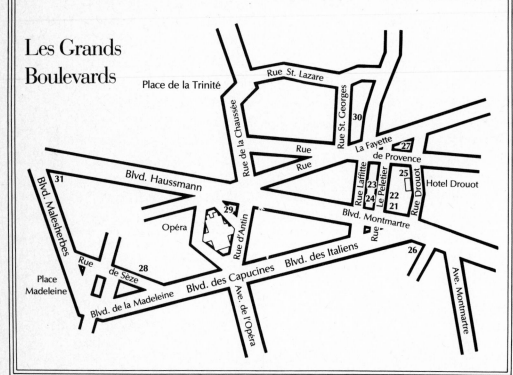

Rue St. Lazare

Place de la Trinité

Rue de la Chaussée

Rue St. Georges

30

La Fayette

27

Rue

de Provence

Rue

Rue Laffitte

23

25

Blvd. Haussmann

24

Le Peletier

22

Hotel Drouot

31

21

Rue Drouot

29

Blvd. Montmartre

Opéra

Rue d'Antin

Blvd. Malesherbes

Rue

28

Blvd. des Italiens

26

Place
Madeleine

de Sèze

Blvd. des Capucines

Ave. Montmartre

Blvd. de la Madeleine

Ave. de l'Opéra

Fig. 12
Map of the *Petit Boulevard* of Montmartre, Paris.

1. Grand Bouillon—Restaurant du Chalet—
   43 Ave. de Clichy
2. Louis Anquetin residence—*atelier*
   (1885-89)—86 Ave. de Clichy
3. Paul Signac residence (1889)—
   20 Ave. de Clichy
4. E. Degas residence—6 Boulevard de Clichy
5. Cafe-Brasserie du Tambourin—
   62 Blvd. de Clichy
6. "Moulin Rouge"—90 Blvd. de Clichy
7. F. Cormon *"atelier libre"*—
   104 Blvd. de Clichy
8. G. Seurat—*atelier* (from 1887)—
   128 Blvd. de Clichy
9. P. Signac—*atelier* (1886-1888)—
   130 Blvd. de Clichy
10. A. Aurier residence (1888-90)—
    26 rue Lepic
11. Vincent and Theo van Gogh apartment—
    54 rue Lepic
12. "Moulin de la Galette"—79 rue Lepic
13. Toulouse-Lautrec—*atelier* (1886-89)—
    27 rue Coulaincourt
14. Toulouse-Lautrec residences (1884-91)—
    19 and 21 rue Fontaine
15. Boutique of "Père" Tanguy—
    14 rue Clauzel
16. Divan Japonais—75 rue des Martyrs
17. Cirque Fernando—
    63 Blvd. de Rochechouart
18. Elysée-Montmartre—80 Blvd. de Rochechouart
19. Chat-Noir-Mirliton—84 Blvd. de Rochechouart
20. Edouard Dujardin residence
    (1885-1887)—79 rue Blanche

(See for other addresses of artists and
establishments in this area in Ph. Huisman
and M.G. Dortu *Lautrec par Lautrec*
1964, p. 249 and B.M. Welsh-Ovcharov
*Vincent van Gogh: His Paris Period
1886-1888*, The Hague 1976, pp.
247-248).

Fig. 13.
Map of the *Grands Boulevards*, Paris

21. Edouard Dujardin residence (1889-90) –
     11 rue Le Peletier
22. Gallery of Le Barc de Bouteville –
     47 rue Le Peletier
23. Gallery Durand-Ruel – 8 rue Laffitte
24. Gallery Bernheim-Jeune – 16 rue Laffitte
25. "Hotel de Vente-Drouot" – rue Drouot
26. Gallery Boussod et Valadon et Cie
     (Theo van Gogh) – 19 Blvd. Montmartre
27. Gallery S. Bing – 22 rue de Provence
28. Galleries G. Petit – 8 rue de Sèze
29. Offices of "La Revue Independant" and
     address for Edouard Dujardin for 1888 –
     11 rue de la Chaussée d'Antin
30. Gallery P. F. Martin – 29 rue St. Georges
31. Gallery of "Père" Thomas –
     43 Blvd. Malesherbes

academic practice. Surviving accounts indicate that all behaved as "intransigents" and that both Anquetin, at one time considered Cormon's chosen successor, and Bernard left after conflict with the master.[18] Nor did the end of attendance at Cormon's terminate further personal contacts. All but Bernard, who lived with his parents in the Paris suburb of Asnières, lived in the Clichy district of Montmartre, and Lautrec's Saturday gatherings are known to have been visited by his old student friends. In particular, Lautrec, Anquetin and Bernard remained close friends and collaborators *circa* 1886-87, and van Gogh, if not so intimate a member of the group, certainly enjoyed a variety of occasions for contact.[19] One place of rendezvous was the café *Le Mirliton*, whose operator, Aristide Bruant, permanently displayed there a number of Lautrec's paintings and drawings and published his illustrations in an eponymous sporadically appearing bulletin.[20] Anquetin was a frequent companion of Lautrec at the café, as were Bernard and Vincent occasionally.

Admittedly these contacts were mostly of an irregular nature during 1886-87. Apart from the question of comings and goings at the *atelier* Cormon, Anquetin, Bernard, and, in 1887, Lautrec followed Impressionist tradition by spending the summer months away from Paris so that contact between these painters and van Gogh, who remained in the city, was limited to the fall-spring periods. Gauguin's absences from the French capital were more prolonged, embracing a June-November stay in Pont-Aven in 1886 and an April-November trip to the Caribbean with Charles Laval the following year. Except for Gauguin's sizable sending of nineteen paintings to the eighth Impressionist Group Exhibition, none of the Cormon-bred group could hope for representation in the official annual Salon exhibitions, let alone significant support by such dealers as Durand-Ruel, Georges Petit or even Vincent's brother Théo, who managed the boulevard Montmartre shop of Boussod and Valdadon (formerly Goupil and Company). Such support was already available in some measure to such older artists as Monet, Renoir, Pissarro and Degas, whom Vincent dubbed the "Impressionists of the Grand Boulevard" (*CL* 468) in recognition of their welcome in the fashionable establishments of the area surrounding the Paris Opera (*fig. 13*). In contrast he called himself and his young acquaintances the "Impressionists of the Petit Boulevard," recognizing hereby their general area of residence and incidental exhibition activities in the Clichy district, then on the northern outskirts of Paris (*fig. 12*).

It was van Gogh who ultimately acted as the principal catalyst for the group to cooperate in a joint exhibition held towards the end of 1887, which Bernard later would describe as having had an "aspect...truly novel" and of having been "the latest thing in Paris."[21] Vincent already possessed some experience in such matters. He had previously arranged for the casual display of his own early Paris canvases and, later, a specific selection of Japanese prints at the café *Le Tambourin*, which was operated by the artists'

18 Welsh-Ovcharov, p. 210.

19 E.g., reminiscence by Suzanne Valadon as given in F. Fels, *Vincent van Gogh* (Paris: Floury, 1928), p. 136.

20 See Joyant, p. 98, and Gauzi, pp. 45-6.

21 *Notes*, p. 678.

model Agostina Segatori (*see cat. no. 3*) with whom Vincent presumably had a brief liaison. Whether or not this exhibition undertaking justified Vincent's later claim to have influenced Bernard and Anquetin "a good deal" with this print exhibition, it certainly provided a prototype for the later exhibition he held at another public locale together with Anquetin, Bernard and Lautrec, which he considered to have been a greater success (*CL*510). Formerly confused with the exhibitions at *Le Tambourin* and thus assigned an earlier date, it is now established that this event took place *circa* November-December 1887 at the commodious *Grand Bouillon-Restaurant du Chalet* located at 43 avenue de Clichy.[22] Bernard has provided the best, if tantalizingly synoptic, accounts of what actually was exhibited. He variously listed: (1) fifty to one hundred works by Vincent, including landscapes, still life subjects (especially flowers) and "flaming self-portraits"; (2) the "Japanese abstractions" of Anquetin (specifically the now missing *Boat at Sunset*); (3) the "prostitute types" of Lautrec; and (4) the "geometric syntheses" by himself, especially *Ragpickers: Iron Bridges at Asnières (Clichy)* (cat. no. 96, pl. 26).[23] He further tells us that several art dealers plus the artists Pissarro, Gauguin, Armand Guillaumin and Seurat visited the exhibition, and that Vincent had wished to include both Seurat and Signac in this manifestation of the "School of the Petit Boulevard."[24] While ignored by the art critics and arousing apparent hostility among the working class patrons of the restaurant, this event scarcely went unnoticed among Impressionists of both the "Petit" and "Grand" boulevards whose knowledge of Vincent's Paris *oeuvre* and the most recent work of his chosen colleagues can be assumed to have been considerable.[25] Finally, we know from Vincent (*CL*510) both that Bernard sold his first painting and Anquetin a study from the exhibition, and that Vincent and Gauguin exchanged paintings there.

This exchange indicates that contrary to accepted opinion, only about the time of the *Du Chalet* exhibition, upon his return from the Caribbean in November 1887, did Gauguin enter into a close personal and economic relationship with the van Gogh brothers. On their part, it was principally the already somewhat Japanist landscape paintings brought back by Gauguin from Martinique, of which Vincent acquired *On the Riverbank* (*fig. 14*) in the exchange and Théo *Among the Mangoes* by purchase (cat. no. 46), which most prompted them to see Gauguin as deserving of meaningful financial support. *Circa* December 1887-January 1888 Gauguin thus received his first of several publicized showings at Théo's gallery when three paintings and a selection of ceramics went on display along with works by the artist's friends Pissarro and Degas.[26] Indeed, from this time until Théo fell fatally ill in October 1890, it was above all to him that Gauguin would look as a source of continuing, if intermittent, income.

Winter 1887-88 was hence a period of uncommonly intense contact between Vincent and the young "Impressionists of the Petit Boulevard," whom he already wished to see united in an association of mutual economic benefit. Gauguin was then brought squarely into this context for the first time, and, as Vincent was to explain later in a letter to Gauguin in Pont-Aven, Vincent and his brother entered into discussions with such artists as Guillaumin, Pissarro and his son Lucien, and Seurat in furtherance of this scheme for a fraternal association of *avant-garde* artists (*CL*554a). Most shocking and unwelcome to

Fig. 14
Paul Gauguin
Au Bord de l'Etang,
1887,
oil on canvas
(Rijksmuseum Vincent van Gogh, Amsterdam).

Gauguin was Vincent's inclusion of the Pointillist Seurat and his new disciples Pissarro father and son in this proposed scheme, an inclination of Vincent's which Gauguin was at pains to correct following his arrival late in October in Arles. At that time Vincent surely became aware, however reluctantly, that there would be no welcome for Pointillism by Gauguin, Bernard and their fellow Pont-Aven associate Charles Laval, all of whom at the time Vincent thought might be joining his Gauguin-led "Studio of the South" in Arles (*CL* 543-44, 549). Yet final proof exists that Vincent's efforts of the winter of 1887-88 to form an association of artists would not remain entirely without issue. For, had Guillaumin, Lautrec and Vincent not declined or been excluded the proffered or expected invitations to attend, the famous Volpini exhibition of late spring-summer 1889 would have comprised as much a reunion of Gauguin and the *Du Chalet* exhibitors as the homage to Gauguin and his own circle that is commonly thought its original intention. We

22   Welsh-Ovcharov, pp. 21, 28, 34-40.

23   Bernard, *Van Gogh*, p. 393, and "Vincent van Gogh," *L'Arte*, February 9, 1901.

24   *P-I*, p. 72, n. 65.

25   Bernard, *Van Gogh*, p. 393.

26   The date of this display is usually given as January, 1888, because of its announcement in that month's issue of *La Revue indépendante*. However, the announcement is unquestionably subject to the heading "Calendrier de Decembre, 1887," when the exhibition must have opened.

Fig. 15
Emile Bernard
Portrait of Breton Girl,
dated 1886,
oil on canvas
(private collection, Paris).

Fig. 16
Emile Bernard
La Place Saint-Briac,
c. 1886-87,
oil on canvas
(Collection Centner, Paris).

shall see that this result was more a product of chance and intrigue than of systematic planning.

As Bernard's enumeration of the contribution by individuals to the *Du Chalet* exhibition implies, personal differences in approach to style and iconography were doubtless readily apparent. Yet, as one might expect from a group of similarly independent-minded artists working in the same *milieu* at comparable stages in their careers, analogies in approach are also discoverable. By 1886, only Gauguin, then in his late thirties, had achieved a degree of public exposure from his participation in several Impressionist group exhibitions, and he, no less than the almost twenty-year younger Bernard, was anxious to achieve recognition in his own right. It is striking how uniformly Impressionism was abandoned or radically transformed by all these artists in the mid-1880s, once its role in freeing them from the strictures of academic or Realist technique was completed. This doubtless reflects in part the dissolution of Impressionism as a group movement, whose original members were showing not only signs of internal dissension but also a tendency to return to stronger compositional emphasis. However, if the times were ripe for change, so were some among the younger generation of artists rapidly ripening for a role in bringing change about.

Moreover, change was already under way in the unmistakable form of the Neo-Impressionist movement led by Georges Seurat and Paul Signac. It was of course the Pointillist style of these painters which both Gauguin and Bernard later vociferously opposed. Twice in 1886 Gauguin had quarrelled with Seurat and by summer 1888 at Pont-Aven he joined with his friends Bernard and Laval in creating the fictional "Ripipoint" (for "rite of the tiny point" as Bernard explained it) as a figure of ridicule.[27] This recorded abrasiveness notwithstanding, there is good evidence to award Neo-Impressionism major credit in bringing about the developments which led to the creation of the Cloisonist style. As Bernard's own accounts testify, he, Anquetin and Vincent all worked quite seriously in a Pointillist vein immediately antecedent to what he describes as their joint evolution during 1886-87 of Cloisonism.[28] He freely admitted to having produced a number of Pointillist-style landscapes which attracted the attention of Signac when they were exhibited locally in Asnières. In fact, a considerably larger number of these, what might be best called quasi-Pointillist canvases have survived (*see* cat. nos. 89 and 90 and *figs. 15 and 16*) than is generally realized. These typically employ the stipple technique merely as a surface patina of uniform brushwork which lends a muted iridescence to an underlying Realist, Impressionist or, in mature examples, geometrizing compositional structure. Anquetin's *Landscape with Trees* (cat. no. 71) is a rare surviving example by his hand of a style suggestive of Pointillism, which, because executed in 1885, presumably derives more from a knowledge of Monet's and other Impressionists' recent works. In the hope of learning how the Impressionists applied Delacroix's laws of colour Anquetin visited Monet apparently in the latter half of 1886 to study Seurat and Signac, only to conclude that it was necessary to arrive at a more scientific theory of

[27]   Bernard, "Souvenirs," *La Rénovation esthetique*, November 1907 and April 1909, pp. 46-9, 331-32.

[28]   *Notes*, p. 381.

Fig. 18
Vincent van Gogh
Still Life: Parisian Novels with a Rose,
1887,
oil on canvas
(private collection, Baden).

colour.[29] Although examples of Anquetin's more fully Pointillist style, upon which Pissarro remarked in spring 1887,[30] have yet to be located, several seemingly Pointillist beachscapes and landscapes may be viewed hanging above the *Avenue de Clichy* in a previously unpublished photograph of Anquetin's studio *circa* 1891-92 (*fig. 17*). Bernard's descriptions of the now lost *Boat at Sunset* as being painted in both a Pointillist and Japanist-Cloisonist style, further substantiate Anquetin's experimentation in this dual stylistic mode by winter 1887-88.[31] Bernard has described Anquetin's interest in Pointillism as more concerned with vibrating effects of colour and light than with the science of optical mixture, that is, the principle of *mélange optique* in which complementary colour spots fuse in the viewer's eye to form a single colour, particularly the "luminous gray" supposedly favoured by Delacroix. The latter he considered an unrewarding and tiresome preoccupation.[32] An end to this temporary involvement with Pointillism, said Bernard, came about through mutual discussions in which he, Anquetin and Lautrec concluded that art should have a mathematical basis and aim at a willfully decorative form of composition.[33] Apart from failing to note that this statement closely approximates what critics like Gustave Kahn and Félix Fénéon by 1886 were describing as the basis of Seurat's art,[34] Bernard in these comments would seem to have defined the approach to composition already apparent in the flattened surface effects and planar divisions of his own Pointillist canvases and the theoretical point of departure for his Cloisonist phase.

The contacts which Vincent and Gauguin had with Pointillist style might easily be considered more tentative than those of Bernard and Anquetin. Vincent's most orthodox examples of this style, such as *View from Vincent's Room in the Rue Lepic* (cat. no. 4) and *Interior of a Restaurant* (cat. no. 5; pl. 13), also employ the stipple technique most notably as a variegated overlay to an essentially Realist depiction. There is little interest in producing effects of optical mixture. In other examples, such as *Still Life: Parisian Novels with a Rose* (*fig. 18*) and *Still Life: Plaster Statuette and Books* (cat. no. 11) the highly personal striated brush technique is scarcely Pointillist, except that the former painting was clearly treated by a critic as belonging with Neo-Impressionism when it was exhibited at the Spring 1888 *Indépendants* exhibition.[35] Like Bernard and Anquetin, Vincent might well have learned about Neo-Impressionism from Signac, with whom he is known to have associated while in Paris, and he most certainly studied Seurat's *La*

Fig. 17
Interior of Louis Anquetin's studio, 62 rue de Rome,
photograph *c.* 1891-2.

29   Bernard, *Anquetin 1932*, pp. 593-94, and *Anquetin 1934*, p. 112.

30   C. Pissarro, *Lettres à son fils Lucien*, ed. J. Rewald (Paris: Albin Michel, 1950), p. 153.

31   Cf. *Notes*, p. 676, and *Anquetin 1932*, p. 594.

32   *Anquetin 1934*, p. 112.

33   *Anquetin 1932*, p. 596.

34   Kahn, "Réponse des Symbolistes," *L'Evénement*, September 28, 1886, apparently was the first to mix mention of Charles Henry and Fénéon's "nouvelle critique d'art . . . sur les impressionistes" (read Neo-Impressionists), and Fénéon himself that year (pp. 35-8) made clear the scientific and mathematical basis of Neo-Impressionist style.

35   G. Kahn, "Peinture: Exposition des indépendants," *La Revue indépendante*, no. 18, April 1888, pp. 160-64; *CL* 474 gives Vincent's undisturbed response.

Fig. 19
Georges Seurat
*Sunday Afternoon on the Island of the
Grande-Jatte,*
1884-6,
oil on canvas
(Art Institute of Chicago, Helen Birch Bartlett
Memorial Collection).

Grande-Jatte (*fig. 19*) and other Pointillist works when they were publicly exhibited during the years 1886-87. Bernard much later recalled having visited Vincent's rue Lepic studio and seeing there his collection of Japanese prints, and his own works of both the dark Brabant period and of a Pointillist persuasion.[36] According to Bernard, Vincent considered the latter two styles not overwhelmingly different in conception. This *aperçu* though clearly intended in jest, unwittingly underlines another affinity of Vincent for the tenets of Neo-Impressionism; namely, the deep interest manifest in his Brabant period for the theories on colour propounded by such writers as Charles Blanc and Félix Bracquemond. Like the Pointillists, Vincent was particularly interested in the heightened intensity gained by colours when juxtaposed in complementary contrasts, as he mentions in numerous letters.[37]

Gauguin, too, is almost certain to have read both these authors. Bracquemond was a personal friend by 1885, and Blanc's influential *Grammaire des arts du dessin* has been recognized as the source of the art theory encapsulated in Gauguin's *Notes synthétiques* (*c.* 1885) and a letter to Emile Schuffenecker (*M*XI).[38] Like Bernard, Gauguin subsequently was reluctant to admit to a fascination with theories associated with Neo-Impressionism and consequently disparaged Pointillism's reliance upon the science of colour as offering a poor alternative to creation according to the force of one's own imagination, intuition and memory. Gauguin's most celebrated Pointillist work, the *Still Life: Ripipoint* (*W* 376) was probably undertaken in a spirit of ridicule in order to illustrate the ease with which the Pointillist technique could be imitated and perhaps to demonstrate its weakness alongside his own maturing personal style in 1889.[39] However, works of an earlier date exist in which Gauguin's use of a brush technique relating to Pointillist stippling cannot be thought perversely intended. More frequently one finds in landscapes from the period 1885-88 a surface encrustation of small brush-stroke daubs which produce a patina effect throughout the composition (*see* cat. no. 49). Whether one interprets this as consciously analogous to Pointillist style or as an organic development from his known model in Pissarro, the fact remains that some canvases by Gauguin dating from 1885-88 display an overall decorativeness in keeping with a chief aim proclaimed on the part of Neo-Impressionism by Fénéon. While this need not lead to the assumption that Gauguin in his pre-Pont-Aven style was a Pointillist in disguise, it does strongly suggest that he was not diametrically opposed to the movement from the start as his later comments would have us believe.

The clear-cut distinction made today between Impressionism and Neo-Impressionism was not as strictly maintained when a rationale for the latter movement was first promulgated. Along with his explanations of the scientific basis of Neo-Impressionism, Fénéon, like Signac later, pictured the Impressionists not merely as naturalists but as already investigating laws of complementary contrast and even optical mixture, albeit in a somewhat irregular manner. The attitude that Neo-Impressionism was no more than an advanced form of its predecessor Impressionism seems also to have been accepted by Bernard and Vincent despite their ultimate disagreement on the compatibility of the Pointillist technique with their own personal styles.

Similarly, it should be remembered that from its inception Neo-Impressionism was strongly linked to the Symbolist movement in literature. Such critics as Fénéon, Kahn and Dujardin were solidly committed to literary Symbolism, the primary cause served by journals like *La Revue indépendante*, *La Revue wagnérienne* and *La Vogue* with which they were intimately connected. Until March 1891 when Albert Aurier's article "Symbolism in Painting: Paul Gauguin" in effect excluded them from this classification, the Neo-Impressionists were as likely to be described in terms of jargon already popular among Symbolist men of letters. As Robert L. Herbert has pointed out, terms such as "essence," "permanence," "the ideal" and even "synthesis" were first applied to the Neo-Impressionists by these critics and, one may add, previous to the adoption in 1889 of the word *synthétiste* by Gauguin and his friends at the Volpini exhibition.[40] Conversely, whereas the offices of *La Revue indépendante* regularly functioned as a public display place for Seurat and the Pointillists, Anquetin's Cloisonist style was displayed there as early as January 1888 and Vincent and Gauguin were invited to show paintings as well. Their refusal in fall 1888 to cooperate had various possible grounds, including Gauguin's disinclination to be associated with this vehicle of Pointillist propaganda. Yet there is no reason to think that men like Fénéon and Dujardin considered Pointillism as necessarily

[36] *Notes*, p. 678.

[37] See Welsh-Ovcharov, Ch. II.

[38] Roskill, pp. 266-67, gives a *résumé* of the issue.

[39] See W376.

[40] Exh. cat. *Neo-Impressionism* (New York: S.R. Guggenheim Museum, 1968), p. 15.

Fig. 20
Georges Seurat
Une Baignade, Asnières,
1883-4,
oil on canvas
(National Gallery, London).

irreconcilable with Cloisonism in the struggle against naturalism in art. Rather, they tended to assign the two phenomena successive roles in the unfolding of a new art which, by implication, was Symbolism in painting.

How then did it come about that the several "Impressionists of the Petit Boulevard" turned away from both Impressionism and Neo-Impressionism in so short a time in order to develop an antagonistic style which was called Cloisonism? The answer must once again be found in large part within the strongly personal styles of individual artists, but it is also possible to discover lingering traces of Neo-Impressionist influence in their post- or non-Pointillist production. The underlying compositional structure of Bernard's *Ragpickers: Iron Bridges at Asnières* (cat. no. 96), for example, is markedly similar to that of Seurat's *Une Baignade, Asnières* (fig. 20), and a looser analogy is sometimes noticed between his *Breton Women in the Meadow* (pl. 9) and *La Grande-Jatte*. Differences in approach are equally noticeable. But in the stress on real or implied silhouette outlines of figures, the overall, tapestry-like sense of composition and the suggestion of what contemporary critics called "the hieratics" (for example, Egyptian, Medievalizing or primitive canons of style) there is at least an affinity of purpose in seeking a mural or decorative effect. Anquetin's *Avenue de Clichy* and Bernard's large, mural-like drawing, *Hour of the Flesh* (cat. no. 87), betray a more specific debt to the figural conception of Seurat's *La Grande-Jatte* and also illustrate the interaction between Bernard and Anquetin in the creation of the Cloisonist style. One must add the study of Japanese prints and experiments with viewing landscape settings through panes of coloured glass, as cited by Bernard, if one is to appreciate the syncratic manner in which Anquetin produced the *Avenue de Clichy* and his other archetypal Cloisonist painting of 1887, *The Mower*.[41] Yet

Fig. 21
Vincent van Gogh
*Japonaiserie: The Bridge in the Rain
(after Hiroshige)*,
summer 1887,
oil on canvas
(Rijksmuseum Vincent van Gogh, Amsterdam).

Fig. 22
Vincent van Gogh
Portrait of Père Tanguy,
autumn 1887,
oil on canvas
(Musée Rodin, Paris).

Fig. 23
Vincent van Gogh
Outskirts of Paris near Montmartre,
summer 1887,
watercolour heightened with white
(Stedelijk Museum, Amsterdam).

Fig. 21

Fig. 23

Fig. 22

even these interests are shared within Neo-Impressionist circles, whether known to Anquetin or not. As so often in the history of art, an attempt to go beyond the peculiarities of style which are being challenged often contains more residual traces of that style than are readily admitted.

In the art of Anquetin and Bernard indebtedness to Japanism, Neo-Impressionism or Cézanne (yet another influence stressed by Bernard) is typically hidden or oblique, functioning to support a general mode of style rather than providing a specific subject or compositional reference point. With Vincent the types of reference are more varied, embracing both overt and less decipherable forms of indebtedness. The overt types include the three late Paris period paintings executed on the basis of specific oriental models (cat. nos. 9 and 10 and *fig. 21*) and the two portraits of *Père Tanguy* (cat. no. 8, pl. 11 and *fig. 22*), which use equally specific prints as background motifs. Such usages are in keeping with the tradition of *Japonaiserie* going back to Whistler and Manet, in which Japanese art objects or their Western imitations are reproduced more or less literally in some decorative context. Nevertheless, the internal framing devices for the single print paintings and the backdrop arrangement of prints in the Tanguy portraits transform these "copies" into designs and colour schemes of the artist's own invention. Equally personal is Vincent's use of a variegated brush technique, which like that in his *Parisian Novels* (*fig. 18*), and the *Italian Woman with Daisies* (cat. no. 13, pl. 12) was seemingly meant to parallel the wrinkled surfaces of the Japanese *crépons* (prints on crepe paper) he so admired. Other paintings of summer or fall 1887 are more obliquely indebted to Japanese art. These include several views of boats and bridges along the Seine, which combine a general debt to Monet—himself under influence from Japan in his depictions of such subjects—with a raking angle point of view related to the perspectival telescoping commonly found in Japanese landscape renderings for example, in the Hiroshige setting used by Vincent in *Japonaiserie: The Bridge in the Rain* (*fig. 21*). Vincent's several watercolour renderings of the fortifications on the then outskirts of Paris (*see* cat. no. 6 and

[41]   Bernard, *Anquetin 1934*, p. 113.

Fig. 24

Fig. 25

fig. 23) follow another popular Japanese habit of design by juxtaposing a dramatically angled foreground bridge or roadway with a vastly panoramic distant landscape view, as found in Hiroshige's *Nihonbashi Bridge* (*fig. 4*). For lack of discernible connecting ground planes, these landscape settings are difficult to read as a harmonious spatial continuum and therefore are suggestive of abstract pictorial structure. It is in these riverscapes and fortification depictions that the artist's closest counterparts to the contemporary, late 1887 "synthetic geometries" of Bernard and "Japanése abstractions" of Anquetin can be found. And whether or not Anquetin and Dujardin would have agreed, these words explain Bernard's statement that rather than deserving classification as a disciple of Gauguin, Vincent "had his beginnings earlier; he was like us a Cloisonist and always remained so."[42]

In contrast, the great majority of paintings by Gauguin and Lautrec from before 1888 could only be called Cloisonist by expanding the definition of this term to include all conceivable traces of Japanist and other exotic influences whatsoever. For both artists, such influences as can be found derive in large part from an intense study of the compositions of Degas, whose Japanist tendencies were widely appreciated. True, the *Four Breton Women* of 1886 (*fig. 24*), several Martinique landscapes of 1887 and a ceramic vase (*fig. 25*) possibly of winter 1887-88 have been forcefully presented as proof

Fig. 24
Paul Gauguin
Four Breton Women,
1886,
oil on canvas
(Bayrische Staatsgemaldessammlungen, Munich).

Fig. 25
Paul Gauguin
Vase with Breton Girls,
winter 1886-87?,
stoneware vase decorated with coloured glazes and lines in gold
(Musées Royaux d'Art et d'Histoire, Brussels).

Fig. 26
Henri de Toulouse-Lautrec
*The Quadrille of
the Louis XIII Chair at the
Elysée Montmartre*,
1886,
canvas and grisaille
(private collection, Paris).

Fig. 27
Henri de Toulouse-Lautrec
*The Refrain of the Louis XIII
Chair at the Cabaret
of Aristide Bruant*,
1886,
papier marouflé on canvas
(collector unknown,
ex-Collection the
Metropolitan Museum of Art,
New York).

Fig. 26

that Gauguin was involved with Japanist and Cloisonist elements of design most likely by *circa* 1886, and certainly before summer 1888 when he saw Bernard's *Breton Women in the Meadow*.[43] However, in his finished paintings Gauguin's Japanist-Cloisonist tendencies remained clothed in still basically naturalist colour schemes and Impressionist brush techniques, even while his figure style (*see* cat. nos. 45 and 46) is clearly tending towards flattened volumes and well defined contour outlines. Gauguin was perhaps not yet ready to be called a Cloisonist nor to call himself a Synthetist in public, but his art was nonetheless moving in a Japanist direction.[44]

Likewise until the end of 1887 Lautrec's mainstream painting style was not characterized by a concerted experimentation with anti-naturalism except for a restricted number of paintings which appear executed virtually as drawings. Some of these have overtones of caricature, such as the 1886 grisaille painting, *The Quadrille of the Louis XIII Chair* (*fig. 26*) and its companion piece, *The Refrain of the Louis XIII Chair* (*fig. 27*), which

42   Bernard, *Notes*, p. 681.

43   M. Bodelsen, "The Missing Link in Gauguin's Cloisonism," *GBA*, LIII, May-June 1959, pp. 329-44.

44   As Gauguin stated in early summer 1888 to Schuffenecker (*M*LXVI), before Bernard arrived in Pont-Aven.

Fig. 28
Henri de Toulouse-Lautrec
The Dancers,
1885,
oil on canvas
(private collection).

were intended as festive decorations for Aristide Bruant's *Le Mirliton* café. Certain ballet subjects painted about the same year (*fig. 28*) incline towards Japanist wide-angle perspective and simplification of figural contours, which perhaps go beyond the models obviously provided by Degas. These traits are more restrained in his studies of one or two figures, such as *At the Café* (cat. no. 116), the *Portrait of Vincent van Gogh* (cat. no. 117) and a drawing *Bar of the Café de la Rue de Rome* (cat. no. 113), which remain naturalistic in conception despite certain simplifications of contour. The drawing *At the Elysée Montmartre* (cat. no. 114) might be considered already Japanist in its sparse outline contours, except that such simplifications of form occur in other illustrations of the period, including examples by Degas.[45] At the least it may be seen as a prognostication of his poster art of the 1890s (cat. nos. 124 and 125), and in this sense is proto-Cloisonist whatever the degree of conscious intention. Some idea of what Bernard meant as Lautrec's "prostitute types" exhibited at the *Du Chalet* restaurant is surely provided by the painted sketch of *Two Prostitutes* (cat. no. 112) which then or later found its way into the collection of Théo and Vincent. This example and a wash drawing variant (Dortu, V, D 2897) include contour outlines which might already be called Cloisonist, although Degas is again the more likely source of inspiration than Japan.

The same can by no means be said, however, of what must be considered Lautrec's most strikingly Japanist and Cloisonist painting of the 1880s, *At the Circus Fernando*: *The Horsewoman* (cat. no. 119, pl. 28). Since this painting figures among the eleven works sent to the *Les Vingt* exhibition held February 1888 in Brussels, it must have been completed before Gauguin and Vincent left Paris that month respectively for Pont-Aven and Arles. Although *Rice Powder* (cat. no. 118) in its subject matter and mixed Realist-Impressionist-Pointillist style was more representative of Lautrec's exhibition contribution, it was *The Circus* which most justified one critic in describing the then just twenty-four-year-old artist as "impelled by the same researches" into modern life as his friend Anquetin.[46] The painting was to be on public display in Paris only when hung permanently at the foyer of the *Moulin Rouge* dance and entertainment hall, which was to open its doors October 5, 1889. This revolutionary canvas by Lautrec fully deserves classification as one of the major initial monuments of the Cloisonist style. The surviving traces of Degas are restricted to the snapshot figural truncations and extreme close-up view, while the asymmetry of the composition, the several areas of bright, flat colouration and even the radically foreshortened horse may derive from a study of Japanese prints, of which Lautrec, too, is known to have been an avid early collector. Sizable though this painting is, Lautrec hereafter worked on an enormous mural-sized version of the theme which, had it been finished and survived, doubtless would be considered the most ambitious Cloisonist painting ever produced.[47] As it now stands, one need only realize that, if not necessarily known to them at the time, *The Circus* clearly predates Bernard's *Breton Women* and Gauguin's *Vision* by a number of months and was yet equally innovative and personal in its creation of a Japanist-Cloisonist canon of style. Not until his lithographic poster work of the 1890s would Lautrec again make so clear a statement in this stylistic idiom.

The Cloisonist-Synthetist Phase: 1888-early 1889

The Cloisonist style, which coalesced principally in the year 1887, matured in the following year and a half. This period is often associated with what is thought to have been the sudden creation of the Synthetist aesthetic with the formation of what Bernard later called the School of Pont-Aven. As with Cloisonism, the term Synthetism was first used as the label for an art movement in reference to a major exhibition event. In this case it was *L'Exposition de peintures du groupe impressionniste et synthétiste* held in the *Café des arts* operated by a certain M. Volpini and located on the Champ-de-Mars, the grounds of the Universal Exposition of 1889. It remains uncertain precisely who first proposed what was clearly intended as a kind of *Salon des refusés* in respect to the official "Beaux-Arts" exhibition of this World's Fair. At the latter exhibition a limited number of works by leading Impressionists constituted the most progressive painting displayed, with Neo-Impressionism as completely excluded as Gauguin and his associates would surely have been.

We can deduce that the organization of the Café Volpini alternative exhibition began late and proceeded at a hectic but fitful pace. It must have been either shortly before or after the fair opened on May 6 that Gauguin's friend Emile Schuffenecker discovered that the proprietor had experienced problems with a promised delivery of mirrors for his walls and was thus willing to accept Schuffenecker's proposal of red drapes and paintings instead.[48] Gauguin was already in Pont-Aven when he learned of Schuffenecker's success;

[45]   See T. Reff, "Degas and the Literature of his Time," in *French 19th Century Painting and Literature*, ill. nos. 126-27, 137.

[46]   E. Verhaeren, "Chronique bruxelloise: l'Exposition des XX à Bruxelles," *La Revue indépendante*, VI, March 1888, pp. 456-57.

[47]   Stuckey, cat. no. 32, fig. 1.

[48]   As recounted in Bernard, *Souvenirs*, pp. 13-15.

he sent (*M*LXXVII) a list of those to be invited (including Guillaumin, Bernard and Vincent and excluding the Pointillists "Pissarro, Seurat etc" with no mention of Lautrec or Anquetin, although the latter, presumably on Bernard's suggestion, did ultimately participate) and then returned to Paris himself. Schuffenecker and Bernard were left to make most of the arrangements. Schuffenecker, soliciting paintings by Vincent from Théo, was turned down, and Guillaumin immediately declined for himself as well.[49] Bernard handled the lion's share of publicity and catalogue publication. In an unpublished letter inscribed "Monday, 10 a.m.," Bernard wrote his friend Aurier that the exhibition was to open the following Thursday. We can deduce that the opening was planned for either Thursday May 23 or 30, since Gauguin, who presumably attended, returned the first week in June to Pont-Aven.[50] In the same letter Bernard urged Albert Aurier to publish a catalogue of the exhibition in a special issue of his journal *Le Moderniste*, but this did not materialize and the eventual separate catalogue was published only sometime after July 6.[51] In fact, Aurier did announce the exhibition in the June 27 issue of *Le Moderniste*, and in subsequent issues he published eight graphics by various participating artists, as well as articles on other topics by both Bernard and Gauguin. The results of the exhibition were revealed in an August 26 letter to Schuffenecker by Bernard, then staying near St. Malo on the northern coast of Brittany. Bernard explained that the exhibition had produced no sales or reviews (sic) and that he had had to deposit a number of excess catalogues with the colour merchant Père Tanguy.[52] All in all the effort seems to have had little immediate impact on the French art world and given little satisfaction to the exhibitors.

The event nonetheless signified the first public emergence of a group of painters with Gauguin as their implicit leader and with the establishment of a counter-tendency to Pointillism as their intended purpose. Despite its disappointing short-term results, this first major manifestation of the Pont-Aven group and what has become known as the Synthetist style rightly deserves attention as a watershed in the history of modern French painting. Apart from the endlessly disputed question whether it was Bernard or Gauguin who first practised the fully developed Pont-Aven style, it was clearly Gauguin, the more mature artist, who had been the guiding spirit of group activities during 1888 in Pont-Aven. During the summer of 1886, he had already been recognized as a leading independent within the multinational artists' colony there. His disciple Charles Laval not only accompanied him to Martinique in 1887 and subsequently to Brittany, but imitated him in style to the point that many critics have described his work as slavish copying.

If on his return in late 1887 from Martinique Gauguin was catapulted into the *milieu* of the "Impressionists of the Petit Boulevard," he soon became their acknowledged leader. During the summer of 1888 in Pont-Aven Bernard freely admitted his awe for the overpowering talent of Gauguin (*CL*539), and late that year Schuffenecker wrote Gauguin a paean: praising him as the equal of Delacroix and Rembrandt, albeit, ironically, not yet Degas.[53] The Volpini exhibition offers further proof of Gauguin's ascendency among his friends and acquaintances represented there. Placing his list of works first in the catalogue was alphabetically unwarranted, and he seems also to have been given the special distinction of a whole wall to himself.[54] Laval, at least, wanted this manifestation to signal the emergence of Gauguin as the recognized leader of the Pont-Aven school (*M*LXXVII). This was the effect produced on several of the future Nabi artists such as Paul Sérusier and Maurice Denis who were profoundly affected in their own art by visiting the Volpini café. In his own writings Denis used the terms "Pont-Aven School" and "School of Gauguin" interchangeably.

However, as contemporary critical reviews document, the exhibition scarcely gave a crystal clear image of what the new *Synthétiste* style was all about, either in practice or theory. Certain participants like Schuffenecker, Leon Fauché and Georges-Daniel (de Monfreid) were better classified by the label *Impressionniste*, and there was some uncertainty as to who best exemplified Synthetism. Jules Antoine, the only critic to address this question systematically, singled out Anquetin and in lesser degree Bernard, as Synthetists while describing Gauguin as still Impressionist, a fact which must have irked the latter as much as Fénéon's attribution of his indebtedness to Anquetin.[55] In fact, Antoine cited Anquetin's *Mower* and *Avenue de Clichy* as the most Synthetist examples in the exhibition, suggesting that these Cloisonist paintings were still perceived as among the most advanced works presented in terms of abstraction of line and use of flat colouration. Significantly, Bernard would once later classify both paintings as already Synthetist, although elsewhere he called them Cloisonist.[56] Why Antoine placed Anquetin before Gauguin as a Synthetist doubtless lies in Gauguin's failure to display his major work *The Vision after the Sermon* (pl.7) at the Volpini restaurant, perhaps because it had been so roundly criticized when presented at the Brussels exhibition society *Les Vingt*.[57] There Gauguin's twelve canvases constituted his largest public display since the final Impressionist exhibition in 1886. Indeed, the consignment of twelve paintings at the 1889 *Les Vingt* was only slightly less imposing than the fourteen paintings and three drawings present at the Volpini café, which in fact included at least seven of the paintings previously displayed

---

[49] On June 16th Théo informed Vincent (*T*10) that he had first agreed to cooperate with the Volpini project, but then decided against sending Vincent's works "to the Universal Exhibition by the back stairs." In Gauguin's letter to Théo (*G*21) sent early June from Pont-Aven he defends the Volpini enterprise and refers to Guillaumin's abstention. It was doubtless Guillaumin to whom Gauguin referred to twice in *M*CVIII as "G," and this letter was likely written to Bernard from Pont-Aven after Gauguin's return in early June, since it clearly defends his own participation in considerable quantity and allows for Bernard's doing the same. *Cf. P-I*, pp. 254 and 288, n. 4.

[50] In *T*10 of June 16 Théo states that "Gauguin went off two weeks ago." The hypothesis that *M*CVIII was written after Gauguin's return to Pont-Aven (note 47 above) implies that the selection of paintings for display was not yet so final that additions by Bernard could not be made.

[51] Fénéon, "Autre groupe impressioniste," of that date still mentions only a "catalogue manuscrit...que vous trouverez sur le comptoir." (Fénéon, I, p. 159).

[52] Information contained in an unpublished letter of August 26 from Bernard to Schuffenecker (cited *P-I*, p. 290, n. 32, but now in the Bibliothèque Nationale, Paris); see also *M*LXXXVI.

[53] English trans. in *P-I*, pp. 236-37.

[54] Bernard, *Souvenirs*, p. 14.

[55] J. Antoine, "Impressionistes et synthétistes," *Art et critique*, *I*, November 9, 1889.

[56] *Cf. Notes*, p. 676, and *Anquetin 1932*, pp. 594-95.

[57] See *P-I*, p. 249.

in Belgium.[58] Taken together, the two selections of work by Gauguin constituted a survey of his production covering principally the Martinique period of 1887 and Pont-Aven and Arles of the following year. The painting *In the Waves* (almost certainly cat. no. 60, pl.1), the watercolour *Eve* (cat. no. 59) and perhaps the two as yet unidentified "decorative" pastel drawings were apparently the only pieces dating from 1889 which were openly displayed at the Exposition Volpini.

Bernard, too, seems to have wished to span the years 1887-88 with his selection of canvases, since his catalogue list included the *Ragpickers: Iron Bridges at Asnières* and *Woman Tending Geese* (cat. no. 92) from 1887 and the *Breton Women* 1888. Notwithstanding the definitive Pont-Aven or Synthetist style of this last named painting, with its curvilinear, medievalizing Cloisonist outlines and "stained-glass window" analogies, the most stylistically advanced work contributed by both Gauguin and Bernard would seem to have been the series of zincographs which each artist had produced early in 1889 (cat. nos. 58 and 109). No public sales of these zincographs are known to have occurred, but circulation among artist friends and publication of several stylistically related drawings in the catalogue and *Le Moderniste* suggest a greater importance for these prints as a sure instance of Synthetist style than is generally appreciated.[59] The exclusively "Breton" subject matter of the Bernard series contrasts somewhat with the Martinique-Pont-Aven-Arles subject references of Gauguin, and the relatively sober treatment by Gauguin of his themes is visibly different from the extravagantly stylized quality of Bernard's production. Despite these differences the collaborative undertaking by Bernard and Gauguin in Paris at the *atelier* of Schuffenecker should be considered the prerequisite effort for eventual collaboration of the three in organizing the Volpini exhibition and the single most important indication that a joint Pont-Aven-Nabi stylistic tradition would shortly coalesce.

Perhaps the most interesting speculation about the Volpini exhibition concerns not what was but what might have been. The alternatives are not only obvious but well documented. Although he may or may not have been invited, Lautrec did not participate, a fact for which Gauguin in early July felt obliged to offer his excuses to Théo (*G*24). Had it been present, his *Circus Fernardo* doubtless would have rivalled Anquetin's contribution in terms of Cloisonist-Synthetist style and provided an interesting comparison to the two studies of horses (*see* pp. 246, 250) which Anquetin also included. Above all, the work of Vincent from the years 1887-early 1889 could have provided a rich assortment of Japanist-Cloisonist-Synthetist canvases. His *Bridges at Asnières* (*fig. 29*) could have offered a tangible point of comparison with the painting of the same subject by Bernard. And the respective versions by Vincent and Gauguin of the "night café" theme (*F* 463, *W* 305) might just as easily have been available for joint display at the Volpini exhibition had the earlier association been more genial and long-lasting. As it was, the exhibited work, while comprising, zincographs included, slightly over one hundred items, scarcely presented a clear picture of the full range of either Cloisonist or Pont-Aven style which had been produced by early 1889 within the full circle of artists who had contributed most to the creation of the Cloisonist-Synthetist movement.

The paucity of truly informative review notices for the Volpini exhibition meant that

Fig. 29
Vincent van Gogh
The Bridges at Asnières,
1887,
oil on canvas
(E.G. Bührle, Zürich).

the term "Synthetism" was not adequately explained in print at the time. Albert Aurier, in a one-paragraph account which appeared late June, limited his explanation of "Synthetism" to the following observation:

> In most of the works shown, and especially in those of Gauguin, Bernard, Anquetin etc., I seem to have noticed a marked tendency towards a synthesis of drawing, composition, and colour, as well as an effort to simplify these means of expression which appears very interesting to me at this particular moment when empty prowess and cheap tricks are the rule.[60]

In this highly tentative explanation Aurier nonetheless attempted to stress the unifying qualities which informed a group effort. It is noteworthy that he defines the Synthetist aesthetic exclusively in terms of elements of style, with an emphasis on line and colour contributing equally to the goal of composition. While neither Cloisonism nor Japanism are specifically mentioned, it is unlikely that these terms were far from the mind of a writer

58   Titles listed in Wildenstein, "Correspondances," preceding p. 1.

59   Among the several drawings from the Volpini catalogue which were reproduced in July and August issues of Aurier's *Le Moderniste* were those illustrated in *P-I*, pp. 260-61, 266-67.

60   Both the present quotation and that given *P-I*, p. 260, were published in "Concurrence," *Le Moderniste*, I, June 27, 1889, p. 74. The latter is listed correctly in *P-I*, p. 290, no. 25, but the former incorrectly as May 26 (*P-I*, p. 289, n. 16) doubtless because of its erroneous inclusion in *Oeuvres posthumes* (pp. 334-35, 344) under a listing of that earlier date. The significance of the late June date for what was the first periodical announcement of the exhibition is to strengthen our impression (notes 48-49 above) that Gauguin had returned to Pont-Aven before the exhibition was completely installed.

Fig. 30
Emile Bernard
A Nightmare—Portraits of Emile Schuffenecker,
Emile Bernard and Paul Gauguin,
c. 1888,
crayon on paper
(Musée du Louvre, Paris).

already in intimate contact with the artists being discussed, particularly with Bernard. The anti-naturalism of this aesthetic stance is equally apparent, if admittedly clothed in the attack upon "empty prowess and cheap tricks" which would become the standard accusation within *avant-garde* circles against the "trompe d'oeil" tradition of Beaux-Arts naturalism. This stance had already been taken in Dujardin's definition of Cloisonism, which clearly anticipates Aurier's pithy outline of synthetist principles. Aurier hardly can be considered to have either championed Gauguin or satisfactorily defined the aspirations of the artists represented at the Volpini exhibition. He nevertheless emerges here as the harbinger of his own later identification of Gauguin as the leader of the Symbolist movement in painting.

Bernard once cited Aurier as having suggested the term Synthetism for use at the Volpini exhibition.[61] It is equally likely that Aurier's use of the term derived from utterances by Gauguin, whether known directly or indirectly from mutual friends like Schuffenecker, whom Bernard, probably at the time of the Volpini show, pictured with Gauguin and himself in a somewhat ironically intended drawing bearing the title "Synthétisme" (*fig. 30*). The appended notation "a nightmare" (*un cauchemar*) is in the spirit of Gauguin's later punning of "symboliste" into "zimbalist" (for cymbal player)[62] and to his virtually caricatural, if well meant, "Soyez Symboliste" (be a symbolist) portrait of Jean Moréas (*fig. 31*), author of the 1886 Symbolist Manifesto for literature.

It is now generally accepted that the brief manuscript called by Gauguin "Notes Synthétiques" was written as early as *circa* 1885.[63] As with his letter to Schuffenecker of

Fig. 31
Paul Gauguin
Be a Symbolist—Portrait of Jean Moréas,
1891,
brush and ink
(collector unknown).

the same year (*M*XI), in which he associates lines of certain directions, colours and even numbers with certain moral or even mystical significances, these "Notes" may nonetheless reflect more his personal interpretation of standard nineteenth century art theory based upon traditional allegorical modes of thought than any involvement by 1885 with the sophisticated aesthetic beginning to emanate from the poets and theoreticians of the Symbolist Movement in literature. In fact, Gauguin's greatest praise at the time was reserved for Cézanne. His anti-music and literature stance in the opening *paragone* section of the "Notes" definitely was at odds with contemporary Symbolist writers such as Dujardin and Téodor de Wyzéwa, co-founders of *La Wagnérienne* in 1885 and forceful champions of the synaesthetic fusion of the various art forms as modelled on the *Gesamtkunstwerk* of Wagner and the *Correspondances* of Baudelaire. Only a half decade later in winter 1890-91 was Gauguin granted the laurel wreath as painter prince of the Symbolist movement by such luminaries as Stéphane Mallarmé. Even then, there is some doubt as to the depth of Gauguin's interest in and understanding of the theories enunciated in these august intellectual circles.

Yet, it would be unwise completely to write off Gauguin as an art theorist. Although sparse, there remain hints, especially in his letters to artist friends written in 1888, that he

[61]   *L'Aventure*, p. 33.

[62]   Quoted in Perruchot, p. 200.

[63]   Found with Eng. trans. in *Paul Gauguin, carnet de croquis*, eds. R. Cogniat and J. Rewald (New York: Hammer Galleries, 1962).

was seriously concerned with finding theoretical justifications for the changes then transpiring in his art style. During that summer, for example, apart from a letter written in July (*M*LXVI) ascribing a Japanese influence to *Boys Wrestling* (*W* 273), he wrote to Vincent in Arles in some detail about the *Vision after the Sermon* (*G*9). After describing the colour scheme and subject matter, Gauguin for the first time indicates his wish to express in the figures "a grand rustic and *superstitious* simplicity." In addition he stresses that his use of scale is arbitrary and that the "struggle" exists only in the minds of those who had heard the sermon on the theme of Jacob's struggle with the angel. This second subject reference thus not only derives from the great fresco with the same subject executed by Delacroix in the church of St. Sulpice in Paris, but involves a dualist theme of vision ("la lutte dans son paysage non nature et disproportionnée) versus reality ("les gens nature") inherent to the Christian theme of the conflict between spirit (the angel) and matter (Jacob).

Confirmation that this dualist preoccupation was not incidental to a single observation or painting is offered by Gauguin's remarks concerning the *Self-Portrait called Les Misérables* (cat. no. 52) which he sent to Vincent, after the latter had requested an exchange of portraits among Gauguin, Bernard and himself. Having already spoken in a letter of August 14 to Schuffenecker (*M*LXVII) of art as "an abstraction" and of his "previous researches where synthesis of a form and a colour does not consider either as dominant," Gauguin in October (*M*LXXI) described his *Les Misérables* as a "complete abstraction." Bernard, too, then working together with Gauguin in Pont-Aven, must have been aware of his older comrade's anti-naturalist ideas on art. The description of his *Les Misérables* to Schuffenecker, like another to Vincent (*G*10), identifies Gauguin as an "impressionniste" painter in the role of Jean Valjean, the bandit hero of Victor Hugo's *Les Misérables*. This self-identification also betrays a penchant for dualistic content on several levels of interpretation. The sitter not only assumes the double role of Jean Valjean and the "personified" Impressionist painter, but contrasts the exterior bandit's mask of the hero with "his nobility and inner gentleness," inevitably calling to mind Gauguin's self-characterization as part civilized and part "a savage from Peru." The background in the painting is credited with having a "symbolist side" suggesting alternatively Persian tapestry and wallpaper of a young girl's room and, on a higher level, the pure artistic virginity of the painter. Whereas a number of other associations will be cited in the catalogue entry below, it is sufficient here to characterize Gauguin's remarks as the earliest known evidence of incipient Synthetist-Symbolist art theory. The intended content in this canvas and other related works is already compounded by iconographic and philosophic associations which approximate the complex suggestiveness of Symbolist poetry.

It is tempting to believe that Vincent had little sympathy for Gauguin's strongly anti-naturalist bias in art, since he made no secret of his great love of Realist painters and writers. Indeed, in a rare surviving letter to Gauguin shortly predating the latter's arrival in Arles (*CL*544a), Vincent stated: "I always think my artistic conceptions extremely ordinary when compared to yours." Thereafter he adds, "I forget everything in favour of the external beauty of things, which I cannot reproduce, for in my pictures I render it as something ugly and coarse, whereas nature seems perfect to me." Yet, to take this literally

Fig. 32
Vincent van Gogh
Self-Portrait [Dedicated to Paul Gauguin],
1888,
oil on canvas
(Fogg Art Museum, Cambridge, Massachusetts,
Maurice Wertheim Collection).

as betokening merely a mixed Realist-Expressionist credo would be to oversimplify. In the same letter, written in reaction to Gauguin's description of the (not yet received) *Les Misérables*, Vincent describes his own *Self-Portrait* (*fig. 32*) which eventually went to Gauguin, as representing "a simple bonze worshiping the eternal Buddha," thus linking his own self-identification consciously or not with the kind of literary-philosophic associations found in *Les Misérables*. The vague halo-effect around the head and the pseudo-monastic garb sometimes noted in the *Self-Portrait* by Vincent are less overtly literary, and thus more Symbolist in their sense of ambiguity, than the title references in Gauguin's work.

Fig. 33
Emile Bernard
Madeleine in the Bois d'Amour,
1888,
oil on canvas
(Musée d'Orsay, Paris).

In this same letter, Vincent described a just completed landscape, which he intended as decoration for Gauguin's room, as "The Poet's Garden" (actually the small park in front of Vincent's Yellow House at Arles; *see* discussion cat. no. 24). He explained that this title was intended to suggest not only the near-by Avignon residence of Petrarch, but "at the same time [the residence] of the new poet living here—Paul Gauguin." As in his slightly earlier *Portrait of the Belgian Painter Eugène Boch* (*F* 462), which he sub-titled "The Poet," Vincent's literary references are as freely inventive, and perhaps less tinged with allegory, than those of Gauguin or Bernard. Little wonder that a year later, Vincent would remonstrate so vehemently with both Gauguin and Bernard (see *M*XCV and *B*21) against their representation of Christian themes with identifiable subjects such as "Christ in the Garden of Olives" and an "Annunciation." Instead he advocated that Bernard return to less overtly "literary" paintings such as *Breton Women in the Meadow* or *Madeleine Reclining in the Bois d'Amour* (*fig. 33*). Like his own "Olive Orchard", "Rising Sun" or "Reaper" subjects, those earlier paintings by Bernard provided sensations of "joy, suffering, anger or a smile" without risking the "counterfeit, affected" quality of what Vincent (*now derogatorily*) calls "abstractions." Doubtless Vincent recalled Gauguin's preference for this term, but feared it had been redefined to include stylized, medievalizing religious allegory at the expense of studying nature itself. Vincent therefore must be considered still Realist in his systematic rejection of overt religious or allegorical imagery in contemporary painting. Yet he was no less intensely interested than were Gauguin and Bernard in pure combinations of, and harmony between, the elements of line and colour as a means of evoking a profoundly human, frequently moral or religious response to the subject depicted.

Cloisonism and Symbolism, summer 1889-early 1891

The long-term after-effects of the Volpini exhibition were as profound as the short-term results had been meagre. This impact was felt in two spheres of activity: painting *per se* and art theory. In the history of French painting it may be considered the primary catalyst for the formation of a circle of stylistically related artists with Gauguin as their acknowledged leader, whether or not the later designation of the group as the "School of Pont-Aven" is truly deserved. Previous to this the school had consisted at most of Bernard, Gauguin and Laval, and it was scarcely identifiable as such at the Volpini exhibition. However, when Gauguin returned in June 1889 to Pont-Aven and subsequently to near-by Le Pouldu on the Brittany coast, within his entourage he added to Laval such disciples as the Dutchman Jakob Meyer de Haan and the co-founder with Maurice Denis of the Nabi fraternity, Paul Sérusier. In this respect, Sérusier's famous small panel painting, *The Talisman: The Bois d'Amour* (cat. no. 137), which in late summer 1888 was painted under Gauguin's instructions, is better understood as a premonition of the style which Sérusier would adopt the following year than as supportive proof that a group style came to maturity in 1888 in Pont-Aven. Even Bernard's *Breton Women* and Gauguin's *Vision* are virtually unique creations in each artist's production of that year, and it is understandable that no proclamation of a common artistic front was forthcoming at the time. Yet in the following year Sérusier credited the Volpini exhibition with having caused the scales of artistic ignorance to fall from his eyes, whereafter he departed to Pont-Aven seeking repentance for having previously failed sufficiently to appreciate Gauguin's genius.[64] Denis has recorded the indebtedness of himself and other Nabi artists to Gauguin, who in turn received their moral support during winter 1890-91 when he was seeking the means to depart for Tahiti.

This group movement coalesced during the approximate year and a half between June 1889 and November 1890, all but four months of which (a Paris visit of early February-early June 1890) Gauguin spent in the relative isolation of Brittany, principally at the inn of Marie Henry in Le Pouldu. Here, accompanied by Meyer de Haan and visited for shorter periods by Sérusier and Laval, Gauguin completed his major wood relief, *Be in Love and You'll be Happy* (Gray 76), which he cited to Vincent (*G*29) as having a "literary aspect" and ironically intended symbolism. Along with numerous still life and landscape subjects, his painted *oeuvre* of late 1889 included several religious or quasi-

---

[64] H. Dorra, "Munch, Gauguin and Norwegian Painters in Paris," *Gazette des beaux-arts*, LXXXVIII, November 1976, p. 180, n. 10, documents that the Volpini exhibition remained open until *circa* early November 1889, thus maximizing its usefulness to receptive artists.

La Belle Angèle

Je 'cherche à mettre dans ces figures désolées, le sauvage
que j'y vois et qui est en moi aussi. Ici en Bretagne
les paysans ont un air du moyen âge et n'ont pas
l'air de penser un instant que Paris existe et qu'on soit
en 1889. Tout le contraire du midi. Ici tout est rude
comme la langue Bretonne, bien fermé (il semble à
tout jamais. Les costumes sont aussi presque symbolique
influencés par les superstitions du catholicisme. Voyez le
dos corsage une croix, la tête enveloppée d'une marmotte
noire comme les religieuses. avec cela
les figures sont presque asiatiques

jaunes et triangulaires, sévères. Que diable je veux
aussi consulter la nature mais je ne veux pas en
retirer ce que j'y vois et ce qui vient à ma pensée.
Les roches, les costumes sont noirs et jaunes; je ne
peux pourtant pas les mettre blonds et coquets.

Fig. 34

Fig. 35

religious themes which grew out of the *Vision* and Brittany Eve themes of the previous
year. Even if one accepts *La Belle Angèle* (*fig. 34*) as being merely a wedding portrait
rather than alluding to sacred imagery as well, his canvases *The Yellow Christ* (cat.
no. 61), *Christ in the Garden of Olives* (cat. no. 66) and the *Breton Calvary: The Green
Christ* (cat. no. 65) testify to Gauguin's intense interest at the time in Christian themes of
personal trial, suffering and martyrdom. This is not to claim that with these examples he
sought or expected approval from literary Symbolist circles, since he scarcely could have
known that precisely these paintings would in 1889 be cited by Albert Aurier as exemplary
of his Symbolist stature. Possibly Vincent's November 1891 injunction against such
Christian themes (see *B*21, *M*XCV, *G*29 and *G*31) had some effect, since such overt
references to traditional Christian imagery virtually disappear from Gauguin's subsequent
oeuvre or are presented obliquely in combination with other, usually exotic iconographic
references.

In December 1889 Gauguin wrote to Vincent again (*G*32) not only denying his deep
involvement with Christian themes, but stating that he could capture a religious sentiment
through presenting scenes of peasant labour in Brittany in terms of appropriate colour
juxtapositions and the regional costumes and facial characteristics, which, thanks to the
force of "catholic superstition," he felt were "symbolic" to the point of sometimes
suggesting a cross (*see fig. 35*). As an instance of rendering peasants at work in native
costumes "as if they were in a church," he cited his *Seaweed Gatherers* (*fig. 36*), which
was further described as combining Japanese stylizations with an observation of nature
transported by the power of dream. Gauguin gave the theme of this painting as "the
struggle of life, its sad or somber quality and submission to laws of misfortune." In this

Fig. 34
Paul Gauguin
La Belle Angèle (*Portrait of Mme Sartre*),
1889,
oil on canvas
(Musée d'Orsay, Paris).

Fig. 35
Letter from Paul Gauguin to Vincent van Gogh,
c. second week of December 1889
(Rijksmuseum Vincent van Gogh, Amsterdam).

Fig. 36
Paul Gauguin
Seaweed Gatherers,
1889,
oil on canvas
(Folkwang Museum, Essen).

anti-allegorical, anti-naturalist and anti-literary approach to art, Gauguin doubtless was hoping to convince Vincent of their common aim. And if his painting style here retained a marked Cloisonist-Synthetist character, the art theory which supported it was already articulated in classically Symbolist terms.

One can surmise that Gauguin was more than mildly surprised that it was Vincent and not himself whose art Albert Aurier chose to celebrate the very first, issue (January 1890) of his new Symbolist journal, *Le Mercure de France*. The young critic, previously unknown to Vincent, was well-known to Gauguin who already had published two articles in Aurier's *Le Moderniste*.[65] It was Bernard who knew Aurier best, having met him during spring 1887 in St. Briac. As early as January 1888 Bernard began to encourage Aurier's support on behalf of Degas, Pissarro and Gauguin, whom he still called Impressionists but mentioned in the same breath as the great Symbolist poets Verlaine and Mallarmé.[66] Hereafter at regular intervals Bernard urged various specific publishing plans upon Aurier until the latter's premature death in 1892. There can be little doubt that it was Bernard who suggested Vincent as the first subject for Aurier's series in the *Mercure* to be devoted to *Les Isolés* ("the isolated ones") and that Bernard supplied at least some of the information

---

65   Cited *P-I*, p. 528, nos. 41-42.

66   *L'Aventure*, pp. 15-24, alas suggests a conflation of events, which *L'Aventure ms.* (ch. IX, p. 68) attributes to both 1887 and 1888. That Bernard and Aurier had met late spring of 1887 (presumably at St. Briac) is indicated by a letter dated January 17, 1888 (*Aurier Archive*), in which Bernard requests Aurier's support in publicizing, via lithographic reproductions in a proposed periodical, the display at Boussod and Valadon of works by Degas, Pissarro and Gauguin.

on which the article was based. By summer 1890 he certainly had urged the same treatment for Gauguin,[67] although since March of that year this apparently already was planned by the critic himself (T29).

Still more surprising than the choice of Vincent for the lead article of the series is the unabashed manner in which he is treated as a member of the Symbolist movement. While not called a Symbolist outright, as Gauguin would be in the March 1891 issue, Vincent was no less the first painter to be so named.[68] Following an extended quotation of freely transposed verses from Baudelaire's *Fleurs du mal*, Aurier presents his readers with a cascade of images which equate Vincent's paintings with the coruscating iridescence of various gems, glazes, metals and crystals. His second analytic salvo, to be sure, gives due credit to Vincent's Realist-oriented Dutch artistic heritage, and with typically incisive critical insight Frans Hals is singled out as Vincent's most noteworthy earlier artist-countryman. Aurier nonetheless proceeded to characterize Vincent as a naturalist who had supremely transcended the "nature viewed through a temperament" aesthetic attributed to Zola and his Realist contemporaries. Aurier, referring to Vincent's illness, explains that the latter perceives "with an abnormal, perhaps even painful, intensity, the imperceptible and secret character of lines and shapes, but still more the colours, tones and nuances which are invisible to healthy eyes and the magic iridescence of forms."

What Aurier said of Vincent hereafter was not as arbitrary in his intention of enlisting Vincent in the Symbolist cause as is usually assumed. He least of all had any external reason to chose Vincent for what amounted to a debut in Symbolist art criticism, and his avowal of personal attraction to the artist remains incontestable; he simply had come to consider Vincent a remarkable artistic personality who deserved designation as "un symboliste." In the same article Aurier specified Vincent as subject to inspiration from the dream and the *Images d'Epinal* (*see* cat. no. 34) and as "simultaneously too simple and too subtle for the bourgeoise contemporary spirit to understand." At the time there was little compulsion for Vincent to consider himself a member of any movement, whether Symbolist or not. Yet, in his letter of acknowledgment for the article to Aurier (CL626a), Vincent objected only that no credit was given to his own indebtedness to Delacroix, Monticelli and Gauguin and not that Aurier was unwarranted in describing Vincent as having transcended his known Realist aesthetic credo.

Aurier's article is more systematic in defining Vincent as a Symbolist than is generally appreciated. He clearly anticipated his study of Gauguin by stating that Vincent loved material reality "only as a kind of marvellous language destined to render the Idea." In what must be considered a conscious paraphrase of a cardinal concept of the literary Symbolist Manifesto of 1886 by Jean Moréas, namely "to clothe Idea in perceptible form," Aurier goes on to describe Vincent as "a symbolist who senses the continual necessity to reclothe his ideas with precise, ponderable and tangible forms, with intensely corporeal and material envelopes." He then calls Vincent's "brilliant symphonies of colours and lines . . . only simple *means* of expression, only simple *methods* of symbolization," concluding that "if one refuses, in fact, to admit these idealist tendencies underlying his naturalist art, a major part of his *oeuvre* which we are examining would remain in large part incomprehensible."

Among the several examples cited in illustration of this interpretation are Vincent's landscapes with figures, the Sower and the Drawbridge themes (see cat. nos. 18 and 27, and 14), and his figural studies of *La Berceuse* (cat. no. 34, pl.19) and the *Zouave* (cat. no. 15). In all of these Aurier discovered a willful tendency towards simplification and naivety in the service of reaching a popular and aesthetically humble audience. We quite likely have Bernard to thank that Aurier had made clear Vincent's greater affinity for his native Dutch Realist tradition than for such late Medieval models as, for example, the "Italian primitives." The whole article, in fact, may be considered an interpretation of Vincent's thoughts on art as contained in Vincent's correspondence to Bernard, but as viewed by Aurier in the light of his rapidly maturing definition of Symbolism in painting. On his part, Vincent merely hinted to Aurier that dividing artists too strictly into categories incurred the risk of engendering unnecessary abrasions among them. At the same time he doubtless pleased the critic when he explained that his two sunflower paintings, then on view at *Les Vingt* in Brussels, in their special qualities of colour "also express an idea symbolizing 'gratitude' " (*see* cat. no. 33, pls.18 and 20). The distinguished Belgian writer and friend of Dujardin, Emile Verhaeren, on viewing Vincent's art as exhibited at *Les Vingt* (February 1891), described him as a Cloisonist, a Japanist and "above all, decorative" in intent. One may herewith better appreciate the degree in which Vincent's aims were understood by leading contemporary critics to be in keeping with the Cloisonist-Synthetist-Symbolist tendency in painting.

This view, moreover, finds support in the writings of Maurice Denis, who in August 1890, shortly before he turned twenty, published pseudonymously the essay "A Definition of Neo-Traditionalism" which opened with the following, now famous injunction:

> Be reminded that a painting—before being a battle horse, a nude woman or some anecdote—is essentially a flat surface covered over with colours assembled in a certain order.[69]

Alternatively viewed as the first clarion call for truly abstract painting or as an attempt to define Symbolism in painting, it was less either of these than a *résumé* of the theories he and Sérusier had discussed at length the previous winter in an attempt to form the theoretical basis for the Nabi movement. Our earliest record of this aesthetic stance is contained in a letter from Sérusier to Denis of *circa* mid-October 1889 which called for an art based upon the "immutable principles" of the "blessed primitives" and the Japanese

---

[67]   Undated letter (*Aurier Archive*) from Bernard to Aurier, which pleads for a supportive article so that Bernard and Gauguin could leave for Madagascar. This latter designation (following Gauguin's discussion with the wife of Redon, who was from this island) and a reference to the *Mercure de France*, which commenced publishing January 1890, ensure the summer 1890 date of this letter.

[68]   Aurier, pp. 257-65; a composite Eng. trans. of this important article is available in L. Nochlin, *Impressionism and Post-Impressionism, 1874-1904* (Englewood Cliffs, N.J.: Prentice-Hall, 1966), pp. 135-39, and B.M. Welsh-Ovcharov, *Van Gogh in Perspective* pp. 55-57, although the latter precedes the former in original sequence.

[69]   *Théories*, p. 1 (first published under the pseudonym "Pierre-Louis" in *Art et critique*, August 23 and 30, 1890); Nochlin, *Impressionism*, pp. 187-97, who observes that the article "might more aptly have been entitled 'A Definition of Symbolism'," publishes a somewhat abbreviated translation of it.

Fig. 37
Louis Anquetin
The Woman in Red,
1890,
pastel on paper
(Musée de Beaux-Arts, Tournai).

(plus, in lesser measure, such "exceptional geniuses" as Rembrandt, Delacroix and Manet). Such models could provide "laws of Harmony in line and colour" and are "innate within . . . all unspoiled men."[70] These principles must be tempered by individual artistic personality or by collective effort (as in Egyptian or Gothic art), which "bestows unity" on the harmony of principles and which can be aided in only a small degree by either science or the right subject choices. Personality is termed an abstract and free quality diametrically opposed to skill, which is merely handicraft rather than art. Although first formulated at a time Sérusier had been sharing a room and discussing art with Gauguin for two weeks, there is no trace in this letter of the words Synthetism or Symbolism. For the structure of Sérusier's thought one is inclined to suppose a Neo-Platonist or Hegelian origin, with which thought systems the artist is known to have been concerned at the time.[71] Denis later described his "Definition" as the "Manifesto of Symbolism," but in his essay the word symbolism appears only once and synthetism only twice without systematic explanation.[72] Furthermore, Denis cites Gauguin's *Soyez amoureuses* and *Green Christ*, Anquetin's *The Woman in Red*[73] (*see fig. 37*), his own drawings intended to illustrate Verlaine's *Sagesse* and Puvis de Chavannes as models of contemporary art worthy of the great "decorative" traditions of the Hindus, Assyrians, Egyptians, Greeks, Middle Ages and early Renaissance. Even his statement that art should aim to achieve the status of "sacred, hermetic, imposing icons" just barely suggests the mystical or occult side of the Nabi movement in art. In its overall argument against all forms of detailed realism in painting, the article might just as well have been given the title "Definition of Anti-Naturalism," and Denis subsequently abandoned "Neo-Traditionalism" as a term for what alternatively had been identified as Cloisonism, Synthetism or Symbolism. In his

[70]   This letter (Sérusier, pp. 42-45; all but complete Eng. trans. in Nochlin, *Impressionism*, pp. 182-84) was written in response to a philosophical statement made by Denis in a now lost letter to Sérusier, whose answer should be considered to constitute the earliest known written formulation of Nabi art theory. It variously has been speculated that Gauguin and Sérusier were together in Le Pouldu as early as spring (*P-I*, pp. 254-55 and pp. 288-89, nos. 4-7) or August (Guicheteau, p. 24 and nos. 25-26) 1889, but the letters from Sérusier to Denis upon which such speculation rests (Sérusier, pp. 39-45) were in fact written just before or during a two to three-week stay with Gauguin during October 1889 at the inn of Marie Henry. The first part of Sérusier's earliest known letter to Denis from Brittany (pp. 39-41) was clearly written from Pont-Aven, when the former was still surrounded by a group of fellow students from the Academy Julian but planning to leave in a few days for what surely was Le Pouldu. The briefer ending of this letter (pp. 41-42) not only attempts to retract some uncomplimentary remarks made four days earlier in the first part, but contains a postscript reporting Sérusier's having inscribed a quotation from Wagner on the wall of the inn at which he and Gauguin were staying. The wall mentioned unquestionably was that of Marie Henry (see cat. nos. 63 and 126) and not *chez* Destais, where Gauguin spent the month of August with de Haan before returning to Pont-Aven for September. The stay *chez* Destais is cited or alluded to in letters from Gauguin to Théo (*G*33), the colour merchant *Père* Tanguy (unpublished letter at Rijksmuseum Vincent van Gogh) and Bernard (*M*LXXXIV), whereas Gauguin's presence at the inn of Marie Henry began only on October 2 according to her records (Chassé, *Pont-Aven*, p. 25). Moreover, since Sérusier recalled accompanying Gauguin by boat trip to Le Pouldu (Chassé, *Pont-Aven*, p. 23) this dates his second letter to Denis, (i.e., pp. 42-45), which was written two weeks following his arrival and several days before his intended departure for the family residence at Villerville and then four weeks of military service, to *circa* the third week of October 1889. Apart from clarifying a much confused issue of chronology, these considerations emphasize just how specifically the initial formulation of Nabi doctrine depended upon a short period of intimate association and intellectual exchange between Gauguin and Sérusier, with Denis' lost letter to Sérusier having played a major catalytic role. Indeed, Sérusier's first visit to Le Pouldu must have involved a virtual conversion to the cause of Gauguin whose art theory and style he had criticized only a few days before. Gauguin, in turn, had complained to Bernard in a letter of *circa* June 1889 (*M*CVIII) from Pont-Aven that "Sérusier has just arrived and speaks only of his evolution," but won't show his work. This chronology was developed in collaboration with my husband, R.P. Welsh, who is planning an article on the decoration of the inn of Marie Henry in Le Pouldu.

[71]   Guicheteau, p. 8, no. 4, documents his early training by a leading scholar of Plato.

[72]   See "Preface," *Théories*.

[73]   M. Denis in *Théories*, p. 10, comments that this portrait figured in the exhibition of La Société National des Beaux Arts (Champs de Mars), which can be further identified here as having been listed in the above exhibition of 1890 as No. 915 "Femme face" (pastel) now in the collection of the Musée des Beaux Arts in Tournai.

later writings he was consistent in preferring such terms as Synthetism or Symbolism. Under these headings he included not only Gauguin and his Pont-Aven-Nabi followers but also van Gogh, whom he did not hesitate to list as a founding father of Synthetism with Bernard and Gauguin, however more "objective" their "decorative deformations" of nature may have been than the "subjective deformations" of Vincent.[74] Notwithstanding Denis' failure to provide a thorough definition of the Synthetist-Symbolist aesthetic by 1890, his dramatic admonition to look upon painting first in terms of abstract design and then only for its subject reference was unquestionably derived from the personal art theory of Gauguin, most probably filtered through the medium of Sérusier.

Gauguin's self-directed emergence as the champion of a "new" tendency in art has frequently been told.[75] Following the disappointment of the Volpini experience his correspondence repeatedly attests to his various schemes to escape France. Presumably he would be accompanied by one or more friends in founding a "studio of the tropics," with successive preference being shown for Tonkin (now Viet-Nam), Madagascar and some Pacific Island such as Tahiti. The plans always foundered for lack of money and perhaps of will, and the year 1890 was one of a relative desultory artistic production. It was also the year of, first, Vincent's death and then Théo's incapacitating illness, which, with its implication of severe economic consequences, jolted Gauguin into action.

Within a month of learning of Théo's situation, Gauguin was back in Paris, where, rather to his surprise, he was increasingly welcomed within Symbolist literary circles and by the Nabi painters as a fraternal spirit. When he asked for published support for his intended auction sale at the Hôtel Drouot this was amply forthcoming and the unexpectedly successful event took place on February 23, 1891. If Emile Bernard was made uneasy by the articles which lavished exclusive praise on Gauguin before the sale occurred, he must have been thunderstruck by Aurier's article in the March issue of the *Mercure*: "Symbolism in Painting: Paul Gauguin."[76] Here Gauguin was implied to be the founder and reigning genius within Symbolist painting. Having promoted such an article in the first place, Bernard must have felt the betrayal to have been intentionally perpetrated. After the sale Bernard never again spoke to Gauguin, who himself left Marseilles on April 1 for a self-declared, if temporary exile in Tahiti.[77]

Like the Brussels *Les Vingt* and Volpini exhibitions of early 1889, the February 1891 auction with its viewing day afforded witnesses a survey of Gauguin's development from his Martinique canvases of 1887 to nearly the then present. Although there is good reason to believe that Gauguin wished herewith to indicate Martinique as the period when his "synthetist" phase had begun, among the thirty paintings put on sale only two Carribean landscapes were present. With no still life and only six to eight predominantly figural paintings included, his landscape *oeuvre* comprised the dominant aspect of the selection. His 1888 production in this *genre* from Pont-Aven and Arles constituted a commanding, and several 1889 Le Pouldu settings a much lesser, proportion of the sale offerings. One might speculate that this conservative emphasis upon picturesque landscape subjects was prompted by a hope for salability in a market place that had yet to reward him in any great measure; it is striking that only the *Vision* and *La Belle Angèle* among his figural pieces bore unmistakable references to religious iconography. Conversely, these two paintings, along with the *Calvary: Green Christ* and *Christ in the Garden of Olives*, had been available for viewing by the end of 1889 at Boussod and Valadon, and in early 1891 Gauguin publically displayed his wood relief *Be in Love* twice and its counterpart *Be Mysterious and You'll be Happy* (Gray 87) once.[78] There is thus little doubt of his willingness to allow this more overtly "mystical" and Symbolist segment of his production to influence his public reputation, especially if it were to be supported by protestations of sympathy from leading critics within the Symbolist movement.

Following complementary appreciations of his art by Octave Mirbeau and Roger Marx,[79] the publication of Aurier's "Symbolism in Painting: Paul Gauguin" not only identified Gauguin as the major figure within this recent phenomenon, but attempted an all-embracing definition of what a Symbolist work of plastic art embodied. Granting that Aurier's five elements necessary to a Symbolist painting suggested to the positivist-socialist Pissarro an errant and backward mysticism and eventually seemed too "metaphysical" and unconcerned with painting *per se* even to Denis,[80] they nonetheless established a definition which has remained a useful critical tool down to the present. His first category, "Ideaist," is the most general and pertains to the Platonic notion of pure forms to which the direct quotation from Plato which heads the article also alludes. The notion that the world of "real forms" is actually illusory is in keeping with the anti-positivist trend of Aurier's whole article, a trend present a year earlier when he described Vincent as an "Idea" artist. As articulated for Gauguin, moreover, it is necessary to understand that the category Ideaist art is ahistorical, which is to say everlasting or as relevant to the art of all historical periods in which realism is subservient to an art of ideas as to late nineteenth century French art in particular. The secondary category, that of Symbolism (and for that matter the other three categories as well) is presented as similarly ahistorical, although Aurier here calls upon the authority of Swedenborg for his version of defining a theory of correspondences between the spiritual and natural worlds which allows the Idea, as with Moréas, to be "expressed by forms." The third or "Synthetic" characteristic of this type of art, on the other hand, clearly derives from contemporary usage of the term within the circle of Bernard and Gauguin. On the other hand, in his designation of it as "a transcription of forms or signs according to a general mode of comprehension," Aurier studiously avoids reference to the specifics of either Cloisonist, Pont-Aven, Synthetist or Gauguin's personal style. This de-emphasis upon the virtue of any individual or group style is continued by the fourth category, the "Subjective" element, which in stressing that

[74] In his "De Gauguin et de van Gogh au classicisme," *L'Occident*, May 1909; reprinted *Théories*, pp. 262-78.

[75] *P-I*, pp. 419-56, remains the most informative account of Gauguin's activities winter 1890-91.

[76] Aurier, pp. 205-19 (although first published in the March 1891 issue of the *Mercure de France*, the author's dateline gives February 9 as date of completion).

[77] Perruchot, p. 214, the date formerly given as April 4 for Gauguin's departure from Paris.

[78] See Gray, pp. 195, 207.

[79] O. Mirbeau, "Chronique—Paul Gauguin," *Echo de Paris*, February 16, 1891; reprinted in Mirbeau, *Des Artistes*, I, Paris: Flammarion, 1922, pp. 119-29. *P-I*, p. 441, translates the Roger Marx account from *Le Voltaire*, February 20, and much of that by Mirbeau, pp. 439-41.

[80] *Théories*, p. 267, n. 2.

objects are not "considered as such, but as a sign of the idea as perceived by the subject," sounds suspiciously like a paraphrase of Zola's famous "nature perceived across a temperament." In any case, the contemporary artist is identified with no particular style of art, either ancient or modern. The final "decorative" element is admittedly illustrated by reference to the ancient Egyptians and, in lesser degree, the Greeks and "Primitives," but universalized nevertheless through definition as merely a simultaneous manifestation of the other four elements. Fittingly in terms of his definitions, Aurier ends his article with an impassioned cry that the French state provide Gauguin the same opportunities that it has Puvis de Chavannes to show himself the great muralist he undoubtedly is.

In reference to particular paintings, Aurier aimed more to evoke than to explain, as one might expect from a Symbolist critic. In his extended opening tribute to the *Vision*, he cited but scarcely elucidated its subject of "Jacob Struggling with the Angel" according to either Biblical or Gauguin's own recorded exegesis. Rather, the critic's statement that it "reveals the ineffable charms of the dream, of mystery and of symbolic veils" implies a world of fantasy and fable which could only be desecrated by traditional iconographic analysis. No less vaguely evocative are his citations of the *Calvary*, *Yellow Christ* and Martinique and Brittany landscapes, which are said to "suggest with completely inexpressible words, all that ocean of ideas which the clairvoyant eye can glimpse." The closest Aurier comes to explaining Gauguin's Symbolism is his implication that both the *Garden of Olives* and the *Be in Love* are devoted to a vanity-of-life theme, while *Be Mysterious*, is said "to celebrate the pure joys of esotericism." Since it can be presumed that, if only in conversation, Gauguin would have explained some of his own personal symbolic associations to Aurier (for example, the fox of *Be in Love* as "perversity"), it is logical to assume that Aurier preferred to give these major pictorial statements by Gauguin the most general of religious-philosophical meanings. Gauguin never responded in print, or, as far as is known, in private, to Aurier's article, and it is intriguing to wonder if he appreciated the author's analysis as much as his praise.

The sequel to this landmark article occurred in April 1892, when Aurier published another essay devoted now to "The Symbolist Painters."[81] Following the death of Seurat and departure for Tahiti by Gauguin within a few days of each other at the end of March 1891, the gulf between Neo-Impressionism and Symbolism which shortly before had seemed so wide again began to narrow. Personal rivalries and intrigues remained, but by December 1891 the enterprising art dealer Le Barc de Boutteville could commence a series of exhibitions under the general title "Impressionists and Symbolists" uniting under one roof paintings in both the Pointillist and the Pont-Aven-Nabi manners.

As Aurier was well aware, the year 1891 had witnessed a veritable rainfall of art nomenclature. This was exemplified in the September 1 special issue of *La Plume* devoted to "Innovating Painters," in which Neo-Impressionism was called Chromo-Luminarism, Gauguin, van Gogh and Denis called Neo-Traditionalists or Deformers, and Cézanne, Pissarro and Anquetin called Independents. If the terms Japanism, Cloisonism, Nabi and even Impressionism are added as still current equivalents for the contemporary *avant-garde*, it is understandable that Aurier would again wish to clarify his own use of the term Symbolism as applied to the plastic arts.

What "The Symbolist Painters" amounts to is the definitive identification, right or wrong, of the Pont-Aven-Nabi group of painters as the legitimate standardbearers of this movement in painting. Quite probably supported by the advice of such artists as Bernard, Sérusier and Denis, Aurier here for the first time defines Symbolism as it applies to late nineteenth century French painting, which he continues to view as a modern analogue to all anti-realist or "primitive" art forms ranging from ancient Assyrian to late Medieval in the West and exemplified by Japanese art in the East. As in his one-year earlier study of Gauguin, the formal elements of art (Synthetism and decoration) are seen to function in the service of more spiritual or mystical realms (Ideaism and Symbolism). The formal aspects of Symbolism are said to be pressaged chiefly in the Impressionist and Neo-Impressionist movements, while the anti-materialist aspects are imputed to such precursors as Puvis, Gustave Moreau, Auguste Rodin and especially Odilon Redon, although both camps are credited in varying degrees with an innate understanding of the "mysterious signification" of abstract elements of line, colour and form. Given Aurier's natural, if very French, bent for clear-cut analysis, the confluence of the two proto-Symbolist currents into a single channel inevitably led to his identification of Bernard, Gauguin, Sérusier, Denis and the other Nabi artists as the true practitioners of a fully Symbolist form of art. It also led to his exclusion of Vincent, Lautrec and (except for acknowledging a subsidiary formative role) Anquetin from membership in the Symbolist fraternity. However ironic this may seem, given Aurier's previous personal and intellectual involvements, it has been his classification, brilliant in its simplicity yet flawed in terms of historical sequence, which has prevailed until the recent past and which the present study seeks to modify.

81   Aurier, pp. 293-309.

Bibliographical References

Adhémar Jean Adhémar, *Toulouse-Lautrec: His Complete Lithographs and Drypoints*, New York: Harry N. Abrams, 1965.

Andersen, *Mummy* Wayne Andersen, "Gauguin and a Peruvian Mummy," *The Burlington Magazine*, CIX, April 1967, pp. 238-42.

Andersen, *Paradise* Wayne Andersen, *Gauguin's Paradise Lost*, New York: Viking, 1971.

Andersen, *Le Pouldu* Wayne Andersen, "Gauguin's Motifs from Le Pouldu—Preliminary Report," *The Burlington Magazine*, CXII, September, 1970, pp. 615-20.

Aurier G.-Albert Aurier, *Oeuvres Posthumes*, 4 vols., Paris: Mercure de France, 1893 (where it has seemed useful, the original place of publication has been noted as well).

B The numbered letters from Vincent van Gogh to Emile Bernard as given in *CL*.

Bernard, *Anquetin 1932* Emile Bernard, "Louis Anquetin: artiste peintre," *Mercure de France*, November 1, 1932, pp. 590-607.

Bernard, *Anquetin 1934* Emile Bernard, "Louis Anquetin," *GBA*, XI, February 1934, pp. 108-21.

Bernard, *Gauguin* Emile Bernard, *Souvenirs inédits sur l'artiste peintre Paul Gauguin et ses compagnons*, Lorient: Imprimerie du Nouvel liste du Morbihan, n.d. (1939).

Bernard, *Inventory* Emile Bernard, *Inventaire de mes Toiles fait le 17 Mars 1893 avant de partir en Italie* (MS at the *Archives Musées Nationaux*, Paris; gift of M. M.-A. Bernard-Fort).

Bernard, *L'Aventure* Emile Bernard, "L'Aventure de ma vie," in *Lettres de Paul Gauguin à Emile Bernard, 1888-1891* (Geneva: Pierre Cailler, 1954), pp. 11-46 (if accompanied by "MS", this abbreviation refers to the complete, unpublished autobiography, "Récit d'un passager voyageant à bord de la vie: L'Aventure de ma vie;" now *Archives Musées Nationaux*, Paris).

Bernard, *Notes* Emile Bernard, "Notes sur l'Ecole dite de Pont-Aven," *Mercure de France*, XII, December 1903, pp. 675-82.

Bernard, *Tanguy* Emile Bernard, "Julien Tanguy," *Mercure de France*, LXXXIV, December 1908, pp. 600-16.

Bernard, *Van Gogh* Emile Bernard, "Souvenirs sur Van Gogh," *L'Amour de l'art*, V, 1924, pp. 393-400.

Bodelsen, *Ceramics* Merete Bodelsen, *Gauguin's Ceramics: A Study in the Development of his Art*, London: Faber and Faber, 1964.

Bodelsen, *Wildenstein* Merete Bodelsen, "The Wildenstein-Cogniat Gauguin Catalogue," *The Burlington Magazine*, CVIII, January 1966, pp. 27-38.

Bowness Alan Bowness, exh. cat. *Vincent van Gogh*, London: Hayward Gallery, 1968-69.

Bremen-Lille H. Bock and J.H. Müller, exh. cat. *Emile Bernard*, Kunsthalle Bremen and Palais des Beaux-Arts, Lille, 1967. (This exhibition catalogue remains the best source of documentation for Bernard's early development, yet is difficult to reference for lack of coordination between the two museums in terms of entry and illustration numbering; thus references below give Bremen first and then when needed the corresponding number or page from Lille.)

Chassé, *Pont-Aven* Charles Chassé, *Gauguin et le groupe de Pont-Aven: Documents inédits*, Paris: Floury, 1921.

Chassé, *Son temps* Charles Chassé, *Gauguin et son temps*, Paris: Bibliothèque des arts, 1955.

CL | *The Complete Letters of Vincent van Gogh*, 3 vols., Greenwich, Connecticut: New York Graphic Society, 1966 (numbers with this designation are exclusively from Vincent to Théo van Gogh).

Cooper | Douglas Cooper, *Drawings and Watercolours by Vincent van Gogh*, New York, Macmillan, 1955.

Cooper, *Lautrec* | Douglas Cooper, *Henri de Toulouse-Lautrec*, New York: Harry N. Abrams, 1966.

Dauchot | Fernand Dauchot, "Meyer de Haan en Bretagne," *Gazette des Beaux-Arts*, LIII, July-August 1954, pp. 355-58 (contains a numbered and annotated check-list of the artist's then known *oeuvre*).

Denis, *Journal I* | Maurice Denis, *Journal I: 1884-1904*, Paris: La Colombe, 1957.

Denis, *Théories* | Maurice Denis, *Théories, 1890-1910: Du Symbolisme et de Gauguin vers un nouvel ordre classique*, 4th ed., Paris: L. Rouart and J. Watelin, 1920.

Dorra, *Arles* | Henri Dorra, "Gauguin's Dramatic Arles Themes," *Art Journal*, XXXVIII, Spring 1971, pp. 12-17.

Dortu | M.G. Dortu, *Toulouse-Lautrec et son oeuvre*, 6 vols., New York: Collectors Editions, 1971.

Dujardin | Edouard Dujardin, "Aux XX et aux Indépendants— Le cloisonisme," *La Revue Indépendante*, VI, March 1888, pp. 487-92.

F | J.-B. de la Faille, *The Works of Vincent van Gogh: His Paintings and Drawings*, posthumously edited by a committee of Dutch scholars, Amsterdam: Meulenhoff International, 1970 (*De la Faille* refers to the book as a whole).

Fénéon | Félix Fénéon, *Oeuvres plus que complètes*, 2 vols., ed. J.U. Halperin, Geneva-Paris: Droz, 1970 (where it has seemed useful, the original place of publication has been noted as well).

G | Exh. cat. *Oeuvres écrites de Gauguin et Van Gogh*, Paris: Institut Néerlandais, 1975 (numbers with this designation refer to the exhibited letters from Gauguin to Théo and Vincent van Gogh, here only scantily excerpted).

Gauzi | François Gauzi, *Lautrec et son temps*, Paris: David Perret, 1954.

GBA Gauguin | Ed. Georges Wildenstein, *Gauguin, sa vie, son oeuvre: Reunion de textes, d'etudes, de documents*, Paris: *Gazette des Beaux-Arts*, January-April 1958.

Goldwater | Robert Goldwater, *Paul Gauguin*, New York: Harry N. Abrams, n.d.

Gray | Christopher Gray, *Sculpture and Ceramics of Paul Gauguin*, Baltimore: Johns Hopkins, 1963.

Guicheteau | Marcel Guicheteau, *Paul Sérusier*, Paris: Side, 1976.

Hôtel Drouot | *Catalogue d'une vente de 30 tableaux de Paul Gauguin*, Paris: Grande Imprimerie, 1891 (the numbering in this Hôtel Drouot auction-house catalogue is followed by a "p.v." number, which refers to the actual February 23, 1891, "procès-verbal," published in Jean Leymarie, exh. cat. *Gauguin: Exposition du centenaire*, Paris: Orangerie des Tuileries, 1949).

H.R.C. | The Humanities Research Center, University of Texas at Austin, which houses the archive of Edouard Dujardin containing unpublished correspondence from Anquetin.

Huisman-Dortu | Ph. Huisman and M.G. Dortu, *Lautrec par Lautrec*, Paris: Bibliothèque des Arts, 1964.

Hulsker, *Complete VG* | Jan Hulsker, *The Complete Van Gogh: Paintings, Drawings, Sketches*, New York: Harry N. Abrams, 1980.

Hulsker, *Théo* | Jan Hulsker, "What Théo Really Thought," *Vincent: Bulletin of the Rijksmuseum Vincent van Gogh*, III: 2 (1974), pp. 2-28.

Hulsker, VGdVG | J. Hulsker, *Van Gogh door Van Gogh: De brieven als commentaar op zijn werk*, Amsterdam: Meulenhoff, 1973 (dates cited in the present text for letters written by Vincent or Théo van Gogh almost invariably follow this authoritative source).

Huyghe *Carnet* | *Le Carnet de Paul Gauguin*, ed. R. Huyghe, Paris: Quatre Chemins-Editart, 1952.

Japanese Prints | Cat. *Japanese Prints Collected by Vincent van Gogh* (with essays by W. van Gulik and F. Orton), Amsterdam: Rijksmuseum Vincent van Gogh, 1978.

Japonisme | G.P. Weisberg, P.D. Cate, G. Needham, M. Eidelberg and W.R. Johnston, exh. cat. *Japonisme: Japanese Influence on French Art, 1854-1910*, The Cleveland Museum of Art, 1975 (contributing authors will be cited as appropriate).

Jaworska | Wladyslawa Jaworska, *Paul Gauguin et l'Ecole de Pont-Aven*, Neuchatel: Ides et Calendes, 1971 (Eng. trans. P. Evans, London: Thames and Hudson, 1972).

Joyant | Maurice Joyant, *Henri de Toulouse-Lautrec*, 2 vols., New York: Arno Press, 1968 (original ed. 1926).

Lautrec, *Corres.* | *Unpublished Correspondence of Henri de Toulouse-Lautrec*, eds. L. Goldschmidt and H. Schimmel, London: Phaidon, 1969.

Lemoisne | Paul-André Lesmoine, *Degas et son oeuvre*, 4 vols., Paris: Paul Brame et C.M. de Hauke, 1947-49.

Leprohon	Pierre Leprohon, *Tel fut Van Gogh*, Paris: Editions du Sud, 1964.
London *P-I*	Exh. cat. *Post-Impressionism: Cross-Currents in European Painting*, London: Royal Academy of Arts and Weidenfeld and Nicholson, 1979-80.
M	*Lettres de Gauguin à sa femme et ses amis*, ed. M. Malingue, Paris: Bernard Grasset, 1946 (*Malingue* refers to the book as a whole).
Mack	Gerstle Mack, *Toulouse-Lautrec*, New York: Alfred A. Knopf, 1938.
Perruchot	Henri Perruchot, *Gauguin*, Cleveland and New York: World Publishing, 1963 (French ed., Paris: Hachette, 1961).
Pickvance, *Drawings*	Ronald Pickvance, *The Drawings of Gauguin*, New York: Paul Hamlyn, 1970.
Pickvance, *Tate Entries*	Ronald Pickvance, exh. cat. *Gauguin and the Pont-Aven Group*, London: Tate Gallery and Arts Council, 1966 (catalogue entries only).
Pissarro	Camille Pissarro, *Lettres à son fils Lucien*, eds. L. Pissarro and J. Rewald, Paris: Albin Michel, 1950.
P-I	John Rewald, *Post-Impressionism: From van Gogh to Gauguin*, 3rd ed. rev., New York: Museum of Modern Art, 1978.
Rewald, *Goupil*	John Rewald, "Théo van Gogh, Goupil and the Impressionists," *Gazette des Beaux-Arts*, LXXXI, January-February 1973, pp. 1-108.
Roskill	Mark Roskill, *Van Gogh, Gauguin and the Impressionist Circle*, London: Thames and Hudson, 1969 (if accompanied by "*Key Works*," this abbreviation refers to the supplementary text to this volume called *A Catalogue Raisonné of Key Works*, which is available in xerographed form from University Microfilms, Ann Arbor, Michigan).
Roskill, *Exchanges*	Mark Roskill, "Van Gogh's Exchanges of work with Emile Bernard in 1888," *Oud Holland*, LXXXVI, nr. 2/3, 1971, pp. 142-79.
Rotonchamp	Jean de Rotonchamp, *Paul Gauguin: 1848-1903*, Paris: Crès, 1925 (1st ed., 1906).
Seguin	Armand Seguin, "Paul Gauguin," *L'Occident*, III, March and May 1903, pp. 158-67, 298-305.
Sérusier	Paul Sérusier, *ABC de la Peinture: Correspondence*, eds. M.P. Sérusier and H. Boutaric, Paris: Floury, 1950.
Stuckey	Charles F. Stuckey, exh. cat. *Toulouse-Lautrec: Paintings*, The Art Institute of Chicago, 1979.
Sutton, *Tate Intro.*	Denys Sutton, exh. cat. *Gauguin and the Pont-Aven Group*, London: Tate Gallery and Arts Council, 1966 (Introduction only).
T	The numbered letters from Théo to Vincent van Gogh as given in *CL*.
Tralbaut	Marc Edo Tralbaut, *Vincent van Gogh*, New York: Viking, 1969.
Venturi	Lionello Venturi, *Cézanne: Son art, son oeuvre*, 2 vols., Paris: Paul Rosenberg, 1936.
Verkade	Dom Willibrord (Jan) Verkade, *Le Tourment de Dieu*, Paris: L. Rouart and J. Watelin, 1923.
Vincent: A Choice	Casper de Jong, ed., *Vincent van Gogh: Paintings and Drawings, A Choice from the Vincent van Gogh Foundation*, Amsterdam: NV't Lanthuys, 1968.
Walter	Elizabeth Walter, "Madeleine au Bois d'Amour par Emile Bernard," *La Revue du Louvre*, XXVIII: 4, pp. 286-91.
Wattenmaker	Richard J. Wattenmaker, exh. cat. *Puvis de Chavannes and The Modern Tradition*, rev. ed., Toronto: Art Gallery of Ontario, 1976.
Welsh-Ovcharov	B.M. Welsh-Ovcharov, *Vincent van Gogh: His Paris Period, 1886-88*, Utrecht-The Hague: Editions Victorine, 1976.
Welsh-Ovcharov, *Angrand*	B.M. Welsh-Ovcharov, *The Early Work of Charles Angrand and his Contact with Vincent van Gogh*, Utrecht-The Hague: Editions Victorine, 1971.
Welsh-Ovcharov, *Petit Boulevard*	B.M. Welsh-Ovcharov, *The "Petit Boulevard" and the Birth of Cloisonism*, M.Phil. thesis: University of Toronto, 1971.
Welsh-Ovcharov, *VG in Perspective*	B.M. Welsh-Ovcharov ed., *Van Gogh in Perspective*, Englewood Cliffs, N.J.: Prentice-Hall, 1974.
W	Georges Wildenstein, *Gauguin, I, Catalogue*, Paris: Les Beaux-Arts, 1964 (*Wildenstein* refers to the book as a whole).
Wil	The numbered letters from Vincent van Gogh to his sister Wilhelmina as given in *CL* (there listed as "W").

N.B.   *French titles included are added in the entry headings only when these derive directly from writings by the artist or his own exhibition catalogue submissions.*

PLATE 1
Paul Gauguin
Undine: In the Waves
1889
oil on canvas: 92 × 72 cm

PLATE 2
Louis Anquetin
Avenue de Clichy: Five O'Clock in the Evening
1887
oil on canvas: 69.2 × 53 cm

PLATE 3
Vincent van Gogh
The Café Terrace on the Place du Forum, Arles at Night
September 1888
oil on canvas: 81 × 65.5 cm

PLATE 4
Louis Anquetin
The Mower at Noon: Summer
1887
oil on cardboard (carton): 69.2 × 52.7 cm

PLATE 5
Vincent van Gogh
The Mowers, Arles in the Background
1888
oil on canvas: 73 × 54 cm

PLATE 6
Emile Bernard
Still Life with Blue Coffeepot
1888
oil on canvas: 55 × 46 cm

PLATE 7
Paul Gauguin
The Vision after the Sermon
1888
oil on canvas: 73 × 92 cm

PLATE 8
Emile Bernard
The Buckwheat Harvesters: Le Blé noir
1888
oil on canvas: 72 × 92 cm

PLATE 9
Emile Bernard
*Breton Women in the Meadow: Pardon at
Pont-Aven*
1888
oil on canvas: 74 × 92 cm

PLATE 10
Vincent van Gogh
Breton Women in the Meadow [after Emile
Bernard]
October–December 1888
watercolour on cardboard: 47.5 × 62 cm

PLATE 11
Vincent van Gogh
Portrait of Père Tanguy
late 1887
oil on canvas: 65 × 51 cm

PLATE 12
Vincent van Gogh
The Italian Woman with Daisies: La Segatori
late 1887
oil on canvas: 81 × 60 cm

PLATE 13
Vincent van Gogh
Interior of a Restaurant
summer 1887
oil on canvas: 45.5 × 56.5 cm

PLATE 14
Vincent van Gogh
Vincent's House on the Place Lamartine, Arles
late September 1888
oil on canvas: 76 × 94 cm

PLATE 15
Vincent van Gogh
Vincent's Bedroom at Arles
October 1888
oil on canvas: 56.5 × 74 cm

PLATE 16
Jakob Meyer de Haan
Breton Women Scutching Hemp
1889
fresco (transferred wall mural): 133.7 × 202 cm

PLATE 17
Paul Gauguin
Joan of Arc
1889
fresco (transferred wall mural): 116 × 58 cm

PLATE 18
Vincent van Gogh
Still Life: Vase with Fourteen Sunflowers
January 1889
oil on canvas: 95 × 73 cm

PLATE 19
Vincent van Gogh
La Berceuse: Madame Augustine Roulin
1889
oil on canvas: 92 × 72 cm

PLATE 20

Still Life: Vase with Fourteen Sunflowers
1888
oil on canvas: 93 × 73 cm

PLATE 21
Paul Gauguin
The Breton Calvary: The Green Christ
c. October-November 1889
oil on canvas: 92 × 73 cm

PLATE 22
Paul Gauguin
The Yellow Christ
1889
oil on canvas: 92 × 73 cm

PLATE 23
Paul Gauguin
Grape Gathering–Human Misery: Vendages à
Arles–Misères Humaines
1889
oil on canvas: 73.5 × 92.5 cm

PLATE 24
Paul Gauguin
Women at Arles: The Mistral
1888
oil on canvas: 73 × 92 cm

PLATE 25
Emile Bernard
Afternoon at St. Briac
1887
oil on canvas: 48 × 54 cm

PLATE 26
Emile Bernard
The Ragpickers at Asnières (Clichy)
late autumn, 1887
oil on canvas: 45.9 × 54.2 cm

Anquetin 89

PLATE 28
Henri de Toulouse-Lautrec
At the Circus Fernando
1887
oil on canvas: 100.3 × 161.3 cm

PLATE 27
Louis Anquetin
The Bridge of Saintes-Pères: Gust of Wind
c.1889
oil on canvas: 119.5 × 126 cm

PLATE 29
Henri de Toulouse-Lautrec
The Ball at the Moulin de la Galette
1889
oil on canvas: 90 × 100 cm

PLATE 30
Louis Anquetin
The Dance Hall at the Moulin Rouge
c.1893
oil on canvas: 169 × 205 cm

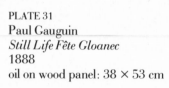

PLATE 31
Paul Gauguin
Still Life Fête Gloanec
1888
oil on wood panel: 38 × 53 cm

PLATE 32
Charles Laval
Going to the Market
1888
oil on canvas: 36 × 46 cm

Vincent van Gogh (1853-1890)

Biographical Data

The published correspondence of Vincent van Gogh (*The Complete Letters of Vincent van Gogh*, 3 vols. London: Thames and Hudson 1959), remains the primary source of documentation for establishing a chronology for the artist's life and artistic development. A more recent publication by Dr. J. Hulsker (*Van Gogh door Van Gogh*, Meulenhoff, Amsterdam, 1973) has produced a thorough ordering and dating of van Gogh's correspondence. The one major period within the artistic career of van Gogh for which there is no record of correspondence, his Paris period of 1886-87, is examined in Welsh-Ovcharov, *Vincent van Gogh: His Paris Period 1886-1888* (Editions Victorine Utrecht-Den Haag 1976). J. Hulsker, "What Théo Really Thought," *Vincent. Bulletin of the Rijksmuseum Vincent van Gogh*, 2, vol. 3. 1974, pp. 2-28 amplifies our knowledge thereof with his study of several unpublished letters from Théo van Gogh to his mother and sister.

EARLY LIFE AND CAREER

1865-1885

Vincent van Gogh is born on March 30, 1853 in the vicarage of the small village of Groot-Zundert in the province of North Brabant in the south of Holland. He is the eldest surviving son of Anna Cornelia Carbentus and Theodorus van Gogh, a Dutch Reformed minister. Four years later a second son Théodore is born who is to remain Vincent's closest friend and his lifelong moral and financial supporter. Shortly thereafter three daughters: Anna Cornelia, Elisabeth-Huberta and Wilhelminien (Wilhelmina) and a son Cornelis complete the pastor's family.

Vincent's early school years (1865-69) are spent in a boarding school in the neighbouring village of Zevenbergen where he exhibits a deep love of nature, and begins to draw. Since the seventeenth century van Gogh's family has practised two distinctive professions: the ministry or dealing in art. At the age of sixteen, on the recommendation of his Uncle Vincent, van Gogh chooses art over religion, becoming the youngest employee at the Dutch art gallery branch of Goupil in The Hague. In 1872 he begins what is to become a rich correspondence (652 letters) with his brother Théo. The following year Théo is employed by the Belgian branch of Goupil in Brussels. Vincent is stationed at the London branch of Goupil where he experiences his first disappointing courtship. In October, transferred for three months to the head office in Paris, he manifests a consuming interest in the Bible. In March 1876 he is dismissed by Goupil and after a short post as teacher-curate in Isleworth and Ramsgate in England returns to Holland to his father's new vicarage in Etten. After a brief period as a clerk in a book store in Dordrecht he attempts in 1877 to prepare for university and a career in the ministry. After a three-month period at a school for evangelism in Brussels he fails to obtain a post as minister and in 1878 departs for the coal mining area near Mons in Belgium, the Borinage, in order to teach the Bible to the poor. He spends two years in Belgium living among the miners, preaching, reading excessively, and admiring the art of Rembrandt, the Barbizon School and The Hague School.

In 1880 he begins to draw with serious intentions of becoming an artist, copies works by Millet and studies perspective and anatomy. From December 1881 to September 1883, financially supported by Théo, he studies art in The Hague and lives with the pregnant and abandoned prostitute Clasina ("Sien") Maria Hoornik, collecting English newspaper illustrations and executing numerous drawings and watercolours of figural studies and landscapes. After less than three months in the isolated Province of Drenthe painting in oils, in December he joins his family in Nuenen.

His stay at his parent's vicarage in Nuenen (December 1883-November 1885) produces the most important mature works of his Dutch years. Vincent corresponds with Théo who has become the manager of the modern art branch of Goupil in Paris and reads by June 1884 about the colour theories of Eugène Delacroix. Inspired by accounts of the latter artist, he begins to experiment with colour orchestrations in his canvases. *Circa* May 1885 he executes his major canvas *The Potato Eaters* and after months of strained family relationships he leaves for Antwerp. Here he visits museums, admires Frans Hals and Rubens and acquires his first known Japanese prints while painting with a considerably lightened palette. After a brief study at the Academy of Fine Arts he leaves in March 1886 for Paris with the intention of studying at the *atelier* of Fernand Cormon.

1886

MARCH

Rather than three months later as planned, Vincent descends peremptorily upon Paris at the outset of this month.

He moves in with Théo whose small bachelor apartment is located on rue Laval close to Montmartre. Here he paints a series of self-portraits and still life paintings in his earlier dark palette.

SPRING

Vincent paints views of Paris out of doors.

Bernard leaves for Brittany by the end of April, precluding any possibility of an early acquaintance with Vincent.

In May Vincent doubtless attends the 8th Impressionist exhibition where he sees works by Monet, Degas, Gauguin and Seurat, especially the latter's *Sunday Afternoon on the Island of the Grande-Jatte*.

SUMMER

In June Théo and Vincent move into more spacious accommodation at 54 rue Lepic in Montmartre where they hire a cook (*CL*462a). Vincent recovers from a dental operation and from stomach problems which he had experienced in Antwerp.

Théo informs his mother that the art dealer A. Portier, living in the same building as the brothers, has taken four paintings by Vincent on commission and has promised an exhibition of the artist's works (Hulsker "Théo," p. 8).

Vincent exchanges canvases with the American artist Frank Boggs and seeks similar exchanges with lesser known artists.

He has as yet no direct personal involvement with Impressionist artists and, although his work progresses in assimilating Delacroix's colour theories through a series of flower paintings, he is unable to sell anything (Hulsker, "Théo" p. 8).

FALL

Vincent studies at the *atelier* of Fernand Cormon, either continuing from late spring or for the first time (Welsh-Ovcharov, pp. 209-212).

Here he works after live models and traditional plaster casts, and becomes an assiduous frequenter of the shop of Père Tanguy.

By this time van Gogh has managed to deposit his canvases for sale with four art dealers: Père Tanguy, A. Portier, P.F. Martin and G. Thomas (*CL*561).

He visits *Salon des artistes indépendants* (August-September) where he sees works by Signac and Seurat, who exhibits again his *Grande-Jatte*.

Bernard returns from his walking trip in Brittany and discovers Vincent working at Cormon's *atelier*.

Vincent meets Bernard in person at the shop of Père Tanguy where the latter has come to deposit some of his recent Breton canvases.

Vincent invites Bernard to the rue Lepic apartment and here they exchange canvases in remembrance of their first meeting (*P.-I.*, p. 56, 72, n. 65).

Bernard introduces Vincent to Louis Anquetin who had left Cormon's by the fall session (Bernard, *Anquetin 1934*, p. 114).

In late October van Gogh paints Montmartre landscapes and meets at the shop of Père Tanguy the Pointillist artist Charles Angrand with whom he wishes to exchange a canvas (Welsh-Ovcharov, *Angrand*, pp. 37-9).

WINTER

Vincent experiences close contacts with Bernard, Anquetin and Lautrec.

In late December he visits the café *Le Mirliton* where Aristide Bruant displays canvases by Lautrec.

Vincent and Théo begin to collect works by Monticelli.

1887

JANUARY

Circa winter of 1886-87 Vincent forms a liaison with Agostina Segatori, the owner of the café *Le Tambourin* where the artist has contracted to take his meals in payment for his canvases (Bernard, *Père Tanguy*, p. 606).

Vincent paints his first portrait of Père Tanguy (F 263).

Sometime in January-February Vincent meets Signac at the shop of Père Tanguy.

He attends Lautrec's weekly open house gatherings, seeing Lautrec's recent works and bringing his own works to be viewed (Welsh-Ovcharov, *VG in Perspective*, p. 35).

Vincent frequents the shop of S. Bing to study and buy Japanese prints.

MARCH-APRIL

About this time Bernard visits Vincent's apartment.

At *Le Tambourin* van Gogh organizes an exhibition of Japanese prints which influences the work of both Bernard and Anquetin.

Lautrec executes the pastel portrait of Vincent in *Le Tambourin* (Bernard, *Van Gogh*, p. 394).

Considerable tension develops between Théo and Vincent.

Théo writes Wilhelmina that Vincent is becoming more skillful every day (Hulsker, "Théo", p. 11).

APRIL

Théo begins to purchase works from Monet and in the successive summer months arranges sales of paintings from other Impressionists, including Sisley, Degas and Pissarro (Rewald, *Goupil*, pp. 89-104). Signac and Vincent paint together on the river banks of the Seine at Asnières and St. Ouen.

MAY

Théo reports to his sister Elisabeth that Vincent's "paintings are becoming lighter and he is trying to put more sunlight into them" (Hulsker, "Théo" p. 12).

By late May, Signac departs for the south of France, while Vincent continues to work on the outskirts of Paris.

SUMMER

Théo handles the canvases of C. Pissarro.

Vincent paints landscapes in the areas surrounding Montmartre and at Asnières "seeing more colour in them than in his previous works." (*Wil* 1).

By the end of July van Gogh breaks his personal and commercial relationship with Agostina Segatori (*CL*461-2).

Vincent informs Théo who is vacationing in the Netherlands that he has seen Lautrec who has succeeded in selling a painting via the dealer Portier (*CL*461).

At the end of July Bernard returns from Brittany and resumes his friendship with Vincent.

Sometime in late summer Vincent and Bernard work together in the studio which Bernard's grandmother has constructed in the garden of his parents' home at Asnières. Here Vincent and Bernard paint together portraits of Père Tanguy (cat. no. 8 and cat. no. 97).

FALL

With the return of Anquetin and Bernard to Paris, Vincent apparently joins them in a productive period of painting and close exchange of ideas on art.

Under the stimulus of van Gogh, plans evolve for a group exhibition of the Impressionists of the "Petit Boulevard."

Vincent announces to Wilhelmina that having painted landscapes at Asnières this last summer he is now working on portraiture (*Wil* 1, see Welsh-Ovcharov, p. 33).

Sometimes in fall-winter 1887-88 van Gogh exhibits one or more paintings in the rehearsal hall of André Antoine's *Théâtre Libre* (*CL*473).

CIRCA NOVEMBER

Van Gogh exhibits between fifty and one hundred paintings alongside those by Bernard, Anquetin, and Lautrec at the group exhibition of the "Petit Boulevard" held in the *Grand Bouillon-Restaurant du Chalet* at 43 avenue de Clichy. A number of artists visit this exhibition including A. Guillaumin, Seurat and Pissarro.

In November Gauguin returns from Martinique and visits the *Du Chalet* exhibition where he meets and exchanges at least two canvases with Vincent.

Vincent visits the Puvis de Chavannes exhibition held at the Durand-Ruel Gallery.

1888
CIRCA JANUARY

Vincent, Théo, Bernard, Gauguin and the Pissarros meet in the "cafés of the Petit Boulevard" and in artists' studios to discuss financial and material problems facing the modern artists (*CL*544a).

FEBRUARY

Vincent, about to depart for Arles, and Théo pay a visit to the studio of Seurat.

Circa February 19 Bernard says goodbye to Vincent who by now is experiencing both physical and mental deterioration (*CL*544a).

On February 21 van Gogh writes Théo that he has arrived in Arles where the winter landscape looks Japanese. He gives his new address as the Restaurant Carrel.

MARCH

On March 3 he receives a letter from Gauguin,

who has been sick in bed for a fortnight; he advises Théo to show two large views of Montmartre in the exhibition of the *Indépendants* (*CL*466, referring to *F*316, 350).

With the aid of Bernard Théo purchases a drawing by Seurat. (*CL*468).

Vincent discusses with Théo plans for a society of Impressionists of the "Grand Boulevards" (Degas, Monet, Sisley and Pissarro) to combine with the artists of the "Petit Boulevard" (Anquetin, Bernard, Lautrec, Vincent and Gauguin) in order to ensure mutual economic benefits, (*CL*468).

He continues to correspond with Lautrec and Bernard (*CL*469-70, *B*2) and dreams of a permanent exhibition of the Impressionists in London and Marseilles.

Vincent describes to Bernard that the Arles countryside is as beautiful as Japan. This month he executes *The Langlois Bridge* (cat. no. 14*A* and *B*).

APRIL

Vincent writes Bernard that he is working out of doors on blooming peach trees (*B*3).

He inquires from Théo (*CL*476) if Lautrec has finished his picture of the woman leaning on her elbows in a café (i.e., cat. no. 118).

Vincent thanks Bernard for sending him some sonnets and a drawing from Paris (*B*5).

MAY

May 1, Vincent's health has improved and he announces he has leased his Yellow House (*CL*480), although he does not move in to sleep there until September, after hearing Gauguin has decided to come to Arles (*CL*507).

Vincent corresponds with Bernard and both admit that Gauguin's *Negresses* (cat. no. 46) as being astonishing (*B*5).

By the end of May he admits to Théo that he hopes Gauguin and Bernard will exchange drawings with him (*CL*490) and is intending to make for both artists little sketchbooks with drawings like Japanese drawing books (*CL*492).

JUNE

Vincent writes Theo outlining a proposal for Gauguin to come to Arles in order to work and share accommodations with Vincent as well as receiving an allowance from Théo (*CL*493) for

the return of one painting by Gauguin to Théo (*CL*494a).

June 10, Vincent announces to Théo that the Yellow House is finished being painted.

By mid June he is working on the *Harvest at La Crau* (*F*412); he thinks of Anquetin and hopes to hear from Gauguin an answer to their proposal of his coming to Arles (*CL*498).

By June 22 Vincent writes from Saintes-Maries on the shore of the Mediterranean that he has already executed three canvases.

The next day back in Arles he informs Théo that an article has appeared in the *Revue indépendante* on Anquetin (i.e. Edouard Dujardin "Le cloisonisme," March 1, 1888) which calls the latter the leader of a new trend (*CL*500).

At the end of July Vincent sends a sketch of his *Sower* (cat. no. 27) and speaks glowingly (*B*7) of Anquetin's *The Mower at Noon* (cat. no. 74).

JULY

Vincent informs Bernard he has painted a seated *Zouave* (cat. no. 15) and thanks him (*B*8) for the sketch of *The Brothel* (cat. no. 100).

On July 7 Vincent is exhilarated to hear from Théo that Gauguin agrees to their plan to join forces and to come to Arles (*CL*507).

At the end of the month Vincent recalls to Théo his two exhibitions at the café *Le Tambourin* and its influence on Anquetin and Bernard and the second exhibition in the room in the boulevard (read: avenue) de Clichy (*CL*510).

He is disinclined to wind up his connections with Samuel Bing, dealer of Japanese prints since these prints never "pass away" (*CL*511). Van Gogh is ready to join Gauguin in Pont-Aven if the latter cannot pay his fare to Arles.

Around the last days of July Vincent thanks Bernard (*B*12) for the ten watercolours which the artist has sent him (e.g., cat. no. 101).

AUGUST

Vincent informs Théo on August 3 that Gauguin has complained of not having money for the trip to Arles (*CL*517). Soon thereafter, Vincent urges Bernard to write Gauguin in Pont-Aven (*B*14).

He confesses to Théo that he is convinced Gauguin will fall in love with Arles (*CL*521). The next day Vincent decides he will go to Pont-Aven only if a house could be found with as low a rent as in Arles.

August 18, Vincent informs Bernard he is pleased the latter has joined Gauguin (*B* 15); the same day Théo is informed that Bernard has joined Gauguin in Pont-Aven some days ago (*CL* 523).

By the third week of this month Vincent is painting three versions of the sunflowers and informs Théo that Bernard and Gauguin are enjoying painting together and that Bernard has shown Vincent's sketches to Gauguin (*CL* 526).

Vincent then announces (*CL* 527) that he is working on the fourth picture of the sunflowers (*F* 454).

This month he paints: *Portrait of Patience Escalier* (cat. no. 21).

SEPTEMBER

Vincent spends a day with the Belgian artist Eugène Boch who has posed for him already (*CL* 531).

He complains to Théo that neither Gauguin nor Bernard have written him.

On the ninth of this month Vincent informs Théo he is busy furnishing his house in anticipation of Gauguin, having bought a bed and some bedclothes, and planning the decoration of its interior (*CL* 534).

By mid-September Vincent informs Théo that Gauguin has written complaining of stomach problems and accruing debts.

On 18 September Vincent writes to Théo that last night he slept for the first time in his Yellow House and that he sees his new lodgings as a studio of the south for all true colourists.

He has received a letter from Bernard who is thinking of coming to Arles this winter and who speaks of Gauguin with great respect (*CL* 538). Vincent urges Bernard and Gauguin to paint each other's portraits, but Bernard is too timid (*B* 16).

By the end of the month he has decorated his downstairs studio with prints by the Japanese, Daumier, Delacroix, Géricault and Millet (*CL* 542) and has thanked Bernard for his drawings of brothel subjects (*B* 17).

He has received a letter from Gauguin who does not commit himself definitely to coming even if his fare should be paid (*CL* 543).

On 29 September Vincent receives a most remarkable letter from Gauguin (*G* 9) which includes a moving description of the latter's *Self-Portrait* (cat. no. 52). In the same letter Bernard includes a message proposing to Vincent on behalf of himself, Laval, Monet and E.

Chamaillard an exchange of self-portraits and an announcement that Bernard has to see his Military Board of Appeal in Paris and Laval will only come in February to Arles. Vincent announces Gauguin will be the head of the studio (*CL* 544).

At the end of the month he receives from Bernard a sketch of *Two Breton Women* and proposes several canvases as exchanges with Bernard, Laval and Monet (*B* 18).

OCTOBER

On October 7 Vincent announces that he has just received the *Self-Portrait called Les Misérables* by Gauguin (cat. no. 52) and the *Self-Portrait* by Bernard (cat. no. 105) and Vincent now has a chance to compare his own *Self-Portrait* (F 476) with them before sending it in exchange to Gauguin (*CL* 545). In the same letter he tells Théo that Bernard has sent him a collection of ten drawings with a daring poem, the whole called "At the Brothel."

Two or three days later Vincent informs Théo that Gauguin plans not to come to Arles until the end of the month (*CL* 549).

By mid-October Vincent receives a letter from Gauguin reporting that he has sent Théo some paintings and studies and that Bernard, Laval, etc. are keeping Vincent's seven studies (*CL* 553).

He sends a sketch of his bedroom to Théo (*CL* 544) and the next day, 17 October, thanks Gauguin for promising to be in Arles as early as the twentieth of the month (*B* 22).

Meyer de Haan has met Théo by this time and Vincent is overjoyed to hear of this new friendship (*CL* 555).

He has gas installed in the studio and the kitchen in anticipation of working with Gauguin every night. He confesses his need to beware of his nerves for if he had not an almost double nature, that of a monk and that of a painter, he would have been reduced to complete insanity a long time ago (*CL* 556).

On 24 October Vincent announces to Théo (*CL* 557) that Gauguin has arrived in Arles in good health and has brought a magnificent canvas by Bernard, *Breton Women in the Meadow* (cat. no. 104).

Three days later Théo informs Vincent that Meyer de Haan is coming to stay with him (*T* 2).

NOVEMBER

Vincent informs Bernard that he and Gauguin are working together and making occasional

excursions to the brothels. Gauguin is busy with his *Night Café* (*W* 305) and Vincent has done two studies of the *Alyscamps* (cat. no. 28).

On November 11 Vincent announces (*CL* 559) that Gauguin is doing a vineyard (cat. no. 56) completely from memory and that he has produced "some women in a vineyard" (F 495).

Vincent receives a letter from the critic Edouard Dujardin asking him to exhibit his works in the offices of the *Revue indépendante*; however, the artist is disgusted with the suggestion of handing over a canvas in payment for the exhibition (*CL* 561).

DECEMBER

Vincent receives the *Self-Portrait* by Laval (cat. no. 136) and a seascape by Bernard (*CL* 562).

Vincent confesses to Théo that he does not dislike working from the imagination since that allows him to stay indoors now that it is winter in Arles (*CL* 560).

During the second half of the month Vincent and Gauguin visit the Montpellier Museum where the former is especially enraptured by the works of Delacroix. Vincent confesses to terribly electric arguments between both artists (*CL* 564).

On Sunday, December 23, Vincent admits that Gauguin is upset with Arles and especially with him (*CL* 565).

The next day Gauguin sends a telegram to Théo to come to Arles since Vincent in a state of extreme excitement has severed a part of his ear.

Théo arrives and stays over Christmas with Vincent who is in the hospital in Arles.

Gauguin and Théo return together to Paris.

By December 31 Vincent feels better (*CL* 565).

1889

JANUARY

January 2, Vincent reassures Théo he is well and is staying in the hospital for a few more days and will then return quietly to his house. He asks Théo to tell Gauguin to write him (*CL* 567).

By January 17 he has started work again and has already finished four studies (*CL* 571).

By the middle of the month Vincent announces (*CL* 571a) he has heard of Théo's engagement. He is again working on his first version of *La Berceuse* (F 504).

Vincent anticipates being an invalid during February and March although he admits sleeping now without any more nightmares (*CL*574).

By January 30 he is working on his third version of *La Berceuse* (*CL*575).

FEBRUARY

He keeps his Yellow House provisionally, feels better and advises Théo which canvases should be exhibited at this year's *Indépendants* exhibition (*CL*576).

By mid-February he experiences mental suffering upon returning to his house (*CL*577).

MARCH

By mid-March Vincent breaks a two-week silence, writing to Théo announcing his recovery, but also the news that a number of people in Arles who considered him a dangerous lunatic have caused the artist to be shut up in a cell by the commissioner of police (*CL*579).

On March 24 he writes Théo that he has seen Paul Signac and that his visit was beneficial for his morale (*CL*581).

Five days later he announces he has returned to working on his portrait of *La Berceuse* for the fifth time and sends Théo his wishes for happiness and serenity in his impending marriage (*CL*582).

APRIL

He works out of doors with renewed physical strength (*CL*583).

Albert Aurier visits the shop of Père Tanguy where Vincent's paintings are on exhibition. The critic writes about this shop and on Vincent's paintings (LUCLEFLANEUR (pseudonym of Aurier) "En Quête de choses d'art," *Le Moderniste*, 13 April 1889, p. 14).

On April 5 Vincent informs Signac that he is working at landscapes around the sanatorium and its environs at Arles (*CL*583b).

By the third week of the month he wishes Théo who has recently been married "a great deal of happiness," but announces that he wishes to go at the end of the month or beginning of May to the hospital in St. Rémy as a resident boarder for a three-month trial period (*CL*585).

He feels deeply that his mental problem has been within him for a very long time and that his repeated attacks necessitate going to an asylum immediately (*CL*586). At the same time he

suggests alternatively the possibility of enlistment in the Foreign Legion (*CL*587).

MAY

On May 2 Vincent sends to Théo the three self-portraits by Laval, Gauguin and Bernard (*CL*589).

He thinks of beginning to draw more with a reed pen which costs less (*CL*590).

ST. REMY

On May 9 Vincent announces to Théo that he is content that he has come to the hospital at St. Rémy and that he has already worked in the garden (*CL*591).

Vincent is given a room with a barred window and an extra room for his studio.

JUNE

He works on landscapes viewed from his bedroom window and comments to Théo on June 9 that he has seen an announcement of a coming exhibition (that is, the *Groupe Impressionniste et Synthétiste*) in which Gauguin, Bernard and Anquetin will figure (*CL*594).

By July 16 his health is gradually returning and he has finished landscapes of the surrounding countryside of the hospital (*Wil*12).

JULY

July 6, Vincent congratulates Théo on the good news of Johanna's pregnancy and announces the doctor's opinion that he should stay at St. Rémy for a year longer (*CL*599).

Théo announces in mid-July to Vincent that Meyer de Haan has joined Gauguin and that the latter has done some very fine things (*T*12).

AUGUST

August 14 Théo telegraphs to St. Rémy to find out why Vincent has not written and discovers Vincent has been ill (*T*14).

Vincent has received, apparently from Gauguin, a catalogue of the Volpini exhibition and finds it interesting. He states (*CL*601) that Gauguin has also written him a kind but rather obscure letter (apparently now lost).

SEPTEMBER

He thinks often of Gauguin and Bernard in

Brittany and feels they are busy creating better work than he.

By 3 or 4 September Théo receives the news from Dr. Peyron at St. Rémy that Vincent has recovered "his lucidity of mind" (*CL*602a).

Upon hearing that Octave Maus, who has seen Vincent's canvases, has invited Bernard and himself for the next exhibition of *Les Vingt* in Brussels, Vincent works incessantly, searching now for not "so much striking effects as once more the half tones" (*CL*604).

In the first half of this month Vincent feels the necessity of restudying the art of Delacroix and Millet and begins to make copies after the two artists (*CL*604-605 and *CL*607).

Théo keeps Vincent informed about Gauguin's activities, and Vincent still thinks that they will perhaps work together again (*CL*605).

Vincent expresses sympathy (*CL*607) with Bernard's and Gauguin's "subjectively deformed use of contour outlines and Gauguin's theory of intensified use of colour."

By the end of the month he is struggling to capture the characteristic essence of the olive trees and hopes perhaps one day to "do a personal impression of them like what the sunflowers were for the yellows" (*CL*608).

OCTOBER

On October 4 Théo informs Vincent that Pissarro finds it impossible to have Vincent live with his family but that the latter knows somebody in Auvers (that is, Dr. Gachet) and adds that Bernard is coming tomorrow to see Vincent's recent canvases (*T*18).

He expresses his longing to see what Gauguin and Bernard have painted in Brittany (*CL*609).

Gauguin writes Vincent that he is not well off and the latter sends letters to both Gauguin and Bernard (*B*20) via Théo (*CL*610).

Van Gogh writes Bernard on October 8 after a year's lapse inquiring anxiously what studies the artist has brought back from Pont-Aven, not realizing that Bernard had not been there this year (*B*20).

Théo informs Vincent that his submission of paintings to *Les Vingt* in Brussels produced positive results (*T*19).

NOVEMBER

Early this month Vincent receives Théo's sending of prints after Millet (*C*613). Vincent learns that Théo has visited Bernard, has seen his recent works and is puzzled by the latter's disturbing abstraction (*T*20).

O. Maus has invited Vincent to participate at *Les Vingt* once again and van Gogh accepts (*C*614).

Gauguin sends Vincent a sketch (*fig. 76*) of the *Christ in the Garden of Olives* (cat. no. 66) and the latter rejects such Biblical representations as being too literary, and avoiding "the reality of things" (*CL*614). On November 17 Vincent writes Bernard (*B*21) thanking the latter for sending him photographs of his recent work; at the same time he laments the counterfeited and affected new style of Bernard, urging him to return to the beautifully ordered earlier works, for example, *Breton Women in the Meadow* (cat. no. 104).

Vincent is working in the olive groves because he considers Gauguin and Bernard's representations of Christ in the Garden of Olives unnerving. He writes both artists urging them to think and not to dream.

DECEMBER

Père Tanguy is exhibiting a great many of Vincent's canvases and Théo informs his brother that Albert Aurier had made a visit to see Vincent's recent canvases (*T*21).

Vincent's work is progressing, but he is resigned to spending the greatest part of next year at St. Rémy (*CL*616-17).

Théo informs Vincent on December 22 that Tanguy is exhibiting his *Sunflowers* (*T*22).

1890

JANUARY

January 1, Aurier's pioneering article on van Gogh, "Les Isolés: Vincent van Gogh," appears in the *Mercure de France*.

Two days before the birth of her child, Johanna writes Vincent that she and Théo wish to name the child after the artist (*T*26).

January 31 Théo and Johanna's child, Vincent Willem, is born and the same day Vincent suffers a relapse (*T*27).

FEBRUARY

February 1 Vincent hears of the birth of Théo's son and sends his congratulations and asks Théo to thank Aurier for his article (*CL*625). February 11 Vincent comments to Aurier on his article (*CL*626a). He writes his mother (*CL*627) that

Théo has announced that one of his paintings was sold at Brussels (*The Red Vineyard*, *F* 495).

February 24 Vincent experiences an attack while visiting Arles and is brought back to St. Rémy.

MARCH

In mid-March Théo transmits to Vincent congratulations from many people who saw his paintings in the exhibition of the *Indépendants* and adds that Gauguin especially noted that his canvases were the chief attraction of the exhibition (*T*29).

At the end of the month Vincent learns from Théo that Bernard and Aurier are coming to see his pictures (*T*30).

Vincent finishes three more copies after Millet's prints and admits to Théo that he is fighting against depression and is thinking of leaving St. Rémy (*CL*623) since life is not always gay there (*Wil*18).

He is beginning to think often of Holland again (*Wil*19). Vincent briefly visits Arles (*T*25).

Théo informs Vincent that Gauguin has arrived in Paris and has asked many questions about him and that Meyer de Haan is experiencing financial hardship (*T*28).

Vincent receives news that Théo has met with Dr. Gachet who finds it necessary to see the artist in order to find out if he can treat him (*T*31).

APRIL

On April 1 Dr. Peyron informs Théo that Vincent has suffered another attack.

After a month-long period of silence Vincent is able to write. He sends Théo recent canvases, a few of which he executed during his period of illness, including a canvas in appreciation for Aurier (*CL*629).

MAY

Vincent writes Théo that he feels certain that if he came north he should recuperate quickly; he wishes to leave St. Rémy (*CL*630). Théo approves (*T*33), and Vincent plans to stay with Dr. Gachet (*CL*632).

By the second week of May Vincent feels calm again, finishes some canvases and packs for his trip (*CL*633-34).

He arrives in Paris on May 17 and stays for three days with Théo and his family.

On May 20 he writes his first letter from

Auvers, letting Théo know that he has seen Dr. Gachet (*CL*635) and has taken lodgings with the family Ravoux (*CL*636).

By the end of the month he is working on landscapes and is delighted by the lush Auvers countryside (*CL*637).

JUNE

By June 3 (*CL*638) he is working on the *Portrait of Dr. Gachet* (cat. no. 43).

JULY

Vincent visits Théo on Sunday July 6 and sees Aurier and Toulouse-Lautrec.

He paints three large landscapes (*F* 776, 778-9) which express his present sense of alienation and sadness (*CL*649).

Théo and Johanna and the baby visit Vincent and lunch at Dr. Gachet's (*CL*640).

By mid-June Vincent plans to make engravings after some of his canvases with the aid of Dr. Gachet's printing press and hopes that Gauguin will engrave some of his canvases, especially his Martinique paintings (*CL*642).

He corresponds with Gauguin explaining that he has not seen his recent canvases while he was in Paris but that he has painted a portrait of Dr. Gachet and hopes to join Gauguin and Meyer de Haan in Brittany for a month (*CL*643).

At the end of the month he informs Théo (*CL*645) that he has painted Dr. Gachet's daughter (*F* 772); Théo in turn explains to the artist that Johanna and the child are experiencing a difficult time and that he is worried over financial matters and is undecided where they should live (*T*39).

On July 24 Vincent sends Théo his last letter which asks for supplies. He ends his correspondence on a note of disillusionment as to the present possibility of individual or collective efforts succeeding on behalf of modern artists (*CL*651).

On July 27 Vincent departs to paint and shoots himself.

On July 28 Théo van Gogh arrives in Auvers-sur-Oise; Vincent dies at 1:30 a.m. the following day.

On July 30 Emile Bernard in the company of Charles Laval joins Théo, Dr. Gachet, Père Tanguy and other artists for the funeral cortege.

Théo, profoundly distressed by Vincent's death, falls ill by late 1890 and dies in Utrecht, The Netherlands on January 25, 1891.

1.
Roadway in a Paris Park
fall 1886
oil on canvas: 37.5 x 45.5 cm
Not signed or dated
Lent anonymously

This painting, here attributed to Vincent van Gogh for the first time, was acquired by the critic Albert Aurier, but after his sudden death in 1892 it remained unrecognized by his heirs as a work of Vincent.[1] In subject matter and style it relates to three other paintings of similarly modest size which also depict the people of Paris strolling in one or another public garden or park. One setting is easily recognizable as the raised *Terrace at the Tuileries* (F 223) and another, *Public Garden in Paris* (F 225, *fig. 38*), probably reflects the same or a similar Paris scene with a formally laid out garden park rather than the suburban Bois de Boulogne as recently claimed.[2] *Roadway in a Paris Park* shares with a signed painting entitled *In the Bois de Boulogne* (F 224) a setting with large, casually dispersed trees suggestive of the

more informal layout of the Bois. Whereas the spring tonalities of the *Tuileries* might well have been executed shortly after Vincent's arrival at the beginning of March in Paris, the yellow, red and brown foliage on the trees in the other three examples places these canvases in fall 1886.[2] The naturalistic colouration of the paintings makes them seem at first glance a holdover of Vincent's Brabant-period preference for earthen colours in the tradition of Millet. Closer viewing reveals a broadly conceived Impressionist brush technique. Our example in particular eschews the residual spatial recessions filtering through beneath the tree foliage and substitutes a pattern of brushwork and colouration which rests largely on a vertical plane in which the foliage and the sky blend harmoniously together. While it would be claiming too much to speak of this 1886 Paris period landscape style as a harbinger of his later adoption of Pointillist or Cloisonist modes, its incipient Impressionism and considerable atmospheric luminosity provide genuine insight into the stage of transition towards a full-blown Impressionism that van Gogh had reached by late 1886. Like the other works of this

subject series it also provides a precedent for those many subsequent paintings in which figures of strolling workers, peasants or couples enliven an otherwise uninhabited landscape with a particular type of human activity.

[1] The current heir of the Albert Aurier legacy has confirmed in writing that this painting was indeed in the possession of the critic at his death, but was not known to have been painted by van Gogh before or at the time of its disposal some time ago.

[2] That the *Tuileries* may have been painted early spring 1886 is suggested by analogy in style and spatial conception between a pencil study of that painting (F 1383) and a drawing executed on the border of a restaurant menu which is dated April 8, 1886 (F 1377). The only alternative to a fall 1886 date for the other three Paris park subjects would be a year later, which is stylistically inconceivable.

Fig. 38
Vincent van Gogh
A Public Garden in Paris
1886,
oil on canvas
(private collection).

2.
Still Life: Absinthe   *F* 339
winter-early spring 1887
oil on canvas: 46.5 x 33 cm
Not signed or dated
Lent by the Rijksmuseum Vincent van Gogh,
Amsterdam

This modest yet striking still life painting featuring a glass of absinthe and a carafe of water has been related in theme to the famous painting of 1876 by Degas.[1] If actually known to Vincent and in his mind when he painted this still life study, it would have been less the social theme of drinkers in a café than Degas' play with encapsulated perspective and radical Japanist "cut off" compositional devices that interested him most. As in a companion piece (*F* 340) in which the still life objects are set off against broad vertical bands of decorative wallpaper design, here Vincent has employed the vertical windowpanes as a rhythmic backdrop for his otherwise static image. It is difficult not to believe that Vincent was alluding to the multi-panelled folding screens of oriental art through his asymmetrical positioning of the figures, tree trunks and boulevard bench within the four principal "panels" of his backdrop. If this Eastern-Western analogy was indeed intended, Vincent would have seen his aim as still basically Realist in conception.

[1]   J. Leymarie, *Vincent van Gogh* (Paris: Pierre Tisné, 1951), p. 103.

3.

Agostina Segatori in the Café Le Tambourin
F 370
c. February-March 1887
oil on canvas: 55.5 x 46.5 cm
Not signed or dated
Lent by the Rijksmuseum Vincent van Gogh,
Amsterdam

Due to the tambourine-shaped table and stools, it
has been recognized that the setting for this portrait was the café *Le Tambourin*, located at 62,
boulevard de Clichy (*fig. 39*) and operated by
Neapolitan-born Agostina Segatori. As an artist's
model she had posed for J.B.C. Corot in Italy
(*Agostina* in the National Gallery, Washington),
often for J.L.G. Gérôme and for her lover the
Swedish painter August Hagborg. The latter's
Realist portrait of her (*fig. 40*) captures her reputed animal sensuality, although not "the profundity in her gaze which bespoke of a malicious
experience, the science, all the science of life,"
which was recognized by Vincent as attributable to
Agostina from a short story by Charles Morice
written in 1888.[1] Although executed in a different
style and up to a decade later, Vincent's seated
female in *Le Tambourin* is close enough in features to allow the presumption that he was depicting Segatori.[2] Given her exotic, presumably
Neapolitan costume, who else could the sitter be
than the proprietress of the then very successful
café-restaurant in Montmartre? Otherwise one
must be prepared to admit the unlikely possibility
that Vincent would have himself proposed the
depiction of one of Segatori's waitresses in a similar
costume, since it is very unlikely that a model
unconnected with the establishment would be so
dressed.

It is also sometimes said that Vincent had
formed a liaison with Agostina during the first half
of 1887. Whatever the relationship it must have
been close, judging from Vincent's summer 1887
account (*CL*461) of the strained circumstances
under which it was falling apart. This letter to
Théo also documents that Vincent at that time still
had a display of paintings at *Le Tambourin* and
that there was a dispute over their return. Perhaps,
as Bernard has written, Vincent had made some
kind of arrangement to exchange art for the
sumptuous dinners for which the restaurant was
famed, and at the least one can say that this was
the first public display of Vincent's painting, either
in Paris or elsewhere.[3] It must in fact have been
considered something of a special privilege, since

Fig. 39
Coll-Toc
Le Tambourin,
1886,
drawing,
illustrated in John Grand-Cartaret, *L'Art dans la
brasserie*, Paris, 1886.

Fig. 40
August Hagborg
Portrait of Agostina Segatori,
c. late 1870s-1880
oil on canvas
(private collection, Sweden).

other artists including Lautrec were confined to
offering of designs on smallish tambourines of the
type illustrated by an advertising vignette of 1886
(*fig. 39*). *Still Life: Bowl with Pansies* (*F* 244)
uses a tambourine seat as a pedestal for the flowers, supporting Bernard's recollection that it was
chiefly flower pieces which Vincent had on display
with Segatori.[4]

When one returns to the portrait itself, it is not
Vincent's art but that of Japan, which is commemorated at upper right. He thus surely here
makes reference to the exhibition of Japanese
prints which he organized early in the spring of
1887 for display at *Le Tambourin* and which he
later credited (*CL*510) with having influenced
Bernard and Anquetin in the direction of their art.
Presumably this would have been fairly early in
the year, certainly before the onset of summer
when Bernard and Anquetin would have departed
Paris. In style, this painting may be considered a

tribute to Degas, not only to his striking *Absinthe
Drinkers*, but also for the Japanist raking-angle
backdrop which Degas above all others introduced
into modern French painting.[5] Vincent's recognition of Degas as model would have been
strengthened by his own current association with
Lautrec, whose veneration for Degas was great
and who also had begun to favour the subject of a
lone woman at a café table by this time (cat.
nos. 115, 116).

Vincent's specific characterization of Agostina
as a modern bohemian is typically a mixture of the
mundane and the exotic. The mundane is present
in the sense of boredom, if not melancholy, which
appears to inform his sitter, pictured here, one
must imagine, during a lull between meal hours.
The exotic is the Italian costume suggestive of a
gypsy life (as is inherent in the "tambourine"
motif). Her use of cigarettes and beer is not exactly
proper in society portraits, but alludes to her inde-

pendent character. Finally, allusions to Japan are to be found in the background print and in the folded but colourful parasol, so often found in prints of Japanese actresses. All in all, Vincent has here incorporated a surprising variety of sources and allusions to give us an image richly suggestive both in its treatment of an established *genre* type and as a document of his own life as an artist and man in Paris.

1   C. Morice, "La Truie bleue," *Courrier Français*, September 16, 1888 to which Vincent alludes to Théo (CL538a).

2   Hagborg arrived in Paris 1875, a decade before Vincent; in the present writer's view *F* 215b, whose sitter wears so similar a coiffure, is the same woman pictured in *Le Tambourin*, thus in all likelihood La Segatori.

3   The Bernard account is in *Tanguy* p. 606.

4   See F. Orton, "Vincent's interest in Japanese prints." *Vincent* I:3 (1971), p. 10 m. 24. The Lautrec Tambourin is Dortu II, p. 316, which if not demonstrably done for the café *Le Tambourin* (see for this possibility G. Coquiot, *Vincent van Gogh*, Paris: Ollendorff, 1923, pp. 126-29); the drawing (*fig. 39*) appeared in J. Grand-Cartaret, *Raphael et Gambrinus ou l'art dans la brasserie* (Paris: 1886), pp. 155-59.

5   However, Vincent would not have been able to see Degas' *Absinthe Drinkers* in the original (see Ronald Pickvance, " 'L'Absinthe' in England," *Apollo*, LXVII, May 1963, pp. 395-98, who establishes that the *Absinthe Drinkers* had entered the collection of Henry Hill of Brighton, England sometime in 1876). He may also have been stimulated by various renderings of similar subjects by such other artists as Daumier, Manet, Renoir, and Forain.

4.

View from Vincent's Room in the Rue Lepic
F 341
early spring 1887
oil on canvas: 36 x 48 cm
Not signed or dated
Lent by the Rijksmuseum Vincent van Gogh,
Amsterdam

This is one of two paintings which Vincent executed of the view from his rue Lepic residence on the slopes of the Butte Montmartre. Whether the other version (F 341a) was executed before or after this one, the two paintings evidence a certain latitude as to which building façades were to be emphasized.[1] A large and detailed sketchbook drawing in horizontal format (F 391) shows that Vincent might have varied his composition even more, had he so wished. The ascription in *De la Faille* of an early spring date for this subject doubtless rests upon the lack of foliage on the tree branches jutting out from behind the foreground building at centre, and the pale blue sky adds to our impression that summer is still some weeks away. It was, in fact, spring 1887 when Vincent must have enjoyed his greatest personal contact with the most active apostle of Neo-Impressionism, Paul Signac, since as usual the latter was to spend the coming summer away from Paris.

Vincent's choice of subject here would seem to have combined the general model provided in such a well-known painting of 1886 by Signac as his *Gas Tanks at Clichy (fig. 41)* with his own penchant manifested throughout his whole Paris stay,[2] for depicting silhouetted architectural subjects. The *View from Vincent's Room* is no less innovative in conception due to these related experiments. Not only is there a daring immediacy in the juxtaposition of unequally scaled and radically truncated foreground and middle distance building components, but the contrast between these looming images and the telescoped view into the far distance, where only the tiny tower of St. Jacques rises above the horizon, doubltess rests upon his then current involvement with the graphic art of Japan. Like certain examples in the work of Hiroshige II, which he either then or shortly thereafter would own,[3] Vincent's combination of a monumentally scaled foreground view involving a raking-angle depiction from above allows no simultaneous viewing into the distance without loss of focus on the foreground building details; the result is a sense of spatial discontinuity common to

much oriental art. Vincent's one means of overcoming this disparity is his use of the Pointillist stipple technique, which despite the intrusion of broader areas of red and green complementary contrast for the window and shutters on the middle building gives the painting a feeling of overall decorative patterning. If still rather Impressionist in its addiction to atmospheric effects, this painting nonetheless signals Vincent's determination to include Neo-Impressionism in his experiments leading to a mature personal style of his own.

Probably Théo had this painting in mind when on July 10, 1887, he wrote to a family friend (T1a) about the magnificient view from the apartment. His statement that "With the different effects produced by the various changes in the sky it is a subject for I don't know how many pictures," could only have Vincent in mind. Also his remark that the view is like one described by Zola in his *Une Page d'amour* must certainly have been shared, if in fact it had not originated, with Vincent. In this respect Vincent's devotion to painterly experiments with the science of colour hindered not at all his association of his depictions of Paris with those in the Realist novels which were his favourite form of reading.

[1] *See fig. 147* for the same view executed by Meyer de Haan *circa* early 1889.

[2] See illustrations in *De la Faille*, pp. 488-93.

[3] *Japanese Prints*, pp. 42-43.

Fig. 41
Paul Signac
Gas Tanks at Clichy,
1886,
oil on canvas
(National Gallery of Victoria, Melbourne).

SEE COLOUR PLATE 13.

5.

Interior of a Restaurant   F 342
summer 1887
oil on canvas: 45.5 x 56.5 cm
Not signed or dated
Lent by the Rijksmuseum Kröller-Müller, Otterlo,
The Netherlands

By any standard this painting (pl. 13) is among
the most orthodox Pointillist-style paintings in
Vincent's *oeuvre*. The stipple technique is
employed throughout, although for the floor area
it is not accompanied by a clear pattern of hues in
complementary contrast. The later "divisionist"
principle is more in evidence in the background
wall areas, where juxtapositions of red and green
dominate. Even here, however, Vincent allows
himself the freedom of one hue having clear
supremacy over the other, as in the pink and red
door, centre rear, and the green transom above it.
The chairs and tables largely resist the Pointillist
overlay giving the scene a sense of underlying
Realist structure, except that here, too, the orange
wood of the chairs and blue tints of the tablecloths
and place settings might be interpreted as another

embodiment of complementary contrast. However
novel may have been Vincent's use of colour
theory and Pointillist style, this is the type of painting with which in 1887 he was most likely to
please his friend Paul Signac and suggest his affinity to the Neo-Impressionist movement.

The setting has been identified with the restaurant *Chez Bataille*, not far from Vincent's residence on the rue Lepic, where he is known to have
taken his evening meals during spring 1887.[1] This
seems less likely than does one of the three restaurants at the Parisian suburb of Asnières which
Vincent depicted from the outside during the
summer 1887.[2] As the present writer has pointed
out elsewhere the unframed painting seen on the
wall of our *Interior of a Restaurant* must be his
own *View in Voyer-d'Argenson Park at Asnières*
(F 276), despite the liberty with which Vincent
has substituted, for the quite Pointillist style of that
painting, the more summarily executed image of
its imitation.[3] It is tempting to read the door at
right as displaying a Japanese print of some sort,
but it is safer perhaps to speak merely of a decorative motif in the Japanese manner. The flower
vases too, suggest a summer rather than spring

1887 date for this painting, and the vase on the
table at right evokes in miniature some of Vincent's still life flower pieces of a comparable date
and style (*see F* 322-323). The top hat hanging
from the wall might easily have been included as a
reference to a well-known item of clothing
favoured by the Neo-Impressionists and such supportive critics as Félix Fénéon.[4] If so, this only
further supports an interpretation of the *Interior of
a Restaurant* as a kind of dedication piece to the
Neo-Impressionist movement and the principles of
colour in which it was based.

[1] A.M. Hammacher with revisions by L. Gans, F.T.
    Gribling and E. Joosten, *Vincent van Gogh
    Catalogue*, 3rd rev. ed., Otterlo, The Netherlands:
    The State Museum Kröller-Müller, 1970, cat.
    no. 205.

[2] Namely, the restaurants called "De la Sirène"
    (F 312-13), "Rispal" (F 355) and "at Asnières"
    (F 321).

[3] Welsh-Ovcharov, pp. 105; 125, nos. 52; 297.

[4] *Ibid*., p. 125, no. 52.

6.
La Barrière with Horsetram F 1401
summer 1887
watercolour, pen and pencil on paper:
24 x 31.5 cm
Not signed or dated
Lent by the Rijksmuseum Vincent van Gogh,
Amsterdam

The subject here and in three companion
watercolours (*F* 1400, 1402-03) represents the
ramparts or fortification walls which at the time
surrounded Paris and defined its outskirts. *La
Barrière* does or should refer to the over one
hundred original gateways through the ramparts
at which taxes could be levied. Horse-drawn trams
provided transportation from the inner city to the
fortifications, although from there on one was
obliged to make one's way by foot or private
carriage. Given Vincent's address on the rue Lepic
it is virtually certain that the specific setting is
either the Porte Clichy or Porte St. Ouen,
depending upon which fork of the road he had
taken at La Fourche near the Place Clichy.
Judging from the similarity of the terrain, the

buildings and the presence of small smokestacks in
the distance (likely representing the industrial area
of Clichy), all four examples very likely represent a
single locale, and the presence of strolling couples
and women with parasols indicate weekend or
holiday rather than workday occasions.

This sense of gaiety amid what middle-class
Parisians would have found rather drab and
unpicturesque surroundings is a theme much
favoured by Vincent. It is as if he were presenting
his viewers with a kind of working-class
alternative to Seurat's *Sunday Aftenoon on the
Island of La Grande-Jatte* (*fig. 19*).

Douglas Cooper has pointed out how in colour
scheme and general style this watercolour
anticipates the watercolour version of *Vincent's
House at Arles* (cat. no. 25).[1] Indeed, Vincent's
use of the three primaries plus green in this linearly
sparse but well structured composition provides, in
its free wash technique, a counterpoint of
spontaneity for the rigours of life and society which
are otherwise inherent in the scene. A similarly
colourful celebration of the fortifications near St.
Ouen as a setting for working-class amelioration of
its miseries occurs in one of Vincent's favourite

novels, *Germinie Lacerteux*, by the De Goncourt
brothers.[2] One cannot imagine that this literary
masterpiece was far from Vincent's thoughts when
he created this particular series of watercolours.
Certainly the ideal of art as a balm for the wounds
of life was more in keeping with his art theory than
any form of social comment.

[1] Cooper, no. 18. Welsh-Ovcharov, *Angrand*, *fig.*
    17, illustrates an 1886 precedent in the art of
    Charles Angrand, which includes a passageway
    through Paris fortifications and which was known
    to Vincent.
[2] The relevant passage is quoted in
    Welsh-Ovcharov, p. 244.

7.

Self-Portrait with Straw Hat   *F* 469
summer 1887
oil on pasteboard: 41 x 33 cm
Not signed or dated
Lent by the Rijksmuseum Vincent van Gogh,
Amsterdam

This *Self-Portrait* was formerly often attributed to the Arles period, one suspects because of the straw hat's associations with the warm, sun-drenched climate of Arles. However, it is now generally attributed to summer 1887 in Paris because, like a number of other examples among his more than two dozen self-portraits now attributed to the Paris period, it employs a loose form of Impressionist brushwork which is fairly common in his paintings from 1887, but quickly disappears after his arrival in Arles when a thicker *impasto* applied more systematically becomes the rule. In style and pose our example is close to two other three-quarter view self-portraits now also attributed to Paris (*F* 61 verso, 526) and also to another self-portrait with straw hat (*F* 524), which might well deserve reattribution from Arles back to Paris, if only because of heavy beard which Vincent is wearing. In mid-summer 1888 Vincent reported to Théo (*CL*514) that he had had his "whole beard carefully shaved off," and in his other known self-portraits from Arles his beard is either quite closely cropped or non-existent. Van Gogh could have perhaps identified himself with his idol, the artist Adolphe Monticelli when he depicted himself wearing a large straw hat. Vincent in August 1888 admitted to his sister his intention to stroll through Monticelli's town of Marseilles "dressed exactly like him, Monticelli, as I have seen his portrait with an enormous yellow hat" (*Wil*8).

In addition we know from Bernard that what he described as Vincent's "enflamed countenances" were strongly represented in the exhibition which the Dutch painter organized at the *Du Chalet* restaurant late in 1887.[1] Although Hammacher rightly has seen an influence of Neo-Impressionist colour usage in the contrast of blue background with yellow-orange figure (there are minor yet vivid contrasts of red and green as well),[2] this painting is most notable for an expressive intensity in the countenance, particularly the somewhat aggressive manner in which the eyes stare directly out at the viewer. It is widely believed that Vincent experienced a mounting sense of frustration and psychological tension during his final months in Paris, and many of his self-portraits of the period seem to border on an expression of hostility. As late as September 1889, he wrote (*CL*604) that in a self-portrait done then he looked "saner *now* than I did then" in Paris, "even much more so." Despite what one may feel about the personal psychology of this painting, its broad areas of colour and simplified contour outlines emphasize how the Cloisonist style of such later paintings as the *Self-Portrait with Bandaged Ear* (cat. no. 32) were first anticipated through experiments like this in a still essentially Impressionist style.

[1]   *Van Gogh*, p. 393. There is a colour illustration in *CL*, III, frontispiece.

[2]   A.M.Hammacher, *Vincent van Gogh: Selbstbildnisse* (Stuttgart: Reklambucher, 1960), no. 13.

8.

Portrait of Père Tanguy　　　*F 364*

c. fall 1887

oil on canvas: 65 x 51 cm

Not signed or dated

Lent by a private collection

TORONTO ONLY

Of the three painted portraits which Vincent made of the humble Parisian colour merchant, Père Tanguy, that bearing the date "January 1887" (*F 263*) incontestably was the first produced. Like his earliest known *Portrait of Alexander Reid* (*F 270*), the earliest *Tanguy* retains the brownish colouration and descriptive naturalism of the artist's initial Paris portrait style. In contrast, the *Tanguy* exhibited here and the version at the Rodin Museum, Paris (*fig. 22*), both belong within Vincent's most advanced portrait style of the Paris years.[1] There is no clear evidence as to which of these two paintings came first, and writers have been divided in their opinions of the matter.[2] A small drawing of the subject's head against a Japanese print depicting Mount Fuji (*fig. 42*) either contributed to or reflects this detail in the Rodin museum canvas, and its execution on the back of a menu of the *Du Chalet* restaurant (*fig. 43*) suggests that the painting was present in the exhibition organized there by Vincent late in 1887 for himself and other painters of the "Petit Boulevard."[3] The Rodin Museum version also includes a detail variation on Vincent's *Japonaiserie: The Courtesan* (cat. no. 10), a painting now generally placed chronologically at the close of the Paris stay, which implies that this version of *Tanguy* post-dates the *Japonaiserie*.[4]

Bernard records that the *Tanguy* which the sculptor August Rodin later owned was begun along with his own (cat. no. 97) when he and Vincent worked together in the wooden *atelier* in the garden of the Bernards' Asnières residence, fall 1887.[5] However, his additional observation that following a dispute with Bernard's father Vincent ceased working at the *atelier* and took the portrait of Tanguy away with him in an unfinished state leaves in doubt which of the two versions with Japanese prints in the background actually was meant. In both the pose is remarkably similar, whereas the selection of prints varies, suggesting that the sitter might have gone to Asnières on one or more occasions and thus have provided the figural image used in the two paintings. Vincent could then have added the accompanying prints in alternate schemes at his own leisure. This freedom would help explain the experimental factor in the selection of prints and also the inclusion, upper left in the version exhibited here, of a framed still life painting by himself.[6] The setting of this portrait thus cannot be identified with any single locale, but should be conceived instead as a composite reference to Tanguy as a colour merchant and art dealer and to Vincent's own well-known love of the art of Japan as a source of inspiration for and oriental equivalent of modern European painting.[7]

1 Both the signed and dated Tanguy portrait and that at the Rodin Museum originally were owned by Tanguy, presumably gifts, but it was surely the latter to which Vincent referred in letters *CL* 50 and 510 as given to Tanguy.

2 Whereas the Editors of *CL* consider the Rodin Museum version the earlier one, Orton (*Japanese Prints*, p. 16) and J. House (London *P-I*, cat. no. 98) think it the last produced.

3 In a manuscript found in the papers of A. Aurier (translated in part in *P-I*, p. 64) Bernard attests to the presence at the *Du Chalet* exhibition of a *Portrait of Père Tanguy*. That he meant the Rodin Museum painting is indicated in Bernard, *Tanguy*, p. 615. Unlike the vague image of Mount Fuji in the version of *Tanguy* here, that behind the sitter's head in the Rodin Museum version and the drawing is likely a free version of a specific print in Vincent's collection (*Japanese Prints*, cat. no. 47c). This drawing could just as easily have been executed (at the exhibition?) after the painting as before it from life.

4 I.e., since Vincent follows the colour of his own painting rather than the colours of the illustrated print (see cat. no. 10) in the *Tanguy*.

5 Bernard, "Introduction," *Lettres de Vincent van Gogh à Emile Bernard* (Paris: Ambroise Vollard, 1911), p. 12. Bernard did not have the *atelier* before fall 1887, and his account makes clear that Vincent stopped visiting it a while before departing Paris. However, since the Tanguy portrait was unfinished, one cannot be absolutely sure that it was the Rodin Museum version as Bernard later presumed.

6 Orton, *Japanese Prints*, p. 16, identifies this still life painting as F 383, which is of additional interest for having an inscribed dedication to Théo.

7 A. Goaziou, "*Le Père Tanguy*" *compagnon de lutte des grands peintres du debut du siècle* (Paris: Floury, 1951), p. 16, asserts that Tanguy actually traded in Japanese prints, but this seems uncertain, even unlikely.

Fig. 42

Fig. 43

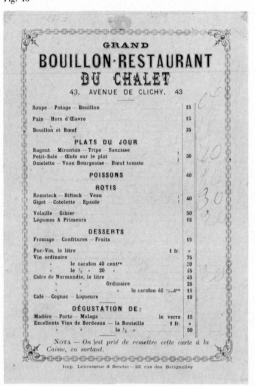

Fig. 44

Fig. 42
Vincent van Gogh
Père Tanguy,
1887,
pencil,
drawn on back of the menu of the
Grand-Restaurant du Chalet
(Rijksmuseum Vincent van Gogh, Amsterdam).

Fig. 43
Menu of the *Grand Bouillon-Restaurant du Chalet,* 43 avenue de Clichy,
(Rijksmuseum Vincent van Gogh, Amsterdam).

Fig. 44
Camille Pissarro
Portrait of Paul Cézanne
c. early 1874,
oil on canvas
(ex-Collection R. von Hirsch).

SEE COLOUR PLATE 11.

That Tanguy had begun to handle paintings by Vincent commercially renders appropriate the inclusion of a still life by the latter in one version. At the same time, it should be recalled that this was the version kept by Vincent (the Rodin Museum canvas went to Tanguy), so that the still life may be considered an oblique form of signature as well.

The use of works of art to provide a decorative background to portraiture was hardly an innovation by Vincent. The *Portrait of Emile Zola* by Manet and that of *James Tissot* by Degas are only the best known examples in which oriental art functioned to indicate a shared taste between the artist and a friend and colleague.[8] Another precedent might have been provided by Pissarro's *Portrait of Cézanne* (*fig. 44*), especially since both these artists were personally associated with either the van Gogh brothers or Tanguy.[9] Even if known to Vincent only by verbal description, and despite obvious differences, Pissarro had presented his friend Cézanne in a similar pose, inelegant workman's clothing, and a close-up background with popular illustrations reflecting the sitter's artistic tastes and producing the same feeling of rough-hewn immediacy inherent to Vincent's conception of Tanguy. Vincent had already experimented with such a mode of portraiture in the above-cited *Portrait of Alexander Reid*.[10] His elaboration of this approach in the case of Tanguy attains a novel intensity by combining a Realist portrait, the pose of a religious icon and an exotic setting to produce an image of enduring humanity.

Our perception of this particular portrait is enriched by the knowledge we have of the sitter. Julien Tanguy was born in 1825 in the hamlet of Pledran near St. Brieuc in Brittany. After marriage and a career as a plasterer, then meat supplier, by 1865 he moved to Paris and represented a firm of colour merchants. During the Paris Commune he became involved with the radical republican side and thereafter spent two or more years in exile under guard from the French capital before establishing himself as an independent colour supplier to the Impressionists by the mid 1870s.[11] Bernard testified later to Vincent's accurate capture of Tanguy's essentially saintly characteristics. The latter's native ruggedness yet gentle and friendly nature is sensed in his flattened Socrates-like nose and benevolent expressive eyes. He is dressed in workmen's clothing and straw hat and posed with the symmetrical frontality of a Buddha.[12]

It would be easy enough to suppose a deep affinity of character between Vincent and "father" Tanguy, especially in their mutual love for the poor, except that Vincent's letters to Théo are replete with suggestions to the relative inadequate quality yet redeeming low prices of Tanguy's pigments. At the same time, Théo's references to Tanguy indicate the growing importance to Vincent of Tanguy as a supplier of paints and potential outlet for sales. More important, Vincent in Arles repeatedly (*CL*506, 514, *B*14) recalls Tanguy in analogy with his new friend Postmaster August Roulin, "terrible republicans" who nonetheless share a certain status with Socrates for their folk wisdom and certainly, in Vincent's mind, for Tanguy's stoic attitude to his shrewish wife. There is of course a basic incongruity in Vincent's surrounding this old Communard with Japanese prints representing idealized images of Japanese courtesans and landscapes, and, however vaguely indicated, the sacred mountain of Fuji behind his head.[13] Such incongruities strangely seem to enrich our perception of the real world, if only because the juxtaposition of this French workman with the "floating world" of the *ukiyo-e* print was as unexpected to late nineteenth century French art as it is still unfathomable to present-day appreciation of Vincent's art.

9.
Japonaiserie: The Flowering Plum Tree (after Hiroshige)   F 371
late 1887
oil on canvas: 55 x 46 cm
Not signed or dated
Lent by the Rijksmuseum Vincent van Gogh, Amsterdam

This is generally considered the earliest of three paintings executed in Paris on the basis of individual Japanese wood block prints (see cat. no. 10 and *F 372*). The principal model in this instance was Hiroshige's *Flowering Plum Tree at the Teahouse at Kameido* (*fig. 45*) from the set of one hundred nineteen sheets called "A Hundred Views of Famous Places in Edo," of which Vincent owned twelve examples including this one.[1] His copying technique was aided by the use of a gridded transfer drawing (*fig. 46*), the Cloisonist outline character of which is only slightly modified by visible brushwork somewhat at odds with the more evenly graded application of colour to the original print. Vincent enhanced the print's forceful complementary colour contrast between the rich green orchard grass and the bright red sky above, by changing the gray bark of the foreground tree into a reddish brown, intensifying the basic opposition of hues. In addition he inserted a secondary complementary contrast by making the whitish sky area near the horizon and the tree blossoms yellow, and the trunks of the middle distant trees purple. This same contrast is present in the little figures strolling in the tea garden. Such alterations as these were consistent not only with Vincent's own strong penchant for complementary colour contrasts, but his belief that strong colour contrasts, above all of complementaries, were equally essential to the art of Japan (*Wil*3-4).

As in his second painting after a Hiroshige print, *Japonaiserie: The Bridge in the Rain* (*fig. 21*), Vincent's additions to the *Plum Tree* of internal framing strips embellished with Japanese characters further augment its overall decorative quality. Although sometimes said to be virtually indecipherable in meaning, certain character sequences have recently been shown to be readable precisely because they were copied from inscribed cartouches on other Japanese prints owned by

8   These precedents are cited in M. Schapiro, *Vincent van Gogh* (New York: Doubleday, 1980), p. 44.

9   On this painting, see T. Reff, "Pissarro's Portrait of Cézanne," *Burlington Magazine*, CIX, November 1967, pp. 627-33. The portrait remained in the collection of Camille Pissarro; *see* exh. cat. *Camille Pissarro 1830-1903* (London: Hayward Gallery, 1980-81), p. 104.

10 Welsh-Ovcharov, *Angrand*, p. 37 n. 43, identifies the setting of this portrait.

11 Bernard, *Tanguy*, provides the biography of this person from which all later accounts derive.

12 *Ibid.*, p. 615.

13 Orton, *Japanese Prints*, pp. 16-17, and "Vincent's interest in Japanese prints," *Vincent*, I (Autumn 1971), pp. 8-10, identify the Japanese prints found in the Tanguy portraits.

1   See *Japanese Prints*, p. 28 (colour ill. of the *Plum Tree*) and pp. 37-38, where all prints owned by Vincent from the set are catalogued, several with illustrations.

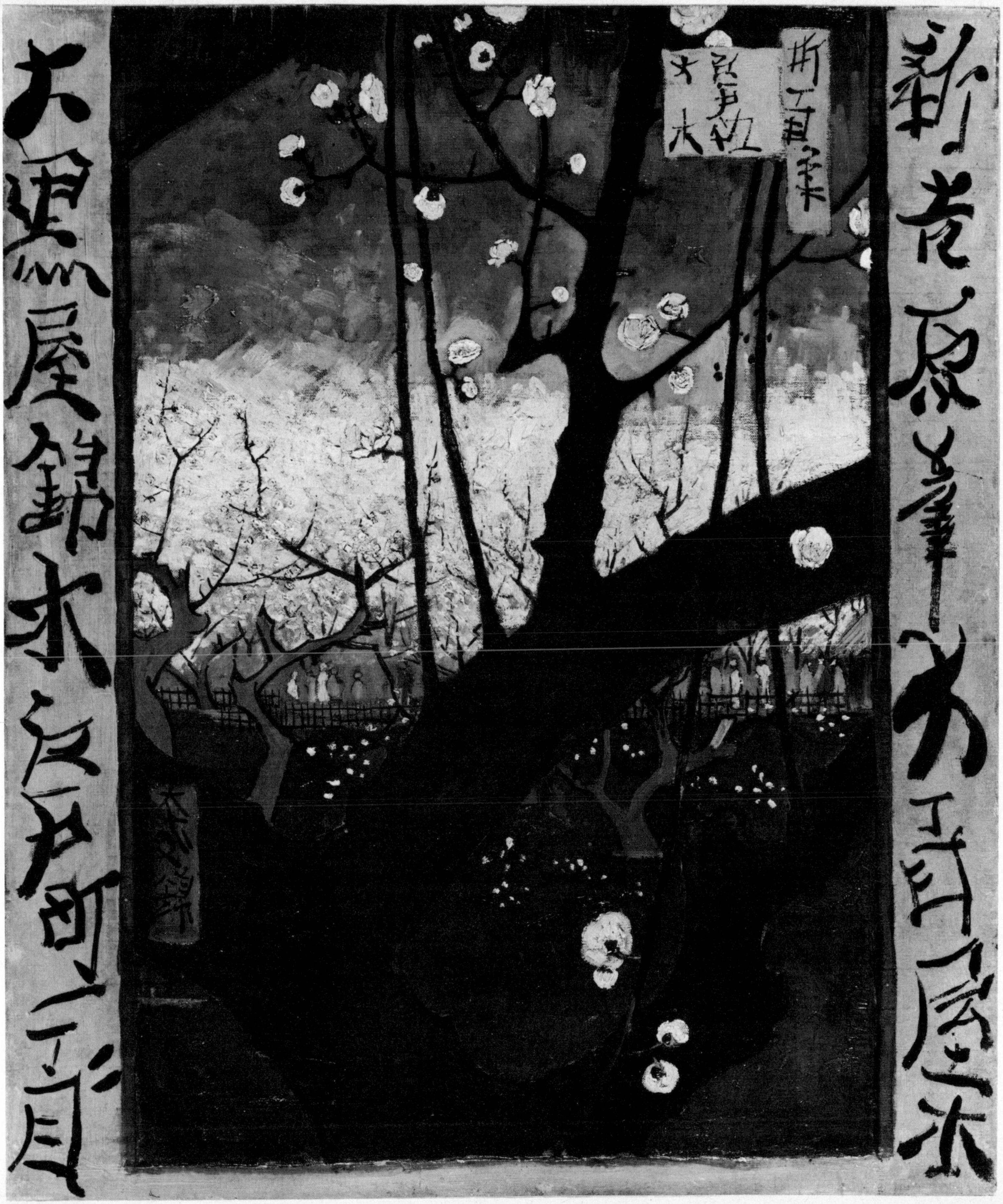

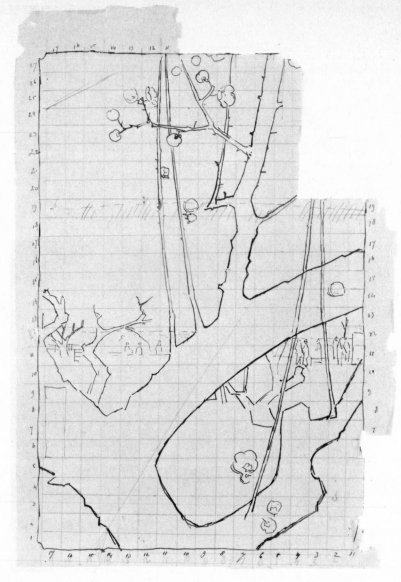

Fig. 45
Hiroshige
The Plum Tree Teahouse at Kameido
1857,
colour print
(Rijksmuseum Vincent van Gogh, Amsterdam).

Fig. 46
Vincent van Gogh
Tracing of Hiroshige Plum Trees in Flower,
1887,
drawing
(Rijksmuseum Vincent van Gogh, Amsterdam).

Vincent.[2] While only rarely extended to form a framing device either at both sides or all the way round the central pictorial image, these Japanese cartouches nonetheless must have been Vincent's source of inspiration. One print owned by the Dutch artist and used in his portraits of *Père Tanguy* (cat. no. 8 and *fig. 22*) included a decorative cartouche extending along the whole right edge.[3] Vincent's invention of these framing strips with characters may also have been the offspring of necessity. In both the *Plum Tree* and *Bridge* the proportions of Hiroshige's scenes, once enlarged and transferred to Vincent's canvases, were slightly too vertical in emphasis to conform to the standardized French formats which Vincent had selected.[4] For the *Plum Tree* a need to fill in left-over space was limited to the edge areas left and right and slightly at the bottom; in the *Bridge* space was left over all the way around.

Like Vincent's other paintings after Japanese prints, the *Plum Tree* is often thought to comprise an aberration from his out-of-door method of painting landscapes, precisely because it is a so-called copy. This implied condescension is not nor-mally extended to his copies after Millet, Rembrandt or Delacroix; it also underestimates the lasting effect of the stylizations of tree form inherent to the Hiroshige print and to Vincent's painting thereof within his own freely created landscapes at Arles. Vincent would certainly have recalled the bold and flattened contours of the truncated image of the foreground tree when he saw a drawing of Gauguin's *The Vision after the Sermon* (*fig. 47*) he shortly thereafter executed a version of his favoured theme, *The Sower* (*see* cat. no. 18), thus combining debts to Gauguin, Hiroshige and himself. An even earlier, if more general, debt to this Hiroshige and to other related Japanese prints in his own collection can be found. This is the series of orchard landscapes which he executed during the period March-April 1888, exemplified in our exhibition by *The Orchard with View of Arles* (cat. no. 35).[5] While such tree formations with their spiky contour outlines can be traced to Vincent's Nuenen period (for example see *F* 1128), no flattened tree silhouettes can be discovered within the Paris period landscape pro-duction. However, immediately upon his removal to Arles he became preoccupied by a variety of orchard subjects with cleanly outlined tree trunks set against quickly receding perspectival views, cut off in the distance by fences or building outlines. Despite differences of style and brushwork, it is scarcely thinkable that he would have entered into this flurry of activity without the art of the Japanese print in mind or without the support of his own well-known identification of Provence as the Japan of Europe (*CL* 500).

2   W. van Gulik in *Japanese Prints*, pp. 11-12.
3   *Japanese Prints*, cat. no. 221 (p. 16 for ill.), which geisha figure, however, when used middle left in the two *Tanguy* portraits, occurs without this extended cartouche.
4   The *Plum Tree* employs a size ten figural format, and the *Bridge* is a size twenty landscape.
5   Hulsker, *Complete van Gogh*, pp. 310-18, con-veniently groups these representations of orchards in the countryside surrounding Arles.

Fig. 47
Paul Gauguin
Vision after the Sermon,
late 1888
drawing sent to Vincent van Gogh in a letter (*G*9)
(Rijksmuseum Vincent van Gogh, Amsterdam).

10.
Japonaiserie: *The Courtesan*
(*after Kesei Eisen*)   *F* 373
c. late 1887
oil on canvas: 105 x 61 cm
Not signed or dated
Lent by the Rijksmuseum Vincent van Gogh,
Amsterdam

This is the largest of three paintings which Vincent
produced principally on the basis of single
Japanese prints. The other two paintings (cat. no.
9 and *F* 373) derive from prints by the well-
known Hiroshige. This example features, in contrast, a work by Kesei Eisen, which Vincent knew
from its illustration on the cover of the May 1886
''special Japanese number'' of *Paris illustré*
(*fig. 48*). The currently ascribed title of this painting and its prototype enjoyed no authority in Vincent's own lifetime, and the frequent identification
of the figural subject as an actor clearly is wrong.[1]
Instead, the female depicted is a courtesan of the
most elevated rank (*oiran*) whose many *kogai* or
hair batons (strips of turtle shell) testify to her
status.[2] Whether or not Vincent recognized this
distinction from the less elevated *geisha* class, he
possessed no less than fifteen prints by Hiroshige,
eleven of which represented these two
entertainer-courtesan types.[3] It is doubtful that the
finer distinctions of Japanese society were familiar
to Vincent, but his knowledge of the general
iconography of such isolated females needs no
questioning.

   The original print source employs a relatively
narrow vertical format, suggesting the function of
a *kakemono*, a Japanese wall hanging. Vincent
employed a still surviving tracing from the print
illustration as a gridded transfer drawing in order
to assure the accuracy of his so-called ''copy'' of
the original.[4] This very accuracy perhaps necessitated the addition of a decorative background of
the kind he devised, since the *kakemono* format
would have had to be accommodated to the somewhat wider framing format he had chosen. At the
same time there was ample precedent for setting
an already exotic female into a doubly exotic background setting, as Whistler already had done in
such paintings as *Rose and Silver*: *The Princess
from the Land of Porcelain*.[5] Closer to Vincent's
own conception are such illustrative precedents as
the cover of *Paris illustré* itself.

   Consciously intended or not, this contrast
between one kind of featured picture image and its
background decor conforms to the tradition of

Fig. 48
"Le Japon," Cover of *Paris illustré*, May, 1886
(Rijksmuseum Vincent van Gogh, Amsterdam).

here transformed his chosen model more radically than in the case of the Hiroshige-based paintings. The result is a painting which rivals in colour intensity those other tributes to the art of Japan from his last months in Paris, the two versions of *The Portrait of Père Tanguy* (*see* cat. no. 8), in one of which (*fig. 22*) the Eisen *oiran* image figures prominently (lower right) and in yet another novel colour selection. Vincent likely was aware that all these print sources conformed to the *ukiyo-e* print tradition with its emphasis upon human happiness enjoyed in the everyday world. In his *Courtesan* Vincent has given us a painting which appears quite literally to embody the ideal of "a picture of the floating world," as the term *ukiyo-e* is translated into English. Metaphorically too Vincent viewed the art of Japan as a mixture of mundane reality and idyllic existence, an ideal he never ceased to cherish in his own painting.

[1] First stated by M.E. Tralbaut, "Van Gogh's Japanisme," *Mededelingen van de Dienst voor Schone Kunsten der Gemeente 's-Gravenhage*, XI (1954), p. 16, who nonetheless produced herewith the first major art historical study on this aspect of Vincent's creativity. However, already in 1885 in Antwerp Vincent did use the term "Japonaiserie" (*CL* 437).

[2] Information kindly supplied in conversation (November 6, 1980) by Mr. Tamon Miki, Chief Curator, the National Museum of Modern Art, Tokyo.

[3] *Japanese Prints*, pp. 30-32, records and in large part illustrates Vincent's collection of prints by Eisen.

[4] Ill. in *Japanese Prints*, p. 18.

[5] Although in his own correspondence Vincent mentions Whistler several times, it is never in the context of Japanism, and *CL* 590 implies that Whistler was seen as a Realist.

[6] Tralbaut, "Van Gogh's Japanisme," and F. Orton in *Japanese Prints*, pp. 18-19, differ slightly in these source identifications. The significance of the cranes may however be more than mere decorative intent for Vincent since "grue" or crane was a popular term for courtesan at the time. See A. Hansen, *Manet and the Modern Tradition* (New Haven: Yale University Press, 1977), p. 87, who discusses this identification in E. Manet's portrait of *Nana* (Kunsthalle, Hamburg).

[7] For obvious prototypes of these bamboo stalks see the Hokusai's print "Fuji seen through a bamboo thicket" from vol. 2 of *One Hundred Views of Fuji*, 1835.

Japonaiserie, which has led some critics to categorize Vincent's paintings in this *genre* as of lesser importance in his *oeuvre* because of their decorative function and derivative character. This type of thinking simply overlooks the fact that except for the linear outline of the courtesan image, Vincent has transformed sources he used, including the frogs (below) and storks (upper left) which were derived from specific Japanese prints. These and the water-lily pond with bamboo background of the landscape setting, are a highly original conglomeration of selectively borrowed motifs and originally conceived composition.[6] Most important, Vincent's heavily laden brushwork and especially his use of colour conform not at all with his source of models. Whereas the *oiran* was printed in a combination of blues, reds, blacks, silver-grays

and whites, Vincent's figure except for the face is treated in colours vastly richer and purer than those of his source. In particular, he has substituted green for blue throughout, doubtless because of his belief that the complementary contrast red-green gave a greater sense of harmony and brilliance to the colour scheme than was found in the illustration. Blue occurs in the hair embellishments, which as seen against the orange-yellow background and newly conceived Western frame for the figure imply a secondary complementary contrast to offset and thus enhance the major one. These same four colours dominate the "waterscape" framing device with both the green foreground bamboo stalks and lily pads given red contours and the bright blue water frequently juxtaposed with yellow-orange stalks.[7] Vincent has

11.

Still Life: Plaster Statuette and Books　　F 360
late 1887
oil on canvas: 55 x 46.5 cm
Not signed or dated
Lent by the Rijksmuseum Kröller-Müller, Otterlo,
The Netherlands

Like the *Still Life: Parisian Novels with a Rose*
(*fig. 18*; *see* cat. no. 12) and *The Italian Woman*
(cat. no. 13), this painting displays a form of
striated and parallel brush strokes which suggest
the wrinkled surfaces of crepe paper on which
some of the Japanese prints in Vincent's collection
were printed.[1] The two books in *Plaster Statuette*
might themselves be thought to lie on a piece of
paper, although the angle of viewing and lack of
ordinary spatial definition in this painting is so
unorthodox that it has rightly been seen as a radical departure in the art of his Paris period.[2]
Whether one attributes this to the influence of
Japanese prints or to that of some such colleague
as Bernard, one cannot imagine any other specific
model having served as a guide to its spatial convolutions and ambiguities. As in certain still life
paintings by Cézanne, logic tells us that the flowers, book and statuette should be sensed as slip-
ping off the presumed table top underneath, but
somehow the composition remains in balance
through the sheer force of the artist's manipulation
of forms, colours and brushwork. While the total
effect can once again be termed decorative, there is
nonetheless a strong sense of real objects being
depicted in their true shapes and colours.

Beyond the question of style, this is one of the
most symbolically charged paintings in Vincent's
total *oeuvre*. What in a number of other treatments of similar plaster statuettes might be considered a student's attempt to master the secrets of
modelling figures in the round is here transformed
into an image of ripe sexuality despite the imitation
of a broken figure from antiquity. This accords
with the subject matter of the De Goncourt
brothers' realist novel *Germinie Lacerteux*, the
heroine of which lives a seemingly placid life as a
domestic servant by day, but is driven by an
uncontrollable biological urge to one desperate
sexual involvement after another by night. Georges
Duroy, the hero of G. de Maupassant's *Bel Ami*,
the novel resting upon *Germinie* in the painting, is
a sexual opportunist, employing his considerable
personal charm in order to further his personal
social aggrandizement. It was not that Vincent
intended to moralize through his identification of

these novels by title, rather, as with his treatment of Parisian novels in general (*see* cat. no. 12), he felt one must read them in order to "be said to belong to one's time" (*Wil*1). Approximately two years after seeing it in an exhibition of late 1887 Vincent described a "Portrait of an Old Man by Puvis de Chavannes" as having "always remained the ideal in figure to me, an old man reading a yellow novel, and beside him a rose and some watercolour brushes in a glass of water. . . . These are consoling things, to see modern life as something bright, in spite of its inevitable sadness" (*CL*617).[3] The fact that the van Gogh family crest featured three roses, which albeit admittedly golden, just conceivably inspired Vincent to include the branch with three roses in his painting, lower left.[4] Whether or not his own identification with the modern life of Paris as depicted in Realist literature is hinted at by the rose branch, we can be sure that throughout his mature life the indefatigable reader Vincent found in them one of most powerful sustaining forces in his life as it was an often cited source of inspiration in his art.

1   F. Orton, "Vincent's Interest in Japanese Prints," *Vincent: Bulletin of the Rijksmuseum Vincent van Gogh*, 13; (1971), p. 8, no. 20, states that only fifteen "crepes" exist in the preserved van Gogh collection of Japanese prints.

2   L. Gans, "Vincent van Gogh en de Schilders van de 'Petit Boulevard'," *Museumjournaal*, 1: 4 (1955), pp. 85-93, ascribed great importance to the *Plaster Statuette and Books* in this pioneering study of the relationships among Vincent, Anquetin and Bernard.

3   A.B. Price, "Two Portraits by Vincent van Gogh and Two Portraits by Pierre Puvis de Chavannes," *The Burlington Magazine*, CXVII, November 1975, p. 714, first illustrated the *Portrait of Eugène Benon* by Puvis and identified it as Vincent's "Old Man."

4   Dr. Anton Frederik Philips, *Nederlands Patriciaat* (The Hague: Central Bureau voor Genealogie, 1964), p. 171, illustrates and describes the van Gogh family crest.

12.
Still Life: Parisian Novels   *F* 358
late 1887 (1888?)
oil on canvas: 53 x 72.5 cm
Not signed or dated
Lent by the Rijksmuseum Vincent van Gogh, Amsterdam

This smaller version of the *Still Life: Parisian Novels with a Rose* (*fig. 18*), which definitely was executed in Paris, presumably in late 1887, was executed either at the same time or, as has been suggested, in Arles as a copy from memory of the earlier work.[1] The *Novels with a Rose* was considered important enough by Théo and Vincent (*CL*468) to be exhibited at the spring 1888 *Indépendants*, where it was described and criticized by Gustave Kahn, who stated, "A polychromatic multitude of books is represented in the manner of a tapestry; while this motif is satisfactory as a study, it cannot serve as the pretext for a painting. . . ."[2] Kahn's comparison to a tapestry seems indeed justified by the rough

striated brushwork which was used throughout to produce a pattern effect further enhanced by the decorative bands of cloth or wallpaper in the background. Since it is known that this version of the subject was produced in the van Gogh apartment, one must assume that Vincent depicted either the existing or a specially arranged decor within that setting. A description of this painting by a visitor to the apartment as Vincent's "first in a series of yellow paintings" and his implication that Japanese prints of crepe paper had influenced Vincent's brush technique provide additional evidence that Vincent's involvement with oriental modes of style already was at a peak during his final year in Paris and involved more

1   C. Nordenfalk, "Van Gogh and Literature," *Journal of the Warburg and Courtauld Institutes*, X, 1947, p. 143, first proposed this thesis, which Hulsker, *Complete van Gogh*, p. 368, follows.

2   Kahn, "Peinture: Exposition des indépendants," *La Revue indépendante*, no. 18 (April 1888), p. 163.

paintings than merely those which reproduce prints in the tradition of *Japonaiserie* (*for example*, cat. no. 13 n. 1).[3]

While lacking the parallel brush strokes in imitation of crepe paper, the Amsterdam *Parisian Novels* may not therefore be thought less devoted to the decorative ideal. Granting the possibility that it was executed from memory at Arles, it is equally plausible to consider it a study for the version exhibited in spring 1888. Many of Vincent's Paris period works are equally intense in their colouration and parallels in his brush technique are also possible to find. The "painting from memory" theory, moreover, carries with it the unfortunate implication of indebtedness to Gauguin's style and working habits, none of whose remarkable still life paintings of summer 1888 (cat. no. 51 and *W* 293) Vincent would have known even after Gauguin arrived in Arles. At least the *Novels with a Rose*, and perhaps the Amsterdam version too, would have been seen by Gauguin in the van Gogh apartment winter 1887-88, when their innovative and striking simplifications of form and colour would have appeared more exceptional than after this had become a norm in *avant-garde* French painting.

For Vincent the bright cover colours of the scattered books had a symbolic meaning. Whereas several of Vincent's paintings with books include their readable titles, this version and its larger companion piece studiously avoid the possibility. One may assume that Vincent wished them to represent French contemporary novels collectively. Writing to his sister Wilhelmina from Paris (*Wil* 1), Vincent recommends the reading of such novels above the Bible as a source of amelioration of life's woes. In fact Vincent speaks of this body of literature as "the light of the world" and as revolutionary as had once been the message of Christianity. For the Dutch artist religion and art retained an essential link.

SEE COLOUR PLATE 12.

13.

The Italian Woman with Daisies:
La Segatori   *F* 381
late 1887
oil on canvas: 81 x 60 cm
Not signed or dated
Lent by the Musée du Jeu de Paume, Paris

The subject of this painting (pl. 12) is often thought to be the same sitter as for cat. no. 3, the artist's model, Agostina Segatori, who operated the café *Le Tambourin* and who is thought to have formed a liaison with Vincent by early 1887. Unfortunately, *The Italian Woman* is so devoid of the pecularities of any concrete setting that identification of the sitter with that locale and its proprietress is more conjectural than with the somewhat earlier painting. In addition, the relationship between Vincent and Agostina had ended in some disillusionment by summer 1887 (*CL* 462), and the Jeu de Paume painting is now widely considered one of Vincent's very final, because most stylistically advanced, paintings from his Paris period.[1] Although it evinces iconographic parallels with a considerable number of precedents in both popular illustration and by artists whom Vincent admired such as Adolphe Monticelli and

Armand Guillaumin,[2] virtually all suggestions of picturesque accompaniment to what is essentially a soberly isolated figure of a generalized folk type, an Italian gypsy, have been eschewed. Even the daisies are held in a desultory fashion in keeping with the impenetrable and impassive gaze of the perhaps bored sitter.

Against all this lack of vivacity in characterization of the principal subject, vibrating clashes of brilliant, saturated pristine colours shriek out. Within the stark framing device top and right, Vincent has as usual insisted upon complementary colour contrasts, here red and green. Apart from the related colour usage found in the *Portrait of Père Tanguy* (cat. no. 8), this painting comes close to a virtual personal exegesis of van Gogh and colour theory. One notices first the total absence from the painting of "unpainted" areas. The background is in fact only a highly coloured version of a background used in early Paris period flower pieces. The brush technique, often called "hatching" by Vincent (*CL* 555), here could be compared to a system of hatchwork, or of systematic striation. At the same time there is evident Vincent's usual fascination with the laws of complementary contrast and graduation (iridescent emanations of the same hue in all its neighbouring variations). As with Vincent's paintings in general, laws give way to expressive effects as soon as they are used. In this instance a putative "gypsy" has served to allow Vincent one of his most daring abstractions before his personal involvment with Gauguin and the "School of Pont-Aven."

[1] See Fred Orton "Vincent's interest in Japanese prints" *Vincent Bulletin of the Rijksmuseum Vincent van Gogh* 3, 1971, p. 8 who gives the source of the composition to "a 'kake-mono-ye' print: a print in kakemono form which was hung for display on a tapestry mount." Orton also relates Vincent's style to imitations of the surface of a Japanese print. However, the same author suggests identification of *The Italian Woman* with either Agostina Segatori or the Italian wife of the artist J.P. Russell (ft. 22, p. 8). Both a description (H. Thannhouser, "Documents inedits Vincent van Gogh et John Russell," *L'Amour de l'art* 7, 1938, 291) of Marianna Russell's long blonde hair and her portrait, dated May 1887 by her husband (Ann Galbally, *The Art of John Russell*, Melbourne 1977, plate XVI p. 40) make this identification for *The Italian Woman* problematic.

[2] See Welsh-Ovcharov, pp. 193-95 and ills. XIVa-d.

[3] A.S. Hartrick, *A Painter's Pilgrimage through Fifty Years*, (Cambridge: University Press, 1939), pp. 45-46.

14A.
*The Langlois Bridge with Women
Washing*   F 397
mid-March 1888
oil on canvas: 54 x 65 cm
Signed lower left: *Vincent*
Lent by the Rijksmuseum Kröller-Müller, Otterlo,
The Netherlands
TORONTO ONLY

14B.
The Langlois Bridge with Road alongside the
Canal   F 400
late March 1888
oil on canvas: 58.5 x 73 cm
Signed lower left: *Vincent*
Lent by the Rijksmuseum Vincent van Gogh,
Amsterdam
AMSTERDAM ONLY

The two versions of Vincent's *The Langlois Bridge*, which are to be exhibited respectively in Toronto and Amsterdam, are the earliest extant treatments of this theme.[1] A third, now at the Wallraf-Richartz Museum, Cologne (*F 570*), was executed in May 1888, thus two months later than these versions, and presents the little drawbridge from the same side but the opposite canal bank as the version in Amsterdam (cat. no. 14b). However, a fourth version was described and sketched in a letter of March 18, 1888 to Bernard (*B2, fig. 49*) and mentioned to Théo at the same time (*CL470*).[2] This version featured a large setting sun and two pairs of lovers heading towards Arles along the same roadway seen in the foreground of the Amsterdam version. The latter was in fact a replacement for the painting described to Bernard, which Vincent admitted to having ruined (*CL471*), when due to inclement weather he tried to finish it at home. This painting, of which only a fragment with one pair of lovers apparently survives (*F 544*), was described on March 18 to Théo as an experimental search for "a good, bold design" and for "colours . . . like stained-glass windows," an aim also inherent in the indications of pure colour for various compositional divisions on the drawing sent to Bernard. These colour choices reflected the particular conditions of weather and time of day at which Vincent had begun his painting, since he described the replacement piece now at Amsterdam (*CL471*) as "the same subject again on another canvas, but, as the weather was quite different, in gray tones and without figures."[3] The Kröller-Müller version provides some indication of the bright sunlight which prevailed when the now lost version was begun *plein air*, but there a yellow sun was intended to contrast with the lilac shadow of the near walls of the bridge, a juxtapostion of complementaries which was accompanied by the dominant green-red juxtapositions planned for the foreground areas. This combination of complementary contrasts and the ideal of stained-glass windows reflect Vincent's preoccupation with a Cloisonist mode of style as he began his life in Arles. It is significant that he instructed his brother to offer one version of the Langlois Bridge to Anquetin in the very letter (*CL500*) in which he reported learning of the Dujardin article about that artist and a new Japanese tendency (*that is*, "Le Cloisonisme").

Neither can there be any doubt that Vincent intended (and probably selected) the Langlois Bridge theme as a tribute to Japan and its art. His March letter to Bernard begins by telling him "this

country seems to me as beautiful as Japan as far as the gay colour effects are concerned," and contains a paragraph which posits that Japanese art, decadent at home, "is being continued in France." Immediately thereupon he mentions the enclosed sketch of the Langlois Bridge and the two oil studies of the subject he had done, thus strongly implying their Japanese character. Not that in this case Vincent had used a particular Japanese print as his model, since we know that these compositions were developed in front of the chosen setting with the help of a framing device he had constructed in order to help him with perspective.[4] While his Japanese print collection did contain several bridge subjects in addition to Hiroshige's *Bridge in the Rain*, which he had copied, none of these has a composition genuinely similar to any of the Langlois Bridge paintings. Yet one senses in them an affinity with Japanese compositional principles such as wide-angle yet deeply receding perspectival thrusts juxtaposed with foreground or middle-distance planar dispositions which interrupt and counterbalance what otherwise would be a feeling of unimpeded flight into the void.

It is also no mere coincidence that Vincent chose Bernard as the recipient along with Théo of the announcement of his first major subject series developed at Arles. Bernard and Vincent, after all, had already painted similar views of the bridges crossing the Seine at Asnières (cat. no. 96 and *fig. 29*). In some ways the destroyed and Amsterdam versions of *The Langlois Bridge* might be thought a tribute to Bernard's *Ragpickers: Iron Bridges at Asnières*, whereas memory of

1 P. Leprohon, *Tel fu van Gogh?* (Paris: Editions du Sud, 1964), pp. 416-17, discovered that the now destroyed bridge was known in Vincent's time as the "Langlois" bridge because of the name of its guard, although Vincent in his letters and the dedication on a watercolour version (*F 1480*) deformed this to "l'Anglois."

2 The Kröller-Müller version as reproduced by Vincent in a watercolour (*see note*), an oil replica (not in *De la Faille*, but reproduced in R. Huyghe, *Van Gogh*; Paris: Flammarion, 1977, p. 42) and an oil variant (*F 571*) made for Théo. Judging from trees, buildings and cast shadows this version would seem to view the bridge from the opposite side from that of the Amsterdam and Cologne paintings. The theme of women washing clothes was used just previously in a painting of another bridge near Arles (*F 396*) and anticipates a subject used the following fall by Gauguin upon his arrival in Arles (*W 302-03*).

3 As noted in Cooper, pp. 60-62, Vincent already had depicted a drawbridge in his Drenthe period, 1883 (*F 1098*), and in May 1888 Vincent commented to Théo (*CL488*) on the similarity between Dutch and Arles subject opportunities. Just possibly the Amsterdam "gray" painting was an illustration of this affinity when Arles was subjected to the overcast skies so common in The Netherlands.

4 See Anne Stiles Wylie, "An investigation of the vocabulary of line in Vincent van Gogh's Expression of Space," *Oud Holland*, IV 1970, pp. 210-235, for a discussion of the artist's use of the perspective frame.

his own variant *Bridge at Asnières* (*fig. 29*) in general composition, colouration, brush technique and the inclusion of boat moorings may have prompted Vincent to attempt the Kröller-Müller and related versions.[5] Vincent and Bernard's suburban bridges of Paris may well in turn have relied upon the example of the Neo-Impressionist Georges Seurat, whose *Une Baignade, Asnières* (*fig. 20*) and *Bridge at Courbevoie* (Courtauld Gallery, London) are only two of the many Neo-Impressionist paintings which embodied a form of geometrizing planar structure featuring a high horizon line and a triangulated foreground wedge of land bordering on a body of water leading to a bridge set along the horizon.[6] Whether or not the perspectival stylizations of Neo-Impressionism were themselves dependent upon a study of Japanese design principles—as is increasingly believed—Vincent's intended employment of complementary colour contrasts with the Langlois Bridge subject is another reason for believing that he also had in mind Seurat, whom he had met personally only about a month earlier, in choosing a bridge subject for his inaugural series of landscapes in his self-styled Japan in southern France.

5   For Bernard, besides *The Ragpickers*, see cat. no. 91 and *fig. 115;* for Vincent, besides *F* 301, the Bührle Foundation *The Bridges at Asnières*, see *F* 302-03, 311 and, though veiled in a mixed Impressionist-Pointillist haze of brushwork, *F* 352, 354.

6   One need only leaf through the illustrations of Ch. II of *P-I*, pp. 73-130, in order to appreciate this usage in Neo-Impressionism, granting that triangular wedges are defined as frequently by curved as by straight lines.

Fig. 50
Vincent van Gogh:
The Zouave: Half-Length,
June 1888,
watercolour
(The Metropolitan Museum of Art, New York).

15.
A Bugler of the Zouave Regiment   *F* 423
end June 1888
oil on canvas: 65 × 54 cm
Not signed or dated
Lent by the Rijksmuseum Vincent van Gogh, Amsterdam

This was one of two versions in oil, which were executed at the very end of June 1888. Whereas to Théo (*CL* 501) Vincent indicated that this bust version of the Zouave bugler was executed before the full-length seated version (*F* 424), to Bernard (*B* 8) he speaks of a "painted sketch" of the full-length version and "finally" the version of "his portrait against a green door and some orange bricks," which only could mean the presently exhibited version.[1] Whatever the exact sequence of paintings and two reed pen drawings (*F* 1485, 1535), there is also a crayon, pen and watercolour version (*F* 1482), which the artist inscribed "à mon cher copain Emile Bernard. Vincent" (*fig. 50*) and presumably sent about this time to his younger correspondent.[2] Since Vincent said to Théo he would not be surprised if Bernard wanted an exchange for the subject of the Zouave's head, we can feel fairly certain that Vincent had Bernard in mind when working "three or four days" and "from the model" on such a subject type. At the very least, Vincent evidently believed that Bernard would be receptive

1   In a letter of early August 1888 to Théo (*CL* 519), Vincent again refers to working on the full-length seated Zouave against a white wall, which could mean that the "painted sketch" mentioned to Bernard is now lost or else that *F* 424 was completed in August.

2   This wash drawing, still more Cloisonist than the painting exhibited here, was done after the painting, as Roskill, *Exchanges*, pp. 151-52, first proposed.

to the kind of portrait conception it exemplifies, which Vincent described to both his brother and Bernard, not without a note of perverse pride, as "horribly harsh and ugly." Nonetheless, in the following letter to Bernard (*B9*) Vincent reports having set aside for exchange this "head of the Zouave," with the idea that it might occur in a brothel of the type found in a watercolour sent in June by Bernard to Vincent (*see* cat. no. 100).[3]

This was the most dramatically Cloisonist-style portrait which Vincent had executed to that date. Having received from Bernard in St. Briac sketches with greater simplification of outline and colour planes than he might have seen back in Paris, Vincent's *Zouave* could be interpreted as a response to the latest development which he sensed in the younger artist. At the same time, the frontal pose, compressed space and abstracted background of this portrait built upon such Paris experiment in portrait icons as the *Père Tanguy* (cat. no. 8) and *The Italian Woman* (cat. no. 13), despite obvious differences of style and iconography. Vincent's observation to his brother that the colour scheme involves "a savage combination of incongruous tones, not easy to manage," and that "vulgar, even loud portraits like this" teach him something, reinforces the belief that this painting was meant as a more radical form of non-tonal painting. As in a still life painting from the previous month, which featured a blue enamel coffeepot (*fig. 125*), Vincent speaks of the colour of the Zouave's jacket as being the "blue of enamel saucepans" (*CL 501*)–another possible veiled allusion to the *cloisonné* tradition. The red cap on a solid green backdrop and the blue versus red-orange-yellow contrast of the other major colour areas suggest that he had complementary contrasts in mind, no matter how incongruous and "difficult to manage" the combinations had been. All in all, these intentionally harsh confrontations of colour match the contrast between the curvilinear contours of the figure and the flat green plane and rectilinear grid of the brickwork. In the vigour with which Vincent describes his harsh stylistic components, one senses that he considered them appropriate to his subject: "a Zouave . . . with a small face, a bull neck, and the eye of a tiger."

3   See Roskill, p. 126 and Pl. 96, which may be considered the original modest instigation which led to the "Night Café" paintings by Vincent and Gauguin.

16.
Boats on the Beach at Saintes-Maries   F 413
last week of June 1888
oil on canvas: 64.5 × 81 cm
Signed below centre: *Vincent*
Lent by the Rijksmuseum Vincent van Gogh, Amsterdam

Vincent spent most of the third week of June at the fishing village of Saintes-Maries on the Mediterranean coast in the swampy region of the Camargue, and as his first effort of his last day of work there (*CL 500*) produced the drawing (*F 1428*) on which a watercolour version (*F 1429*) and the present painting are based. The brilliant coloured watercolour version preserves the composition of the drawing intact, but, as Vincent said in his letter to Théo, the oil version added "more sea and sky on the right."[1] He might easily have added that this was derived from a series of three drawings of boats on the open sea (*F 1430, 1430a, 1430b*). Whereas the watercolour (now unfortunately lost), viewing the beached boats from much closer and with more evenly distributed bright colouration, may be considered one of Vincent's most genuinely Japanist and Cloisonist works, in the painted version these analogies are preserved chiefly in the depictions of the boats.[2] As noted by Meyer Schapiro, this contrast between the luminous Impressionist landscape background and the firm contours and flat colouration only enhances the contrast between structural elements in the art of van Gogh. Although no specific Japanese wood block print has been identified as the source of this painting, the general indebtedness is indicated in more than one letter (*CL 487, 495*), which supports the identification of this painting as one of Vincent's most Japanist-inspired works.[3]

1   For a colour illustration of this watercolour see R. Treble, *Van Gogh and His Art* (New York: Galahad, 1975), pp. 64-65, Pl. 46.

2   Schapiro, pp. 56-57.

3   One thinks especially of models in the art of Hiroshige, of which Vincent and Théo had collected several examples; see *Japanese Prints*, especially p. 36. Roskill, p. 45, has pointed to Monet as another primary source for this comparison.

17.
View of Saintes-Maries   *F* 416
last week of June 1888
oil on canvas: 64 × 53 cm
Not signed or dated
Lent by the Rijksmuseum Kröller-Müller, Otterlo,
The Netherlands
TORONTO ONLY

At the time Vincent visited the fishing village of
Saintes-Maries-de-la-Mer on the Mediterranean
coast in the Camargue (the third week of June
1888) it consisted, according to the artist's account
(*CL* 499), of perhaps one hundred houses
huddled around the old church, an ancient fortress
and the barracks.[1] The impression of this town in
Vincent's painting is more that of a typical citadel
village of southern France rather than a fishing
village. In this respect, it reminds one of such
Cézanne treatments as his well-known views of
Gardanne or more significantly Cézanne's *The
Harvest*, which was on Vincent's mind shortly
before his departure by coach on the
fifty-kilometre trip from Arles to Saintes-Maries
(*CL* 497)[2]. It is not only Cézanne's dense massing
of the building forms in his views of Gardanne
which are called to mind in Vincent's
Saintes-Maries but also that master's simplified
use of colours, reflected in Vincent's restriction to
orange and blue hues for the sunlit and shadow
areas of building façades. Of course this use of a
basic complementary contrast has Vincent's own
stamp on it, having been employed just previously
in his series of landscapes done at La Crau (for
example, *F* 412, *Harvest at La Crau: The Blue
Cart*). Furthermore, we know that the

[1] The name of the village derives from a legend that
following Christ's death and resurrection the
"three Maries" on a sea journey touch and thus
consecrate French soil at this location. The
barracks presumably housed a body of the Zouave
mercenaries who guarded the region.

[2] In his letter, Vincent recalled seeing this painting
with Théo at the Paris apartment of the art dealer
Portier. M. Bodelson, "Gauguin's Cézannes,"
The Burlington Magazine, CIV, May 1962, p.
211 and fig. 45, thinks it may have been owned
by Gauguin and left with Portier during the trip to
Martinique. Roskill, p. 45, thinks it influenced
Vincent's *Harvest at La Crau* (*F* 412), whereas
the present writer would suggest an influence on
Saintes-Maries for the "citadel and field" views
depicted.

Saintes-Maries was one of only three paintings executed on the spot (CL499), his aim in visiting Saintes-Maries having been to work on his drawing technique in order that it should become "more spontaneous, more exaggerated" (CL495). We thus may assume that the painting was executed after nature, although Vincent remarked upon the rapid changes of colour his subjects underwent on the coast due to the constantly changing light (CL499).[3] At the same time the sky in this painting may be thought to represent a more generic colouration typical of the region of Provence in summer, which Vincent credited Cézanne with having best understood, and described as "the green azure sky blanched with heat" (CL497).

In addition, Vincent found in the flat, often boggy countryside of the Camargue an area analogous to both his native Holland (he points out similarities with the landscapes of Rusydael and the house types of Drenthe; CL496, 499) and to Japan (CL500). Except for the common occurrence in these general sources of wide expanses of foreground land areas similar to the vineyard of the Saintes-Maries, one need not expect to find a specific model for the quite striking and original composition of this painting. As always Vincent clothes an underlying Realist depiction of an actual setting with the ever purer hues of his Arles period palette, thereby producing an image combining the fairy-tale charm of Japanese prints without losing hold on the naturalistic traditions in the West exemplified in Dutch seventeenth century landscape painting.

[3] However, this statement was made in specific reference to the sea itself. The fairly large horizontal drawing of the View of Saintes-Maries (F 1429) as pointed out in De la Faille (F 1439) was probably that mentioned in CL499. The large and intensely radiating sun seen upper left behind the citadel in the drawing, although absent from the painted version, nonetheless indicates that the religious associations of this "holy city" (see note 1) were not unknown to its Dutch visitor.

18.
The Sower with Yellow Sun   F 422
end June-early July 1888
oil on canvas: 64 × 80.5 cm
Not signed or dated
Lent by the Rijksmuseum Kröller-Müller, Otterlo, The Netherlands
TORONTO ONLY

Following Vincent's visit to *Saintes-Maries* during the third week of June 1888 (cat. nos. 16, 17), he returned to Arles and produced a rich assortment of paintings relating to the then germane theme of the spring harvest and reseeding. Although many of these creations are rightly considered among Vincent's finest paintings, he himself singled out only one, *The Sower* from the Kröller-Müller Museum, as a breakthrough painting. His observations at the time reflect both pride in his accomplishment (CL501-03) and anxiety that Pissarro, for example, might not find it acceptable (CL533). Although he clearly considered himself to have achieved a major advance, he also felt that this was merely a prelude of things to come (*see Patience Escalier*, cat. no. 21). Like the related painting *The Mowers, Arles in the Background* (cat. no. 19) the impetus to this subject series may well have been Anquetin's *The Mower at Noon* (cat. no. 74).

In his letter to Bernard which mentions *The Sower* subject (B7), Vincent both acknowledges the debt to Millet and the Dutch Barbizon tradition, and insists upon his departure from them. He then relates the painting to Anquetin's experiments into simplification which he had witnessed in Paris. Significantly he emphasizes to Bernard that he has "played hell somewhat with the truthfulness of the colours" in order to produce a "wholly primitive manner" which is to be found in popular prints out of "old farmer's almanacs, like the one Anquetin has hit upon so well in his *Harvest*" (*see also* cat. no. 74 and *fig. 85*). Yet Vincent's explanation presents us with his favourite colour analogy, a complementary contrast—the "chrome-yellow" of the sun versus the "frankly violet" shadows of the field, which he equates with the ripeness of the wheat (sun-ripened) in contrast to the "colds of earth, for the most part frankly violet" as the antipode to the sun-wheat.

This same letter to Bernard emphasizes the absolutely novel symbolism which Vincent attached to this particular painting. The upper half, yellow, was associated with the sun, whereas the lower half, violet, correspondingly must be associated with the "nether regions," however specifically this was meant. No one, least of all the present author, would claim that this painting was Cloisonist in the literal sense of imitated Medieval or Japanese precedents in style. At the same time, it is noteworthy that this earliest intrusion of the classic "light-dark" contrast (in this case of course only light) occurs in a painting which Vincent was to see as the first in a series of innovative essays in style which at times he associated with popular prints (cat. no. 19). He found no problem in employing one of the most personally expressive brush techniques in the service of a vision of the South of France as a Western counterpart to Japan. Strange bedfellows though they might seem to be according to normal art historical standards, Millet here strides through the Japanese gardens of Southern France with all the confidence which Vincent could afford him.

19.

The Mowers, Arles in the Background   F 545
end June-July 1888
oil on canvas: 73 × 54 cm
Not signed or dated
Lent by the Musée Rodin, Paris; collection
Auguste Rodin

This painting (pl.5) was one of a series representing the wheat fields during spring harvest at Arles, painted after van Gogh had returned in late June from Saintes-Maries and before he sent drawings made after that trip to Bernard, John Russell and his brother (*F* 1490-92) *circa* late July 1888.[1] The same setting with Arles in the background was rendered in a version in horizontal format, *Summer Evening* (*F* 465), of which he sent Bernard a sketch on or about June 28 (*B*7) and which even includes the train entering the scene from the right near the horizon line, as in the Rodin Museum version. Whereas *Summer Evening* included a large setting sun and a distant couple walking in the field there is no trace of the mistral winds which Vincent said were raging when he painted it, easel pinned to the ground. In contrast, *The Mowers* is visibly a daytime setting with the sun presumably still high in the sky and working couple well advanced towards harvesting the whole field of wheat.

This not only suggests a slightly later date of execution for the Rodin Museum version, but is reflective of the now well-known major compositional source of this version in vertical format; namely, *The Mower at Noon* (cat. no. 74) by Anquetin. Our authority for making this connection is none other than Bernard, who in writing on Vincent and on Anquetin recorded Vincent's gladly admitted indebtedness to this much admired painting by Anquetin which he had known from winter 1887-88 in Paris.[2] As Bernard indicates, there is some reason to think that Vincent had the single Anquetin painting in mind when beginning his series of wheat field paintings during the last week of June. We know that Vincent had heard about, although not read, Dujardin's article on Anquetin entitled "Le cloisonisme" by June 23, when he wrote to Théo (*CL*500) that Seurat, not Anquetin, was the leader of the new tendency in art and that Bernard had gone further in the Japanist direction than Anquetin. He had preceded this comment with an identification of Southern France as the "equivalent" of Japan, thereby implying his own "studio of the south" as the proper home of the

whole group of the "Petit Boulevard." A few days later Vincent refers specifically to Anquetin's *The Mower* in a letter to Bernard (*B*7), praising it as reflecting "naive pictures out of old *farmer's almanacs* in which hail, snow, rain, fair weather are depicted in a wholly primitive manner." Unwittingly or not, Vincent here was citing for Anquetin's Cloisonism a source closely related to the Images of Epinal as given by Dujardin. Probably within days of making this statement, Vincent's own print collection was to include a calendar for July from the *Paris illustré* (*fig. 51*) which, if not of the primitive type sold to farmers, featured a mowing scene with the background landscape predominantly in yellow-orange tones.[3]

Bernard also asserts that Vincent was fully aware of the origin of Anquetin's *The Mower* in colour experiments, viewing landscape settings through differently coloured panes of glass as a means of avoiding the theories of Pointillism and achieving the flat hues of "what one then called Cloisonism." Bernard claimed that Vincent was so struck by this "discovery" that he thereupon abandoned Pointillism and through involvement with Japanism and Cloisonism soon achieved a mature personal manner, which was more "grand, simple and contoured."[4] Although Vincent preferred to take credit for himself introducing Bernard and Anquetin to Japanese prints (*CL*510-11), this claim occurred in July shortly following his completion of the Anquetin-inspired series of wheat field paintings and the most intense references to that painting in his correspondence.

Vincent's *The Mowers* is the closest in composition to the model in Anquetin, but by no means a copy. Apart from having to rely upon his memory alone in order to recapture its spirit, Vincent departed from his model in a more agitated overlay of personal brushwork, included a blue-violet haze for the city outline along the horizon and, by analogy with his account of *Summer Evening*, must have executed the painting before the out-of-doors actual site. Vincent's indebtedness may also have included the painters Monet and Charles Angrand, whose landscape art he is known to have admired greatly,[5] and a general debt to the art of Japan is also implied by the high horizon and flat, decorative and asymmetrical composition. Yet all this richness of a assimilated influence aside, the painting offers strong support that by summer 1888 in Arles, as Bernard quoted Vincent (*B*3), the latter had developed a personal style based on no particular method except being served by "as much flat colour, as much contour, as many brush strokes as is needed."

1   Hulsker, *Complete van Gogh*, pp. 331, 340, 344-46, deduces from *CL*501 that at least most of the ten or more Arles wheat field paintings were produced during the last week of June and, on the basis of Roskill, *Exchanges*, pp. 143-57, lists many of the small drawings relating to these paintings (including all three sharing the subject of the *Mowers*; namely *F* 1490-92) which were produced from the paintings and sent either late July to Bernard or early August to Russell or Théo.

2   In both *Van Gogh*, pp. 399-400, and *Anquetin 1932*, p. 595.

3   See *fig. 85* for a more "primitive" image of the type also used with "farmer's calendars." See also H.B. Werness *Essays on van Gogh's Symbolism*, PhD diss. University of California at Santa Barbara, 1972, pp. 135-67, 269-70, for a useful illustrated discussion of the sources of Vincent's Mower and Harvesting themes, especially in reference to medievalizing or "primitive" imagery. The citation in B7 to "old farmer's almanacs," however, was made in reference to *The Sower with Yellow Sun* (cat. no. 18).

4   *Van Gogh*, p. 400.

5   See Welsh-Ovcharov, *Angrand*, pp. 44-49.

SEE COLOUR PLATE 5.

Fig. 51
July calendar from *Paris illustré*, July, 1888
(Rijksmuseum Vincent van Gogh, Amsterdam).

20.

Flowerbed with Sunflowers   F 1457
early August 1888
pencil, reed pen and brown ink on Ingres paper:
60 × 48.5 cm
Signed lower right (on bucket): *Vincent*
Lent by the Rijksmuseum Vincent van Gogh,
Amsterdam

The *Flowerbed with Sunflowers* is one of three
large drawings representing gardens in or near
Arles, which Vincent sent to Théo on August 8,
1888 (*CL*519). The other two (*F* 1455-56)
represented farm or cottage gardens containing a
mixture of flowers and fruit trees, but Vincent
wrote of our example, "The one with the
sunflowers is a little garden of a bathing
establishment." This description explains the
presence of the water bucket with Vincent's
signature, lower right, towards which the little cat
is looking with such undisguised curiosity. All three
drawings were intended as "guides" for intended
paintings, although this plan was carried out in
only a single instance, not ours.[1] Nonetheless, in
creating them, Vincent felt that they afforded the
pretext for "a whole school of men working
together in the same country" like the old Dutch
masters, and that "it was all a poem, and the
eternal bright sunshine too, in spite of which the
foliage remains very green." This rhapsodic
outpouring of enthusiasm for these quintessential
Provençal garden and architectural settings thus
included reminders to Théo of Vincent's national
artistic heritage and his thoughts of at last
founding a Studio of the South.

Inclusion of this drawing in the present study
is intended to provide an archetypal example of
Vincent's mature Arles period drawing style.
Vincent developed this style through execution of
"a *tremendous* lot of drawings, because I want to
make some drawings in the manner of Japanese
prints" (*CL*474). The result was not necessarily
compositions which remind one of specific
Japanese print models, which until September
1888 he did not have with him in Arles (*CL*540),
telling his sister (*Wil*7), "I don't need Japanese
prints here, for I am always telling myself *that
here I am in Japan*." This attitude could lead him
to interpret the wide Ruysdael-like vistas which he
found at La Crau (*F* 1420, 1424) as depictions
"*which do not look Japanese*, but which really
are, perhaps more so than some others"
(*CL*509).[2] It is sometimes thought that Vincent
was alluding indirectly to his use of a reed pen in
these and many other Arles drawings including the

Flowerbed; he had earlier explained the adoption
of this homemade graphic utensil to Théo
(*CL*478). However, Vincent's account suggests
merely that, due to the quality of the reeds
available in Provence, he prefers this to the
exclusive use of the similarly sharpened goose-quill
pen, and it is therefore unwise to lay too much
emphasis upon the choice of drafting tools.

Instead one may note the systematization of
brush or pen strokes which informs the mature
Arles drawings. In our example this is evident
from the contrasts among the stipples used for the
sky, garden border and wall at right; the clusters
of parallel hatchings for the ground areas and,
more darkly applied, much of the foliage; and the
curvilinear enclosures for the flower blossoms and
leaves. Whereas the use of stippling immediately
suggests a personalized version or remembrance of
Pointillist technique, this and the various other systems of hatching are paralleled in the art of the
Japanese wood block print, albeit without the den-
sity of application by Vincent which imparts to his
late drawing style its compelling sense of overall
surface decoration and *horror vacuii*.[3] In the
Flowerbed, a Japanist design quality is nonetheless
found in the asymmetry, side-to-side and front-
to-back, of the pictorial components. In addition
his employment of these various graphic insignia
in relationship to the sometimes wave-like, sometimes architectural or sometimes vegetal configurations commonly found within the Japanese prints
he owned adduces the argument that Vincent was
guided more by his general appreciation of
Japanist principles than by the memory of specific
prints. Indeed, the fact that he had departed Paris
without a portfolio of Japanese prints is proof
enough of Vincent's determination to utilize the
lessons of the Orient "without a crutch," so to
speak. The *Flowerbed*, apart from its being Vincent's first and only depiction of this subject *in
situ*, is a typically daring experiment in the use of
various drawing techniques, the study of which
except for Vincent's example might be considered
academic. Given Vincent's previous and subsequent addiction to the depiction of cut sunflowers, this drawing of a radiant cluster of the growing
plant must be considered unusual.

[1] *F* 1456, *A Garden*, Vincent's first preference for a
painting, was the basis of *F* 578, *Garden behind
a House*. However, *De la Faille* seems to confuse
the functions of *F* 1454 and 1455, the former of
which served for the painting, *F* 429, *Flowering
Garden with Path*, and the latter of which was
one of the three large drawings mentioned in
*CL*519. Thus *F* 1454 was the compositional
study upon which *F* 429 was based, thereby leaving *F* 1455 and the at present exhibited *F* 1457,
Flowerbed, as final study drawings without issue
in oil.

[2] See Orton, *Japanese Prints*, pp. 20-22, for this
general question, although the following interpretation disagrees as to Vincent's incorporation of
Japanist elements of design.

[3] For the Japanese use of "Pointillism," see
Japanese Prints, no. 330; article-length analyses
could be written on the relationships of Vincent's
Arles magnificent drawings to his Japanese
sources, but this is neither called or wished for in
the present context.

This would seem to be the second of the two paintings of this subject which Vincent executed in August 1888. In the one done during the first half of the month (*F* 443), Vincent employed a rather agitated brush technique for the background, and he considered (*CL* 522) his colour usage to be as "strange" as that of *The Sower* (cat. no. 27). The version exhibited here, although probably executed during the last week of the month (*CL* 528-29), may be thought to embody the same symbolic allusions listed by Vincent for the other version.[1] As well as describing the subject as "Master Patience Escalier... formerly cowherd of the Camargue, now gardener at a house in the Crau" (*CL* 520), Vincent calls him a "sort of man with a hoe," an obvious reference to the famous painting by Vincent's early idol, J.F. Millet. In a description of the painting to Bernard (B15), along with a small drawing of the subject (*F* 1461), Vincent spoke of the *Escalier* as "an absolute continuation of certain studies of heads I did in Holland," which he further amplified with a reference to his own *Potato Eaters* (*F* 78, 82), a version of which Bernard had seen in Vincent's Paris residence and which he doubtless knew to have been heavily impregnated with intimations of Millet. Claiming that, unlike most others who would consider it merely ugly, Gauguin and Bernard would surely understand why this member of the "true peasant race" so strongly reminiscent of "a wild beast" would have a colour background suggesting "the blazing air of harvest time right in the south, in the middle of the dog days." Vincent is even more specific about his colour symbolism in a reference of late August (*CL* 529) to Théo in which he describes what must be this version of "the old peasant" *Patience Escalier*: "I am doing him this time against a background of vivid orange which, although it does not pretend to be the image of a red sunset, may nevertheless give a suggestion of one." Little wonder then that Vincent subsequently will list his peasant from Provence (*CL* 533) in a sequence of recent and innovative development which had begun with the Kröller-Müller Museum *The Sower* (cat. no. 18) and was to include his *Portrait of Eugène Boch, a Belgian Painter* (*F* 462), which he referred to as "the poet" and finally the famous *Night Café* (*F* 463) as well. Because of its overtly Cloisonist style and its implied symbolism, this painting illustrates how effectively Vincent in Arles was able to develop in a direction comparable to that which would be undertaken in Pont-Aven by Gauguin and

21.
Portrait of Patience Escalier   *F* 444
late August 1888
oil on canvas: 69 × 56 cm
Not signed or dated
Lent by a private collection
AMSTERDAM ONLY

Bernard, although direct communication was then limited to the exchange of correspondence and illustrative drawings and watercolours.

As usual with Vincent, his use of Cloisonist stylistic principles is limited to the clothing and background of the figure, with the hands and face retaining a high degree of expressive Realism. The resulting characterization of this sun-wizened, yet undefeated toiler remains in the tradition of Millet. Vincent's mixture here of Realist portraiture and abstract colour and contour lines has been most effectively evoked in the powerful exegesis of Meyer Schapiro, who describes it as "focused upon a face of an unsoundable depth and complication" and composed as "a world with its own shapes, colours, movement, and character..." and as "perhaps the last realistic portrait of a peasant in the tradition of Western painting. It is perhaps also the only great portrait of a peasant."[2]

Another reference by Vincent to this subject is even more surprising.[3] After stressing the "Potato Eaters" analogy to Théo and the need for more paintings "en sabots in Paris" (that is "wooden shoe" peasant paintings), he suggested that Théo hang the *Patience Escalier* next to Lautrec's *Rice Powder* (cat. no. 118) which Théo owned. His rationale for this unlikely juxtaposition was that the contrast would be mutually beneficial, with Lautrec's figure looking "even more distinguished" and his own peasant even more "sun-burned..., tanned and air swept" through the comparison. Quite possibly in the contrasts of age, sex and profession of the two sitters Vincent wished to imply that, these differences notwithstanding, each figure represented a life hardened and limited by its respective *milieu*. Whether or not Théo took his brother's advice in this instance is unknown, but the present exhibition provides an excellent opportunity to test Vincent's acumen in this matter of taste.

---

[1] *CL* 520, 522 and *B* 15 (the last two containing drawings *F* 1460-61) thus would refer to *F* 443, while *CL* 528-29 would seem to refer to *F* 444. However, since *F* 1461 includes the walking stick or tool handle on which the figure of this version leans, this could mean that it wasn't the drawing sent with *B* 15 to Bernard.

[2] M. Schapiro, *Vincent van Gogh* (Garden City, New York: Doubleday, 1980), p. 64.

[3] I.e., in *CL* 520, which thus refers to the earlier version, *F* 443 (cf. Stuckey, p. 121).

22.
The Café Terrace on the Place du Forum, Arles at Night   *F* 467
September 1888
oil on canvas: 81 × 65.5 cm
Not signed or dated
Lent by the Kröller-Müller Museum, Otterlo, The Netherlands

This painting (pl.3) was executed in September 1888, thus without dependence upon the summer 1888 joint efforts of Bernard and Gauguin in founding a common Pont-Aven style. Its debt to the prototypal *Avenue de Clichy* of Anquetin (cat. no. 76) was already implied by Bernard in 1932, although only in 1958 did Gans posit a direct connection.[1] The imputed indebtedness doubtless is correct, as the first juxtaposition ever of the two paintings in the present exhibition should substantiate. Bernard specifically related the painting by Anquetin to that artist's experiments with landscape seen through coloured panes of glass, in this case "blue" for the colour of evening.[2] Vincent's own association of blue with the colour of night is well known, although this painting, the portrait of Eugène Boch (with its similarly starred background) and *Vincent's House* (cat. no. 24) are, it would seem, Vincent's earliest usage of this particular colour association. One is tempted to suspect that Vincent remembered the Anquetin painting almost a year later at least as much for its symbolic as for its scientific use of colour theory. This is not to deny the profound debt to Anquetin but only to emphasize that the relationship was not based upon a one-sided tribute. How instrumental the study of Japanese prints was for Vincent's and Anquetin's Cloisonist style can be noted here in both artists' adaptation of Hiroshige's *Scene of the Saruwakacho Theatre Street by Night (fig. 52)* into their respective night street scenes. This print, owned by Vincent and almost certainly known to Anquetin, displays not only a night street scene but also a funnel-like perspective and dominant blue-yellow tonality to be found both in the *Avenue de Clichy* and the *Place du Forum*.

In terms of the relationship in colour theory implied by Bernard's comments, Vincent's painting exhibits both dependency and aberration. The profoundly enriched blue of the Anquetin prototype forms only part of the more

[1] *Anquetin 1932*, p. 595.
[2] *Anquetin 1934*, p. 113.

SEE COLOUR PLATE 3.

Fig. 52
Hiroshige:
Scene of the Saruwakacho Theatre Street by Night,
1856,
colour print, from "One Hundred Views of Edo" (Rijksmuseum Vincent van Gogh, Amsterdam).

multicoloured reincarnation by Vincent. Instead, what are minor elements of contrast in the Anquetin painting, namely the major orange-yellow versus blue opposition, is transformed by Vincent into a clear-cut polarization between the orange-yellow of the gas-lit café terrace and the star-lit blue sky and also the red-green contrast of the terrace tiles and its presumed complementary reflection (otherwise inexplicable) on the wall. Vincent's own ultimate tribute to the painting by Anquetin was summed up in his observation (*CL*550) that "if I ever see Paris again, I shall try to paint some of the effects of gaslight on the boulevard."

Vincent (*Wil*7, *CL*537) characterizes this painting as dominated by the blue-cold versus yellow-warm analogy and attendant contrasts. It is alive with both subtle and glaring colour contrasts, which Vincent himself, despite the blue-black of the descending street, describes to Wilhelmina as "a night picture without any black in it, done with nothing but beautiful blue and violet and green, and in these surroundings the lighted square acquires a pale sulphur and greenish citron-yellow colour. It amuses me enormously to paint the night right on the spot."[3]

The record of Vincent's creation of this painting includes a reed pen drawing (*F* 519) which might well have recorded rather than preceded Vincent's oil version of the *Place du Forum*, since it scarcely seems an on-the-spot sketch, but rather an afterthought *résumé* of the painting. This interpretation not only enhances Vincent's own account of the painting as having been executed *in situ* (that is, *Wil*7), but also supports his claim that his fascination for the subject was the colour gamut it provided. All these factors combine to create a starngely dramatic yet truthful image of Vincent's Arles environment, whether one views it from within or outside the chosen café.

---

[3] Vincent's repeated use of candles on his hat in painting such scenes as the *Café Terrace* and the *Starry Night* (*F* 474) rests on oral tradition (G. Coquiot, *Vincent van Gogh*; Paris: Ollendorff, 1923, p. 180). This has been accepted Rewald (*P.I.*, p. 218) and Tralbaut (pp. 244-50) but rejected by Hulsher (*Complete VG*, p. 360).

23.
Interior of a Restaurant in Arles   *F* 549
mid-September 1888
oil on canvas: 54 × 64 cm
Not signed or dated
Lent by an anonymous lender

It is an understatement to say that the determination of the actual sites of Vincent's few café subjects in Arles is as yet not resolved. The disagreement has been concerned chiefly with the famous *Night Café*, which traditionally was identified as the Café de l'Alcazar, but which Leprohon with persuasive evidence has denied.[1] He rightly further challenges the identification of the *Interior of a Restaurant in Arles* here exhibited and a slightly larger companion version (*F* 549a) as representing the Restaurant-Hôtel Carrel, where Vincent had stayed upon his arrival in Arles, since the artist had departed that place after a disagreement over cost with the owner considerably before these two paintings were executed *circa* summer 1888.[2] However, Leprohon himself clearly was mistaken in connecting these interiors with that described in a letter by Vincent of early August (*CL*521), since, apart from other dissimilarities, the "little tables . . . with white cloths" and the "two women waitresses, both in gray" do not conform with the long tables and three waitresses in white and blue costumes present in the *Restaurant in Arles*. In this letter, moreover, Vincent contrasts the old-fashioned type of Provençal restaurant at which he was dining with the other local restaurants "so much modelled on Paris," by which one may interpolate a reference to larger restaurants for a mass public without the intimacy of the one he was describing located quite near his own Yellow House.

This should not lead us to believe Vincent was painting a hostile environment in this *Restaurant in Arles*. Since the *Night Café* did not yet exist in two versions (see *B*19) when an earlier letter of September 18, 1888 (*CL*539) mentions completion of "two cafés," this subject reference almost certainly indicates our exhibited and the companion version of the *Restaurant in Arles*.[3] This narrowing of the date of these paintings to the period when Vincent finally was furnishing and moving into his Yellow House, but still taking his meals elsewhere, is perhaps further enlightened by the appearance of six paintings hung on the rear walls of the restaurant. Unquestionably his own work, although none is well enough defined to

allow for identification, the logical supposition is that the restaurant belongs to his friends, M. and Mme Ginoux, the latter of whom sat for the *L'Arlésienne* (cat. no. 30), and both of whom were among those few friends close enough to Vincent for one to imagine them allowing Vincent to display his paintings on the walls of their café-restaurant.[4] As noted by Hulsker, neither of the two versions is necessarily a preliminary study for the other, and it is speculation to decide which version came first.[5] Even if it is unprovable that this *Interior* represented a restaurant owned by the Ginoux family, the display is nonetheless determined by Vincent, and above all represents a memory of his organization late 1887 of an exhibition at a similar "café-bouillon" at the *Du Chalet* restaurant on the avenue du Clichy, a year earlier. Significantly the artist had chosen a similar subject in his Paris *Interior of a Restaurant* (cat. no. 5) associating a popular eating establishment with the display of his art. This painting may therefore be considered emblematic of Vincent's determination to continue displaying his paintings in popular places of assembly, as well as of his conviction that such places were as noteworthy of attention as the respectable galleries of Paris.[6] No major artist in Western tradition has chosen such humble surroundings for the display of his own works of art; one must add that no major artist has been so well served by his humility—the very anonymity of so many of his subjects serves silent witness to the universal appeal which they are accorded. The presentation of this painting in a major exhibition for the first time in recent years is warranted by more than the usual reasons of convenience. It exhibits Vincent's most significant qualities as an artist: namely, a striking choice of subject, a Realistic depiction thereof and richly conceived colours added thereto. It also presents us with a view across tables which could only have been conceived by the artist himself. The overall impression relates to the café subjects and treatments of the whole circle of the "petit boulevard," despite the transference of this locale to the south of France. These two paintings therefore may best be interpreted as a reminder (to Théo) of things past, and to Vincent himself of his hopes of things to come.

Because it was created upon the brink of Gauguin's and perhaps Bernard's arrival in Arles, *Restaurant in Arles* presents a special moment of optimism, even gaiety, within Vincent's *oeuvre*. The gay colours of the flowers (red versus green) and the yellow-green versus blue (pictures) docu-

ments Vincent's adherence to strong, whether or
not complementary, contrasts, in one of Vincent's
most complex yet subtly structured paintings of its
period. The slice-of-life aspect to the painting is
enhanced by the feeling that "life goes on" and
may in fact provide its central theme.

1 Leprohon, pp. 414-15, points to Vincent's situation of this café as out of view to the left of the pink
   building with green shutters at far left in *Vincent's
   House* (cat. no. 24), whereas the Alcazar would
   have been out of view, but to the right.

2 *Ibid.*, p. 415; presumably the *Restaurant in Arles*
   paintings traditionally were assigned to summer
   1888 because of the flowers seen on the tables.

3 Vincent's reference to "café," like French usage in
   general, allows for an overlap between this term
   and "restaurant." An alternative identification for
   the second cafe is *The Cafe Terrace* (cat. no. 22),
   which admittedly would leave this *Interior of a
   Restaurant* unmentioned in Vincent's known
   correspondence.

4 Tralbaut, p. 238, asserts that Vincent took his
   meals at the Café de la Gare operated by the
   Ginoux family and slept at the Alcazar while waiting to move into the Yellow House, but this author
   does not document his assertion which may be
   based on family recollection only, and Vincent's
   correspondence gives no clear evidence on the
   question.

5 Hulsker, *Complete van Gogh*, p. 356; F 549a,
   however, is there considered less finished than the
   version here exhibited.

6 As early as Antwerp van Gogh already had this
   idea of displaying works of art in working class
   cafés and restaurants (*CL* 439).

24.
*Vincent's House on the Place Lamartine,
Arles*   W 464
late September 1888
oil on canvas: 76 × 94 cm
Not signed or dated
Lent by the Rijksmuseum Vincent van Gogh,
Amsterdam

SEE COLOUR PLATE 14.

The story of this modest structure in Arles which has become known as Vincent's Yellow House (pl.14) is celebrated world wide, but its exact situation in the immediately surrounding environment remains unclear. In a letter of May 1, 1888 (*CL*480) Vincent announces renting the structure for fifteen francs per month; he describes it as painted yellow on the outside and obtaining two large and two smaller adjoining whitewashed rooms. By the end of the month (see *CL*491) he had induced the proprietor to repaint the façade and the doors and windows, inside and out, with a ten-franc contribution from himself. Yet only in early September (*CL*533-34) did he prepare in earnest to move into this would-be "studio of the south" and begin the much more arduous and expensive task of furnishing the rooms according to his taste and the expected visits from fellow artists. Without doubt Vincent undertook these tasks with the expectation that one or both of Gauguin and Bernard would be arriving from Pont-Aven, although he made clear (*CL*534) that the house was equally well suited as a summer residence for Théo. With its known address as Place Lamartine 2, and the clear view of the railway overpasses in the distance at right, the location of this now destroyed building is

ascertainable, although Vincent's own painting might well be considered the best extant record of the immediate ambient.

Painted late in September (*CL*543 and accompanying sketch *F* 1453), this canvas represents "the house and its surroundings in sulphur-coloured sunshine, under a sky of pure cobalt." This equation between Vincent's colours from the tube and daylight-night contrast is reinforced by his juxtaposition of this daylight painting with *Starry Night* (*F* 474), which he admitted in this letter as resulting from "a terrible need – shall I say the word – religion?" A reference in the same letter to his *Night Café* provides a further polarity in which a place of escape, in this instance one of temptation and despair, is contrasted with a sense of security and hospitality reigning supreme. Indeed the Yellow House itself was rented, furnished – and rendered in this famous painting – as no less than Vincent's Utopian answer to the woes that had beset himself and, as he pictured it, the whole group of Impressionists of the Petit Boulevard whom he would gladly have welcomed in Arles.

Nor may one think that Vincent painted his picture of the Yellow House without a reference to literature, however indirect. The innocent

consideration that he wished to plant "two oleanders before his door" (*CL*540) should be seen in the context of his immediately preceding reminder (*CL*539) that these were the flowers of Petrarch (whose present-day surrogate, Gauguin, was now imminently expected). His more direct references to his own painting of the house include a defence against the criticism of his friend the Zouave lieutenant Milliet (*see F* 473), who could not understand Vincent's wish to depict "a dull grocer's shop" (presumably the similarly gabled wing of Vincent's building with pink awning, at left). Vincent's answer to Théo was a reminder that the novelist Zola in *L'Assommoir* and Flaubert in *Bouvard et Pécuchet* had incorporated such descriptions of streets without being "mouldy" as yet. With this comment by Vincent to his brother in mind, it is less than surprising that at approximately the same time he wrote to Bernard (*B*18) about this painting calling it "view of the house, which might be called 'the street'." Without hesitation one may describe this painting as one of the most symbolically laden, colouristically intense, yet realistically accurate in the artist's total production.

25.
Vincent's House at Arles   *F* 1413
c. October 1888
chalk, pen, brown ink and watercolour on paper:
25.5 × 31.5 cm
Not signed or dated
Lent by the Rijksmuseum Vincent van Gogh,
Amsterdam

This single watercolour version of the Yellow House was formerly ascribed to as early as May 1888, when Vincent first rented the structure with green shutters seen at the corner both here and in the painted version (cat. no. 24), or else to the summer months. However, in composition, colour and most details (for example, the little train on the bridge at right) the two versions are so close that one must have been executed on the basis of the other. Since the watercolour seems hardly a preliminary study for the painting it is, as the Editorial Committee of *De la Faille* surmised, the "better drawing" of the motif which in late September (*CL*543) Vincent promised after sending a smaller sketch "made from memory" (*F* 1453) upon completion of the painting. It thus served a function analogous to that of another major Arles period wash drawing, *The Night Café* (*F* 1463).

This should not be taken to mean that this version of *Vincent's House* is any less an original work of art. Vincent was a practised master in the watercolour technique by this time, and the relative blondness of his tonalities is as appropriate to this work on paper as is the more heavily saturated colouration and thick impasto to the version in oil. His use of a pastel-like blue for the lamppost at left, the curb surrounding the buildings, and the sky subtly enlivens what might otherwise have appeared a too broad expanse of uninterrupted yellow wash.

As one distinguished critic of van Gogh has noted, it is impossible not to think of both renderings in colour of the Yellow House, and the Arles version of his 1885 *Vicarage at Nuenen* (*F* 182) as linked with the Dutch tradition of the seventeenth century cityscape painters as exemplified by the famed Old Town Hall of Amsterdam by Pieter Saenredam.[1]

1   Cooper, *Watercolours*, no. 23.

SEE COLOUR PLATE 15.

26.

Vincent's Bedroom at Arles   F 482
October 1888
oil on canvas: 56.5 × 74 cm
Not signed or dated
Lent by the Rijksmuseum Vincent van Gogh,
Amsterdam

Fig. 53
Edgar Degas:
Interior,
1868-70,

oil on canvas
(Collection Henry P. McIlhenny, Philadelphia;
photograph: Philadelphia Museum of Art).

Although this painting (pl.15) is sometimes
known as the Yellow Bedroom at Arles, this is a
misnomer, since all three versions (this and
F 483-84) are multi-coloured. Such is the power
of Vincent's art and recorded statements that they
are too often confused in respect to specific
paintings. Vincent in fact seems to have wished to
represent his own bedroom from the moment that
he furnished it. In a letter of September 9, 1888
(*CL*534) Vincent not only describes his Yellow
House as, by implication, the intended "studio of
the south," but also states his intention to "paint
his own bed: there will be three subjects on it,"
which he indicates indecisively as "perhaps a nude
woman...or perhaps a child in a cradle."
Ultimately he decorated the bedroom with a
landscape painting, seen near the window, and
two portraits which can be identified (*CL*553b) as
that of Eugène Boch (*F* 462), "the poet," and
Vincent's officer friend of the Zouave regiment,
Milliet (*F* 473). Vincent's various decorative
schemes for his bedroom alternated from Japanese
prints, to sunflowers, to various combinations of
his own paintings, and the paintings depicted at
right over his bed are similarly less specific in the
two later variations.

Apart from the likelihood that Vincent's
various colour contrasts here record his ongoing
love of using complementary contrasts in his own

highly inventive manner,[1] Vincent's colours may
easily reflect his concern, in this painting and its
descendants, that his art is not without humanistic
content. As early as July 1888 Vincent had
observed (*CL*511) that Pierre "Loti's book *Mme
Chrysanthème* taught me this much: the rooms
there are bare, without decorations or
ornaments," whereupon Vincent launches upon a
defence of simplicity and directness in the use of
prints as decorative motifs. While he may also
have recalled the well-known *Interior* by Degas
(*fig. 53*) as a more sophisticated source for his
own composition, the likelihood that Vincent's
original painting of his bedroom was executed *in
situ* helps explain the tilted-up perspective as
much as the equally persuasive explanation of
impending emotional instability.[2] Whatever the
viewer feels about Vincent's insistence in
mid-October (*CL*554) that this painting was
meant "to be suggestive of *rest* or of sleep in
general," it is to be remembered that the canvas
was executed in a period of relative calm for the
artist, when he had many a reason to expect that
his idea of founding a studio of the south would
shortly materialize. Thus it is just as reasonable to
look at Vincent's *Bedroom* as a promise of
harmonious cooperation among artists living in an
ideal community, far from the infectious debility of
urban Parisian society, than as the harbinger of

pyschological instability which is its most
frequently attributed meaning.

[1] See *CL*554-55 and especially *B*22, where he even
   lists black and white as the fourth set of
   complementaries.

[2] T. Reff, "Degas's 'Tableau de Genre'," *Art
   Bulletin*, LIV, September 1972, pp. 316-24,
   discusses the possibilities of literary content in the
   Interior by Degas. By late 1887 Théo had
   established a commercial liaison with Degas
   allowing for either Théo or Vincent to have seen
   this work, which seems to have remained in
   Degas' studio until at least 1897 (Reff, *ibid.*, p.
   316; *see also* Reff, *Degas: The Artist's Mind*;
   New York: Metropolitan Museum of Art—Harper
   and Row, 1976, Ch. V). For explanations of
   perspective usage in the *Bedroom see* H.P.
   Bremmer (in Welsh-Ovcharov, *Van Gogh in
   Perspective*, pp. 85-87), and Schapiro, *Van Gogh*
   (as in cat. no. 21 n.2), p. 78. For two
   contradictory intrepretations of van Gogh's
   pictorial space in this painting *see* P.A. Heelan,
   "Toward a New Analysis of the Pictorial Space of
   Vincent van Gogh," *Art Bulletin* LIV, September
   1972, pp. 478-492 and J.L. Ward "A
   Reexamination of van Gogh's Pictorial Space,"
   Art Bulletin, LVIII, December, 1976, pp.
   593-603.

functioning as halo for his hard-working peasant as saint. And of course, the sower theme itself is a much used parable of spiritual endeavour in the Christian as in other religions. It is also difficult not to see an intended equation between the new shoots growing from the pollarded tree stump and the action of the equally sturdy farmer, whose devotion to the land involves a lifetime of morning to evening labour. It is unlikely that Vincent would have seen anything incongruous in this multiple wedding of various stylistic and thematic borrowings. While responding to the challenge of Gauguin's most recent discoveries in art, Vincent here produced one of his most compact, emotionally charged and, in reference to both style and meaning, Synthetic paintings of the Arles period.[6]

27.
The Sower　　*F* 451
late November 1888
oil on canvas: 32 × 40 cm
Not signed or dated
Lent by the Rijksmuseum Vincent van Gogh, Amsterdam

This is the smaller copy of the painting now at the E.G. Bührle Foundation, Zurich (*F* 450), which Vincent executed in late November 1888.[1] Whether done at that time or closer to late May 1889, when it is first mentioned (*T* 9), this smaller painting is slightly compressed from the more horizontal format of the Bührle version. This exaggerated the Japanese effect of the silhouetted foreground images of man and tree against the swiftly receding perspective of the ground plane. Its smaller size also accounts for the somewhat more agitated brushwork of this version which heightens its expressive intensity. Like the late June 1888 painting of the same theme now at the Kröller-Müller Museum (*F* 422), the Zürich and Amsterdam versions apparently were produced without preliminary drawings, since only letter sketches of them for descriptive purposes survive (for example, in *CL* 558a). This in part is explained by Vincent's long familiarity with the theme, which was dependent upon the model of J.F. Millet as witnessed in a number of drawings from Vincent's earlier Dutch periods.[2] The tree too is quite reminiscent of a much earlier image (*F* 947), as is the use of a wide-angle perspectival recession. The Kröller-Müller *Sower* quite consciously returned to Millet for inspiration, although in this instance Vincent stressed (*CL* 501) that there was still needed "a sower, in colour and large-sized."

Alan Bowness first suggested that the *Sower* was influenced by a knowledge of Gauguin's *The Vision after the Sermon* (*see fig.* 47).[3] However, the oil version was sent from Pont-Aven to Théo in Paris, but his theory is strengthened by the availability of the composition from a hitherto unpublished drawing of *The Vision* sent to Vincent from Pont-Aven in a letter (*G* 9) of late September.[4] This formal debt to Gauguin and Japan notwithstanding, Vincent has impregnated an otherwise Cloisonist-style canvas with a thematic contrast between the life-giving radiance of what he calls the "immense citron-yellow disk" and the sombre violet and blue colouration he has given the figure, tree and ground.[5] Rather than producing an inventive paraphrase of a Biblical story as had Gauguin, Vincent only obliquely alludes to religious content with the sun

1　Hulsker, *VGdVG*, p. 167, provides a thoroughly argued and convincing case for redating *CL* 558a to *c*. November 21, 1888, and therefore at least the Bührle version of the *Sower* to about the same time.

2　E.g., *F* 830, 852, 1035 (plus the related oil sketch *F* 11) and 1143.

3　Bowness, exh. cat. *Vincent van Gogh* (London: The Hayward Gallery, 1968-69), cat. no. 140.

4　For two additional drawings of *The Vision* see Bodelsen, *Ceramics*, p. 180, figs. 132 and 133. Significantly, immediately upon Gauguin's expressing admiration for his earlier *Sower* (cat. no. 18) Vincent commenced work on the Amsterdam or Bührle Foundation (*F* 450) version. Vincent's earlier *Japonaiserie: The Flowering Plum Tree* (cat. no. 9) provides a major precedent both in style and theme for the late 1888 *Sower*.

5　R. Rosenblum, *Modern Painting and the Northern Romantic Tradition: Friedrich to Rothko* (New York: Harper & Row, 1975), p. 91 sees this canvas "for all its indebtedness to Gauguin and Japanese prints" as belonging in its spirit to the tradition of Northern Romantic painting as found in the paintings of artists such as Samuel Palmer and D.C. Friedrich, where peasants "inhabit... an enchanted landscape... magically vitalized by blazing golden suns...."

6　A painting (*F* 738) with the same setting as this version of *The Sower* has not been accepted as authentic in the last two editions of *De la Faille*, but was recently accepted in Roskill, *Exchanges*, pp. 162-63, as a *Red Sunset* sent in an exchange to Bernard.

28.
Les Alyscamps   F 486
early November 1888
oil on canvas: 72 × 91 cm
Not signed or dated
Lent by a private collection
TORONTO ONLY

The subject is one of the most frequented promenades in Arles, a thoroughfare lined with poplar trees and, most conspicuously, rows of Roman tombs interspersed with modern benches. Four variants of this subject were produced by Vincent, of which three were reported in a letter to

Théo (*CL* 559) of *circa* November 11. It is customary to see the four canvases as divisible into two sets of companion pieces. This division actually holds only insofar as this example and its counterpart at the Kröller-Müller Museum (*F* 486) employ Japanist raking-angle perspective, whereas the other two versions incorporate the scene with equal effectiveness according to a deeply penetrating perspective (*F* 568-69). The letter to Théo makes clear, however, that the distinctions between versions are real and meaningful, which clearly is true for our example and its companion piece. For example, Vincent's description to Théo of this setting as

lined by Roman tombs is clearly accompanied by references to the "falling leaves" which are scattered along the roadway, but which continue to flutter down. As Vincent said, "And then the earth is covered with a thick carpet of yellow and orange fallen leaves. And they are still falling like flakes of snow."

The exhibited version of the theme was the first executed. It alone includes what Vincent described as "little black figures of lovers" and in "the upper part of the picture . . . a bright green meadow, and no sky, or almost none." It must have been the version now at the Kröller-Müller Museum (that is, *F* 486) of which he stated, "The second canvas is the same avenue but with an old fellow and a woman as fat and round as a ball." In theme the Alyscamps series goes back to a subject series first systematically exploited in Paris (*see* cat. no. 1 and *F* 314); namely, strollers—frequently pairs of lovers—along an avenue or in a park (*see also* cat. no. 39). The Alyscamps subject thus represents a kind of Arlesian "Bois d'Amour" (cat. no. 94). It is significant that Gauguin too chose to paint this subject (*W* 306-07) probably following Vincent's example, since to Bernard (*B* 19a, postscript) he reported seeing the two "falling leaves" paintings hanging in Vincent's room, without mentioning his own version.

There is thus a certain irony in the popular view that Vincent's two *Alyscamps* paintings are an instance of his submission to the spatial distortions of Gauguin when they worked together in Arles. Not only are Gauguin's subject treatments still within the naturalistic picturesque tradition, when compared with the Japanist truncations of the trees and tilted ground planes, but there is simply no specific precedent for Vincent's composition in his friend's *oeuvre*. Moreover, Vincent's love of bold contrasts of complementary colours (in this case blue-lilac tree trunks and tombs versus the yellow-orange bed of leaves, as he reported to his brother) was by now anathema to Gauguin, whose colour choices admitted no such simple oppositions. There is nonetheless an identifiable source influence for Vincent's *Alyscamps*, Bernard. In July Bernard had sent Vincent several watercolour drawings, of which the *Lane in Brittany* (cat. no. 101) includes a strolling couple and an iconography similar to that of Vincent. If known to Vincent, Bernard's 1887 painting *Promenade in the Bois d'Amour* (cat. no 94) would have provided a powerful prototype for what Vincent described as "some . . . trunks in lilac cut by the frame where the leaves begin." It was surely such paintings as the *Promenade* which elicited from Vincent the comment (*CL* 500) that "young Bernard has perhaps gone further in the Japanese style than Anquetin." In so great an artist as Vincent such indebtedness is not a sign of weakness but of strength. The Alyscamps paintings remain one of his most forceful and independent artistic statements produced during Gauguin's visit to Arles, all the more so for having been produced so shortly after the latter's arrival.

SEE COLOUR PLATE 10.

29.
Breton Women in the Meadow
(after Emile Bernard)   *F* 1422
watercolour: 47.5 × 62 cm
Signed lower right: *Vincent*
Inscribed lower left: *d'après un tableau d'E. Bernard*
Lent by the Galleria Civica d'Arte Moderna di Milano; Grassi Collection, Milan

It is not possible to date this watercolour copy (pl.10) after Bernard's *Breton Women in the Meadow* (cat. no. 104) with great precision and certainty, since the model painting was available to Vincent throughout Gauguin's stay in Arles. Within a few days of the latter's arrival Vincent reported (*CL* 557) Gauguin's acquisition of the painting in an exchange with Bernard and described it as "a magnificent canvas . . . Breton women in a green field, white, black, green and a note of red, and the dull flesh tints. After all, we must all be of good cheer." Given this degree of enthusiasm and his impulsive nature, it is quite possible that Vincent's copy was executed about this time. Alternatively, it may have been done in December, when Vincent advised Théo to think of acquiring a painting by Bernard, since "Gauguin

has a *superb* one" (*CL* 562), by which only the *Breton Women* could have been meant.[1] A year later Vincent received from Bernard photographs of his latest work, the overt religious subject matter and medievalizing style of which Vincent found repellent. Vincent was so frank in stating this to Bernard (*B* 21) in mid-November 1889 that it ended their correspondence. Significantly his initial and most telling contrast with what he termed Bernard's "counterfeit, affected" latest work was with "that picture which Gauguin has, those Breton women strolling in a meadow, so beautifully ordered, so naively distinguished in colour." About a month later in December he advised Wilhelmina (*Wil* 16), who was planning a

[1] Hulsker, *Complete van Gogh*, p. 380, prefers this *c*. November-December 1888 date and rightly draws analogies in style with Vincent's Bernard-influenced *The Dance Hall* (*F* 547) and *The Arena in Arles* (*F* 548). Unfortunately, neither of these paintings is documented as to exact date, nor, any more than the copy of the *Breton Women*, mentioned in Vincent's one letter to Bernard written during Gauguin's stay in Arles (*B* 19a).

trip to Paris and had inquired as to who Bernard was, that despite the "bizarre" nature of his recent religious paintings he was a young artist of great talent who had earlier produced a "Sunday afternoon in Brittany, Breton peasant women, children, peasants, dogs strolling about in a very green meadow; the clothes are black and red, and the women's caps white." This description makes clear that Vincent had not heard from Gauguin of any religious context for the representation, and he went on to explain to his sister: "But in the crowd there are also two ladies, the one dressed in red, the other in bottle green; they make it a very modern thing." Vincent further explained that he had considered Bernard's painting "so original" that he had made a watercolour copy of it for himself which she could see at Théo's. On his part, Bernard was appreciative enough of Vincent's gesture of tribute that he apparently acquired the copy for himself.[2] What this record of comment lacks in specifics about date and circumstance of origin for Vincent's copy of the *Breton Women* it gains by the magnitude and consistency of Vincent's admiration for this one major Cloisonist and Pont-Aven style painting by Bernard which he surely saw in the original.

Considering the degree of Vincent's praise and his proven exactitude as a copyist of his own work when he so wished, one is all the more struck by the liberties in colouration which the artist allowed himself in his self-proclaimed "copy." Having described the field as green, he painted it yellow, and the "red and black" clothes of the peasants are changed to brown, with only minor accents of red and blue remaining to offset a colour conception tending toward the monochromatic. Conversely, Vincent did retain Bernard's use of Cloisonist outlines for the figures, if anything strengthening this aspect of Bernard's approach to style.[3] While one may not consider this a "free" copy, there are enough variations of details of poses and figural proportions that one can observe Vincent's own design sense coming to the fore as he makes minor adjustments to the composition. There is no reason to believe that in making these changes Vincent was consciously attempting to improve upon his model.[4] Instead, one may note the many similar minor changes which occur when he made copies of his own paintings and hence consider such variations as an irrepressible component of his native genius.

[2] Although not cited in *De la Faille*, Bernard, *Notes*, p. 680, no. 2, clearly states that he had been the first owner of van Gogh's copy.

[3] This may have been due in part to Vincent's possession of several Bernard watercolours executed in a comparable figural style (*see* cat. no. 101) which contain similarly emphasized contour outlines.

[4] However Orton, *Japanese Prints*, p. 22, advances the position that the version by Vincent exhibits "a much more organic unity."

30.
L'Arlésienne: Madame Ginoux with Books
F 488
November 1888
oil on canvas: 90 × 70 cm.
Not signed or dated
Lent by the Metropolitan Museum of Art, New York;
Bequest of Sam A. Lewisohn, 1951

The sitter for this portrait was Mme Joseph Ginoux, who with her husband operated the Café de la Gare, in Arles[1]. Mme Ginoux agreed to sit for what Vincent called (CL559) his first portrait of a woman of Arles, which here and in another letter (CL573) he stipulated had been done in an hour or less. Vincent's remark suggests some difficulty in getting local females as opposed to men to sit for him and that he perhaps feared she would not agree to a second sitting. It may in fact have been her one and only sitting, since the famous drawing (Pickvance, Pl. 27) made by Gauguin employed in *Au Café* (*W* 305) and by Vincent in St. Rémy for a series of four portraits of Mme Ginoux (*F* 540-43) depicts the same head-propped-against-arm pose as had Vincent, but, as would have been natural with two artists working together, from a different angle. At least one can deduce that the sitting was held in the Yellow House, since she sits in what clearly is what Vincent identified as "Gauguin's armchair" (*CL*563), when he described the painting of this subject (*F* 499) late in the year. The same chair was also used for *La Berceuse* (*see* cat. no. 34)

[1] Although Tralbaut, p. 228, claims that Vincent rented his Yellow House from the Ginoux family and, p. 238, took his meals at their Café de la Gare, this account, presumably based upon family memory, must be flawed. In *CL*534, Vincent distinctly connects his painting of the *Night Café* (*F* 463) with payment of a debt to his landlord, clearly the owner of that establishment, not the Ginoux family. In *CL*543 of end September, moreover, Vincent clearly identifies the restaurant where he takes his evening meals as that pink house with the green shutters to the left in the painting of his *House* (cat. no. 24), with the "night café" further to the left and not in the picture. Whether or not this location coincides with that of the now destroyed "Alcazar" café is much disputed, but in any case the "night café's" owner undoubtedly was Vincent's landlord.

and two other portrait studies of Mme Roulin executed respectively by Vincent (*F* 503) and Gauguin (*W* 298), again perhaps at joint sittings because of the differing angles of view.

It is often claimed that the Metropolitan Museum painting testifies to the substantial indebtedness of Vincent to Gauguin at this time through adoption of the latter's method of painting "abstractions" on the basis of memory. Yet Vincent states explicitly that the painting was "slashed on in an hour," whereas Gauguin produced only the drawing from a different angle and could hardly have been offering much advice to Vincent at so furious a pace. Vincent's famous statement a year later to Bernard (*B*21) about having given in to the "charming path of abstraction," that "enchanted ground" leading to a "stone wall," referred specifically to *La Berceuse* and *The Novel Reader* (*F* 497), where, unlike *L'Arlésienne*, the background does contain invented decorative motifs. Most important, there is no single portrait produced by Gauguin to this date which compares in the purity and forcefulness of its Cloisonism to this starkly outlined and richly coloured example by van Gogh. In this respect Bernard's *Self-Portrait* (cat. no. 105) sent to Vincent, more than that by Gauguin (cat. no. 52), represents a studied Cloisonist approach to portraiture, although Vincent's *Bugler of the Zouave Regiment* (cat. no. 15), his *Patience Escalier* (cat. no. 21) and depictions of the *Postman Roulin* (*F* 432-34), all of which predate the famous exchange of portraits between Pont-Aven and Arles, show how independently Vincent had developed a modern portrait art combining Cloisonist style with a powerful characterization of the subject's physiognomy based upon natural appearance. Had Gauguin not been present when Vincent painted this particular *L'Arlésienne*, the result likely would not have been as different as is generally thought.

In one other respect, that of implied symbolic content, the contrast with Gauguin is of some interest. Vincent by November was quite familiar with Gauguin's emerging stress on double or ambiguous literary references in his art through receipt of and explanations about Gauguin's *Self-Portrait called Les Misérables*. Yet, in this *L'Arlésienne*, apart from the single flower motif "embroidered" on her, Vincent was not prepared, as he would be with the *Berceuse* in December, to employ Gauguin's background of floral patterns as suggesting "the room of a pure young girl." Nor did he give his painting a title containing an easily

recognizable literary reference, as well he might, so rich was the region of Provence in literary associations. Vincent even gainsays inscribed titles on the "novels" she presumably is reading, as if this former usage (*see* cat. nos. 11, 12) now seemed extraneous to the more generalized and archetypal image of "a woman of Arles" Mme Ginoux was intended to personify. Indeed, like the harmonious complementary colour contrasts exemplified by the red book on green tablecloth[2] and blue figure against yellow-orange ground, Mme Ginoux somehow expresses a sense of thoughtfulness, patience and quiet strength of character which

Vincent would have admired in his sitter as the regional virtues she was intended to embody. That Vincent took little liberty with the regional costume and hairdo is substantiated even in the illustration of a postcard (*fig. 54*) postmarked 1913, which unfortunately largely hides the bun of hair (*chignon*) better visible in *L'Arlésienne*. Yet the flower decoration at her waist provides the rationale for the flower drollery on his sitter's white blouse.

[2] Due to his unabated love of complementary colour contrasts, Vincent goes so far as to paint the pages of the open book green and to reflect this up onto the sitter's white chemise as well.

Fig. 54
An Arlésienne,
postcard *c* 1913, Paris
(Collection B.M. Welsh-
 Ovcharov).

28 - *Arlésienne*

31.
Portrait of Camille Roulin F 538
December 1888
oil on canvas: 37.5 × 32.5 cm
Not signed or dated
Lent by the Rijksmuseum Vincent van Gogh,
Amsterdam

Vincent preferred almost always to depict
single-figure portraits rather than group portraits.
Both traditions were well established within Dutch
tradition, with Rembrandt and Frans Hals being
the principal protagonists. Considering how close
the Roulin family had become to Vincent in Arles,
a group portrait might have been expected.
Instead (by mid-December; *CL* 560) Vincent,
with greater pride, represented individually "a
whole family . . . all characters and very
French. . . ." This family almost certainly will
eventually be seen as one of the most privileged
series of sitters that world art history ever had
witnessed.[1]

    This smallest male member of the Roulin
family is no less an exemplar of Cloisonist style for
the evidence of brush technique which is visible as
a patina overlay to the clear divisions into blue
(hat), green (jacket), yellow-green (background)
and the more multicoloured face of this
peasant-putti figure within Vincent's circle of
friends. The red-brown outlines of the colour
divisions only reinforce the impression that Vincent
was here applying his own sophisticated
knowledge of earlier art forms and techniques to
what he considered a new form of portrait
painting.

[1] Only the two versions of *Mother Roulin with her
Baby* (*F* 490-91) slightly modify this preference
for single portraits.

32.
Self-Portrait with Bandaged Ear and Pipe F 529
January 1889
oil on canvas: 51 × 45 cm
Not signed or dated
Lent by an private collection
AMSTERDAM ONLY

Following a period of tension with Gauguin, on the night of December 23, 1888, Vincent mutilated his own ear and then offered the ear part to a certain Rachel, a prostitute in an Arles brothel. Gauguin called Théo to Arles and on December 26 or 27 returned with him to Paris, leaving Vincent to recuperate in the local hospital, Vincent soon returned to his Yellow House, where he remained several months before voluntarily entering in the mental hospital at St. Rémy. This *Self-Portrait* must have been completed by about mid-January, since a letter of that date (*CL*571) refers either to this or an alternative version (*F* 527). The two versions were executed coincidentally, even if the iconographies of the artist seen before an open window and with a Japanese print and this composition with an abstract background and with Vincent smoking a pipe are scarcely related. From our painting one can most easily deduce a wish by the artist to project a feeling of "calm after the storm," although the inclusion of the bandaged ear, may also have been a reminder to Théo and through him to Gauguin (*CL*571) of the latter's unnecessarily hasty flight from Arles without first speaking again to Vincent. In this sense, it represented less a call for pity than a possible reminder to the two persons then closest to the artist's feelings that their arbitrary handling of his situation had not been helpful but instead a waste of time, as his subsequent letter implies (*CL*566-69).

The importance of this painting rests upon its quality as a work of art, which has been overshadowed by the biographical attention focused upon the tragic human story that it records. Vincent here obviously wished to project his own sense of relief that the ordeal was over and that he was ready to start painting again. In it one senses introspective uncertainty despite his wish to reassure Théo of his own emotional equilibrium. From the point of view of psychology, this is one of Vincent's most neutral self-portraits, suggesting neither overt aggressiveness nor anguished self-doubt. At the same time it is a summation of the artist's will, whatever his personal situation, to

persevere in his assigned role with or without the comforts of material and fraternal support.

The painting truly embodies the Cloisonist aesthetic, albeit with Vincent's typical retention of Realist depiction of the facial features. This incredibly simple self-portrait thus contrasts the blue cap with its orange background and the green jacket with an equally inexplicable red ground. The placement of the artist's eyes so close to the division of colour areas was no less intentional than the, as usual, complementary contrasts which the artist here embodied. Perhaps this was meant as a gesture of protest to Gauguin that such contrasts of complementary hues were at the base of

contemporary art or, equally plausible, that Vincent no longer found Cloisonism and Divisionism irreconcilable.

[1] Gauguin's account of the dramatic and tragic event of Vincent's temporary mental breakdown is told in *Avant et après* (Eng. trans. Van Wyck Brooks, *Paul Gauguin's Intimate Journals*; Bloomington: Indiana University Press, 1958, pp. 33-38), which was written almost fifteen years after the event and doubtless contains a degree of distortion and exaggeration: see also Roskill, pp. 269-70.

SEE COLOUR PLATE 18.

33.
Still Life: Vase with Fourteen Sunflowers
F 458
late January 1889
oil on canvas: 95 × 73 cm
Signed (on vase): *Vincent*
Lent by the Rijksmuseum Vincent van Gogh,
Amsterdam

Although other subjects treated by Vincent are equally loved, none is considered more symbolic of the artist himself than the sunflower theme (pl. 18). Not only did he produce more versions of this subject than any other, but he himself once stated "the sunflower [theme] is mine in a way" (*CL*573), this in contradistinction to specialists in peonies and hollyhocks whom he admired.[1] Vincent's concentrated involvement with the subject began late in his Paris period, when he produced three major treatments of large cut sunflowers, one with four (*F* 452) and two with only two blossoms (*F* 375-76). These latter two canvases are unusual in being both signed and dated, doubtless because they were given in an exchange to Gauguin, winter 1887-88.[2] Vincent would have remembered this when he wrote from Arles to Bernard (*B*15), who by August 1888 had joined Gauguin in Pont-Aven, that he was "thinking of decorating my studio with half a dozen pictures of 'Sunflowers'," a plan he soon shared with Théo and his sister Wilhelmina as well. To Théo he confided (*CL*526) that the three paintings of sunflowers upon which he was then at

work were part of a planned dozen with which he wished to decorate the studio in his Yellow House which he expected soon to share with Gauguin. By early September, what he had described to Bernard as "a symphony in blue and yellow" had been transferred in his mind to the smaller guest bedroom (for Théo or Gauguin) and reduced to the two large sunflower paintings with respectively twelve (probably *F* 456) and "fourteen" (probably *F* 454, which actually represents fifteen flowers) blossoms in a vase, which in fact was how Gauguin's room actually was decorated (*CL*574). Already in September Vincent described to Théo how the room's occupant would awake to "a decoration of great yellow sunflowers" on the white walls of the room and a view out the window to "the green of the public gardens and the rising sun. . . ." About the same time he wrote to his sister (*Wil*7) that the guest or second bedroom upstairs was to be decorated "in the Japanese manner," with "at least six very large canvases, particularly the enormous bouquets of sunflowers," this on the theory that the Japanese decorate large rooms with small pictures and small rooms with large.[3] If one recalls that he had earlier said in the letter to Bernard that his projected series of sunflower paintings would seek "effects like those of stained-glass windows in a Gothic church," one may realize how steeped in the Cloisonist aesthetic Vincent was when conceiving this formidable decorative scheme.

The Arles sunflower paintings signified for Vincent a new departure in several respects. As Vincent explained to Théo when he began the series in August (*CL*527), he was following the example of "solid impasto" used in a still life with peonies by Manet, and was attempting to develop a new and simplified brush technique which would be "without stippling" and feature "nothing but the varied stroke." As to colour, he now sought, as he explained to Bernard, an exclusive use of "raw or broken chrome yellows," which "will blaze forth on various backgrounds." Such paintings were to include a blue in the form of a "pale malachite green" (*F* 455-56) or, for those canvases with fourteen blossoms, (*F* 454, 457 and the here exhibited Amsterdam painting), two tones of chrome yellow. These latter examples are as exemplary of monochromatic painting as Vincent ever achieved, which is one more reason for their singular expressive effect. The Amsterdam painting was executed in late January and was possibly intended as a copy for Gauguin (*CL*573), who preferred Vincent's sunflower paintings to one by Monet (*CL*563) which he, but not Vin-

cent, had seen. The *Sunflowers* was also intended to serve as a wing of *La Berceuse* triptych (see cat. no. 34). Here, its virtually pure chrome yellow colouration would have been intended as a foil for the similar colour of Madame Roulin's hair and a brilliant contrast to the other colours of the central panel.

Vincent considered his sunflower paintings as crucial in his development, which is substantiated by allusion to them in reference to his avowed hero Adolphe Monticelli (*CL*573) to whom, unexpectedly, he compares himself favourably. Along with his late offering to Gauguin and Bernard of copies of *La Berceuse* (*CL*592), Vincent insisted (May 1889) that Gauguin be obliged to an exchange in reference to the sunflower subject (*CL*592). It is uncertain whether or not Gauguin ever received from Théo a version of the Arles Sunflower subject as directed by Vincent. One may at least say that Vincent remembered the importance of this subject when he submitted it in duplicate at the *Les Vingt* exhibition of 1890. At the time he expressed to Albert Aurier (*CL*626a) that his "two pictures of sunflowers which are now at the *Vingtistes* exhibition, have certain qualities of colour, and that they also express an 'idea symbolizing gratitude'."[4] This reference, made long after the sunflower paintings were conceived, recapitulates the feelings Vincent had expected his guest Gauguin to feel awakening each morning flanked by the sunflower paintings and confronted with the natural inspiration for them through his bedroom window. Whether or not such feelings were reciprocated at the time, one can say that Vincent's sunflower paintings comprised the most intimate artistic link between himself and Gauguin throughout their association beginning in Paris, consummated in Arles and having further repercussions in 1889.

1 Namely G. Jeannin and E. Quost; see also Welsh-Ovcharov, pp. 45, 151.
2 See A. Tellegen, "Vincent en Gauguin," *Museunjournaal*, XI, nos. 1-2, (1966), pp. 42-44.
3 *CL*544a (in Hulsker, *VGdVG*, cited as 553a) however records Vincent's intention to include in the decoration of Gauguin's bedroom his then preferred theme of "the poet's garden" (e.g., *F* 468, 479).
4 Aurier, pp. 262-3 saw no pictorial precedents for Vincent's sunflowers; *cf* K. Hoffmann "Zu van Goghs Sonnenblumenbildern," *Zeitschrift Fur Kunstgeschichte*, XXXI, 1968 pp. 27-58, where the whole question of sunflower iconography is discussed.

SEE COLOUR PLATE 19.

34A.
La Berceuse: Madame Augustine Roulin
F 508   (pl. 19)
February-March 1889
oil on canvas: 92 × 72 cm
Inscribed lower right: *La Berceuse*
Lent by the Boston Museum of Fine Arts
TORONTO ONLY

34B.
La Berceuse: Madame Augustine Roulin
F 507
March 1889
oil on canvas: 91 × 71.5 cm
Not signed or dated
Lent by the Stedelijk Museum, Amsterdam
AMSTERDAM ONLY

The first of the five versions of this subject theme was begun shortly before Vincent's crisis at the end of 1888 (*CL*573).[1] Given the dedication of the artist to this theme and his "freedom within exactitude" in its copying, qualitative comparisons among the several versions seem redundant. Upon his temporary recovery in January 1889, Vincent immediately recommenced upon the *berceuse* subject, with the added understanding that this would include his replicas of his two August 1888 sunflower paintings in some arrangement as a triptych, with the portrait of Madame Roulin as the central icon and the two sunflower pieces as the wings to act as "torches or candelabra" (*CL*574 of January 28). His first mention of the subject as "La Berceuse" (the Lullaby) had come in a letter to his friend and former colleage A.H. Koning (*CL*571a), where he refers to the lullaby theme in a work by the Dutch writer Frederik van Eeden.[2] In his second reference (*CL*574) Vincent refers to conversations he had had with Gauguin about the hard life of Icelandic fishermen, which he indicates had inspired his conception of *La Berceuse* as a kind of mother figure for all "sailors, who . . . at once children and martyrs, seeing it in the cabin of their Icelandic fishing boat, would feel the old sense of being rocked come over them and remember their own lullabys." Only days after Gauguin's arrival in Arles, Vincent, having learned of Gauguin's past career as a sailor, compared him (*CL*558b) to "that *Pêcheur d'Islande* by Loti" which work of literature may also have inspired discussions between the two artists about the "mournful isolation, exposed to all dangers, alone on the sad sea," of Icelandic fishermen that prompted Vincent's initial conception of *La Berceuse* (*CL*574).[3]

   The relationship to Gauguin was important to *La Berceuse* in other ways as well. Both men had already painted a portrait of *Madame Roulin* (*F* 503, *W* 298) probably by mid-December when Vincent reported to Théo (*CL*560) having done individual portraits of the whole Roulin family. In the two earlier portraits Madame Roulin is seated in the same wooden armchair which Vincent was to use again in *La Berceuse* and which can be identified as "Gauguin's armchair" from Vincent's painting of this subject as a main motif (*F* 499) and his statements about it (*CL* 563, 571). Vincent produced this *ersatz* portrait of Gauguin at about the time that Gauguin was doing his *Van Gogh Painting Sunflowers* (*W* 296), both of which are rightly considered charged with an element of implied tension—the chair as a presentiment of Gauguin's threatened departure and the portrait as Vincent interpreted it, "It's I all right, but I gone mad."[4] Vincent's December 1888 portrait of *Madame Roulin*, while no slavish imitation of Gauguin's style, was produced at a time when Vincent admitted adopting Gauguin's practice of "working from memory" (*CL* 563) and both this preliminary version and the *La Berceuse* portrait of Madame Roulin show her against a flat background containing a frankly decorative motif arbitrarily inserted. With *La Berceuse* the imaginary wallpaper with flower motifs of dahlias inevitably calls to mind Gauguin's *Self-Portrait called Les Misérables* (cat. no. 52), then in Vincent's possession, although both Madame Roulin and her background are even more reminiscent of Bernard's *Portrait of the Artist's Grandmother* (cat. no. 95), another of Vincent's favourite paintings. Finally one should not forget the precedents within the painter's own *oeuvre* for this icon of maternal reassurance. Already in Paris Vincent posed both *Père Tanguy* (cat. no. 8) and the *The Italian Woman* (cat. no. 13) in a similar frontal fashion with hands clasped, in the former instance with a backdrop at least as decorative as that in *La Berceuse* and in the latter with a wedding band and carnations functioning in a comparable manner to the rings and rope held by *La Berceuse*.[5] The proliferation of more or less Cloisonist portraits in the Arles period (*see, for example*, cat. nos. 15, 30 and 31) is such that one might better interpret *La Berceuse* as the culmination of more than a year of experimentation in a form of highly stylized and intensely colouristic portraiture. It retained its roots in Vincent's Realist outlook while yet achieving a suggestiveness of spiritual or even religious content that adumbrates, perhaps attains, genuine Symbolist portraiture.

Vincent's decision in January 1889 to combine the portrait of his friend's wife with flanking paintings of sunflowers as a pseudo-triptych was a masterstroke of imagination insofar as he thereby gained an allusion to traditional religious art without giving in to overt story telling of either a religious or secular kind. Whether Vincent's presumable faith that Icelandic sailors would be comforted by this pictorial lullaby was justified, it doubtless provided some such comfort to himself following his mental crisis. And his subsequent offer (*CL* 592) to provide copies of *La Berceuse* to both Gauguin and Bernard indicates his faith that they would appreciate the gift on similar grounds. They would also have grasped Vincent's embodiment of a strong red-green complementary colour contrast, which Vincent had outlined in a letter to a Dutch painter friend, A.H. Koning (*CL* 571a) and which along with the green clothing against the red tile floor was said to include the secondary contrast of orange dots within blue ovals as part of the imaginary wallpaper design. Vincent was willing to leave to the critics whether he "really sang a lullaby in colours," hereby alluding to the analogy between musical tones and the colour scale that slowly was becoming popular in Symbolist art circles. In May (*CL* 592) the artist observed that when *La Berceuse* was arranged between the pairs of yellow sunflowers "it makes a sort of triptych . . . then the yellow and orange tones of the head will gain in brilliance by the proximity of the yellow wings."

As time passed Vincent's recollection of the *Berceuse* and Sunflower themes became increasingly tinged with Symbolist overtones. When two sunflower paintings were exhibited in early 1890 in Brussels, Vincent, while denying they could be considered different in nature for such flower subjects by other artists, described them (*CL* 626a) to Albert Aurier as expressing "an idea symbolizing 'gratitude'." A few months earlier he had returned to the meaning of *La Berceuse* (*CL* 605). Whatever its weaknesses, said Vincent of this painting, had his strength permitted he would "have made portraits of saints and holy women from life who would have seemed to belong to another age, and they would be middle-class women of the present day, and yet they would have had something in common with the very primitive Christians." Thus van Gogh saw this *Berceuse* as a modern madonna of the common people whose strident colouration and naive image was likened elsewhere by the artist to cheap coloured popular prints of "chromos" which were available in the little shops in Paris (*CL* 576). Later Aurier astutely recognized this genial image of Madame Roulin as an "image d'Epinal."[6] One can only add that never before or after did Vincent come closer to realizing this dream of Realist portraiture which was nonetheless a religious icon than in the five versions of his justly honoured *La Berceuse*.

1. In *De la Faille* both examples exhibited here are given to late January-early March 1889.

2. Van Eeden's *De Kleine Johannes* (1885) was famous in the Netherlands for its fairy-tale recounting of the emergence of an introverted child who, through voyages of the imagination into the world of elves and talking animals, attains to maturity, self-knowledge and love of mankind in the model of Christ.

3. Roskill, p. 155 and 260, no. 40, interprets *CL* 558b and 574 to indicate that Gauguin had observed the life of Icelandic fishermen first-hand. This seems highly unlikely, given his service with the French merchant marine and navy, although, significantly, one trip (Perruchot, pp. 57-58) did take him up the Norwegian coast beyond the Arctic Circle. Tales of this voyage could only have enriched Vincent's knowledge gleaned from Loti's book.

4. Recounted by Gauguin in *Avant et après* (*see* W 296).

5. *Woman with Cradle*, F 369, comprises a naturalistic predecessor for the motherhood theme of *La Berceuse* (see Welsh-Ovcharov, p. 195) and provides a precedent for the clasped hands as well.

6. Aurier, p. 263, speaks of "La Berceuse cette gigantesque et géniale image d'Epinal."

35.

The Orchard with View of Arles   *F* 515
early April 1889
oil on canvas: 50.5 × 65 cm
Not signed or dated
Lent by the Rijksmuseum Vincent van Gogh,
Amsterdam

In late March-April 1888, not long after his arrival in Arles, Vincent devoted himself to painting approximately fifteen studies of orchards. His letters (*for example*, *CL*474, *B*3) make clear that the subjects reminded him of Holland at the same time that they aimed at a mixture of Impressionism and the gaiety of Japanese art.[1] A year later, shortly before leaving Arles for the asylum at St. Rémy, he returned to the orchard theme, and one day in early April he produced a large peach orchard study near La Crau (*F* 514) and this smaller painting, in which a range of buildings of Arles including the church tower of St. Julien (*compare F* 1480a) appear in the background. The day's work is described in a letter to Paul Signac (*CL*583b), where he specifically cites the Japanese character of *La Crau with Peach Trees*, an association one may presume equally valid for *The Orchard with View of Arles*. The Cloisonist outlines of the tree trunks and branches are strongly reminiscent of his Paris period painting after Hiroshige's *Flowering Plum Tree*, as is the broad expanse of emerald green orchard meadow and the "lilac" of the tree trunks. He explained to Signac that this painting included gray as a result of the rainy day on which it was painted. This reference suggests that Vincent was again associating his painting with the weather of his native Netherlands (see cat. no. 9), and there is a striking resemblance between this orchard at Arles and an 1884 drawing of *The Vicarage Garden at Nuenen in Winter* (*F* 1128). Along with an analogous disposition of spiky, heavily pruned trees in a flat, deeply receding landscape, the Nuenen drawing also includes a little church tower in the background. It is noteworthy that Vincent had wished (*CL*477) to group his orchard paintings of spring 1888 in a series of three, thus like a triptych, and projected this usage for the following year's orchard blossom time as well. One may conclude that Vincent's choice of blossoming orchards for so significant a segment of his landscape production in Arles embodied an age-old symbolism of cyclic rebirth after death, which the triptych idea and, in this instance, the church tower were meant to reinforce.

[1] In *B*3, Vincent gave an account of his working method in these orchard studies which scarcely could have expressed the Cloisonist approach more fully:

> Working directly on the spot all the time, I try to grasp what is essential in the drawing–later I fill in the spaces which are bounded by contours–either expressed or not, but in any case felt–with tones which are also simplified–.

Not only does this description follow upon Vincent's receipt of Bernard's Cloisonist drawing *Girl in a Street: Paris* (*fig. 107*), but its credo seems especially embodied in his own *Flowering Plumtree* of late 1887 and the *Orchard at Arles* of spring 1889.

A

36A.
*Window of Vincent's Studio at Saint Paul's
Hospital*   F 1528
late spring 1889?
black chalk and gouache on Ingres paper:
61.5 × 47 cm
Not signed or dated
Lent by the Rijksmuseum Vincent van Gogh,
Amsterdam
TORONTO ONLY

36B.
The Vestibule of Saint Paul's Hospital   F 1530
late spring 1889?
black chalk and gouache on Ingres paper toned
pink: 61.5 × 47 cm
Not signed or dated
Lent by the Rijksmuseum Vincent van Gogh,
Amsterdam
AMSTERDAM ONLY

Along with a third gouache, *A Passage at Saint
Paul's Hospital* (*F* 1529), these two depictions of
complementary interior views of Saint Paul's
Hospital at St. Rémy were executed with identical
materials and in a style so similar that they were
conceived as a closely knit series. Although
undated and not mentioned in Vincent's
correspondence, they are generally attributed to
shortly after the artist's voluntary entrance into the
asylum for treatment. His condition was there at
first diagnosed as epilepsy but, since then it has
been described as virtually every mental illness
known without any true consensus having been
reached.[1] The spring or, at the latest, summer of
1889 date of these depictions is further suggested
by the green foliage seen through the window and
door. It also seems reasonable that they were made
in order to supply Théo with an immediate
impression of Vincent's new surroundings, visual
supplement to his verbal descriptions (especially
*CL*592 of May 22).

   Vincent has here once again combined
naturalistic accuracy in terms of perspective and
architectural detail, as photographic evidence
attests, with simplified contour outlines filled in
with flat areas of colour according to Cloisonist
principle.[2] The imitation of reed pen technique in
those brush strokes which are visible only fortifies a
sense of clarity and order within these gouaches.
However, his previously brilliant colour
experiments are here gradually replaced by such
earthy tones as red ochres and raw sienna, a return

to his Dutch palette. Vincent deleted from all three depictions the iron bars which were present, one can only assume in order to spare the sensibilities of his brother. It has been erroneously suggested that Théo generously had provided Vincent a second cell-room for use as a studio; the artist himself informed Théo that because the asylum had more than thirty empty rooms he had been given an extra one to work in.[3] It is a part of this room that Vincent rendered in the *Window* gouache as evidenced by the presence of his working tools and four displayed canvases, alas not identifiable with any certainty.[4] One can find inside the door and at right in *The Vestibule* a painting and perhaps a drawing portfolio. The inclusion of these objects may again be interpreted as reassurance to Théo that during confinement in the hospital, his older brother remained capable of working outside as well, and as symbols for the recuperative powers of artistic creativity. Although it is tempting to read the railroad-track perspective of *The Passage* as reflecting psychological instability and a flight into an unknown infinity, both *The Window* and *The Vestibule* represent the everyday places from which Vincent could see the hospital gardens which he often depicted.[5]

B

[1]   Both Cooper, p. 84, and Bowness, cat. nos. 154-55, consider the gouaches as the product of Vincent's first weeks in St. Rémy.

[2]   Tralbaut, pp. 289, 291, juxtaposes photographs of the three subjects with illustrations (two in colour) of the gouaches.

[3]   Tralbaut, *ibid*. However in *CL* 592 Vincent clearly attributes the new studio to the availability of empty rooms in the asylum.

[4]   The painting at right above bears a generic resemblance to *F* 640, *The Park of Saint Paul's Hospital*, of October 1889, but one cannot be at all certain. R. Rosenblum, *Modern Painting* (*see* cat. no. 27, n. 4), p. 97 observes the artist's materials and pictures on the wall should be viewed as a projection of van Gogh's personality ''rather than a decorative component.''

[5]   E.g., F 1531, *The Fountain in the Garden of Saint Paul's Hospital*, which can be seen through the doorway of *The Vestibule*.

37.

Death's-Head Moth   *F* 610
c. late May 1889
oil on canvas: 33 × 24 cm
Not signed or dated
Lent by the Rijksmuseum Vincent van Gogh,
Amsterdam

The subject of this painting was mentioned in one of Vincent's very first letters from St. Rémy to Théo of late May 1889 (*CL*592), in which was included a tiny sketch of the moth. This Vincent called a "rather rare night moth, called the death's-head" and praised for its size and "colouring of amazing distinction." This identification is sometimes challenged, both the emperor moth and the peacock butterfly having been suggested as a more accurate zoological designation.[1] Retention of Vincent's title remains justified nonetheless, since this is what he thought he was representing and, above all, because in both his preparatory drawing (*F* 1523) and this painting an image of a death's-head is clearly visible at the very centre of the moth as seen from above. Vincent's sensitivity to the peculiar beauty of this fragile creature was tinged by regret at having had to kill the "beautiful beast" in order to paint it. While such a statement might all too easily be over-interpreted in reference to Vincent's later suicide, the hint at the fragility of biological existence cannot be altogether overlooked, in particular considering the fact that this painting was produced immediately following Vincent's voluntary incarceration in what, let us be frank, was a jail-like institution.

The most striking stylistic aspect of this painting is its inventive mixture of accurate observation of nature, a forceful and dramatic stylization thereof, and his once again well-documented involvement with the art of Japan. For this painting Vincent employed the most minute rendering of nature and its colours, yet hinted, as so often, that these involved a tendency towards monochrome green enlivened by the usual complementary contrast with red which he found inherent to the colours of the moth itself. His other analogy was with the plants which it was his first instinct to depict upon arrival at St. Rémy. Just previous to his move from Arles to the asylum at St. Rémy, Vincent (*CL*590) had Japanese prints hanging on his walls. Upon his arrival he was immediately drawn to representations of vegetation, perhaps as a sign of life amid the signs of decay in the humanity with which he was surrounded (*CL*593). The convolutions of line and nuanced compartmentalization of green colouration is no less Cloisonist for the intimations of Art Nouveau *flamboyant* which this miracle of minor design evinces. This provocative image of a hopelessly vulnerable, yet seminally productive harbinger of the night flitting about the infinitely attractive pistils and stamens of the flowers depicted is deeply evocative of the hope-in-despair theme of Vincent's avowal to his brother and his new bride (to whom Vincent sent his assurances of affection and encouragement upon his arrival at St. Rémy) that things would get better rather than worse. That this small study of a moth and vegetation was discussed in the first letter in which Vincent explained his "Berceuse Triptych" indicates the "macrocosm within a microcosm theme" which so preoccupied Vincent at the time and which is evident in this deceptively simple image of a night moth in flight.

---

[1]   See Bowness, cat. no. 153, L. Jampoller, "Observations of nature 2: butterflies," *Vincent*, I:3 (1971), pp. 30-31, and *Vincent: A Choice*, p. 101.

38.

The Walk: Falling Leaves   F 651
early November 1889
oil on canvas: 73.5 × 60 cm
Not signed or dated
Lent by the Rijksmuseum Vincent van Gogh,
Amsterdam

This painting would seem to be the one cited in
early November 1889 as "falling leaves"
(*CL* 613) and is thus reminiscent in theme to the
Alyscamps paintings of a year earlier (cat.
no. 28). Though lacking internal evidence which
makes this certain, the setting is almost surely the
park with fir trees at Saint Paul's Hospital at St.
Rémy, which Vincent depicted in ten other
canvases and a number of drawings during
autumn 1889.[1] Whether the little blue figure is
meant to symbolize his own or some other
inmate's peregrinations in this informally laid-out
woodland setting, the long coat indicates chill
weather in keeping with the approaching winter
season. In his letter mentioning this painting,
Vincent in fact says that with most leaves having
fallen the countryside reminds him of the north,
which he would see "more clearly than before,"
should he return.

   In apparent reaction to Théo's warning (*T* 19)
that too much stylistic experimentation by Vincent
could prove harmful and that Gauguin's Japanism
might be inappropriate in treating Breton women,
Vincent answers forthrightly: "I feel strongly
inclined to seek style, if you like, but by that I
mean a more virile, deliberate drawing. I can't
help it if that makes me more like Bernard or
Gauguin." That this allusion to the two painters
was not merely incidental to his current artistic
tendency is indicated by his closing remark. There
he refers to "a big landscape with some pines,
trunks of red ochre defined by a black stroke,"
which he says has "more character" than some
earlier examples. Except for the reference to a
large size, Vincent could easily have been
describing *The Walk*, with its several "red-ochre"
tree trunks defined with Cloisonist outlines.[2]
Although the artist referred to Delacroix's "Jacob
Struggling with the Angel" as his model for this
new development, it is permissible to believe that
he also had in mind the style exemplified by
Gauguin's treatment of the same theme, no matter
how far removed in subject from the subject
matter of the park at Saint Paul's.

   Nor should one overlook the likelihood that
Vincent in his landscapes of autumn 1889 was

seeking to profit by and keep abreast of
developments in the art of Bernard. In an October
1889 letter (*B* 20) – the first to Bernard in a year's
time – Vincent assured his younger colleague that a
painting he himself had done of an "Entrance to a
Quarry" (that is, *F* 635), which he likened to
"certain Japanese drawings," shows "In the
design and in the division of the colour into large
planes . . . no little similarity to what you are doing
at Pont-Aven." This observation probably was
based upon his earlier experience in studying the
Cloisonist style of Bernard, as embodied for
example in the *Breton Women*, of which he made
a copy (cat. no. 29), or in the *Promenade in the
Bois d'Amour*, (cat. no. 94) which seems a
particularly likely possibility to have been
remembered in Vincent's *The Walk*. Although the
park at Saint Paul's Hospital scarcely functioned
as a "garden of love," it nonetheless provided to
Vincent a place of respite, however temporary,
from his recurring fear of psychological relapse.

1   *Cf. F* 640, 642-43, 659-60, 731-33, 742, and
   for the related drawings *De la Faille*, pp. 538-41.
   Many of these depictions include building façades,
   benches or fences which allow for the identification
   of the setting as Saint Paul's Hospital.
2   Colour illustration in *Vincent: A Choice*, p. 100.
   The "big landscape with some pines" is likely *The
   Garden of Saint Paul's Hospital* (F 659-60), one
   version of which Vincent described in a letter to
   Bernard (*B* 21) as dominated by the "red-ochre"
   colouration also mentioned to Théo.

39.

*Still Life: Vase with Irises
against a Yellow Background*   F 678
early May 1890
oil on canvas: 92 × 73.5 cm
Not signed or dated
Lent by the Rijksmuseum Vincent van Gogh,
Amsterdam

Along with two flower pieces with roses (F 681-
82), this vertical format painting of *Irises* and a
companion piece in horizontal format (F 680)
were executed during Vincent's last week at the
asylum in St. Rémy (*CL* 633), when a desire to
produce these final testimonials of his stay in the
south of France competed with a wish to complete
his packing for the trip to Paris and Auvers. The
special compulsion to paint the subject of irises
surely owed something to the modest success
which his first treatment of this subject (*F* 608),
painted almost immediately upon his arrival at the
institution, had enjoyed at the *Indépendants* exhibition of September 1889.[1] It is probably too fan-
ciful to believe that a critic's comment that the
earlier *Irises* "violently slash their petals to pieces
upon swordlike leaves," was remembered in the
slain flower stalks falling to the right in our later
example, but the characterization nonetheless
remains apt.[2]

　　This canvas represents a final tribute by Vincent to St. Rémy where these flowers bloomed in
rich profusion in the garden of the asylum in contradistinction to the *Sunflowers* (cat. no. 33)
which in the mind of the artist were associated
with Arles.[3] The *Irises* also comprised another
tribute to two of the major conceptual loyalties
which sustained his spirit to work while there. One
of these loyalties, that to the art of Japan, is substantiated by a comparison of the Amsterdam
Irises (and even more so, *F* 608) to the *Irises and
a Grasshopper* (*fig. 55*) from a set of ten prints
by Hokusai known as the "Large Flowers" (the
sword-like petals of which appear even more
menacing than in Vincent's treatments of the subjects of irises).[4] In the same letter to Théo that he
described these flower pieces in some detail, he
also mentioned looking forward to visiting an exhibition of Japanese prints then on view in Paris, a
coincidental reference Théo would have been the
first to understand.

　　The second important reference in this letter
was to Georges Seurat, a visit to whose studio with
Théo on the eve of his own departure for the south
Vincent specifically recalled. Vincent wished to

Fig. 55
Hokusai:
Irises and a Grasshopper,
colour print
(Fitzwilliam Museum, Cambridge).

make the parallel between that departure and the
impending one quite specific, stating, "just as we
were so struck by Seurat's canvases on that day,
these last days here are like a fresh revelation of
colour to me." The connection between this utter-
ance and the colour conception of these final
flower studies from St. Rémy is contained in his
description of them. Whereas the red-green complementary contrast is dominant in a study with
roses and that of irises in horizontal format, in our
example it is the purple-yellow contrast which is
most essential. Here a "violet bunch of flowers
(ranging from carmine to pure Prussian blue)
stands out against a startling citron background,
with other yellow tones in the vase and the stand
on which it rests, so it is an effect of tremendously
disparate complementaries, which strengthen each
other by the juxtaposition." Such was the fierce-
ness of Vincent's loyalty to the colour usages he
assigned to Seurat and yet to the principles of the

Japanese wood block print as well that he fails to
mention his own unique ability to synthesize his
various sources of inspiration in so powerful a personal style that no trace of dependence upon the
art of others remains.

[1]　Theo reported (*T* 20) that, "the 'Irises' was seen
　　by a lot of people, who now talk to me about them
　　every once in a while."

[2]　Fénéon, I, p. 168 (from *La Vogue*, September,
　　1889).

[3]　*F* 601, given there to Arles, 1889, most possibly
　　was executed along with *F* 608 after his arrival in
　　St. Rémy, when van Gogh was forced at first to
　　paint such subjects in the hospital garden from his
　　studio window (*CL* 592-3).

[4]　Vincent's appreciation of this and similar Japanese
　　flower depictions which included visible insect
　　forms is also reflected in cat. nos. 10, 37 and 38 of
　　the present exhibition.

40.

Roses and a Beetle   F 749

c. June 1890

oil on canvas: 32.5 × 23.5 cm

Not signed or dated

Lent by the Rijksmuseum Vincent van Gogh, Amsterdam

This little painting is one of four flower pieces in a similar style which Vincent executed in Auvers, giving one of them to his friend Dr. Paul Gachet.[1] In this example the conception is so devoted to a decorative ideal that one cannot determine whether a still life or an outdoor rose bush was depicted. The latter is perhaps implied by the presence of the beetle so prominently displayed on the rose blossom at bottom. However, this was doubtless done independent of any natural setting, since sketches of beetles and other insects by Vincent have been preserved which date from as early as his nineteenth year and as late as July 1888 (*CL* 506), when he wrote Théo that the insects in Arles reminded him of those one sees in Japanese sketchbooks.[2] The beetle's inclusion in this painting thus probably is as much emblematic of Vincent's love of Japanese art as it was of his observation of nature. In late May 1889 the artist had already painted the *Death's-Head Moth* (cat. no. 37) which documented Vincent's similar inventive mixture of nature and the art of Japan. Even while the painterliness of Vincent's surface gains new freedom in his final Auvers period, the thick contour lines with which the leaves are defined remind us of his protracted involvement with Japan and Cloisonism.

[1] See the Editorial Commission of *De la Faille* (*F* 595, 597, 748-49) for discussion of this question of chronology.

[2] See V.W.v.G. "Observations of Nature: Insects." *Vincent*, I, (Spring 1971), pp. 46-47.

41.
View at Auvers   *F* 799
June-July 1890
oil on canvas: 50 × 52 cm
Not signed or dated
Lent by the Rijksmuseum Vincent van Gogh,
Amsterdam

"Auvers is very beautiful, among other things a lot
of old thatched roofs which are getting rare...it is
the real country and picturesque" (*CL* 635); so
van Gogh described his first impressions of his new
surroundings to Théo and his young wife on May
20, 1980 upon his arrival at this village which he
admitted was far enough from Paris and its noise
to be the "real country" (*CL* 637). In this canvas
Vincent expresses his first days of calm there and
directly characterizes the "lush well-kept
greenery" and quiet surroundings in particular its
many cottages and middle class dwellings
(*CL* 637) which description however, builds upon
the simplicity and defined Cloisonist lines of his
Arles-St. Rémy periods. In recent months Vincent
had confessed a nostalgic yearning to see his native
Netherlands again, and in "northern" Auvers
such desires perhaps were being reawakened. He
suggested to Théo that he saw in the landscapes of
Auvers a "quiet like a Puvis de Chavannes, no
factories" (*CL* 637), only verdant abundance, but
he then also must have been aware of such
panoramic views of Auvers as painted by Cézanne
and Pissarro during their respective earlier sojourns
at this village on the river Oise. In the last days
before his suicide on July 29, Vincent's nervous
intensity increased, obliterating such bucolic and
tranquil views, producing instead canvases of fields
of wheat which, he wrote, are placed "under
troubled skies." He thereafter added "I did not
need to go out of my way to try to express sadness
and extreme loneliness" (*CL* 651).

   This depiction of Auvers eschews the
well-known views of an earlier generation, but also
includes a view of the ridge of fields symbolically
represented in the *Portrait of Dr. Paul Gachet*,
the leading citizen of the village (*see* cat. no. 43).
It stresses instead Vincent's preferred arrangement
of a foreground grain field, a middle distance
configuration of buildings and a distant landscape
background, components of the picture aligned
vertically as if to question the issue of rendering in
depth. The resulting image is one of the most
tranquil which Vincent produced of this village
where he was to experience his final triumph in art
and self-abnegation of life.

42.

Trees, Roots and Branches   F 816

c. July 1890

oil on canvas: 50.5 × 100.5 cm

Not signed or dated

Lent by the Rijksmuseum Vincent van Gogh,
Amsterdam

In this, one of Vincent's final dozen or so
paintings, he paradoxically points dramatically
towards the future in Western art, yet remembers,
however subtly, his own earliest beginnings as a
painter. Forest undergrowth – what the French call
"sous-bois" – had already been depicted in one of
his very earliest paintings (*F* 8). That same year,
1882, a major mixed media drawing called *Study
of a Tree* (*F* 933 recto) depicts a silhouetted
assortment of tree trunks, branches and exposed
roots in a manner which remarkably anticipates
the convoluted organic configurations found in the
eight-year-later *Trees, Roots and Branches*.
Vincent's return to northern France was
predicated upon his self-avowed abandonment of
prismatic colours for the "broken" or mixed
colours of his native Dutch tradition, present in
Trees, Roots and Branches in the tan-to-brown
hues indicating the "earth" tonalities inherent to
the setting.

At the same time, this painting combines with
reminiscences of Vincent's naturalist beginnings
one of the most extraordinary degrees of a
decoratively conceived quasi-abstraction which
can be discovered in his total *oeuvre*. Cloisonist
outlines, areas of distinct, if slightly muted,
colouration and a visible pattern of individual
brush strokes are here so inexplicably integrated
that the final effect is one of ordered chaos.
Whereas intimations of the elegant stylizations of
the international Art Nouveau movement are thus
obviously present, Vincent's emotionalized, yet
controlled, use of his artistic means should remain
the focus of our attention. Not the least of those
who paid devoted attention to the late style of
Vincent as embodied in this painting were the
Fauves, whose typical brush technique is predicted
so forcefully in this and its companion paintings
from the final weeks in Auvers. One of these, the
endlessly celebrated *Crows in the Wheat Field*
(*F* 779), is certain to retain its reputation as the
single most important harbinger of Fauve
expressionism, but the here exhibited painting
with its one by two height versus width
proportions should be equally celebrated for the
prediction of twentieth century style which it
represents.[1]

[1]   See *De la Faille*, pp. 297-99, plus *F* 793, 809,
      811, for the widespread use at Arles of this
      horizontally extended "marine" and hence
      panoramic landscape format.

43.

Portrait of Dr. Paul Gachet   *F* 753
June 1890
oil on canvas: 66 × 57 cm
Not signed or dated
Lent by a private collection, New York
AMSTERDAM ONLY

The subject of this portrait was a most remarkable figure within the Impressionist circle. Addicted to a wide variety of radically modern causes of his day, he had befriended such artists as Courbet, Manet and the Impressionists, especially the artist Camille Pissarro, and in some instances had become their patron.[1] He was an amateur etcher himself on whose equipment Vincent produced his only essay in this medium, a portrait of the Doctor smoking a pipe (*F* 1664) executed by Vincent on May 25, 1889, only four days following his arrival in Auvers. Dr. Gachet, who was clearly an eccentric, lived in a large house in Auvers, where he kept a sizable assortment of domestic and farm animals, but still practised medicine several days a week in Paris. Pissarro had recommended him as a medical overseer for Vincent, and Théo described him to Vincent in St. Rémy (*T*31) as "physically . . . a little like you," which allusion doubtless included the red hair of the two men. Vincent's often cited first impression of Gachet as in combat with a "nervous trouble from which he certainly seems to me to be suffering at least as seriously as I" (*CL*635) may be considered an extension of Théo's comment on the physical similarity of the two men into the realms of personal psychology. On June 3 Vincent announced to Théo (*CL*638) both that he was at work on a painted portrait of Gachet and that Gachet was so "absolutely fanatical" about his last *Self-Portrait* (*F* 627) from St. Rémy that he, wished a copy of it; this perhaps suggests that the new sitter, too, felt a spiritual kinship with his portraitist. There is no doubt that by this time Vincent had come to see himself profoundly reflected in Dr. Gachet, whom he described the same day in a letter to his sister as "something like another brother, so much do we resemble each other physically and also mentally" (*Wil*22).

Vincent's conception in this portrait depends upon a far greater variety of sources and personal interpretations than is commonly thought. The depiction is both Realist and Symbolist without any conflict between the two approaches. The subject is shown in the white cap with visor and blue overcoat which Gachet wore even in summer,

and, as with the etching, can be identified here as seated leaning on his "red garden table" (*Wil*22), even if the "rustic scenery with a background of blue hills" (*Wil*22) is difficult to fathom without help from the quoted remark. A. Brown Price has recently established that Vincent was in part induced to include the blue background, books, glass and flowers because of similar features in the *Portrait of Eugène Benon* by Puvis de Chavannes, which he had seen in late 1887 and remembered in late 1889 (*CL*617) as "the ideal in figure to me" for the consolation it offers among the "inevitable griefs" of modern life.[2] For Gachet's pose, however, we must turn to two other paintings, which are also mentioned by Vincent, although not in direct reference to the *Portrait of Gachet*. Intimations of the Gachet portrait conception are already contained in a letter of late summer in Arles (*CL*520) in which, on the basis of Delacroix's supposedly "arbitrary" use of colour, Vincent outlines his idea of painting the portrait of an artist friend being at first "as faithful" as he could but then painting "infinity, a plain background of the richest, intensest blue that I can contrive." This concept was realized not long thereafter in the *Portrait of Eugène Boch, a Belgian Painter* (F 462), a work also known as "The Poet," which Vincent linked in a subsequent letter (*CL*531) "with what Eug. Delacroix attempted and brought off in his 'Tasso in Prison' . . . representing a *real* man . . . [but with] the soul of the model in it." That Vincent continued to harbour thoughts of Delacroix's portrait of the mentally ill Tasso is proven by yet another Arles letter (*CL*564), written after he had visited the Montpellier museum with Gauguin and seen there both the collection assembled by Courbet's friend and patron Alfred Bruyas as well as the latter's portrait by Delacroix.[3] Vincent herein asks his brother to secure an inexpensive lithograph after *Tasso in the Hospital* (*fig. 56*), since he thought "the figure there must have some affinity with this Delacroix's fine portrait of Brias (*sic*)." However justified this association in actual fact, due to the fundamental similarity of the poses of Delacroix's *Tasso* and Vincent's *Gachet*, it is difficult not to believe that the one was a consciously employed source for the other.[4] Indeed, just before announcing to Théo (*CL*638) that he had begun work on the *Portrait of Gachet*, he mentions that Gachet had known Bruyas in Montpellier.

The theme of this symbolic portrait is also deducible from the combination of associations which these sources on Gachet himself suggested

for Vincent. Since Vincent in describing the *Portrait of Benon* by Puvis to Bernard (*B*14) coupled a reference to the "Yellow Novel" the subject is seen reading to that artist having also painted "a

[1] The extraordinary character, liberal Republican and socialist politics, and wide range of intellectual convictions of Dr. Gachet are conveniently given in *P-I*, pp. 362-66.

[2] A. B. Price, "Two Portraits by Vincent van Gogh and Two Portraits by Pierre Puvis de Chavannes," *The Burlington Magazine*, CXVII, November 1975, pp. 714-18, where the *Portrait of Benon* was first illustrated.

[3] The *Portrait of Alfred Bruyas* by Delacroix is illustrated in colour in R. Huyghe, *Delacroix*, (New York: Harry Abrams, 1963), p. 386. Vincent identified (*CL*564) Bruyas as a benefactor of artists whose portrait "by Delacroix . . . with red beard and hair" has an uncommon resemblance to the van Gogh brothers. Elsewhere (*CL*570) Vincent claimed that he and Théo were continuing in the south what Monticelli and Bruyas had begun.

[4] L. Johnson, *The Paintings of Eugène Delacroix, A Critical Catalogue I*, (Oxford: The Clarendon Press, expected date of publication 1981), pp. 91-93, discusses the earliest of two versions of *Tasso in the Hospital of St. Anna, Ferrara* (1824) and points out that van Gogh wished to attain in his own portraits in Arles a similar conception as found in Delacroix's *Tasso*. It is not certain which painting had inspired van Gogh, since he could have seen prints after both this earlier and the 1839 version now in the Oscar Reinhart Foundation, Winterthur.

Van Gogh clearly recalls to Théo a painted version of *Tasso* (*CL*531). The present author presumes that it was the second version which was known to Vincent in one form or another, whether or not Théo acquired and forwarded the "inexpensive lithograph" requested by Vincent, since the inverted figure in this painting here reproduced in reverse (*fig. 56*) conforms so closely to that in *Dr. Gachet*. As Johnson documents, by the early nineteenth century Tasso was considered a genius unjustly "imprisoned" in a madhouse despite the lucidity of his thinking most of the time. This conception, if known to Vincent, would have intensified his inclination to both a physical and spiritual self-identification with the similarly red-haired Tasso and, by extension, with the red-haired Alfred Bruyas and Dr. Gachet.

Fig. 56
Eugène Delacroix
Tasso in the Hospital of St. Anna, Ferrara,
1839,
oil on canvas
(Oskar Reinhart Foundation, Winterthur).

fashionable lady, as the Goncourts have depicted them," we can better understand why he has identified the two yellow books in the *Gachet* as *Germinie Lacerteux* and *Manette Salomon* namely in order to heighten the theme of consolation despite the inevitable griefs of modern life in France that the Goncourt brothers had predicted in these two Realist novels.[5] The foxglove or digitalis flower which is employed in the treatment of heart disease, seemingly refers to an area of specialization by the doctor.[6] Another area of the sitter's interest was the study of "melancholia," on which he had written a thesis for the medical faculty of Montpellier University.[7] This may be considered the most essential theme of the portrait. Vincent referred to Gachet as a very nervous and broken man in describing this or the companion version to Wilhelmina (*Wil*23), and in a reference to it written to Gauguin (*CL*643) he said it contained "the heartbroken expression of our time" and further compared it in intention with Gauguin's *Christ in the Garden of Olives* (cat. no. 66), the dolorous theme of which Gauguin had described to Vincent in a letter. It was this painting which prompted Vincent to cite (*Wil*22) "the modern portrait" as his greatest passion and to specify this with the wish "to paint portraits which would appear after a century to the people living then as apparitions." In this his most melancholy and apparitional painting of all, Vincent has fused so many sources so successfully that its, for some, hallucinatory attraction was manifested long before the predicted wait of a century.

5   Jules and Edmond de Goncourt, *Germinie Lacerteux* (1865) explores the social and physical temperament of a working class girl in Paris whose character leads her to nymphomania, alcoholism, theft and finally death, while *Manette Salomon* (1867) concerns mid-nineteenth century modern art in France as Vincent noted in *CL*604 and exposes the suffering caused when a talented artist in Paris fails in his desperate search for the ideal through art. Vincent credits Gachet as having "extended much friendliness to the artists of the new school" (*Wil*21), a fact which explains the inclusion of *Manette Salomon* on the table.

6   See exh. cat. *Van Gogh et les peintres d'Auvers sur Oise* (Paris: Orangerie des Tuileries, 1954), no. 46.

7   Cited in *P-I*, p. 366. It is also possible that Vincent had Dürer's famous engraving *Melancolia I* in mind in conceiving Gachet in a similar rueful pose.

The melancholy of the theme and expressive freedom of the brushwork do little to compromise the Cloisonist colour usages which are present. To his sister he indicated that the purple of the foxglove was meant to complement the yellow of the books, and this aim is present as well in at least the red-green of the garden table top. In this final portrait example of a blue-jacketed seated older male friend, which classification includes such notable portraits as those of *Père Tanguy* (cat. no. 8), *L'Arlésienne* (cat. no. 30) and *The Postman Roulin* (for example, F 432), we have not only a powerful climax to the subject series but a fitting terminus to the van Gogh portion of the present study.

Paul Gauguin (1848-1903)

Biographical Data

The primary sources for the life of Gauguin include governmental archives, dated or otherwise datable works of art (for example, as documented by his surviving sketchbooks, listed *Wildenstein*, opposite p. 1), surviving contemporary accounts (unfortunately, *Avant et après*, which includes accounts of Gauguin's pre-Tahitian periods, like his other surviving texts, was written after his departure of the South Pacific and is not entirely trustworthy as to fact) and his own and related surviving correspondence. Gauguin's pre-Tahitian letters are most conveniently collected in *Malingue*, whose ascription of dates is sometimes open to question. A number of other letters have yet to be published in full, including those to Vincent and Théo van Gogh, now at the Rijksmuseum Vincent van Gogh and shortly to be published as edited by Douglas Cooper. Roskill, pp. 268-77, provides valuable assistance in reference to the movements and correspondence of Gauguin, Bernard and van Gogh in 1888. I should like to thank my husband, R.P. Welsh, for sharing several discoveries about the movements of Gauguin, Meyer de Haan and Séusier in late 1889, which he will present more fully in a forthcoming article on the decorative scheme created by these artists for the inn of Marie Henry at Le Pouldu.

The most important secondary accounts of Gauguin's life are those provided by Rotonchamp, Chassé (*Pont-Aven* and *Son temps*), Perruchot and *P-I*, although numerous other authors have made valuable contributions.

EARLY LIFE AND CAREER
1848-1885

On June 7, 1848, "under the barricades" in Paris, Paul, the first son but second and last child, is born to Clovis and Aline Gauguin (the latter née Chazal and daughter of Flora Tristan, of mixed French and Spanish-Peruvian parentage and a notorious free-thinker and propagandist for revolutionary working-class causes). During 1849-55 he lives with his mother and sister Marie in Peru, his father having died on the journey there. An intermittent career follows (1865-71) first as merchant seaman, then as sailor in the French navy. In 1871, with encouragement from his godfather, Gustave Arosa, he joins the stockbroking firm of Paul Bertin and there meets Emile Schuffenecker and begins painting as an amateur. On November 22, 1873 he marries Mette-Sophie Gad, a Dane who bears him five children: Emil (1874), Aline (1877), Clovis (1879), Jean-René (1881) and Paul-Rollon or Pola (1883). Following a desultory artistic production throughout the 1870s, in the last year of the decade Gauguin executes an increased number of landscape paintings in a Realist-Impressionist style, and exhibits a statuette at the fourth Impressionist exhibition. By spring 1881 he is able to send eight canvases to the sixth Impressionist exhibition following which he spends his summer vacation painting at Pontoise with Pissarro and Cézanne, an activity reflected in the submission of twelve canvases or pastels to the Impressionist exhibition of 1882. In January 1883, Gauguin resigns his position as stockbroker and begins to paint "every day." During June-July he visits Pissarro in Osny. Late in the year, accompanied by his family, he follows Pissarro to Rouen, staying there until November 1884, when he accompanies Mette and the children to Copenhagen for a period of strained family relationships. Pressure from the academy (*M*XXII) closes his one-man exhibition of spring 1885 in Copenhagen after five days, and *circa* June he returns to Paris with Clovis, leaving Mette and the other children behind. On September 19, during a short stopover in Dieppe where he is said to have met and quarrelled with Degas, he announces a three-week visit concerning hoped-for Spanish business contacts in London (*M*XXV). He is back in Paris by early October, where his economic situation remains critical. (Except where noted, the above account derives from Perruchot.)

1886

JANUARY–MAY
PARIS

A period of austerity culminates with the sickness of Clovis, which *circa* early April forces Gauguin, still hoping (*M*XXXV) for a business career in Spain, to work as a bill poster. On May 15 the month-long eighth Impressionist exhibition opens with nineteen canvases of *circa* 1884-85 by Gauguin, who thereafter quarrels with co-exhibitor Georges Seurat over the use of Paul Signac's studio (Pissarro, p. 112).

In late spring Gauguin meets the French ceramicist Ernest Chaplet through the engraver Félix Bracquemond (*M*XL).

JUNE–NOVEMBER
PONT-AVEN

Gauguin lodges Clovis in the countryside and departs *circa* late June for Pont-Aven where he resides at the artists' pension of Marie-Jeanne Gloanec until mid-November (*M*XLIV). Here he befriends Charles Laval and makes the passing acquaintance of Emile Bernard. His landscape painting remains essentially Impressionist in brushwork, but figural depictions become increasingly stylized (*see fig. 24*).

NOVEMBER–DECEMBER

Upon his return to Paris, Gauguin works in the *atelier* of Chaplet on his first "ceramic sculpture," although illness imposes a hospital stay of almost a month (*M*XLV). He probably produces *Vase with Breton Girls* (Introduction, *fig. 25*), and again becomes friendly with Degas, but remains hostile to the Neo-Impressionists, who now include Pissarro (Pissarro, pp. 111-12).

1887

JANUARY–APRIL
PARIS

Apparently the artist remains preoccupied with ceramics, fifty-five of which he fires one day in January, rather than painting (only W 215-16 dated 1887 could have been pre-Martinique) and with various "get rich quick" business schemes (*M*XLVII/XLVIII). During this time he is preparing for an extended visit to Panama, which his sister seems to have suggested upon his return from Pont-Aven (*M*XLV).

APRIL–NOVEMBER
CENTRAL AMERICA

Gauguin leaves Paris April 9 with Charles Laval for Panama, where he stays with his brother-in-law at Panama City, before leaving for the island of Tobago (*M*L). Finding no means of sustenance here, he works on construction of the Panama Canal in order to earn funds for a stay in Martinique. Let go after two weeks' labour, he and Laval are nonetheless established and working in St. Pierre, Martinique, by late June (*M*LIII). On August 25 Gauguin writes to Schuffenecker that he has fallen seriously ill and needs help for repatriation to France, where he expects to make a living through collaboration with the ceramist Chaplet. Leaving Laval behind, Gauguin regains Paris by late November by serving as a seaman, but finds to his dismay that Chaplet has sold his Paris workshop (*M*LVIII).

DECEMBER
PARIS

While lodging temporarily with the Schuffenecker family, he begins his association with the Boussod and Valadon gallery operated by Théo van Gogh, by exhibiting three paintings and five ceramics in December. Possibly this exhibition was arranged by Gauguin's friends Pissarro and Guillaumin, with whom he exhibited here. Gauguin also sees the Du Chalet exhibition organized by Vincent van Gogh (*CL*510), whom he may or may not have known previously. His artistic activity (winter 1887-88) is apparently largely limited to ceramics (*M*LIX), produced in collaboration with Chaplet (Bodelsen, p. 72).

1888

JANUARY–FEBRUARY
PARIS

Gauguin seems to have produced no new paintings during this period (none are cited in *Wildenstein*, for 1888 except those with Pont-Aven or Arles subjects), but he probably continued to work on his ceramics, while preparing for a long stay in Pont-Aven. In contrast to the assurances of eventual reconciliation offered Mette before and during the Panama-Martinique trip (*M*XLVII,XLIX, LII-LIII, LV), he now insists upon a protracted separation (*M*LX-LXII).

FEBRUARY–JULY
PONT-AVEN, BRITTANY

On Thursday, either February 9 or 16, Gauguin departs for Pont-Aven, where until late March he remains plagued by sickness (*M*LXII-LXIII) a situation which only gradually improves but is by no means at an end in July (*G*4, *M*LXVI). In the meantime he commences a correspondence with the van Gogh brothers (*G*1-4) which indicates his hope of commercial success through aid from Théo.

In early June Vincent and Théo propose that Gauguin stay with Vincent at his newly rented "Yellow House" at Arles (*CL*493-94a, 496, 498), to which Gauguin, having lived on credit for three months at the Pension Gloanec, agrees in early July (*G*5, *CL*507, *M*LXVI). However, he continues to live and paint landscapes in and near Pont-Aven, reporting, *circa* July (*G*6), to Vincent the completion of the Japanist *Two Breton Boys Wrestling* and to Théo (*G*7) the commencement of *The Three Breton Girls Dancing* (*W*251). Laval arrives in Pont-Aven in July (*G*6).

AUGUST–OCTOBER
PONT-AVEN, BRITTANY

Bernard, after ascertaining Gauguin's continued presence in Pont-Aven from Vincent (*B*14 of *circa* 4 or 5 August), arrives there by August 14, bringing along from St. Briac what Gauguin describes to Schuffenecker as "interesting things" (*M*LXVII). Although his health vacillates, Gauguin is productive in terms of landscape, figural and still life studies. In September he produces *The Vision after the Sermon* and the *Self-Portrait called Les Misérables* (cat. no. 52) upon request from Vincent (and described late that month respectively in *G*9-10), having earlier exchanged thoughts with Vincent on "colouration suggestive of poetic ideas" (*G*8). During the first week of October he agrees to leave for Arles where Théo will support him and Vincent jointly; arrives on October 23.

LATE OCTOBER–DECEMBER
ARLES, PROVENCE

Having arranged for the transport of his Pont-Aven canvases to Paris, especially to Théo (see *G*12, written one or more days after his arrival in Arles), Gauguin takes charge of communal relationships and, despite initial and continuing tensions with Vincent, begins another of the most fruitful, if short-lived, periods of his career. Not long thereafter (13 November) he learns from Théo that a first one-man and commercially successful exhibition of his work has opened at Boussod and Valadon; without delay he dispatches several Arles canvases to Théo in the hope of capitalizing further upon this opportunity. He thereupon turns down an opportunity to exhibit works at the offices of *La Revue indépendante*, but readily accepts an offer to participate at the *Les Vingt* exhibition of 1889 in Brussels (*G*15). By mid-December, Gauguin considers himself "tempermentally incompatible" as a companion to Vincent (*G*16) but, following a joint visit to the Montpellier Museum (Ingres, Delacroix, Courbet), reneges on his determination to return to Paris (*G*17). This period of concord proves only temporary and on or about December 23 occurs the unfortunately most-remembered event of Gauguin's Arles period, the confrontation which leads to Vincent's self-mutilation. Gauguin immediately calls Théo to the scene; both, once knowing that Vincent's physical health is no longer in grave danger, return together to Paris a day or two after Christmas.

1889

JANUARY–MARCH
PARIS

The record of Gauguin's exact whereabouts during the first nine months of this year has proved confusing, but can be established with relative certainty nonetheless. In January he writes three times to Vincent (*G*19-20 and a missing letter of January 30 mentioned in *CL*575) while again staying *chez* Schuffenecker. Upon urging by Théo he begins the series of "lithographs" eventually presented at the Volpini exhibition and speaks of planning to do the *Schuffenecker Family Portrait* (*W*313). Whether or not Gauguin visits the *Les Vingt* exhibition in Brussels as he had wanted (*G*19), he likely waits out much of February only to learn that his twelve submitted paintings have been roundly criticized and remain unsold. *Circa* February 20-21, Théo reports to Vincent (*CL*578) Gauguin's completion of the series of lithographs; his departure thereafter for Pont-Aven likely occurs sometime in March or possibly even early April. Since, apart from the lithographs, only two portrait paintings (*W* 313-14) are almost certain to date from before his first trip this year to Pont-Aven, it is again likely that his major creative effort while in Paris has been directed toward his ceramic sculptures.

APRIL–MAY
PONT-AVEN, PARIS

If it remains uncertain when in early 1889 Gauguin left for Pont-Aven, it can at least be assumed that he received Schuffenecker's announcement that the Café Volpini was available for a group exhibition either shortly before or at the latest, just after the opening of the Universal Exposition on May 6. Théo van Gogh's May 21 announcement to Vincent (I9) that he had seen Gauguin "not long ago" implies that the latter was back in Paris by mid-May, and a spring 1889 letter from Pont-Aven (*M*LXXVII, there misdated to Arles, December 1888) documents that he did not return to Paris immediately upon hearing of Schuffenecker's "success." One may thus safely say that the artist was back in Paris during the final two weeks of and perhaps even earlier in May. Fortunately, Gauguin's date of subsequent departure can be fixed with greater exactness to Tuesday June 4, since on Sunday June 16, Théo stated that Gauguin had left for Pont-Aven "two weeks ago" and since the artist himself informed Bernard (*M*LXXXI) of his intention to leave "next Tuesday," which would coincide but for two days with Théo's recollection.

The most striking aspect of this early 1888 period of heightened itinerancy is Gauguin's relative lack of productivity as a painter. As might be expected, his return to Paris meant another return to sculpture, but a virtually complete lack of landscape paintings with Pont-Aven subjects for 1889 is less accountable. At the Volpini exhibition in effect only the *Breton Eve* and *Undine* themes (cat. nos. 60, 59; *see* discussion above, pp. 41-42) were added to the type of work he had exhibited earlier at *Les Vingt*. Moreover, only the six works of this subject series (*W* 333-38) can be viewed as a major pictorial innovation of the immediate pre-Volpini period, which the artist himself signalized by its incorporation into the lithographic frontispiece, *Aux Roches noires*, of the Volpini exhibition catalogue (fig. 60).

JUNE-JULY
PONT-AVEN

Upon his return to Pont-Aven, Gauguin spends another two months at the Pension Gloanec without producing any body of known paintings. Perhaps again his personal optimism outstrips rational expectations, sinc the Volpini exhibition had scarcely produced concrete personal benefits. Instead, twice during this period he feels obliged to justify the event to Théo (*G*21, 24), and one presumes that this is yet another period of artistic infertility for Gauguin. Two Gauguin articles appear (July 7 and 13) in A. Aurier's *Le Moderniste* on the Universal Exhibition (ceramics).

AUGUST
LE POULDU

Gauguin and Meyer de Haan spend the month at the inn *chez* Destais in the coastal hamlet of Le Pouldu, within easy walking, carriage or sea transport from Pont-Aven. While there, Gauguin writes to his wife (*M*LXXXII), to Père Tanguy (unpublished at Rijksmuseum Vincent van Gogh), to Théo (*G*33) and Bernard (*M*LXXXIV), in the latter case announcing his return in three days to Pont-Aven, where he still enjoys credit and a convenient *atelier* ("Les Avians"). It remains speculative as to how many of the numerous Le Pouldu landscape paintings dated 1889 (see *W* 340-74) are produced at this time, although the letter to Théo suggests a period of non-productivity.

SEPTEMBER
PONT-AVEN

Having announced to Bernard his imminent return from Le Pouldu to Pont-Aven, with the intention of staying there until winter, Gauguin upon his arrival writes September 1 to Schuffenecker (*M*LXXXVI) and shortly thereafter to Bernard (*M*LXXXVII), with reports of his preliminary work on the carved wood relief *Soyez amoureuses et vous serez heureuses* (Gray, 76) and of his intention now to return to Le Pouldu, where De Haan has found a rentable *atelier* overlooking the sea (that is, the present hotel Castel Teeaz, then the villa of a certain M. Mauduit of Quimperlé; see Jaworska, p. 88).

OCTOBER–DECEMBER
LE POULDU

On October 2, 1889, Gauguin inscribes himself as resident at the inn of Marie Henry in Le Pouldu, a record of official residence not terminated until his final departure on November 7, 1890. The fall spent at Le Pouldu produces not only the rich harvest of landscape paintings which bear dates of this year, but also sees the completion of his wood sculpture, *Soyez amoureuses*, and the decoration with paintings, sculptures and graphics of the "salle" of the inn of Marie Henry itself (*see* cat. no. 63). Admittedly the "religious" paintings (*see* cat. nos. 61, 62, 63, 65 and 66, for examples) of this period provoke Vincent to a mixture of disappointment and scorn (*see* discussion, pp. 51-52 above). Yet it is one of the most prolific periods in the life of Gauguin, not to mention the impact his art has upon such figures as Meyer de Haan, Sérusier and, later, other Nabi initiates.

1890

JANUARY
LE POULDU

Following his fruitful production of the previous fall, the new year seems to have ushered in another period of uncertainties. Plagued by winter storms at Le Pouldu and uncertainty that de Haan can continue to provide the joint living expenses as he has in the past three months, Gauguin at the end of this month actually proposes the possibility of again living together with Vincent, albeit at Antwerp where a studio might be founded under Gauguin's own name (see *T*28, *G*35,

*CL*625-26). Simultaneously, with funds supplied by Schuffenecker (*M*XCVIII) he returns to Paris, arriving on February 8 (*T*28), where he hopes to find the means to re-establish himself in some far-off French colonial paradise such as Tonkin.

FEBRUARY–MID-JUNE
PARIS

Gauguin's artistic somnolence during these months in Paris is witnessed not only by the dearth of thereto datable works of art, but also by Théo's June 13 observations that Gauguin is leaving for Brittany because he is doing scarcely any work while staying at the home of Schuffenecker (*T*37). Gauguin had been much struck with the ten paintings by Vincent which had been exhibited in March at the *Indépendants* (*T*29, *G*36), and he is prompted to suggest another exchange of paintings. His attempts at governmental support for a trip to Tonkin apparently failing, his thoughts turn to Madagascar, which, thanks to a description by the wife of Redon, he now sees as the appropriate seat of the "studio of the tropics" he plans to found with one or both of Meyer de Haan and Bernard (*M*CIICV). This is to be accomplished with the sum of 5,000 francs promised by a doctor and inventor named Charlopin in payment for a collection of Gauguin's paintings and ceramics. Activity in this latter medium is again recorded for this latest Paris interlude (*M*CI), whereas activity as a painter is not.

LATE JUNE–OCTOBER
LE POULDU

Gauguin's intention to spend only two months with Meyer de Haan in Le Pouldu while waiting for the Madagascar trip to become practicable is thwarted by the failure of Charlopin to realize his promise. Gauguin's career in France also appears in jeopardy when, following the death of Vincent in late July, Théo in October becomes incapacitated by illness. Gauguin returns to Paris early the following month with the help of Bernard and Schuffenecker (*M*CXIII). In the meantime, he has once again completed a major sculpture, *Soyez mystérieuses* (Gray 87), and a fair number of landscape, figural and still life paintings. In the autumn his preference for a colonial existence shifts to Tahiti, to which abode he presumably still will be accompanied by Bernard and Meyer de Haan.

NOVEMBER–DECEMBER
PARIS

Upon arriving in Paris, Gauguin once again resides with the Schuffenecker family until, apparently sometime in January 1891, personal tensions demand his departure (*P-I*, p. 432). While with Schuffenecker, Gauguin meets his future French correspondent Georges-Daniel de Monfreid and, through him, the milliner Juliette Huet, who is thought to have served for the reclining figure in *Loss of Virginity* (cat. no. 70) and who is later to bear Gauguin a child. Gauguin paints or sculpts very little, spending his time planning for the *Les Vingt* exhibition to which he will send only wood and ceramic sculpture, and seeking an opportunity for sale or exhibition of his painted *oeuvre*. He is befriended by the circle of Nabi painters, by Eugène Carrière and, increasingly, by the Symbolist poets who meet Monday evenings at the Café Voltaire, Place de l'Odéon.

1891

JANUARY–MARCH
PARIS

Before Gauguin on April 4 departs Paris for Tahiti, alone, despite minor setbacks such as the adverse criticism received in Brussels (*P-I*, p.431), he enjoys critical and financial successes as never before. The February 23 auction at the Hôtel Drouot brings him approximately 9,000 francs. It is accompanied by the favourable critical accounts of Octave Mirbeau, Albert Aurier and others (*P-I*, p. 439 ff.) which, to the lifelong chagrin of Bernard, establish Gauguin as the Symbolist painter *par excellence*. A month following the sale, during which period he may have briefly visited Mette and the children in Copenhagen, he is given a testimonial banquet by the Symbolist poets at the Café Voltaire, further enhancing his prestige and the romantic aura surrounding his imminent departure for Oceania. Three days thereafter on March 26 the artist is entrusted by the Ministry of Fine Arts with an unsalaried mission and thus a reduced fare for his voyage.

Despite the death or alienation of most of his former closest painter colleagues, Gauguin now enjoys a singular moment of personal triumph, which few of his companions would ever experience, but which, alas, must sustain him for the twelve years of troubled existence that are to follow.

1891-1903

Subsequent to his first departure for Tahiti, Gauguin returned to France for a nineteen-month stay during 1893-95, but completed his career in Tahiti, 1895-1901, and the Marquesas Islands, 1901-03. One might argue that his Cloisonist tendency was gradually submerged within rather than replaced by the more plastically conceived figures and painterly rendered landscapes of his final periods. In any case a few specific late works, including oil paintings (for example, W 476, 513) and, of course, paintings on glass (W 509-11), retain direct reminders of this earlier involvement. Nevertheless, in his 1897 or later "Diverse Choses" additions to a *Noa Noa* manuscript, he included an intended florid tribute to the beauty and significance of Japanese *cloisonné* vases, probably in memory of the role they had played in his earlier evolution.

44.

The Field of Derout-Lollichon I: W 199
Church at Pont-Aven
summer 1886
oil on canvas: 73 x 92 cm
Signed and dated lower right: *P. Gauguin [18]86*
Lent by a private collection, Switzerland

The site of this painting and five other paintings
contained in Wildenstein has been established by
photographic evidence as a sloping piece of farm-
land just on the outskirts of Pont-Aven known as
the Field of Derout-Lollichon.[1] This and one other
example (W 200) were executed in 1886,
whereas the other four date from summer 1888.
The second 1886 example presents a view of the
farm building from approximately where the cow
at right grazes in this painting, whereas those from
1888 include the famous *Breton Girls Dancing a*
Rondel (fig. 57), two hay-gathering scenes
(W 269-70) and a reprise of our exhibited example (W 271), seen from further up the slope and
thus slightly more panoramic in conception.
Derout-Lollichon I can be traced back in
provenance to Gauguin, who *circa* 1887 repaid a
loan of three hundred francs from a banking
friend named Mirtil which had allowed him to set
out on his first trip to Pont-Aven in June 1886.
This story derives from the banker's son and is
corroborated in a notebook annotation which,
along with the owner's name and sum received,
cites the painting as *Eglise Pont-Aven* (*see*
W 199). Indeed, the typically Breton crocketed
spire of the Pont-Aven church rises up behind the
complex of farm buildings, although this is more
in keeping with picturesque tradition than because
of any obvious intention to impregnate the iconography with symbolic meaning.

The *Derout-Lollichon I* is presented here as an
excellent example of the starting point in the development of Cloisonist or Synthetist style. Our most
trustworthy account derives from the painter
Henri Delavallée, who fortunately knew Gauguin
only that one summer before the latter's departure
for Tahiti and thus refers to a specific time frame.[2]
Delavallée's key word in reference to Gauguin's
technique was "zébrée" or striped brush strokes,
which he felt still showed the influence of Pissarro.
This witness also emphasized Gauguin's stress on
laying on these stripes in contrasting colours in
order to heighten the luminosity of the painting.
Although his style thus remained basically Impressionist, the wish to avoid mixed or broken colours
is analogous to the Neo-Impressionist technique

Fig. 57
Paul Gauguin
Breton Girls Dancing a Rondel,
1888,
oil on canvas
(National Gallery of Art, Washington. Lent by
Mr. and Mrs. Paul Mellon; photograph National
Gallery of Art).

with which he had occasionally experimented in
the previous spring. This analogy was actually
mentioned in other eye-witness accounts, those by
the English painter A.S. Hartrick and by Armand
Seguin, and has been followed up in more recent
analysis.[3] The *Derout-Lollichon I* is a splendid
example in which to rediscover such usages as
described by Delavallée, with its clearly visible
"zebrated" parallel hatchings and equally apparent contrasts of adjacent hues of colour. Areas of
bright green for the shadow cast by the main farm
building, the bright yellow-orange of the sunlit
gabled end wall and the rich dominant blue of the
roof do seem to approximate "cloisons" of pure
colour which will emerge fully as the basis of a
Cloisonist-Synthetist style only in 1888. Delavallée
also tells us that Gauguin already in 1886
employed the word "synthèse" in reference to his
artistic aims, but without any attempt at a credo.
Finally, he tells us that Gauguin executed many of
his landscape paintings in the studio, being satis-
fied to apply merely the finishing touches on the
site out-of-doors.[4] While this cannot as yet be

termed painting from memory, as Gauguin would
advocate to Vincent in fall 1888 in Arles, it does
show that he was already reacting against the
extreme *plein airisme* of Impressionism in favour
of more constructed forms of composition, of
which the solidly planted wall planes of this farmhouse in a meadow give us a particularly suitable
example.

[1] See the unsigned "Pont-Aven: Dans le Champ
Derout-Lollichon, 1886-1888," in *GBA*, *Gau-*
guin, Reunion, pp. 83-87, where photographs of
the actual site are included.

[2] As recorded in Chassé, *Son Temps*, pp. 40-47.

[3] Hartrick, p. 32 and Seguin, pp. 164-65; see also
Chassé, *ibid.*, p. 44, and J. House in London *P-I*,
nos. 80-81.

[4] Hartrick, pp. 32-33, independently confirms that
Gauguin had a studio at Pont-Aven (namely, at
"Les Avians"), explaining that this resulted from
the patronage of a well-off student who defected
from his academic *atelier* to the cause of Gauguin
and Impressionism.

P Gauguin 86

45.
Still Life with Profile of Laval W 207
late (?) 1886
oil on canvas: 46 x 38 cm
Signed and dated lower left: *P Gauguin* [18] 86
Lent by a private collection, Switzerland

This still life is one of the most intriguing, yet difficult to explain paintings of its *genre* in the artist's career. Everything about it seems to look both backward and forward in his development at the same time. The primary subject matter, fruit spread on a table with a white cloth seen against a decorative background, is above all indebted to Cézanne, as is the type of scumbled brush technique which allows for a varied nuancing of the equally Cézannesque colour scheme.[1] The intrusion at right of the head of Gauguin's painter-friend Charles Laval is doubtless chiefly indebted to another, at the time much admired, model: Edgar Degas, who had employed this device in a pastel drawing of 1878, *Dancer with a Bouquet* *(fig. 7)*. Apart from this in itself rather unexpected combination of influences, the painting is additionally intriguing for the inclusion of a ceramic object doubtless executed by Gauguin himself but now lost. It is recorded only in this and another portrait of 1886 attributed to Gauguin (W 184) and in a tiny sketch in a letter of December 6, 1887, to his wife (*M*LIX) where, upon his return from Martinique, he asks her if she might not have taken it with her back to Copenhagen the previous spring.[2] The ceramic as represented surely appears more a sculpture than a vessel, with its large opening allowing only for some such use as incense burning. The equivocal suggestion of a half-open doorway behind, and the closed eyes of Laval further enhance the ambiguity of the multiple subject references of this painting. One may not be justified in supposing a truly Symbolist intention with this painting, but the closed eye profile of Laval is a striking anticipation of the priest's face (lower right) in *The Vision after the Sermon* (pl. 7) and the first time it has occurred in the figural art of Gauguin.

The general presumption that this canvas was executed while the two painters were initially forming a friendship during the summer months of 1886 in Pont-Aven is open to some question. Unless, contrary to accepted opinion, the two men had known each other previously which would allow for execution of the painting in Paris during the spring, it seems unlikely that, presuming it was already extant, Gauguin would have had any reason to carry such a bulky yet fragile ceramic to Pont-Aven, where it had less chance of sale than if left back in Paris. Thus there seems some likelihood, if admittedly no certainty, that the *Still Life with Laval* was painted during the last six weeks of the year, when Gauguin was back in Paris, in fact devoting himself to ceramics and mending his interrupted friendship with Degas.[3] The question of whether the ceramic sculpture represented was produced before or following his stay in Pont-Aven is not crucial to this question of date for the painting, but there is no reason to rule out an end of 1886 date of execution (or of firing of an earlier moulding) for the ceramic as well.

This extended analysis is only justified if it illuminates the place of this painting in a special historical context. A *circa* December dating of the *Still Life with Laval* facilitates a number of happy coincidences. On the personal level it commemorates the friendship with Laval and the strengthening of the Degas-Cézanne wing of Impressionism about which issue the normally benign intermediary Pissarro was so nervous. The combination here is unique, a friend of the artist as portrait subject seen contemplating the Cézannesque apples without the slightest desire to reach for them, and the inclusion of a personally executed ceramic as an adjunct to this contemplation. Whether executed at Pont-Aven or later in the year, this still life asks the questions which were answered later on in a variety of ways, the metaphorical and rhetorical "who am I, where am I, whither am I going?" If it does not provide the answers, it at least asks a number of appropriate questions.

46.
Among the Mangoes: Martinique W 224
c. late July-early August 1887
oil on canvas: 89 x 116 cm
Signed and dated bottom centre in the pail:
P Gauguin [18] 87
Lent by the Rijksmuseum Vincent van Gogh, Amsterdam

As one of three large landscape paintings (with W 226, 232) executed during Gauguin's approximate four-month stay on the Island of Martinique in the French Antilles, this example was almost certainly selected for presentation in December 1887 at Boussod and Valadon as representing his latest development of style. At the time it was reviewed as such in *La Revue indépendante* by Félix Fénéon, whose generally favourable characterization did not, however, overly please Gauguin when he received a copy of the review in Pont-Aven by March.[1] Probably Gauguin was sensitive to a characterization of his painting which included such words as "atrabilious," "barbaric," "little atmospheric" and "troublesome" and which stated that he was more a potter than a painter. Ironically, in the May 1888 issue of *La Revue indépendante*, Fénéon was to cite another Martinique canvas by Gauguin on view at Boussod and Valadon and call for a one-man general exhibition of his "powerful and individual" art.[2] It is unknown whether or not Gauguin learned of this supportive gesture by Fénéon, but he seems never to have considered the critic as particularly friendly to his own cause.[3]

The date and intended meaning of *Among the Mangoes* and two related Martinique subjects (W 217-18) is best found in a Gauguin letter of July 14, 1887, to Schuffenecker in which he describes the idyllic life he and Laval had been leading at Martinique since escaping the ruinous experience they had shared in Panama.

> For the past three weeks we have been at Martnique, land of the creole gods. In truth we have lodged in a Negro cabin located on a large property two kilometres from the city. Below us is the sea with a sandy beach suitable for bathing, and to each side are coconut and other fruit-bearing trees admirably suited to a landscape artist.
> What agrees with me the most are the human figures which each day continually come and go attired with coloured finery and moving with an infinitely varied grace. At present I restrain myself to making sketch after sketch with the aim of penetrating their char-

acter until finally I shall have them pose. Even while carrying heavy loads on their heads they chatter away without stopping. Their gestures are very special and their hands play a great role in harmony with balancing the hips.[4]

Exactly how many weeks these ideal living and working conditions were enjoyed is uncertain, although a month was the maximum, since in a second letter to Schuffenecker dated August 25, Gauguin stated that for at least a week he had been sick unto death with dysentery and begged for help in repatriation to France.[5] Hence the *Mangoes* and probably most other Martinique landscapes were executed between mid-July and mid-August following the initial period of sketching and before the onslaught of debilitating sickness.

No other Martinique painting sums up better than *Mangoes* Gauguin's intentions and implied iconography as stated in his July letter to Schuffenecker, and one can imagine the setting as situated between the Negro cabin residence of the two artists and the sandy beach below. Several goats and a dog share in the life of abundance provided by the mango grove, a veritable tropical paradise in which the natives work or rest and enjoy the fruits of their labour at will. The artist's references to the infinite grace of the native people, their colourful costumes and their expressive hand gestures in balancing the hips are manifestly present, especially in the foreground standing figure seen from the rear.[6] The existence of a pastel study of the two foreground figures confirms that Gauguin produced studies from posed models following a period of sketching, as he explained he would.[7] Whereas the major paintings produced

---

1   See *P-I*, p. 169, for colour illustration of this painting and pp. 167-68, where a joint debt to Cézanne and Degas is predicated. Roskill, p. 43 also credits Cézanne as a probable source for this canvas.

2   Bodelsen, *Ceramics*, p. 154, discusses this issue of the pot in detail, whose discussion in fact provided my point of departure for disagreement.

3   This activity is documented in Pissarro, p.111.

1   See Fénéon, *Plus que complètes* I, pp. 90-91; Gauguin's sarcastic responses was stated to Schuffenecker (*M*LXIII): See also Rewald, *P-I*, pp. 168-71, on other responses to the exhibition.

2   Fénéon, *ibid.*, p. 111.

3   See Roskill, pp. 277-79.

4   This letter excerpt was quoted in A. Alexandre, *Paul Gauguin: sa vie et le sens de sa oeuvre* (Paris: Bernheim Jeune, 1930), pp. 58,60.

5   I.e., *M*LVI.

6   See also the Martinique-derived lithographs (cat. no. 58, i and j) for additional celebrations of these habits of the Martinique natives.

7   Bodelsen, *Ceramics*, figs. 115-16, reproduces both the more developed and one of the notebook sketches of the figures for *Mangoes*, which she discusses on pp. 167, 170; on p. 203 she lists other related sketches.

subsequently in Brittany and Arles would often be laden with suggestions of human suffering and doom, the paintings of Martinique are remarkably free of such associations. As exemplified by the *Mangoes*, they present the human condition as one of unimpeded relaxation and fecundity, at least in such rural and pristine locations as Martinique. It was here that Gauguin first expressed his dream of a tropical paradise, which ultimately led to his exile in the South Pacific, where his chosen themes would so often echo those of this earlier experience of the tropics.

Within the context of the present study, the *Mangoes* offers proof of Gauguin's involvement by 1887 with Japanist modes of design. A specific type of Japanese print has been convincingly demonstrated to have inspired other depictions of the Martinique seaside, and, while this is unlikely the case for the *Mangoes*, if only because of the featuring of figures based on live models, a Japanist quality of design is nonetheless present.[8] This is implied by the use of a cut-off figure *à la Degas*, the extremely high horizon, the compression of near and far distances and the hint of Cloisonist flattening of the figural content. These aspects should not be overstressed, since the uniformly patterned brushwork remains at base Impressionist and, in both the preparatory pastel drawing and the painting itself, the figures retain an appreciable degree of modelling in the round by means of light and shadow effects. Similarly, the colour scheme definitely features broad areas of single dominant hues, held in check from becoming too independent from the overall even tonality of the painting, still dominated, as Fénéon felt, by a "heavy green." Fénéon's further remark that the painting reminded one of "those old illustrated engravings from the Islands," offers a final note of support for believing that outline and colouration were becoming increasingly distinct in the art of Gauguin.

[8] *Ibid.*, p. 178 and figs. 128-29, for the inspiration of a Japanese print for *W* 217.

47.
Breton Boys Bathing: Les Baigneurs W 275
c. June 1888
oil on canvas: 92 x 73 cm
Signed and dated lower left: *P. Gauguin* [*18*]88
Lent by the Hamburger Kunsthalle, Hamburg
AMSTERDAM ONLY

Although not identified specifically, this must have been one of the paintings which Gauguin referred to as "some *nudes*" in a July 8, 1888 letter to Schuffenecker (*M*LXVI). It thus probably slightly preceded *Two Breton Boys Wrestling (fig. 58)* and *W* 274) which he described as "made completely according to the Japanese, by a savage of Peru." The setting for both subjects is the bank of the Aven River with the dam of the *Moulin David* (on the shore opposite) seen at upper left.[1] Both paintings had been anticipated by a painting of two years earlier, which contained a greater number of figures and more ample setting and which carried an inscription *verso* identifying the mill as that of the *Bois d'Amour*, which is in fact located behind the *Moulin David*.

[1] A photograph of the setting of the *Moulin David* is illustrated in *GBA* Gauguin, p. 93, fig. 5, but unfortunately allows no easy comparison of the angle of view chosen by Gauguin.

Gauguin stressed to Schuffenecker that these paintings of nudes were no longer based on the example of Degas. This may be true in the literal sense that the poses were not directly derived from specific models in Degas but, as his negative reference itself proves, that master was fully in mind when he chose to do bathing scenes in the Japanese manner. Whether or not Roskill is correct in seeing Hokusai's representations of wrestlers in the *Mangua* as the source of Gauguin's pose for his own wrestling boys,[2] this is certainly not the case for the Hamburg *Boys Bathing*, for one of which figures there exists a drawing in sanguine and coloured chalks that obviously was executed from a posed live model. This drawing was squared up with the figure approximating that in the painting, so there can be little doubt of its functional use for the canvas of 1888. Pickvance (*Drawings*, Pl. 15) has argued persuasively that the drawing was executed in 1886, which, if true, offers additional indication that Gauguin produced his figural studies and landscape settings separately, combining them in individual canvases to produce a greater variety of compositions than otherwise would be allowed. Thus there is every likelihood that the figural studies were executed in the studio and perhaps much of the landscape background as well, with only the final touches added *plein air* and *in situ* according to his practice in summer 1886, as described by the painter colleague Delavallée (*see* cat. no. 44).[3] As with the *Boys Wrestling*, there is here also a general subject reference to the art of Puvis de Chavannes, whose suggestions of timeless Arcadia may have provoked Gauguin's imagination in the local context of ageless Brittany.[4]

[2] Roskill, p. 79, whose assertion is not supported by a figural comparison. Andersen, *Paradise*, pp. 53, 281 and figs. 29-30, offers a comparison with Puvis' *The Gentle Land* which seems convincing, although obviously no exact quotation was attempted by Gauguin.

[3] There is some confusion and disagreement in the literature about just where Gauguin had his studio summer 1888, but most authors presume that he had one.

[4] See note 2 above. The subject of nude bathing figures is so ubiquitous in the art of Puvis that a specific source seems hardly necessary to suppose. However, one might speculate that Gauguin had in mind a paraphrase of the well-known female figure leaning on her raised right leg as found in *Repose* and *At the Fountain* (Wattenmaker, no. 11).

48.
Breton Girls Dancing a Rondel: Study
summer 1888
pastel: 22 x 41 cm
Not signed or dated
Lent by the Rijksmuseum Vincent van Gogh, Amsterdam

This pastel[1] would seem to have been a working study for the painting now in the National Gallery, Washington (*W* 251 and *fig. 57*). The latter is dated 1888 and was sent in November of that year to Arles from Paris by Théo for retouching as demanded by a prospective buyer (*T*3a), and both it and the present drawing date from the previous summer spent in Pont-Aven.[2] Whereas the painting is little advanced towards a mature Cloisonist-Synthetist style over certain examples of 1886 and 1887 (*fig. 24* and cat. no. 46), the pastel drawing, perhaps because of its function as an experiment in colour (the notation "vert" appears on the girl at right) and design, allowed for a fuller exploitation of Cloisonist principles than was embodied in the painted version.

It is also rewarding to compare this drawing of August with a presumably contemporary water-colour (cat. no. 101) and a slightly earlier painting of the same summer by Bernard (cat. no. 99). Distinctly profiled female heads adorned with regional Breton head-dress had clearly assumed a special importance in the style and iconography of both artists by the time of their summer 1888 meeting. It may be less important to decide which of the two artists first became obsessed with the stylistic and iconographic implications, than what the emphasis on such folkloristic vestments meant in the career of each.

[1] See Pickvance, "Drawings," Pl. IV (in colour).

[2] Bodelsen, *Ceramics*, p. 184 and fig. 132, has shown that the *Rondel* figures were illustrated on the back of an August 14, 1888, letter from Gauguin to Schuffenecker (*M*LXVII), which allows for the completion of the painting either before or shortly after Bernard's arrival in Pont-Aven early that month.

49.
The Fiancée W 242
Summer 1888
oil on canvas: 33 x 41 cm
Signed, dated and inscribed (in red) lower right:
P. Go [18] 88 La Fiancée
Lent by a private collection, Switzerland

As pointed out in Wildenstein (*W* 242) this painting employs the same view from a window as in *Window Opening on the Sea* (*W* 292 and *fig. 59*), a painting executed upon the reverse side of *Hay-making* I, a work, dated 1888. Wildenstein also identifies *La Fiancée* with the painting exhibited at Copenhagen in 1893 under the title, "La Gudu, fille d'auberge," which if accurate further intimates a portrait executed spontaneously on one or another excursion from Pont-Aven to some coastal inn. As the subject's somewhat suspicious gaze suggests, she may have been skeptical of the honour of sitting for the artist, and it seems unlikely at this late date that her true identity ever will be uncovered.

The painting is of greatest interest for the mixture of Impressionist and quasi-Pointillist style which it incorporates. This diversity in brush technique is accompanied by a comparable catholicism in the inclusion of bright colour areas juxtaposed with others in shadow, and the traditional modelling for the face contrasting with a compromise of perspectival orthodoxy on behalf of a Japanist asymmetry of design. In composition this painting approximates the *Self-Portrait called Les Misérables* (*see* cat. no. 52), *vis-à-vis* which it may best be considered an intriguing and enigmatic prelude.

Fig. 59
Paul Gauguin
Window Opening on the Sea
c. 1884-88?,
reverse of a painting dated 1888
(Musée d'Orsay, Paris).

50.

Above the Precipice: Au-dessus du Gouffre W 282
summer 1888
oil on canvas: 73 x 60 cm
Signed and dated lower left: P Gauguin [18] 88
Lent by the Musée des Arts Décoratifs, Paris

This painting is illustrative of Gauguin's
continuing willingness to combine Impressionist
brushwork with Cloisonist colour intensity and
principles of design. In this case, some specific
source in the art of the Japanese wood block may
have been operative, since such an example as the
Shoheibashi Bridge in the Snow Japanese Prints,
cat. no. 532, by Hiroshige II employs a steeply
descending, V-shaped foreground gorge in a
manner strikingly similar to the composition of
Above the Precipice. Yet Gauguin provides no
psychological relief to his vertiginous setting while
the Oriental artist includes a more restful view, a
flat landscape receding into the far distance. In
Gauguin's painting both the boat at top and cow
at bottom appear to flirt with disaster on the
surging eddy and rock formations at the foot of the
precipice[1], an effect heightened by darkish
colouration underlying the reddish (one presumes
sunset) glow in which the cliffs of rock, like the
two large mounds of hay at right, are bathed.

As so often in Gauguin's work, the figural
imagery, here the cow, seems to have repeated a
pose used both earlier (*W* 206) and later (cat. no.
58, f and g), and probably taken from a
sketchbook drawing as was the composition of
Above the Precipice. This painting of summer
1888 almost certainly reflects the rock cliffs at Le
Pouldu, and not a coastal setting at the mouth of
the Aven river as sometimes previously thought.[2]
Its radically descending, bird's-eye perspective is
also found in a bathing and fishing scene depicting
a smaller precipice[1] at Pont-Aven (*W* 264). This
further indicates that he already was able to
impose what in a letter of July (*M*LXVI) he called
his post-Degas and Japanist manner according to
his own artistic will as much as from what the
natural setting offered him.

The painting is subject to interpretation as an
initial investigation of the theme of the two early
1889 lithographs to which he gave the title
"Dramas of the Sea," (that is, cat. no. 58 g and
h). Not only does the cow reappear in the version
with three female figures, but the two cliffside
settings with hay mounds are likely identical but
seen from differing angles. The title *Au-dessus du
Gouffre* derives from the 1891 Hôtel Drouot sale

aux
Roches
noires
P90

Fig. 60
Paul Gauguin
Aux Roches noires,
frontispiece of the Volpini exhibition catalogue,
1889.

(no. 29) and evokes the opening scene of Poe's "A Descent into the Maelstrom," expressing feelings of vertigo at the edge of a coastal cliff rising above "a sheer unobstructed precipice of black shining rock." Whether or not this passage also inspired Gauguin's title "Aux Roches noires" for the Volpini exhibition catalogue frontispiece (*fig. 60*), it is significant that Poe's "horribly black and beetling cliff" was accompanied by a "surf which reared high up against it, its white and ghastly crest, howling and shrieking forever." The story also describes, far out to sea, a sailing vessel plunging in and out of the surf. Gauguin's combination of a "giddying cliffside" and a "storm-tossed ship" inevitably recall this, his favourite story by Poe, and the general association of such imagery with human mortality within romantic tradition.[3] One could easily exaggerate

the implication of danger and gloom underlying the otherwise decorative character of Gauguin's composition, but, like two thematically related paintings from 1889 (*W* 360-61) neither should one altogether overlook the prickling emotive suggestiveness of Gauguin's precarious setting.

1 Cogniat, *Carnet*, pp. 18, 25, 57 as cited in *W* 206, 264, 282.

2 Andersen, "Le Pouldu," pp. 619-20, argues for a summer 1886 stay at Le Pouldu. But only indirectly, by including in his Le Pouldu works *The Wave* (*W* 286), a painting dated 1888, does he imply a 1888 visit as well. In fact most, if not all, "coastscapes" dated 1888 (*W* 281-86) were very likely executed during or following a summer sojourn there that year. Apart from the evidence of a reference to a Le Pouldu female figure in

Human Miseries of 1888 (*see* cat. no. 56), her appearance in typical Le Pouldu rather than Pont-Aven costume in the early 1889 lithograph *Dramas of the Sea* (cat. no. 58g), presuming the setting represented is also that of *Above the Precipice*, further identifies the latter painting with Le Pouldu as visited the previous year.

3 As late as 1897, after his friend Daniel de Montfreid had accepted the gift of a painting by Gauguin representing another storm-tossed boat (*W* 551) because the recipient found it "romantic," Gauguin merely replied, "Why not?": see Gauguin, *Lettres à Daniel de Montfreid*, ed. A. Joly-Segalen (Paris, Falaize, 1950), p. 109.

51.
Still Life Fête Gloanec W 290
early August 1888
oil on canvas mounted on panel: 38 x 53 cm
Signed and dated lower right: *Madeleine B.*
[18]88; also inscribed: *Fête Gloanec*
Lent by Le Musée des Beaux-Arts, Orléans

SEE COLOUR PLATE 31.

The origin of this painting (pl. 31) as told by Maurice Denis in 1934 was the annual name-day celebration ("fête de la patronne") of Marie-Jeanne Gloanec, hostess of the inn in Pont-Aven where Gauguin lodged.[1] Each of her artist guests normally presented her with a painting on this festive occasion, but the conservative painter G. de Maupassant advised her that accepting the proffered canvas by Gauguin would make her look ridiculous. Gauguin thereupon devised the subterfuge of saying that the novice painter Madeleine, the younger sister then visiting Emile Bernard, had actually executed it; hence the counterfeit signature. The painting was in any case mounted on a panel in the inn, presumably until acquired by Denis himself, who also acquired a two-year earlier still life painting by Gauguin (*W* 208) which bore the label "Pension Gloanec" and thus might have served a similar function.

The outrage of de Maupassant is quite understandable considering the painting's radically Cloisonist simplification of form and intensification of colour. Since the Fête Gloanec took place on August 15 in celebration of the Assumption of the Virgin Mary, the wide expanse of vermilion table

top must have anticipated a similar much celebrated usage for the crimson field in *Vision after the Sermon* (pl. 7).[2] Although the perspectival ambiguity of the tilted-up table top is not in itself a novelty, Vincent having employed such abrupt foreshortening in *Still Life: Plaster Statuette* (cat. no. 11) the year before, the arbitrariness of Gauguin's telescoping and hence truncation of the table setting must have been upsetting indeed for M. de Maupassant. Similarly enigmatic truncations are found in the related summer 1888 still life paintings, *Still Life with Fruits* (*W* 288) and *Still Life with Three Puppies* (*fig. 61*), the latter of which employs the same kind of round table edge found in *Fête Gloanec* but with even greater licence in the ambiguity with which the spatial and the iconographical program were imposed.[3] Whereas both these related paintings are subject to interpretation in reference to implications of religious symbolism, the search for some underlying profundity of meaning in the *Fête Gloanec* is less susceptible to convincing proof.

For the present writer, this masterpiece of forceful decoration reflects a rare moment of total harmony among the friends Bernard, Gauguin and Vincent, all of whom were joined at this moment in planning the ideal of a working "studio" for their group. The composition may thus depend upon the two sunflower paintings by Vincent which Gauguin then owned (*F 375-6*), although Gauguin has wished to clothe any such reference in a stylistically independent garb. No reference to this painting so far has included a guess at the identity of the major floral and, one may presume, bakery product represented at right. One possible interpretation is that both were meant to be shown as symbolic of the name-day celebration, since the white around the flower might be read as paper wrapping for a bouquet of homage (as in Manet's *Olympia*, but without ironic sexual meaning), and the brown object at right could easily indicate a form of Breton pastry suitable to the festive occasion.[4] Above all, despite holdover traces of Cézannesque brushwork, this is one of the earliest and finest examples of Gauguin's adoption of a highly Cloisonist mode of style.

1 M. Denis, "L'Epoque symboliste," *GBA* I (1934), p. 189. However, Bernard, "Souvenirs," p. 17, simply describes Gauguin's fictitious signature as "in veneration of my sister." See also David Ojalvo, *Nouvelles acquisitions du Musée d'Orléans*, Musée du Louvre, Pavillon de Flore, Paris, 3 decembre 1976 - 27 mars 1977, cat. no. 18, pp. 36-38.

2 Perruchot, p. 154, gives the date of the name-day of the hostess: House, London, *P-I*, 85, cites the use of a bright red field of paint in both the *Fête Gloanec* and the *Vision*, but his further suggestion that the flowers and two pears at left were meant as surrogates for Madeleine's head and breasts is highly conjectural indeed.

3 Thirion, p. 106, has convincingly suggested the Japanese source for Gauguin's conception of the three dogs. The mock trinitarianism of the three dogs, goblets and eggs (?) becomes even more enigmatic, if one asks why the animals are allowed to eat on such a smartly dressed table top. Andersen, *Paradise*, p. 88, interprets the figure in *Still Life with Fruits* (*W* 288) as an Eve before the Fall, which if true would make it the earliest example of this iconography (*see* cat. no. 56), since the dedication to Laval implies summer 1888 in Pont-Aven when the two worked together.

4 E.g., a Breton *gâteau*: the French phrase, "*trouver la fève au gâteau*," means "to have good luck in something."

Fig. 61
Paul Gauguin
Still Life with Three Puppies,
1888,
oil on wood
(The Museum of Modern Art, New York,
Mrs. Simon Guggenheim).

52.

Self-Portrait called Les Misérables   W 239
late September 1888
oil on canvas: 45 x 55 cm
Entitled, signed and dated lower right:
les misérables à l'ami Vincent P. Gauguin
Lent by the Rijksmuseum Vincent van Gogh,
Amsterdam

This painting is rightly considered to have manifested a breakthrough in the development of
Symbolist portraiture, as Gauguin himself claimed
in letters explaining it to Schuffenecker (*M*LXXI)
and to Vincent (*G*10). As discussed above (*see*
Introduction, pp. 48-49), this involved self-
identification as the Jean Valjean of Impressionist
painting and of this "completely abstract" portrait
with its pure yellow background decorated with
children's bouquets. This floral analogy extended
to the features of his face, the eyes, mouth and
nose which he likened to "flowers of a Persian
tapestry and which involved symbolic personifica-
tion," as he told Schuffenecker. The latter would
also have understood Gauguin's following com-

parison between the unnatural reds and violets of
the face and baked pottery, producing a sense of
radiating glow "to the eyes, seat of the mental
struggles of a painter," since Schuffenecker had
been a witness to Gauguin's activities with ceramic
pottery. The metaphor for the reddish face
changes to "blood in turmoil" for Vincent, but by
and large Gauguin's two descriptions correspond
and testify to a well-defined, even programmatic
portrait conception having been achieved.

Upon receiving it in early October, Vincent
was taken back by what he saw as an unnecessary
degree of despair and lack of gaiety in Gauguin's
characterization which gave the "impression of. . .
representing a prisoner" (*CL*545). In contrast his
own *Self-Portrait Dedicated to Paul Gauguin*
(*F* 476), which was also intended as himself and
"an Impressionist in general," but further as "a
simple worshipper of the eternal Buddha." Unlike
Gauguin, Vincent avoided any reference to literature, especially the alienated outcast hero of Victor
Hugo's famous Romantic novel. Vincent would
have realized that the inclusion of the image of
Bernard in profile, upper right, was in honour of

Vincent's initial request that Gauguin and Bernard
do each other's portrait, which both preferred not
to do as such. Whether or not Bernard was
painted from life, he is depicted in a starkly
Cloisonist manner, more in keeping with the style
of Bernard's *Self-Portrait* (cat. no. 105) than
with the still forceful modelling of Gauguin's own
visage. Perhaps it was this painting which Bernard
had in mind when he raised the question of the use
of shadows in modern painting in a letter to Gauguin in Arles. The latter's answer (*M*LXXV) equiv-
ocates somewhat by allowing it as a necessary
compositional element, but not as a trick of the
trompe l'oeil tradition. Yet it is precisely the contrast between the powerfully sculpted head of
Gauguin, with its hawk-like aggressiveness in
expression, and the pristine frail decorative patterns of the background, which lends this painting
its peculiar fascination and makes it so innovative
an example of modern portraiture.

53.
Maker of Wooden Shoes W 280
1888
oil on canvas: 58 x 49 cm
Not signed or dated
Lent by a private collection, Switzerland

This painting has been described as "unfinished" by Wildenstein (*W* 280), presumably because it is neither signed nor dated, in contrast to *The Cove II*, (*W* 285 and *fig. 62*), a painting which was executed on the reverse side of the present canvas and bears the inscription, "To my Friend Moret, P. Gauguin [18]88." If anything, *The Cove II*, which Wildenstein rightly described as a study for the larger and more finished looking *The Cove I* (*W* 284), employs a sketchier brush technique than the *Maker of Wooden Shoes*, which itself appears no more unfinished than several stylisti-

cally related studies (for example, *W* 278-79 *bis*, 281), which are signed and in some cases dated. While the use of both sides of the canvas further indicates Gauguin's conception of both as studies—and alas his treatment of one in vertical and the other in horizontal format prevents simultaneous exposure in any kind of double display frame—this should not imply any denigration of a "final compositional study," considering the respectability of such a designation in French artistic tradition and the fact of Gauguin's dedication to a friend and artist-colleague.

The painting likely had a personal meaning for Gauguin, who not only wore wooden shoes ("sabots") but would carve at least three pair *c.* 1889-90 (Gray nos. 81-83). His painting of the "sabotier" thus might have been a tribute to one he considered a kind of fellow craftsman and from whom he might even have learned a few tricks of the trade. However, the painting is more impor-

tant as an indication of Gauguin's concentrated experimentation in "abstract," which is to say two-dimensional, Japanist elements of design, rather than for a profound imputed meaning. The subdued yet distinct areas of colour concentration, while not executed in a Pointillist style, nonetheless evince an interest in clearly enunciated areas of a single colour dominant which are further enlivened by contrasting highlights in sometimes complementary but always harmonious colour contrasts.

54.

Farmhouse with Haystack, Arles W 308
(*Ferme à Arles*)
Autumn 1888
oil on canvas: 91.4 x 72.4 cm
Not signed or dated
Lent by the Indianapolis Museum of Art;
Gift in memory of William Ray Adams
TORONTO ONLY

There is some uncertainty about the early exhibition record and provenance of this painting. Wildenstein was the first to correct an ascription of a Breton subject on the basis of type of vegetation, and this is supported as well by the type of farm building represented. Its high walls, low-pitched roof and no chimney are not typical of Brittany. The painting might be one of several citations of "Farmhouses at Arles" by Gauguin in exhibition listings between 1889-93, except that the lack of signature and date renders this less likely than for the only other two paintings with a similar subject matter (W 309-10), both of which are signed and dated and enjoy some evidence in support of an exhibition record.[1] Yet no one would doubt its attribution to Gauguin and it is widely considered a painting of very high quality and one displaying a unique synthesis of stylistic influences for the moment in Gauguin's career it represents.

Goldwater in particular has singled it out as evidence that Gauguin "was an artist who, without copying, understood and absorbed what he needed from the work of the great men around him."[2] What this writer had in mind was the continuing use of a Cézanne sense of colouration and ordered composition and a minor intensification of colour and brushwork borrowed from van Gogh. How restrained in all respects Gauguin remained in this painting from Arles is obvious when one compares it to *Haystacks in Provence* (*F* 425) by Vincent, where in contrast to the balance and placidity of Gauguin's canvas the land and its burden appear to heave and writhe in the broiling sun. In the Gauguin all is order, and, had they known it, the Cubists might well have thought it as meaningful a precedent to their own style as many a landscape by Cézanne. Clearly the orange, green and blue colour scheme is a conscious tribute to the modern master from Aix, even if the tendency towards a decorative overall flatness to the design is more in keeping with the precepts of the so-called Pont-Aven Synthetist tradition. Finally, this painting may be compared with the Houston *The Breton Goose Boy* (cat. no. 64) of a year later. The style and methods used at Le Pouldu for such paintings as that seem so strikingly anticipated in *Farmhouse with Haystack* that one is again reminded of Gauguin's independence of vision and technique while undertaking an experiment patently intended to benefit from the experience of others.

1 Bodelsen, *W-C, Wildenstein*, p. 36, has argued persuasively that the Houston painting (i.e., W 308), is more likely to have been no. 13 (p.v. 14) *Les Mas* sold in the 1891 Hôtel Drouot sale to M. Daniel (de Monfreid) than was W 309 or 310. This author points out that W 309 apparently was exhibited in 1893 in Copenhagen as "Autumn Landscape from Arles," and W 310, as Wildenstein surmised, was the painting owned or kept by Schuffenecker which was exhibited in 1889 at the Volpini exhibition (as per instructions in *M*LXXVII, no. 7 of list, "Le paysage d'Arles que vous avez avec buissons.") as no. 37, *Paysage d'Arles*. Roskill, p. 134 and n. 8, points out that Vincent in his second letter to Théo after Gauguin's arrival in Arles (558b) speaks of the latter artist as already at work upon "a large landscape of this region." This author's choice of W 310 as the designated painting is possible, yet W 308 and 309 are of the same size and deserve equal consideration.

2 Goldwater, p. 86.

55.

Women of Arles: The Mistral W 300
oil on canvas; 73 x 92 cm
Signed and dated lower left: *P. Gauguin* [*18*]88
Lent by The Art Institute of Chicago; Gift of Annie
Swan Coburn to the Mr. and Mrs. L. L. Coburn
Collection

For so famous a painting (pl. 24) as this, surprisingly little has been ascertained as to its exact date of execution, subject matter and iconography. Gauguin did not refer to it specifically in his correspondence, and there is no known record of exhibition until as late as 1925. His one reference to it is found in his Arles notebook (p. 223), where it is listed as "Van Gogh Arlésiennes (Mistral) 300," the latter figure presumably being the number of francs paid for it by Théo. Since the Boussod and Valadon firm ledgers do not list a transaction, it seems likely that Théo bought the painting privately, perhaps as a means of giving Gauguin a fresh financial start following his hasty and embarrassing retreat from Arles. Indeed, since it provided the subject for one of the eleven lithographs executed in January-February 1889 at the Schuffenecker residence but under instigation from Théo (*see* cat. no. 58k), this coincidence might be explained as a gesture of gratitude by Gauguin toward Théo, whose friendship and support he assuredly wished to keep.

A second reason for Théo to have taken special interest in this painting was its probable setting: the public park entrance located opposite the Yellow House, which he would have seen during his brief visit at the end of December 1888. It is incorrectly cited by Wildenstein (*W* 300) as the garden of the Arles hospital, a formal garden in a walled enclosure (*see F* 519) with very little in common with the imagery found here, in Vincent's companion painting "Memory of the Garden at Etten" (*F* 496) or, more instructively, in the several paintings (*F* 468, 470-72, 479) he had executed in September-October 1888 which represent the little public park opposite his house (*see* cat. nos. 24, 33). The chief characteristics of this park were its variety in species and shapes of trees and bushes, and the bifurcation of its central pathway into two curved walkways encompassing an oval grass lawn from which grow two "bottle-shaped" cypresses (*CL* 551) and several other tree forms. Two versions (*F* 470-71) depict the pathway and oval lawn area from within the park with the entrance gate seen at rear. The height and type of

open slatted fencework appear so similar to the red gate seen lower right corner in the Chicago *Women at Arles* that the coincidence is telling. The bush form, lower left, also likely represents what Vincent described to his brother as "a clipped round bush of cedar or cypress" (*CL* 541), and there is no problem of identifying such forms in his own *oeuvre* (for example, *F* 468, 1465). Finally, the two elongated conical shapes which have been identified tentatively as "hay-frames with drying hay," are equally likely Vincent's two or another pair of "bottle-shaped" cypresses wrapped in burlap or thatching for protection against the fall mistral.[1] We know from a series of notebook studies that Gauguin developed his imagery as separate pictorial components (*fig. 63*),[2] and it is obvious from a comparison among the paintings, these little studies and the subsequent lithographic version (*see* cat. no. 58k) that he allowed himself considerable freedom in the scale and placement of individual images. The result was another of Gauguin's most fully Cloisonist style paintings, the colour compartments of which are sharply defined in contour and largely filled in with uniformly saturated and bright hues.

Although the exact date of this painting is now known, the accepted opinion that it was executed at about the time of Vincent's *Garden at Etten* or even together with it should be maintained. Hulsker's researches document completion of Vincent's canvas to the first day or so of December 1888.[3] Whereas Vincent chose to depict his mixed memory image of the Etten setting and the Arles Public Garden with its cypresses as a summer idyll, Gauguin insisted on a late fall season as his virtually shivering foreground figures, the absence of summer verdure and the sub-title of *The Mistral* all indicate. Ironically this argues for at least a partial reversal of the general tendency to see Gauguin in this context as having exercised the stronger influence on his colleague, whose painting evinces in fact a highly personal combination of Pointillist and Cloisonist features. What should be recalled here is that Vincent's *L'Arlésienne: Madame Ginoux with Books* (*see* cat. no. 30) was painted early in November shortly after Gauguin's arrival in Arles; surely the heads of one or both of the foreground women in Gauguin's *Women of Arles* may be read as indebted to Vincent's earlier conceptualization of a classic Arlesian female portrait. The representation of Mme Ginoux in Gauguin's *Night Café* (*W* 305), and the attendant drawing (Pickvance, *Drawings*, Pl. 27) which subsequently inspired a painting and three near-

Fig. 63
Paul Gauguin
Notebook studies for the *Women at Arles*,
1888,
Arles notebook.

replicas by Vincent (*F* 340-43), may well have been done at or about the same time as Vincent produced his first painting of Mme Ginoux (*CL* 559, 573).[4] Their common subject, though seen from different angles, is depicted in exactly the same head on hand, elbow on table pose, and it is difficult to avoid concluding that the New York and Moscow paintings were the product of a single sitting for the model. It is also risky to claim that one or the other artist was more radical in his adherence to Cloisonist principles in any of these compositions featuring one or more Arlesian women in regional costume. If Vincent was self-consciously accepting Gauguin's stress on working from memory or imagination in the *Garden at Etten* (*W* 9), Gauguin to some degree was still working on the basis of posed figures and objects studied in their natural surroundings.

Iconographically, this painting has remained one of the least decipherable, yet most intriguing among Gauguin's major statements. All recent commentators have found a portrait, usually a

SEE COLOUR PLATE 24.

self-portrait, disguised in the bush lower left, although no one has ventured a guess as to why.[5] Andersen has ventured the most suggestive interpretation so far, stating that "In their dark garb, gray-faced, with shawls clutched close to the mouth in a grief-checking gesture, the women make a strangely funereal procession," although this assertion of a thanatos theme is unsupported by any known reference by Gauguin. Coming as it did after the more famous "Café at Arles" scenes of the two artists, this painting presumably had the charged content which each artist attributed to any representation of Arles women in native dress. Certainly the women suggest the pictorial metaphor of "crossing over" which was a preferred image of Gauguin particularly in 1889 (*for example W* 321-22, 353). In addition the stark "black against white" contrast at left unavoidably suggests the age-old life-death confrontation, although the assumption of a specific moral for the painting should be avoided.

Ultimately this painting would seem to have

been intended more as an essay in style than as a statement of some profound human truth. Shortly after his arrival, Gauguin wrote back to Bernard in Pont-Aven (*M*LXXV) that the women of Arles with their "elegant hairdos" and "pleated shawls like the primitives" give the impression of a procession of beautiful Greek virgins. The Arles women are characterized by Gauguin as a blend of a "colourful Puvis de Chavannes," of Japan and of Greece which provides, as he said, "a source of a beautiful *moderne style*." Whatever its thematic content, the stylistic elegance and cohesion of this composition guarantee its masterpiece status within his *oeuvre*.

1   Andersen, *Paradise*, p. 81. This setting, called by Vincent either "the public garden" or "the poet's garden," is discussed at length in J. Hulsker, "The Poet's Garden," *Vincent* III: 1 (1974), pp. 22-32.

2   All are conveniently reproduced by Roskill, Pls. 129-31, 133, or else *Arles Notebook*, pp. 51-52,

56, 60.

3   VGdVG, no. 562, *W* 9, and VGW, pp. 374-76.

4   *G*14 of late November lists Gauguin's *Night Café* as being sent to Théo, which strengthens the supposition of a similar date for the stylistically related *Women of Arles*. Although Vincent mentioned in late spring 1889 (CL 638, 643) that he had then executed his second set of portraits of Mme Ginoux after the drawing of her for the *Night Café*, which was left behind in Arles by Gauguin, there is some speculation that at least one version was executed from life (*see* F 540).

5   Bodelsen, *Ceramics*, p. 104, tentatively, and Roskill, p. 147, without qualification, have read this presumed face in a bush as referring to Gauguin's own features, the latter author claiming there was a precedent for this usage, which, however, he does not cite. Andersen, *Paradise*, p. 81, is certainly incorrect in identifying the features as those of Meyer de Haan, whom Gauguin met only the following year.

SEE COLOUR PLATE 23.

56.

Grape Gathering-Human Misery:
Vendanges à Arles-Misères Humaines W 304
oil on canvas: 73.5 x 92.5 cm
Signed and dated lower right: *P. Gauguin* [*18*]88
Lent by the Ordrupgaard Museum, Collection of
William Hansen

Fig. 64
Paul Gauguin
sketch for the *Grape Gathering*,
sent to Emile Bernard in November 1888,
illustrated in D. Lord (Cooper) *Vincent van Gogh*
Letters to Emile Bernard (Letter XXIII),
New York, 1938.

The alternative titles under which this painting (pl. 23) is known both originated with Gauguin. In a letter (*G*14) of late November 1888 to Théo he cited it as "*La Vendange* or *la pauvresse*" among the five paintings he was forwarding from Arles to Paris.[1] Along with some advice on the stretching of this still wet canvas, he expressed fear that it and the companion piece *Les Cochons* (that is, cat. no. 57) might frighten off prospective purchasers, being "somewhat unpolished" (*un peu grossières*). He nonetheless asserted his own love of these paintings, calling them "rather masculine" perhaps because "the sun of southern France makes us want to rut." Having described it slightly earlier to Théo (*G*13) as "a poor woman, fully bewitched in a field of red vines," he subsequently entitled it *Misères Humaines* when it was exhibited first at Brussels and then at the Café Volpini in 1889.[2]

Gauguin also described this painting in an illustrated note to Bernard, which must also date from November 1888 (*fig. 64*).[3] After giving the background colours as "purple vines forming a triangle against the chrome yellow above," Gauguin characterizes the standing figure at left as

a Breton woman of Le Pouldu in black and gray, the two bent-over figures as Breton women in blue-green and black (the head-dresses, in fact, suggest Pont-Aven) and the seated figure as "pauvresse" in orange, white and earth-green against a pink terrain. Apart from the support this passage provides for the supposition that Gauguin in summer-fall 1888, likely accompanied by Bernard, had from Pont-Aven visited the coastal hamlet of Le Pouldu and there found several landscape motifs (*see* cat. no. 50), it also shows that his sub-title "the poor woman" in the letter to Théo was more than an off-hand means of identification. Gauguin then stated, "The whole was made with strong outlines filled with virtually uniform tonalities," adding that the execution had been with a palette knife producing a very thick layer on the coarse sackcloth beneath. While admitting that the setting represented "an effect of vines he had seen at Arles," he stressed that the figures were Breton and therefore not "exactly correct" in this his best painting of the year. Bernard almost certainly would have been familiar with the head of the seated figure, which Gauguin had employed already in the upper left corner of

his *Still Life with Fruits* (*W* 288), executed and dedicated to Charles Laval presumably before Gauguin left Pont-Aven for Arles.[4] This head type has been rightly seen as a variation on that found in the lower right corner of Bernard's *Breton Women in the Meadow*, and one may speculate that Gauguin would have expected Bernard to appreciate this self-admission of indebtedness from both Pont-Aven and Arles.[5]

A final source for understanding Gauguin's intentions in *Grape Gathering* is his references to it in an important letter of November 1889 to Vincent (*G*29). Before discussing his more recent *Christ in the Garden of Olives* and the wood sculpture *Soyez amoureuses*, he states that his current work is taking a new course, which, however, was anticipated in the *Grape Gathering* of Arles.

Claiming that he had been "led to search for a synthetic form and colour in this order of abstract ideas," he mentioned in passing that this was beyond the comprehension even of Degas. Since Gauguin also credits Vincent with having provided the composition (*dessin*) for his own *Grape Gathering*, we can be certain that the latter's *The Red Vineyard* (*F* 495) was meant, despite the manifest differences in compositional structure, deployment of figures and brushwork. The dominant red-purple versus yellow colour contrast and starkly outlined figural concept are similar in the two paintings nonetheless, so here too we can sense Gauguin reminding a colleague of a still appreciated relationship. On his part, when reporting completion of their respective vineyard canvases to Théo (*CL* 559), Vincent mentions his determination "to work from memory," indicating thereby his temporary acceptance of Gauguin as artistic mentor. At this period of initial cooperation in Arles between these two great painters, it is unusually significant that both artists should have recorded the relationship in such mutually appreciative terms.

The *Grape Gathering: Human Miseries* has duly received a great amount of critical attention in recent publications. Most of this discussion has centred upon the iconographic sources of Gauguin's figural imagery. The breakthrough identification was provided by Andersen, who convincingly identified the pose of the seated figure in *La Vendange* as related to the image of the "Peruvian mummy" (*Fig. 65*).[6] Other associated pictorial sources include Dürer's woodcut *Melancholia*, a graphic print by F. Rops, and even Vincent's own drawing *Sorrow* (*F* 929),[7] all of which imply a victimized-to-bestialized condition of female humanity.[8] Whereas all such sources may be supported or challenged according to one's inclination, it remains that the image preferred by Gauguin was that of a chagrined female, albeit so modified that the inclusion of an "orientalized" head derived from Bernard was scarcely noticeable. The symbolism of her "slanted eyes" could have either a "happy" or a "sinister" connotation. Gauguin's usage, however, is uniformly negative in the belief that "misères humaines" constitute a universal human condition.

Gauguin's most emotional description of *Grape Gathering* occurred in a letter of December 1888 to Schuffenecker in which he asked rhetorically if the seated figure was not "a poor disconsolate being? It is not a nature deprived of intelligence, grace and all the gifts of nature. It is a woman. Her two hands under her chin she thinks of few things, but feels the consolation of the earth (nothing but the earth) which the sun spreads with its red triangle. And a woman dressed in black goes by, looking at her like a sister."[9] Since Gauguin elsewhere in this letter identifies black as the colour of mourning, Dorra has convincingly suggested that the standing figure in black functions as a symbol of death and as such anticipates a usage which becomes overt in such Tahitian paintings as *The Spirit of the Dead Watches* (*W* 457). She is quite literally a reaper, however "grim" or not we may choose to think her, and Andersen has expanded this analogy to specify the girl as a virgin before her meditated fall.[10] This interpretation is given more plausibility by the presence of a male figure in later versions of this theme (cat. no. 58E, *W* 523), although only when transformed into a nude Eve accompanied by a serpent (*see* cat. no. 59) is the theme of the Fall assigned an overt religious connotation. Her role is in any case a dolorous one, which Gauguin seems to have considered inevitable for his virgin mother and wife images, however painful his own associations with the state of marriage.

1   *G* 14 is the second letter which Gauguin sent Théo in quick sequence from Arles after learning from him in a letter of November 13, 1888 (*T* 3a) that his exhibition at Boussod and Valadon had enjoyed some commercial success. The five paintings sent were *W* 251, 301, 304-05, 307.

2   I.e., no. 9 at *Les Vingt* (his top price listed as 1500 fr.) and no. 43 at Volpini's (there listed as owned by Emile Schuffenecker, who had bought it for 300 fr. according to a listing as "Splendeur et misère" in Huyghe, *Carnet*, p. 223).

3   First reproduced along with the note in Vincent van Gogh, *Letters to Emile Bernard*, ed. and trans. D. Lord (Cooper), New York, Museum of Modern Art, 1938, pp. 106-07 and Pl. 31.

4   Laval's presence in Pont-Aven was reported by Gauguin to Vincent in a letter of late September (*G* 9, which Vincent discussed as just received in *CL* 543 of *c*. September 28). Gauguin's dedication of this still life painting dated 1888 logically reflects this late summer period when he, Bernard and Laval worked together at Pont-Aven rather than a remembrance from Arles.

5   Andersen, *Mummy*, p. 241, first credited the head types in Bernard's *Breton Women* with having inspired those in Gauguin's *Fruits* and the *Grape Gathering*.

6   *Ibid*., pp. 238-41, where, however, only a similarity of pose is claimed between the seated figure in *La Vendange* and the mummy, whose earliest true reincarnation in the art of Gauguin comes only the following spring with the *Eve* watercolour (cat. no. 59).

7   The latter two sources are adduced in Dorra, *Arles Themes*, pp. 13-15.

8   Andersen, *Mummy*, p. 241, was the first to relate the various instances of "slanting eyes" within Gauguin's art with its presumed "oriental" associations, especially as these refer to "sinful" instincts. The most obvious source for associating specific ethical meanings with the racial slant of eye alignments was again Charles Blanc, who reproduced a diagram of his predecessor, D.P. Humbert de Superville, in such theories. (See W.I. Homer, *Seurat and the Science of Painting*, Cambridge, Mass.: The M.I.T. Press, n.d. [1964], pp. 198-205.) However, these theoreticians associated "upward" slanting eyes with "gaiety," which contrasts with the negative, fox-like connotations of Gauguin, perhaps because the latter was inclined towards more sinister themes at the time.

9   As quoted, translated and discussed in Dorra, *Arles Themes*, p. 12 (here dated late December, according to Roskill, p. 273).

10   Andersen, *Mummy*, p. 241.

Fig. 65
Peruvian mummy
(Musée de l'Homme, Paris)

57 A.
Woman in the Hay:
Pigs: In Full Heat W 301
Early December 1888
oil on canvas: 73 x 92 cm
Signed and dated lower left: *P. Gauguin* [*18*]*88*
Lent by a private collection
TORONTO ONLY

57 B.
Study for Woman in the Hay:
Pigs: In Full Heat
early December 1888
charcoal and watercolour on paper: 26.3 x 40 cm
Not signed or dated
Lent by the Rijksmuseum Vincent van Gogh,
Amsterdam
AMSTERDAM ONLY

The correct title of this painting has remained uncertain. *Woman in the Hay* derives from its description by Vincent in a letter to Théo (*CL* 562) written shortly before the painting was finished and sent to Paris in early December 1888 and from the title used for the 1891 sale at the Hôtel Drouot (no. 6; p.v. 7). Yet at the *Les Vingt* exhibition of early 1889 Gauguin chose to call it *En plein chaleur*, reasonably translated into English as "In the Heat of the Day."[1] This respectable title, however, conceals a *double entendre*, since *en chaleur* means "in heat" for female animals. That Gauguin's intention was to imply this state of sexual disquiet in his human figure even more than in the two truncated pig forms (upper right and lower left) is strongly suggested by his private reference to it as *Les Cochons* to Théo (*G* 14) and in a notebook listing.[2]

Andersen has rightly seen the pose of the female figure as anticipating the Woman in the Waves or Undine theme of the following year (*see* cat. nos. 59, 60). It is not without precedent, since beginning *circa* 1886 Gauguin had shown a penchant for depicting female figures from the rear, both clothed and nude.[3] Although many of these Pont-Aven-Martinique settings remain true to the picturesque nineteenth century tradition of showing peasants as hard-working but happy harvesters of earth's bounty, this Impressionist idyll occasionally had been interupted by intimations of more serious content. The *La Baignade* (*W* 215), a painting dated 1887 and exhibited the last month of that year at Théo's gallery, was Gauguin's first major exercise in the exploitation of female figures discovered, naked, in a landscape setting and depicted voyeuristically from the rear. In his self-chosen role as David spying on a continuing parade of seemingly willing Bathshebas, the artist had rediscovered a modern equivalent to Renaissance tradition, even if these Venuses of Brittany and Arles evoke a mixture of attraction and repulsion. The figure lower left in *La Baignade* is the obvious prototype of the Woman in the Hay and of the Undine figure in the "Aux Roches noires" lithograph of the Volpini exhibition (*see fig. 60*).

As first discovered by Pickvance, the central figure of the "Woman in the Hay" bears a general resemblance to a similarly "flagellated" female nude in the *Death of Sardanapalus* by Delacroix, the macabre sexual connotations of which are quite obvious.[4] In *Les Cochons* the debasement of the female is quite apparent, although it remains moot whether Gauguin intended to degrade woman or rather to view woman as an inevitable victim of degradation. His explanation to Théo that this and a companion painting were born of the influence of the Southern French Sun, "which encourages us to rut," (*G* 14) thus may be interpreted as total anti-feminism or alternatively as a call for liberating women from the toils and frustration of their existence. As in the *Breton Calvary* (cat. no. 62) there appears a mysterious black being, in this instance apparently a dog with a collar, which further and somewhat surreptitiously insinuates the idea of death (the colour black) into an otherwise image of procreation. Certainly this image was the predecessor of the "black sheep" which figures in the *Green Christ* (cat. no. 65) of the following year. One need not impose a strictly Freudian interpretation of this "penetrating intrusion" in order to agree that the painting somehow reflects sexual frustration.

The painting continues Gauguin's investigations into the Cloisonist dialogue between three-dimensional and two-dimensional conceptions of design. His surfaces continue to undulate, whatever the subject, in a manner that suggests the flow and ebb of time and transcends allegorical association. In the context of his progression from the overt Cloisonism of *Jacob Struggling with the Angel* to his mature *Synthétiste* works of 1889, this investigation of frustrated female sexuality may be considered Gauguin's agonizing testimony of transition from Impressionist tranquillity to Symbolist subterfuge.

The Amsterdam watercolour representing this subject provides an intriguing problem of intended function. Although considered by a leading authority on Gauguin's drawings as possibly a copy after the painting executed in January 1889, this is ruled out by the artist's having finished the painted version by early December 1888.[5] Moreover, the setting of the watercolour is clearly an interior with the semi-nude model leaning against, and even grasping, a cloth suspended against a decorated wall surface. It is inconceivable that a model would have agreed to pose in the open as pictured in the painting, especially in Arles, and, if one had, then why the reversion to a studio setting for a watercolour copy, in which one might have expected to find some landscape elements included as well? The drawing in fact suggests not only a study from the live model, but one in which the application of coloured wash bears all the earmarks of a preliminary experiment for the painting, where the hues of the figure but not of the background generally correspond to the watercolour.[6] Most intriguing of all is whether Gauguin didn't possibly invent his background, by inserting his landscape and figural element according to his imagination and the felt needs of the composition as determined by the figure. There would seem to be no other known paintings or published drawings of such a landscape background with pigs, dog and pitchfork, which would present a rather uncomfortable pictorial combination, if the figure were to be imagined as lacking. Given the experimental nature of this work, one is not surprised to read Vincent's observation (that is *CL* 562): "Gauguin is working on a very original nude woman in the hay with some pigs. It promises to be very fine, and of great distinction."

1 Andersen, *Paradise*, 91.

2 *Arles Sketchbook*, 72.

3 See for example: W 201, 215, 224 and 302/03.

4 Pickvance, *Tate Entries*, no. 16, first suggested this female figure by Delacroix as a source for Gauguin's *Woman in the Hay*. At the latest Gauguin would have known this famous painting when it was exposed at the Durand-Ruel gallery at the time of the Puvis de Chavannes held there, late 1887 (see M. Serullaz, *Memorial de l'exposition Eugène Delacroix*, Paris: Editions des Musées Nationaux, 1963, cat. no. 99).

5 Hulsker, *VGdVG*, assigns a date for *CL* 562, which mentions the Gauguin painting as underway, to December 2, 1888, and *G* 14 which mentions it as just sent to Paris should accordingly be dated perhaps a week later, but before midmonth, when Gauguin declares to Théo (*G* 16) his "incompatibility" with Vincent. The view of Pickvance, *Drawings*, Pl. 26, that the watercolour in this case might follow the oil, is reasonably based on analogies between oil and watercolour versions of other Arles subjects, but is less acceptable for the reasons stated in the entry text.

6 It is also possible that this watercolour was executed in Pont-Aven, where Gauguin had his own studio and, according to one report (see Sutton, *Tate Intro*., p. 11), a model who, "while prepared to take off her shift, she would retain her *coiffe*." The report also mentions her use for the major figure in the wood relief *Soyez mysterieuses* (Gray 87), which, being the "Undine" variation of the figure of this watercolour, further suggests a Pont-Aven rather than Arles female as the model for this study.

57A

57B

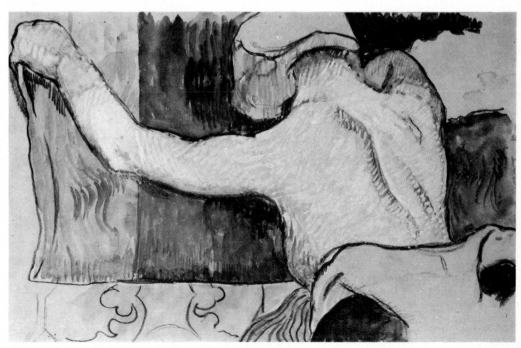

58.

Eleven Lithographs from an Album
early 1889
lithographs from zinc plate on yellow paper
Lent by The Art Institute of Chicago

The eleven lithographic prints of the present catalogue entry represent a set of those made available, along with six by Bernard (see cat. no. l09), at the Volpini exhibition under the catalogue rubric "visible on request." They are now also known as zincographs due to their execution on zinc plate. Gauguin preferred to call them "lithographic drawings" (*Dessins lithographiques*) as he individually inscribed with pencil the "Design for a Plate" (cat. no. 58a), which he cut down and mounted as the cover illustration on at least several sets presented in portfolios covered with marbled paper. Although no albums are believed to have been sold during the exhibition, the so-called Arles sketchbook lists five sales at between twenty-five and forty francs apiece.[1] The cover illustrations seem typically to have been given watercolour additions, but whether this occurred as a single effort before the exhibition opened or as occasion demanded with individual subsequent sales is unclear. The original edition by the printer Ancourt is thought to have been less than fifty, and perhaps considerably less, since this printing on yellow wove paper is now quite rare. A subsequent edition from l894 or later by Ambroise Vollard, who bought the plates from Schuffenecker, was printed on imitation Japanese paper of a lesser quality.

Vincent had considered surviving as an artist through the production of inexpensive prints as early as 1882 (*CL* 241). Shortly before Gauguin's arrival in Arles he wrote to Vincent proposing that, once Bernard and Laval had also moved to Arles, the four of them could work on lithographs in the evenings. Vincent's somewhat negative reply (*CL*549) was that this would be fine if done for their own pleasure, but that publication for sale carried too heavy financial risks. Gauguin may have had this response in mind when in late January, 1889, he wrote Vincent that he had "commenced a series of lithographs for publication in order to make himself known," adding that this was undertaken "according to the counsel and under the auspices of your brother."[2] In a still unpublished manuscript, Bernard amplifies our knowledge of this collaborative effort:

Gauguin came to Paris a short time thereafter. He landed at the house of his friend Schuffenecker. I went to see him often. We made our lithographs. . . . He had finished his album when I showed him mine. They pleased him so much that he remade two, executing them in the manner which I had discovered.[3]

Taken together, these references clearly place the joint project in the first month or two of 1889 at the home of Schuffenecker, which means that it occurred before plans were completed, and perhaps even begun, for the exhibition eventually held at the Volpini café.

Bernard's memoir, while obviously intended to suggest indebtedness by Gauguin to his own stylistic innovations, should not be overlooked for this reason. Whereas the majority of Gauguin's Volpini lithographs reflect his own painted *oeuvre* (or in one instance, Guerin no. 8, clearly constitutes a novel composition), three others (Guerin nos. 2, 4, 6,) display exaggerations of contour which may best be explained as at least a tribute, if not necessarily subservience, to the series of Bernard with its greater degree of exaggerated figural contours and Cloisonist integration of figural imagery and background. Coming as it did at a fate-filled moment of Gauguin's reappearance in Paris after the cataclysmic events of Arles, this renewed contact between Bernard and Gauguin, under the joint sponsorship of Théo and Schuffenecker, should be recognized for what it was; the immediate renewal of the association the two artists had formed the previous summer in Pont-Aven and thus the essential link between their mutual influence of that time and their close cooperation in the Volpini enterprise. It was surely this collaboration in graphics at the Schuffenecker residence which forged the triumvirate of organizers of the Volpini manifestation. As indicated above (p. 42), the exhibition produced no immediate benefits to any party involved. Yet involvement in this event afforded all participants a chance to expose their works in a collective manifestation, which was epitomized in the "Album of Lithographs by Paul Gauguin and Emile Bernard visible upon request." Only future research will disclose just how far-reaching was the effect of the Volpini exhibition for individual artists, but the "Album de Lithographie" of Gauguin and Bernard must have played a greater disseminating role than heretofore imagined.[4]

It should be understood that the numeration by Guerin has no basis in any recorded sequence by Gauguin, who presumably felt no urge to arrange his lithographs in any chronological or inconographic order.

[1]   Huyghe, *Carnet*, p. 223, where those listed as purchasers of the "album" include "Jean" de Rotonchamp (?), "Chamaillard," a Pont-Aven artist, "Portier," an art dealer, and Théo "van Gog." In addition, albums were listed as given to the artists Schuffenecker, Charles Filiger and Auguste "Delaherche." This record of buyers and recipients of gifts may have been expanded subsequent to this listing of *circa* 1889, but even this "short list" indicates the availability of these prints as a ready informer of "Pont-Aven" style.

[2]   *G*19; since 572 of January 19 transcribes contents of *G*19 received by Vincent "yesterday," the latter must date *circa* January 17.

[3]   This MS, "L'Aventure de ma vie," (excerpt is p. 79), was recently given by Bernard's son, M. M.-A. Bernard-Fort, to the Archives, Musées Nationaux, Paris. Although Bernard remembered many years later the production of the Volpini lithographs occurring just before Gauguin's Arles episode, the actual occurrence only three months later is not far off.

[4]   The eight drawings were reproduced in Aurier's *Le Moderniste* (nos. l5-22, Aug.3-24, 1889) from the Volpini exhibition catalogue, another major source of dissemination of the "Pont-Aven-Synthetist" style which calls for further elaboration.

Dessins Lithographiques

Paul Gauguin

58A.
Design for a Plate
Guerin No. 1
zincograph plus watercolour:
now matted on 55.9 x 71.1 cm board

This image employs the head of a would-be bathing girl found in a painting and pastel-watercolour both dated 1887 (*W* 215-216). It is most likely that the head was copied from the drawing now at the Art Institute of Chicago (Pickvance, *Drawings*, Pl. 16), naturally represented in mirror reverse.[1] The other images (swan, geese, snake and flowers), can be presumed improvisations. The inscription "homis (sic) soit qui mal y pense" (the French equivalent of "those in glass houses shouldn't throw stones") is sometimes thought to anticipate the theme of Gauguin's ceiling decoration of the inn of Marie Henry, which reportedly bore the same inscription, but when first created the circular design was intended as a plate design (ergo the *Projet d'asiet* [sic.]) inscribed below. This is not to gainsay the obvious Leda and the Swan iconography of this representation and its mock erotic implications, but rather to implicate Gauguin in a system of iconography in which an image of clandestine love is so dissimulated that it was intended to serve the most domestic of functions, an ordinary dinner plate. The style of this "drawing-lithograph" emits strong affinities with painted Breton ceramic ware, with which Gauguin was familiar. Two companion designs dedicated respectively to the Joys and Follies of Love (ills. in *P-I*, p. 276) were produced to employ a more elaborate assortment of indecipherable decorative images.

[1] The illustration of this lithograph in *Post-Imp.*, p. 276, would seem to be a photographically corrected reversal of the original print in order to allow the inscription to be easily read.

58B.
Joys of Brittany
Guerin No. 2
zincograph on paper (black on yellow):
20.4 x 24 cm
Signed lower left: *Paul Gauguin   Joies de Bretagne*

The two girls of this graphic correctly could be
seen as variations on the theme of *La Ronde des
Petites Bretonnes* (*W* 251), although the pastel
drawing of this subject (cat. no. 48) would seem a
more likely candidate for direct inspiration. The
fact that the painting was sent by Théo to Arles for
retouching must only enhance the iconographic
association of these two with the three of the "Breton Rondel" theme. At the same time, these figures and their background tend to substantiate
Bernard's claim that his own series of lithographs
had encouraged a degree of imitation by Gauguin.

58C.
Bathers in Brittany
Guerin No. 3
zincograph on paper (black on yellow):
23.3 x 19.7 cm
Signed lower left: *P Gauguin*

The Guerin title "Bathers in Brittany" for this
image seems justified, although the central image
was in all probability derived from a drawing at
the Art Institute of Chicago. This is the first
demonstrable reference to the Black Rocks of
Brittany as a source of reference for Gauguin's
iconography, and here the juxtaposition of an
earlier figure from Pont-Aven with the Black
Rocks only intensifies one's suspicions that this
image expanded rather than contracted an
iconographic tradition. How other to explain the
frolicking female bather, upper left in the
lithograph, except as an innocent bystander in the
"Terrors of the Sea" theme which is the central
motive of the lithographic series.

58D.

Breton Women at a Fence Gate
Guerin No. 4
zincograph on paper (black on yellow):
17 x 21.5 cm
Signed lower left: *P Gauguin*

The figure lower right derives from the painting
Four Breton Women (*W* 201), a work now
generally accepted as dating from 1886 rather
than 1888 as formerly supposed. It more directly
derives from the chalk drawing at the Glasgow Art
Gallery (Pickvance, Pl. II), although the landscape
background unites elements from too many
sources to be enumerated. The costumes and
setting are of a Pont-Aven character.

58E.

Human Misery
Guerin No. 5
zincograph on wove paper (sanguine on yellow):
28.2 x 22.7 cm
Signed lower right (inverted): *P Gauguin* [*18*]89

The *Misères Humaines* title by Guerin recognizes
the Arles painting of this name (cat. no. 56) as the
formal and iconographic source of this lithograph.
Dorra has explained the addition of a male figure
in the lithograph in terms of "a sordid village
drama" involving infanticide, although his identifications of the head seen among the branches as
a village priest and of a serpent on the trunk of the
tree appear to this viewer unconvincing.[1] Nonetheless his general interpretation that the issue of sexuality is more exactly specified here seems justified.
Certainly Gauguin's well-known love of pointing
to the hypocrisy of conventionalized social mores is
here embodied in an image of ultimate suspicion
and mistrust between the two central figures.

[1]   Dorra, "*Arles* Themes," p. 14.

Washerwomen
Guerin No. 6
zincograph on paper (black on yellow):
21.2 x 26.1 cm
Signed lower right: *P. Gauguin*

The setting clearly is that of Arles, since this lithograph derives directly from a painting (*W* 303)
which represents women in Arlesian costume.[1]
The goat image paradoxically is found in a Martinique member of the series (cat. no 58I and
W 219, albeit a work questioned by both Cooper
and Bodelsen)[2] and also strangely resembles the
animal seen lower right in the title piece illustration
of Bernard's series of "Bretonneries"
(cat. no. 109). Again the Gauguin zincograph
seems to accommodate Bernard's greater expansion of contour and thus more Cloisonist flatness in
design.

[1] Pickvance *Drawings*, Pl. 28, reproduces a watercolour on silk variant of *W* 303 and the present
zincograph, albeit without the goat.
[2] Anon. (D. Cooper?), "Not All Painted with the
same brush," *The Times Literary Supplement*,
August 19, 1965, and Bodelsen, "Wildenstein
Catalogue," p. 28.

58G.
Dramas of the Sea: Brittany[1]
Guerin No. 7
zincograph on paper (black on yellow):
16.9 x 22.7 cm
Signed lower left (inverted): [*18*]*89 Paul
Gauguin*
Inscribed centre below: *Les drames de la mer
Bretagne*

The title of this lithograph refers to the Edgar Allen
Poe short story, "A Descent into the Maelstrom,"
which is more directly depicted in a companion
lithograph (see following item). The image here is
one of three women situated on the edge of a
precipice, one standing, one kneeling and one with
her back to the apparent danger. The general
setting of this piece is Le Pouldu as in *Above the
Precipice* (cat. no. 50), which was executed the
previous summer. As usual Gauguin has
employed his repertory of figures in a new
accommodation. The cow is a variation of that in
Above the Precipice, the standing figure at left was
the "dark presence" in *Misères Humaines* (cat.
no. 56) and the kneeling figure appears in *Breton*

Calvary: Pardon in Brittany (cat. no. 62). The costumes worn derive from both Pont-Aven (figures at right) and Le Pouldu (figure at left).

The iconography of "Three Maries above the Watery Tomb" also recalls the theme of *La Berceuse* (cat. no. 34) and *Breton Calvary* (cat. no. 65) with their remembrance of the waiting daughters-sisters-mothers of this insular female population.[2] Certainly the inscribed sub-title was intended to underscore the precarious nature of all human existence, as symbolized in the three women at the edge of the black rocks of the Brittany coast.

[1] Thanks to the special and fraternal generosity of the Albright-Knox Gallery, Buffalo, we are privileged also to present one of Gauguin's hand-coloured versions of this lithograph. Only further research will reveal the degree of variety with which Gauguin enriched his lithographs in this series with colour.

[2] It should be remembered that economic circumstances sent many of Brittany's young men to sea, which had the effect of producing a kind of matriarchy (ergo the inns at Pont-Aven and Le Pouldu run by women, who were therefore receptive to the idea of visiting artists).

58H.
Dramas of the Sea: Descent into the Maelstrom
Guerin No. 8
zincograph on paper (black on yellow):
18 x 27.5 cm
Signed left of centre below: *P Gauguin*
Inscribed lower left: *Les Drames de la Mer*

More even than 58g, above, this lithograph may be recognized as derived in theme from the Edgar Allen Poe story "A Descent into the Maelstrom." This story, which has been characterized thematically as "salvation through terror," involves a sailor's hair-graying experience of being swept into the seemingly endless and mortal grips of a whirlpool, a confrontation with almost certain death, which induced a series of psychological reactions including initial terror, fascination and relief[1]. Gauguin's use of an inverted fan image is not only a clever conceit for the conversion of Impressionist gaiety into Post-Impressionist seriousness, but appropriately substitutes intimations of the underworld for that of heavenly transcendence. The Poe story is paralleled in many respects by another of Gauguin's favourites, Balzac's

Fig. 66
Sadahide:
Seaweed Gatherer,
c. 1850,
coloured print
(Victoria and Albert
Museum).

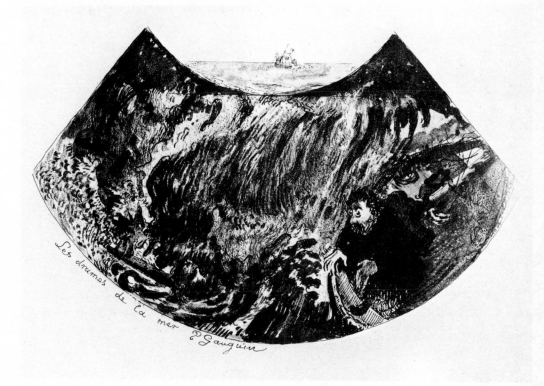

esoteric novel *Séraphita*, which also juxtaposes the spiritual ascent of mountainous fiord cliffs with the threat of an unfathomable plunge below, and Gauguin's use of the cliffs, beach and sea found at Le Pouldu in the service of such literary-philosophic themes is hardly surprising.

As Whitford discovered, Gauguin likely derived his own inverted-fan composition from a print by Sadahide (*fig. 66*). The humourously intended subject of *Seaweed Gatherer*, if known to

Gauguin, would have had a double irony, given his familiarity with its importance to the peasants of the Brittany coast.[2]

[1] See E.A. Poe, *The Short Fiction of Edgar Allen Poe*, eds. S. and S. Levine (Indianapolis: Bobbs-Merrill, 1976), pp. 32-50.

[2] F. Whitford, *Japanese Prints and Western Painters* (London: Studio Vista, 1977) pp. 173, 176.

581.

Martinique Pastorale
Guerin No. 9
zincograph on paper (black on yellow):
17.8 x 22.4 cm
Signed below centre: *Paul Gauguin*
Inscribed lower left: *Pastorales Martinique*

In theme, this lithograph could be considered a variation on the theme "Tropical Conversation" as embodied in a painting which Gauguin included in his *Les Vingt* exhibition of early 1889 (*W* 227). The tree and goat at right occur in a disputed painting (*see* 58f, note 1) and the goat is also present in a member of the same lithographic series (58f.). In general, the contrast between the casually embracing figures at left and the root-grubbing yet milk-giving goat at right suggests the fascination with "sin in paradise" which would preoccupy Gauguin for the rest of his creative life. Although representing a Martinique subject, this is yet another illustration of Gauguin's attraction to Cloisonism *circa* 1888-89, although less depend-ant upon the "cloisonisme flamboyant" (*see* cat. no. 109) of Bernard in his accompanying series.

58J.

The Grasshoppers and the Ants
Guerin No. 10
zincograph on yellow paper (black on yellow):
20 x 26.3 cm
Signed lower left: *Paul Gauguin*
Inscribed lower left: *Les Cigales et les fourmis*

Based on one of La Fontaine's most popular tales, "The Ant and the Grasshopper," this lithograph contrasts industriously working ants and the only too lazy grasshoppers. Those in the foreground of Gauguin's setting, although not singing and strumming a guitar as in the actual fable, nonethe-less are wasting away the summer months with no apparent thought for putting food in their lar-ders for the winter ahead. In contrast those at the rear are collecting their food and may be expected to turn down the eventual request for assistance from the now idle grasshoppers. One need not suppose a profoundly ethical intention for Gauguin in his choice of title. In a letter written 1887 from Martinique to his wife (*M*LIII), he associated fruit with sexual temptation by superstitious female negresses with no little malice aforethought. The title thus could have been intended to provide to a French audience a pleasantly innocuous subject

reference for a depiction of exotic life in the colonies which otherwise might not have carried any particular meaning.

The seaside setting is similar to those of two Martinique paintings (W 217-18), which in their decorative aspect and contrast between a foreground web of tree trunks and background panorama have been shown to contain a Japanese principle of design.[1]

[1] Bodelsen, *Ceramics*, pp. 178-79.

58K.
Women of Arles: The Mistral
Guerin No. 11
zincograph on yellow paper (black on yellow):
18.9 x 21 cm.
Signed lower left: *P. Gauguin*

In executing this zincograph after the painting (see cat. no. 55) Gauguin left out several details (fountain, park bench and gate), added a small tree and rearranged the two cones. The result is a less

elaborate composition than typical of the print series as a whole, and an even starker simplification of outline according to Cloisonist principles than in the painting. Like the other series members with figures or compositions executed after earlier paintings or drawings, this print is naturally seen in reverse to its source of inspiration, although here as usual the artist took the trouble to make his signature come out correctly.

59.

Eve   W 333
early 1889
pastel and watercolour: 33 × 31 cm
Signed and dated lower right: *P. Gauguin* [18]
89
Lent by the Marion Koegler McNay Art Institute,
San Antonio
TORONTO ONLY

This justly famous mixed-media example of
Gauguin's graphic art has nonetheless been treated
as a final version of the seated Eve with a serpent
theme (*W 333*). It was in fact signed and dated
by the artist doubtless because of its inclusion at
the Volpini exhibition, where it was listed merely
as "42. Eve–Aquarelle." This identification is
based on Antoine's review in *Art et critique* of the
Volpini showing in which he took Gauguin to task
for having inscribed the picture with the pidgin
French caption, "Pas écouter li...li...menteur"
(that is, "Don't listen to the liar"). Antoine's
rhetorically facetious accompanying question–
"From what document does Mr. Gauguin base his
supposition that Eve spoke Negro?" was answered
in turn by Gauguin in a letter to Bernard (*M*XCI)
with the retort that who could know in what
language she and the serpent communicated.[1] The
"Breton Eve" label given by Wildenstein thus has
no basis in any known Gauguin reference and
most probably derives from the use of this same
Eve figure in a painting (*W 335*) he designated
Bathing Women, which includes a background
view of the Brittany coast with its seaweed- or
lichen-bedecked "black rocks," a phrase Gauguin
used for the frontispiece illustration of the Volpini
exhibition catalogue (*fig. 60*). Here Gauguin
included the seated Eve and a second female figure
throwing herself at the waves, to which he gave the
name "Undine" when the painted version (cat.
no. 60) was exhibited and sold in 1891 at the
Hôtel Drouot (no. 14, p.v. 15). Since this painted
Undine was almost certainly present at the Volpini
exhibition as No. 44, "In the Waves," this
indicates that his "Aux Roches noires" catalogue
illustration was derived from the exhibited
watercolour and painting, albeit with a rock form
substituted for the tree and serpent in the *Eve*
watercolour. The exhibited watercolour and
painting are the only two identifiable examples to
bear inscribed dates of 1889, which strongly
suggests that he used them in the catalogue
frontispiece as an indication that they constituted a
recent and important innovation in his art.

It is quite probable that one or both of these
examples were produced either during Gauguin's
spring 1889 visit to Pont-Aven or even after his
return to Paris in order to help arrange for display
and to see the Universal Exposition. Before his
departure he had been chiefly concerned with his
lithographic series and *Les Vingt* exhibition,
neither of which contain the Eve or Undine image.
That the latter and the "Aux Roches noires" illustration probably represent a setting at Le Pouldu
cannot be used to situate their place of execution,
since he definitely had already visited there in
1888, if not 1886 as well (see cat. no. 50), and it
was already his established practice to combine
images from diverse sources according to his "synthetist" or painting from memory credos. In this
respect, one might even question if the seated Eve
figure of the San Antonio watercolour or a variant
pastel version (*W 334*) probably used for the
Bathing Women was executed from a live model.[2]
The pose of all three variant figures after all is
considerably closer than had been the central figure of the *Misères Humaines* to the Peruvian
mummy (*fig. 65*) which Andersen discovered as
the source of the seated Eve image.[3] In other
words, in these cases painting from memory may
well have entailed painting or drawing with one's
imagination. We know that his *Exotic Eve*
(*W 389*) of 1890 featured a female figure based
upon photographs of his mother for the head and
of a Buddhist frieze on the Javanese temple at
Borobudur for the body, and there is no reason to
doubt his ability to effect such transformations as
were necessary from the mummy to the seated
Eve a year earlier, granting the more radical
change of "style" that was demanded in this
instance.[4] This is not to claim, of course, that
Gauguin had altogether abandoned use of live
models by 1889, but only to suggest the likelihood
that the *Eve* figure was less a study after nature
than an image of tormented humanity which he
had composed according to his maturing synthetist
philosophy.

The Volpini *Eve* is thus, one might say,
Gauguin's full revelation of the "naked truth" of
the degradated female condition. The Christian
reference to the Fall notwithstanding, her obviously ineffectual hear-no-evil attempts to forestall
self-knowledge are little more pathetic than those
of the Peruvian mummy, a literally bound and
sexless figure, which inspired this psychologically
unsettling icon of death. Indeed, the death association of the mummy has been confirmed by the
Bodelsen and Pickvance identification of the *Bath-

ing Women with the painting exhibited under the
title "Life and Death" at Copenhagen in 1893.[5]
The juxtaposition in this painting of the seated Eve
with a female bather seen frontally and drying
herself implies a before and after the Fall contrast
which only the absence of the snake of the Eve
watercolour leaves inexplicit. Significantly, the
seated Eve was also used as a harbinger of female
doom and mortality in such Gauguin masterpieces
as the late 1889 wood relief *Be in Love and You
Will Be Happy* (*fig. 67*, Gray 76) and the 1897
painting *Whence Cometh We, Who Are We,*

1   This identification was first made in Dorra, "The
First Eves in Gauguin is Eden," *Gazette des
Beaux-Arts*, VI:41 (1953), p. 192. Pickvance,
Drawings, pl. 33, however, believes that both figures in *W334* were based on drawings from the
nude model, which, if true, does not of course tell
us whether this occurred in Brittany or Paris. The
"Aux Roches noires" Volpini catalogue frontispiece illustration has been variously categorized as
a wash drawing (e.g. Pickvance, p. 27, pl. 41) or
a woodcut (e.g., Andersen, *Paradise*, p. 87,
whose fig. 58, however, is clearly reversed from
the Volpini catalogue illustration and doubtless a
later reprise). Even if the illustration was reproduced from a lithograph (Gray p. 43) this was
surely produced after Gauguin had returned to
Paris from Pont-Aven, since only then was the
catalogue format determined (*see* p. 42).
Both Pickvance, p. 26, pl. 33, and Andersen,
"Peruvian Mummy," p. 241, cite the presence of
an influence from Degas in these seated Eves
despite the use of the pose of the Peruvian
mummy, which hypothesis, while quite acceptable, only further complicates the issue of whether
or not a live model was also used.

2   I.e., Andersen, "Peruvian Mummy," p. 238, and
Paradise, p. 89 and fig. 57.

3   On the *Exotic Eve*, see Dorra, "The First Eves,"
pp. 193-200, and Andersen, *Paradise*, pp.
123-27.

4   Bodelsen, "Wildenstein Catalogue," *Wildenstein*
p. 37, and Sutton, *Gauguin*, Pickvance, *Tate
Entries*, discovered this independently in 1966.
This painting nonetheless is dated 1889 and like
the related Eve and Undine themes may well have
been executed during the first half of the year. The
use in this painting of a towel by the "Life" figure
possibly already symbolizes "after the Fall," as
Dorra has shown for the early Tahitian period
("The First Eves," pp. 200-01).

5   For Gauguin's statements about the *Be in Love*,
see *M*LXXXVII, *G*29, *G*31; those on *Whence Cometh We* are collected under *W* 561.

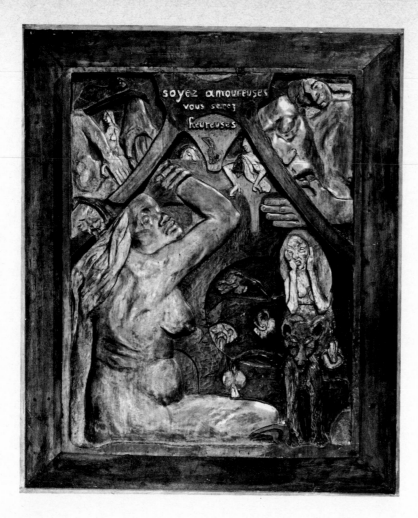

Fig. 67
Paul Gauguin
Be in Love and You Will be Happy,
polished polychromed linden wood, late 1889
(Museum of Fine Arts, Boston, Arthur Tracy
Cabot Fund; photograph courtesy of Museum of
Fine Arts, Boston).

60.
Undine: In the Waves   W 336
oil on canvas: 92 × 72.4 cm
Signed and dated below middle: *P. Gauguin* [*18*]
89
Lent by The Cleveland Museum of Art;
Gift of Mr. and Mrs. William Powell Jones

Unlike the companion *Eve* watercolour (cat. no.
59), there is no absolute proof that the painting
Undine (pl.1) was present at the Volpini
exhibition. That it was present as "44. Dans les
vagues," however, is rendered virtually certain by
the absence from Gauguin's 1887-89 *oeuvre* of
paintings for which the title, with its implication of
one or more bathing figures, would be better
suited. The use of this figure in the catalogue
frontispiece (*fig. 60*) along with that of the *Eve*
watercolour, would seem totally unwarranted had
not both images been represented in the actual
exhibition. Moreover, since neither the *Eve*
watercolour nor the present *Undine* had been
present at *Les Vingt* exhibition in February, both
were likely to have been executed either during
Gauguin's spring visit to Brittany or possibly even
after his return to Paris by early May. There is
even less reason than with *Eve* to associate the
origin of the *Undine* figure with a particular site,
Breton or otherwise, since posing a live model in
the waves as depicted is unthinkable and since the
only way a live model could hold such an
off-balance pose would be lying down or on an
incline, neither a very satisfactory position for the
artist to work with. Andersen has viewed the
female of *Woman in the Hay* (cat. no. 57) as
providing a precedent in pose for the *Undine*. If
one adds the figure, lower left, of the 1887
Bathing Girls (W 215), one might feel that only
the study of the head and shoulders known as
Undine II (W 337) was needed rather than a live
model, to enable Gauguin to execute the Cleveland
painting and a watercolour version in the shape of
a fan (W 338) apparently derived therefrom. The
use of an unusual, somewhat awkward pose and
the residual modelling in the round of the nude
retain a general indebtedness to Degas, as does the
Japanist close-up, asymmetrical and truncated
view of the figure. For its simplification of contour
outlines and bold use of green, red and white
colour areas, the *Undine* may be considered one of
the most genuinely, if originally conceived,
Cloisonist examples in the artist's total *oeuvre*.

Apart from its excellent condition and
extremely high artistic quality, the *Undine* is of

Whither Are We Going? (W 561)[6]. According to
Gauguin's account this latter painting was executed as a philosophic testimonial piece prior to his
attempted suicide, and in it the seated Eve has
become a gray-haired crone who in accepting
imminent death "terminates the legend" of this
many-figured composition. The seated Eve was
hence for Gauguin equally at home in Arles, Brittany, Peru and Tahiti, which further universalizes
her symbolization of human anguish when confronted with the knowledge of impending death.
Perhaps the vivid primary hues in which the San
Antonio *Eve* is rendered were meant to suggest a
last vestige of earthly Paradise before she begins
her life of trial and torment leading to death and
burial according to the ancient traditions of Peru.

6   Pickvance, *Drawings*, p. 27, pl. 41, has pointed
out in *Nirvana* (cat. no. 68) the serpentine configuration looping the arm of Meyer de Haan ends
as a large "G" of Gauguin's signature. Similarly
one may speculate that the snake of the San
Antonio *Eve* should be equated with the same type
of open "G" as found in the actual signature. If so,
this would suggest that Gauguin considered himself the "liar" of his pidgin French inscription,
which would constitute a disguised element of
iconography more blatantly contained in the
well-known self-identification of the *Be in Love*
and the *Loss of Virginity* (cat. no. 70).

SEE COLOUR PLATE 1.

Fig. 68
Paul Gauguin *Be Mysterious* 1890, linden wood carved and painted (Musée d'Orsay, Paris).

intriguing interest as to its originally intended content. Andersen, in the light of his overall Freudian interpretation of Gauguin's art, has seen this Woman in the Waves as yet another "fallen Eve" condemned by "her shame and guilt. . ." to a life "courting death rather than truth, maturing to the stage of Contemplative Anguish before proceeding along a fixed route to the movement of Abandonment, at which point she throws herself with a cry into overwhelming waters."[1] In these and other similar passages Andersen suggests that this God-abandoned image of doomsday is pictured at the point of a watery suicide, but in this instance the evidence is less congenial to such an interpretation than for numerous other cases he cites. For one thing, the title *Undine*, which Gauguin himself gave this painting as early as the 1891 Drouot sale (no. 14; p.v. 15) refers not to a fallen mortal, but to a sea nymph who remains soulless only so long as she hasn't married a mortal and borne him a child. The earlier title "Dans les Vagues" also overlaps with the Latin root of "Undine," which means "wave" as might well have been known to the artist. Indeed, his figure "undulates" as much as the waves which surround her, and if she is uttering a cry, who can say whether it is one of despair or of joy?

There is further reason to believe this image to be suggestive, however temporary, of joy rather than pain. Gray argues that both the pre-Christian menhirs for which Brittany is famous and, by extension, the lesser "black rocks" found along its coastline were treated by the superstitious though Christianized inhabitants with veneration and used as the "centre of rites performed to assure marriage and fertility."[2] This lingering survival of ancient European phallic worship was certainly well known to Gauguin as must have been the widespread mythological association, ancient and modern, between water, especially the ocean, and childbirth. The Undine image in the "Aux Roches noires" illustration is thus better interpreted as an antipode to the fearful Eve, as an image of life renewing vitality rather than sin and death, even if this is to be her ultimate fate. In the Cairo painting *Life and Death* (*W* 335; *see discussion* cat. no. 59), the female symbolizing life has in fact successfully returned from an encounter with the waves and is obviously not fear-ridden in contrast to her Eve-death-mummy companion. The Undine of both catalogue illustration and painting functions as a metaphor of procreation, somehow intermediate between the two figures of *Life and Death*. Her iconography is hence in keeping with

the Western Venus of the Sea iconography, and her spiritualized intercourse with the waves of the sea is no less evocative of ritualized love-making for being viewed voyeuristically from behind. Just as the seated Eve image was incorporated in the *Be in Love* panel of 1889, the Woman of the Waves became the central and largest image of *Be Mysterious* (*fig. 68*), the pendant piece executed the following year. Whether Aurier was fully justified in describing this latter work in 1891 as a celebration of "the pure joys of esotericism," (*see* p. 59, *above*), his characterization occurred only following personal discussions with Gauguin and about the time the painter assigned the "Undine" title to his 1889 painting. In its multiple references to Breton folk superstition and the more exalted connotations of the Undine and Venus of the Sea myths, Gauguin here evokes a sense of mystery about woman in her procreative role. Animality blends with spirituality, as is appropriate to Undine's status as a soulless being seeking salvation through marriage and childbirth and to the related rites which Breton women still practised among the black rocks of their coastal shores.

[1] Andersen, *Paradise Lost*, p. 90.

[2] Gray, pp. 43-44.

61.

The Yellow Christ   *W* 327
c. September 1889 (finished later?)
oil on canvas: 92 × 72 cm
Signed and dated lower right: *P. Gauguin* [18]
89

Lent by the Albright-Knox Art Gallery, Buffalo.
TORONTO ONLY

There is very little contemporary documentation about this painting's (pl.22) creation and intended meaning. Gauguin himself did not refer to it in his preserved correspondence, and it was never exhibited in his lifetime. Both these facts are in part due to its having entered the collection of Emile Schuffenecker, probably upon Gauguin's return to Paris from Le Pouldu in February 1890, and Gauguin's not wanting to advertise the fact to Théo van Gogh who had been sent his *Breton Calvary: The Green Christ* (cat. no. 65) the previous November.[1] By this time Gauguin certainly knew that Vincent heartily disapproved of the reintroduction of traditional Christian iconography in contemporary painting and that this attitude would be shared within Impressionist circles.[2] Ironically, although he chose not to include either this painting, the *Calvary* or the *Christ in the Garden of Olives* in the Hôtel Drouot auction of February 1891, it was these paintings and the *Vision after the Sermon* which Aurier cited in his contemporary article on Gauguin as exemplary of Symbolism in painting.[3] Equally ironic, in the second most important article written about Gauguin at the time of the sale, Octave Mirbeau, who shortly thereafter purchased the *Garden of Olives*, singled out *The Yellow Christ* for exclusive discussion of what he termed Gauguin's "disquieting and savory mixture of barbaric splendor, of Catholic liturgy, of Hindu reverie, of Gothic imagery, of obscure and subtle symbolism."[4] Despite certain exaggerations and inaccuracies in his account, Mirbeau, who received and returned a visit from Gauguin as research for the article, thus provides our only and best account of what the artist himself intended.[5]

The author begins by describing the crucifix as "a badly squared calvary" supporting a "Papuan divinity" made from a tree trunk by a local artisan and painted a sad autumnal yellow similar to the Breton hillside. This "piteous and barbaric Christ" is surrounded by kneeling peasant women who do not pray or look at the Calvary despite their enactment of a Pardon ritual, the obligations of which are only too gladly over for the three other figures fleeing between the red apple trees. The Christ

figure, for Mirbeau, has such an effect of "indescribable melancholy" that he seems to look down at the figures representing a "miserable and uncomprehending humanity" as if to say, "And yet, if my martyrdom was in vain?" While one senses a degree of literary licence in the thoughts or lack thereof attributed by Mirbeau to the figures of *The Yellow Christ*, his general interpretation of it as suffused with melancholy and resignation can hardly be challenged. Certainly the autumnal setting is appropriate to this interpretation and, like the identification of Breton crucifix types, costumes and religious customs, is all but sure to have been supplied by Gauguin's own verbal accounts.

Various other points of information about the subject matter of *The Yellow Christ* have become known over the years. At first confused with crucifix images at Nizon and Le Pouldu, it is now generally accepted that both the Christ figure and

his support derive from a polychrome wood sculpture found on the left nave wall of the Chapel at Trémalo (*fig. 69*), a rural district located on an

[1] See *W* 327 for record of provenance and early citations; the present interpretations of the issue of provenance rests on the absence of any mention of the canvas to Vincent, Théo, Bernard and Schuffenecker, which implies that Gauguin had the painting with him in Le Pouldu, autumn 1889, and presumably brought it to Paris in February 1890.

[2] See cat. no. 66; *P-I*; p. 441, illustrates this reaction by Pissarro.

[3] Aurier, p. 218.

[4] Cited and translated in *P-I*, p. 440; see also p. 456, nos. 56, 59.

[5] *P-I*, p. 439.

Fig. 69
Polychrome Crucifix,
date unknown,
in the chapel at Trémalo
(photograph B.M. Welsh-Ovcharov).

Fig. 70
The Passion of Christ, colour print popular early
nineteenth century
(Picard-Guerin, Caen).

SEE COLOUR PLATE 22.

elevated plain just to the north of Pont-Aven.[6] An extant pencil drawing of the crucifix may be all that Gauguin produced in the chapel itself, since a small watercolour was probably produced after the painting, which of course was realized with a landscape background setting.[7] Pickvance has noted that it is the town of Pont-Aven behind which rises the Hill of Saint Margaret which is depicted here and in *The Swineherd* (*W* 255), and the latter painting includes the tower of the church of Pont-Aven, which is perhaps purposefully blocked from view by the crucifix in *The Yellow Christ*. The same author has also observed that the two figures to the left of the crucifix are variations on the small figures upper left corner of the *Vision*, and one is struck by the coincidence that in our 1889 painting the single figure lower right is viewed from the rear and cut off at the shoulders, as were the foreground figures of its 1888 predecessor.[8] As with the crucifix drawing, Gauguin likely laid his three foreground females in from his stock of outline drawings in sketchbooks, whether or not these were once done from a live model.

This hypothesis of working from outline drawings for the figures is not so easily extended to the landscape. No such landscape drawing has as yet come to light, and *The Swineherd* was executed in 1888 and therefore presumably stored in Paris when Gauguin produced the Buffalo example. One can say nonetheless that the scene was quite familiar to Gauguin, whose Pont-Aven *atelier* was located on the slope, just outside the town, known as "Lezaven," not far below the spot from which the view of *The Swineherd* and *The Yellow Christ* were demonstrably taken.[9] This does not rule out the possibility that the latter painting was completed along with the *Green Christ* late in the year in Le Pouldu, but at least demonstrates that the composition was likely determined and perhaps the final canvas at least already begun while he was still in Pont-Aven. And unless the yellow autumn colouration be considered an afterthought from Le Pouldu, the logical period of origin would be September, after returning from his August stay and before his definitive move in October to Le Pouldu. Since one can also specify July 1888 as the month in which Gauguin executed his archetypal Cloisonist portrait, *La Belle Angèle: Mme Sartre* (*fig. 34*), neither can one claim that *The Yellow Christ* should be considered the first painting of 1889 to be involved with a combination of religious and secular iconography.

This subtle ambiguity between the here-and-now and the eternal makes *The Yellow Christ* an effective witness of the turn Gauguin's art was taking in the last half of 1889. Where the *Vision* had to be explained by Gauguin to his closest colleague before the conflation of Biblical story and contemporary experience became apparent, *The Yellow Christ*, with its iconic simplicity of form, suffers rather than benefits from Mirbeau's literary embellishments regarding the thoughts and behaviour of the various figures depicted. His mention of a Pardon celebration, while interesting as possibly supplied by Gauguin, is not as crucial to the interpretation of this painting as it is for Bernard's *Breton Women in the Meadow* (cat. no. 104). What Mirbeau missed in Gauguin's "obscure and subtle symbolism" is as important as what he revealed. It is difficult for this reader, for example, to avoid reading the three kneeling women as Breton peasant surrogates for the "three Maries" iconography as found and more easily recognized in the *Green Christ*. And does not their isolation in a relatively bare field, set off by a stone fence over which one must climb for entrance or exit suggest a holy terrain atop a mountain, in contrast to the secular world of the town below? For Gauguin himself this iconography would have been fortified by the knowledge that the hill in the distance at right was named after a saint and that the chapel of Trémalo, although not depicted, was located in the distance at the left.

In an 1885 letter to Schuffenecker (*M*XI), Gauguin had already speculated on the iconography of abstract geometric forms, attributing both expressive and symbolic qualities to various lines, directions and two-dimensional shapes. In particular, the straight line is said to suggest infinity and the curved line to delimit creation, ideas which it is possible to coordinate with the "infinite" nature of the Christ on his crucifix and the closed or material forms of the women, apple trees and landscape contours. Immediately hereafter Gauguin observes rhetorically, "The numbers three and seven, have they been sufficiently analysed?" Given the traditional religious associations of these "mystical" numbers, is it not possible that the two groups of three persons, which with Christ added make seven, would have reflected this early preoccupation on the artist's part? Finally, as is frequently noted, Gauguin's slightly later *Self-Portrait with the Yellow Christ* (*W* 324) makes clear his dual nature by including both the crucifix image and his grotesque self-portrait stoneware pot as symbols of his divine and earth-bound qualities.[10] For the artist then and for viewers ever since, *The Yellow Christ* has represented one of Gauguin's most compelling images, in which Cloisonist-Synthetist elements of style blend harmoniously with a Symbolist approach to iconography and content.[11].

6   Chassé, *Pont-Aven*, p. 25, instigated the Nizon confusion, and in *Son temps* compounded the issue with the citation of a possible *Le Pouldu* model, p. 84 (see *W* 327). F. Dauchot, "Le Christ jaune de Gauguin," *Gazette des Beaux-Arts*, XXXXIV (July-August 1954), pp. 66-68, first identified the source as the Trémalo image. Fig. 69 also shows that Gauguin consciously excluded the "death skull" image seen there from his painted version.

7   Pickvance, *Drawings*, Pls. 38-39, reproduces and documents both variants of *The Yellow Christ*. That the drawing (Pl. 38) was done *in situ* is proved by the inclusion of the animal lower right, which is to be seen upper left in my photograph of the Trémalo "Yellow Christ" in its original and present setting.

8   Pickvance, *Tate Entries*, no. 26.

9   *GBA Gauguin*, pp. 88-94, with a map and photographic evidence, provides the basis for but strangely does not reach the conclusion of the present author, which were arrived at originally by visits to the area.

10 E.g. Pickvance, *Tate Entries*, no. 29, and Andersen, *Paradise*, p. 7.

11 Among other pictorial associations for the present painting which can be cited are: *cloisonné* crucifixes in the Byzantine tradition (*fig. 2*), *Puvis de Chavannes*, Japanese prints for the female figures (see Wattenmaker, p. 120) and the many *Images d'Epinal* (*fig. 70*) upon which his conception may have also depended (see exh. cat., *Images populaires françaises*, Paris: Paul Proute, 1979, *passim*).

62.

Breton Calvary: Pardon in Brittany
fall 1889
gouache on board; 26 × 32.4 cm
No signature or date
Lent by a private collection, New York

Chassé was the first to publish this Gauguin
gouache rendering of a subject which he called
with understandable equivocation "Breton
Calvary" and "Pardon in Brittany."[1] Long before
the issue had been joined as to whether Bernard's
Breton Women in a Meadow (cat. no. 104) was a
religious subject or just, iconographically speaking,
another "Sunday afternoon on the island
peninsula of Brittany," the present painting proves
that the issue was never so clear cut. Presumably
executed in fall 1889 at the inn of Marie Henry at

Le Pouldu, it includes a praying figure at left of the
sepulchre which patently derives from the same
image as represented in a zincograph of early 1889
in Paris (cat. no. 589).[2] At the same time the
central image of mourning is a conflation of the
Breton Calvary: Green Christ and an as yet
unknown source in Breton sarcophagus image of
the dead Christ.[3] In the background is an
unequivocal, albeit free, quotation from Bernard's
Breton Women, which indicates the ambiguity of
religious *vs* secular imagery, especially for the
artists who were attempting to deal with this issue.

This modest-sized painting may indeed be of
greatest interest for its iconographic make-up, but
it is also one of Gauguin's purest examples of
Cloisonist style.[4]

1 Chassé, *Pont-Aven*, ill. p. 27, is labelled *Calvaire
   Breton*, while the text (p. 43) describes the subject

as a *Pardon en Bretagne*.

2 The provenance is given *ibid.*, p. 43. Although
   overlooked in the first edition of Wildenstein, it is
   planned for inclusion in the revised edition. M.
   Malingue, "Du Nouveau sur Gauguin" *L'Oeil*,
   no. 55/56 (July-Aug., 1959), p. 35, gives the
   same provenance.

3 However, the type of Calvary is that illustrated in
   Andersen, *Paradise*, fig. 69. Chassé, *ibid.*,
   although recognizing the unity of the sarcophagus
   and mourners from their common gray
   colouration, was nonetheless misled by Gauguin's
   conflation into detailing the subject matter of this
   central image as three souls of the dead behind the
   tomb of a saint.

4 It was thus first exhibited in *Japonisme*; see
   discussion by G. Needham, pp. 124, 136, cat. no.
   186.

63.

Breton Peasant Girl Spinning:
Joan of Arc   W 329
autumn 1889
fresco (transferred to canvas): 116 × 58 cm
Signed and dated lower right: *en l'an*
[18] 89 P Go
Lent anonymously
TORONTO ONLY

This is one (pl.17) of two paintings by Gauguin
(the other is *The Goose*, W 383) which he added
to a wall of the inn of Marie Henry in Le Pouldu
(*fig. 71*) as complements to Meyer de Haan's
Breton Women Scutching Flax (cat. no. 126).
Probably because she knew these paintings to be
covered over with wallpaper at the time, Marie
Henry did not include them in her *circa* 1920-21
description of the decorative scheme for the dining
room of her inn which she had previously disman-
tled and taken with her when the inn was sold in
1893.[1] The frescoes came to light again only in
1924, when a reported seven layers of wallpaper
were removed during a refurbishing of the building by its current owners.[2] Because the two Gauguin paintings and that by Meyer de Haan went to
different owners, they have not been seen together
again until the present exhibition in which the two
major paintings are reunited.

The fresco by Gauguin has become known as
Joan of Arc, but without the authority of any
known earlier source or, until very recently, any
supportive explanation. That the angel is bringing
Joan the sword with which she will drive the English from France, that the spinning materials she
holds symbolize her virginity and that the tree may
refer to the stake at which she was martyred are all
plausible suggestions but only if one is first convinced that the attributed title had some basis in
the time of Gauguin.[3] Hence, it is necessary to
question the appropriateness of this title until new
evidence of a compelling nature is offered in its
support.

There is, moreover, one heretofore unpublished reference to it by Gauguin, which does not
mention Joan of Arc or any other legendary per-
sonage. In describing the undertaking to Vincent
in mid-December 1889 (*G32*), Gauguin merely
states that, having been so impressed with de
Haan's wall painting, he "made in turn a peasant
girl spinning at the edge of the sea, her dog, her
cow." In remarking further that he had done only
a single religious painting that year—he must have
meant either the *Christ in the Garden of Olives* or
the *Green Christ*, both of which he had sent to

Fig. 71
Photograph of the dining room of the inn of Marie
Henry,
from left: Gauguin: *Joan of Arc*; Meyer de Haan,
Scutching Flax.
(photograph *c.* 1924 by Victor Honoré,
Quimperlé).

Théo—Gauguin was clearly dissimulating about
the inclusion of an angel along with his "peasant
girl spinning," but this is not enough to prove that
the painting was intended to illustrate a specific
sacred or historical legend.[4]

Instead one is inclined to look for a role in
which the figure could be interpreted, according to
Gauguin's habit, as emblematic of some general
condition of mankind, usually a tragic or doom-
filled one. In this context, the theme of spinning
not only logically follows upon de Haan's *Scutching Flax*, but is a further instance of his general
theme of *Labour*. It is thus more likely that the
angel is symbolic here of the expulsion from the
Garden of Eden, which ensures a life of toil at
spinning and cow-herding, than of a promise of
glorious martyrdom. This theme was in fact

treated explicitly in another painting on display at
the inn of Marie Henry with another angel per-
forming his appointed role to order.[5] The bare
tree, so similar to that in the *Garden of Olives*,
might well have been meant to suggest some kind
of martyrdom in this land of calvaries, but again
on a more general level than reference to a specific
legend would entail. The landscape background in
this painting is related to those in the *Green Christ*
and the *Garden of Olives* (probably showing a
view of the Grand Sables beach at Le Pouldu),
which also encourages an interpretation of the girl
as projecting the "passive acceptance" of her
dolorous fate that Gauguin several times pointed
out about this time in reference to both himself
and the Breton peasantry.

In style, too, no one single source dominates.

As the mural decoration might have implied to the artist, there is a sense of late Medieval style, which then was summed up in the idea of the "Italian primitives" of the age of Giotto and was highly respected by Symbolist poets and painters. One thinks as well of both Egyptianizing and Japanist tendencies, which Théo van Gogh, not all too admiringly, felt had become dominant in Gauguin's art in late 1889 (*T*19). Egypt and the Orient help explain the sharply silhouetted outlines and flatness of the girl's body, whereas the Japanese wood block print best explains the dramatic contrast between the looming foreground and tiny background images, symbolized in the Japanese regatta which populates the horizon upper left.[6] Admittedly, chance determined the elongated proportion of Gauguin's mural undertaking, but the resemblance to a *kakemono-e* Japanese wall hanging is nonetheless striking. Informed as it is by remembrances of Cézannesque brush work as well, this fortuitously preserved painting by Gauguin records the brilliance of imagination with which he managed to "synthétise" so many influences into a style all his own.

SEE COLOUR PLATE 17.

1   This description was provided at his request to Chassé for *Pont-Aven* published 1921.

2   See Chassé, *Son temps*, which text of 1955, unfortunately, does little to correct the earlier account. *P-I*, p. 290, no. 40, perpetuates the myth (*Life*, May 1, 1950) that the American painters Abraham Rattner and Isidore Levy actually discovered the paintings. See *W* 329 for obviously correct contrary evidence.

3   V. Jirat-Wasiutynski, *Gauguin in the Context of Symbolism* (New York: Garland, 1979), pp. 212-14, was the first to this writer's knowledge to attempt a justification of the Joan of Arc title in terms of its iconography, which he sees as involving the hermetic tradition with its emphasis on the androgyny (in his opinion, as exemplified by the saintly Madeleine Bernard, see *M*LXIX). The present writer's reservations do not preclude this possibility but only await their further substantiation.

4   For this type of peasant girl spinning see Robert Herbert 1, exh. cat. *Jean François Millet*, London: Arts Council of Great Britain–Hayward Gallery, 1976, no. 128, *Goat Girl of the Auvergne* (Musée d'Orsay, Paris).

5   I.e., *W* 390, a work now owned by the Yale Art Gallery.

6   Such "regattas" are found in Vincent's Japanese print collection (*Japanese Prints*, p. 36), and in *Japonisme* (p. 10, fig. 7).

64.

The Breton Goose Boy   *W* 367

c. October 1889

oil on canvas: 92 × 73 cm

Signed and dated lower left: *P. Gauguin* [*18*] *89*

Lent by Mrs. Catherine B. Taylor, Mrs. Camilla B. Royall and Mrs. Sarah B. Hrdy on loan to the Museum of Fine Arts, Houston.

This painting does not occur on any of Gauguin's lists of sales, exhibitions or ownership and is first recorded as having been sold by the firm of Bernheim in 1906. The Wildenstein catalogue designation *Breton Goose Boy* is nonetheless quite accurate since there is little besides the boy and goose in the painting which is distinctive enough as subject matter to warrant inclusion in a title. In 1888 at Pont-Aven Gauguin produced two paintings featuring geese (*W* 277-78), one of which (probably *W* 277, the larger canvas) is likely to have figured as No. 9, *A Painting* (p.v., "Geese at Play") of the 1891 Hôtel Drouot sale. This fact is only of interest in reference to the 1889 Houston *Goose Boy* insofar as it highlights the more restrained mood which informed the majority of Gauguin's paintings executed in Le Pouldu, an isolated locale in which the life of the peasantry, young and old alike, was devoted to the hard task of survival in a harsh and sombre environment. That the setting is Le Pouldu rather than Pont-Aven, where Gauguin had spent most of summer 1889, is indicated by the broad expanse of pasture presumably sloping towards the sea and the yellow foliage of the three deciduous trees which suggest the fall season after his October 2 arrival at the coastal hamlet.

There fortunately has come down to us an eye-witness account of Gauguin's working methods in producing his landscape paintings while at Le Pouldu; namely, that of Marie Henry, keeper of the inn where Gauguin and Meyer de Haan stayed beginning in late 1889.[1] As she recalled, they worked both mornings and afternoons out-of-doors, weather permitting, choosing between drawing in sketchbooks or painting with full equipment according to the conditions of light. Only after long hours of study of a chosen subject setting and its analysis in terms of "abundant sketchbook notes," was it considered appropriate to begin work with paint on canvas, and then only when the most preferred conditions of light were present. However, once the setting had been so studied that Gauguin could claim it already had been completed in his

imagination, he then could commence to execute his composition in short order and preferably without interruption. After tracing in the compositional outlines in Prussian blue, he thereafter filled in the areas with brush strokes on either a vertical or oblique axis. Although he painted in front of nature, he never used live models, both for the sake of economy and because he had built up a repertory of figural types in his notebook studies.

One could scarcely ask for a better example to illustrate the results of this method than the Houston *Goose Boy*. Not only are the outlines of his compositional design in blue in large part visible, but the infilling conforms in general to his preference for parallel hatching in vertical and oblique directions. Several pages from a contemporary notebook (*fig. 72*), though not used specifically in this painting, document the accuracy of Marie Henry's memory in reference to

both individual figures and general composition.[2] These bare outline studies thus would have performed a major function in Gauguin's working procedure which their diminutive size would not normally lead one to expect. They must often have provided the artist a complete figure for use in an appropriate setting, which otherwise would have been bereft of figural imagery altogether. To what extent Gauguin's choice of colours was based on natural appearance or else involved intuitively arbitrary preferences by the artist is difficult to say. Some combination of imitation and self-assertion must have been operative in the Houston painting, where abstract decoration and observed natural appearance so harmoniously combine.

1   This account, as told by her long-time confidant, a M. Mothéré, was produced *c*. 1920-21 upon request for C. Chassé, *Pont-Aven*, pp. 33-34.

2   -Huyghe, *Carnet, e.g.*, pp. 160, 173, 202.

Fig. 72
Paul Gauguin
Notebook, three studies of Breton subjects, 1889,
Arles notebook.

65.

The Breton Calvary: The Green Christ   *W* 328
c. October-November 1889
oil on canvas: 92 × 73 cm
Signed and dated lower left: P. Gauguin [18]89
Musées Royaux des Beaux-Arts de Belgique,
Brussels
AMSTERDAM ONLY

Although often seen as a pendant to *The Yellow Christ* (cat. no. 61) and thus popularly known as the *Green Christ*, Gauguin's own citation of this painting (pl.21) as "Calvaire breton"[1] is a more exact and significant title. Just as *The Yellow Christ* was presented as a roadside crucifix despite its origin in the polychromed wood sculpture from within the chapel of Trémalo located just outside Pont-Aven, so the stone Calvary sculpture adjacent to the church at the inland village of Nizon which was also located near Pont-Aven (*fig. 73*), was transferred by the artist's power of imagination to the dunes of the coastal hamlet of Le Pouldu. Gauguin further transformed his source by eliminating the *ecce homo* and crucifix images from the upper levels of the sculpture in order to concentrate upon the *pietà* at the base. As in his so-called *Pardon in Brittany* (cat. no. 62) gouache of probably the same date, an even more Cloisonist variation on a theme of lamentation, he employs his group of three Maries as a foil for the mixture of sacred and profane activities depicted as typical of the living Breton population. Since it was cited along with three other paintings having religious themes in Aurier's article on Gauguin, *The Breton Calvary* may be considered one of the

handful of paintings which allowed Aurier to associate Gauguin with his definition of "Symbolism in painting."

Gauguin apparently sent the *Breton Calvary* to Théo along with the wood relief *Soyez amoureuses* sometime in November 1889, and, upon hearing that both Théo and Degas were uncertain of his intended content, provided some comment on the two pieces in a fourteen-page, still largely unpublished letter (*G*21). After stressing that his art is one of suggestion and generality rather than specific explication and summarizing the symbolism of *Soyez amoureuses* as he did in letters to Bernard and Vincent (*M*LXXXVII, *G*29), Gauguin refers to the *Breton Calvary* as follows:

> The same goes for the picture of three women in stone holding Christ. Brittany—simple superstition and desolation. The hill is guarded by a cordon of cows disposed as a calvary [procession]. I have sought in this picture that which fully breathes of belief, passive suffering, a primitive religious style and the cry of a majestic nature. I am at fault for not being strong enough to express this better, but not at fault *for having the thought*.

Whether or not here, as is often thought for his other representations of Christ, Gauguin has suggested his own personal features, he clearly identifies unavoidable suffering with the lot of the Breton peasantry as expressed both in its regional sculpture and present hard mode of life.

A second more detailed exegesis of this painting by the artist has been published by M. Malingue, based on the annotations found along

Fig. 73

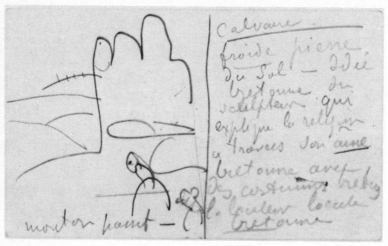

Fig. 74

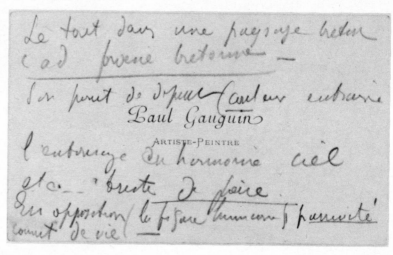

Fig. 75

with an identifying sketch of the figural composition on a calling card (*fig. 74*) the artist left with Aurier in Paris, either during the first months of 1890 or, equally possible, during winter 1890-91 when the critic finally was preparing his article on Gauguin for the *Mercure*.[2] Here Gauguin comments (*fig. 75*):

Calvary, cold stone of the earth—Breton idea of sculpture which explains religion according

[1] Apart from Gauguin's descriptions of it cited below, it was listed as "Le Calvaire breton" when sold in 1891 and 1893 by Boussod and Valadon (Rewald, "Goupil," p. 91), and Aurier, "Gauguin, *Mercure*, p. 218, used *Calvaire* in juxtaposition to *Christ jaune*.

[2] Gauguin doubtless met Bernard's friend Aurier at the time of the Volpini exhibition, whereafter he published articles in Aurier's journal *Le Moderniste*. However, his paintings with overt religious symbolism were executed only later in the year in Brittany, and Gauguin would not have had any particular reason to explain the meaning of the *Breton Calvary* or *Christ in the Garden of Olives*, especially in such urgent fashion as the calling card notations imply, before Aurier had committed himself to the article on Gauguin for the *Mercure de France*. From winter 1889-90 both paintings were on consignment to Théo's Boussod and Valadon Gallery, and on March 19, 1890, Théo wrote Vincent (*T29*) of Aurier's intention to visit the shop in order to see paintings by Gauguin in connection with the planned article, which only appeared, however, a year later.

Fig. 73
Breton Calvary at Nixon near Pont-Aven, front view
(photograph B.M. Welsh-Ovcharov).

Fig. 74
Paul Gauguin
Sketch of and notes on the *Breton Calvary* to Albert Aurier on the back of the artist's calling card, 1890-1
(Rijksmuseum Vincent van Gogh, Amsterdam).

Fig. 75
Paul Gauguin
Notes on the *Breton Calvary* for Albert Aurier on the artist's calling card, 1890-1
(Rijksmuseum Vincent van Gogh, Amsterdam).

SEE COLOUR PLATE 21.

to the Breton soul, with Breton costumes [and] the local Breton colour. A passive lamb. All this in a Breton landscape, which is to say, Breton poesy. Its point of departure (colour animates the setting in harmony [with the] sky, etc. . . . a sad undertaking). In contrast (the human figure)—poverty known in life—.

In these words Gauguin comes as close as he ever would in defining what he meant as a Synthetist-Symbolist work of art. A Calvary is not a narrative; it represents the Breton soul, its costumes and landscape. This poetic interpretation of all of Brittany ancient and modern may not seem objective today, but it doubtless informed Gauguin's title of this important canvas as "Breton Calvary."

There is one more possible, indeed likely, iconographic source for this unusual painting, which deserves special attention: the reference and tribute to Vincent's *La Berceuse* (cat. no. 34). Vincent's painting of this subject was well known to Gauguin, who doubtless would have remembered that Vincent had been working on this very painting when "the incident of the ear occurred" and who thereafter may have been offered one version thereof.[3] In fact two out of the three praying figures in the *Yellow Christ* employ the type of hand-grasp of the *La Berceuse*, whose surrogates in patience and moral steadfastness they may be presumed to be. The *La Berceuse* was, of course, itself a notorious instance of Gauguin influence on Vincent of a year earlier. From a letter of late January (*CL* 574) to Théo we know that Vincent had just written to Gauguin and explained his idea that *La Berceuse* should be seen as the central panel of a triptych arrangement with sunflower images serving as the two "wings." He also reminded Gauguin of their former conversations about "the fishermen of Iceland and . . . their mournful isolation, exposed to all dangers, alone on the sad sea," a situation he doubtless felt Gauguin in former times had personally experienced. Since a letter (*CL* 558b) of the previous October associates Gauguin with the novel *Pêcheur d'Islande* by Pierre Loti, we can be sure of Vincent's source for the spiritual meaning of *La Berceuse* in which he intended "to paint a picture in such a way that sailors, who are at once children and martyrs, seeing it in the cabin of their Icelandic fishing boat, would feel the old sense of being rocked, come over them and remember their own lullabies" (that is, CL 574).[4] With Vincent's intended meaning for *La Berceuse* so well-known to him, one can understand how Gauguin might

have expected both van Gogh brothers to recognize his maritime setting and the cord held by his own Breton shepherdess as a subtle tribute to Vincent's painting, even if his inclusion of a pietà reference lends his *Calvary* a more overt symbol of universal melancholy and suffering.[5] In contrast to Vincent's aim to relieve human misery, Gauguin of course depicts it here as something borne stoically by the people of Brittany and, so his words imply, by himself in a period of personal hardship and disappointment. We may never be certain if Gauguin identified himself more with the black "passive lamb" extreme lower right, with the martyred Christ, or with both, but we can feel sure that he expected his audience to sense the theme of suffering which he had sought to convey.

3 In *CL* 573 and 574 of late January, Vincent spoke of his illness having occurred when the first *La Berceuse* was underway and in *CL* 592 of May 1889 he instructs Théo to offer versions to both Gauguin and Bernard.

4 Roskill, p. 197, first cited Gauguin's inclusion of a woman holding ropes for rocking a cradle in his own *Green Christ*.

5 Wattenmaker, pp. 120-21, has suggested that a figure in *The Childhood of Saint Genevieve* by Puvis de Chavannes may have played a supportive role in the Christ image of the *Breton Calvary* and also the *Nude Breton Boy* (*W* 339). The latter figure might itself be thought a paraphrase of the Christ figure from Nizon.

66.
Christ in the Garden of Olives   *W* 326
c. November 1889
oil on canvas: 73 × 92 cm
Signed and dated lower right: *P. Gauguin* [18] *89*

Lent by the Norton Gallery and School of Art, West Palm Beach, Florida

This well-known painting by Gauguin clearly was felt by the artist to have had a considerable importance within his personal development. Having outlined in a letter (*G* 29) of mid-November 1889 to Vincent his current artistic credo as the pursuit of abstraction and synthetic form and colour, he went on to describe this painting as follows:

> I have at my residence a thing which I have not sent (to your brother) and which would irritate you I believe. It's a Christ in the Garden of Olives: a blue-green evening sky, inclined trees in shades of purple, violet earth and Christ enveloped in a sombre ochre garment with vermilion hair. This canvas is not intended to be understood. I shall keep it for a long while. Herewith included is a drawing which will give a vague idea of the thing.

One may suspect that, despite these words, Gauguin was fishing for Vincent's approval of a painting in which he doubtless would have recognized Gauguin's features in the Christ figure, and hoping that Vincent would encourage Théo to accept it at least on consignment, if not purchase. This was not to be the case since immediately upon receipt of this letter with sketch (*fig.* 76) Vincent wrote November 17 to Théo (*CL* 614) that he was "not an admirer of Gauguin's *Christ in the Garden of Olives*, for example, of which he sent me a sketch." Vincent also stated here "that it is better to attack things with simplicity than to seek after abstractions" and makes clear his own answer to the reintroduction of religious imagery by Gauguin and Bernard would be embodied in a series of "Women Picking Olives" (*F* 654-66) which would reflect a scene experienced in a natural setting. Vincent's premonition of even greater disillusionment with Bernard's Medievalizing treatment of the same subject (*fig.* 77), once a promised photograph of it was received, was well borne out as he stated in letters to his brother (*CL* 615) and to Gauguin (lost) and Bernard (*B* 21), the latter of which was so negative in its criticism that it appears to have terminated correspondence between the two men.

Handwritten letter text:

verdâtres - Car malgré l'inscription les personnes ont l'air triste en contradiction avec le titre. Sur ce bois ciré il y a des reflets que donne la lumière sur les parties bosses qui donne de la richesse -

Je vais l'envoyer à Paris dans quelques jours. Peut être celui plaira plus que ma peinture. De Haann vous dit bien des choses.

Cordialement à vous

P. Gauguin

P.S. Je sais que vous fatiguez quand vous écrivez aussi je ne demande pas de lettre (malgré tout le plaisir que j'ai à vous lire -

Le service militaire de Bernard a été remis à un an pour (Santé) -

au Pouldu près Quimper (finistère)

Fig. 76
Paul Gauguin
watercolour of *Christ in the Garden*,
part of a letter November 1889 to Vincent van
Gogh
(Rijksmuseum Vincent van Gogh, Amsterdam).

Vincent's disappointment aside, the Norton Gallery *Christ* manifests precepts of composition and content which were at the heart of Gauguin's own most progressive thinking about art. The retention of still somewhat Cézannesque brushwork notwithstanding, the unbalanced asymmetrical composition and the flattened contortions of the Christ figure give the design a Japanese quality which Gauguin spoke of approvingly in his letter to Vincent. Probably based on a general sensitivity to widely used modes of figural depiction within Japanese popular prints rather than a specific model (however, compare the Christ with *fig.* 5), the pose is also rather similar to that of the Breton peasant women in the *Breton Calvary*. While the inclined pose of Christ must in part reflect the fact that Jesus fell in prayer during this episode in the Biblical accounts, it also contains a hint at the *pietà* theme of the *Breton Calvary*, especially since his leaning is echoed in the storm-induced inclinations of the trees seen at rear which contrast with the upright position of the central tree trunk, itself so obviously suggestive of the pole of Breton crucifixes. Indeed, the setting of the Christ approximates that of the *Breton Calvary* and presumably is a dune landscape at Le Pouldu, although the Biblical account of Gethsemane scarcely allows for an ocean in the background. In iconographic type, then, Gauguin's self-identification with the Christ figure includes allusions to not only the sorrowing Christ in the Garden of Olives, but also the Crucifixion, Pietà and (thanks to the hands crossed in front) the Ecce Homo (Man of Sorrows) pilloried after judgment as well.

Gauguin's most personal interpretation of this painting was provided on the calling card left for Aurier (*fig.* 78) in which he gave the following brief summary of its meaning:

> Christ: special sorrow of treason and of the
> heart applying to the Jesus of today and
> tomorrow. A small explanatory group. The
> whole [forms a] *sombre* harmony: sombre
> colours and supernatural red.

While the "supernatural red" of the hair may refer to the bloody drops of sweat experienced by Christ in his Agony according to *Luke* (XXII: 44), it is also a generalized metaphor for the whole agony of the passion. In identifying his own trials and sorrows as a man and artist with the figure of the agonized Christ, he was laying himself open to the charge of either impiety or self-pity even if such an identification had historical precedent in no lesser an artist than Albrecht Dürer.[1] Whatever reservations Vincent might have felt, Gauguin's notations for Aurier clearly were reflected in the latter's appreciation of this painting: "in this sublime *Garden of Olives* where a Christ with blood-red hair, seated in a desolate site, seems to mourn with the ineffable sorrow of the dream, the agony of chimeras, the treason of contingency, the vanity of the material and of life, and perhaps, of the beyond. . . ." In this characterization Aurier not only spoke with Gauguin's authority; he spoke as a brother spirit, who shared in Gauguin's philosophy of life and art as no one before. This painting can only be considered one of the most important for Aurier's definition of "Symbolism in Painting" in terms of the style of Gauguin. Although Gauguin had written to Vincent that he did not expect to sell the painting for a long time to come, it was in fact sold immediately preceding his first departure for Tahiti in March 1891. The purchaser was, appropriately enough, Octave Mirbeau, the critic who along with Aurier helped most to lionize Gauguin within and without Symbolist literary circles and to assure his success at the Hôtel Drouot sale.[2]

Fig. 77
Emile Bernard
Christ in the Garden of Olives
1889,
oil on canvas
(private collection).

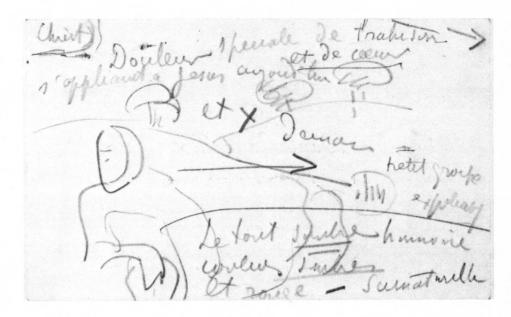

Fig. 78
Paul Gauguin
Notes on the *Christ in the Garden of Olives* to
Albert Aurier on the artist's calling card, 1890-1
(Rijksmuseum Vincent van Gogh, Amsterdam).

[1]   There is no documentation for this analogy, which might best be seen as art historical coincidence. Yet the similarly conceived ideas of these two artists as "men of sorrows" is too striking to be excluded from consideration. At the least it indicates that German and French artists more than three hundred years apart could have felt similar thoughts about identification with Christ while both were apparently having thoughts of impending mortality. See E. Panofsky, *Albrecht Dürer* (Princeton, N.J.: University Press, 1948), vol. 1, frontispiece and p. 241.

[2]   See Rewald, *Goupil*, p. 91.

67.

Cows in a Landscape   *W 343 bis.*
late 1889
oil on board: 26.4 × 32 cm
Signed lower left: *P Go*
Lent by a private collection, New York
TORONTO ONLY

Although quite different in subject matter, this watercolour is related to the *Breton Calvary: Pardon in Brittany* (cat. no. 62) in size, medium, style and common provenance from the inn of Marie Henry at Le Pouldu, where they probably served as wall decorations.[1] Indeed, the Cloisonist style of this work is so marked that one writer has considered it to anticipate Art Nouveau curvilinearity, and has pointed to the wit with

which Gauguin has echoed the forms of the pair of horned cows in the equally bulbous contours of the pollarded willows in the background.[2] This harmony of design is maintained in the equally flat and round contours of the female figure and in the stones of the retaining wall of the roadway cut. The overall decorative effect is achieved here by a combination of evenly distributed parallel brush strokes, with the Cloisonist elements of broad areas of only slightly modulated colouration contained within strongly outlined contours.[3] Along with the gouache *Breton Calvary*, it relates in style to another watercolour depicting two cows and a woman (*W 343*) and to a series of designs for plates, which would seem to be free variations on the themes of animals, flowers, fruit baskets and

figures in native costume used in the hand-painted decorations of traditional Breton faience tableware.[4]

[1] *W 343 bis* ascertains that Marie Henry once owned this watercolour, which implies that Ganguin left it with the numerous other items decorating her inn when he departed Le Pouldu in late 1890. The present writer's ascription of a late 1889 date is from analogy with other Le Pouldu willow tree subjects (*W 343, 346-47, 356-57* and Pickvance, *Drawings,* Pl. VIII), all of which are dated 1889.

[2] Pickvance, *Drawings,* Pl. 46.

[3] Colour ill. in Goldwater, p. 57.

[4] *P-I,* p. 276, illustrates three such plate designs.

68.
Nirvana: Portrait of Meyer de Haan   *W* 320
1889 (1890?)
oil and turpentine on silk: 20 × 29 cm
Signed lower middle on the hand: [*G*]*auguin*;
inscribed lower right: *Nirvana*
Lent by the Wadsworth Atheneum, Hartford;
Ella Gattlup Sumner and Mary Gatlin Sumner
Collection

This pastel-like painting on silk must postdate the use of the background "Aux Roches noires" image as found in the Volpini frontispiece (*see fig. 60*) and cat. nos. 59, 60. Since it bears no inscribed date and was never exhibited in Gauguin's lifetime, there is apparently no easy way to resolve the conflict in the Gauguin literature as to whether this painting was executed in the year 1889 or 1890.[1] Any argument for 1889 would be based upon the use that year of the "Aux Roches noires" as the Volpini catalogue frontispiece, but there is no reason to question the use of this same background at a later date. Indeed, the free yet compositionally so effective use of the Meyer de Haan portrait against the reassembled "Aux Roches noires" background suggests a sophistication of understanding, which

[1] However, the present writer does favour a date of either summer or fall 1889, or shortly following Gauguin's intense involvement with the Eve and Undine imagery in connection with the Volpini exhibition. It must be admitted that the wood panel *Be Mysterious* (*fig. 68*) shows employment of the Undine figure again in summer 1890 (*M*CXXII and G29). This latter letter to Vincent should be redated to summer 1890 because the "bois sculpté" cited there as "plus beau que le premier" was clearly *Be Mysterious*.

could hardly have been achieved in the short period during which De Haan and Gauguin became personally acquainted. It is thus likely that this carefully and exquisitely rendered oil on silk painting was done some time between the period summer 1889 and fall 1890 when the two painters were in intimate contact. The assigned date of 1889-90 thus encompasses a wide range of possibilities, which involve a consideration of Meyer de Haan's production as well.

The use of the imagery of the "Aux Roches noires" Volpini catalogue frontispiece (*fig. 60*) as background for this Cloisonist-Synthetist portrait may be taken for a sign of related but not exactly similar content. Whereas the seated Eve remains a metaphor of Temptation and Death, the Undine has been removed from the waves and placed against a vague rock configuration. Perhaps this latter placement is a veiled allusion to a known fertility ritual, although the interests of compositional balance may also have had an effect. In any case, the small nude female on the beach at left presumably is on her way for an immersion in the sea, thereby hinting at the Undine theme as related to the black rock rituals. At the least one may suppose that some sense of contrast between *thanatos* and *eros* is suggested in the two female figures, one cringing in apprehension and the other baring herself to some elemental natural force. The cycle of life and death relates to the Buddhist and Hindu concept of Nirvana, which brings this cycle to a close when earthly passions are extinguished and the individual soul is absorbed into the Supreme Spirit.

A more troublesome problem is what to make of the slant-eyed state of the main figure, which has been interpreted as a symbol of sinful desire wherever found within Gauguin's *oeuvre*.[2] This is certainly true for its occurrence in the face of a fox, which Gauguin employed as what he termed "an Indian symbol of perversity" (*M*LXXXVII) in the *Be in Love* panel (*fig. 67*), a wood female figure he called *Lewdness* (Gray 88) and the painting *Loss of Virginity* (cat. no. 70).[3] With this interpretation Meyer de Haan is seen as governed by wily thoughts and lewd designs and the title *Nirvana* is logically seen as intended perversely in the manner Gauguin admitted to with *Be in Love*. His sinister desires might also be thought symbolized by the serpentine vine which is wrapped around his arm and which could be read as a disguised snake with the associations it has in the *Eve* watercolour. Meyer de Haan is sometimes said to have been used by Gauguin on several occasions (for

example, Gray 86 and *W* 317, 625) as a symbol of base cupidity, either because of his deformed stature or Gauguin's supposed jealousy over his sexual liaison with Marie Henry, keeper of the inn where they both resided in Le Pouldu. Certainly this painting does not immediately evoke a sense of other-worldly blessed repose and cessation from psychological torment for the beings depicted, and the Nirvana of the title must therefore be considered a goal less than fully achieved.

Arguing conversely, it is equally difficult to think of this painting as merely containing thematic ironies, as a kind of satirical joke played by the cynical Gauguin upon his follower and financial supporter. For one thing, Meyer de Haan is thought to have been a generally learned person, with accomplishments in the area of music, languages, and both Jewish and Oriental philosophies. Especially in the relative isolation of Le Pouldu, it seems unlikely that such areas of knowledge would remain undiscussed by two men who invariably spoke well of each other in correspondence to others. It is even possible that Meyer de Haan participated in selecting the title and in clarifying for Gauguin the ramifications of this term as understood in the chief religions of India. It may be assumed at the least that he was receptive to playing the assigned iconographic role whatever was intended. As Andersen points out, in Hindu tradition the snake is both a symbol for water and "an invincible life force set in a mortal sphere."[4] Unlike "the monster" Gauguin himself in *Be in Love*, Meyer de Haan does not participate directly in the deception or degradation of woman but, to the extent that this may exist among the black rocks, he turns his back on it. Indeed, his gesture of hand clasped to heart represents an almost universal, even child-like symbolization of honest resolution, if not religious faith as well. Whether or not the slanted eyes are thought suggestive of a fox, they may also be read as a sign of shrewdness of mind, which is further symbolized in the robe and cap that lend him the appearance of a philosopher-priest. Although elsewhere Gauguin did depict his Dutch colleague more overtly as a faun or satyr, his depiction here seems more that of Faust than of Mephistopholes. If still situated within a world of earthly passions and torments, he nonetheless comprehends that ultimate release comes only through attaining the state of Nirvana.

2 See Andersen, "Peruvian Mummy," p. 241, and *Paradise*, pp. 120-22, where the author admits the validity of the title *Nirvana* as suggestive of rebirth, yet characterizes the figure of Meyer de Haan as a vampire. See also Sutton, *Gauguin*, pp. 12-13.

3 The title *Lewdness* rests on the account of its first owner, the Danish painter, J.F. Willumsen, who received it in an exchange with Gauguin (see Pickvance, *Tate Entries*, *Gauguin*, cat. no. 67).

4 Andersen, *Paradise*, p. 120.

69.

Harvest: Le Pouldu   W 396
late summer or fall 1890
oil on canvas: 73 × 92 cm
Signed and dated lower right: *P. Gauguin [18] 90*
Lent by The Trustees of the Tate Gallery, London

Although signed and dated as a finished painting, the current title does not derived from Gauguin, who failed to include it in the Hôtel Drouot sale.[1] The accepted date of late summer or early fall is predicated upon the normal harvest season and Gauguin's known departure from Le Pouldu on or about November 7, 1890. The exact location of the scene depicted has been established by Andersen as some fields and a now unfortunately levelled dune promontory south of the hamlet Kerzellec, which is within a kilometre of Le Pouldu.[2] A south-easterly view is depicted, with the water leading at left towards the port of Bas Pouldu on the Laïta River and at right out to sea. As Gauguin's painting shows, the dune promontory rising above the Beach of Porguerrec was then cultivated to the very edge of the ocean so as to form a triangulated hillock of green pastures outlined against the bright blue sea. Whether or not this strikingly pyramidal land mass might

[1] The dealer A. Vollard seems to be the earliest known owner of this painting, which he sold in 1912 to C. Maresco Pearce (Pickvance, *Tate Entries*, cat. no. 34).

[2] Andersen, "Le Pouldu," pp. 615-66.

already have been meant to harbour associations with the "magic mountain" of romantic tradition, it does anticipate a recurring compositional element found in several paintings with religious overtones from the Tahitian years, not least of all the Boston *Whence Cometh We, Where Are We, Whither Are We Going?* (*W* 561).

A more contentious issue is raised by Andersen's assertion that contrary to the opinions of Sutton and Pickvance, this painting could not have served as the basis for the landscape background in the *Loss of Virginity*, which therefore must also have been painted on site in Le Pouldu before Gauguin's return to Paris.[3] Andersen certainly is right in pointing out significant differences in the precise point of view employed and in details either included or excluded, but given the large size of the Chrysler Museum painting it is unlikely in any case, to have been executed *plein air*, and Gauguin did clearly employ the same general setting in both paintings to produce quite similar compositional formats. For the present writer the validity of Andersen's lengthy and well-informed interpretation of the *Loss of Virginity* (*see* cat. no. 70) is little affected by whether it was painted in Brittany or Paris, and the Tate *Harvest* inevitably must be considered a major precedent for the style and composition of the version with a nude girl and fox. Andersen himself stresses the relationship of the harvest theme and the reaping or raping of virginity, so that the Tate painting may be thought an iconographic precedent as well. In style, as Pickvance notes, the *Harvest* already manifests stylizations of shape and outline bearing a relation to the emerging Art Nouveau.[4] While not quite as Cloisonist in its colouration as the vividly hued *Loss of Virginity*, the *Harvest*, with its extremely high horizon and structured compartmentalization of surface areas, is decidedly an exemplar of the same stylistic tendency.

70.
The Loss of Virginity: La Perte du pucelage
W 412
winter 1890-91
oil on canvas: 90 × 130 cm
Not signed or dated
Lent by the Chrysler Museum at Norfolk, Virginia;
Gift of Walter P. Chrysler, Jr.

Our knowledge of the origins of so large and important a painting is surprisingly sparse, and the one account which derives from Gauguin's lifetime has been disputed. This was provided by Gauguin's friend, Jean de Rotonchamp (alias "Brouillon") in his biography of the artist.[1] By this date the painting had disappeared into prolonged inaccessibility through ownership by the mystically inclined Count Antoine de la Rochefoucauld, who must have acquired it at or just prior to the time of Gauguin's second sale at the Hôtel Drouot in 1895.[2] Marred though it is by minor errors of fact, the Rotonchamp account deserves respect as coming from a first-hand witness who doubtless was presenting his best memory of the artist's own explanations. One puzzling aspect of the recollection by Rotonchamp has been his reference to a certain "ex-helmsman of Desaix" as having provided the "provisional title" *The Loss of Virginity*. However, by this the author could only have meant Gauguin himself, who had served in the French navy during the Franco-Prussian war on a ship named *Desaix*.[3] The explanation of the theme of the painting as "a virgin seized in her heart by the demon of lubricity" accords with our independent knowledge of Gauguin's use of the fox as a symbol of sexual enticement (see cat. no. 68), all the more so because of Rotonchamp's ventured opinion that a lion might have served the artist better. The characterization of the procession of diminutive figures at right as revelling celebrants of a marriage ceremony dancing their way home to the accompaniment of fiddlers obviously exaggerates. But the observation that, "This was complementary to the allegory of the foreground plane as the image of its normal denouement," cannot therefore be completely disregarded, since the foremost of the two groups of figures contains a distinct contrast of children and adults. Rotonchamp also was obviously in error in describing the painting as ruined by ceaseless retouching (it is actually evenly painted and in excellent condition) and since lost because left to rot in an attic. At the same time, his description of the painting as too

much influenced by the artist's contact with the literary Symbolists might well reflect a certain frustration with it by Gauguin, who after all neither signed nor chose to exhibit it in public. As several commentators have felt, it represents Gauguin's final major canvas in an overtly Cloisonist and Symbolist vein and as such constitutes both the culmination and termination of his pre-Tahitian development.

In the view of the present writer, the least questionable part of Rotonchamp's account should be his ascription of it to Gauguin's final months in Paris and that the nude girl represented was a quite young, thin and not particularly pretty model found there. Rotonchamp not only was in personal contact with Gauguin during winter 1890-91, but used as the principal outside source of information the records and verbal accounts of another long-time friend of Gauguin, the painter Daniel de Montfreid.[4] It was this latter friend who introduced Gauguin to his presumed model, the seamstress Juliette Huet, who would bear Gauguin a daughter following his departure for Tahiti.[5] From the present distance in time, it is hopeless to speculate whether Gauguin knew of this pregnancy before or while he was working on the *Loss of Virginity*, but it is difficult not be believe that self-identification with the seducer-fox was by that time an association that came automatically.

The arguments advanced by Andersen against Rotonchamp's ascription of the canvas to Paris, winter 1890-91, and for his own preference for Le Pouldu, fall 1890, are unconvincing and seem hardly necessary in support of that author's rich

3 *Ibid.*: Sutton, *Tate Intro.*, cat., p. 13, and Pickvance, *Tate Entries*, cat. no. 34.

4 Pickvance: *ibid*.

1 Rotonchamp, pp. 81-82, whose account has been challenged in Andersen, *Le Pouldu*, pp. 615-16, and *Paradise*, p. 99 ff.

2 See D. Sutton, "*La Perte du pucelage* by Paul Gauguin," *The Burlington Magazine*, XCI (April 1949), p. 104.

3 Rotonchamp, p. 15, and Perruchot, pp. 58-59, document Gauguin's service on the *Desaix* (formerly the *Jérôme-Napoléon*), although the former's reference to a position as "helmsman" generously euphemizes Gauguin's actual position as a stoker, then member of the quarter-master's section.

4 As cited in *P-I*, p. 530, item 95.

5 Rotonchamp, p. 82; Perruchot, p. 204, improving in chronological accuracy on the first report of this liaison in Chassé, *Son temps*, pp. 87-88; and *P-I*, p. 433, sequentially revealed the identity of this model and her relationship to Gauguin.

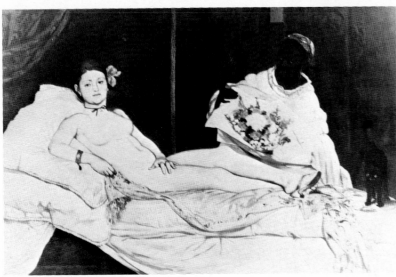

Fig. 79
Edouard Manet:
Olympia,
1863,
oil on canvas,
(Musée d'Orsay, Paris).

and fruitful examination of Breton artistic and folkloristic sources for this painting.[6] Why challenge, for instance, the assumption that Gauguin relied on another landscape painting (*that is*, cat. no. 69) for his landscape background in *Loss of Virginity* when it is patently unthinkable to imagine a Breton female model lying naked in a field while the artist produced an out-of-size painting *plein air* and a sizable number of properly attired Sunday worshippers approach? And if not *plein air*, why not Paris rather than Brittany, considering Gauguin's avowal of "painting from memory" and his well-documented use, often many years later, of a model from his notebooks, graphics or paintings.

Rather, the Breton sources listed by Andersen merely reinforce an interpretation of this painting as involving a final *résumé* of Gauguin's Breton experience at the moment of his impending departure, perhaps forever, to the far-off shores of Tahiti. The most fundamental of Andersen's discoveries is his recognition that the position of the virgin is not only sepulchral, but also a surrogate for the supine Christ often found at the base of Breton Calvaries—a discovery felicitously summed up in his "Calvary of the Maiden" appellation for this painting.[7]

Along with his thorough exploration of the various Breton connations for the use of a devious fox as seducer, which effectively belie Gauguin's own exclusive crediting of the Indian tradition, Andersen rightly stresses precedents in Bernard for the conflation of the reclining female figure with the dead Christ, although one of these may offer additional proof that the Gauguin painting was executed in Paris (*see* cat. no. 111).

His final analogy between the death and resurrection of Christ and the Greek myth of Demeter is equally suggestive, whether or not it was a consciously understood source for Gauguin.[8] He is also doubtless right in viewing the overlapping feet as hinting at Christ nailed to the cross, with the flower held in the hand as a perhaps Puvis de Chavannes symbol of rebirth, an iconography incidentally reinforced by the configuration of the fingers in a classic form of priestly blessing. All in all, Andersen's interpretation of Gauguin's art as fundamentally based in an eros-thanatos confrontation could find no better example than in this evocatively Symbolist painting.

One final source of iconographic inspiration for the *Loss of Virginity* which has gone unnoticed is the *Olympia* by Manet (*fig. 79*). That the comparison is germane is proven by Gauguin's late 1889 (*M*CVI) interest in the offer to the French state of this notorious painting thanks to Monet's organization of a subscription and Gauguin's having arranged, at no inconsiderable effort, to copy it (*W* 413) during the same winter 1890-91 in which the *Loss* was produced.[9] The two paintings in fact constitute his only known serious efforts at painting during this more than four month period. It would be easy enough to contrast the two paintings as respective paradigms of Realist and Symbolist treatments of the "modern Venus themes." Yet both examples, apart from a comparable rigidity in the pose and unrelieved white colouration of the body, employ animal (cat and fox), flower (bouquet and iris) and less than gentle settings in which the fallen (or about to fall) mundane goddess is ensconced in order to present an image highly disruptive of conventional acceptance. There is thus a very real possibility that Gauguin's *Loss of Virginity* was conceived of as a simultaneous tribute and challenge to Manet's notorious *Olympia*, just after its reluctant state acceptance as a "masterpiece" of French art. Fittingly, both paintings have evoked enigmatic responses among viewers and critics alike, which offers additional reason to suppose Gauguin's interest in the *Olympia* as a standard of accomplishment just before his departure for Tahiti.

6   Andersen, *Paradise*, pp. 99-106 and then for the question of the chronology, "Le Pouldu," pp. 615-16. Given Gauguin's well known use of figural notebook sketches over a number of years and his "painting from memory" technique, there hardly seems any reason to doubt his ability to combine a Breton landscape with a Paris studio-posed nude for the *Loss of Virginity*.

7   Andersen, *Paradise*, p. 98 and fig. 69.

8   *Ibid.*, p. 105, certainly overstates matters, however, in claiming that Edouard Schure's *Les grands Initiés* "gave equal attention to Christ, Buddha, and Persephone," even if one presumes knowledge of this volume by Gauguin.

9   See Rotonchamp, pp. 82-3, who records a week of work at the Luxembourg Palace, where it was housed, and completion *chez lui*. Gauguin would have seen the Manet painting in the original at the latest when it was present at the Universal Exposition of 1889. The Gauguin copy has reappeared in auction recently (Sotheby's Parke Bernet and Co., London, July 1, 1980, "Preview Calendar of Sales, June-July 1980," p. vi. for colour illustration).

Louis Anquetin (1861-1932)

Biographical Data

A general idea of Anquetin's formative years can be gathered from several published accounts on his life, especially those by his close friend and colleague, Emile Bernard. Apart from his several articles about Anquetin, Bernard's own partially published manuscript *L'Aventure de ma vie* remains an important document on the development of Anquetin's Cloisonist style during 1886-1888. No known letters between the two artists seem to have survived, nor much early correspondence from Anquetin to his family and friends, with the notable exception of a series of letters exchanged during the years 1884-1891 between Anquetin and the Symbolist writer and critic Edouard Dujardin. A number of references by Lautrec on Anquetin have been recently published (Lautrec *Corres.*) which enable us to ascertain the close friendship between the two. Anquetin's record of exhibition and certain critical appraisals also add to this nonetheless scant amount of biographical source materials.

EARLY LIFE AND CAREER

1861-1884

Louis Anquetin is born in Normandy on January 26, 1861 in the town of Etrépagny near Gisors where his father and mother operate a prosperous butcher shop. An only son, he is taught to ride at the age of four by his father and spends much of his childhood and mature years riding through his beloved Normandy. In this manner he discovers the sea and develops an appreciation for the beauty of the region. Throughout his life, these two passions, the love of horses and the natural landscape, are profoundly reflected in his activities as a painter. From an early age he displays a great passion for drawing and art. In 1872 he enters the Lycée Corneille in Rouen where he meets the young Edouard Dujardin with whom the artist remains in extremely close contact during the years 1884-91 in Paris. As a schoolboy he has already acquired a reputation as an artist. After completing his *lycée* diploma in July 1880, he is employed briefly as a clerk in a relative's drapery business. Anquetin, however, begs his parents to allow him to study painting in Paris. Having completed his military service sometime in 1882, he enters the "atelier libre" of Léon Bonnat where he meets and befriends Toulouse-Lautrec, who becomes his closest friend. When Bonnat closes his *atelier* in September, Anquetin moves with Lautrec to the studio of Fernand Cormon at 104 boulevard de Clichy. In October 1884, the sixteen-year-old Emile Bernard enters Cormon's and is befriended by Anquetin who introduces him to Lautrec. By this date the students in the studio already consider the twenty-four old Anquetin a master and Cormon's possible successor, and Lautrec lauds his already developed Impressionist landscapes (Lautrec, *Corres.* p. 85).

1885

Anquetin experiences a period of close friendship with Symbolist writer Edouard Dujardin. He spends his time between Etrépagny and at Cormon's in Paris. Together with Emile Bernard and Lautrec, he visits the Louvre and explores modern art at the gallery of Durand-Ruel on the rue Lafitte. He frequents the shop of Père Tanguy where he studies the works of Paul Cézanne, Camille Pissarro and Armand Guillaumin.

He continues to experiment with an Impressionist style (cat. no. 71).

In late autumn, Anquetin invites Lautrec to hunt at Etrépagny (Lautrec *Corres.*, p. 96).

1886

While working at Cormon's, Anquetin admires paintings by Monet, Manet and Velásquez.

In early April Emile Bernard departs Cormon's *atelier* for good.

In May Anquetin visits the last Impressionist group exhibition where he would have seen canvases by Seurat, Gauguin, Signac, etc. He is portrayed in two works by Lautrec depicting Montmartre night life (*figs. 26 and 27*).

In the summer after a student uprising, he leaves the studio of Cormon.

According to Bernard (*Anquetin 1932*, p. 593) Anquetin visits Claude Monet who provides lessons on Impressionist technique and colour theory.

By the fall he encounters Bernard who has returned from Brittany. Bernard introduces him to the newly arrived Vincent van Gogh. A close artistic relationship with Bernard follows.

Anquetin paints with new prismatic palette of the Impressionists (cat. no. 73).

In the autumn Anquetin probably sees the exhibition of the *Indépendants* (Aug.-Sept.) which includes Neo-Impressionist works by Angrand, Pissarro, Signac, Seurat, etc.

Late 1886 (October) he exhibits at the Salon Municipal in Rouen where he is noted by the art critic Joseph Delatre for his remarkable simplifications (letter no. 97, 22 October, 1886, Delatre to Charles Angrand, Collection Musée Andelys).

By this date he is living at 86 avenue de Clichy in the heart of Montmartre where he often gives *soirées* to which are invited Lautrec and Bernard (Bernard, *L'Aventure de ma vie* MS, pp. 66-67).

In the company of Lautrec, he attends the café-cabaret *Le Mirliton*.

1887

In the winter of 1886-87 he exchanges ideas on art with Bernard and works on a large project *The Interior at the Cabaret Bruant* (later abandoned). Bernard acts as a model for one of the figures (Bernard, *Anquetin, 1932*, p. 593) and in February again poses for Anquetin (*fig. 80*).

Anquetin studies and paints according to Pointillist theories and with Bernard visits Signac's studio (Bernard, *Anquetin 1932*, p. 594).

MAY

In May Camille Pissarro meets the artist at the Millet exhibition (Ecole des Beaux-Arts) and notes that Anquetin is working in Pointillist manner (letter *circa* 20 May 1887, *Pissarro*, p. 153).

Anquetin begins to turn away from Pointillism and to simplify his art under influence from Japanese prints, *images d'Epinal* etc.

Vincent takes Anquetin and Bernard to the attic of the shop of S. Bing in order to study the dealer's vast holdings of Japanese prints (*CL* 511).

SUMMER

Anquetin spends the summer in Etrépagny where he produces studies based on the surrounding countryside and experiments independently in his chromatic researches. By late summer (late July-August) he paints *The Mower at Noon* (cat. no. 74), his earliest known Cloisonist painting.

SEPTEMBER

Anquetin, back in Paris (letter September 8, 1887 H.R.C.), contacts Bernard and with Lautrec frequents Montmartre cabaret life.

Fig. 80
Louis Anquetin
(here attributed to):
Portrait of Emile Bernard
c. early 1887,
pastel (collection unknown).

NOVEMBER-DECEMBER

Bernard and Anquetin work together towards abstraction. In late 1887 he paints his second known Cloisonist work *Avenue de Clichy: Five O'Clock in the Evening* (cat. no. 76).

At the same time he continues to experiment, combining a new simplification with Pointillist colour theory, for example, *The Boat at Sunset* (now lost).

Vincent van Gogh organizes the first exhibition of the "Petit Boulevard" at the popular restaurant *Du Chalet*, 43 avenue de Clichy. Anquetin, Bernard, Lautrec and van Gogh hang their canvases in this restaurant. Anquetin shows possibly both *The Mower at Noon* and the *Avenue de Clichy: In the Evening* and also (as remembered by Bernard) *The Boat at Sunset* (*see* cat. no. 76). According to van Gogh, Anquetin sells a study from this exhibition (*CL* 510).

1888

JANUARY

During the winter 1887-88 he exhibits three works, one of which is *The Boat at Sunset* (as recalled by Bernard), at the offices of Dujardin's *La Revue indépendante* (Bernard, *Anquetin, 1932*, p. 594). Pissarro, Seurat and Signac also exhibit works there (Fénéon, *Oeuvres plus que completes*, p. 92). Early the same month Octave Maus, on the recommendation of Théo van Rysselberghe, invites Anquetin to participate at the exhibition of *Les Vingt* in Brussels.

He accepts the invitation and informs Maus of his intention to be in Brussels two days prior to the opening to hang his paintings personally (two unpublished letters from Anquetin to Maus in the Archives de l'Art Contemporain, Musées Royaux de Beaux-Arts, Brussels). He sends his personally designed exhibition list (fig. 81) after Maus urges him to send the drawing as quickly as possible (letter January 20, 1888, H.R.C.).

FEBRUARY

Anquetin exhibits eight works at the fifth exhibition of *Les Vingt* in Brussels:

1. *Backdrop for a Punch and Judy Show* (unlocated),
2. *The Mower: Afternoon* (cat. no. 74),
3. *Fan* (unlocated),
4. *Street at Five O'Clock p.m.*, *sketch* (cat. no. 76),
5. *Boat at Sunset* (unlocated),
6. *Some Studies for "chez Bruant"* (destroyed?),
7-8. *Horses* (probably the paintings upper centre of *fig. 17*).

MARCH

He exhibits the same eight works in Paris at the Salon de la Société des Artistes Indépendants (March-May). Van Gogh, Seurat, Signac also exhibit their paintings here.

Edouard Dujardin reviews Anquetin's paintings and baptises the latter's new style of painting "Cloisonism" (*see* Introduction, pp. 23-24).

APRIL-MAY

Anquetin is unable to work due to a severe bout of rheumatism.

He writes Dujardin from Etrépagny that he has been ill for six weeks (letter May 12, 1888, H.R.C.).

SUMMER

Able to work again, he corresponds from Etrépagny with Dujardin in Paris. By July the dealer Thomas buys his study "The Peasant" (*B* 11). In August he executes a pastel drawing of his mother (cat. no. 79). In early October, back in Paris, he sees Théo van Gogh (*B* 19).

WINTER

He spends his time between Paris and Etrépagny. By late winter he is working on a dry point etching (fig. 82) for a frontispiece for Dujardin's symbolist work *Pour la Vierge du roc arden* (published in *La Revue indépendante* 1889).

Fig. 81
Louis Anquetin
Illustration for exhibition list of the catalogue of "Les Vingt,"
1888,
drawing.

1889

JANUARY-FEBRUARY

In Etrépagny, he takes care of his mother, who has typhoid fever, and continues to work on the frontispiece for *Pour la Vierge du roc ardent*. By early February, he informs Dujardin that he is sending the proofs (letter February 11, 1889 H.R.C.).

MARCH

From Etrépagny Anquetin informs Dujardin that his mother is close to death (letter March 5, 1889 H.R.C.). By the end of this month his mother dies. (letter to Dujardin March 24, 1889 H.R.C.).

APRIL

This month is spent in Paris with frequent trips to Etrépagny to settle his mother's estate.

LATE SPRING-SUMMER

On the recommendation of Bernard, he exhibits seven works at the exhibition of the "Groupe Impressionniste et Synthétiste" at the Cafe Volpini (mostly the works exhibited in 1888).

Fascinated by horse subjects, he does paintings and drawings (cat. no. 78?).

He probably spends part of summer in Etrépagny but also works in Paris.

FALL-WINTER

By the end of the year he has moved to a more sumptuous studio-apartment on 62 rue de Rome near the Gare Saint-Lazare in Paris. He begins a new and more elegant Parisian existence and ceases his earlier bohemian life (Bernard, *Anquetin*, *1932*, p. 596). He sees Bernard rarely and visits the shop of Père Tanguy less frequently. He has begun to paint portraits of fashionable ladies, nudes, Parisian street scenes (cat. no. 80) and horse-race themes. His enthusiasm is centred in capturing "la vie moderne" in the manner of Manet and Daumier. From this period on, Anquetin, Lautrec and Edouard Dujardin frequent the recently opened Moulin Rouge dance hall.

1890

MARCH-APRIL

Anquetin exhibits one work at the Salon de la Société des Artistes Indépendants.

MAY-JUNE

He exhibits one painting and two pastels (e.g. *fig. 83*) at the first exhibition of the Société National des Beaux-Arts (Salon de Champs de Mars).

SUMMER

His favourite subjects continue to be high fashion portraits of ladies (cat. no. 81) and subjects from modern life in Paris, e.g. horse-race scenes.

WINTER

Anquetin begins to renounce his earlier modernism for study of classical art. He becomes especially enamoured by the art of Rubens and Michelangelo.

Fig. 82
Louis Anquetin
Frontispiece for Edouard Dujardin's Pour la Vierge du roc ardent
1889,
dry point etching heightened with colour
(Paris: La Revue indépendante, 1889).

Fig. 83
Louis Anquetin *At the Bar* *c*. 1891-3, pastel (private collection).

1891

MARCH-APRIL

He exhibits ten works at the *Salon de la Société des Artistes Indépendants*.

MAY

One pastel, *Woman in front of a Japanese Background (fig. 96, first row, centre)*, is exhibited at the *Salon des Beaux-Arts*. He continues to paint portraits of modern men and women.

OCTOBER

Lautrec writes his mother that Anquetin still suffers from rheumatism (Huisman-Dortu, p. 88).

WINTER

In December Anquetin exhibits four works at the gallery of Le Barc de Boutteville in the first exhibition of the "Peintres Impressionnistes et Symbolistes" (works by Bernard, Lautrec, Gauguin, van Gogh and Signac are also included).

1892-1932

From 1892 to 1900 Anquetin begins a period of intense research into the art of Rubens, resulting in the replacement of modern subjects with mythological themes. His contacts with Edouard Dujardin, however, continue unabated. Lautrec's friendship and their joint admiration for Montmartre night-life remain equally strong and result in Anquetin painting sometime by late 1893 a large canvas *The Dance Hall at the Moulin Rouge* (cat. no. 86), as a "swan song" to his Cloisonist years. His close artistic ties with Emile Bernard are considerably loosened due to both Bernard's absence from France for several years and the independent researches of each artist into the renewal of a classic art. By 1894 Anquetin's interests widen to include new acquaintances such as the artists Charles Conder and Armand Point. He also begins to meet regularly with a newly founded group of poets and writers including Dujardin, Paul Magritte, Aristide Marie, Stuart Merril and Camille Mauclair at Marlotte in the Forest of Fontainebleau. Yet he continues to exhibit regularly (1893-1896) with the artists "Impressionnistes et Symbolistes" at the gallery of Le Barc de Boutteville. Impassioned with a new study of anatomy and by the art of Rubens, Titian and Tintoretto he produces such allegorical works as *The Combat* (1896) and the theatre curtain for the Theatre Antoine (1897), and works on cartoons for tapestries for Beauvais and the Gobelins. His multiple resources as a unique colourist and painter in a series of portraits of his friends and paintings of Parisian life (1897-98) continue to be admired by the critics. In 1900-01 he undertakes the decoration of Dujardin's summer retreat at Val Changis with a series of mythological mural paintings. In 1909 France bestows the Legion of Honour upon Anquetin. During the years 1912-13 he publishes a series of articles in *Comoedia* which define and urge renewal of the techniques of the ancient masters (for example, Rubens and Poussin) and compares them to modern art. In 1924 he is commissioned by Gustave Geffroy to write a book on Rubens. On August 19, 1932, after a lengthy illness Anquetin dies and is buried in his native Etrépagny.

Louis Anquetin
71.
Landscape with Trees
spring 1885
oil on canvas: 72.7 × 59.4 cm
Signed and dated lower right:
L. Anquetin [*18*] *85*
Lent by a private collection, Paris

This previously unpublished landscape by
Anquetin is of unrivalled value to our knowledge
of the artist's early experimentation in Impressionist style. Because of its inscribed date and the presence of new foliage on the trees, one may deduce
a spring 1885 date of execution. The subject very
likely was one found during a visit to Etrépagny,
where he was free to paint *en plein air* in an
Impressionist style, in contrast to his concentration
upon figural style while working at Cormon's in
Paris. Nor should this be thought an exceptional
experiment, since Bernard recalled Anquetin's
avenue de Clichy apartment having once been
filled with Impressionist works representing
"effects of morning, of evening, of sunlight etc."[1]
In a letter of late 1884, Lautrec documents that
Anquetin already had produced a body of Impressionist landscapes, which were said to have
"amazed everyone" and were much better than
his own "feeble stuff."[2] This achievement would
have contributed to Anquetin's growing reputation
as the leading student in the *atelier*, whether or
not Cormon himself approved of this aspect of his
favourite student's activities.

The *Landscape with Trees* fully substantiates
Lautrec's opinion of the precocity of Anquetin's
talent as a landscape artist. The technical control
of a stippled paint application, the strong sense of
underlying composition and the fine sense of
atmosphere display remarkable maturity for a
young artist of limited experience as a landscapist.
The sense of morning haze and an overcast sky
conforms to Bernard's description of Anquetin's
search for particular effects of lighting, atmosphere
or time of day in his Impressionist phase. Apart
from its grayish overall tonality, the *Landscape
with Trees* may be considered a decorative work of
art, both for the clear rhythms of its ordered composition and for the surface patina of its encrusted
dabs of paint.

[1]   Bernard, *L'Aventure* ms., p. 66.
[2]   Lautrec, *Corres*., pp. 84-85.

72.

Portrait of Henri de Toulouse-Lautrec
c. 1886
oil on canvas: 40.3 × 32.5 cm
Signed lower left: *Anquetin*
Lent by a private collection, Paris

This virtually unknown painting by Anquetin portrays his close friend and fellow student at the Bonnat and Cormon studios, Toulouse-Lautrec, whose memorable physiognomy allows for easy identification of the sitter.[1] Judging from the impetuosity of the brush technique, the artist would seem to have worked in some haste, possibly in emulation of Lautrec's own habits, but more probably in keeping with the Impressionism which he had begun to practise in reaction to the laborious studio techniques mastered in his student apprenticeship.[2] The image itself is suggestive of a momentary pose, since the turned-up collar and hat which casts a shadow over the face imply an out-of-doors setting in chilly weather. Despite the looser brushwork, this painting is close in style and in the emphatic white background to *The Kiosk* and therefore may be dated to *circa* 1886 as well.

Anquetin's characterization of his friend, in keeping with Realist-Impressionist tradition, is relatively impersonal. He neither flatters through idealization nor caricatures Lautrec's blunt features, preferring to emphasize the colour contrast between the ruddy ear and face and the white of the strongly illuminated neck. As the only truly Impressionist portrait by Anquetin which is known, this oil study may be taken as a guide to the numerous other such portrait studies he is said to have executed *circa* 1885-86.

At a somewhat later date, Anquetin executed a portrait of his diminutive friend in charcoal (*fig. 84*). In this drawing the figure is described within expressive contour lines which capture the essential character of his subject's unfortunately abnormal body.[3] Here Impressionism is limited to interior modelling of the figure, and the only undoubted remembrance of the earlier portrait in oil is the subject's preference for wearing a derby hat.

Fig. 84
Louis Anquetin
Portrait of Toulouse-Lautrec,
c. 1887-88,
charcoal drawing
(Musée Toulouse-Lautrec, Albi).

[1] The only known record of exhibition for this painting is *Exposition: les premiers Indépendants*, 1884-1894 (Paris: Grand Palais, 1965), cat. no. 8. Bernard, *Anquetin 1932*, p. 592, recalled of this period that "Lautrec rarely left Anquetin's side." The strong friendship between Lautrec, Anquetin and Dujardin is recalled as well in the recollections of William Rothenstein, *Men and Memories*, I, (London: Faber and Faber, 1931), esp. pp. 63-65, and J.E.S. Jeanes, *D'après Nature* (Besançon: Editions Granvelle, 1946), pp. 18-19.

[2] Bernard, *Anquetin 1932*, p. 592, recalls how he and a certain Tampier often sat for Anquetin at the time.

[3] Dortu, I, no. Ic. 95 assigns the date 1889 to this drawing; however the style suggests a *circa* 1887-88 date for its execution.

The painting was known to a former owner as "Boulevard des Batignolles," which is accurate insofar as the title reflects one of the "exterior" boulevards of Paris which then abutted on the Place Clichy.[1] Thanks to a description by Bernard, who received this painting as a gift from Anquetin, we can be more exact as to its actual subject and place in the artist's career.[2] According to Bernard it was executed *circa* 1886 after Anquetin had become preoccupied with contemporary art and had paid a visit to Monet in the country. The result was a "complete transformation of his palette and new restlessness in his spirits." Bernard considered this painting, which represented a view from the second story of a café on the boulevard de Clichy frequented by a circle of Cormon students,[3] to show Anquetin's complete adherence to Impressionism, and the sacrifice of his personal temperament, which was alleviated only when Bernard converted him to a more decorative mode of painting based upon the models of tapestries and Gothic windows.

Valuable though this account is, it oversimplifies the novelty of design imparted to the composition by its author. Surely the raking angle view is a mixture of Impressionism and a favourite mode of viewing street scenes in Japanese prints. And whereas Bernard described the subject as "a kiosk with posters illuminated by the light reflected from the street," he only partially explains the combination of Impressionist luminosity and the complementary contrast between yellow reflected sunlight and purple shadows in the foreground street area. Winter landscapes with brightly illuminated snow surfaces were favoured subjects of Monet, to whose example Anquetin may have been paying a tribute in this rare example of his Impressionist phase.

73.
The Kiosk: Boulevard de Clichy
c. 1886
oil on canvas: 44.2 × 36.5 cm
Not signed or dated
Lent by Mr. and Mrs. Arthur G. Altschul,
New York

[1] The title "Boulevard des Batignolles" was supplied by the vendor when the painting was sold July 8, 1971, lot 25, at Sotheby and Co., London.

[2] Bernard, *Anquetin 1932*, pp. 593-94.

[3] *Ibid.*, p. 594. Given the winter setting one might presume a very early 1886 date based on Anquetin's presumed departure from the Cormon *atelier* in summer of the same year (Hartrick, p. 42, implies this), but one could also imagine that his fraternization with fellow students outlasted this event.

SEE COLOUR PLATE 4.

74.
The Mower at Noon: Summer
c. August 1887
oil on canvas: 69.2 × 52.7 cm
Signed and dated lower right:
L. Anquetin [*18*] *87*
Lent by Professor and Madame Léon Velluz, Paris

The Mower (pl. 4) is the earliest datable example of Anquetin's Cloisonist style. Its inscribed date of 1887 ensures that it must have been executed the previous summer that is, *Eté*, which is the title that the artist chose to employ when it was exhibited at the Café Volpini in 1889 (no. 3). When exhibited in 1888 it had been entitled successively "The Mower: Afternoon" (*Les Vingt*) and "The Mower: Noon" (*Indépendants*), both of which specify a time of day, when the effects of the day's heat and accompanying warm light were at their apogee. The place of execution inevitably was Etrépagny, where Anquetin spent most of his summer months and to which place Bernard attributed his friend's discovery of a new principle of colour harmony, derived from viewing the local landscape through a pane of coloured glass at his family residence.[1] While Bernard's cites the colour of the glass as yellow, and Dujardin refers to orange, these hues are frequently interchanged in nineteenth century colour theory, but are always seen as emanations of bright and warm sunlight appropriate to daytime, especially in summer. Bernard may have been ingenuous in his anecdotal

reference (cat. no. 76) to the panes of coloured glass at Etrépagny having supplied the sole incentive for Anquetin's Cloisonist colouration—given the depth of his interest in scientific colour theory—but in this case the painting itself bears witness to the general accuracy of Bernard's account. His description of this usage as producing an "extraordinarily decisive effect of one colour dominating all the others, assimilating them by its influence," is borne out by the manner in which the yellow-orange sunlight so inundates the setting that the blue sky is turned green and the green grass along the foreground roadway yellowish, in conformity with the dominant general tonality of the summer sun.[2] Although the interaction of blue sky and yellow light to produce green strongly suggests an analogy with the "optical mixture" of colours favoured within Neo-Impressionist circles, Dujardin, who was well informed in such matters, was careful to point out that here Anquetin had studiously avoided the use of complementary contrasts in favour of the "general contexture."[3] In Dujardin's account this did not declassify the canvas as one executed "by compartments," according to his definition of Cloisonist style, but only rendered it subject to the overpowering impression of full sunlight.

Albeit not mentioned directly, the composition of this painting is suggestive of Dujardin's other criteria for a modern Cloisonist work of art. These of course are concerned with the basic sources of the style, namely Japanese art and various West-

Août est venu! les épis gonflés se balancent lourdement au soleil avec des reflets d'or. La moisson est prête : la terre a récompensé ses durs travailleurs. La joie règne sur tous les fronts! c'est la vraie fête de la nature.

ern forms of "primitive" art such as the "Images d'Epinal." The oriental influence in this case was clearly not a specific Japanese landscape print, but rather the general tendency of such prints to favour clearly defined planar components, scenes of everyday life and, frequently, high horizon lines. Western counterparts to the Japanese print were to be found in the inexpensive coloured prints which, whether produced in Epinal or elsewhere, remained popular among the poorer classes of the French population as household decorations and sources of religious or other instruction. The most likely type of popular print to have inspired Anquetin in his *Mower* was that devoted to recording the four seasons or twelve months and the duties and activities appropriate to them. One need not presume a specific example as source; and that shown here (*fig. 85*) has been selected chiefly because of the coincidence of an August (cited by Dujardin for Anquetin) wheat harvest inundated by "golden sunlight," and the general simplification of forms and contours which are apparent in both examples.[4] Although Anquetin's painting might be considered more important as a harbinger of abstraction in modern art than as a celebration of the fruits of agrarian labour, there is no reason to doubt that the phrase with which the illustrative print caption ends, "It's a true celebration of nature," should be considered equally appropriate for *The Mower* by Anquetin. The appeal during summer 1888 of this painting to Vincent van Gogh is well documented, and he commemorated it in at least two major landscapes at the time (cat. no. 18 and *F* 465). Vincent's appreciation was conditioned by his association of this painting with "old farmer's almanacs" (*B*7) and who is to say his information was wrong?

[1] Bernard, *Anquetin 1934*, p. 114.

[2] Bernard, *Anquetin 1934*, p. 595.

[3] Dujardin, p. 491.

[4] Illustrated from "Ce qu'on fait avec un Grain de blé," *Images d'Epinal de la maison Pellerin*, Série encyclopédique, feuille no. 8, 1882 (Bibliothèque Nationale, Paris).

75.

Profile of Young Boy with Images of Fire
c. late 1887
oil on canvas: 58 x 40 cm
Signed centre left: *Anquetin*
Lent by the Musée d'Orsay, Paris

This canvas contains three separate oil sketches,
which may or may not have been executed in
reference to one or more planned paintings. The
"unfinished" corner lower left and the continuation of similar colouration throughout the composition suggest, as does the presence of a signature,
that the tripartite division of the composition into
separate "tableaux" was something of a fiction or
rather a conceit regarding the nature of art and
illusion.

The outlining of the child's head, neck and
shoulders is in keeping with the compartmentalization of the canvas divisions. Anquetin later recalled
his fascination with the mystery of light: "My
studio was a palace of light and shadow—warm
and moving light... flaming light concentrating on
a face, a hand, a torso."[1] The artist's recollections
of shadows in his apartment studio were no less
Romantic in their evocation of shadow with the
"echoes of basses and of trombones of
orchestras."[2] The general effect of this painting is
of experimentation in colour and induced light
effects, with an accompanying symbolism which is
appropriate to the artist's investigations into the
nature of colour (see cat. no. 74).

[1] Quoted in Anquetin, *De l'Art* (as in cat. no. 76,
     n. 7), p. 21.

[2] *Ibid*.

76.
Avenue de Clichy: Five O'Clock in the Evening
c. November-December 1887
oil on canvas: 69.2 x 53.5 cm
Signed and dated lower left: *L. Anquetin 1887*
Lent by the Wadsworth Atheneum, Hartford,
Connecticut:
Ella Gallup Sumner and Mary Catlin Sumner
Collection

This painting (pl. 2) and *The Mower at Noon* (cat. no. 74) are the artists' best known canvases, doubtless because of the attention focused upon them and the now lost *Boat at Sunset* when they were displayed in Brussels and Paris in early 1888 and treated as the artist's quintessential examples of what E. Dujardin first called his Cloisonism.[1] The fame of the *Avenue de Clichy* has been further enhanced by Vincent van Gogh's having remembered it in producing in Arles his *Café Terrace, Place du Forum* (cat. no. 22) which until the present exhibition has never been seen together with its model. It is possible, however, that Vincent first came to know the *Avenue de Clichy* through its inclusion in his own exhibition organized at the *Du Chalet* restaurant towards the end of 1887, or else either at the offices of *La Revue indépendante* or the artist's studio.[2] The warm clothing worn by the figures and the descent of evening by five in the afternoon indicate its execution in late fall 1887 or not long before it was exhibited beginning February 1888 at *Les Vingt* in Brussels.

For this exhibition the title was given as *Rue (soir. 5 heures). Ebauché* (Street, five o'clock in the evening; a sketch). A description followed with variations in other catalogue and critical references.[3] Apart from the misnomer of "sketch" for so finished a painting, as Dujardin, pointed out, the title fails to specify the exactitude of locale and personal iconographic associations inherent to the scene.[4] The actual setting has been identified

[1] Dujardin, pp. 488, 492.

[2] Bernard is inconsistent in his memory of where Anquetin exhibited specific paintings winter 1887-88. For a fan and two landscapes exhibited January 1888 at the offices of *La Revue indépendante* (Fénéon, I, p. 92), Bernard first cited the *Avenue de Clichy* and *The Mower* (*Notes*, p. 676) but later mentioned instead the *Boat at Sunset* (*Anquetin 1932*, p. 594) for this event. Neither citation precludes the possibility that one or more of these Cloisonist paintings also had been exhibited at the *Du Chalet* restaurant among what Bernard called (*Van Gogh*, p. 393) Anquetin's "Japanese abstractions."

[3] See fig. 81 and "Anquetin, biographical data," p. 230, above. This title varied only slightly in the 1888 *Indépendants* and 1889 Volpini exhibition catalogue and was also maintained by Dujardin, p. 488.

[4] Dujardin, p. 492.

by Bernard, who named it the *Avenue de Clichy*.[5] The accuracy of this designation can be substantiated *in situ* even today; the background is clearly the intersection known as *La Fourche* ("the fork") where the avenue de Clichy veers to the left at the intersection with the avenue de St. Ouen, which descends to the right. Not only was the setting thus "a stone's throw," as Bernard said, from Anquetin's residence at 86 avenue de Clichy, but the butcher shop was situated even closer to the *Du Chalet* restaurant, at number 43 on the same street.[6] If in fact present at Vincent's exhibition, the patrons of the restaurant would not have far to go to test the accuracy of Anquetin's powers of representation. A final personal association of the site for the artist must have been the inclusion of a subject reference which relates to his parents' family business at Etrépagny, which he still regularly visited during the summer months.[7] Doubtless meant as a private allusion and not mentioned in any of Bernard's accounts, this indirect iconographic reference lends greater weight to an interpretation of Anquetin's approach to subject matter as remaining within Realist tradition.

Yet the painting involves more than that. Bernard's insistence that he and Anquetin were adamant foes of Neo-Impressionism notwithstanding, the painting betrays a deep indebtedness to the theoretical concerns upon which that movement was founded. Possibly the artist himself wished to acknowledge this debt when he included several bustled female figures which seem to paraphrase similar figures found in Seurat's *La Grande-Jatte* (fig. 19). In its streetside setting illuminated by gaslight there is also a parallel with Seurat's *La Parade* (fig. 86), perhaps coincidentally, since it has not been proven that the latter was begun before the winter 1887-88 or, if so, known in any fashion to Anquetin.[8] Of course the two paintings are quite dissimilar in style and composition and were treated as such by one critic who saw them both at the spring *Indépendants* exhibition of 1888.[9]

Most telling, the *Avenue de Clichy* embodies Neo-Impressionist principles of colour usage while venturing in an antithetical stylistic direction. Bernard's accounts would have us believe that the dominant blue colouration for this canvas was the result of a chance observation of how the mood of landscape subjects changed if viewed through differently coloured panes of glass.[10] But this somewhat simplified explanation overlooks the various scientific texts which may have encouraged

Anquetin in this usage, and fails to point out the areas of warm red, orange and yellow hues which are scarcely altered by the blue sky and ambiance of the imputed chilly evening hour. Among art theorists both Charles Blanc and Félix Bracquemond devoted attention to the effects of dominating warm and cool overall colour, mentioning moreover the special cases of gas or electrical light in contrast to natural lighting.[11] And if Anquetin here consciously avoids Impressionist and Pointillist techniques of seeking "optical mixture" by juxtaposing numerous small brush strokes of complementary colour, what better indication could be provided that colour interactions were on his mind than the green streaks of illumination reflected on the underside of the shop marquee and the suspended hams? Certainly this is predicated as an interaction between the yellow gaslight and the blue ambiance, whatever theory of colour mixture is thought to be operative. And if the warm colours in this instance are fighting a losing battle against the forces of the "dark cold night," it seems nonetheless predictible that the Parisian denizens of this *quartier* will eventually be cheered by the warmth of their own ovens.

Colour theory aside, this painting is the arch example of Anquetin's involvement with Japanism. Early reviewers and more recent discussions have stressed this aspect of the artist's 1887 production, albeit with quite divergent views as to the quality and historical importance of this particular example.[12] While no single Japanese print may be singled out as the compositional source of this painting, Hiroshige's *Saruwakacho Theatre Street* (fig. 52) from his famous series "A Hundred Views of Famous Places at Edo," is the most likely candidate for specific comparison.[13] The deeply receding perspective, the stark contrasts of warm versus cold colours and the rush of figures to and fro in both compositions suggest a more than casual affinity. Anquetin's Japanism may also have owed a debt here to the example of Degas, as one critic noted,[14] but his own achievement in this instance also had a generative effect most notably in the subsequent *The Trace Horse of the Bus Company* (fig. 143) by Toulouse-Lautrec. Anquetin's striking use here of Cloisonist outlines and colouration makes the *Avenue de Clichy* one of the most influential examples of this style which its then heralded originator produced.[15]

5   Bernard, *Notes*, p. 676, introduced the "Avenue de Clichy" label.

6   Bernard, *Anquetin 1932*, p. 595, uses the comparable French phrase "à deux pas" to describe this proximity; his previous reference (p. 592) to Anquetin's apartment being situated above the juncture of the avenues de Clichy and St. Ouen (at *La Fourche*) indicates its greater distance from both the *Du Chalet* and its neighbouring "boucherie."

7   See L. Anquetin, *De l'Art*, ed.: C. Versini (Paris: Nouvelles Editions Latines, 1970), p. 11.

8   Orthodox opinion (see H. Dorra and J. Rewald, *Seurat*, Paris: Les Beaux-Arts, 1959, pp. 225-27) dates this painting *c*. winter 1887-88, since it was first exhibited March 1888 at the *Indépendants*. However, R. Herbert, exh. cat. *Neo-Impressionism* New York: S.R. Guggenheim Museum, 1968, no. 82, leaves open the possibility that it was begun earlier, with his "1886-88" dating. One can only speculate which artist first conceived of a night street scene in Montmartre.

9   G. Geffroy, "Chronique: Pointille–Cloisonisme," *La Justice*, April 11, 1888, although the coincidence of mention of the two paintings is worth noting.

10 Bernard, *Anquetin 1932*, p. 595, and *Anquetin 1934*, p. 113; however, this type of experiment was scarcely without precedent, not the least of which was provided by Goethe's *Farbenlehre* (for example, numbers 55, 70-71, 763, 769, 778, 782-85, seem applicable to either *Avenue de Clichy* or *The Mower*, cat. no. 74).

11 C. Blanc, *Grammaire des arts du dessin* (Paris 1867), pp. 571-73, and F. Bracquemond, *Du Dessin et de la couleur* (Paris: 1885), pp. 69-96 (a copy of the latter being in the Anquetin archive, Paris), discuss this issue.

12 Cf. Roskill, p. 107, M.A. Stevens, London *P-I*, cat. no. 7, for recent views, the divergence of which was already apparent in 1888 (*see* L., "Correspondance de Belgique," *Chronique des arts*, March 3, 1888, who speaks of "le pseudo. japonisant M. Anquetin," and E. Verhaeren, "Chronique Bruxellois," *La Revue indépendante* March 1888, pp. 454-62, whose review was altogether more favourable.

13 See *Japanese Prints*, cat. no. 46i.

14 J. de Gesures, "Chroniques: Les Artistes indépendants," *Le Salon pour tous* (March 31, 1888), p. 114.

15 The present wood frame painted blue was possibly added by Anquetin and, if so, adds another form of complementary colour contrast with the enclosed "orange-yellow" harvest scene.

Fig. 86
Georges Seurat
La Parade,
1887-88,
oil on canvas,
The Metropolitan Museum of Art, New York,
Bequest of Stephen C. Clark, 1960.

77.

Boat at Night
c. 1887-88
pastel on paper: 49.5 x 64.5 cm
Signed lower right: *Anquetin*
Lent by a private collection, Paris

This image of a sailboat by night isolated against
the vastness of the ocean and sky was deeply
entrenched within Romantic and Realist tradition.
The Green Wave (*fig. 87*) by Monet and several
paintings of fishing boats by Millet would have
provided sufficient stimulation for Anquetin to try
his hand at such a subject.[1] Like the now lost
painting *Boat at Sunset*, which was exhibited by
early 1888, this pastel is basically monochromatic
in conception, substituting for the reported red of
the *Sunset*, an overall bluish tonality appropriate
to a nocturnal theme. Apart from its reminiscences
of Romantic-Realist pictorial conceptions, the
Boat at Night evinces a tendency toward a
compression of space at the service of decorative
aims. The light highlights of the twinkling stars
seen elsewhere also serve this function as do the
indications of water swell in the foreground. A
previously unpublished fan painting by Signac
(*fig. 88*) offers a parallel to Anquetin's interest in
depicting different times of day with one
appropriate colour dominant. Signac's *Sailboats:
Day and Night* thus involves the same contrast as
between Anquetin's *Mower* (cat. no. 74) and
Avenue de Clichy (cat. no. 76), although there is
no certainty as to whether it was painted before or
after the works by Anquetin.[2] The latter's *Boat at
Night* is decidely unpointillist in style, but an
affinity of concerns about colour dominants is
present nonetheless.

[1]   C. Pissarro in a letter of May 20, 1887 (Pissarro,
      p. 153) reports having met Anquetin at an
      exhibition, which a previous letter (pp. 149-50)
      makes clear was the major Millet retrospective of
      that spring.

[2]   The Signac is certainly in the style already
      practised *circa* 1887-88 (cf. F. Cachin, Paul
      Signac, Paris: Bibliothèque des Arts, 1971, fig.
      nos. 23-24, 26), and Pissarro's statement about
      Anquetin cited *ibid*., p. 153, is followed by the
      inference that this artist too wishes to join the
      Neo-Impressionist movement (i.e., "marcher
      dans la voie").

Fig. 87
Claude Monet:
The Green Wave,
1865,

oil on canvas
(The Metropolitan Museum of Art, New York,
Bequest of Mrs. H.O. Havemeyer, 1929, The
Havemeyer Collection)

Fig. 88
Paul Signac:
Boats; Night and Day,

late 1880,
oil on canvas (private collection, Japan).

78.

Equestrian Self-Portrait
1887-89 (?)
oil on canvas: 88.3 x 51.4 cm
Signed at lower right: *Anquetin*
Lent by a private collection, Switzerland

This oil sketch shows the bearded artist mounted bareback on a brown unbridled horse. This probable lack of realism is most easily explained by the presumption that the painting was done largely from imagination. It seems unlikely that he had had a photograph made of himself astride the animal and he could not have otherwise seen let alone painted himself in this position. The background house could have been painted from nature, especially if one assumes that the setting was found at or near the family residence in Etrépagny, or even was that residence itself.

It is difficult to assign a date of execution to this painting, for lack of documentation or as yet uncovered stylistically similar examples. On the one hand, it reflects somewhat the loose brushwork and muted colours found in certain paintings of Daumier and Courbet, artists Anquetin is known to have admired greatly from an early date. There is also present a sense of Anquetin's mature decorative style of the late 1880s. Some black curvilinear contour lines, for example used to define the musculature of the horse's chest and the rider's body, are of a type used more extensively in a wash drawing of two men riding a plow horse (*fig. 89*) which bears an 1887 date. Hence, while *circa* 1887-88 seems the safest guess, at this point in the study of Anquetin's career, it is no more than just that.

Fig. 89 Louis Anquetin: *Riders*, 1887, gouache (private collection).

79.
Portrait of the Artist's Mother
August 1888
pastel with pencil on paper: 50 x 35 cm
Dated upper left: *Août 1888*
Inscribed upper right: *Oeil* [drawing of eye with colour notes] *noir, jaunvert* [sic] *bleu, blanc Lèvres violacées.*
Lent by a private collection, Paris

The mother of Anquetin, born Rose-Félicité Chauvet, came from a family of horse breeders, but married a butcher who was famed locally for his physical prowess, his horsemanship, and his musical talent. Anquetin, an only child, was deeply attached to his mother, who brought him up "as a prince" and at her death in 1889 she left him an inheritance which made him financially independent for life. Although little in the portrait speaks of this personal relationship, the very objectivity of the rendering is itself a silent tribute.[1]

The portrait conception here is strongly reminiscent of Renaissance tradition, in which profile views were more common than in later periods. His mother's elaborately braided coiffure adds to a feeling of noble distinction as does the steadfastness of her gaze. However, Anquetin has superimposed upon the pencil underdrawing thin but distinctly Cloisonist outlines for her major contours. The rich blue-green background and the violet of the blouse (and lips as indicated in the colour notes upper right) enhance the feeling of clarity and simplicity in this portrait desgin, which lacks the exaggerations and mannerisms of his "high fashion" female bust portraits of *circa* 1889-91 (*see* cat. nos. 80, 81).

[1]   The above information is chiefly derived from the exh. cat. *Hommage à Louis Anquetin* (Etrépagny: Hotel de Ville, 1977), as prepared, alas only in mimeograph, by C. Clerembaux (anonymously).

80.
The "Rond Point" of the Champs Elysées
c. summer 1889
pastel on paper: 153 x 99 cm
Signed and dated lower left: *Anquetin [18] 89*
Lent by a private collection, Paris

The title of this large pastel drawing was first published in a 1960 exhibition catalogue, but may
reflect Anquetin family tradition.[1] In any case, the
reference to the rondabout where the avenues
Franklin Roosevelt and Montaigne meet the
Champs Elysées conjures up one of the most fashionable promenades in Paris. It is difficult to
decide which of the modishly dressed woman,
gilt-harnessed horses or carefully groomed and
beribboned dogs most deserves the viewer's attention. The gushing fountain adds to the splendour
of the scene and also indicates a summer setting
for the drawing, which when combined with the
inscribed 1889 date makes this one of the artist's
earliest documented examples of his 1889-91
depictions of women and scenes of Parisian high
fashion.

   It is tempting to imagine that the physically
vigorous horseman Anquetin found the manicured
elegance on view along the Champs Elysées artificial or pretentious. However, following the death
of his mother in spring 1889, he seems to have left
his student and apprentice years behind in order to
lead a life dedicated to both earthly and aesthetic
pursuits, which came as a disappointment, if not a
shock, to the mystically inclined Bernard.[2] The
amenities of female companionship became a
major part of Anquetin's gay bachelor existence.
At the same time, an element of caricature does
enter into some of his depictions of high society,
and a slight trace of it may be present in the
haughty pose and rather ridiculous hat of the
woman in the *Rond Point*.

   The principal attraction of this elaborately
finished pastel is in the brilliance of the artist's
stylizations of form. Logically it is difficult to imagine that even the best trained carriage horses could
prance in such rhythmic unison as do the pair
portrayed here, especially given the contrast
between their rampant and bowed heads. Such
rhythms are enhanced by the counterpoint of the
lines of the harness and where necessary the overtly Cloisonist outlines of the horses' bodies. Here
even more than in the painting with horses on *The
Bridge of Saints-Pères* (cat. no. 82) Anquetin
seems to anticipate the style which Toulouse-
Lautrec developed for his advertising posters of the

1890s. This is less than surprising considering the
extremely close personal and artistic relationship of
the two men which culminated *circa* 1889-91.[3]
For the interaction of these two artists, compare
this pastel by Anquetin from 1889 with *Riders
Approaching the Bois de Boulogne*, 1888
(*fig. 90*) by Toulouse-Lautrec. One can also
imagine Anquetin having learned from the example of his friend's *At the Circus Fernando* (cat.
no. 119) of winter 1887-88, although differences
are obvious. At the least, this brilliantly executed
and richly coloured composition deserves consideration as not merely a harbinger of the Art Nouveau
movement, but as one of its major early examples.

Fig. 90
Henri de Toulouse-Lautrec
Riders Approaching the Bois de Boulogne
1818,
gouache
(private collection, New York).

1   Exh. cat. *Les Amis de Van Gogh*, Intro. by A.M.
    Hammacher (Paris: Institut Néerlandais, 1960),
    cat. no. 8, the then owner of which was a step-
    granddaughter of Anquetin.
2   Bernard, *Anquetin 1932*, pp. 595-96.
3   See W. Rothenstein, *Men and Memories*, I (Lon-
    don: Faber and Faber, 1931), pp. 63-65.

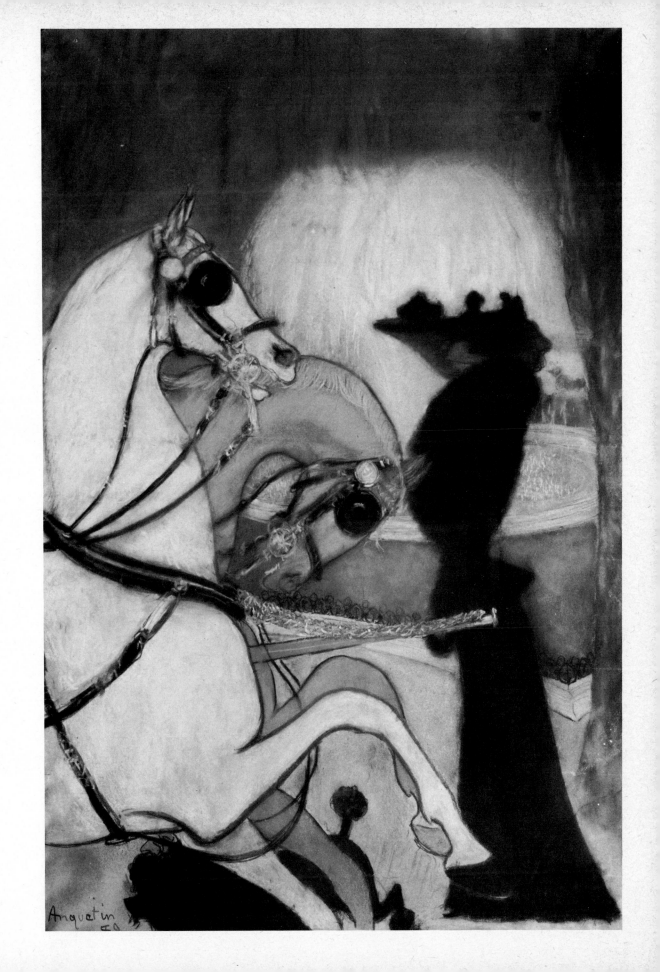

81.
Woman in a Carriage
summer 1889
pastel on paper: 55.5 x 50.5 cm
Signed and dated lower left: *L. Anquetin* [18] 89
Lent by a private collection, Paris

This pastel drawing represents the type of fashionable subject matter to which Anquetin dedicated
himself beginning *circa* summer 1889. The
woman depicted seems to view through her eye-
glass the entrance to *Longchamps* rather than the
actual races. Her attention to events outside the
arena implies that her interest in racing is pre-
eminently social.

   Apart from this modest element of social comment, the artist has here revealed his talent in
using subtle colour combinations along with strong
contrasts. Thus olive-drab greens accompany the
brighter blues of the carriage upholstery without
any apparent conflict.

   This pastel, dated 1889, probably is to be
identified with no. 17, "Femme," of the 1891
Indépendants catalogue.[1] Highly finished, with an
inscribed signature and date it was obviously
intended for either exhibition or sale, a prospect
noted by Bernard in his letter to Boch reporting
Anquetin's success at the exhibition.

   That this painting was not a single example of
its genre is reflected in such related works of art as
the *Dame à l'ombrelle* of 1890 (*fig. 91*) cited by
Bernard and the *Dame au carrick* (*Lady Wearing
a Cape*) (*fig. 92*), which was exhibited in spring
1891.[2] In all three, Anquetin has depicted fash-
ionably dressed modern women, apparently hurrying to an appointment.

Fig. 91
Louis Anquetin:
Woman with Umbrella,
1890,
oil on canvas
(private collection).

Fig. 92
Louis Anquetin: *Lady Wearing a Cape*,
c. 1889,
oil on canvas
(private collection).

[1] J. Leclercq, "Aux Indépendants," *Mercure de
    France*, II (May 1891), p. 299, refers to "a pro-
    file," and Bernard (letter to E. Boch, mentioned
    cat. no. 82n.2) calls it "a pastel."
[2] The *Dame à l'ombrelle* (*Women with Umbrella*)
    is cited in Bernard, *Anquetin 1932*, p. 597, while
    the *Dame au carrick* is described in Fénéon, I,
    pp. 194-95.

82.

The Bridge of Saints-Pères: *Gust of Wind*
autumn 1889
oil on canvas: 119.5 x 126 cm
Signed and dated lower right: *Anquetin* [18] 89
Lent by the Kunsthalle, Bremen

SEE COLOUR PLATE 27.

First exhibited at the 1891 spring *Indépendants* exhibition (no. 15) under the title *Le Pont de Saints-Pères*, this painting (pl. 27) was executed more than a year earlier. The inscribed date of 1889 in all likelihood refers to autumn as suggested by the bare trees in the background and warm dress of the figures, and because at the beginning of this year Anquetin was preoccupied with the illness and death of his mother.[1] The alternative descriptive title *Gust of Wind* has no known justification from early documents, but was used by Bernard when he described the painting in a letter to the Belgian painter Eugène Boch as "very successful, very delicate" and as having "the most perfect colouration that I know in his work."[2] Denis, too, must have been quite taken with this painting, which he acquired, after having already in 1890 cited Anquetin along with Gauguin and himself as practitioners of "Neo-Traditionalism" in art.[3]

Gunther Busch has revealed that the bridge known in Anquetin's day as that of "Saintes-Pères," after the street to which it leads on the left bank of the Seine, was rebuilt in 1939 and henceforth was called the Pont du Carrousel which leads on the right bank to the Place du Carrousel in the courtyard of the Louvre.[4] With the Ile de la Cité and its towers of Sainte Chapelle and Notre Dame in the background, Anquetin's setting was situated at the very heart of Paris. Beginning with Bernard, most accounts have stressed that Anquetin in this and related works of the years 1889-91 was at pains to become a, and perhaps *the*, contemporary "painter of modern life" in the tradition of Manet and Daumier.[5]

In the *Saints-Pères* he thus relegates the view of the Ile and the intervening Pont des Arts and Pont Neuf to a background corner of the composition, while featuring two elegantly dressed modern women and heads of tram horses hurrying across the bridge in the foreground. The contrast between the old and the new Paris surely is not fortuitous and provides the central iconographic theme to this otherwise secular scene of everyday life in Paris.

It is in the realm of style that this painting was most innovative. It has recently been described as being indebted to Japanese prints,[6] presumably meaning the use of cut-off figures, Cloisonist outlines, asymmetrical design, a simplified colour scheme and perhaps the bridge subject. One may note that the inclusion of cut-off horse images also owes a generic debt to Degas, although that master kept his equine specimens at the race tracks rather than, like Anquetin, placing them in the streets of downtown Paris.[7] The large scale of Anquetin's heads of horses is one of the most striking features of this painting, if not quite so striking as in a large pastel drawing of essentially the same subject (*fig. 93*), but which shows more clearly the *troika* of horses entering the scene from the left and substitutes a strolling couple and another horse entering from the right for the two female figures of the exhibited version. Whereas the horses of the pastel with their expressive vigour reflect Anquetin's lifelong respect for Michelangelo and the Romantic tradition, those of the painting are more stylized into flattened patterns and, like the women, reflect in their wind-tossed manes the subduing power of the natural elements. The flowing manes and garments of the manneristically elongated full-length figures have been seen as anticipating the stylizations which are found in the Art Nouveau posters of Lautrec two or more years later.[8] The wilful reduction of the colour scheme to clearly defined areas of black, white, mauve and turquoise further add to the proto-Art Nouveau style of this painting. One contemporary critic described this painting as a fresco without fresco-like colours, a judgment facilitated by the style, the almost square format and flat frame with hand-painted grid design.[9] Within Anquetin's *oeuvre* and the Cloisonist tendency in late nineteenth century French painting the *Saints-Pères* remains a highly personal, indeed unique, yet classic statement of this aesthetic.

Fig. 93
Louis Anquetin
Horses on the Bridge of Saints-Pères,
c 1889,
pastel
(private collection).

1 See "Louis Anquetin: Biographical Data," p. 230, above.

2 This unpublished letter from Bernard to Boch (Letter 3.970, *Archives de l'Art Contemporain*, *Musées Royaux des Beaux-Arts*, Brussels) is undated, but must be from *circa* late March 1891, since it is a report of the Paris *Indépendants* exhibition which opened March 20.

3 Denis, *Théories*, p. 10, although it was Anquetin's *Femme en rouge* (*fig. 37*, above) which the author cited.

4 G. Busch, "Louis Anquetin: *Der Windstoss auf der Seinebrucke*," *Neue Zürcher Zeitung* (November 2, 1969), p. 53.

5 Bernard, *Anquetin 1932*, p. 596.

6 M.A. Stevens, London P-I, cat. no. 8.

7 Lemoisne, nos. 461, 646, 649, 680, 702, provide examples of this usage which might have influenced Anquetin.

8 As pointed out by Busch, "Louis Anquetin."

9 J. Lerclerq, *Mercure de France*, II (May 1891), p. 299. O. Mirbeau, "Vincent van Gogh," *Echo de Paris* (March 31, 1891) spoke of Anquetin's *Saints-Pères* as containing "a pleasing streak of light along that Parisian horizon."

83.
The Actor
c. 1889-91
oil on canvas: 70 x 58 cm
Not signed or dated
Lent by a private collection, Paris

The title of this work derives from an illustration in
Bernard's 1934 article on Anquetin and thus
might reflect a personal recollection by the writer
from his early association with his artist friend. It
might also derive from the whiteness of the man's
countenance containing suggestions of facial
make-up for the bright red lips and darkly
accented eyebrows. Although the formal dress
could be that of a member of Parisian high society,
it would also be appropriate for one or another
type of public performer, whether in the legitimate
theatre or more popular forms of entertainment.
While by no means Anquetin's only known
portrait in strictly frontal view, this is his most
rigidly formal in pose.[1] With its flat, pale blue-gray
background features held still as if for a prolonged
photographic exposure and tightly fitting clothing,
this portrait would seem to emulate the format of a
religious icon except for the hint of parody in the
artificiality of the pose and contemporary habits of
dress. Yet during the period *circa* 1889-91, when
the artist was most concerned with creating a novel
personal idiom that accurately reflected modern
French society, this painting was one more
example of that many faceted investigation.

[1]   Bernard, *Anqetin 1934*, p. 112, fig. 7, where it
     was misdated to *circa* 1880. The same year it was
     listed as no. 1, ''Portrait de jeune homme en
     chapeau haut de forme,'' in exh. cat. *Gauguin et
     ses amis* (Paris: La Gazette des Beaux-Arts,
     1934).

84.
Walking Old Woman in Profile
facing right: The Bigot (?)
c. 1889-90
pastel mounted on board: 141.3 x 57.4 cm
Not signed or dated
Lent by Mr. and Mrs. Arthur G. Altschul, New
York

The title "La Bigote" may reflect no more than
the closed-eyes and clenched-hands pose of this
aging female figure. Her uniformly black clothing
could indicate a woman in mourning rather than
some adherence to religious orthodoxy which the
term "bigot" implies in French. The artist was
clearly more interested in formal design values
than with any specific depiction of human character beyond the general qualities of sex, age and
dress. A related work, *Seated Woman with
Umbrella* (*fig. 94*), displays similar characteristics, having the dark figure starkly outlined
against the lighter background. Possibly Anquetin
had Manet in mind as a prototype for these elongated studies of single figures, since we know that
he was a master to whom Anquetin looked for
inspiration in his own attempt to become "a
painter of modern life."[1] At the same time, the
long narrow format of the *Walking Old Woman*
may reflect this general usage for single figures in
Japanese art and in such Western derivations as
the standing figures of J.A.M. Whistler. In fact, if
Whistler's famous mother had been painted standing rather than seated, she might have looked
something like this old lady executed by Anquetin.
Despite her wizened appearance, she represents
another attempt by the artist to produce a decorative, mural-like painting which yet reflects the
types of human beings found in contemporary life.

[1]   Bernard, *Anquetin 1932*, p. 596.

Fig. 94
Louis Anquetin:
Seated Woman with Umbrella,
c. 1889-90,
oil on canvas
(private collection, Switzerland).

expanse of cheek area, the sallowness of which
contrasts with the foppish elegance of the coiffure
and head-dress. If unflattering to the sitter,
Anquetin's forceful simplification of design and
powerful colour effects provide further confirmation as to why at the time he was widely considered the most promising young artist in his circle.[3]

1   W. Rothenstein, *Men and Memories*, I (London:
    Faber and Faber, 1931), p. 63. See London P-I,
    cat. nos. 9, 29. The *Female with Blue Hat* when
    exhibited June 1891 apparently was described by
    Fénéon, I, p. 194, as "cheveux roux, que mate
    une capote violet et rose-courge prolongée en folle
    poupe par des plumes . . . ."
2   That virtually if not in fact all pictures in this
    photograph date from the period *circa* 1890-91,
    is demonstrable from the following list of
    identifications:

    A: lower left, *Seated Nude Woman in Profile*
    (probable description in June 1891 by Fénéon, I,
    p. 194, when he states "Anquetin présente des
    femmes à poses de cataleptiques, de manequins et
    de statues");

    B: left centre, *Woman with Exposed Breasts*, pas-
    tel, signed and dated: *Anquetin [18] 91* (now
    Norton Simon Inc., Museum of Art, Pasedena);

    C: "Females in the street with lampposts" both
    conform to April 1893 description by Fénéon, I,
    p. 227, of a work which could have been executed
    one or more years earlier, as "une grenouille qui
    joue de la prunelle, dans la rue, pour embobiner
    les passants");

    D: upper right, *Nude Woman Kneeling among
    Flowers* (see no. 1 in present list);

    E: lower right, *Reclining Woman* (apparent
    description in June 1891 by Fénéon, I, p. 194, as
    "un autre pastel décèlent, dans l'ombre de cour-
    tines, une femme couchée, là l'épaule, là la gorge
    découvertes.");

    F: bottom centre, *Femme sur fond Japonais*, pas-
    tel, signed and dated lower left: *Anquetin [18] 90*
    (exhibited as no. 953, *Société Nationale des
    Beaux-Arts: Champ de Mars* in 1891). Moreover,
    the two female images seen at centre above the
    couch level in fig. 96 are, at left, *Torse de jeune
    fille*, signed and dated lower right: *Anquetin,
    [18] 90* (exh. *Indépendants*, 1891, no. 22) and,
    at right, *Femme à sa coiffure* (exh. *Indépendants*,
    1891, no. 12). For a work of a greater similarity
    in subject medium and style see cat. no. 81.
3   Jacques-Emile Blanche. *Les Artes plastiques*
    (Paris: Les Editions de France, 1931, p. 125.

85.
Female Head in Profile with Blue Hat
1890
pastel on paper: 37.5 x 40.5 cm
Signed and dated lower left: *L. Anquetin [18] 90*
Lent by a private collection, Paris

This pastel has been called *La Goulue* ("the
glutton"), referring to the famous entertainer at
the Moulin Rouge dance hall depicted by Lautrec
on several occasions (*see fig. 138*). However, this
woman's coiffure differs from the distinctive
knobbed pompadour worn by La Goulue. The
title could also refer to the woman's ample proportions which Anquetin has forcefully caricatured in
her profile. The model used by Anquetin was
nonetheless likely found in the environment of the
Moulin Rouge or another Montmartre locale, since
a memoire of William Rothenstein recalls how
Anquetin produced a number of "striking pastels
of men and women, vigorously coloured and
amply drawn," from models (*fig. 95*) he found

within Montmartre café life.[1] A selection of
Anquetin's work in this vein is displayed in a
photograph of his studio (*fig. 96*), where this pastel is included among several other treatments of
women in differing poses and settings.[2] Despite the
range of styles employed for these works, the
dominant preoccupation visible is a search for a
decorative form of art with the female figure as its
basic subject matter.

Only close scrutiny discloses that our *Female
with Blue Hat* is depicted outside against a fuzzily
indicated park setting in green. The dominant colour contrast is the orange hair and the blue hat
with the red-green bow providing a second set of
complementary hues. These of course are
employed without any intent related to Pointillist
precepts, and the high intensity of the hues
throughout was extremely daring at the time. This
is one of the artist's most obviously caricatural
female studies, with the pointed nose, pursed lips
and tiny chin descending in a row to the fatty
pouch of flesh protruding below. Neither do the
tiny eye and ear do much to embellish the formless

Fig. 95
Louis Anquetin:
Girl Reading a Newspaper,
1890,
pastel
(The Tate Gallery, London).

Fig. 96
Interior of Louis Anquetin's studio, 62 rue de
Rome,
photograph *c*. 1891-2.

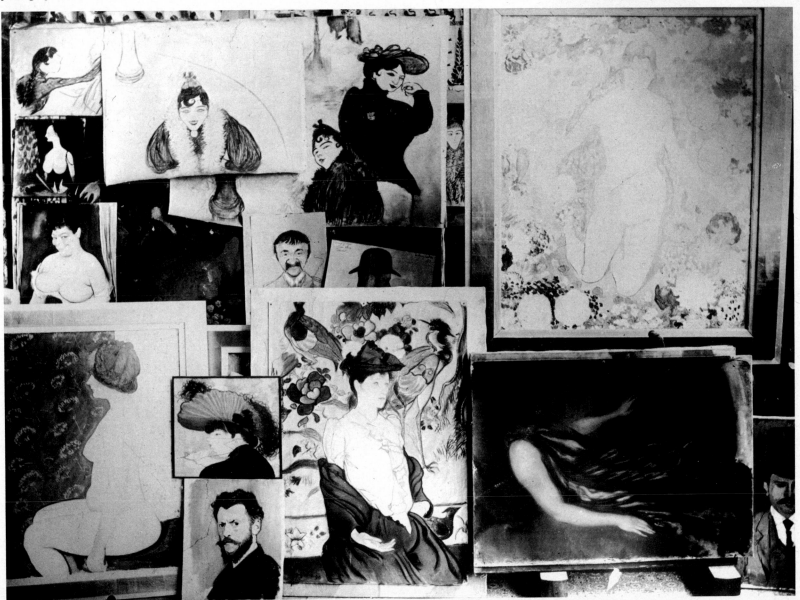

86.
The Dance Hall at the Moulin Rouge
c. 1893
oil on canvas: 168.3 x 206.4 cm
Not signed or dated
Lent by a private collection, Switzerland

This canvas (pl. 30) is mural in conception not only for its considerable size but because of the variety of its figural content. Its relatively late date in the "moderniste" work of Anquetin is based on the supposition that the central image of Jane Avril doing a "kick" is derived from the study (*fig. 97*) or the lithograph poster itself of Jane Avril which is

dated 1893.[1] That the gouache study was the specific model is suggested by the technique of the painting, which carries the use of elongated brush strokes throughout the composition.

Anquetin has here quite consciously remembered another painting by Lautrec. This is the 1890 *The Dance at the Moulin Rouge* (*fig. 98*); Anquetin has adopted its essential composition while substituting a variety of figures for those used by Lautrec.[2] It is in this respect difficult to decide whether Anquetin here wishes to pay tribute to Lautrec's achievements in style and iconography, or to impart an element of parody to the type of scene which by 1893 had become popular within French art of that decade.

Without doubt the figural conception is caricatural. One discovers a variety of bourgeois couples observing what must have been then considered the risqué antics of Madamoiselle Avril

[1] The lithograph poster is catalogued in L. Delteil, *Le peintre graveur illustre*, X-XI, Toulouse-Lautrec (Paris: 1920), no. 345, and E. Julien, *Les Affiches de Toulouse-Lautrec* (Monte Carlo: 1950), Pl. VII. Also *see* Adhémar.

[2] The poster based on this painting dates from 1891 and was Lautrec's first and largest of such commissions. It includes La Goulue as the central figure; catalogued *ibid.*, Delteil 339, Julien I and Adhémar.

Fig. 97
Henri de Toulouse-Lautrec:
Jane Avril,
1893,
oil on cardboard
(private collection).

Fig. 98
Henri de Toulouse-Lautrec:
The Dance at the Moulin Rouge
1890,
oil on canvas
(Collection Henry P. McIllhenny, Philadelphia;
photograph Philadelphia Museum of Art).

SEE COLOUR PLATE 30.

with a variety of haughty indifference bordering on disdain. She fascinates her largely aged audience without one person being inclined to remove, not to say tip, a hat in recognition of her widely acknowledged talents. Avril, the centrepiece of this modern *tableau vivant*, is as much a prey to the society which gave her momentary prominence, as she was—considering her role as a notorious *femme fatale*—its symbol of innocent decadence. Between the productions of these two friends, Lautrec and Anquetin, we have a rich assortment of reactions to this world of fleeting excitement and pleasure, of which their pictorial characterizations are the most lasting and evocative. On the extreme right is the artist Joseph Albert, a close friend of Lautrec; he is also depicted on the extreme right in the *Ball at the Moulin de la Galette* (cat. no. 121).

This large canvas may also have been Anquetin's final embodiment of his long-standing wish to produce a major painting of Parisian café life. The challenge to such an achievement had been laid down in Zola's novel *L'Oeuvre*, which has been variously interpreted, but in general is seen to have criticized Impressionism for having failed to produce a masterpiece of figural composition. Anquetin had this challenge in mind when he began his project for an interior of the "Café Bruant" which so excited the younger painters Bernard and Lautrec.[3] The project was abandoned at the time, but perhaps was revived in this final major painting by Anquetin in a style involving the "vie moderne." Caricature apart, it shows us a view of Parisian night life which is essentially sardonic. In this respect the colours of the painting may have been considered virtually "lurid," but today remind us that Anquetin was among the fundamental instigators of such colour radicalism in modern art.

[3]   See Bernard, *Anquetin 1932*, pp. 592-93, and *Anquetin 1934*, p. 114.

Emile Bernard (1868-1941)

Biographical Data

SOURCES

There is not as yet available a fully reliable
published biography of this artist. Jean-Jacques
Luthi, *Emile Bernard l'Initiateur* (Paris: Editions
Caractères, 1974) covers the years 1886-93 in
eleven not always accurate pages of text. Among
primary sources Bernard summarized his early
development in "Lettre ouvert à M. Camille
Mauclair," *Mercure de France*, XIV (June 1895),
pp. 332-39, and in *Notes* from 1903. His longest
account was *Récit d'un passager voyageant à bord
de la vie: L'Aventure de ma vie* (recently given by
M. M.-A. Bernard-Fort to the Archives Musées
Nationaux, Paris) of which random excerpts have
been published without scholarly identification as
the Introduction to *Lettres de Paul Gauguin à
Emile Bernard* (that is, *L'Aventure*). This
important account is supplemented by surviving
unpublished letters from Bernard to his sister
Madeleine (Archives Musées Nationaux), to his
parents (collection M. Bernard-Fort), to
Schuffenecker (Bibliothèque Nationale) and to A.
Aurier (private collection, France). These sources
along with the published letters from Vincent van
Gogh (*CL*) and Gauguin (*M*) to Bernard have
provided the basis for the following chronology.

EARLY LIFE AND CAREER

1868-1884

Emile Bernard is born April 28, 1868, in the city
of Lille in the north of France. His father is a cloth
merchant who, bankrupted by the war of 1870,
becomes a representative of a cloth mill at
Roubaix. After a period with his family at Rouen
and the birth of his sister Madeleine (1871),
Bernard begins in 1877 to live with his
grandmother, who operates an important laundry
in Lille. His deep admiration and love for his
grandmother remains a great support during later
years of strife with his parents in Paris. During his
stay in Lille Bernard begins to frequent the *atelier*
of a glass merchant. By 1882, he executes his first
painting and does drawings (*fig. 99*), including
some after Gustave Doré (*fig. 100*). Shortly
thereafter he resumes his formal education in
Sainte-Barbe College in Paris (*fig. 101*). During

the next three years he draws incessantly
(*figs. 100, 101*). At the college Bernard meets
fellow student Louis Libaude and together they
found a small student journal. Despite his father's
insistence on a business career, some time in October 1884 Bernard, on the recommendation of a
Russian artist, at the age of sixteen becomes a
pupil of Fernand Cormon. At this studio he begins
to draw after plaster casts and live models
(*fig. 102*). Louis Anquetin introduces Bernard to
another studio comrade, Toulouse-Lautrec. These
three begin to spend time together admiring such
masters as Velásquez, Michelangelo and Luca
Signorelli.

Fig. 99
Emile Bernard:
Madeleine,
1881,
pen and pencil drawing
(Kunsthalle Bremen).

Fig. 100
Emile Bernard:
Study of the Don Quixote by Gustave Doré,
c. 1882,
pen drawing
(Kunsthalle Bremen).

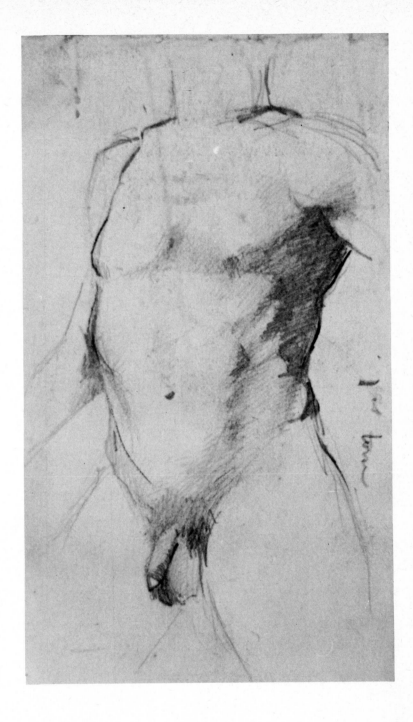

Fig. 101
Emile Bernard:
The Courtyard of Sainte-Barbe College,
1882,
pen drawing
(Kunsthalle Bremen).

Fig. 102
Emile Bernard:
First torso executed at Cormon's,
c. 1884,
pencil drawing
(Kunsthalle Bremen).

1885

Bernard lives with his parents in a rented house between Asnières and Courbevoie. He continues to work daily at the Cormon "atelier libre" and produces, according to his recollections, his first painting there, *Portrait of the Artist's Grandfather* (*fig. 103*). He is on close personal terms with fellow students Louis Anquetin, Toulouse-Lautrec, François Gauzi, Tampier and Eugène Boch. With Anquetin and Lautrec he frequently visits the Louvre and also commences to know the works of the Impressionists (especially Manet, Monet and Renoir) at the Durand-Ruel Gallery. At the colour shop of Julien "Père" Tanguy on 14 rue Clauzel he is overwhelmed by the canvases of Paul Cézanne. Lautrec paints Bernard's portrait (*fig. 136*). Bernard spends the summer in Lille with his grandmother where he paints many studies. He returns to Paris after the summer and paints landscapes in the Impressionist style along the Seine, at Asnières (*fig. 104*) and on the Island of the Grande-Jatte.

1886

FEBRUARY-MARCH

He quarrels with Cormon over his progressive artistic experiments in colour theory and the use of Pointillist technique (Welsh-Ovcharov, p. 210) and quits the *atelier*. While waiting to depart for Brittany, he spends one month visiting galleries and such friends as Toulouse-Lautrec and Anquetin. He sees the paintings of Camille Pissarro at the Gallery of Durand-Ruel (unpublished letter to his mother, February 28, 1887). On April 6 Bernard leaves on his first "voyage à pied" for Britanny. His route is in the direction of Mont St. Michel and he stops over at Cancale. He is attracted by the Gothic churches and Calvaries and reads poetry by Baudelaire, Poe and Villiers de L'Isle-Adam. He spends six months in northern France (*L'Aventure de ma vie* MS, p. 59).

APRIL-JULY

From April on he records his journey on foot by a set of drawings of Normandy landscapes (cat. no. 89 *fig.* nos. 112, 113, 116). His first major Breton stop is in St. Briac near St. Malo where he stays for two months (*L'Aventure*, pp. 50-51). Here he paints, draws and makes his living quarters a "véritable atelier" at the inn of Madame Lemasson. Bernard continues on foot through Lamballe; Tréguier; Morlaix and Landerneau. He reaches Douarnenez and heads for Faouët and then to Quimper (*L'Aventure de ma vie* MS, pp. 55 ff.).

END OF JULY

At Concarneau, Bernard first meets the painter Emile Schuffenecker who was then employing the technique of Pointillism; he gives Bernard a card of introduction to Paul Gauguin. The next day Bernard arrives in Pont-Aven at the pension of Marie Gloanec and meets Paul Gauguin.

Fig. 103
Emile Bernard:
Portrait of the Artist's Grandfather,
1885,
oil on canvas
(Collection Clément Altarriba, Paris).

Fig. 104
Emile Bernard:
Bank of the Seine at Asnières, 1885, oil on canvas
(private collection).

AUGUST-SEPTEMBER

He stays two months in Pont-Aven, where he becomes acquainted with Gauguin and Laval and paints landscapes and other Breton subjects. (cat. no. 90). He arrives at the end of September in Rennes via Lorient, Cavuesca, Auray and Vannes, and returns to Paris by train.

END SEPTEMBER-DECEMBER

He possibly returns to Paris in time to visit the second exhibition of the *Salon de la Société des Artistes Indépendants* (Aug.-Sept.) where he would have seen the Pointillist paintings of Seurat and Signac. He paints along the Seine and at Asnières, working in an Impressionist and Pointillist manner.

In Paris he resides with his parents and visits his friends at Cormon's. There he first observes Vincent van Gogh at work. He deposits some of his "retouched" paintings from the Breton trip at the shop of Père Tanguy; here he meets Vincent van Gogh.

1887

JANUARY-FEBRUARY

In the winter of 1886-1887 he cements his friendship with Vincent van Gogh, to whom he had introduced Anquetin.

Sometime in the winter 1886-87 Bernard poses for Anquetin's large painting *The Interior of the Cabaret Bruant*. In February Bernard announces in a letter to his parents that he is posing for Anquetin (*fig. 80*), that he is working in the environs of Paris and that he frequents the shop of Père Tanguy (unpublished letter, Archives Musées Nationaux).

On February 28 (unpublished letter to his parents) he first meets Lucien Pissarro at the shop of Père Tanguy where he has gone to leave again some recent "retouched" canvases of his Breton trip. On the same day he meets the Neo-Impressionist artist Charles Angrand. Possibly by this date, or by December, Bernard executes a large pastel (cat. no. 87) accompanied by a series of preparatory sketches (*fig. 111*).

MARCH-APRIL

In March Bernard's parents lease a house in Asnières (unpublished letter February 27, 1887). He continues to work out-of-doors along the

banks of the Seine and paints a large canvas, *The Boating Party* (unlocated) and diverse views of Asnières. By this time Bernard has become a close friend of van Gogh and visits the latter's apartment at 54 rue Lepic where he sees Vincent's collection of Japanese prints and his paintings including canvases from the Dutch period. Probably he sees the opening of the third exhibition of the *Indépendants* (March 26—May 3) where Seurat, Signac and related artists exhibit their Pointillist works. At a small exhibition in Asnières, Bernard exhibits his recent Pointillist canvases, and Paul Signac seeks him out.

Bernard and Anquetin discuss Pointillist theories and pay a visit to Signac's studio on 130 boulevard de Clichy.

At the café *Le Tambourin*, situated at 62 boulevard de Clichy, Vincent van Gogh organizes an exhibition of Japanese prints. This exhibition, according to van Gogh, impresses Bernard and Anquetin deeply and influences their respective researches into simplification (*CL* 511). At Tanguy's shop Bernard continues to study the paint-

ings by Paul Cézanne, which aid him in his research into abstraction.

Van Gogh takes Bernard and Anquetin to the attic of the shop of S. Bing in order to study Japanese prints (*CL* 511). By the end of April-May both Bernard and Anquetin begin to move away from Pointillism towards Japanese "abstraction."

At the end of April he announces to his parents his arrival in Ribay, Normandy (unpublished letter April 27, 1887).

MAY-JUNE

He works in St. Briac. He stays for two months at the inn of Madame Lemasson. There he paints his room with "frescoes" depicting pastoral scenes, covers his windows in imitation Gothic stained-glass and decorates the door of the inn's "salle" with a stained glass motif. He becomes acquainted with the young Symbolist writer Albert Aurier (*see* Intro. above, p. 53). During this period he paints portraits and landscapes of St. Briac and such Breton subjects as *Breton Interior* (*fig. 105*).

Fig. 105   Emile Bernard: *Breton Interior*, 1887, oil on canvas   (private collection).

1888

Fig. 106   Emile Bernard: *Village Park*, 1887, oil on canvas (private collection).

JANUARY

Bernard writes Aurier that he has a project for a publication of lithographs by certain artists such as Bernard, Degas, Gauguin as well as his poems and that he wishes Aurier to participate (unpublished letter, January 17, 1888). The influence of Cézanne is especially noteworthy in Bernard's still life paintings of this period (cat. no. 98).

FEBRUARY

Circa February 20, Bernard spends some hours with Vincent, who departs for Arles that day.

MARCH

Bernard's first letter from van Gogh in Arles (*B*2) inaugurates an intensive correspondence.

APRIL

In early April, Théo van Gogh visits Bernard, who sends a drawing (*fig. 107*) to Vincent in Arles (*B*5). At the end of April Bernard leaves Paris for Brittany.

MAY-AUGUST

By some time in May, Bernard arrives in St. Briac for a three-month stay, where he falls in love with the innkeeper's daughter, Marie Lemasson. He paints and draws Breton subjects.

In late June, Bernard sends Vincent a watercolour sketch of a brothel (*CL*502) and in July invites him to St. Briac (*CL*501b). At the end of July Bernard sends a group of ten drawings to Vincent.

AUGUST

In early August Bernard informs Vincent that he is studying the art of Italian and German primitives, for example Giotto and Holbein (*B*14). By August 14, Bernard arrives in Pont-Aven and at the inn of Marie Gloanec encounters Gauguin (*B*14), to whom he shows his work from St. Briac. He begins to work in the company of Gauguin and Charles Laval (*L'Aventure* MS, p. 75) and exchanges ideas on Synthetism with Gauguin. He paints many studies including two panels for the post office of Pont-Aven (*figs. 108, 109*).

Some time before mid-August Madeleine Bernard and her mother arrive in Pont-Aven for their holidays.

JULY

He arrives via Quimperlé in Pont-Aven and is informed of Gauguin's voyage to Martinique. By this time he produces paintings of Breton and Normandy landscapes (*fig. 106*) rendered in a highly simplified manner (cat. no. 94).

FALL

By the fall he is back in Paris and working at his parent's new house on 5 avenue Beaulieu, Asnières. His grandmother has arrived from Lille and lives with them; she has ordered the construction of a wooden *atelier* for Bernard. (*L'Aventure* MS, p. 74). Bernard, Anquetin and Vincent work together toward the latter's idea of exhibiting as a group which Vincent calls the "Petit Boulevard."

Bernard paints portraits of his grandmother and of Tanguy (cat. nos. 95 and 97).

C. NOVEMBER

He exhibits canvases which he calls his "synthèses géometriques" alongside those of Vincent, Anquetin and Lautrec at the first and only manifestation of the "Petit Boulevard" in the working class Grand Restaurant-Bouillon du Chalet at 43 de Clichy.

Bernard sells his first painting at this exhibition (*CL*510).

By this date he paints mature Cloisonist canvases depicting the environs of Asnières (cat. no. 96).

WINTER

Bernard participates in heated discussions on art in the cafés of Montmartre with Vincent, Gauguin, Camille and Lucien Pissarro (*CL*498). He admires and remarks on the Martinique paintings brought back by Gauguin then on view at Théo van Gogh's shop.

SEPTEMBER

Bernard begins a month of intense creativity; he executes his *Breton Women in the Meadow* (cat. no. 104) and Gauguin paints his *Vision After the Sermon* (pl.7).

Late in this month Bernard dispatches six drawings to van Gogh illustrating four brothel subjects (*B*17, *CL*543) and two watercolours depicting Asnières subjects.

Bernard paints several portraits of his sister Madeleine (cat. nos. 102 and 108).

Late in the month Bernard paints his *self-portrait* (cat. no. 105) to be sent to Vincent as part of a planned exchange of portraits among Gauguin, Bernard, Laval and Vincent.

For the post office at Pont-Aven, Bernard paints several works directly on the wooden partitions, windows and doors.

OCTOBER

Early this month Bernard sends twelve drawings from Pont-Aven depicting brothel scenes with a

Fig. 107
Emile Bernard:
Girl in a Street: Paris,
1888,
pen drawing
(Rijksmuseum Vincent van Gogh, Amsterdam).

Fig. 108
Emile Bernard:
Woman with a Red Umbrella,
1888,
oil on panel
(Collection John A. and Audrey Jones Beck, Houston).

Fig. 109
Emile Bernard:
Fireworks on the River,
1888,
oil on panel
(Yale University Art Gallery, New Haven, Gift of Arthur G. Altschul, B.A. 1943).

Fig. 108

Fig. 109

title page and a poem to Vincent (*B*19). Bernard sends his *Self-Portrait* to Vincent (*B*19).

Bernard writes van Gogh that seven paintings sent by Vincent as exchanges have arrived.

NOVEMBER

Bernard arrives in Paris *circa* November 10 (*M*LXVIII). He renews his friendship with Albert Aurier (unpublished letter November 25, 1888).

DECEMBER

Gauguin, who has returned from Arles, visits Bernard (December 27), informing him of Vincent's hospitalization after he had mutilated his ear.

1889

JANUARY-FEBRUARY

January 1 Bernard writes Aurier and informs him of Gauguin's news about Vincent's "madness".

Bernard sees Gauguin often at Schuffenecker's during these months. He completes his six zincographs *Les Bretonneries* and shows them to Gauguin, who at the same time completes his eleven zincographs. During this period Bernard is in great conflict with his father (*CL*572) and seeks exemption from military service.

MARCH-APRIL

Bernard is living and working in Asnières. Some time in March Gauguin leaves Paris.

MAY

Circa mid-May, Bernard is contacted by Gauguin who has arrived back in Paris from Pont-Aven (*T*9) to see the World Exposition which has opened May 6.

Monday, May 20 or May 27, Bernard writes Aurier about the plans for a catalogue for the exhibition, indicating that on Thursday, May 23 or 30, the exhibition of the "Groupe Impressionniste et Synthétiste" was planned to open at the Café des Arts owned by M. Volpini.

JUNE

By June Bernard had on view at the Café Volpini twenty paintings along with a set of his zincographs *Les Bretonneries* (*see* Introduction, (p. 44, n. 48).

He now writes Aurier about plans for a

catalogue of the Volpini exhibition which is to contain eight reproductions of drawings and urges Aurier to have these reproductions appear also in the latter's journal *Le Moderniste*. Meanwhile, Bernard is working on the publication of the Volpini catalogue.

JULY

The article "Au Palais des Beaux-Arts, notes sur la peinture" by Bernard appears in *Le Moderniste* (No. 14, July 27).

At the end of July he leaves for St. Briac anxious to renew his friendship with Marie Lemasson and he stays there after his father forbids him to go to Pont-Aven.

AUGUST

Bernard spends this month working in St. Briac and nearby St. Malo.

On August 3 appears the first of four weekly issues of *Le Moderniste* which reproduces eight drawings by Bernard, Gauguin, Schuffenecker, Roy and de Monfreid which had been illustrated in the Volpini catalogue.

Bernard receives a letter from Gauguin, who is staying in Le Pouldu with de Haan and Laval, informing him that Gauguin is returning to Pont-Aven in three or four days (*M*LXXXIV).

He writes to Schuffenecker explaining the consequences of the Volpini exhibition, especially that catalogues of the Volpini show remain unsold (letter August 26), and invites Schuffenecker to St. Malo.

SEPTEMBER

Bernard is back in Paris, Gauguin is in Pont-Aven for one month and writes to Bernard inviting him to Le Pouldu (*M*LXXXVII).

Vincent is puzzled that Octave Maus has invited Bernard as well as himself to show at the next exhibition of *Les Vingt* (*CL*604).

OCTOBER-NOVEMBER

On October 5 Bernard visits Théo to see Vincent's recent paintings (*T*18). He corresponds with Gauguin in Le Pouldu.

Gauguin writes Bernard that he has decorated his *atelier* at the villa "des Grandes-Sables" with his and Bernard's Volpini zincographs as well as Japanese prints (*M*LXXXIX).

Bernard arranges with Aurier (unpublished

letter October 11) for the latter to write an article on van Gogh (which ultimately appeared in *Mercure de France*, January 1890); Bernard sends Aurier a set of his Volpini zincographs.

In mid-November Théo visits Bernard to see his recent works (*T*20). *Circa* mid-November, Bernard sends to Gauguin two photographs from Paris of his recent paintings. *The Adoration of the Magi* and *The Annunciation*. Van Gogh acknowledges receipt from Bernard of these or similar photographs in November, but refutes these works as too abstract and mannerist, saying he prefers Bernard's earlier, more naive works (*B*21).

In late November, Gauguin writes from Le Pouldu to Bernard (*M*XCV) and to Madeleine Bernard (*M*XCVI) in Paris, approving of Bernard's use of religious themes.

DECEMBER

By December, Bernard is in Lille, attempting to earn a living as a designer of textiles. He corresponds with Aurier and asks him of any news on Gauguin.

1890

JANUARY-MARCH

By the second half of March Théo informs Vincent that Bernard and Aurier intend to come to see his latest paintings (*T*29).

MAY-JUNE

By the end of May, Bernard writes a joint letter to Gauguin and Schuffenecker in Paris, describing his state of depression on feeling abandoned by his friends (letter May 28 or 29, 1890, Bibliothèque Nationale, Paris). He writes to Schuffenecker again in late May, announcing his intention to marry a young girl in Lille May 31, 1890.

Early in June, he returns from Calais to Lille and replies to a letter from Gauguin that he is willing to depart for Madagascar (letter June 9, 1890); in the same letter he includes a note to Schuffenecker.

JULY-AUGUST

Bernard back in Paris, hears of the death of Vincent van Gogh on July 27 and attends the funeral in Auvers on July 30. He writes Aurier the next day of this tragedy.

On the advice of Schuffenecker, Bernard writes in early August to Daniel de Monfreid informing him that his parents have cut off his financial support. He asks him to buy some tickets for a lottery on one of his paintings (letter *circa* August 10, 1890, Jean Loize "Les Amitiés du peintre Georges-Daniel de Monfreid et ses reliques de Gauguin," Paris, n.d., p. 89 no. 113).

Bernard writes Aurier of his plans to go to Madagascar with Gauguin and asks Aurier to write an article for the *Mercure de France* on Gauguin as he had done on Vincent.

On September 18 Théo writes asking Bernard to aid him in hanging in his apartment a small exhibition of the canvases of the late artist ("Emile Bernard et Vincent van Gogh," Art-Documents, no. 17 [February, 1952], pp. 13-14).

1891

JANUARY-FEBRUARY

In early January Bernard writes Schuffenecker that he is staying with his friend, Eugène Boch at Couilly until May (letter January 19, 1891). By this time Bernard has again written to urge Aurier to do an article on Gauguin.

Circa February 22, Bernard and his sister Madeleine encounter Gauguin at the latter's benefit sale at the Hôtel Drouot. An altercation arises over Gauguin's proclamation as the leader of Symbolism. This is the last known contact between Bernard and Gauguin.

MARCH-MAY

In March-April, Bernard exhibits six works for the first time at the *Indépendants*.

In April and May he writes Schuffenecker suggesting changes on the article which the latter is doing on Bernard (the article dated and signed June 6, 1891 is now in the Bibliothèque Nationale, Paris).

AUGUST-OCTOBER

Bernard, in St. Briac, corresponds with Schuffenecker about his artistic projects and speaks of the Italian primitives and of the Symbolist writer Sar Péladan.

NOVEMBER-DECEMBER

In November, Bernard writes a letter from Asnières on Filiger and his art which is published in *La Plume* (Dec. 15, p. 447). By this time Bernard has dedicated a set of his *Bretonneries* zincographs to Filiger (cat. no. 109).

In December he exhibits three paintings at the gallery of Le Barc de Boutteville in the first exhibition of the "Peintres Impressionistes et Symbolistes," which also includes works by Gauguin, van Gogh, Sérusier, Signac and Lautrec.

1891 to 1941

In 1892 Bernard organizes the first van Gogh retrospective in France at the gallery of Le Barc de Boutteville. The same year he participates at the *Salon de la Rose-Croix*.

Maurice Denis and Bernard sever relations because of the former's critique of Bernard's works in this exhibition. He executes a tapestry (1892) and illustrates the "Cantilènes" (1892) by the Symbolist poet Jean Moréas. During the period 1893-95 and in 1897, Bernard publishes in the *Mercure de France* extracts both from the twenty-one letters he had received from Vincent and from a limited selection of Vincent's letters to Théo van Gogh. His works of this period exhibit a mannerist extension of his previous Cloisonist style and the artist is now inspired by themes based less on Breton life than on romantic visions of the Middle Ages and mystic Catholicism.

In 1893 he embarks for Italy and then travels to Samos, Constantinople, Bayreuth and Jerusalem; by the end of September he arrives in Egypt. In August 1896 to May 1897, Bernard leaves Egypt to visit Spain where he experiences a serious spiritual crisis and meets the Spanish artist Zuloaga. His art begins to return to a more traditional style of the sixteenth and seventeenth century. In 1901 Ambroise Vollard organizes an important exhibition of Bernard's work.

In 1904, after eleven years in Egypt, Bernard returns to France and visits Paul Cézanne in Aix-en-Provence. In July he publishes in the journal *L'Occident* his first article on the art of this master. The next year Bernard pays a final visit to Cézanne and finds a new journal *La Renovation esthétique* which becomes the principal organ for his defence of a return to classical art. In 1911 he publishes in Paris a luxury edition of the *Letters of Vincent van Gogh to Emile Bernard* (editor Ambroise Vollard). In the night of April 16, 1941 he dies in his *atelier* on 15 quai de Bourbon in Paris.

87.

Hour of the Flesh:
L'Heure de la viande
c. 1885-87
pastel and gouache on wrapping paper
(mounted on linen): 125 × 170 cm
Not signed or dated
Lent by Clément Altarriba, Paris

Previously unexhibited and unpublished this work represents a cabaret interior and finds its title in an ink drawing of the same subject to which Bernard added the inscription "l'heure de la viande" (*fig. 110*). The setting relates to that typified by the Café *Le Mirliton* of Aristide Bruant which was planned to serve as the basis for a major representation occupying Anquetin for some time *circa* 1885-87 before he abandoned it and apparently destroyed his preliminary studies.[1] It is likely that Bernard conceived this major composition in some relationship to Anquetin's Bruant project, since he repeatedly implied that it was the earliest major experiment in this subject *genre* among Anquetin, Lautrec and himself, at the time regular visitors to the famous singer's café. A smaller preliminary

sketch for his own mural-like pastel and gouache drawing (*fig. 111*) displays an affinity in subject treatment and style to Lautrec's *Bar of the Café de la Rue du Rome* (cat. no. 113), indicating the close interrelationship of style and subject interests within the little group of ex-Cormon students called by Vincent the "Petit Boulevard." Whereas Bernard would later turn his back upon the Bohemian café life led by Anquetin and Lautrec, it is here treated as a subject proper to the creation of monumental decorative art.[2]

This noticeable attempt at a complex and large-scale figural composition also can be considered both a tribute and a challenge to the work of Seurat. The bustled female figures in profile, like those in Anquetin's *Avenue de Clichy* (cat. no. 76) are decidedly like those in Seurat's *La Grande-Jatte* (*fig. 19*), albeit here placed in a setting far removed from the idea of Sunday afternoon promenading. The artificial lighting of Bernard's drawing is one more element of this scene which shows a relationship to the contemporary interests of Anquetin.[3]

[1] Bernard, *Anquetin 1932*, pp. 592-93, where Bernard recalls having posed on numerous occasions seated at a table of the Café Bruant (before it opened because of his young age). This likeness was to be used in the foreground of the composition. One such study is likely to have been the *Portrait of Bernard at a Table* (*fig. 80*), formerly thought a self-portrait by Bernard (Tralbaut, p. 210), but here attributed to Anquetin as a study for the "*chez* Bruant" (the inclusion of a transfer grid suggests this function). The *L'Heure de la viande* follows Anquetin's recorded usage of wrapping paper for his pastels.

[2] In an unpublished letter dated February 1887 to his parents, Bernard already states his intention of going to Brittany in order to escape the "unsavoury" (*fade*) life of the Paris cafés and taverns.

[3] Except for Bernard's report of Anquetin having destroyed all preliminary studies for the project (Bernard, *Anquetin 1932*, p. 593) and because of Bernard's other studies of the Hour of the Flesh subject, it would be tempting, as this writer once did from a photograph (*Petit Boulevard*, pp. 29-30) to attribute the *Viande* pastel to Anquetin.

Fig. 110
Emile Bernard:
Hour of the Flesh,
1885,
pen drawing,
(ex. Collection Clément Altarriba, Paris).

Fig. 111
Emile Bernard:
The Tavern,
c. 1885-87,
pen drawing
(ex. Collection Clément Altarriba, Paris).

88.
Beach and Cliffs at Cancale
May 1886
oil on canvas: 45.5 × 55.5 cm
Signed lower right: *Emile Bernard*
Inscribed and dated lower left: *Cancale 30 Mai
[18]86*
Lent by the Musée Petit Palais, Geneva

With its exceedingly specific inscribed date, this painting provides an excellent guidepost for appreciating at least one tendency in Bernard's painting style during the early stages of his first trip to Brittany.[1] As he was anxious to see the ocean he started off in the direction of Mont St. Michel, which he eventually by-passed in order to stop over at Cancale. Here he began to paint his first Breton studies, which included *Beach and Cliffs*. Describing the view from his bedroom at the inn named La Houle ("the swell"), he stated "The sea was underneath my window where I observed daily the beached fishing barges and the comings and goings of the local wives and daughters going out for oysters."[2] Although the terrain presented in his painting is viewed from the beach below the cliffs, he has clearly sought to capture the rugged essence of the setting.

The painting is more broadly significant within the context of Bernard's stylistic interests at the time. Shortly before this trip Bernard had been dismissed from the Cormon studio due to his conversion to Impressionism and interest in scientific colour theory, and this canvas may be considered a further extension of these interests.[3] The relatively high pitch of the overall tonality is in the Impressionist tradition of Monet, who this same summer was to concentrate upon a series of coastal subjects similar to this one by Bernard but at Belle-Ile sur-Mer. Whereas direct contact between the older and younger artist therefore cannot be assumed, the presence of a uniform brush technique throughout and treatment of the cliff and rock formations as if flattened planes of colour hint at the search for compositional order both within and outside Impressionism. Along with the painting's allegiance to *plein air* Impressionism, there is also a sense of seeking a rational basis for its use. As the artist wrote of this period of transition, he had to work "with the aid of theory and nature to become an original artist."[4] The same search is embodied in a small drawing of the *Beach at Cancale* (*fig. 112*) dated May 19, 1886, in which the divisions of ground planes and silhouetting of the figural imagery are more striking still than in the slightly later painting.

Quite possibly Vincent was referring to such paintings as this when from St. Rémy in late 1889 he recalled (*Wil*16) that Bernard "had also painted cliffs and beaches in Brittany."

1   *L'Aventure*, ms., p. 47.
2   *Ibid.*, p. 49.
3   *Ibid.*, p. 45-47.
4   *Ibid.*, p. 46.

Fig. 112
Emile Bernard:
The Beach at Cancale,
19 May 1886,
drawing
(Kunsthalle Bremen).

Canal 30 mai 86   Emily Bernard

89.

Landscape with Trees, Pont-Aven
August 1886
oil on panel: 52 × 53 cm
Signed and dated in blue lower right:
Emile Bernard [18] 86
Inscribed in red lower left: *AOUT*; lower right:
1886
Lent by Le Glouannec, Paris

Bernard painted this landscape during his first month in Pont-Aven, conceivably as part of some interior decor since it is painted on joined slats of wood that might originally have been part of room furnishings. Of the three paintings from summer 1886 exhibited here (*see* also cat. nos. 88 and 90) this example displays the closest affinity to Pointillist style. It recently has been advanced that Bernard became acquainted with Neo-Impressionism when, just previous to his arrival in Pont-Aven, he met Emile Schuffenecker in Concarneau, who was working in that idiom.[1] That is an attractive theory, since Bernard had left for Brittany before the opening of the eighth Impressionist exhibition which contained the first full-scale manifestation of the Neo-Impressionist work of Georges Seurat

including *The Grande-Jatte*. However, Bernard calls Schuffenecker's style of that period Impressionist, and little is known of how extensive the contact was at either Concarneau or Pont-Aven.[2] Moreover, it is possible that *La Place Saint-Briac* (*fig. 16*) was painted *circa* June-July 1886 rather than the following year, as has been supposed.[3] This possibility is strengthened by the existence of a group of drawings executed at that date and place, such as the *Landscape with Villa, St. Briac* (*fig. 113*) dated July 7, 1886. In these, one finds not only a pattern of striated strokes of charcoal evenly distributed throughout the sky areas, but also uniform patterns of other graphic techniques in other areas of the composition. Conceivably this tendency towards a uniform appliqué of brush or graphic technique could have been evolved more on the model of the mid-1880s Impressionism of Monet or Pissarro without much knowledge of the Neo-Impressionist movement in its latest manifestations.

Yet there is a general contrast of the dominantly orange sunlit and blue shadow areas throughout the *Landscape with Trees* so that an interest in the science of colour cannot be completely ruled out. Bernard several times admitted

to a temporary involvement with Pointillism and its colour theories. This previously unpublished panel painting is one of the rare surviving examples of the *genre* which allow us a glimpse into this passing but important moment of experimentation. As elsewhere in his early work, the patina of brush daubs overlying the painting surface is combined with a relative simplicity of pictorial structure which seems to be a trait native to Bernard's talent whatever his chosen style.

[1] M.A. Stevens, London *P-I*, cat. nos. 12, 184.
[2] Bernard, *L'Aventure*, p. 11.
[3] I.e., R. Herbert, exh. cat. *Neo-Impressionism* (New York: S.R. Guggenheim Museum, 1968), cat. no. 109, whose suppostion of a 1887 date, if correct, would indicate that the artist wished to prolong his involvement with the Impressionist-Pointillist tendency, even after his geometrizing Cloisonist landscape style of 1887 was well advanced (*see* cat. no. 92).

Fig. 113
Emile Bernard:
Landscape with Villa, St. Briac,
July 7, 1886,
charcoal drawing
(Collection Clément Altarriba, Paris).

AOUT

Émile Bernard
1886

90.
Breton Girl Seated in a Landscape
summer 1886
oil on canvas: 79.2 × 55.2 cm
Signed and dated lower right: *E. Bernard [18]86*
Lent anonymously

During 1886 Bernard spent six months in Brittany producing many drawings and oil studies in various locales. By late July he left St. Briac, where he had established an *atelier* for two months, and after passing through Brest, Quimper and Concarneau he spent most of August and September in Pont-Aven.[1] In Concarneau he had met by chance Emile Schuffenecker, who provided a card of introduction to Gauguin, but Bernard recalled not having become intimate with the latter subsequently in Pont-Aven and not even showing him his work from the early summer.[2]

Despite Bernard's disclaimer of serious contact this summer with Gauguin, *Breton Girl* evinces a definite affinity of style with, for example, Gauguin's *Field of Derout-Lollichon 1* (cat. no. 44), in which one finds a quasi-stippled brush technique rather like that used here by Bernard. We now know that the latter approached even closer to Pointillist style in another work from this first stay in Pont-Aven (cat. no. 89), although there too we scarcely have a classic use of Neo-Impressionist principles of colour. Bernard's subject, a seated girl wearing the local head-dress and broad white fichu and viewed from the rear, is also common to Gauguin's 1886 Pont-Aven iconography (*see W* 196, 201-03), and it is difficult to believe Bernard would not have seen examples of such paintings during a two-month stay.

At the same time, Bernard's sense of composition differs from Gauguin's contemporary style, tending towards simplification of contour and spatial divisions whereas Gauguin appears to favour lush vegetation and complex spatial rhythms. It is tempting to believe that this particular canvas by Bernard already betrays a Japanist design element. The wood block print *Fuji Seen from the Outskirts of Koshigaya in Musashi Province* by Hiroshige (*fig. 114*) is only one of many oriental prototypes which might have influenced Bernard's sense of composition and subject selection even at this early date. Though written in 1903, Bernard's account of his development along with Anquetin of a Cloisonist style places this in 1886 and lists "the study of Japanese prints" (*crépons*) as its single direct cause.[3] Moreover, a similar sense of Japanese simplification is already present in a

drawing (*fig. 116*) dated May 1, 1886. This example indicates that Bernard had begun to evolve a personal design sense tending towards bold simplification before his arrival at Pont-Aven and the meeting with Gauguin.

The *Breton Girl Seated in a Landscape* was somehow acquired by the critic Albert Aurier some time after he had met Bernard in 1887, and it remained in the Aurier family's possession for many years thereafter.

[1] *L'Aventure* MS., p. 57.
[2] *Ibid.*, pp. 58-59.
[3] *Notes*, p. 676.

Fig. 114
Hiroshige:
Fuji Seen from the Outskirts of Koshigaya in Musashi Province,
print
(The Rijksmuseum Vincent van Gogh, Amsterdam).

91.

Quai de Clichy on the Seine
beginning (?) 1887
oil on canvas: 39 × 59 cm
Signed and dated lower left: *Emile Bernard 1887*
Lent by Lenoir M. Josey Inc., Houston

No known early record of exhibition or other documentation by the artist for this painting seems to
have survived. A recent exhibition title, *Quai de la
Seine à Asnières*, is approximately correct, since
the setting depicted is the Quai de Clichy located
opposite Asnières on the Paris side of the Seine.
The barges clustered about the elevated loading
dock with cranes in the middle distance are also
found in a previously unpublished painting, a
View from the Pont d'Asnières (*fig. 115*) north-
ward toward the Ile Robinson and the Pont de
Clichy, which may be vaguely indicated along the
horizon in both paintings.[1] In the latter painting
one can also see the smokestacks of the industrial
areas of Clichy and Saint Ouen. The Pont
d'Asnières across which the two girls in the foreground of this painting walk is the more distant
one in Bernard's *The Ragpickers* (cat. no. 96) and
in van Gogh's painting (*F 301*) from the same
setting on the Asnières side of the river.

Since the *Quai* and *View* depict scenes of winter, it is tempting to see them as executed approximately at the same time. Yet the *Quai de Clichy* is
rendered in still Impressionist brushwork, despite
the geometric quality of its underlying composition. It is thus possible to believe it was executed at
the beginning of 1887 before Bernard's departure
for Brittany, especially since such canvases as
Woman Tending Geese (cat. no. 92) and *Afternoon at St. Briac* (cat. no. 93) indicate just how
advanced was the artist's commitment to a
geometric basis for his compositions by spring
1887. In contrast, the *View from the Pont
d'Asnières* is still more developed in terms of
Cloisonist outlines and colour areas and flat, virtually invisible brushwork than either of these two
paintings of early 1887 or the *Ragpickers* from the
fall. The *View* painting is therefore likely to date
from the very last months of 1887, when Bernard's devotion to the ideal of "synthèse géomet-
rique" had reached its apogee.

The *Quai de Clichy* is, in contrast probably
one of the earliest manifestations of a radically
geometrizing approach to composition in the history of late nineteenth century landscape painting.
The distance already travelled from his own
Impressionist involvement is evident when one

looks at the 1885 *Bank of the Seine at Asnières*
(*fig. 104*) with its charming variety of brushwork
and almost complete dissolution of solid or outlined forms. The *Quai de Clichy* substitutes for
this picturesque compositional disarray a forceful
contrast of straight linear elements: vertical, horizontal, and diagonal.[2] The foreshortening of the
perspective lines of the roadway is so dramatic that
here, once again, the influence of Japanese prints is
to be presumed. The sense of oriental compression
of space is accompanied by the "slanted eyes" of
the two figures, centre foreground, whom the artist
has encompassed in frankly Cloisonist contours.
Although a minor expressive factor, Bernard has
included streaks of red with the olive green of his

figures, the trees and wall at right and the piers of
the dock, as if he wished with this contrast of
complementaries to somewhat enliven the otherwise bleakly overcast winter setting.

[1] I wish to acknowledge my thanks to M. Réne
    LeBihan, curator of the Musée de Brest, for show-
    ing me this work and allowing me to take photo-
    graphs of the painting.

[2] E. Bernard, *Inventory*, includes several canvases
    of the period 1887-88 which he entitles
    "recherches décoratives de rythmes correspond-
    ants et couleurs (analogie de contraires)."

Fig. 115
Emile Bernard:
View from the Pont d'Asnières, winter 1887, oil on
canvas (Musée de Brest, photograph B.M.
Welsh-Ovcharov).

92.

Woman Tending Geese: *Femme aux oies*
spring 1887
oil on canvas: 33 × 41 cm
Signed and dated lower left:
Emile Bernard [18]87
Lent by a private collection, Bremen

By the end of April 1887 Bernard had departed Paris for his second walking trip to Brittany. In a letter dated April 27 to his parents he announced his arrival at the village of Ribay in Normandy. Bernard's personal inventory of canvases annotates the *Femme aux oies* as "Ribay 1887, voyage au pied."[1] In the same letter Bernard spoke of the atrocious weather he was encountering and asked that Tanguy be requested to send some Veronese green to Ribay where he was working on two canvases, one of which must have been this landscape, in large part coloured green.[2]

The spring 1887 date of this painting is of paramount importance in documenting Bernard's arrival at a style which he characterized as "mes synthèses géometriques."[3] His earlier flirtations with Impressionist and Pointillist style have here been abandoned for painting in clearly defined, silhouetted forms set against the flat, geometrically defined planes of the landscape elements. A drawing dated May 1 (*fig. 116*) and thus executed a year earlier at a similar site indicates just how radical Bernard's negation of the atmospheric effects of Impressionism had become by early 1887. One possible explanation for this shift was that offered by Vincent (*CL*511), namely the exhibition of Japanese prints the latter had organized at the café *Le Tambourin*, which Bernard presumably saw before his departure. While not of course the direct model for this painting, such an example of Japanese prints as Hiroshige's *Fuji seen from the Outskirts of Koshigaya in Musashi Province* (*fig. 114*)[4] provides parallels of silhouetted trees against a backdrop of well-defined planar landscape compartments of a type Bernard could have had fresh in his memory as he set off for another painting expedition in the north of France. This painting was probably shown at the exhibition of the Café Volpini under the title *Woman and Geese*.[5]

1   Bremen-Lille, cat. no. 14, assigns this work to St. Briac, but see E. Bernard, *Inventory*, where no. 5, format 6, is *Femme aux oies*.

2   See Bernard, biographical data, p. 263.

3   I.e., in Bernard, *Van Gogh*, p. 393.

4   A copy was owned by Vincent; see *Japanese Prints*, no. 47b.

5   Volpini exhibition catalogue no. 86 "Femme et oies (collection M. Régis Delboeuf)."

Fig. 116
Emile Bernard:
Landscape with Trees at Ribay,
May 1, 1886,
charcoal drawing
(Collection Clément Altarriba, Paris).

93.
Afternoon at St. Briac
late spring 1887
oil on canvas: 45.5 × 55.5 cm
Signed and dated lower right: *L. Nemo 1887*
Lent by the Aargauer Kunsthaus, Aarau,
Switzerland

This (pl. 25) is one of two canvases which Bernard presented at the Volpini exhibition of 1889 under the pseudonym Ludovic Nemo. It was listed as no. 87, *Après-midi à Saint-Briac*, belonging to Emile Schuffenecker, and as a "peinture pétrole," a turpentine-thinned oil medium less glossy and therefore more matte and dry in appearance than is normal in oil paintings. From the artist's 1893 inventory we can identify the site as a view of the bay from the chapel of St. Briac.[1] The artist stayed at this village on the northern coast of Brittany during at least parts of May and June, where, presumably at the hostelry operated by Madame Lemasson, he decorated his bedroom with wall frescoes representing landscape scenes from the surrounding countryside and Biblical subjects such as the "Adoration of the Shepherds."[2] He also recalled having painted several window panes as simulated stained glass. These Medievalizing techniques are echoed in the distinct areas of even colouration found in the *Afternoon at St. Briac*.

It was during this sojourn that Bernard met Albert Aurier, who was staying in a neighbouring village with his mother and sister.

Afternoon, despite its modest size, recalls several imposing artistic precedents. One thinks of Monet's *Terrace at the Seaside near Le Havre* (Metropolitan Museum, New York) and Bernard later recalled the influence of Puvis de Chavannes *circa* 1886 in the development of Cloisonist style and the flat tones of the school of Pont-Aven.[3] Most of all, the *Afternoon* recalls the subject matter, spatial organization and strong even colours of Japanese prints. The *Shirasuka: The Legend of Onnaya* by Kuniyoshi (*fig. 117*) is an example of oriental design which Bernard might have known from the collection of Vincent van Gogh and recalled when working alone in St. Briac.[4] The Bernard painting does not picture a courtesan mourning a dead lover as does the *Shirasuka*, but a sense of longing for the unknown is present in young Bernard's image of a single female figure looking towards far distant shores.

1   I.e., *Inventory*, no. 33, "la mer et la vue de village de la chapelle en St. Briac (peinture au petrole 1887, voyage au pied)."

2   Bernard, *L'Aventure* MS, p. 69.

3   Bernard, "Le Symbolisme pictural: 1886-1936," *Mercure de France* (June 15, 1936), pp. 526-28.

4   *Japanese Prints*, no. 272m; in *CL* 510 Vincent recalls having given some Japanese prints to Bernard when they exchanged paintings in Paris, which could have been as early as winter 1886-87 (*see P-I*, pp. 56, 72 n. 65).

Fig. 117
Kuniyoshi:
Shirasuka: The Legend of Onnaya, c. 1843-45, print (Rijksmuseum Vincent van Gogh, Amsterdam).

94.

Promenade in the Bois d'Amour
summer 1887 (later retouched?)
oil on canvas: 65 × 54 cm
Signed and dated lower right: *E. Bernard 1887*
Lent by Durand-Ruel et Cie., Paris

Beginning in July 1887, Bernard worked for at
least two months in Pont-Aven, during which time
Gauguin and Laval were in Martinique.[1] That the
subject was the Bois d'Amour in Pont-Aven is
documented in the artist's 1893 inventory of his
oeuvre.[2] Previous to his arrival Bernard had
experimented with highly abstracted landscapes
including Cloisonist colour divisions (cat. nos. 92,
93) and with the subject of upright trees with
elongated trunks in a grassland setting (*fig. 118*)
where a directionalized form of Impressionist
brushwork is preserved.[3] A combination of both
approaches is present in the *Promenade*, which
displays a form of Cézanne-derived brush
technique for the grass areas, despite the high
degree of Cloisonism in the bright even colouration
for the various design components and the strong
contour outlines of the tree trunks.[4] Since it is
possible, even likely, that this canvas was
displayed late 1887 at Vincent's *Du Chalet*
exhibition, where it could have been seen by
Gauguin, the latter artist's *The Blue Trees*
(*fig. 119*) of late 1888 might be considered a
conscious or unconscious stylistic heir to the
Promenade. Bernard, too, in 1888 recapitulated
the theme of this painting, albeit now with a
horizontal format necessitated by the inclusion of
his sister reclining in the supine position of much
traditional tomb sculpture (*fig. 33*).[5]

Apart from its importance to the development
of the distinctive Pont-Aven movement, the
painting calls to mind the idyllic spirit and the
"sacred grove" iconography of Puvis de
Chavannes. Later in life Bernard attached great
importance to inspiration by Puvis in the evolution
of the Symbolist movement, and the *Promenade*
may be accounted an instance of this general
indebtedness in his own case.[6]

Fig. 118
Emile Bernard:
Landscape in Brittany,
1887,
oil on canvas
(private collection).

[1] Bernard, *L'Aventure* MS., p. 68.

[2] Bernard, *Inventory*, "no. 70, format 15, *Le Bois
d'amour à Pont-Aven* (*voyage au pied*)." This
painting was included in exh. cat., *De Pont-Aven
aux Nabis: Rétrospective 1888-1903*, (Paris:
Société des artistes indépendants, Grand Palais,
1971), no. 7, *Promenade au bois d'amour*,
which title is used in the present despite the
anomaly of "promenade" for two seated and one
standing woman.

[3] This painting is dated 1887 and was listed
Sotheby and Co., cat. 32 (sale April 26, 1967)
no. 447, as *Le pré à Saint-Briac*; the flat terrain is
indeed unlike the rolling hills surrounding
Pont-Aven, which indicates that the work was
produced before his arrival there, quite possibly at
or near St. Briac where the artist stayed *circa*
May-June.

[4] Possibly the contour line of the tree trunks were a
later addition, since they are not characteristic in
other paintings certain to date from summer 1887
or before, but they do nothing to change the
composition and essential style of this painting. To
the degree that the generally ordered brushwork
here and in other related landscapes may be called
Cézannesque, it justifies Bernard's later statement
that in 1887 he and Anquetin "perfected
Cloisonism under the influence of Paul Cézanne"
(*Notes*, p. 676).

[5] This work of summer 1888 is more decidedly
Cézannesque in character than the *Promenade*;
for various interpretations of the *Madeleine*, see
Roskill, pp. 95, 100; Andersen, Paradise, pp.
98-100, and Walter, pp. 286-91, where it is
illustrated in colour as fig. 3.

[6] Bernard, "Le Symbolisme Pictural, 1886-1936."
Mercure de France, June 15, 1936 p. 527.
Bernard would have known the *Sacred Wood* by
Puvis from either its exhibition in 1884 or the copy
by Lautrec which that artist had in his studio from
1886 (Wattenmaker, cat. nos. 25, 45), or both.
Although in Breton rather than Greek dress,
Bernard's three "promenaders" are as quietly
meditative as the figures in the arcadias of Puvis.

Fig. 119
Paul Gauguin:
The Blue Trees,
1888,
oil on canvas
(The Ordrupgaard Collection,
collection Wilhelm Hansen).

95.

Portrait of the Artist's Grandmother
fall 1887
oil on canvas: 53 × 64 cm
Not signed or dated
Lent by the Rijksmuseum Vincent van Gogh,
Amsterdam

The sitter for this portrait was Bernard's much beloved maternal grandmother, Madame Sophie Bodin-Lallement, who had operated a laundry establishment in Lille, but who, recently widowed, by late August-September 1887 had joined the artist's family in their new Asnières residence 5, avenue de Beaulieu. She financed the construction of the wooden *atelier* in the garden which was used by Bernard, and also Vincent, during the fall.[1] Bernard had sketched his grandmother as early as 1884 in Lille (*fig. 120*), but the painting shown here and the portrait actually dated 1887 (now at the Museum of Fine Arts, Boston) were both likely the product of Bernard's activities in fall 1887.[2] The Amsterdam painting was present at the *Du Chalet* exhibition, when Vincent, one may presume, acquired it in exchange (*CL* 553) for a *Self-Portrait with Straw Hat* (*F* 526), a variant of that in the present exhibition (cat. no. 7).[3] One may assume that Vincent had met Bernard's grandmother during one or more of her sittings for young Emile, and that Vincent's acquistion of her portrait was based in part upon his knowledge of this intimate Bernard family relationship, which in some respects paralleled his own with Théo.

On several occasions Vincent's letters refer to this portrait. He described it to his sister Wilhelmina (*Wil* 16) as follows: "It is the portrait of his grandmother, very old, blind in one eye; the background is the wall of a room covered with chocolate-coloured wallpaper and a completely white bed." His stress on the sitter's age and physical infirmity testifies to Vincent's love of realistic depiction. He reminded Bernard (*B* 14) that the latter's two portraits of his grandmother were perhaps the best things he had done: "Have you ever done anything better than that, and have you ever been more *yourself* and a personality? I think not. The profound study of the first thing that came to hand, of the first person who came along was enough to *create* realistically."

Vincent's memory of this painting was as usual acute, erring only in calling what appears to be drapery "wallpaper" and leaving out mention of the cylindrical hat box at right. In the same letter to Bernard (*B* 14) Vincent mentions the

portrait in analogy with the Realistic artist Daumier and the old Dutch masters, but fails to cite two other likely sources of inspiration. One of these is Cézanne, whose use of patterned floral backgrounds in a number of still lifes and some portraits is a possible general model for Bernard's backdrop for his grandmother.[4] A second even more obliquely incorporated model may have been a style of bust portrait found in Japanese prints, such as that of the *Matsushimaya Actor* by Kunisada (*fig. 121*) of which Vincent owned a copy.[5] These actor portraits are typified by three-quarter bust poses, simplified and intensely concentrated facial features and either head-dress or hair arrangements which seem strangely echoed in Bernard's forceful portrait. Perhaps the analogy is fortuitous, but by late 1887 the artist had become deeply devoted to the study of the Japanese print.

[1] *L'Aventure* MS., p. 71.

[2] Another version of his grandmother exists (private collection) dated 1889. Roskill, *Key Works*, p. 216, indicates that the Boston version (ill. in Pickvance, *Tate Entries*, cat. no. 75) is much overpainted, but Vincent had seen both versions and acquired the Amsterdam version before his own departure from Paris in February 1888, and presumably considered both complete (*B* 14).

[3] Roskill, *Exchanges*, p. 142 n. 2, identified the Vincent *Self-Portrait* which Bernard received in the exchange.

[4] Bernard, *Tanguy*, p. 609, mentions having seen *circa* 1886-88 at the shop of Père Tanguy, the *Achille Empéreire* (Venturi, I, no. 88), where one such usage occurs.

[5] *Japanese Prints*, cat. no. 177 (see. also nos. 176, 178).

Fig. 120
Emile Bernard:
Portrait of the Artist's Grandmother, 1884,
drawing
(Kunsthalle Bremen).

Fig. 121
Kunisada:
Bust Portrait of the Matsushimaya Actor,
1859
(Rijksmuseum Vincent van Gogh, Amsterdam).

96.

The Ragpickers: Iron Bridges at Asnières:
late fall 1887
oil on canvas: 45.9 × 54.2 cm
Signed and dated lower right: *E. Bernard 1887*
Lent by the Museum of Modern Art, New York
(Grace Rainey Rogers Fund, 1962)

SEE COLOUR PLATE 26.

The Ragpickers (pl. 26) is rightly considered a pivotal work for any interpretation of Bernard's contribution to modernist tendencies in French art of the late 1880s. It is nonetheless sometimes held suspect because of the visible presence of over-painted areas upon one of which the signature, lower right, appears to have been added.[1] This over-painting if done later than 1887 may have been intended to strengthen the Cloisonist aspect of its colour components, but critics agree that this would not have altered the underlying linear and planar design.

The main subject is easily established as the two bridges, that in the foreground for trains and that behind for pedestrian and vehicular traffic, which connect metropolitan Paris with the suburb of Asnières.[2] The same site was represented in van Gogh's *Bridges at Asnières* (*F* 301), but a widespread opinion that the two men worked together is obviated by the summer atmosphere which Vincent stressed in contrast to the late fall scene pictured by Bernard.

Since 1885 Bernard had lived in the area with his parents during the winter months. Returning from Brittany to Paris in late 1887, he found them established in a new residence at 5, avenue de Beaulieu, Asnières, located adjacent to the rail line and only a five to ten minute walk from the bridges seen in *The Ragpickers*. This residence was commemorated in *The House of the Artist's Parents at Asnières* (*fig. 122*), a painting which because of the bare trees and inscribed 1887 date must be thought contemporaneous with *The Ragpickers*. The oval shield, centre left, in the *House at Asnières* represents a railway signal which rises out of the sunken and shadowed railroad bed forming the triangular wedge, lower left, in this highly geometrical composition.[3] The woman *silhouetted* against the wall in this painting, like the women in *The Ragpickers*, enhances by way of contrast the viewer's appreciation of the degree of abstraction in the artist's treatment of his landscape subject. This pair of paintings from late 1887 offer convincing testimony that Bernard had

attained a highly stylized form of geometrizing design as one tendency in his art by that date.

Bernard himself identified *The Ragpickers* as the arch example of his early Cloisonist style, and he accordingly exhibited it late in 1887 at the *Du Chalet* restaurant and again in 1889 at the Volpini café.[4] Vincent van Gogh thus likely had this and its companion landscapes in mind in August 1888 when he wrote to Bernard (*B* 14), "I most certainly do not despise your researches relating to the property of lines in opposite motion, . . . to the simultaneous contrasts of lines, forms." This commendation was admittedly less warm than that which he had for Bernard's *Portrait of the Artist's Grandmother* (cat. no. 95) and two still life paintings (cat. no. 98), but he at least preferred Bernard's exercises in geometry to his avowed interest in the art of the late Middle Ages.

The conception of *The Ragpickers* was not limited to a novel experimentation with abstract canons of design. The subject reference draws upon tradition well established within Realist circles and the popular illustrations which artists like Manet sought out for inspiration.[5] Bernard had depicted the ragpicker-type with his stock high hat on several earlier occasions, including, I believe, in an unsigned and previously unattributed painting of a *Ragpicker Fishing* (*fig. 123*) from the collection of Vincent and Théo van Gogh.[6] This *circa* 1886-87 still Impressionist painting is of interest not merely for the motif of a ragpicker or ne'er-do-well type, but also for the extreme asymmetry of the composition, which indicates that Bernard was experimenting with Japanist design principles

before their occurrence in such paintings as the Museum of Modern Art *Ragpickers*. Moreover, Louis Anquetin is reputed to have posed for the tall figure of the ragpicker in the New York painting.[7]

A final aspect of this painting is the considerable similarity of its composition with Seurat's *Une Baignade, Asnières* (*fig. 20*), which may include in the background the Asnières train bridge rather than the Pont de Courbevoie as is generally thought.[8] Bernard admitted on occasion to a passing interest in Neo-Impressionism and could easily have learned something about its theories of line and colour through his recorded contact with Paul Signac.[9] It was within Neo-Impressionism that what Vincent referred to as "the simultaneous contrasts of line, forms" was first systematically investigated in reference to the "scientific" theories of such men as Charles Blanc and Charles Henry.[10] While *The Ragpickers* evinces little affinity in the use of colour and brush technique to the Pointillist style, the approach to linear compositional structure is remarkably similar.

The provenance of *The Ragpickers* has remained unclear; Bernard however records that he gave the painting to his Belgian artist friend Eugène Boch with whom he had formed a close friendship from his school days at the *atelier* Cormon.[11]

1   The present writer has discovered traces of an earlier signature and 1887 date in red embedded in the paint surface, lower left, which would corroborate both that the painting was first completed

Fig. 122
Emile Bernard:
The House of the Artist's Parents at Asnières,
1887,
oil on canvas
(Mr. and Mrs. Edgar B. Miller, Chicago).

Fig. 123
Emile Bernard (here attributed to):
Ragpicker Fishing,
c. 1886-87,
oil on canvas
(Rijksmuseum Vincent van Gogh, Amsterdam).

in 1887 and that it was subsequently overpainted to some extent.

2   At the time there were three bridges connecting Asnières to Clichy across the Seine. The two pictured are properly known as the Bridges at Asnières, whereas the Bridge of Clichy is located further downstream. Unfortunately, Bernard's one known catalogue reference to this painting, the Volpini exhibition, "no. 7, Chiffonnières–Clichy," has until now gone unrecognized as referring to the "Bridges at Asnières." It is recorded in the 1893 *Inventory* as "No. 35, format 10, *Ponts de fer à Asnières*, 1887," but, to confuse matters, in the *Notes*, p. 676, and *L'Aventure* MS., p. 68, as "Chiffonnières du pont de Clichy," by which Bernard confuses the two Asnières-Clichy vehicular bridges (incidentally, this reference lists that painting as given to Eugène Boch).

3   This building still exists at 5, avenue de Beaulieu. However, either because of restorations or because Bernard altered features for the painting, there are now only two sets of windows to each façade and the canopied entrance is on the avenue de Beau-

lieu, which runs at a right angle to, not parallel with, the railway tracks.

4   Its presence at the *Du Chalet* is mentioned in "Vincent van Gogh," *L'Arte*, XIII (Feb. 9, 1901).

5   A. Hanson, "Popular Imagery and the Work of Edouard Manet," in *French 19th Century Painting and Literature* (Manchester, England: Manchester University Press, 1972), pp. 133-39. On the ragpicker theme in Realist art *see* also G. Weisberg, *The Realist Tradition: French Painting and Drawing 1830-1900*, Cleveland Museum of Art and Indiana University Press, 1981, no. 164.

6   This attribution is made on the basis of stylistic similarities with several unpublished drawings and paintings by Bernard, one of which is a signed oil painting in a private collection, New York. I also take the *Ragpicker Fishing* as the "marine" which Vincent cited (*CL* 562) as acquired from Bernard in an exchange.

7   Auriant, "Souvenirs sur Emile Bernard," *Maintenant*, 7, 1947, p. 127.

8   Like the other pedestrian and vehicular bridges situated along this area of the Seine, the bridge at

Courbevoie up river from Asnières has low arches between the piers, features found in only a single small oil study for the *Bathers*. All other studies which include a visible bridge, and the final large painting show a straight truss surmounting the piers as is unique to the train bridge at Asnières. One suspects that Seurat purposefully left out even the Pont de Levallois, which crosses the northern or downstream tip of the *Ile de la Grande-Jatte*, but kept the latter feature visible at right in the painting and adjusted scale and distances to suit his compositional needs. The sub-title "Asnières" would be misleading, unless the adjacent bridges (there do seem to be two sets of piers indicated) at that site were the ones included.

9   Mentioned in *Anquetin 1932*, p. 594, and *L'Aventure* MS., p. 67.

10 See on this general subject W.I. Homer, *Seurat and the Science of Painting* (Cambridge, Mass.: The M.I.T. Press, 1964) and H. Dorra, "Charles Henry's 'Scientific' Aesthetic," *Gazette des Beaux-Arts* (Dec. 1969), pp. 345-56.

11 *See* n. 2 above.

97.
Portrait of Père Tanguy
late 1887
oil on canvas: 36 x 31 cm
Signed and dated upper left: *Emile Bernard 1887*
Inscribed upper right: *à mon ami Tanguy*
Lent by the Kunstmuseum Basel

Bernard has recalled that he and Vincent van
Gogh painted portraits of Père Tanguy in the
wooden *atelier* which had been constructed in the
garden of his parents' house in Asnières.[1] Presuming that this painting and not a smaller and sketchier study (*fig. 124*) was meant, this implies a date
of execution fairly late in the year, given the
advanced style of Vincent's two paintings of Père
Tanguy with Japanese backgrounds (*see* pl. 11
cat. no. 8). Bernard's account also allows us to
presume that he painted the wallpaper background either from imagination or elsewhere than
the garden *atelier*, which was not likely so decorated. A similar flowered backdrop appears in a
portrait of his grandmother executed in a style
similar to that of the *Père Tanguy* (cat. no. 95).

In contrast to the vague features of the other
version, this *Tanguy* is presented with strongly
modelled and clearly outlined features. This does
not detract from the sympathetic characterization
of the sitter as a man of determined will yet kindly
disposition. It is from Bernard's 1908 article on
the then deceased Tanguy that most of our knowledge of the man and his role in the art life of Paris
derives. Bernard stressed both his generosity in
extending credit to those who bought his paint
supplies and his sympathy to Impressionism and
other modernist tendencies. The clients for whom
he stored and displayed paintings at his small shop
at 14 rue Clauzel included Pissarro, Renoir, Gauguin, van Gogh, Anquetin, Signac, Lautrec and
especially Cézanne. Bernard assigned so great a
role to the shop of Tanguy as a meeting place of
artists and source of knowledge of each other's
work that he once stated that the "Pont-Aven"
school should more properly be known as that of
the "rue Clauzel."[2] In the portrait, Bernard has
preserved a Realist approach by emphasizing what
he described as a "nose, like that of Socrates,
being very flat" and eyes which were "small and
without malice, being full of emotion."[3] The year
following Bernard's departure from Paris, Tanguy
succumbed to cancer of the stomach on February
6, 1894, and seven days later was eulogized by the
critic Octave Mirbeau in the *Echo de Paris*.

Fig. 124
Emile Bernard:
Portrait of Père Tanguy,
1887,
oil on canvas
(private collection).

Despite its Realist features, the *Père Tanguy*
betrays elements of Cloisonist style,[4] in certain
delineations of the face and ear and in the even
tonality of the decorative background. In its
succint characterization it is a major accomplishment for the young painter in 1887 and a worthy
companion to the *Portrait of the Artist's
Grandmother*.

[1] E. Bernard, Introduction to *Lettres de Vincent van
Gogh à Emile Bernard* (Paris: A. Vollard, 1911),
p. 12. This must have been fall 1887 following
Bernard's spring-summer trip to Brittany where
he returned to find his parents residing at a new
address, 5 rue Beaulieu, in Asnières just outside
Paris.

[2] *Notes*, p. 677.

[3] Bernard, *Tanguy*, p. 615.

[4] M.A. Stevens, London *P-I*, cat. no. 13.

SEE COLOUR PLATE 6.

Fig. 125
Vincent van Gogh: *Still Life: Blue Enamel Coffeepot, Earthenware and Fruit,*
May 1888, oil on canvas (private collection, Paris).

98.
Still Life with Blue Coffeepot
early 1888
oil on canvas: 55 x 46 cm
Signed and dated lower right: *Emile Bernard 1888*

Lent by the Kunsthalle Bremen

Vincent van Gogh had seen this painting (pl. 6) before he left Paris in February 1888 for Arles, since in April (*CL*478) he reported having viewed it in an unfinished state and called it "magnificient." Vincent's enthusiasm was so great that the following month he executed a free variation of Bernard's composition (*fig. 125*) with a similar blue coffeepot as the centrepiece and immediately sent sketches thereof in letters to Bernard and his brother (*CL*489, *B*5).[1] The Cloisonist aspect in Vincent's painting is contained not only in the overall division between the bright blue of the table top and yellow background, but in the coloured glass effect of the enamel coffeepot, majolica jug and other crockery depicted.

The Bernard *Blue Coffeepot*, by comparison, employs a muted colour scheme doubtless on the model of Cézanne, whose subject preferences and brush technique made up of parallel and even strokes are also imitated in this painting.[2] Other still life paintings of *circa* winter 1887-88 evince a pictorial conception analogous to this one and equal indebtedness to Cézanne. The well-known *Pots de grès et pommes* (*fig. 126*), although visibly overpainted later, is structurally similar to the *Blue Coffeepot*, and at some point was inscribed on the back by the artist "first attempt at synthetism and simplification."[3] A previously unpublished *Still Life Blue Flower Vase and Cup* (*fig. 127*), which also went into the collection of the van Gogh brothers, would seem to be a modest variation of Cézanne's *The Blue Vase* (Venturi 512), which canvas Bernard later acquired. The inevitable conclusion is that Bernard's still life paintings executed *circa* winter 1887-88 in Asnières were based upon a profound study of the canvases in this *genre* which he was able to see at the shop of Père Tanguy.[4]

Apart from their Cézannesque derivation, these still life paintings were, as Bernard claimed for the *Pots de grès*, among his initial experiments in abstract stylization which he described as the essence of his Synthetism. In them one finds a strong sense of reduction of the imagery to clearly outlined configurations containing areas of relatively pure colours, what he called "recherche à teinte plate" in reference to the *Pots de grès*.[5] He also assigned a major role to Cézanne as a source for his own Cloisonism and elsewhere described the master from Aix as a practitioner of an abstract mode of painting realized in terms of harmonious colour.[6] Because it shows no traces of overpainting the Bremen *Blue Coffeepot* remains incontestably our best witness of the species of painting and moment in his career which it represents. Remembering them in August 1888 Vincent, who was well aware of Bernard's unbridled admiration for Cézanne (*B*11), urged him to turn away from his fascination with late Medieval art and return to the virile portraiture and still life paintings which Vincent had seen before leaving for Arles (*B*14).

[1] Gans (as in cat. no. 11 n. 2) was the first to deduce the Bremen painting was meant in *CL*478 and inspired Vincent's version. Like this letter reference, the sketches and descriptions of his own *Coffeepot* imply that Théo in a now lost letter had described seeing the painting by Bernard after it was finished. Vincent's *Coffeepot* is illustrated in colour in exh. cat. *Alex Reid & Lefevre,* 1926-1976 (London: Lefevre Gallery, 1976), p. 83, uniquely including his hand-painted white frame; cf. Roskill, pp. 108, 125.

Fig. 126
Emile Bernard:
Pots de grès et pommes, late 1887,
oil on canvas
(Musée d'Orsay, Paris).

Fig. 127
Emile Bernard
(here attributed to):
*Still Life,
Blue Flower Vase and Cup,
c.* winter 1887-88,
oil on canvas
(Rijksmuseum Vincent van Gogh,
Amsterdam).

2   See for example Venturi, nos. 337-40. Colour ill.
    of Bremen *Coffeepot* in *Bremen-Lille*, p. 68.

3   In French, "Premier essai de Synthétisme et de
    Simplification 1887," which inscription with its
    retrospective flavour was probably added later.
    However, see note 5 below. The *Pots de grès* has a
    solid blue tablecloth and yellow wall, which might
    well have been remembered in Vincent's *Cof-
    feepot*, since the latter visited Bernard at Asnières
    "often" in late 1887 (*see* cat. 97 n. 1) and in
    another letter (*B*14) refers to his admiration for
    "two still life" paintings by Bernard.

4   However, his inventory entries for both the Paris
    Pots de grès (no. 23) and Bremen *Coffeepot* (no.
    34) cite Asnières as place of execution, which
    seems to preclude his having worked with a
    Cèzanne still life painting before his eyes.

5   *Ibid.*, no. 23, which reads "format 10, *Nature
    morte* (*pot flammand*, pommes) première
    recherche à teinte plate, Asnières (1887) – (app. à
    Madame Huot)." The entry for the Bremen *Cof-
    feepot* reads," no. 34, format 10, *Nature morte –
    cafetière bleu et oranges sur table verte* (Asnières
    1888)".

6   Respectively in *Notes*, p. 676, and *Tanguy*, p.
    607.

99.
Three Breton Women at the Coast
May-June 1888
oil on paper (mounted on canvas): 53 x 64 cm
Signed lower right: *Emile Bernard*
Lent by Clément Altarriba, Paris

This painting has become known as "Three Breton Women at Le Pouldu," presumably because
the setting calls to mind paintings by Gauguin with
a similar view out to sea (*see* cat. no. 69). However, Bernard may never have visited Le Pouldu
and, if so, only fleetingly.[1] Most telling, the costumes have little in common with those worn at Le
Pouldu (cat. no. 63 and *fig. 36*) or with the

elaborate *coiffes* and fichus of the women of
Pont-Aven. Instead, the triangulated or otherwise
peaked type of head-dress was favoured in the
region of the "Emerald Coast" near St. Malo, near
Bernard's frequent lodging, the village of St. Briac.
Long black dresses and black shawls were also
popular along the northern coast of Brittany, and
this is the combination of head-dress and gown
which Bernard has given to his three women looking out to sea.

The style of this painting suggests that Bernard
was on the brink of producing such full-blown
examples of the "Pont-Aven" style as the *Breton
Women* (pl. 9, cat. no. 104) and the *Buckwheat
Harvesters* (cat. no. 106), but without yet having

adopted the systematically rounded and often
bulging contours of his figures employed there. In
his reminiscences, Bernard recalls Gauguin's having found "much personality" and having "loved
the rich colouration and simple execution" of the
studies which Bernard had brought from St. Briac
to Pont-Aven in summer 1888.[2] Quite possibly
this painting was among them.

1   Ironically, the most likely visit would have been
    summer 1888, to which year I propose dating this
    painting (it is usually given to 1889), but such a
    supposition of a trip is tentative (*see* cat. no. 56).

2   As recorded in *L'Aventure*, p. 25 (MS. p. 76).

Fig. 128
Emile Bernard:
The Saltimbanques, 1887,
oil on canvas
(Museo Nacional de Artes Plasticas, Montevideo).

100.
Brothel Scene
mid-June 1888
watercolour on paper: 30.5 x 19.7 cm
Signed and dated lower left: *E. Bernard [18]88*
Inscribed lower left: *A mon ami Vincent ce croquis bête*
Lent by the Rijksmuseum Vincent van Gogh, Amsterdam

As in his earlier large gouache, *Hour of the Flesh* (cat. no. 87), Bernard in this *Brothel Scene* shows his fascination with the cabaret-tavern-brothel subjects also favoured by his friend Lautrec (cat. no. 113). This watercolour, executed in St. Briac,

can be dated to on or just before June 19, 1888, the date accompanying the poem by Bernard written out on the reverse. Vincent received the *Brothel Scene* as a gift on July 1; describing it in a letter to Théo (*CL* 502) he stated that the accompanying poem was in "just the same tone as the drawing." The opening lines of the poem do attempt to reflect the subject and colour of the watercolour:

C'est dans un coin très retiré
Un cabaret sombre qu'cet triste
Le jour bas d'un volet tiré
La marchande est specialiste
Et vena comme les un débil clair
De la banon et de la chair...

The setting is doubtless a bordello, with one prostitute standing and drinking—her bright red vest perhaps symbolic of her profession—and two others at the right rear. The figure style is a further development of the *Girl in a Street: Paris* (*fig. 107*) of *circa* April 1888, which has been related to the iconography and funnel perspective of Anquetin's *Avenue de Clichy*.[1] In his description to Théo of the *Brothel Scene*, Vincent indicates expressly that it should be hung "beside the clowns, which you already have." The enigma of this reference is solved by the existence of a

[1]   Roskill, p. 125.

hitherto unpublished Bernard painting of *The Sal-timbanques* (*fig. 128*), which the artist dedicated "A l'ami Vincent" and dated 1887. Although Bernard retrieved this painting, presumably following the death of Vincent, it can be considered an important 1887 Cloisonist precedent for the *Brothel Scene*, a stylistic relationship Vincent immediately recognized, and also for the several paintings and related drawings of Bernard's Pont-Aven style which came to maturity in the summer of 1888. The Breton head-dress of the "audience" lower left raises the possibility that this painting was executed summer 1887 in Brittany. In style, however, it and several smaller drawings of café-concerts are closely related to the type of painting Lautrec was doing as exemplified in his *Two Prostitutes* (cat. no. 112) *circa* 1886-87, presented late in 1887 at the *Du Chalet* restaurant.[2]

Moreover, Vincent felt (*B*9) that his portrait of the *Zouave* (cat. no. 15) was a response to Bernard's *Brothel* watercolour. At the end of July he sent (*B*10) a watercolour of this head to Bernard (*fig. 50*).

Bernard's *Brothel* watercolour is thus not an isolated work created without precedent but a link in a chain of development which extends back to Bernard's early Cloisonist experiments and forward to his Pont-Aven style of late 1888 and thereafter. Significantly, it also served as inspiration for Vincent when the latter in October 1888 produced an oil sketch of a *Brothel* (*F* 478) "from memory for Bernard" (*CL*548), which undertaking reflected a long exchange between the two artists concerning this particular subject matter.[3]

[2] Several of Bernard's thematically and stylistically related drawings (coll. Kunsthalle Bremen) are illustrated in Welsh-Ovcharov, *Petit Boulevard*, figs. 46-51. Bernard, *Van Gogh*, p. 393, cites "les types de prostitution de Lautrec" as that artist's featured *genre* at *Du Chalet*.

[3] On April 21, 1888, Vincent wrote Bernard (*B*4) a description of a brothel at Arles, which might have inspired the latter's June watercolour sent to Vincent. By the time Vincent produced his oil sketch in October he also was in receipt of two more groups of brothel drawings by Bernard, only one of which (Roskill, *fig. 99*) would have influenced Vincent's *Brothel* (*F* 428) to a degree comparable to his memory of the exhibited example here.

101.
Lane in Brittany
July 1888
watercolour on paper: 30.5 x 20 cm
Signed and dated lower left: *Emile Bernard* [*18*] *88*
Inscribed lower left: *Esquisse;*
lower right: *Pont-Aven*
Lent by the Rijksmuseum Vincent van Gogh, Amsterdam

At the very end of July 1888 this and nine other drawings arrived in Arles as a gift from Bernard to Vincent (*B*12), and a few days thereafter Bernard left St. Briac (after a three-month stay) in order to join Gauguin in Pont-Aven.[1] This and several other watercolours among the group sent to Vincent thus remain as incontestible evidence that Bernard had indeed developed the rudiments of the Synthetist style which he would embody in his *Breton Women in the Meadow* (cat. no. 104) before his second and most artistically eventful meeting with Gauguin in Brittany. This is not to support unreservedly Bernard's later claim to have been the chief, if not sole architect of that style, with Gauguin relegated to the role of imitator. One could argue conversely that the largest figure of Bernard's watercolour reflects a knowledge of the similarly placed central figure in Gauguin's *Four Breton Women* (*fig. 24*) of 1886, which was likely to have been on deposit with Théo at Boussod and Valadon from winter 1887-88.[2]

While it would be too rash to assert that Bernard surely had Gauguin's painting in mind when producing his *Lane in Brittany*, it would be in keeping with his developing tendency to work from memory according to Gauguin's precept. It would also explain the anomaly of his having inscribed the watercolour "Pont-Aven," when it is all but certain that the *Lane* was executed in St. Briac, where the artist stayed May-July 1888. The seaside setting with a three-masted sailboat offshore is totally incongruous with Pont-Aven but congenial to St. Briac on the north coast of Brittany, just as the archetypal head-dress (*coiffe*) and fichu of Pont-Aven are out of place in a St. Briac setting. The imagery has a general feeling of idyllic, fairy-tale fantasy about it, in keeping with Bernard's tendency to romanticize the Breton folk and their costume in terms of a hypothetically still surviving Medieval spirituality. No wonder that in his *A Corner of the Chapel* (*fig. 129*) sent to Vincent at the same time as the *Lane in Brittany*, the association between a religious setting and

crucifix and the meditation of a Breton woman in her exaggerated Pont-Aven costume becomes explicit. Symptomatic of his aversion to such openly religious subjects, Vincent fails to mention it in his letter of thanks to Bernard (*B*12).

[1] Roskill, *Key Works*, pp. 219-20, has identified all ten works sent to Vincent. In *B*12 Vincent expressed his particular appreciation for this watercolour by stating, "I greatly like the avenue of plane trees on the seashore with two women chatting in the foreground and people strolling about." Roskill, p. 126, thinks the *Lane* influenced Vincent's *Dance Hall* (*F* 547) of fall 1888 in terms of figural style, and it is also possible that Vincent had this watercolour in mind as a precedent for his treatments of the Alyscamps theme (cat. no. 28).

[2] Rewald, *Goupil*, p. 90, identifies this painting as sold in October 1888 (apparently the painting mentioned in *T*2). Given its 1886 date and Gauguin's early 1888 departure for Brittany, a consignment to Théo winter 1887-88 is implied. W 201 unfortunately confuses the title and provenance of this painting. Bernard might conceivably have also known Gauguin's major chalk drawing, *Breton Girl* (Pickvance, *Drawings*, Pl. II).

Fig. 129
Emile Bernard:
A Corner of the Chapel,
1888,
watercolour
(Rijksmuseum Vincent van Gogh, Amsterdam).

102.
Portrait of My Sister
late summer 1888
oil on canvas: 61 x 50 cm
Signed and dated lower left: *Emile Bernard 1888*
Lent by the Musée Toulouse-Lautrec, Albi

In contrast to his depiction of his sister recumbent
in the Bois d'Amour in the larger painting at the
Musée d'Orsay (*fig. 33*), this portrait shows her
as a bust effigy but, one must suppose, situated
within that same semi-sacred wooded setting. A
photograph taken of Madeleine at the time (*fig.
130*) shows her not only in Breton festive costume,
but with a consciously arranged backdrop which
included a virginal *Image d'Epinal* with Bernard's
Buckwheat Harvesters (cat. no. 106) seen above.[1]
While this photograph probably reflects the conception which Bernard and his sister shared of her
role as a present-day saint, the portrait shows
Madeleine in a more enigmatic role. Dressed in
secular costume, so sober as to suggest a religious
habit, Madeleine is pictured as a mysterious,
near-frontally posed icon. The rigid horizontality
of her mouth and eyes evokes the mystery of eternal repose. The three purple tree trunks which
embellish and yet seem to rise from her head
inevitably evoke the idea of the Trinity, especially
as this was embodied in the three tree-like staffs of
the regional Calvary tradition.[2] The relatively
sombre tones of this painting do not obscure its
essential construction in terms of Cloisonist colour
compartments. It represents both an important
foundation stone in the creation of the Pont-Aven
movement, and in iconography as well as style
anticipates the quietistic Catholicism of the Nabi
movement. It has been strangely overlooked that
Bernard in his 1887 (cat. no. 94) and 1888 depictions of the *Bois d'Amour*, with or without representations of Madeleine, did at least as much as
Gauguin in his famous lesson to Sérusier (the
Talisman, cat. no. 137) to provide a basis in style
and veiled religious imagery for the Nabi movement. In his portrait of Madeleine, Bernard has
again enlisted the help of Cézannesque brushwork,
Cloisonist simplification of form and the impersonal sphere of iconic imagery to produce one of
his most subtle and suggestive portraits.[3]

Fig. 130
Madeleine Bernard in Breton
Costume in Pont-Aven,
1888,
photograph
(Archives Musées Nationaux,
Paris).

[1]   At this time, Madeleine presumably met Charles
       Laval to whom she later may have become
       engaged, but, as documented in Walter, n. 18, p.
       290, she neither was followed to Egypt by nor
       married to Laval, as continues to be asserted in the

relevant literature (e.g., M.A. Stevens, London
P-I, cat. no. 14 and p. 88).

[2]   Cf. cat. nos. 62, 65; some of the more famous
       Breton Calvaries show the threefold crucifixion
       (Christ with the good and bad thieves) with the

vertical staff represented as a barked trunk.

[3]   Illustrated in colour, R. Shone, *The Post-
       Impressionists* (London: Octopus Books, 1979),
       fig. 69.

103.
Breton Women in the Meadow at Pont-Aven
September 1888 (?)
gouache over black chalk on paper:
50.4 x 63.5 cm
Signed and dated lower right: *Emile Bernard
1886 Pont-Aven*
Inscribed upper left: *Mercredi—Basse*
Lent by the Kunsthalle, Bremen

Just when Bernard dated this fairly large wash drawing "1886" and inscribed it "Pont-Aven," is open to doubt. In this writer's opinion the advanced Cloisonist outlines for the figures and the broad areas of high colouration are more in keeping with the style which came to maturity during summer 1888 than with known work of summer 1886 (*see* cat. nos. 88-90), in comparison with which it appears a complete anomaly. Whether the inscribed date can be considered a later memory lapse or, as is sometimes claimed, a conscious antedating of works in order to prove his own precedence in the invention of the Synthetist style, is evidence not in itself conclusive.

The setting is approximately that of the watercolour *Woman under an Umbrella*, one of ten drawings sent by Bernard from St. Briac to Vincent in Arles in late July 1888, which therefore must have depicted in an act of memory and imagination the Pont-Aven hilltop view with the village church tower in the distance.[1] In contrast to the highly simplified and generalized character of that watercolour, the Bremen gouache has all the appearance of an on-the-spot sketch, an impression reinforced by the inscription "Mercredi" (Wednesday). Its subject and style is related to a previously unpublished work by Bernard in an elongated horizontal format. It is known to the present writer only from a photograph (*fig. 131*), but is dated 1888 and includes a group of figures in Pont-Aven dress seated in a field overlooking the river valley from which the village church spire once again rises.[2]

Bernard himself may have provided an explanation of the function and meaning of the Bremen *Breton Women*. He claimed not only to have produced his oil painting *Breton Women in the Meadow* (cat. no. 104) before Gauguin executed *The Vision after the Sermon* (pl. 7), but also to have contributed the knowledge which allowed Gauguin to achieve this breakthrough to Synthetist style.[3] According to Bernard, Gauguin was so struck by the novelty and power of Bernard's use of solid areas of undivided colour in *Breton Women* and its accompanying sketches that his *Vision* was painted in imitation of Bernard's model. He indicated that he had specifically urged Gauguin to adopt the use of Prussian blue which as an Impressionist Gauguin had abandoned. Certainly the strong blue colouration used with the figures of the *Breton Women* gouache is a salient feature which, although not maintained so forcefully in the *Breton Women* canvas, might nonetheless have impressed Gauguin in this and related preliminary studies.[4] Despite similarities of poses among several individual figures, the Bremen example cannot be considered the basis of the final composition. The group of isolated and seated female figures is echoed in the smaller group upper right in the oil painting, the discussion of which sheds light on the meaning of the gouache as well.

[1] Collection Rijksmuseum Vincent van Gogh, Amsterdam. Illustrated in Pickvance, *Tate Entries*, as Pl. 13c (for cat. no. 110); Roskill, *Key Works*, pp. 219-20, documents its provenance and situation in Bernard's production.

[2] My thanks to N.J. de Jong of E.J. van Wisselingh & Co., Amsterdam, for supplying a photograph of this work.

[3] Bernard's account is given in *L'Aventure*, p. 26 (MS. p. 76).

[4] It would be unfair to Gauguin to imagine that he depended heavily upon Bernard's figural style for the evolution of his art in summer 1888, since for example *Breton Girls Dancing a Rondel* (*W* 251) and its preparatory colour sketch (cat. no. 48) were underway, if not finished, by the time of Bernard's arrival in Pont-Aven (*MLXVII*).

Fig. 131
Emile Bernard:
Five Bretons on Hill Overlooking Pont-Aven,
1888,
oil on panel (?).
(private collection).

104.

*Breton Women in the Meadow: Pardon at
Pont-Aven*

c. September 1888
oil on canvas: 74 x 92 cm
Lent by a private collection

Bernard's *Breton Women in the Meadow* (pl. 9) is
both his best known and most controversial painting. Its fame and disputed importance stem from
its execution during the same two to two and a half
month period, summer 1888, when Bernard was
working in close contact with Gauguin at Pont-
Aven and the latter produced his even more
famous *The Vision after the Sermon* (pl. 7).
When Aurier in early 1891 cited Gauguin's *Vision*
as the foundation stone of a Symbolist movement
in painting, Bernard was thunderstruck by the
critic's failure to consider his own role and immediately broke off relations with Gauguin.[1] Beginning in 1903, Bernard repeatedly claimed in print
that the *Breton Women* had preceded the *Vision*
in date of execution and provided the basis for its
style.[2] Partisans of one or the other artist have
continued the dispute down to the present.[3] The
following investigation will be centred on the *Breton Women*, discussing the *Vision* only insofar as
this helps to interpret Bernard's canvas.

In reference to early documentation the chief
problems have been when exactly the *Breton
Women* was executed in relation to the *Vision* and
whether, like the latter, it was intended from the
first to celebrate a religious event or custom in
Brittany. In Bernard's case this would have been
the annual "Pardon at Pont-Aven," which has
served as a secondary title to the *Breton Women*,
the relevance of which some writers deny but
others accept on the basis of Bernard's own references and an explanation he added on the reverse
of the canvas.[4] A Pardon is a Breton religious
festival differing in detail according to local customs and patron saints, but typically involving
devotional processions, penitence and hoped-for
absolution for the participants—not to mention the
possibilities of faith healing or miracles extended
from above to the truly deserving. Pardons also
involved related social customs such as wrestling
matches or horse races among the young men or
merely socializing among friends and acquaintances. By the late nineteenth century these Pardons, large and small, had begun to attract the
curiosity of the outside world, so that the presence
of what today would be called tourists was already
noticeable.[5]

Although Bernard's claim that his *Breton
Women* were participants in a "Pardon at Pont-
Aven" has been discounted as unwarranted by his
chosen imagery, the late 1903 date of his first
reference to a Pardon, and the absence of such an
event at Pont-Aven, the actual facts are not so
harsh to his claim. His arrival during the second
week of August would have allowed him to celebrate the "fête Gloanec" (cat. no. 51) which coin-
cided with the celebration of the Ascension of the
Virgin Mary in mid-August, and there was an
annual Pardon at Pont-Aven on the third Sunday
of September, which in 1888 would have meant
September 16.[6] Admitting that Bernard's first title
for his painting was merely "Les Bretonnes" (Volpini, cat. no. 14), he did call it "Pardon à Pont-
Aven" as early as the 1892 *Indépendants* exhibition (no. 98), which would be inexplicable had
there been no Pardon in Pont-Aven or if this
would have seemed unwarranted in the eyes of the
Pont-Aven and Nabi circle of artists. Finally, an
artist need not include traditional Christian iconography in order to justify the title Pardon. Jules
Breton had already (1869) depicted the subject as
an elaborate religious procession, but in the *Breton
Women at a Pardon* which P.A.J. Dagnan-
Bouveret exhibited at the official *Salon* of 1887 a
group of Breton women are seated in a circle in the
foreground with other groups and a church spire
to the rear, just as in the Bremen watercolour
Breton Women in the Meadow at Pont-Aven (cat.
no. 103).[7] In the painted *Breton Women* the
church steeple is missing, but Breton costumed
men and women are there and, the inclusion of
two men and a child dressed merely in their "Sunday best" is no reason to rule out depiction of a
combined religious and social event.

In allowing the justice of Bernard's entitling his
"Les Bretonnes" alternatively "Pardon à Pont-
Aven," one need not attribute to it the full com-
plexities of reference in Gauguin's *Vision*, the
interpretation of which is vexed enough in itself.
Yet, Bernard's iconography is not quite so devoid
of religious connotations as recent analogies drawn
between his *Breton Women* and Seurat's *La
Grande-Jatte*—in themselves quite appropriate—
might tend to suggest.[8] One fundamental aspect of
the Bernard painting is its solid yellow-green background, suggestive of the art of tapestry or stained-
glass windows. The absence of a horizon and a
visibly receding ground plane with the resulting
ambiguities of scale and figure placement produce
a greater effect of generalized Medieval style than
in the *Vision*, for example, where a relatively

higher degree of spatial recession remains. The
more visible use of dark Cloisonist outlines by Bernard is, perhaps intentionally, suggestive of the
lead tracery of stained-glass windows, as was
noted as early as 1889 by Félix Fénéon.[9]

In sum, at this stage of his career and in this
painting, Bernard did not yet consider it necessary
to employ traditional religious iconography or even
indirect allusions to sacred text in order to produce
a form of art with religious overtones. Breton folk
life was thought by many contemporary outside
witnesses to contain an inherent religious quality
which continued Medieval, if not pre-Christian,
sacred tradition. As did Gauguin (*see fig. 35*),
Bernard romanticized the Breton *coiffes* and costumes within this same context, considering them
evocative of sacerdotal experience.[10] Given the
ethos of the time and place, and his own religious
sensibilities, it was inevitable that he would have
considered the titles *Breton Women in the Meadow*
and *Pardon at Pont-Aven* quite interchangeable.[11]

1   See pp. 59-60, above.

2   As argued in *Notes*, pp. 678-80 and *L'Aventure*,
    pp. 25-27.

3   Roskill, pp. 103-06, and *Key Works*, pp. 221-22;
    M.A. Stevens, London, *P-I*, cat. no. 15.

4   Stevens, *ibid.*, which inscription by its very nature
    must have been added later.

5   G.P. Weisberg, "Vestiges of the Past: The Brit-
    tany 'Pardons' of Late Nineteenth-century French
    Painters," *Arts Magazine* (November 1980), pp.
    134-38, conveniently summarizes the character of
    Breton Pardons in relation to painting of the
    Realist and Symbolist movements.

6   Bernard presumably departed St. Briac upon
    being reassured in a letter of August 4 or 5 from
    Vincent (*B*14) that Gauguin was still in Pont-
    Aven. On August 18 Vincent wrote Théo that he'd
    just heard from Bernard who had joined Gauguin
    in Pont-Aven "some days ago." Moreover the use
    of Madeleine Bernard's name on the *Still Life Fête
    Gloanec* (cat. no. 51) would have been impossible
    had not both she and Emile been in Pont-Aven by
    August 15. This "fête," whether for Marie
    Gloanec or the Virgin Mary, could have been what
    Bernard referred to in *L'Aventure*, p. 26, rather
    than the month later actual Pont-Aven Pardon.
    This is identified as September 16 in Perruchot, p.
    155, the accuracy of which is confirmed in M.
    Herban III, "The Origin of Paul Gauguin's *Vision
    after the Sermon: Jacob Wrestling with the Angel*
    (1888)," *Art Bulletin*, LIX (September 1977), p.

SEE COLOUR PLATE 9.

418 n. 23. Herban, therefore, inexplicably draws the conclusion that this excludes the Pont-Aven event for consideration with Gauguin's *Vision* "which was begun in August." In fact, Gauguin's letter (*G*9, partially translated *P-I*, pp. 181-82, and Herban, *ibid.*, p. 415) to Vincent describing the *Vision* (just finished, since Gauguin begins his account, "Je viens de faire un tableau religieux") was mentioned as just received by Vincent on or about September 28 (i.e., *CL*543). The *Vision* was thus executed during the last half of September and, if Bernard was correct in claiming for his *Breton Women* both that it was based on the Pardon at Pont-Aven (*Notes*, p. 679) and executed before the *Vision*, then the latter must be dated just after September 16 in the third week of September. Otherwise, one should date the *Breton Women* to late August-early September, with the *Vision* remaining late September.

7   Illustrated and discussed Weisberg, "Vestiges," p. 76, and Stevens, London, *P-I*, cat. no. 58. Having left already for Brittany, Bernard would not have seen the 1887 *Salon* which opened as usual

in May, but Dagnan's composition could have been known to him by hearsay. Most important, it depicts an aspect so typical of Breton Pardons that Bernard could have chosen a similar motif independently.

8   As suggested by, in chronological sequence, Pickvance, *Tate Entries*, cat. no. 83; Roskill, p. 88; Stevens, London *P-I*, 41. However, the reference by Vincent to it (*W* 16) as a "Sunday afternoon in Brittany," even if it meant as an oblique reference to the Grande-Jatte, merely betokens Vincent's disapproval of religious iconography and not of Cloisonist style.

9   Fénéon, p. 158, described his work at the Volpini exhibition thusly: "Les larges traits dont M. Bernard cerne accidents de terrain et êtres sont le réseau de plomb d'un vitrail."

10   In *L'Aventure* MS., pp. 58-59, Bernard recalls how in 1886 at the Quimper Museum he associated Breton costume with the Middle Ages and (p. 83) how he became a man of the Middle Ages in Brittany; his sister actually adopted the local dress (see cat. no. 106).

11   The early provenance of this painting has remained as uncertain as its date. It was taken by Gauguin to Arles, where Vincent produced a copy of it (pl. 10, cat. no. 29) and indicated it was owned by Gauguin through an exchange with Bernard (*CL*557). It next appeared in the Volpini catalogue as no. 14 *Les Bretonnes* owned by Madame Berthe, a designation quite possibly thought up as a subterfuge for Gauguin's tentative ownership of the painting. Some time in the early 1890s the painting was evidently returned to Bernard, who exhibited it at the 1892 *Indépendants* and eventually sold it to Arsène Alexandre from whom it went to the art dealer Vollard (*Notes*, p. 680, n. 2). Thereafter, it was acquired by Maurice Denis, however this record of acquisition is beyond the scope of the present investigation. It should be noted that Vincent's copy of this painting apparently went to Bernard (*Notes*, p. 680, n. 2), although this transfer remains otherwise unrecorded.

105.

Self-Portrait dedicated to Vincent
c. late September 1888
oil on canvas: 46 x 55 cm
Signed and dated upper right:
Emile Bernard 1888 à son copaing Vincent
Lent by the Rijksmuseum Vincent van Gogh,
Amsterdam

Vincent had requested in early September (*B*16)
that his friends Bernard and Gauguin produce portraits of each other, explaining that Japanese artists
who also lived and worked together in harmony
very often exchanged works among themselves
(*B*18). The two painters in Pont-Aven preferred
to produce self-portraits instead, each of which
nonetheless included an imaginary portrait of the
other artist on the background wall (cat. nos. 52,
105). Both were received by Vincent in the first
week of October 1888 (*CL*545) and therefore
may be presumed to have been executed in the
latter weeks of September. Examination of the
paintings lends little credence to any theory that
either painting was a collaborative effort. The
background "alter ego" images may have been
derived from images supplied by the artists to each
other, but each is so schematic in conception that
neither can be considered a key device to understanding the total painting. Gauguin totally ignores
Bernard in describing his own self-portrait to Vincent (*G*10 as described in *CL*544), and Bernard
has left no first-hand description of his own *Self-
Portrait* sent to Vincent.

Vincent, apparently appreciated the *Self-
Portrait* by Bernard in equal if not greater measure than that of Gauguin. He described it as "the
inner vision of a painter, a few abrupt tones, a few
dark lines, but it has the distinction of a real, real
Manet" (*CL*545). The portrait Vincent had in
mind with this allusion was inevitably Manet's
Portrait of Emile Zola (*fig. 132*), with its three-
quarter view of the artist seated left and the pas-
tiche of Japanese and Spanish art works pictured
upper right.[1] Whether or not Bernard had based
his painting largely upon this one model, his combination of respect for Manet, Degas (in the cut-off
image) and, by implication, Gauguin, is evident in
the asymmetry of the composition, even while the
Cloisonist outlines witness his continued allegiance
to Japanese principles of design. Having been so
deeply involved with similar concerns in his own
art, Vincent would quickly have appreciated their
manifestation in a Bernard *Self-Portrait* dedicated
to himself.[2]

Fig. 132   Edouard Manet: *Portrait of Emile Zola*, 1868, oil on canvas (Musée d'Orsay, Paris).

[1] Manet's *Portrait of Zola* was exhibited in 1884 as
no. 42 at Manet's posthumous exhibition at the
Ecole des Beaux-Arts.

[2] On this painting see, *P-I*, pp. 185-86; Pickvance,
Tate Entries, cat. no. 84; Bodelsen, *Ceramics*, p.
182; Roskill, pp. 101-02; and Stevens, London
P-I, cat. no. 16.

106.

The Buckwheat Harvesters, Pont-Aven:
Moissonneurs de blé noir, Pont-Aven
c. September-October 1888
oil on canvas: 72 x 92 cm
Signed and dated lower right: *Emile Bernard
1888*
Lent by a private collection, Switzerland

A major painting in Bernard's *oeuvre* and the development of Synthetist style, *The Buckwheat Harvesters* (pl. 8) was almost certainly shown at the Volpini exhibition as "no. 19, Moisson—Bretagne," and it is clearly the painting "no. 99, Moissonneurs de blé noir, Pont-Aven 1888," at the *Indépendants* exhibition of 1892.[1] At both exhibitions it was a companion piece to *Breton Women in the Meadow* (pl. 9, cat. no. 104) in size and in the epitome of Cloisonist-Synthetist style each represents. The addition of "Pont-Aven" to the one title ensures that the painting was done there late summer or fall 1888, since Bernard arrived there by mid-August and departed some time in November.[2] This departure date is important, since, despite Bernard's claim in 1907 that it had influenced Gauguin's *Grape Gathering* produced at Arles (pl. 23, cat. no. 56), the *Buckwheat Harvesters* could have been executed either at the same time or following Gauguin's *Vision after the Sermon*, in which a similarly red field occurs. Gauguin's *Still Life Fête Gloanec* (pl. 31, cat. no 51) anticipates both these paintings in its dominant red colouration, since it was painted just before or at the time of Bernard's arrival. Of greater importance, Bernard's subsequent claims of having influenced Gauguin towards the adoption of uniform and anti-Impressionist colour usages conveniently forget the precedent of Anquetin's earlier Cloisonist landscapes inspired by looking through a pane of uniformly coloured glass (cat. nos. 74 and 76). Most appropriate in this instance would have been the now lost *Boat at Sunset*, which Bernard variously described as "un grand crépon japonais." It was the artist's first Cloisonist work and was a brilliant uniform red associated with the setting sun.[3] This use of colour based upon time of day could have been a factor in Bernard's choice of red as well, since in describing the *Breton Women* as in "une prairie ensoleillée de parti pris jaune," he indicates why he has modified the green grass there with touches of yellow.[4]

The ultimate reason why this painting was finished in red, is the subject itself. Buckwheat was at one time so common a form of grain in Brittany that one writer in 1901 described Brittany as the country of buckwheat (*blé noir*), explaining how the ripening kernels turn from white to vermilion before turning to black.[5] In an 1888 account Madeleine Bernard described the buckwheat fields of Brittany as turning "blood red" in the fall, which is further reason to think that the painting was finished only then.[6] Since in the same account Madeleine tells how she had adopted the local costume of Pont-Aven, in part as an example to the village girls to resist the lure of Paris fashions and retain their traditional costumes, this explains why she is posed in Pont-Aven costume along with both an image of the Holy Virgin and her brother's painting of the *Buckwheat Harvesters* (*fig. 130*). Not incidentally, her own *coiffe* and costume reinforce the thematic juxtaposition of the large peasant head, lower left, in the painting and the shrouded Madonna of the tapestry or print suspended below.

As in a wash drawing of this theme (*fig. 133*), which seems to be a concise recapitulation of the painting rather than a study for it, the mood of the painting is free of the sense of "human misery" which is announced in the title of one work by Gauguin (cat. no. 56) and implied in the subjects of numerous other Breton landscapes by the same artist. Bernard's farm workers perform their tasks as if in rhythm with the stacks of hay some of them are shaping. If the expression on the one face with delineated features cannot be called exactly joyful, neither does its slightly oriental character bespeak a feeling of burden and woe. Rather, Bernard has wished by the very neutrality of his approach to the theme of human labour to evoke the timelessness of this annual ritual. It is said that the Host of the Holy Communion was sometimes made from the buckwheat crop, and the theme of harvesting in general implies a variety of Christian connotations.[7] Knowing that this must have been one of the paintings which were compared to stained-glass windows when exhibited in 1889, it is almost as likely as with the *Breton Women* that for Bernard the *Buckwheat Harvesters* represented a religious painting in secular guise.

---

[1] The only other candidate for the *Harvesters* is the painting now at the Musée d'Orsay (*Bremen-Lille*, cat. no. 22; Lille 24), but the *Buckwheat Harvesters* accords better with Fénéon's allusion to stained-glass windows; see cat. no. 104 n. 9, and Stevens, London *P-I*, cat. no. 17 where this work was discussed at some length for the first time. Stevens has astutely noted that the final layer of dominantly red paint was superimposed upon a green undercoat. However, given the considerations listed in my text (and the hats of the male figures are definitely from Pont-Aven), her suggestion that this painting was brought to Pont-Aven in mid-August cannot be accepted. Yet her further suggestion that the red was added after Bernard saw Gauguin's *Vision* is possible, even likely, given the association of red buckwheat and fall.

[2] See Bernard chronology, p. 264, for data on arrival; *M*LXVII from Gauguin in Arles to Bernard must date from November since he refers to Bernard's plans to leave Pont-Aven for Paris "about the tenth," and he had left Pont-Aven himself only October 21 (Roskill, p. 269).

[3] Bernard's references occur respectively in *Anquetin 1932*, p. 594, and *Notes*, p. 676; Dujardin, p. 492, describes "la tonalité générale de rouge" of the *Bateau*.

[4] *Notes*, 679.

[5] E. Herpin, "Au pays de blé noir," *Au pays de légendes* (Rennes, 1901), p. 114 (as quoted in Herban, "The Origin of Paul Gauguin's *Vision after the Sermon: Jacob Struggling with the Angel* (1888)," *Art Bulletin*, LIX (September 1977), p. 419.

[6] Quoted in Bernard, *Gauguin*, p. 15.

[7] See Herban, "Gauguin's *Vision*," p. 419.

Fig. 133

Fig. 133
Emile Bernard:
Study: the Buckwheat Harvesters,
1888,
ink drawing
(collection unknown).

107.

Portrait of Madeleine with Blue Background
late 1888
oil on canvas: 41.5 x 32.5 cm
Signed (monogram) and dated lower right: *1888*
Lent by the family of Maurice Denis, Alençon,
France

Upon her arrival at Pont-Aven in the company of
her mother in late summer 1888, Madeleine Bernard immediately became the muse of Gauguin,
Laval and her brother Emile.[1] Apart from
Gauguin's persiflage in adding her name as signature to his own *Fête Gloanec* (cat. no. 51), he
produced the well-known half-length study at the
Grenoble Museum (*W* 240) which evokes interpretations characterizing her as alternatively
satanic or virginal, according to the author's inclination. Emile's portraits of his sister from approximately this date including the reclining and bust
images set in the *Bois d'Amour* (*fig. 33* and cat.
no. 94) are among his best known portrait
images.[2] This previously unpublished bust portrait
hence can only amplify our knowledge of this
extraordinarily concentrated record of portraiture,
despite the generally impersonal expressions worn
by the sitter.

　　This treatment of Madeleine is particularly
devoid of emotion. She is depicted with an utter
simplicity of contour and colouration and also with
a feeling of inner spiritual strength and mystery
which defy easy characterization. It is impossible
to decipher the yellow and darker blue configurations of the background except as abstract decorative motifs which enhance the idea of her other-
worldliness. Although cast in three-quarter view,
this image of Madeleine is even more iconic than
either portrait with the Bois d'Amour as background, yet is more suggestive of the Art Nouveau
movement which was to come.

　　No other portrait by Bernard represents so
completely the principal aims of the artist, to
found an art of his time which would be "the
simplest of simple" and to be accessible to all
people—an art which he hoped would re-establish
a style, a sort of "modern hieraticism" as Bernard
believed was to be found in the Gothic, Egyptian
and Assyrian styles.[3]

　　After the death of Laval in 1894, Madeleine
worked for the library in Geneva. A year later she
joined her brother in Cairo where she succumbed
to tuberculosis on November 19 at the age of
twenty-four.

[1]　Bernard, *Gauguin*, p. 17.

[2]　Bernard, *Inventory*, 1893, no. 57 indicates
　　another portrait of his sister on a divan, 1889,
　　which remained unfinished. His *Inventory*, 1901,
　　notes another portrait of his sister at the piano in
　　the evening in Asnières, 1888. Two other known
　　portraits of Madeleine given to 1889 and 1890
　　remain respectively in the collection of the Univer-
　　sity of Kentucky Art Museum and a private collec-
　　tion in Stockholm.

[3]　Bernard, *Gauguin*, p. 11.

Fig. 134
Emile Bernard: *Study for the Seaweed Gatherers*, 1888 (later?)
crayon drawing (private collection).

108.
The Seaweed Gatherers: *Les Goëmons*
1888 (later?)
oil on canvas: 81 x 63.5 cm
Signed lower left (fragmentarily visible): *Emile Bernard*
Lent by a private collection, Switzerland

The Seaweed Gatherers apparently went unrecorded in the exhibition record or literature by or about Bernard. An alternative version in an extended horizontal format was first published in a 1939 article by Bernard, in which the title "Les Goëmons" occurs.[1] In neither version is there a clear reflection of the "Seaweed Gatherers" theme, although hints of the "black rocks" and breaking waves of the Breton coast are present in the painting exhibited here.[2] A surviving drawing (*fig. 134*), dated 1888 and inscribed "Ière idée des Bretonnes au goëmon, E. Bernard," would seem to resolve the problem of chronology, if the nature

of the inscription itself did not suggest that it was an afterthought.

Nonetheless, this painting may be considered one of Bernard's most pristine examples of the Cloisonist style. The clear use of independently coloured areas, the emphasis on figural outlines and the harmony between figural and background images is so complete that, in style, the painting is one of the artist's most harmonious from his "Pont-Aven" years. Despite the artist's own title of "Seaweed Gatherers," the subject reference is less evocative of physical labour than of seated initiate nuns receiving instruction from the standing figure (the fuller composition adds three seated females at right, making a mystical three-plus-one-plus-three equals seven composition). This ambiguity between the sacred and profane realms is so fundamental to the Pont-Aven and Nabi movements that its occurrence here should be considered the norm rather than the exception.[3]

[1] Bernard, *Gauguin*, p. 14, illustrates and entitles this work "Les Goëmons," and attributes it to 1888.

[2] As early as 1888 Emile Schuffenecker had painted the subject of *Seaweed Gatherers at Yport* which was exhibited a year later at the Volpini exhibition no. 61 with accompanying drawing for this work; for reproduction of this now presumed lost painting see Numero Special "Pont-Aven," *Bulletin des amis du Musée de Rennes*, no. 2, summer, 1978, p. 58. In November 1889 Gauguin painted his famous *Seaweed Gatherers* (*fig. 36*).

[3] R. Goldwater, *Symbolism* (New York: Harper and Row, 1979), p. 97 and fig. 87, chose to date this painting 1892, probably in analogy with other paintings by Bernard of that year (Cf. *P-I*, ill. p. 443). While four years later than that of Bernard, Goldwater's ascribed date has the virtue of suggesting the interrelationship of the Pont-Aven and Nabi groups in relation to both style and iconography, which the *Seaweed Gatherers* implies.

109.

Bretonneries
January-February 1889
lithographs on zinc plate: 33 x 25 cm
(or in reverse order)
Frontispiece signed (centre)
and dated (lower left): *E. Bernard* [18] 89
Dedicated: *à l'ami Filliger* (sic)
Lent by the Musée des Beaux-Arts, Quimper

These five lithographs derive from the collection of
Marie Henry, where Gauguin and Meyer de Haan
stayed and worked for much of the period late
1889–late 1890.[1] An inscription by the artist "à
l'ami Filliger" (sic) indicates that Bernard had
given a set of these prints to that artist sometime
between 1889 and 1892, which is to say before
Marie Henry gave up her inn at Le Pouldu and
took this set of prints with her. Present scholarship
favours seven prints in the set, although there is no
recorded order of execution or public presentation
of this important series.[2]

Yet there should no longer be any doubt as to
the time or circumstances under which these
lithographs on zinc plate were created. The circumstances are set out above in reference to
Gauguin's companion print series (cat. no. 58),
which makes clear the collaboration between Gauguin and Bernard, at the instigation of Théo van
Gogh, for this graphic production. Bernard's
account is, as always, a bit self-flattering, claiming
that Gauguin was so impressed upon seeing Bernard's series, that he altered two of his own
designs in order to make them conform more to
the examples of Bernard.[3] Only a close comparison
of style between the two series would resolve this
issue of interpenetrating influence which, given the
complication of wash added to some versions of
both series, is obviously a serious research undertaking in itself.

In style these prints exaggerate and further
flatten the figures in his *Breton Women* (cat. no.
104) and *Buckwheat Harvesters* (cat. no. 106). It
is as if the already narrow spatial confines of the
paintings had been so pressed together that the
result was an ironed-out appearance which in fact
is metaphorically signified in the iconography of
one of the images, *Three Women Hanging Wash*
(cat. no. 109b). The same effect is present in
Women Feeding Pigs (cat. no. 109c) and in
Women Gathering Grain with Geese (cat. no.
109d), where contours of landscape, vegetation,
figures, animals and grain stacks are so similarly
conceived that subject matter is hopelessly subor-

dinant to the overall decorative effect. One of these
graphics, the *Sailing in Brittany* (cat. no. 109e),
was considered by Bernard so successful a composition that he used the composition for a painting.[4]
The frontispece *Three Women and a Cow in a
Meadow* (cat. no. 109a) is the most classically
balanced member of the series, befitting Bernard's
intention of capturing not so much the appearance
as the "character" of his chosen subjects.[5]

Whereas the dispersion of Bernard's *Bretonneries* is even less documented than that of the
comparable series produced by Gauguin, there is
little doubt that this joint effort at the beginning of
1889 signified the high point of collaboration
between the two artists. The juxtaposition of the
two graphic series in the present exhibition has
been intended to present an all but complete representation of the "Album on request" of lithographs as listed in the Volpini catalogue.[6] While the
series by Bernard may have been less influential in
the history of the Pont-Aven and Nabi movements
than that of Gauguin, without its presence at that
exhibition, the impression that a common style
between the two men and their associates existed
would not so easily have been created.

[1] As documented in exh. cat. *L'Ecole de Pont-Aven
dans les Collections Publiques et Privées de Bretagne* (Quimper: Musée de Beaux-Arts, 1978),
nos. 12-16.

[2] *Bremen-Lille*, cat. nos. 198-204, illustrates the
whole series, including the two prints not included
in the present exhibition (i.e., nos. 201-02).
Hand-coloured versions of this series also exist,
possibly executed later by Bernard (Bremen
Kunsthalle has an incomplete hand-coloured set).

[3] As quoted in cat. no. 58, above.

[4] Now owned by The Fine Arts Gallery of San
Diego.

[5] Bernard, *Gauguin*, p. 11.

[6] An exhibition of these series in their various states
would be of great importance in helping to clarify
such questions of precedence and influence.

A

B

C

D

E

110.
The Apple Harvest
1890
oil on canvas: 105 x 45 cm
Signed and dated lower right: *E. Bernard* [*18*] *90*
Lent by the Musée des Beaux-Arts, Nantes

Little is recorded of Bernard's activities during
1890, and few of his known works bear that date.
We know from his own account that he spent
approximately three months in Lille with his
grandmother, who had returned there at his urging, and that his purpose was to learn the trade of
"industrial design" in order to have a regular
income which would allow him to marry.[1] After
producing a number of decorative floral designs in
gouache for which a lace maker paid him only
thirty francs, Bernard became disillusioned and
decided to return to painting, abandoning his
plans for marriage.

   To some extent his Lille activities are reflected
in the Nantes *Apple Harvest*, the narrow format of
which suggests a decorative function such as that
of a tapestry. The painting's Cloisonist style and
uncomplicated subject matter might be expected
to have the pleasing effect of a wall hanging.[2] The
subject matter refers to the grain fields and apple
trees of Brittany, in this case because of the woman's dress in all likelihood the area of St. Briac,
where he had spent the summer of 1889.[3]
Although foreshadowed in one of his illustrations
for the Volpini exhibition catalogue which he
signed with the pseudonym "Ludovic Nemo," the
elongated proportions and slightly mannered poses
reflect his then current interest in the Italian and
German "primitives" as the late Medieval artists of
the thirteenth to fifteenth centuries were then
called.[4]

[1]   Recounted in Bernard, *L'Aventure*, pp. 34-44.

[2]   In fact Bernard conceived several works based on
     the theme of fruit harvesting *c*. 1890-92 for both
     a stained-glass window and a wall hanging, see
     P-I, p. 279.

[3]   The woman's costume *cf*. cat. no. 99, and the
     costume of the man with the pole is definitely not
     that of Pont-Aven.

[4]   The Volpini illustration "Two Women Walking"
     is reproduced *P-I*, p. 261. This little known *Apple
     Harvest* was first illustrated and discussed exh.
     cat. *L'Ecole de Pont-Aven dans les Collections
     Publiques et Privées de Bretagne* (Quimper: Musée
     des Beaux-Arts, 1978), cat. no. 4. Here reference
     is made to the discovery that this canvas had been
     conceived as a larger composition, which Bernard
     later reduced to the present format.

111.
Christ at the Foot of the Cross: Lamentation
1890
oil on canvas: 90 x 150 cm
Signed and dated below left: *Emile Bernard*
[*18*] *90*
Lent by Clément Altarriba, Paris

By the time Bernard painted his *Lamentation* he
had become "very believing; with my profound
love and mysticism having reappeared, Brittany
had made of me a Catholic ready to struggle for
the church." Or as he continued, "I was intoxi-
cated with incense, with organ music, with
prayers, with old stained-glass windows, with
hieratic tapestries, and I re-ascended the centuries... Little by little I became a man of the
Middle Ages."[1] Late in 1889 Bernard sent to both
Gauguin and Vincent photographs of religious
paintings based on such traditional themes as the
*Adoration of the Magi, Christ in the Garden of
Olives* (*fig.* 77) and the *Annunciation* (*fig.
135*).[2] Gauguin, despite a suspicion that he was
portrayed as Judas, approved (*M*XCV) of the

1   *L'Aventure*, p. 38.

Fig. 135
Emile Bernard:
The Annunciation,
1889,
oil on canvas
(private collection).

2   The *Adoration* is known, as far as the present
writer is concerned, only by this reference.

Christ in the Garden, while Vincent was aghast at the figural imagery, complaining of the *Adoration* that Mary should be giving suck to the Christ child rather than praying, and describing some attendant figures as "fat ecclesiastical frogs kneeling down as though in a fit of epilepsy" (*B21*). Although Vincent admitted to liking certain landscape elements, for example the "terrace with two cypresses" of the *Annunciation*, he expressed himself forcefully against what he saw as Bernard's attempt "to revive Medieval tapestries" with an art of "mystification." Given the intensity of Bernard's religious sentiments at the time, it is not surprising that he did not ever again write to Vincent, although he continued to admire his art fervently.

This canvas of 1890 shows that Bernard did not immediately desist from his essays in Medievalizing religious art. The *Lamentation* was a standard theme in late Medieval narrative cycles of the Life of Christ; a famous version by Giotto is in the Arena Chapel, Padua. Bernard's figures however, are so attenuated and elongated that even the most elegantly stylized of Gothic figure types would seem normally proportioned by comparison. In addition, Bernard has complicated his iconography by including two groups of three Maries each, so adding a "consolation" episode to that of "grieving." These two groups of three plus Christ make seven, so that, as with Gauguin (cat. no. 62), one suspects that sacred numerology was intended as part of the iconographic program.

Somewhat ironically, Vincent's opposition to Bernard's use of traditional religious imagery was coupled with an admonition to recall a painting he had done the previous year in Pont-Aven, which represented a girl stretched out full-length on a grassy forest floor before a barrier row of vertical tree trunks. Despite knowing this painting only from Gauguin's verbal description, and not realizing it represented Bernard's sister *Madeleine in the Bois d'Amour* (*fig. 33*), Vincent, in his letter to Bernard, improvised a sketch of it which is remarkably accurate as to the body and arm positions.[3] We know from Bernard that he had consciously posed Madeleine "in the attitude of a reclining tomb effigy" (*gisante*), which is analogous to the image of the dead Christ in the *Lamentation*.[4] Yet, Vincent quite likely would have approved Bernard's indirect allusion in the *Madeleine* to Medieval sepulchral statuary, since it was embodied in a figure and a landscape based on nature.

It is uncertain whether Bernard's *Lamentation* became known to Gauguin and, if so, to what extent he admired it. Gauguin doubtless had the reclining *Madeleine* in mind as one prototype for his own *Loss of Virginity* and possibly the *Lamentation* as well. He himself had not shied from inclusion of Medieval symbolism in his *Self-Portrait with a Halo* (*W* 323), although the skull and crossbones motif had been expressly excluded from his *Yellow Christ*.[5] As the *Loss of Virginity* was for Gauguin, Bernard's *Lamentation* was the culmination of his efforts to combine a Cloisonist landscape background with figural content of inherently religious and Symbolist significance. It is hence fitting that they are being seen together in the present exhibition, apparently for the first time ever.

3 Andersen, *Paradise*, p. 95 ff. discusses this question in great detail.

4 Bernard, Gauguin, p. 11, and Andersen, *ibid.*, ills. pp. 304-05.

5 See fig. 68, where the skull and crossbones image appears in the Trémalo chapel just above and behind the head of Christ.

Henri de Toulouse-Lautrec (1864-1901)

Biographical Data

SOURCES

Despite the extensive literature about Henri de Toulouse-Lautrec, his failure to date many works, a restricted record of exhibition and the paucity of eye-witness accounts have combined to hinder the emergence of a fully dependable account of the development of the man and his art. Lautrec's first biographer, Maurice Joyant, was a childhood friend, who renewed this acquaintance only in 1890 when he assumed the position formerly held by Théo van Gogh at Boussod and Valadon. Joyant's uncertainties about Lautrec in the 1880s are in part ameliorated by the biography of François Gauzi, a friend from the artist's student days. The recent publication of a volume of Lautrec letters to family members (Lautrec, *Corres.*) provides some useful information, but unlike Vincent van Gogh, Lautrec only occasionally spoke of specific paintings and not very often of art in general. Although not accompanied by systematic documentation or discussion of the works of art included, the six-volume complete *oeuvre* catalogue of Lautrec's production by Dortu provides the basis for an examination of his art through comparative stylistic analysis. The recent exhibition catalogue by Charles Stuckey and assistants, *Toulouse-Lautrec: Paintings* (Chicago: The Art Institute of Chicago, 1879), with its detailed discussions of 109 items, constitutes the most up-to-date monograph on the artist's painted *oeuvre*.

EARLY LIFE AND CAREER

1864-1885

Henri-Marie-Raymond de Toulouse-Lautrec is born November 24, 1864 in the Hôtel de Bosc, the house of his paternal grandmother at Albi, in the south of France. His eccentric father, Count Alphonse de Toulouse-Lautrec, is descended from one of the oldest and most important families in France and his mother, Adèle Zoë Tapie-de-Céleyran, is a first cousin of her husband. In 1872 Henri moves with his parents to Paris where he pursues his studies at the Lycée Fontanes (today Lycée Condorcet). There Lautrec meets Maurice Joyant, later to become one of his best friends and his biographer. At Albi an accident in 1878 and another in 1879 arrests the growth of Lautrec's legs. After receiving his *baccalauréat* in 1881 at Toulouse, and with support from his parents, Lautrec begins seriously to study art. From age fourteen to eighteen he studies with the academic equestrian painter René Princeteau, who contributes to the development of his early style and his continued interest in animal subjects, especially the horse. By March 1882 Lautrec, on the advice of Princeteau, is working in the academic *atelier* of Léon Bonnat in Paris, and there meets the artist Louis Anquetin. Bonnat closes his *atelier* in September (*Corres.*, pp. 67-8), and Lautrec, like other students, immediately joins the *atelier* of Fernand Cormon who has taken over Bonnat's premises (*Corres.*, p. 69). His close friendships with Louis Anquetin and fellow-students René Grenier, Henri Rachou and François Gauzi continue.

By the summer of 1884, Lautrec moves in with René and Lili Grenier, at 19 bis rue Fontaine, a building where Edouard Degas occupies a studio. In October, Lautrec meets via Anquetin the young Emile Bernard who has been accepted into Cormon's *atelier* (Bernard, *Anquetin, 1932*, p. 591). In the winter Lautrec executes a large canvas parodying Puvis de Chavannes' masterpiece *The Sacred Grove*. During 1885, he continues to paint and draw at Cormon's in the mornings, a procedure he had evidently informed his mother of by the summer of 1884 (Joyant I, p. 75). He begins to lead a bohemian life in Montmartre, and in the company of Anquetin and Bernard frequents the gallery of Durand-Ruel (Bernard, *Anquetin, 1932*, p. 591). In the company of Anquetin and Grenier, he patronizes the dance halls *L'Elysée Montmartre* and *Moulin de la Galette* and the café *Chat Noir* at 84 boulevard de Rochechouart, which by the second half of 1885 becomes the café-cabaret *Le Mirliton* operated by the popular singer and songwriter Aristide Bruant (Joyant I, p. 93). In late autumn Lautrec visits Anquetin's family home in Etrépagny (*Corres.*, p. 96). In the winter he paints four murals for the Auberge Ancelin at Villiers-sur-Morin (Dortu II, p. 239-42). At this time he admires above all the art of Degas, Velásquez, Ingres, Renoir, Forain and Japanese prints (Gauzi, pp. 26-7). He begins to paint portraits of the women of Montmartre, dancers and cabaret subjects. *Circa* late 1885 or winter 1886 he paints the *Portrait of Emile Bernard* (*fig. 136*).

Fig. 136
Henri de Toulouse-Lautrec
Portrait of Emile Bernard,
c. 1885-86,
oil on canvas
(The Tate Gallery, London).

1886

Lautrec works infrequently at Cormon's.

Bruant begins to hang Lautrec's work on a permanent basis at *Le Mirliton* (Joyant I, p. 98). The selection includes *At Saint Lazare*; *The Refrain of the Louis XIII Chair* (fig. 27); *At Grenelle*; *At Bastille*; *At Montrouge*; *At Batignolle* and *The Hangover*. After resisting his father's wish to locate him in an *atelier* near the Arc de Triomphe (*Corres.*, p. 99), by the summer he takes a larger studio on the fourth floor of 27 rue Coulaincourt (corner of 7 rue Tourlaque) in the heart of Montmartre (Huisman-Dortu, p. 86), and lives with Suzanne Valadon. Some time by the second half of this year he meets Vincent van Gogh at Cormon's *atelier* (Gauzi, p. 28). By late fall, Lautrec quits Cormon's altogether (Welsh-Ovcharov, p. 210).

August-September he visits Villiers-sur-Morin and Arcachon (*Corres.*, p. 307).

In September, Lautrec sees his first drawing published, *Gin Cocktail*, in the magazine *Le Courrier français* (Sept. 26).

Lautrec exhibits for the first time in October-December at the *Salon des Arts Incohérents* under the name "Toulou Segroeg."

In December Bruant publishes in *Le Mirliton* (Dec. 29) Lautrec's *Le Quadrille of the Louis XIII Chair* (fig. 26).

1887

During winter 1886-87 Lautrec, Bernard and Anquetin are closely associated. Lautrec is exposed to Anquetin's and Bernard's researches into Pointillist colour theory and emerging ideas on simplification of form. He observes Anquetin working on *The Interior of the Cabaret Bruant* (Bernard, *L'Aventure* MS., p. 66).

In both February and March issues of his journal *Le Mirliton*, Aristide Bruant publishes a drawing by Lautrec on the front cover.

Lautrec rents an apartment at 19 rue Fontaine with his friend Dr. Bourges (Huisman-Dortu, p. 87).

By the spring Lautrec sees the Japanese print exhibition organized by van Gogh at *Le Tambourin* on 62 boulevard de Clichy.

He executes the pastel portrait of Vincent van Gogh (cat. no. 117).

Lautrec holds weekly gatherings at his *atelier* where Suzanne Valadon recalls seeing Vincent van

Gogh among those present (Welsh-Ovcharov, *VG in Perspective*, p. 35).

Before spending the late summer in Arcachon (*Corres.*, p. 307), in July Lautrec sells a painting via the art dealer Portier (*CL*461).

In late November-December the first and only manifestation of the "Petit Boulevard" group is held in the popular restaurant *Du Chalet*. Lautrec exhibits paintings of his "prostitute types" (Bernard, *Van Gogh*, p. 393).

1888

The Belgian artist Théo van Rysselberghe visits Lautrec, which leads to an invitation for Lautrec to exhibit at *Les Vingt* in Brussels (*Corres.*, p. 107). The same month Lautrec reports to his mother that he will exhibit at *Les Vingt* (*Corres.*, p. 106).

On January 12, Lautrec completes the sale of his painting *Poudre de Riz* (cat. no. 118) to Théo van Gogh.

In February he exhibits with Louis Anquetin at the fifth exhibition of *Les Vingt*. He personally designs his exhibition list for the catalogue (*fig. 137*) which records eleven paintings and one drawing, including his major canvas *At the Circus Fernando: The Horsewoman* (cat. no. 119).

In March Lautrec receives correspondence from van Gogh in Arles (*CL*470).

In June Théo sends the *Poudre de Riz* to Vincent which the latter admires greatly (*CL*501).

Except for one or more brief excursions, the summer is spent in Paris (*Corres.*, p. 110).

On July 7, the French journal *Le Paris illustré* publishes four drawings by Lautrec to illustrate Emile Michelet's article "L'Eté à Paris:" *The Laundress* (cat. no. 120), *The Trace Horse of the Bus Company* (*fig. 143*), *Riders Approaching the Bois de Boulogne* (*fig. 90*) and *Day of First Communion* (Dortu II, p. 298).

In October, Théo van Gogh sells for Lautrec, a "Study of a Head" (Rewald, *Goupil*, p. 104).

October-December, Lautrec visits the Greniers in Villiers-sur-Morin (*Corres.*, p. 302).

1889

In January Lautrec returns to Paris (*Corres.*, p. 308). During this year he develops his mature style.

In June he exhibits with the "Cercle Artistique et Littéraire Volney;" on June 16 Théo van Gogh

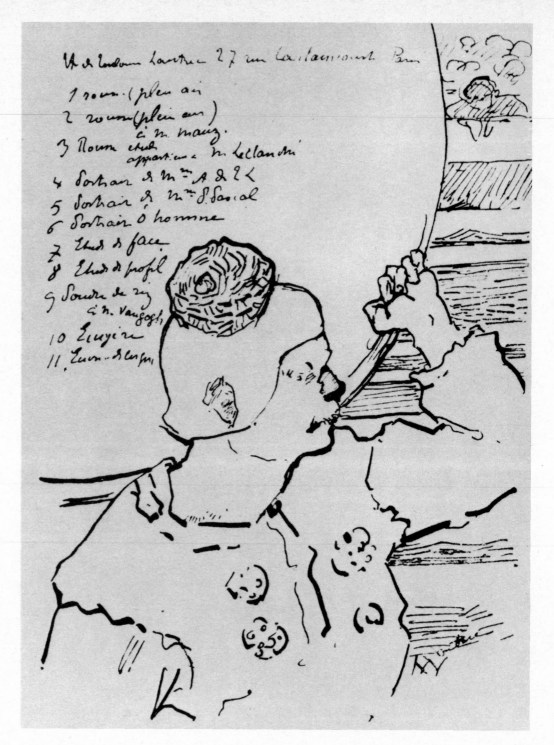

Fig. 137
Henri de Toulouse-Lautrec:
Illustration for the exhibition list of the catalogue of "Les Vingt"
1888.

Fig. 138
Henri de Toulouse-Lautrec:
La Goulue at the Moulin Rouge,
1891,
four-colour lithograph posters.

informs Vincent (*T*10) that for this reason Lautrec was not invited to participate in the Volpini exhibition.

Gauguin justifies the exclusion of Lautrec from this group by insisting that Lautrec only thinks of himself (*G*24).

The summer is spent once again largely in Paris with a possible trip *circa* August to Arcachon (*Corres.*, p. 112).

In September Lautrec exhibits three paintings including *Moulin de la Galette* (cat. no. 121) in the fifth *Indépendants* exhibition, along with works by Louis Anquetin, van Gogh, Georges Seurat and Paul Signac. On October 5 the dance hall Moulin Rouge is opened; it becomes Lautrec's favourite dance hall.

Lautrec is invited to exhibit at *Les Vingt* in Brussels along with Vincent van Gogh (*T*20).

1890

In February Lautrec exhibits five paintings at *Les Vingt*, and travels to Brussels for the opening.

From March through April, Lautrec exhibits ten works, including his canvas *Au Moulin Rouge* (Dortu II, p. 361) in the sixth *Indépendants* exhibition, along with works by Louis Anquetin and van Gogh.

In May, along with Anquetin, he contributes to the first exhibition of the *Société Nationale des Beaux-Arts* (*Salon du Champ de Mars*).

On July 6 he lunches in Théo van Gogh's apartment with Vincent van Gogh who has come from Auvers-sur-Oise.

In early fall, Théo experiences a sudden illness and Maurice Joyant replaces him as manager of the Boussod and Valadon Gallery. Among Théo's stock of canvases are paintings by Gauguin, Redon, Pissarro and others; Joyant also discovers there some works Lautrec left on consignment (Joyant I, p. 118).

1891

Lautrec changes his living quarters in January from 19 to 21 rue Fontaine which he continues to share with Dr. Bourges. The next month he exhibits at the *Cercle Artistique et Littéraire*.

March through April Lautrec shows nine works at the seventh *Indépendants* exhibition along with works by Anquetin, van Gogh, Seurat and Signac.

In the autumn he creates his first lithographic poster *La Goulue at the Moulin Rouge*: (*fig. 138*).

In December he exhibits seven works at the *Salon des Arts libéraux* along with Anquetin, Bernard, Gauguin, van Gogh, Sérusier and Signac in the first exhibition of "des Peintres Impressionnistes et Symbolistes" at the gallery of Le Barc de Boutteville.

1892-1901

During these years Lautrec continues to paint café figures such as Jane Avril and creates his brilliant and innovative posters.

In 1893 his first one-man show at Boussod and Valadon, of which Maurice Joyant is the director, takes place.

He begins by 1894 to be the painter of bordellos such as those on the rue Moulins in Paris.

In 1895 he exhibits both at the *Société Nationale des Beaux-Arts* and at S. Bing's *Maison de l'Art Nouveau*, a Tiffany stained-glass window (*Fig. 139*) along with other stained glass by Vuillard, Bonnard and Sérusier.

He travels to London, Lisbon (1895) and Holland (1897).

By 1898 he is drinking heavily, working less and suffering from acute alcoholism. In February 1899 after a delirium crisis, Lautrec is taken to a treatment centre at Neuilly. In order to demonstrate his sanity, he executes thirty-nine drawings based on his earlier circus theme. By autumn he returns to drinking and in August 1901 is struck by paralysis.

Lautrec dies at the Château Malromé at the age of thirty-seven, surrounded by his parents and immediate family.

Fig. 139
Henri de Toulouse-Lautrec:
At the Nouveau Cirque: Father Chrysanthemum,
1895,
stained-glass window
(Musée d'Orsay, Paris).

112.
Two Prostitutes in a Café
late 1885-1886
oil on panel: 24 x 17 cm
Not signed or dated
Lent by the Rijksmuseum Vincent van Gogh,
Amsterdam

Although not mentioned in the correspondence
between Vincent and Théo van Gogh, this small
painting on panel nonetheless entered their possession, most likely at the time of the *Du Chalet*
exhibition where Lautrec was featured with his
"types de la prostitution."[1] A drawing of the same
subject (Dortu V, D.2.897), signed with the
pseudonym "Tréclau," that disappeared in the
course of 1886, may indicate the probable date of
execution of the panel painting, although neither
may be identified as a definitive version.[2]

The apish features of the seated woman are
only slightly less unattractive than the visage of the
standing figure reflected in the mirror. Both
women may be characterized as "prostitutes"
chiefly because of their brazen and unsociable confrontation. In a major gouache of a related theme,
The Artilleryman and a Woman (Dortu II,
p. 272), the woman depicted appears close in
dress, hairstyle and wanton décolletée to the seated
figure in *Two Prostitutes*. Such sketches of *circa*
1886-87 witness the incipient emergence of Lautrec as an innovator of Cloisonist style and of his
personal direction within this tendency. The stylistic affinity of this painting with Bernard's *The
Saltimbanques* (*fig. 128*) is striking enough that
a community of effort cannot be ruled out.[3]

[1] Bernard, *Van Gogh*, p. 393.
[2] This painting is included in Dortu III, as S.P. 6.
     On the verso of this panel is a sketch representing
     a woman in a mountainous landscape, not by the
     hand of Lautrec. Mark Roskill in conversation
     with the author has also expressed doubts that it
     can be by the same artist.
[3] A watercolour of a *Brothel Scene* by Bernard of
     1888 which the artist sent to Vincent in later Sep-
     tember of that year (ill. Roskill, *fig. 99*) should be
     seen as a possible derivation from this panel.

113.
Bar of the Café de la Rue de Rome
c. 1886
charcoal with estompe and scraping,
heightened with white chalk: 34.3 x 46.3 cm
Not signed or dated
Lent by The Art Institute of Chicago,
Gift of Mr. and Mrs. Carter H. Harrison

Following 1886 this type of relatively worked-up
drawing largely disappears from the *oeuvre* of
Lautrec. In some respects it may be considered a
holdover from his student drawings at the Cormon
atelier. Indeed, the man seated at the bar with his
high hat is said to be Lautrec's fellow student at
Cormon's, G. Claudon, and the Café de la Rue de
Rome was located within easy walking distance
from the Clichy district.[1] The "finished" nature of
this drawing is confirmed by a preliminary compositional sketch (Dortu II, D.2.982), a practice
paralleled in the existence of both a preliminary
and a final version of the *Gin Cocktail* (Dortu V,
D.2.964, 2.965), a subject treatment which
closely relates to the *Café de la Rue de Rome*. Since
the *Gin Cocktail* was illustrated in September
1886, the *Café* may be assigned a roughly comparable date.

In theme and graphic style this drawing also
relates to Bernard's *Hour of the Flesh* (cat.
no. 87), although Bernard's overtones of sexual
encounter are here muted to the man's implied
fascination with the absent-minded charm of the
blasé barmaid. Lautrec's drawing probably was
related to, and may to some effect reflect,
Anquetin's destroyed project on the theme of the
café Bruant.[2] The high quality and compositional
sophistication make one wish that more such
examples of this style, medium, date of execution,
and state of finish had also survived from the hand
of Lautrec. Despite the reminders of academic
canons of figure modelling and realistic detail,
there is present a freedom of chalk stroke and
search for a unified decorative effect which pres-
ages the fuller emergence of these concerns in the
years to follow.

[1] Joyant I, p. 58, n. 1, lists Claudon as a Cormon
student and elsewhere (p. 189) cites him as the
seated figure in *Au Bar*. I wish to thank H.
Joachim, curator of Prints and Drawings at the Art
Institute of Chicago, for allowing me to consult the
Lautrec notes in the Drawings Catalogue. Mr.
Joachim gives the current title of this drawing (no.
77 of the "Checklist of Prints and Drawings in the
Exhibition," which accompanied Stuckey). It
derives from correspondence between a former
owner, Henri Cottereau, and Joyant, who previously had not known of its existence but learned
that it (Dortu VI, S.D. 14) was executed in
Lautrec's studio, rue Tourlaque, on the basis of
the preliminary sketch (i.e., Dortu V, D.2.982).

[2] Bernard, *Anquetin 1932*, pp. 592-93, documents
the close relationships among himself, Lautrec and
Anquetin *circa* 1885-87, which included modelling for each other and many discussions of art
theory and practice, while Anquetin worked on his
Bruant subjects.

114.

At the Elysée Montmartre
c. 1886
crayon on tracing paper: 33 x 30 cm
Stamped monogram lower left
Inscription lower right: *84-86 Montmartre* (by
Lautrec?)
Lent by the Musée Toulouse-Lautrec, Albi

A version in charcoal (Dortu V, D.2.970) may
have been done on the spot and have provided this
distilled version on tracing paper. It was apparently never used as a transfer medium in the manner of a similar drawing (fig. 140) with the basic
figural content of the 1886 *The Quadrille at the
Elysée Montmartre* (fig. 26) and of comparable
size to the painting. However, a man in top hat
seated with two women at a round-top table was
the foreground image of the grisaille painting
dated 1888 (Dortu II, p. 301), which is called the
Masked Ball. If never employed for the execution
of an oil painting, this charming "cartoon" of a
group of three figures seated around a table
nevertheless provides an insight into the distinction
of Cloisonist figural outlines and implied in-filling
with colour which was a part of Lautrec's working
habits by *circa* 1886-87.

The setting of these and numerous related
drawings by Lautrec was the fashionable dance
hall, *L'Elysée Montmartre*, located at 80

boulevard Rochechouart, two doors down from
the tiny *Chat Noir* café, which in the summer of
1886 the singer Aristide Bruant took over from
Rodolphe Salis and turned into *Le Mirliton*.[1]
These two virtually adjacent sites were home terri-
tory to Lautrec, Anquetin and Bernard *circa*
1886-87 when they were most intimately associated.[2] A previously unpublished ink drawing by
Emile Bernard (fig. 141) almost certainly represents the same dance hall, where the *quadrille*
was danced to an extravagant degree of perfection.
While perhaps dating to 1887-very early 1888,
despite the added inscribed date of 1886, this
compositionally innovative drawing further cor-
roborates the intimacy of the artistic exchanges
which seem to have been endemic among the Petit
Boulevard group of the Clichy ambiance.[3]

[1] On the character of the *Chat Noir–Mirliton*, see
G. Mack, *Toulouse-Lautrec* (New York: Alfred
A. Knopf, 1838), pp. 92-94, and Joyant I,
pp. 92-96.

[2] See Gauzi, pp. 67-70, and Mack, pp. 111-18,
for accounts of this entertainment centre and its
denizens.

[3] Although known to the present writer only in photographic reproduction, the provenance goes back
to the Bernard family (see Welsh-Ovcharov, *Petit
Boulevard*, pp. 63-64).

Fig. 141
Emile Bernard:
Woman with High Hat in a Dance Hall,
1887-88,
ink drawing
(collection unknown).

Fig. 140
Henri de Toulouse-Lautrec
Elysée Montmartre,
1886,
pencil drawing
(Musée Toulouse-Lautrec, Albi).

115.
Waiting at Grenelle
c. 1886-87
oil on canvas: 56 x 46.8 cm
Signed upper right: *HLautrec*
Lent by the Sterling and Francine Clark Institute,
Williamstown, Massachusetts
TORONTO ONLY

It recently has been established that this was not
the painting *A Grenelle: La Buveuse d'Absinthe*,
which, originally was displayed above the piano in
Aristide Bruant's café *Le Mirliton*.[1] It now
appears to be a second version of the same or a
related theme, which Lautrec sold from an exhibition in Reims to the father of Frederic Wenz, a
fellow student at the Cormon studio.[2] The title *A
Grenelle* is taken from a song by Bruant about an
aging and disillusioned prostitute who had spent
her best days in service to the military personnel
stationed in the Grenelle district of Paris. Nothing
in the painting alludes specifically to the song, and
it is obvious from the mounted canvas upper left
and the round-top café table (*guéridon*), one of
which the artist owned, that the painting was executed in the artist's own studio. However, the original version of *A Grenelle* is equally notable for its
lack of reference to the Grenelle area of Paris, and
the Clark Institute painting evokes a sense of disil-
lusion similar to that of Bruant's ballad. Though
the face is half-hidden, the down-turned mouth
and set of the body suggest a weariness with life
that is as much mental as physical. The placement
of the glass of absinthe next to the nose and lips of
the sitter, despite her apparent disregard of it, renders more poignant this image of a wasted life for
which there is no hope of redemption.

The association between absinthe drinkers and
the down-and-out way of life was of course well
established by major treatments, first by Manet
and then by Degas.[3] The 1876 *Absinthe Drinker*
(Louvre, Paris) by Degas would have provided a
precedent not only in subject but in the angle of
view and brush technique as well. Lautrec
nonetheless creates a novel and highly personal
version of this theme by showing the woman in a
less formally posed and publicly situated stance.
As if the ambiguity of her setting—café and artist's
studio—were not enough, Lautrec depicts his
absinthe drinker as seemingly so lost in thought
that she is unaware of the artist's presence.

1 Gauzi, pp. 45-46, recalled that the *Le Mirliton*
painting was hung near the piano behind a statue
of a golden angel praying on its knees. It is thus
the painting seen hanging in a photograph of the
Mirliton café (fig. 142) in which Lautrec is seated
next to Anquetin but, unfortunately, the painting
is too indistinct to allow for recognition. For contemporary accounts of *Le Mirliton* see "Lanterne
de Cabaret," *Le Mirliton*, no. 32, February
1887, p. 2, where Lautrec and Anquetin are listed
as clients; *see* also John Grand-Cartaret, *L'Art
dans la brasserie, Paris, 1886.*

2 *Whereas Gauzi, ibid.,* believed that Lautrec
retrieved the Mirliton *A Grenelle* for exhibition at
Reims, Stuckey (and co-author N.E. Maurer)
cat. nos. 26, 29, have demonstrated that the Mirliton version was sold by Bruant in 1905 (see
Joyant I, p. 265; not an estate sale since the singer
died only in 1925) and that the Clark Institute
version must have been the one exhibited at
Reims. Stuckey and Maurer also point to a drawing with the figure of the Mirleton absinthe drinker
(Dortu V, D.2.947), which is inscribed by the
artist lower right "1886, à Grenelle Mirliton" and
which thus suggests a date earlier than that of
1888 assigned by Joyant (I, p. 265). Whether the
Clark Institute painting was exhibited at Reims
under the title "A Grenelle," seems not to have
been documented as yet, so it remains uncertain
whether this title is genuinely applicable.

3 Manet's *Le Buveur d'absinthe* (Ny Carlsberg
Glyptotek, Copenhagen) was available as an etch-
ing, but how Lautrec would have known the
Degas painting is uncertain.

Fig. 142
photograph of
Louis Anquetin and
Henri de Toulouse-Lautrec
in Bruant's Café *Le Mirliton*,
c. late 1880s.

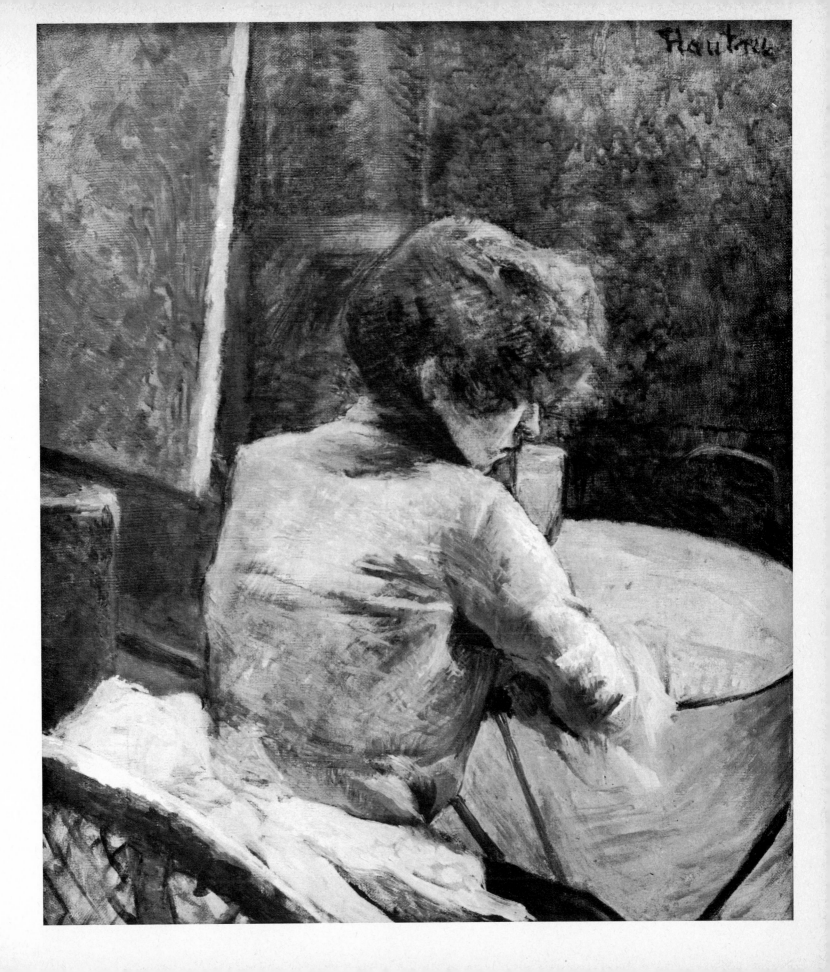

116.
At the Café
c. winter 1886-87
oil on canvas: 61 x 50 cm
Not signed or dated
Lent by Mrs. C. van der Waals-Königs,
The Netherlands
AMSTERDAM ONLY

That this painting truly represents a café scene would be uncertain, except for the existence of a crayon and ink drawing on yellow paper of the subject, equal in size to the painting, and including a glass of cold coffee (*un mazagran*) with accompanying sugar cube on a saucer placed on the foreground table (Dortu V, D.2.968).[1] The drawing's great clarity of outline suggests a version derived from the painting, rather than a final compositional study for it. The drawing itself may have been preceded by other sketches, since there is some reason to believe it identical with one of several drawings which Lautrec produced for illustration in *Le Courrier français* but which, unused for this purpose, was sold at auction in 1891.[2] Since one such drawing, *Gin Cocktail* (Dortu V, D.2.965) was published as early as September 1885 and relates in style to the more sparsely executed *At the Café* drawing, a comparable date of origin is suggested. Because the girl of the latter subject is warmly dressed with a scarf and fur borders to her sleeves, the subject likely dates from winter 1886-87, but could be either a year earlier or later.

In subject and style the painting remains strongly indebted to Impressionist tradition where women reading or at café tables were common themes.[3] The angled close-up view may derive from Lautrec's intense interest in Degas, whom he apparently met about this time, although an interest in Japanese design principles may also help explain the tendency to simplification of form which characterizes the painting. While lacking a figure, Vincent's *Still Life: Absinthe* (cat. no. 2) relates in style and composition to the *At the Café* and is not far removed in date. Within Lautrec's own career, the painting anticipates the style and subject developed in the series containing his 1887 portraits of his mother and Madame Aline Gibert (Dortu II, p. 277, 280), his 1888 study of *Hélène V* (Dortu II, p. 318) and his 1889 *The Reader* (Dortu II, p. 439).

[1] Joyant I, p. 189, identifies the glass as containing coffee, while only the saucer outline is visible in the painting.

[2] Joyant I, p. 10, illustrates this drawing, but when cataloguing it (p. 189) does not connect it with the *Courrier français*-owned "Jeune fille lisante" auctioned in 1891 (p. 187). This drawing remained unlocated and thus unmeasured in Dortu V, D.2.927, which, given its similarity in style and signature to another *Courrier français*-owned drawing (e.g., Dortu V, D.2.928) which was auctioned in 1891 without having been published, argues further for an identification between "Jeune fille lisante" and "At the Café."

[3] Stuckey, p. 107, fig. l; p. 117, fig. 1; p. 119, fig. 3; and p. 123, fig. 1, illustrates some obvious subject precedents, albeit not in the context of *At the Café*.

117.

Portrait of Vincent van Gogh
c. early 1887
pastel on cardboard: 57 x 46.5 cm
Not signed or dated
Lent by the Rijksmuseum Vincent van Gogh,
Amsterdam
AMSTERDAM ONLY

According to Bernard this pastel *Portrait of Vincent van Gogh* was executed by Lautrec at the *Le Tambourin* café.[1] If this was the case, the portrait would date from the first half of 1887, when Vincent's association with Agostina Segatori, the café proprietress, was at its height before ending abruptly in July.[2] While Vincent never became a close companion of Lautrec, he is known to have attended the weekly gatherings at Lautrec's studio, and not only did Vincent continue to ask about Lautrec from Arles (*CL* 470, 476) but they lunched together as late as July 1890, when Vincent visited Paris from Auvers.[3]

It may be that in this drawing Lautrec was adopting Vincent's own use of varied and highly visible hatching strokes. The use of such intense colours was also unusual for Lautrec, who at the time still preferred a more restrained palette. Yet the style accords with other Lautrec portraits datable to 1887 (for example, Dortu II, pp. 277, 279), and it is also likely that Vincent was attentive to the transformation of style then being achieved by Lautrec.[4] In his *Portrait of Vincent* a clearly outlined figure is seen in profile against a geometrically subdivided background with single colours generally dominating the individual areas of the composition. In this sense it can be characterized as quasi-Cloisonist in conception, although Lautrec is not thereby led away from capturing the febrile intensity of Vincent's super-charged personality.

[1] In *Van Gogh*, p. 394. Vincent is not seated at one of the round imitation *tambourin* tables, as found in his own *Agostina Segatori* (cat. no. 3), but the café also served hot meals so that Vincent may have been depicted with his absinthe aperitif in the restaurant area.
[2] See Welsh-Ovcharov, p. 251, for the date the relationship ended.
[3] Susan Valadon recalled Vincent's presence at these gatherings in a reminiscence published 1928 (Eng. trans. in Welsh-Ovcharov, *VG in Perspective*). The July 1890 visit by Lautrec is mentioned *CL*, p. 1ii.
[4] Welsh-Ovcharov, pp. 174-77.

118.
Rice Powder: Poudre de riz
c. late 1887
oil on cardboard: 65 x 58 cm
Signed bottom left: *H.T. Lautrec*
Lent by the Rijksmuseum Vincent van Gogh,
Amsterdam

The title *Poudre de Riz* was furnished by Lautrec
himself, when he sent the painting to the *Les Vingt*
exhibition of February 1888. In Lautrec's own
catalogue submission (fig. 137) occurs the listing
"no. 9, Poudre de riz, à m. van Gogh." That
Théo van Gogh was the owner is proven by the
extant receipt date-marked January 12, 1888
which Lautrec sent Théo for payment of 150
francs for his painting "femme assis devant un
tableau."[1] Vincent, too, had known this painting
by Lautrec in an unfinished state before his departure for Arles (*CL*476) and remembered it again
the following summer (*CL*520), when he
suggested it would be a fitting companion piece to
his own just finished *Portrait of Patience Escalier*
(cat. no. 21). Vincent's reasoning was, as usual,
simple and direct: his own rough-hewn portrait
and the elegant Parisian of Lautrec would each
gain in distinction by the contrast between urban
artificiality and rustic simplicity. However unlikely
the contrast may seem today, its realization in the
present exhibition grants viewers a special opportunity to observe Vincent's context of reference.

While admittedly speculative, the identification of Lautrec's model as Suzanne Valadon can
be supported on several grounds. She sits in a
chair which is likely the round-backed rattan
which was used for *Waiting at Grenelle*
(cat. no. 115). Her features are, despite the differences in Lautrec's style of execution, similar to
those of the *Portrait of Madame Suzanne Valadon* (Dortu II, p. 250). The widely spaced eyes,
accented eyebrows, rather plain nose and thin,
pursed lips are found in both portraits, and a similar feeling of *ennui* is present. If either sitter aspires
to the role of *femme fatale*, her expression of boredom scarcely discloses the fact.

The pose of this figure is similar to that in the
Agostina Segatori (cat. no. 13) which presumably preceded it in execution. The similarities in
conception are more striking than the contrasts,
whatever the order of sequence of the two paintings. Both display a certain indebtedness to Degas
and the general influence of Japanism, whereas the
portrait by Lautrec comes as close as he ever did to
the technical strictures of Pointillism. The *Poudre*

de Riz is thus a watershed example of Lautrec's
transition from Impressionism, via a flirtation with
Pointillism, to his mature Art Nouveau style
(cat. no. 123). In this respect his sitter's "rice

powder" make-up anticipates Lautrec's general
tendency towards abstraction.

[1] Preserved at the archive of the Rijksmuseum Vincent van Gogh, Amsterdam.

119.
At the Circus Fernando: The Horsewoman
late 1887
oil on canvas: 100.3 x 161.3 cm
Signed lower left: *HTLautrec*
Lent by The Art Institute of Chicago;
The Joseph Winterbotham collection

The *Circus Fernando* (pl. 28) has already been discussed (Introduction, pp. 40-41) as a major monument in the development of Cloisonist style, and Charles Stuckey's analysis of the painting in terms of its origins and related studies in Lautrec's *oeuvre* is most thorough.[1] Suffice it to say that the *Circus Fernando* is universally considered Lautrec's major debut painting for exhibition in February 1888, and no one doubts that Seurat meant to pay it tribute when painting his own *Circus* (Louvre) of 1890-91.[2]

Gauzi has related that in early 1887 Lautrec became interested in producing a major painting of a female horse rider. To this end his friend, the painter Zandomeneghi, introduced him to a model called Maria, later better known under the pseudonym Suzanne Valadon.[3] It was she who posed for the figure atop the horse by which time it is possible she had also become Lautrec's mistress. The painting depicts the ringmaster at the Fernando, M. Loyal, directing a dappled stallion toward the truncated figure of a clown on a pedestal. The clown holds a hoop through which the rider will jump from her cushioned saddle pad, a stunt Lautrec must have particularly admired.[4] Yet the artist has intentionally played down the drama of the act with the rider not yet poised for her feat, the sparse audience and two circus ushers at the ring entrance showing no visible signs of excitement and the little clown at left sauntering away with equal unconcern. Psychological interest is present in the implied confrontation between the ringmaster and the horse with rider. M. Loyal, with his caricatural fish-like face, pivots towards the horse holding his whip in a manner recalling the stylized postures of samurai figures in Japanese prints. His implied sadism may be directed at either the horse or the girl, who looks back at him with an expression which could be read as either a forced smile or haughty disdain. The powerful masculinity of the lumbering beast heightens our awareness that the circus world is not only one of artifice and escape from reality, but embodies certain darker aspects of the human psyche as well. Penetrating psychological analysis was not Lautrec's chief concern in this highly decorative painting, but neither can he be thought a totally neutral observer. His stunted leg growth having prevented his becoming a horseman himself, in the family tradition, his attention in art to horse subjects in various guises assumes a compensating intensity of personal interest.

[1] Stuckey, pp. 124-29.
[2] The *Cirque Fernando* was purchased by Joseph Oller, one of the directors of the *Moulin Rouge*, and displayed in the entrance hall of that establishment after its opening in October 1889.
[3] Gauzi, pp. 131-32; see also Joyant I, p. 86. The true name of Suzanne Valadon was Marie-Clementine Valade; Lautrec has been credited with suggesting the change to Suzanne (J. Storm, *The Valadon Drama; The Life of Suzanne Valadon*, New York: E.P. Dutton, 1959).
[4] See Stuckey, p. 126.

120.

The Laundress
June 1888
brush and india ink, heightened with white lead,
on scratchboard: 76.2 x 63 cm
Signed lower right: *HTLautrec*
Lent by the Cleveland Museum of Art;
Gift of Hanna Fund

This was one of four drawings illustrating an article by Emile Michelet, "L'Eté à Paris" (Paris
illustré, July 7, 1888). The theme of "Summer in
Paris" was treated in terms of street scenes, three
of which include horses and the fourth, *First
Communion* (Dortu II, p. 298) a baby carriage.
The Trace Horse of the Bus Company (fig. 143)
shows a scene analogous to the *Avenue de Clichy*
(cat. no. 76) by Anquetin, with its image of the
bustling everyday life of metropolitan Paris. *Riders
Approaching the Bois de Boulogne* (fig. 90)
depicts a more elegant diversion of city life, and
Lautrec's picture-edge curtailment of one of the
horses not only betrays an indebtedness to Degas
and the art of Japan but itself provides a precedent
upon which Anquetin would capitalize a year later
in the pastel *The "Rond Point"at the Champs
Elysées* (cat. no. 80). *The Laundress* also employs
a sharply receding perspective combined with a
tilted-up ground plane suggestive of an influence
from Japanese wood block prints, as is the large
scale and bottom truncation of the central figure.[1]
Lautrec already had employed these Japanist
devices to great effect in *At the Circus Fernando*
(cat. no. 119).

The *Laundress* has its most immediate precedents within Lautrec's own graphic *oeuvre*. In
Young Woman with a Wine Bottle (Dortu V,
D.2.928) and *In the Street* (Dortu V, D.3.001),
settings, figures and a sparcely accented linear style
strongly anticipate the theme and style of the
Laundress.[2] The seemingly facile sketchiness of
this 1888 drawing is deceptive, since a preliminary
study exists (Dortu V, D.3.028) which shows how
carefully Lautrec worked out the juxtaposition of
the woman and her basket against the horse and
carriage at left. One may also presume that the
female figure derived from a studio situation, since
vehicular traffic would have precluded a pose *in
situ*. This exquisitely sensitive and subtly balanced
composition forms a striking prologue to the even
more simplified style of Lautrec's poster art of the
1890s.

[1] With its storefront and awning canopy at left and
   kiosk at right in the distance, Lautrec's setting is

Fig. 143
Henri de Toulouse-Lautrec: *The Trace Horse of the Bus Company*,
1888, drawing (private collection, Paris).

reminiscent of that in Anquetin's *Avenue de Clichy*
as well.

[2] The *Woman with a Wine Bottle* of *circa* 1886-87
   was intended for illustration in the *Courrier français* but never used, and *In the Street*, with its
   theme of aged lechery, appeared as the cover
   illustration of Bruant's *Le Mirliton*, no. 33,
   February 1887. In this form the drawing includes
   a brief dialogue in which the old "gentleman"
   asks the delivery girl for a milliner's shop her age,
   and upon learning it is fifteen, declares that to be a
   trifle old for his taste. E. Lipton, "The Laundress
   in Late Nineteenth Century French Culture:
   Imagery, Ideology and Edgar Degas," *Art History
   III* (September 1980), pp. 295-313, discusses in
   depth the social condition of Parisian laundresses,
   especially as this pertains to art and literature in
   the Realist-Impressionist tradition. *See also*
   T. Reff, *Degas: The Artist's Mind* (New York:
   Harper and Row 1976) pp. 164-70.

121.

The Ball at the Moulin de la Galette
c. winter-early spring 1889
oil on canvas: 88.9 x 101.3 cm
Signed lower left: *H.T. Lautrec*
Lent by The Art Institute of Chicago;
Mr. and Mrs. Lewis L. Coburn Memorial
Collection

Lautrec first exhibited this painting (pl. 29) in September 1889 at the fifth *Indépendants* exhibition, where Théo van Gogh singled it out for mention in a report to Vincent (*T*16). Lautrec attended the opening day with members of his family and was quite excited by the event.[1] It was Lautrec's first important exhibition participation in Paris, since he had chosen not to contribute to the 1888 *Indépendants* and was excluded by Gauguin from the 1889 Café Volpini display. The *Moulin de la Galette* was not a last minute effort for the 1889 *Indépendants*, having been finished in time to serve as the basis for a drawing reproduced in the magazine *Courrier français* of May 19, 1889 (Dortu V, D.3.091).

The painted version was described at some length by Félix Fénéon, albeit more for its variety of human types than for its style, which he summed up as a mixture of influences from J.-L. Forain and Degas without being a copy of either.[2] Fénéon's designations of the seated male figure at right as "Alphonse the lawyer," and the uniformed figure standing beyond him as a "municipal officer," while somewhat hypothetical, suggest the "policing" which seems to have been occasionally necessary to keep order in a centre of Montmartre night-life noted as a place of sporadic outbreaks of violence. Lautrec's artist-friend and later biographer, François Gauzi, claimed that the reputation of the area was such that Lautrec never visited the establishment at night but only on Sunday afternoons, when daylight offered protection against attack.[3] According to Gauzi, apart from artists and their models, the dance hall was frequented by a variety of working-class types and included a proportion of pimps. One paid for the privilege of each dance, with differing prices for the waltz, mazurka or quadrille, and each dance stopped midway for the collection of the small fee. Whether or not Lautrec ever did visit the *Moulin de la Galette* at night, he has invested his scene with a sense of frenetic pleasure-seeking and a candidly sinister atmosphere which conforms to Gauzi's characterization of the ambiance.[4]

The intense observer at right has regularly

been identified as a certain Joseph Albert, a painter-friend of Lautrec, who is said to have introduced Lautrec to Degas and to have been the original owner of this picture.[5] His presence in the scene is more than that of an interested observer. He here acts as a surrogate for Lautrec, the absent observer, whose saucers are seen stacked high on the foreground table surface.[6] Albert's inclusion in this painting may or may not support the theory of his original ownership, but it does indicate that Lautrec produced the canvas at home and not in the enervating circumstances of an actual "bal." The striking absence of well-known dancers in this painting confirms the proletarian and low-life iconography. Although Lautrec would subsequently raise the level of his social vision in his paintings of the *Moulin Rouge*, this important canvas witnesses his devotion during winter 1888-89 to dance-hall themes, which both he and Vincent van Gogh had been investigating during the previous years.[7]

The question of Lautrec's sources for this painting is involved and likely to provoke controversy for years to come. Recently Charles Stuckey has listed Manet, Degas, Renoir and Gauguin as probable sources of Lautrec's painting[8]. Stuckey's most convincing analogy is that with Renoir's *Moulin de la Galette* there is the virtue of a coincident subject and an execution a decade earlier. Gauzi had cited this precedent, which Lautrec must have had in mind, not only in theme but in composition, with the seated figures right foreground and dancing figures to the area at left.[9] Lautrec, while paying tribute to Renoir's formidable precedent, has replaced that artist's delight in innocent social pleasures with an image of fugitive excitations and unfulfilled longings which border on the sinister.

[1] *Corres.*, pp. 112-13.

[2] Fénéon, p. 169 (from *La Vogue*, September 1889). For a protype café-scene by Forain see Stuckey, p. 108, fig. 2.

[3] Gauzi, pp. 84-89.

[4] *Ibid.*, p. 86, however, in keeping with the account of Lautrec restricting his visits to Sunday afternoons, describes the setting as a sunlit garden. While this description fits the *Moulin de la Galette* by Renoir (Louvre), which Gauzi mentions as having inspired Lautrec to treat the same subject, the latter's version included board flooring, a wall at rear but no trees and, judging from the heavy coat with upturned collar of the tall man with high hat entering the scene at upper right, represents the winter season when the garden would be

closed. The uniformed figure upper right could be, rather than Fénéon's "municipal officer," the doorman or "barker" of the establishment (Gauzi, p. 88), who announced each dance and collected the fees.

[5] Both Joyant I, p. 126, and Arsène Alexandre (cited in Cooper, p. 76) identify this figure as Joseph Albert, who is listed in several repertories as a student of Bonnat and Puvis de Chavannes and who exhibited at the *Salon* 1887-89. Gauzi, p. 86, apparently confused Joseph with Adolphe Albert, who had been a fellow student with Lautrec at the Cormon *atelier*, exhibited at the *Indépendants* regularly beginning in 1886, drew a portrait of Lautrec in 1897 (ill. in A. Alexandre, "Toulouse-Lautrec," *Figaro illustré*, April, 1902, p. 2) and was himself rendered by Lautrec as "The Good Engraver" lithograph of 1898 (Adhémar, no. 301). The same figure who appears in the *Moulin de la Galette* occurs in a Lautrec lithograph of 1893 (Adhémar, no. 48) and seems to be present standing at right in Anquetin's *Moulin Rouge* (cat. no. 86). However, although Joseph Albert has been called the first owner of Lautrec's *Moulin de la Galette* (Alexandre as cited in Cooper, *ibid.*), and his figure is absent from a preliminary compositional study (Dortu II, p. 334), the painting was not listed as owned by anyone when exhibited fall 1889 at the *Indépendants*, but was owned by the collector Montandon when exhibited again a few months later at the *Les Vingt* exhibition of February 1890.

[6] As suggested by Stuckey, pp. 144-45. One should not assume that Lautrec painted or perhaps even drew Albert's portrait at the dance hall, since the girl in profile lower left clearly derives from an oil sketch executed in his studio (Dortu II, p. 351).

[7] Lautrec's own most striking precedents are *The Quadrille of the Louis XIII Chair at the Elysée Montmartre (fig. 26)*, *The Refrain of the Louis XIII Chair at the Cabaret Aristide Bruant (fig. 27)* and *Bal Masqué* (Dortu II, p. 302). During Vincent's stay in Paris 1886-87, he and Lautrec would have been aware of each other's use of café interiors as settings for figural depictions (*see* cat. nos. 3 and 116). While in Arles we know that Vincent was sent the *Poudre de Riz* (cat. no. 118), and Lautrec would have seen some of Vincent's production, most of which was sent to Théo in Paris. Possible influences by Vincent in 1888 on the *Moulin de la Galette* might have included *Vincent's Bedroom* (cat. no. 26) or *The Night Café* (*F* 463) for the perspective (the latter work is related in theme as well); *The Dance Hall* (F 547) for the theme (Stuckey, p. 146,

incongruously considering their respective dates, has Lautrec's *Moulin* influencing Vincent's *Dance Hall*); and the *Interior of a Restaurant* (cat.

no. 5) for the idea of foreground benches at raking angles.

8   Stuckey, pp. 144-45, with good illustrations.

9   Gauzi, as in note 3, above.

122.
The Hangover: The Drinker
Gueule de Bois: La Buveuse
c. March 1889
india ink, blue crayon and conte crayon on paper:
49.3 x 63.2 cm
Signed lower right: *HTLautrec*
Lent by the Musée Toulouse-Lautrec, Albi

The model for this figure study is again thought to
have been Suzanne Valadon.[1] The title "Gueule
de Bois," according to Joyant, was given by Aristide Bruant, who had the painted version hanging
in his café.[2] The drawing was produced on request
for the *Courrier français*, where it appeared in the
April 21, 1889 issue. The painting could have
been executed some time earlier, since its style of
loose coruscating hatching throughout is already
found in portraits executed in 1887 (for example,
Dortu II, p. 277-79). One of these, the pastel rep-

resenting *Vincent van Gogh* (cat. no. 117), is so
similar in pose, setting and style that the painted
Gueule de Bois must be thought either a companion piece to or a derivation from it. The subject of
a woman drinking alone was used by Lautrec on a
number of occasions, and here, as with *Waiting at
Grenelle* (cat. no. 115), it remains ambiguous
whether the setting is truly meant to be read as a
café or as the more casual ambiance of the artist's
studio. The woman wears a working-class white
chemise similar to that worn by *The Laundress*
(cat. no. 120) and is thus not specified as a prostitute or other denizen of Montmartre night-life.[3]

In style the drawing relates most closely to
other *Courrier français* commissions of spring
1889 (Dortu V, D.3.089-91), one of which, *A la
Bastille*, shows another female drinker seated at
the round-topped table which Lautrec had in his
studio.[4] In these drawings there is a noticeable
simplification of contour *vis à vis* the paintings,

and Lautrec emphasizes a contrast between those
areas he has filled in with parallel hatching and
others left largely bare. This contrast between dark
and light areas in the composition looks forward to
his related usages in the posters of the 1890s for
the realization of which drawings such as the
Hangover provide a distinct presentiment.

[1] A photograph of her is reproduced in Huisman-
    Dortu, p. 59.
[2] Joyant I, p. 98
[3] See Dortu II, p. 305, 317, 345, and 346 for simi-
    lar portraits of girls wearing white shirts, which
    were especially popular among working-class girls
    in Montmartre during this period.
[4] I.e., Dortu V, D.3.089 based on the painting
    Dortu II, p. 307, the title of which, *A la Bastille*,
    refers to a well-known song by Bruant (see also
    Stuckey, p. 111).

123.

At the Nouveau Cirque: Father Chrysanthemum
c. November 1892
watercolour, tempera and oil on wove paper
backed with Japanese paper: 118.7 x 87.6 cm
Signed lower left with monogram
Lent by the Philadelphia Museum of Art;
The John D. McIlhenny Fund
TORONTO ONLY

The style of this painting is so similar to that of
Lautrec's poster art of the early 1890s that it has
been considered an unfinished project for an
advertising lithograph. Yet, there is no area suitable for insertion of a title large enough in scale to
serve as advertising.[1] The event depicted is theatri-
cal: the ballet production *Père Chrysanthème*
which took place in November 1892 at the fashionable Nouveau Cirque located on the rue Saint-
Honoré near the Place Vendôme.[2] The event was
perhaps more a spectacle than a classic ballet. A
lily pond had been improvised in the circus ring,
and coloured lights enhanced the appeal of the
nymphs in diaphanous gowns who swirled
around it. The story was of a Japanese prince who
returned to his homeland with a Western bride,
who is seen in Lautrec's painting as presenting
herself to her husband's court in a solo dance.[3]
The five seated figures in stiff shirts, formerly
called clowns, on closer inspection appear as caricatured members of the court in Western dress. A
drawing of the same scene (Dortu VI, D.4.556)
but from another angle, includes three cut-off
female figures, seen from the rear, who must be
members of the French *corps de ballet* in Japanese
costumes and hairdos. The foreground seated figure in the Philadelphia version wears contemporary Western dress, which is no less sumptuously
flamboyant than the costumes found in the drawing. In contrast to the relative sobriety of what
may have been preliminary studio studies of this
seated figure (Dortu II, p. 403-04), the serpentine
linear outlines of the two females in the painting
are so patently Japanist in character that one
scarcely hesitates to classify this work of art as an
early example of the Art Nouveau movement. The
label Cloisonism is equally applicable, and by
1895 it was suitably realized in the form of Lautrec's only stained-glass window by the workshops
of Louis Tiffany (fig. 139).[3] The fact that this
elegant image of high fashion in a theatre setting
could be considered equally suitable for use as a
lithographic poster and as a stained-glass design
testifies to the homogeneity of style which Lautrec

achieved in his decorative output of the 1890s and
also to how deeply it was indebted to the Cloisonist
and Japanist ideals.

[1] The assumption of an intended function as a
poster design has been made by Stuckey, p. 194,
and Cooper, p. 92, but there is no record of Lautrec's having received a commission, and it is possible that this painting was executed in reference to
the stained-glass commission by Tiffany (see note
3, below).

[2] See Mack, pp. 217-18, and Stuckey, p. 193, for
details of the performance, which is also reflected
in Dortu II, p. 430-31, 515.

[3] Mack, p. 218, gives details of the Tiffany project
which included windows by a number of Nabi artists, including Paul Sérusier. See G. Mauner (*as in*
cat. no. 142 n. 1) for illustrations of these windows,
figs. 37-40, 42, 43. These works in glass were
presented in the April 1895 exhibition of the *Société
Nationale des Beaux-Arts*, where Lautrec's submission was singled out for praise by J.-E. Blanche,
La Revue blanche, May 15, 1895. This version in
glass is now at the Musée d'Orsay, Paris (exh. cat.
*Cinq années d'enrichissement du Patrimonie
national*, 1975-1980; Paris: Grand Palais,
1980-81, no. 214).

124.
Aristide Bruant in his Cabaret
1893
coloured lithographic poster: 127.3 × 95.2 cm
Signed lower left: *HTLautrec* plus monogram
Lent by the Museum of Modern Art, New York;
Gift of Emilio Sanchez

The relationship between Lautrec and the popular
singer and composer Aristide Bruant was a lasting
one. The latter had opened his café *Le Mirleton* in
the summer of 1885, and Lautrec was not only an
early frequenter but supplied numerous decorations for the cabaret itself, a number of which
were illustrated in the eponymous pamphlet which
appeared irregularly from 1885 to 1892. Bruant's
songs were rich in Parisian *argot*, and his habit of
bantering insults at his customers contributed to
his popularity. As the poster indicates, Bruant was
impressively handsome, and his habitual costume
of flowing dark cape, red scarf and large soft felt
hat complemented his physical assets. He appears
as a troubadour in the best tradition of both the
Middle Ages and the Romantic era of Victor
Hugo. He had been raised amidst the squalour of
Parisian working-class districts, and his songs
reflected the self-defeating misery of the victims of
this *milieu*. He might as easily have identified
himself with Hugo's Jean Valjean as did Gauguin
(cat. no. 52) and was apparently more concerned
with bringing attention to the evils of the working-
class quarters of Paris than Gauguin ever was.[1]
It was strangely the aristocrat Lautrec, himself
little inclined to political or social reform, who
epitomized the seemingly heroic stature of Bruant
in the several posters which he produced in celebration of this long-term friendship and the admiration he felt for the singer's talent.[2] Both Lautrec
and Bruant had a penchant for simplicity in their
respective artistic work. Restricting his colours to
the green-trimmed black of the cape and hat and
the red of the scarf against a pale yellow ground,
Lautrec has here produced one of the purest
embodiments of the Cloisonist spirit provided
in the whole of late nineteenth century French
painting.

[1] Mack, pp. 92-104, provides a convenient sum-
    mary in English of Bruant's career and outlook on
    life. A contemporary account is provided in 0.
    Metenier, "Aristide Bruant," *La Plume*, no. 43,
    February 1, 1891.

[2] See also Adhémar, nos. 6, 7.

125.
The Divan Japonais
1892-April 1893
coloured lithographic poster: 77.5 × 59.2 cm
Signed lower right: *HTLautrec*
Lent by the Albright-Knox Gallery, Buffalo

Traditionally dated 1892, this poster has been
reassigned to early 1893 by Adhémar, who states
that the *Divan Japonais* artists' café opened only
in 1893; he points out that the poster drew critical
praise on the last day of April of that year and yet
didn't prevent the establishment closing by July.[1]
Whatever the case may be, the *Divan Japonais*
was for a time a place much frequented by Lautrec and his circle of friends. (*fig. 13*) Apparently a
mixture of a *cabaret artistique* and café concert, it
was located in relatively confined quarters seating
no more than two hundred people, to which was
added a cellar appendage which allowed for spe-
cialized entertainment into the early hours of the
morning. Singing and dancing performances were
provided, and, judging from Lautrec's poster, the
orchestra was large enough to include two bass
fiddles. It has been presumed that the name of the
establishment derives from its decorative motifs,
and this penchant would have augmented Lautrec's interest in providing a suitable poster design.

The personages present in this *affiche* are well
known. The dancer Jane Avril seated in the foreground is accompanied by their mutual friend the
music critic and writer Edouard Dujardin—not
only the author of the article "Le Cloisonisme"
but a featured figure in Lautrec's *circa* 1892
painting *Au Moulin rouge* (Dortu II, p. 427).
Dujardin in this instance is represented as a shaggy
leonine figure of dapper and, with his monocle,
rather English appearance. This was appropriate
for a companion of Mademoiselle Jane Avril,
whose first name and general appearance often
caused her to be considered English.[2] The third
figure represented was the most appropriate for
this poster, since it is Yvette Guilbert, whose comi-
cally lascivious songs made her the star of this and
other cabarets, but whom Lautrec has here
decapitated leaving her identification to the long

[1]   Adhémar may be right about the date of the
poster, but he certainly underestimates the period
when the cabaret flourished; see the accounts in
Mack, pp. 105-10, and Gauzi, pp. 103-04, who
recounts an initial visit with Lautrec during their
student days at the Cormon studio.

[2]   Mack, p. 149.

black gloves which were her trademark. It is not recorded that Avril was a performer at the *Divan Japonais*, but her prominence in this poster at the expense of a reputed rival shows at least partiality if not downright hostility to Guilbert on Lautrec's part[3].

It was at about this time that Lautrec achieved his reputation as a significant artist, especially for such graphic essays as this. A final sketch for this lithograph exists (Dortu V, D.3.223) which documents that the artist took great pains at working out the composition to his satisfaction.[4] One account exists however, which stresses both the concerted preliminary effort which went into Lautrec's lithographic achievements, and also the immediacy with which the artist executed these compositions from memory on the lithographer's stone block.[5] Whether or not accurate in all respects, it substantiates both the freedom with which Lautrec applied his talents to this medium and his appreciation of its reductive tendencies. The restriction in colour to olive green, yellow and orange (for Avril's hair) plus a variety of white, gray and black may derive in part from Lautrec's sobriety in the use of his medium, but it also reflects a comparable simplification in the use of colour in the Japanese prints which he here so effectively assimilated into a highly personal stylistic usage.

[3] On Guilbert see *ibid.*, pp. 194-204, where is translated into English the singer's plea in another instance that Lautrec make her a little less ugly. That this entreaty was fully justified is apparent from photographs of her even when compared with those of Avril (see Huisman-Dortu, pp. 97, 102-05).

[4] A preliminary watercolour exists as well, Dortu III, A.201.

[5] Gauzi, pp. 161-62; however, as explained in the sale catalogue of the Robert von Hirsch collection, vol. 4, *Impressionist and Modern Art*, p. 195 (Sotheby Park Bernet and Co., 27 June 1978) the technique, especially in this case, was considerably more complicated.

Jakob Meyer de Haan (1852-1895)

Biographical Data

SOURCES

Since the de Haan family itself and pertinent
records were victims of the Nazi occupation of The
Netherlands in World War II, our present scant
knowledge of Meyer de Haan's life either before or
after his stay in France (1888-91) is unlikely to be
augmented. Even these years are best documented
by references to him in letters by others, especially
Gauguin and the van Gogh brothers, and in an
odd remembrance. Only four letters written by
Meyer de Haan himself are known to the present
writer, one each to Vincent and Théo and two as
yet unpublished letters to Théo's widow, Johanna
van Gogh-Bonger (Rijksmuseum Vincent van
Gogh, Amsterdam). F. Dauchot, "Meyer de Haan
en Bretagne," *Gazette des Beaux-Arts*, XL (July-
December 1952), pp. 355-58, and W. Jaworska,
"Jakob Meyer de Haan: 1852-1895," *Nederlands Kunsthistorisch Jaarboek*, no. 18 (1967),
pp. 197-221, remain the basic studies of his life
and art, and each contains a checklist of chiefly his
French *oeuvre* (Jaworska, pp. 95-106, is this article without checklist). For the French period it is
the surviving body of paintings by de Haan—
restricted in numbers, but it would seem relatively
intact—which provides our best record of his personal contribution of the Cloisonist-Synthetist
movement.

Fig. 144
Jakob Meyer de Haan:
Portrait of a Girl,
c. 1880,
oil on canvas
(private collection, Amsterdam).

ARTISTIC CAREER IN THE NETHERLANDS

circa 1878-88

Jakob Meyer de Haan is born into a successful Jewish family of biscuit manufacturers, but is more inclined towards the study of religion, music and art. His musical talent is reported to have led to a guest concert by himself and his brothers before the royal family in The Hague, which is considered such an honour that the group never again appears in public. De Haan is reported to have studied under the painter P.E. Greive (Jaworska, p. 242 n. 63) and beginning *circa* 1878-80 he is known to have produced portraits (*see fig. 144*) and several paintings that raise questions about aspects of rabbinical practice or history: *Examining a Chicken for its Dietary Laws* (1880) and *A Dispute over the Talmud* (1878-79). His most ambitious painting in this vein is *Uriel Acosta* (*fig. 145*), a canvas he works on dilatorily for about a decade before presenting it in an exhibition at the Panorama Building, Amsterdam. Despite his stylistic indebtedness to the Lowland artists Teniers and Rembrandt the work clearly provokes resentment in conservative Jewish circles in Amsterdam for depicting sympathetically a free-thinking seventeenth century Dutch Jew of Portugese origin who had been repeatedly excommunicated by rabbinical courts for heresy and died, a martyr to his beliefs, by suicide. Although de Haan's painting is defended in a pamphlet (J. Zürcher, *Uriel Acosta*, Amsterdam, 1888), the negative reaction is apparently such that the artist leaves for Paris by fall 1888 with one of his students, J.J. Isaacson, who not long thereafter is to write the first critical notice on Vincent van Gogh in The Netherlands (*De Portefeuille*, August 17, 1889).

Fig. 145
Jakob Meyer de Haan:
Uriel Acosta,
1878-88,
oil on canvas
(private collection, the Netherlands).

1888

In October Théo reports the arrival in Paris of de Haan and Isaacson, their meeting (probably through himself) of Pissarro, their plans to stay in Paris for the winter, and the character of *Uriel Acosta* (*CL*555, *T*1, 2). On October 27 Théo announces (*T*3) that de Haan is moving in with him the next day, following which date de Haan executes a portrait drawing of Théo (*fig. 146*) and a painting *View from Théo van Gogh's Window, Rue Lepic* (*fig. 147*). On November 11 Vincent writes Théo (*CL*559) how much he likes the Rembrandtesque qualities apparent in the photographs of drawings by de Haan he has received. He encourages de Haan's intention of exploring Impressionist style systematically, adding the advice that de Haan should abandon *chiaroscuro* in favour of painting in colour alone and that Gauguin would advise his working in the tropics towards that end.

During December Vincent merely sends his compliments to de Haan.

Fig. 146
Jakob Meyer de Haan:
Théo van Gogh,
c. early 1889,
pencil drawing
(Rijksmuseum Vincent van Gogh,
Amsterdam).

1889

In January and February Vincent repeats his greetings to de Haan, who is presumably still staying at Théo's, and expresses regret that present conditions (Gauguin's abrupt departure from Arles) do not allow for a visit from de Haan and Isaacson (*CL*568, 570-71, 575, 577). By early April de Haan must have vacated the apartment of Théo, who is about to marry, and for lack of accommodation in the neighborhood apparently has sought in vain to visit with Pissarro (*T*17). By late May Théo reports (*T*9) that de Haan is already in Pont-Aven, with Gauguin soon to follow.

Towards mid-July Théo and his wife Johanna report an evening visit from de Haan with Pissarro and his son present, from which one might deduce that de Haan has returned to Paris in order to visit the Volpini exhibition, which opened after his departure in May.

De Haan spends the month of August at Le Pouldu with Gauguin, who in an unpublished letter (Rijksmuseum Vincent van Gogh, Amsterdam) requests Père Tanguy to send some paints there *chez* Destais, care of M. de Haan (a visit also reported as with de Haan to Bernard in *M*LXXXIV). Possibly de Haan does not return to Pont-Aven for September with Gauguin. Gauguin reports that month to Bernard (*M*LXXXVII) de

Fig. 147
Jakob Meyer de Haan:
View from Théo van Gogh's Window, Rue Lepic,
c. winter 1888-89,
oil on canvas
(Collection L. and S. Leger, Paris).

Haan's plans to rent a large *atelier* in Le Pouldu for the winter (that is, the second floor of a villa owned by M. Mauduit of Quimperlé, now the *Castel Teeaz*).

October through December, Meyer de Haan resides with and pays the costs of Gauguin in Le Pouldu at the inn of Marie Henry. Gauguin reports to Schuffenecker and Bernard (*M*LXXXIX, XC) that "his student" de Haan is making excellent progress. Towards mid-November Gauguin writes Vincent (*G*29, forwarded by Théo to Vincent in *T*20 of November 16) that he and de Haan have a large *atelier* and inexpensive lodgings on the coast of Brittany and that de Haan now works in "our manner," but without losing his own personality or his love of Rembrandt and the Dutch masters.

In mid-December Gauguin writes Vincent (*G*32) and de Haan writes Théo (*T*49, not in *CL* but cited cat. no. 126, below) about the decoration that they have completed in the dining room of the inn of Marie Henry. Here de Haan speaks of having completed a "very large number of studies," among them "five large completed still life paintings."

1890

De Haan apparently remains in Le Pouldu for most of the year, despite the early February departure for Paris of Gauguin, who reports to Théo that de Haan's family is trying to force his return home (*T*28). In late January Gauguin has raised the possibility of having a studio in Antwerp with de Haan and Vincent (*G*35, mentioned by Vincent in *CL* 624-625), but nothing comes of this. Before Gauguin's return in June, de Haan is apparently living alone with Marie Henry, with whom he is presumed to have formed a liaison. Upon his return to Le Pouldu in mid-June, Gauguin, having reported that he plans to stay two months with de Haan in Brittany before departing for the tropics (*G*38, forwarded in *T*37 of June 15), receives from Vincent a request to visit himself and de Haan, a trip Gauguin firmly advises against (*G*39). In this letter Gauguin reports having just spent five days with de Haan on a visit to Pont-Aven. When Vincent dies at the end of July, Gauguin immediately sends a brief, almost cold, letter of condolence; on October 8 Meyer de Haan writes a longer and more heartfelt letter calling Théo his best friend (unpublished letter, Rijksmuseum Vincent van Gogh).

During the summer Gauguin reports (*M*CX, CXII) that de Haan is resolved to accompany him to Tahiti.

Circa October Gauguin writes (MCXIII) that de Haan is now in Paris trying to arrange for the resumption of the allowance from his family which had been cut "for some time." Since Gauguin leaves Le Pouldu shortly hereafter for good, there exist no further reports of de Haan's presence. However, by October Marie Henry would have known she was carrying de Haan's child (born June 7, 1891), so the trip to Paris might have been occasioned by this crisis situation. (Her family tradition blamed Gauguin for intriguing to separate her from de Haan, but the latter's family may have been a factor as well, and in any case he never accompanied Gauguin to Tahiti; see Jaworska, p. 71, 242-43 n. 52.) It is also possible that Meyer de Haan never learned Marie was pregnant.

1891-93

De Haan is at least briefly in Paris in early 1891, since he meets there the future Nabi artist Jan Verkade (see Verkade, pp. 68-9).

How soon hereafter de Haan leaves France for good is uncertain, but is established as some time in 1891 by an unpublished letter from Hatten, The Netherlands, dated October 12, 1893 from de Haan to Théo Gogh's widow, Johanna van Gogh-Bonger (Rijksmuseum Vincent van Gogh). Herein de Haan claims that he had left Brittany two years ago in order to say farewell before accompanying Gauguin to Tahiti, a statement consistent neither with the October 1890 departure cited above nor his further observation that this was "a long time after the death of my unforgettable friend, your husband" (Théo died January 1891, as de Haan certainly would have then learned). However, his further account of having fallen gravely ill on the trip to see his family in Amsterdam appears trustworthy, as does that of having, since November 1891, received treatment in Germany (Bad Wildungen) and The Netherlands for a debilitating kidney ailment which had precluded his wish to visit Johanna and her child.

1895

De Haan dies, presumably not having seen or

heard from Gauguin, whose only known mention of this Dutch painter after 1890 occurs in a letter of *circa* November 1891 written shortly after his arrival in Tahiti to Paul Sérusier (see Sérusier, p. 54). Herein Gauguin inquires after "Meyer," from whom he had heard nothing, and asks "The Woman, has she got him in her clutches?" The source of de Haan's death date apparently is Johanna van Gogh-Bonger (*CL*, p. 88).

126.

Labo(r): Breton Women Scutching Flax
fall 1889
fresco (now transferred to canvas):
133.7 x 202 cm
Not signed, but dated lower left: *TEN JARE 1889*
Inscribed lower right (on jug): *LABO(R)*
Lent Anonymously, San Diego Collection

It has been known since 1924 that this large painting (pl. 16) functioned as the central decoration of
one wall of the dining room of Marie Henry's inn.
In that year it was discovered under several layers
of wallpaper during a restoration of the inn by its
owners.[1] Before being removed and sold at auction
into private hands, where it remained little known
in the original until quite recently, it was photo-
graphed *in situ* (*fig. 71*) in 1924 with two
smaller adjoining paintings by Gauguin (cat.
no. 63 and *W* 383).[2] Perhaps because she had left
them behind or presumed them to have been
mutilated by the wallpaper effacement, Marie
Henry did not mention these mural paintings in
her *circa* 1920 account of the room decoration,
nor do other early eye-witness descriptions.[3] As
with the so-called *Joan of Arc* by Gauguin, which
is seen in the photograph of the inn wall to the left
of de Haan's painting, this lack of early accounts
renders uncertain the accuracy of the titles which
have accrued to the two paintings. Hence it is less
likely hemp, native to Asia, that the two women
are scutching than flax, which is more common to
Europe and is a slender plant, closer in shape than
is hemp to what the women grasp.[4]

More fundamentally, both by his inscription
on the large jug lower right and in a little studied
letter to Théo van Gogh (*T*49), de Haan specifies
the title of this painting as *Labo(r)*.[5] The letter is
dated December 13, 1889, and as in one of a
comparable date from Gauguin to Vincent (*G*32),
he indicates that they had decorated the whole of
the dining room by that date. Whereas Gauguin,
who sent a now lost sketch of it in his letter to
Vincent, described it merely as "local peasants
working fanatically against a background of piles
of hay" and as "very good and finished," de
Haan was even more synoptic calling it "Labour,
Pouldu at high harvest time," adding that he had
"finished it very quickly." Unlike Gauguin, de
Haan failed to sign his painting, unless one considers his use of the Dutch term "ten jare" (in the
year) with the date a subtle means of self-
identification.

De Haan's observation that Gauguin had done
an accompanying smaller painting which was
"totally and unbelievably different" from his own
relates rather more to the contrast in settings and
Gauguin's inclusion of an angel than to any profound contrast in style. De Haan's setting appears
to be a telescoped view of the haystacks found in
the landscape painting used as backdrop for his
Motherhood (cat. no. 127) or in the related painting *The Harvest in Brittany* by Gauguin
(*fig. 150*). Possibly de Haan's comment about
differences refers to the compression of space
which this close-up view imposes, in contrast to
the distant view out to sea included by Gauguin.
De Haan's composition is more self-consciously
simplified and monumentalized than that of his
French colleague, one supposes in the service of
ideals associated with the fresco tradition. At the
same time, the Cloisonist-Synthetist ideal is more
purely realized than anywhere else in de Haan's
oeuvre, with the colour areas reduced to several
basic hues and the contour outlines remarkably
distinct. Granting that in his choice of title and lack
of religious symbolism de Haan remains, unlike
Gauguin in his appended painting, loyal to Realist
tradition, the heraldic placement of his two figures
together with the theme of harvest imply that
labour is sacred and worthy of depiction in terms
of mural painting with its age-old sacerdotal associations.[6]

[1] In that year M. Henri Tromeur, a painter from the
neighbouring hamlet Clohars-Carnoët, discovered
under seven layers of wallpaper the wall paintings.
The widely circulated story that these paintings
were actually discovered by the American painter
Abraham Rattner and D.M. Lévy is almost certainly a fiction (see references in *W* 329, 383),
although Rattner apparently engineered their
detachment from the wall surface. The *Labo(r)*
was sold to a M. de Rochefort. Years later this
fresco was sold at Sotheby Parke Bernet, 2 July
1969.

[2] The existence of this collaborative wall decoration
became widely known only with the publication of
this photograph by Rewald in the first edition of
P-I (1956). In the original hanging, as evidenced
in this photograph, these two works were in
reverse order to that in the colour plates published
here.

[3] Marie Henry's account is found in Chassé, *Pont-
Aven*, pp. 46-50, and, slightly abbreviated, in
Jaworska, p. 90 (or 1972 Eng. trans.).

[4] Jaworska, *ibid.*, was the first to substitute "flax"
for "hemp."

[5] This letter in Dutch is strangely absent from *CL*,
but included in the standard original language(s)
edition of the letters, *Verzamelde Brieven van Vincent van Gogh*, 2 vols., eds., J. van Gogh-Bonger
and V.W. van Gogh, Amsterdam-Antwerp:
Wereld Bibliotheek, 1955. "Labo(r)" presumably
is Latin.

[6] Although not a pictorial prototype, de Haan would
have had the large, mural-like painting *Le
Travail* by Puvis de Chavannes (now National
Gallery of Art, Washington, D.C.) in mind when
choosing his theme.

127.

Motherhood: Marie Henry and Her Child
fall 1889
oil on canvas: 73 x 65.1 cm
Not signed or dated
Lent by a private collection, Switzerland

It was formerly thought that Gauguin too had done a portrait of Marie Henry (*W* 387), but *Motherhood* by de Haan remains the only known representation of this almost legendary figure. She is thought to have been about thirty years of age when Gauguin and de Haan in 1889 became residents in the inn, not far from the Grand Sables beach, which she had operated since about 1886. Known under the sobriquet *Marie Poupée* ("the doll"), she has been described variously as diminutive in stature and also as tall and strong of build.[1] From the painting it is difficult to decide the issue, although she is represented as having attractive if not finely chiselled features. To a degree these may have been generalized in keeping with the simplification of forms characteristic of the Synthetist style, but one senses the artist's basic realism in his approach to portraiture with its roots in his pre-French experience (*fig. 144*).

The date when this portrait was executed can be determined as fall 1889. Marie's first daughter Léa had been born in the first days of March 1889 and would certainly not have continued suckling into the following year. In addition, this painting was accorded the place of honour at the centre of the wall opposite the entrance in the dining room of the inn, and all four walls had been decorated by the end of 1889.[2] From an account given by Marie herself, we know that de Haan resisted Gauguin's wish to see the portrait before it was finished. When finally shown it Gauguin was so pleased with this painting by his "student" that he produced a hand-decorated frame and hung it in the most visible place in the room.[3]

De Haan's iconography would have pleased both Vincent van Gogh and Gauguin. De Haan shared Vincent's love of realist painting from nature and is said to have disliked the term "Symbolism" to the point of lampooning it.[4] His mother and child thus are unadorned with any visible sign suggestive of the Madonna and Christ Child, except that Marie is clothed in a robe of blue according to standard usage for the Biblical "Marie." Yet the traditional Christian connotation of the suckling child is impossible to forget completely, and Marie's blue-black garb could also be thought suggestive of Mary's knowledge of eventual mourning. The inclusion of a landscape with great mounds of grain as its principal feature is also unavoidably symbolic, whether only of the general theme of fecundity or possibly of the eucharistic bread as pan-European tradition within Christian peasant communities would have reinforced.[5] The backdrop painting probably did not exist as a separate creation, since it presumably would have survived in the collection of the sitter. However, it does remarkably approximate the subject and general style of surviving paintings by Gauguin (*fig. 150*) and Sérusier (cat. no. 138), and de Haan conceivably wished to indicate his own authorship of the version included in *Motherhood* by what could be read as an "H" at the lower right corner of the farm scene.

Apart from its retention of a sculpturally modelled head for Marie, this painting employs a form of Cloisonist-Synthetist style almost as pure as that of the *Labour* mural (cat. no. 126), which the artist executed at the same period of time and for the same place of display. Although in some places overpainted, heavy Cloisonist outlines are used to define the major contours of the images depicted, and the in-filling with colour is in large part with uniform hues, according to the same stylistic principle. The retention of a relatively heavy *impasto* and painterly brush technique, while providing an element of individuality to the general Gauguinesque style, does not compromise de Haan's allegiance here to the precepts of his "teacher." The *Motherhood* must be considered a cardinal instance of what Gauguin had in mind when he wrote, November 1889, to Vincent (*G*29), "De Haan has done everything to work in our manner (*sens*) and is progressing very well without losing his personality, and I assure you that he now understands Rembrandt better than before."

1   Verkade, p. 113, who, writing many years later, approximated Marie Henry's age as about thirty when he visisted Le Pouldu in 1891. He described her physique as tall and robust (*grande et forte*) and her face as having "two black eyes which enlivened a rugged (*rude*) and energetic countenance." However, her daughter Marie-Ida Cochennec has insisted Marie Henry was of small foot and thin waist (Jaworska, p. 243 n. 70).

2   *G*32, which Vincent received by *circa* December 18, 1889 (it is mentioned in *CL*617), describes all four walls as already decorated.

3   This reminiscence was provided by Marie Henry *circa* 1920 via her companion M. Mothéré, a teacher of philosophy, for Chassé, *Pont-Aven*, pp. 46-47.

4   Jaworska, p. 98.

5   Andersen, *Paradise*, pp. 101-02, discusses the dual death and resurrection connotations of grain in Breton folklore.

128.

Self-Portrait with Japanese Background
c. late 1889
oil on canvas: 32.4 x 24.5 cm
Not signed or dated
Lent by Mr. and Mrs. Arthur G. Altschul,
New York

This justly famous self-portrait by de Haan is likely to have been produced winter 1889-90, dated thanks to the presence of a Japanese print in the background.[1] This was apparently an insignia which Gauguin preferred to assign to the walls of the Le Pouldu studio, and its occurrence here, if not necessarily an exact reproduction, is symbolic of this setting. The background of the portrait is more likely to be fictional than realistically accurate. The blue ground with red areas may be interpreted as a reference to the Pont-Aven canvases of Gauguin and Bernard (*cf*. cat. no. 108). The general impression is that of a solitary and self-possessed figure, intent upon investigating the nature of this contemporary art and its historical antecedents. It is tempting to see this *Self-Portrait* only in these terms. Yet a compositional relationship exists between this off-centre portrait with decorative background and a figural representation on the wall, and the self-portraits supplied by Gauguin and Bernard to Vincent (cat. nos. 52 and 105).[2] It is possible that de Haan saw these paintings during his stay at Théo's apartment, presuming they had been forwarded from Arles. Otherwise, Gauguin could readily have described them verbally or with a sketch for de Haan.

At the same time, de Haan has presented himself here not as the hunchback he was, but as the independent Jewish free-thinker whom he had lionized in his controversial *Uriel Acosta* (*fig. 145*). His philospher's skull cap was therefore as much a symbol of his own emancipation from conventionality as his insistence upon his Jewish intelligence. In this *Self-Portrait* Meyer de Haan has asked us, as viewers, to look at him objectively as a man of learning and perhaps also of suffering, only incidentally indicating the sources of this pictorial conception in the background curtain.

[1] The decoration of the large *atelier* with Japanese prints and the Volpini lithographs is mentioned in a fall 1889 letter from Gauguin to Bernard (*M*LXXXIX). Since it is also recorded (Chassé, *Pont-Aven*, p. 28) that by spring 1890 the villa Mauduit *atelier* had been given up and replaced by a reconstructed attachment to the inn of Marie Henry, this *Self-Portrait* presumably dates before that time.

[2] The *Self-Portrait* of Charles Laval (cat. no. 136) was the last item in this exchange, reaching Vincent in Arles by the first days of December 1888 (*CL*562) and Théo in Paris by early May 1889 (*CL*589). Thus the self-portraits by Gauguin and Bernard also could have been forwarded to Paris by spring 1889 and seen there by de Haan before his departure for Pont-Aven in May.

129.
Still Life with Two Flowers in a Glass
summer 1890(?)
oil on canvas: 34.6 x 27.3 cm
Not signed or dated
Lent by a private collection, Switzerland

The *Still Life with Two Flowers in a Glass* is one of the two variant versions of the same subject and has been described as "investigation into lightness and precision, a bluish harmony," whereas the other example was called merely "a good coloured sketch."[1] Whatever the functional relationship between the two equally sized oil paintings, the other version has been readily identified as depicting two blossoming roses, while this would only be a likely surmise in the present instance. Since the paintings were among those left by the artist at the inn of Marie Henry, and a summer setting can be deduced from the flower subject plus the open window with a gentle breeze blowing aside the diaphanous curtain, it seems likely that this painting was executed summer 1890 from a second storey window of the inn.[2] That de Haan probably shared this bedroom with his hostess lends it a certain biographical significance. In contrast to his other surviving Brittany flower paintings, which are realistically modelled despite the bright colours employed, this canvas aspires to a decorative flatness which relates to the style of Sérusier's *The Talisman* (cat. no. 137) of 1888. This usage is somewhat ironic, since when de Haan in fall 1889 painted a *Still Life with Onions and a Pot* (*fig. 148*), it was so similar in style to a compan-

[1]   In Dauchot, "Meyer de Haan." Checklist nos. 7-8; Jaworska in *Nederlands Kunsthistorisch Jaarboek*, p. 222, identifies the other version, which is not known to me even by photograph, as depicting roses.

[2]   This presumes that de Haan's residence at Marie Henry's inn began too late in 1889 (October) for it to have been likely that he then painted a summer subject, especially in so advanced a Synthetist style.

Fig. 148
Jakob Meyer de Haan
(here attributed to):
Still Life with Onions and a Pot,
fall 1889,
oil on canvas
(Ny Carlsberg Glyptotek, Copenhagen).

ion piece painted by Gauguin (illustrated as *W* 380) that until now it has been accepted as an authentic work by the latter artist.[3] In comparison to the still rounded forms of the *Onions and a Pot*, the *Two Flowers* appear so two-dimensional and abstract that without its known provenance, it would be difficult to attribute this painting to de Haan rather than his Nabi friend Sérusier, for instance.[4] The fact that both artists had been so profoundly influenced by Gauguin should not blind us to the possibility of interaction between these two "disciples" when they were working together at Le Pouldu.

[3]   The painting wrongly reproduced in *W* 380 as in the collection of the Ny Carlsberg Glyptotek, Copenhagen, is actually the one cited in the catalogue entry as a replica in a New York private collection, which is signed *P Go* and dated [*18*] *89*. In contrast, the Copenhagen painting (the present fig. 148) bears, lower right, a quite dubious "P.G." signature and is quite close in style to the Quimper Museum *Still Life with Onions* which is unquestionably by de Haan (no. 131, ill. 24b, in Pickvance, *Tate Entries*). Possibly Wildenstein had his photographs confused when he referred to the New York painting as close in technique to "certain works of Meyer de Haan." In any case the mystery is solved by the report on February 9, 1890, from Théo to Vincent (*T*28) that de Haan had sent (presumably via Gauguin) for forwarding to his brother a picture with "pink and orange onions, green apples and an earthenware pot." This substantiates the late 1889 date of the Copenhagen painting, but alas not the attribution to Gauguin.

[4]   Yet, apart from the fact that Sérusier signed his other paintings of 1889-90, there are differences of style between this painting and his still life works of the early 1890s, and there is no reason to doubt the traditional attribution going back to Marie Henry.

130.
Still Life with Profile of Mimi
c. summer 1890(?)
oil on canvas: 50.5 x 61.5 cm
Not signed or dated
Lent by a private collection

The child in this painting was the first daughter of Marie Henry, who was named Marie-Léa but called affectionately Mimi. Since the birth was registered on March 4, 1889, the child would scarcely be able to sit at the edge of a table ogling the fruit as she does before she had reached the age of one, if not later. Thus, unless one assumes she is pictured as held suspended by her mother, the painting would seem to date from 1890, probably the summer given the non-storable nature of the grapes present in one fruit dish.

Visibly worked on over a period of time, this painting reflects the example of Gauguin in several ways. His 1888 *Still Life with Fruit* (*W* 288) sets a subject precedent even if its implied temptation theme could hardly be imputed to Mimi's innocent desires.[1] Gauguin had done a somewhat similar still life painting at Le Pouldu in fall 1889 (*W* 378), which, apart from depicting differing objects similarly stresses a sharp angle view from above and an asymmetrical composition with truncated objects in the tradition of Degas and Japanese prints. This is also one of the few paintings by de Haan to include overtly Cloisonist outlines. Because they occur in the head of the infant, it is possible that de Haan was following a specific model by Gauguin; namely, the previously unpublished wash drawing which represents *Man with Cap—Head of Mimi* (*fig. 149*) and includes heavy figural outlines in the manner of de Haan's oil *Profile of Mimi*.[2] This painting is thus an intimate portrait of a family situation and, at the same time, an image of eternal infantile domesticity.

[1]   On the Gauguin painting, see Andersen, *Mummy*, p. 241.
[2]   Gauguin's wash drawing was auctioned at Hôtel Drouot, March 16, 1959, no. 111, as "L'Homme à la calotte—Tête de Mimi."

Fig. 149
Paul Gauguin:
Man with Cap—Head of Mimi,
late 1889-90(?),
india ink and black crayon
(collection unknown).

131.
Landscape at Le Pouldu
fall 1890(?)
oil on canvas: 58.5 x 71.7 cm
Signed lower left: *Meyer de Haan*
Lent by Mr. and Mrs. Arthur G. Altschul,
New York

In this undated landscape, Meyer de Haan displays his talent for profiting by the example of Gauguin, while not completely abandoning his inherited Dutch naturalism. The Gauguin version of this same setting, dated 1890 (*W* 398) is more broadly conceived, with the house given less attention and the landscape divisions more evenly distributed. Gauguin's painting is one of his most majestic landscape paintings of 1890, and whether or not it was the inspiration of the variant painting by de Haan, it stands as a masterpiece of the Pont-Aven/Pouldu style.

The painting by de Haan, in comparison, must be considered a student exemplar, albeit a student in a minor form of rebellion. Only photographs taken at the time would tell us of the relative exactitude of the two paintings in representing the setting. Certainly the de Haan version is more suggestive of the rhythms of the Brittany landscape than is Gauguin's version. De Haan is also highly inventive in reference to the bands of colour representing fields, which the scene allows. His spatial structuring is in some ways Cézannesque, employing a variety of techniques in order to suggest spatial recession while at the same time denying it. If somewhat eclectic in his choice of sources, Meyer de Haan has here displayed an incredible talent for combining his Dutch past with the most advanced developments in France without doing great harm to either tradition.

Charles Laval (1862-1894)

Biographical Data

SOURCES

The life of Charles Laval is one of the least documented within the circle of Gauguin and Bernard. Not a single letter written by the artist has so far come to light. Primary source materials are thus largely limited to letters which mention him, written by Bernard, his sister Madeleine (only a few and still unpublished in the Archives Musées Nationaux, Paris) and Gauguin (those to Vincent, which have yet to be published in full, but which are often recapitulated in the latter's letters to Théo). The next most important source is Bernard (namely in *L'Aventure* and *Gauguin*), who is more accurate than generally appreciated. More recently Jaworska, pp. 43-47, with some unpublished accounts at her disposal, was the first to attempt even a brief summary of Laval's life and career. In 1978 Walter provided accurate information on the relationship between Laval and Madeleine Bernard, showing that they were indeed engaged for a time, but never married and died within one year of each other in separate places.

1886

Born into a well-to-do family in Paris, and having attended the studio of Bonnat, Laval arrives during the summer of 1886 in Pont-Aven and becomes the friend and disciple of Gauguin (Chassé, *Son temps*, p. 45). The closeness of this relationship is uncertain, and Laval is not mentioned again in Gauguin's correspondence until their joint arrival in Central America (*M*LI of end April 1887).

1887

Following a disappointing reception in Panama and dismissal from the work force on the canal, Gauguin and Laval repair to Martinique and presumably begin a productive period of communal work together (see *M*LIII of June 2 to his wife). Subsequent reports (*M*LIV-VII) are less optimistic, and it remains dubious, given his health problems, that the tubercular Laval, also ridden by yellow fever, could have had a productive summer.

Gauguin departs Martinique in the fall of this year, leaving behind Laval presumably at the latter's own choice.

1888

Laval is first reported again in France in Gauguin's letter to Vincent of *circa* 30-31 July 1888 (*G*6), and it is likely that on disembarking he spends little time in Paris (*cf.* Jaworska, p. 43).

Laval is shortly hereafter introduced to Emile Bernard and his sister and apparently stays in Pont-Aven until departing towards mid-November with Bernard for Paris. During the period at Pont-Aven Laval is reported to Vincent as a willing participant in the studio of the south, but this plan never is consummated and these two artists never meet.

1889

It is possible that Laval accompanies Gauguin to Pont-Aven in early spring 1889, since his residence is listed as such in the Volpini catalogue. Doubtless his inclusion in the Volpini exhibition (ten items) is a result of this close friendship as is attested by Gauguin's initial authorization of those to be included (*M*LXXVII, to be redated to late April-early May 1889).

According to Bernard (*Gauguin*, p. 15) Laval helps paste posters announcing this exhibition.

Laval apparently spends the summer in Pont-Aven, where he receives a letter from Bernard and shares it with Gauguin (*M*LXXXIV); he is included in the September plans of Gauguin and de Haan to establish themselves in the villa Mauduit at Le Pouldu (*M*LXXXVII). There is no further record of Laval's presence in Brittany in this year, and it is therefore likely that he returned to Paris. Late this year, Gauguin complains to Schuffenecker and Bernard of no word from Laval (*M*LXXXIII, to be redated to late 1889, *M*CII-III).

1890

Throughout this year Gauguin receives no news from Laval (*M*CXIII) and writes him off as a companion to the studio at Madagascar (*M*CIII).

In late July he departs with Bernard by train for Vincent's funeral at Auvers.

By August illness forces Laval into a country retreat (unpublished correspondence dated August, 1890, between Madeleine and her family, Walter, p. 290 n. 19); late in the year he and Madeleine become engaged (unpublished letter, Madeleine to her brother, Archives Musées Nationaux, Paris).

1891

Laval is in Paris, when Bernard returns from Lille, having heard confirmation of his sister's engagement (*L'Aventure* p. 44).

1892-1894

By 1892 Laval's relationship with Madeleine is broken due to his inability to earn a living (*L'Aventure*, p. 39), and she leaves for Nottingham, England (Walter, p. 290 n. 11).

On April 27, 1894, Laval dies, aged thirty-two, in Paris, listed a bachelor (Walter, p. 290 n. 18). Madeleine dies November 19, 1895 while visiting her brother in Cairo.

132.
Martinique Panorama
summer 1887(?)
oil on canvas: 60 x 73 cm
Not signed or dated
Lent by the Rijksmuseum Vincent van Gogh,
Amsterdam

For many years this Martinique landscape was
attributed to Gauguin on the basis of its presence
in the Théo and Vincent van Gogh collection, and
included in the catalogue of Gauguin's painted
oeuvre (*W* 225), although Wildenstein stated that
he otherwise would have thought it by Laval.
Bodelsen pointed out that Théo van Gogh quite

easily could have come into possession of a painting by Laval, and Vincent acquired a *Self Portrait*
of Laval (cat. no. 136) in an exchange agree-
ment.[1] It is moot whether the current attribution
to Laval is due to a cognizance of his personal
stylistic approach or rather to a feeling that, if not
by Gauguin, then obviously it must be by his companion in Martinique.

Until the various attribution problems concerning Gauguin and Laval can be systematically
studied, conclusions reached now are necessarily
tentative. Nonetheless, the single most striking feature of this painting, distinguishing it from the
uncontestably authentic Martinique paintings of
Gauguin, is its overall integration of figural, floral
and landscape contours in the service of a decor-

ative pattern. Despite a certain undulating effect in
the surface planes, which seem to anticipate similar qualities in *The Bathers* (cat. no. 134), the use
of areas of uniformly parallel brush strokes in
order to distinguish the objects depicted is sys-
tematized further than in Gauguin's Martinique
paintings and implies an analogy with tapestry.
While still fundamentally Impressionist in
approach, this *Martinique Panorama* already
incorporates elements of the style which two years
later would be presented under the banner of
Synthetism.[2]

1   Bodelsen, *Wildenstein*, p. 28.
2   The Volpini exhibition catalogue lists five works
    out of the ten exhibited as Martinique subjects.

133.

Martinique Women
summer 1887-early 1889
oil on canvas: 62 x 92 cm
Not signed or dated
Lent by a private collection

It seems more than likely that this painting was present at the Volpini exhibition as "no. 91, Femmes au bord de la Mer: Esquisse."[1] Unfortunately, this does not guarantee a date of summer 1887 for the painting. One may consider it Laval's counterpart to Gauguin's *Among the Mangoes* (cat. no. 46), whose description to his wife (*M*LIII) of the setting and behaviour of the local negresses seems equally applicable to Laval's representation.[2] But Laval not only stayed in Martinique through winter 1887-88, but also brought back to France a number of "very curious watercolours," which works so favourably impressed Gauguin (*G*9) that he wished Vincent to see them, and which could have been employed in the creation of this relatively large oil sketch. The style of the *Martinique Women*, moreover, is rather advanced in its employment of Synthetist design elements. The even distribution of vertical brush strokes in the background water and sky and the uniform colouration of these areas plus the red of the garment of the middle figure may be thought to betray an assimilation of the style he had first adopted from Gauguin and Bernard in his *Going to the Market* of late summer-fall 1888. In iconography and style Laval's closest counterpart in the art of Gauguin may be the latter's *The Grasshoppers and Ants* lithograph (cat. no. 58j), executed as a souvenir of Martinique at the beginning of 1889.[3] Certainly Gauguin's parade of women in flattened profiles, widely considered one of his most blatantly Japanist designs, bears some relationship to the similarly stylized outlines and hand gestures of the two standing figures in Laval's oil sketch. The independence of Laval's personal style is quite apparent as well. Once again analogies with the art of tapestry come to mind, and the undulant sway and swirls of drapery of the figure at left are already evocative of Art Nouveau.

[1] Apart from the unfinished, sketchy quality of the lower right area of the canvas, no. 97 was sandwiched between two Martinique subjects in Laval's list of catalogue entries and another "bord de la mer" (no. 96) was designated a "Martinique watercolour." For colour illustration of *Martinique Women* see Roger Cucchi, *Gauguin à la Martinique*, Vaduz-Leichtenstein: Calivran Anstalt, 1979, pl. VIII.

[2] *W* 217-18 likely reflect the same beach setting with the same spit of land sloping towards the sea from distant right.

[3] Rewald, *P-I*, p. 171, juxtaposes the Laval *Martinique Women* and Gauguin's *Grasshoppers* lithograph, but his 1887 date for the former would seem to imply its precedent position.

134.
The Bathers
summer 1888
oil on canvas: 46 x 55 cm
Dated and signed lower left: *1888 C Laval*
Lent by the Kunsthalle, Bremen

Laval is the most frequently cited disciple of Gauguin, and to some degree this painting proves the point. Having rejoined Gauguin for the summer in Pont-Aven, following their artistically frustrating and physically enervating period in Martinique the previous year, Laval regained his status as the close colleague of Gauguin and, after Bernard's arrival in early August, continued as the third horse in this troika of like-minded artists. It was then that Gauguin gave and dedicated to Laval an important still life painting (*W* 288) and also informed Vincent (*CL* 543) that Laval too was also making plans to join the studio of the south in Arles.

The Bathers provides an interesting test case of the artistic relationship between Gauguin and Laval. The subject relates to a major preoccupation of Gauguin that summer, as evidenced by the Hamburg *Breton Boys Bathing* (cat. no. 47). More to the point, Laval has chosen for his treatment of this theme the rugged coastline of Brittany with its variegated configurations of rock formations around which swirl the treacherous waves of the Atlantic. Gauguin recorded this perilous terrain in his *Above the Precipice* (cat. no. 50) and, with greater relevance to this canvas by Laval, *The Cove II* (*fig. 62*). This coincidence of site, incidentally, strengthens the impression (*see* cat. no. 56) that Gauguin along with Bernard and, it now seems, Laval as well may have visited the area of Le Pouldu in summer 1888, where such eddies swirling around the "black rocks" at the foot of coastal precipices are more common than at the estuary of the Aven river. Given the notoriously limited production of the sickly Laval, it is probable that this painting figured as "no. 94, Dans la mer (appartient à M. Bernard)" in the Volpini exhibition catalogue, one further indication of an artist's exchange within the circle of Gauguin during the period 1888-89 when the Pont-Aven group was at its most cohesive.

On close inspection all three figures in this *Bathers* are female, and it therefore appears that Laval has anticipated a theme which Gauguin would utilize the following spring (cat. no. 60). In the present instance there is little of the weighty meaning concerning temptation and death which would concern Gauguin in 1889. Instead Laval seems concerned more with a reconciliation between Impressionist and Pointillist proclivities of style, colour usage and brush technique than with a statement on the nature of human fate. Nonetheless his ebb and flow of sparkling colour patterns achieve an imaginative synthesis of linear and orphic elements appropriate to the "female" connotations of the sea, and there is no hint of slavish imitation of Gauguin in this iridescent painting by a too often maligned and underrated artist.

SEE COLOUR PLATE 32.

135.

Going to the Market Brittany
c. September-October, 1888
oil on canvas: 36 x 46 cm
Signed and dated below centre: *C. Laval 1888*
Lent by a private collection, Switzerland

In a letter of late July 1888 to Vincent, Gauguin first reported the return from Martinique and presence in Pont-Aven of his friend Charles Laval.[1] By mid-August Emile Bernard also had arrived, and the three painters formed a small coterie of artists who in the following two-month period would work closely together and produce such archetypal examples of the so-called Pont-Aven style as Gauguin's *Vision after the Sermon* (pl. 7) and Bernard's *Breton Women in the Meadow* (cat. no. 104). The contribution of Laval to this development is best, and perhaps exclusively, contained in *Going to the Market Brittany* (pl. 32) which all but surely was that work shown the following year at the Volpini exhibition under the title *Allant au marché, Bretagne* (cat. no. 85). Both male and female head-dress in the painting are those worn locally in Pont-Aven, and with the title allusion to

a market day we can in this instance avoid discussion of possible religious symbolism or associations.

When exhibited at the Volpini café and ever since, Laval's paintings have been criticized as little more than competent imitations of the style of Gauguin.[2] There is some justification to this opinion, for the twenty-six-year-old Laval freely modelled himself upon the example of his older and more experienced colleague—just as for several years Gauguin had followed the example of Pissarro and Cézanne. The in part red background, perspectival compression and Japanist truncation of forms are likely to derive in large part from a knowledge of Gauguin's *Vision*, no matter how the two paintings differ in other respects. *Going to the Market* owes at least as much to the example of Bernard's *Breton Women*, an indebtedness Laval may have wished to signalize by his inclusion, upper right, of a bright green area of meadow. The painting also includes a related brush technique and the emphasis upon a large female head with an outsized *coiffe* in the lower right corner. This dependence upon the other two artists notwithstanding. Laval characterizes the faces according to individual physiognomy to a greater degree

than either Gauguin or Bernard. And neither in choice of subject nor in compositional embodiment is Laval anyone but his own mentor. The conception of this canvas is inventive in its juxtapositions of various figural poses without attendant loss of concentration upon the central seated female. It is a welcome recent addition to the small body of works surviving from Laval's hand, and it can only be hoped that more such examples will come to light in the future.

[1] This letter (*G*6) was reported by Vincent in a letter to Théo (*CL*515) of the last day or two of July and reads as if Laval's arrival in Pont-Aven had been quite recent. Moreover, Gauguin first mentions the return of Laval to his wife Mette only in a letter of circa October (*M*LXVI), but not in his previous letter to her of *circa* mid-June (*M*LXIV) in which he speaks of his fortieth birthday on June 7 as having passed.

[2] Whereas Fénéon I, p. 158 (*La Cravache*, July 6, 1889) merely calls attention to a general indebtedness of Laval to Gauguin, J. Antoine (*Art et critique*, November 9, 1899, p. 370) berates Laval for "une imitation trop littérale" of his master.

à l'ami Vincent
C. Laval 88

136.
Self-Portrait dedicated to Vincent
c. October-November 1888
oil on canvas: 50 × 60 cm
Signed and dated bottom centre:
à l'ami Vincent C. Laval [18] 88
Lent by the Rijksmuseum Vincent van Gogh,
Amsterdam

Following several preliminary mentions of their
friend Laval in letters by Bernard and Gauguin

written in August and September 1888, Gauguin
at the end of the latter month wrote twice (*G*9,
10) in quick succession to Vincent (duly reported
in *CL*543, 544 to Théo) recommending Laval as
someone who would like to join the studio of the
south and has the financial means to provide his
share of the expenses. Bernard too recommended
to Vincent Laval's acceptance into the studio and
advised his willingness to join in Vincent's program of exchanges of paintings among fellow artists (the now lost Bernard letter is recapitulated in

*CL*544). This flurry of correspondence was followed by Vincent's acceptance in principle of the
expanded circle of exchanges (*B*18), which he
specifies *circa* October 7 as most pleasing to himself if realized in the form of a self-portrait. The
intensity of this discussion, which did not include
correspondence between Vincent and Laval who
had never met, nonetheless explains the origin of
this *Self-Portrait dedicated to Vincent* and the
phrase "à l'ami" (to my friend), certainly in any
literal sense an overstatement. On or about

December 2 Vincent could report receipt of the painting (*CL*562), and on January 17, 1889, Vincent complained (*CL*571) that in returning to Paris Gauguin had not bothered to take along his own self-portrait intended for Laval.

Vincent displayed an ongoing appreciation of this portrait, which he sent to Théo at the beginning of May 1889 (*CL*589). Vincent's final mention of this painting occurred in September of that year (*CL*604), when he eulogized it as "amazing, the look of the eyes through the glasses, such a frank look." Many years later, Bernard, doubtless disillusioned that Laval had inadvertently infected and thus caused the death from tuberculosis of his fiancée, Bernard's sister Madeleine, described Laval as "a failed Don Quixote," flawed by an excess of "mundane manners" bordering on "degeneracy."[1] Whether Laval in fact deserved the various charges of a wasted youth, professional lassitude and general self-indulgence which Bernard and Gauguin on several occasions raised against him, it is just as possible to interpret his character as sensitive, noble and self-effacing, which is how these same friends alternatively described him.

As a stylistic exercise this *Self-Portrait* is modestly innovative within the Synthetist movement.[2] Featuring the same displacement of the portrait image to one side of the composition, as had his two friends in their portraits sent to Vincent (cat. nos. 52 and 105), Laval substitutes an open window with a natural landscape for the portraits of each other included in the paintings by Gauguin and Bernard.[3] The colouration and brush technique employed by Laval remains essentially Impressionist, and it would be difficult to choose among Gauguin, Pissarro and Cézanne as a source of general influence. The innovative aspect of the painting lies in its sense of underlying compositional structure, with the geometrical framing device of the window divisions and the silhouetted tree trunk at left providing an antidote to the then increasingly decried "formlessness" of Impressionism.

[1] Bernard, *L'Aventure*, p. 39.

[2] Another modified version of this portrait dated 1889 exists in the Musée d'Orsay, Paris.

[3] Presuming that his landscape was at least begun in Pont-Aven before Laval and Bernard returned to Paris in November, the setting depicted may have been a view from the window of the "Les Avians" studio used by Gauguin, which still extant building is situated on such a hillside slope.

Paul Sérusier (1864-1927)

Biographical Data

For many years the principal source documents on the years 1888-91 during which Sérusier enjoyed periodic contact with Gauguin were Gauguin's letters (Malingue) and a handful of his own to Maurice Denis (Sérusier): both sets, largely undated, have produced more disagreement than solution of outstanding chronological problems. Chassé, *Pont-Aven*, records several interviews with Sérusier containing information on his contacts with Gauguin. Maurice Denis, in *Théories* and the Introduction to the 1942 edition of Sérusier, *ABC de la Peinture* was Sérusier's most important early biographer. The chapter on Sérusier in Jaworska, pp. 123-38, provides a useful summary of his early career (also in Eng.). The recent monograph by Guicheteau in French is based on a wealth of documents not previously known or readily available, but these are sometimes open to differing possibilities of interpretation.

EARLY LIFE AND CAREER

1864-87

Louis Paul Henri Sérusier is born November 9, 1864, in Paris, where his father is a prosperous glove manufacturer and merchant. During the years 1876-83 he is a highly successful student at the Lycée Condorcet, interesting himself especially in philosophy and mathematics and passing two baccalauréat examinations.

In 1885 he enters the Académie Julian, where he eventually becomes *massier* (chief student proctor). Since he attends the 1885 opening of Agostina Segatori's *Le Tambourin* café, it is possible that in 1887 he sees the works displayed there by Vincent van Gogh, whom, however, he never seems to have met. He sees Anquetin's *Boat at Sunset* (Chassé, *Pont-Aven*, p. 72) which he calls "un tableau...cloisonné de vermillion," but mislocates to (Segatori's) "restaurant Italien." His own work remains conventionally Realistic.

1888

His *Tisserand* (*Weaver*: ill. in Guicheteau, p. 196) wins an honourable mention in the spring *Salon*. He spends part of the summer at Concarneau in Brittany and briefly meets Gauguin in Pont-Aven, where he paints the *Bois d'Amour* (cat. no. 137). Returning to Paris and the Académie Julian, he begins with Maurice Denis to found the Nabi group (with Pierre Bonnard, H.G. Ibels, Paul Ranson and eventually others).

1889

At the Volpini exhibition he is converted to the cause of Gauguin, and *circa* the end of June sends a note to Denis (Sérusier, pp. 38-39) indicating his departure for Brittany. He spends the summer in Pont-Aven (in *M*CVIII, to be redated to July 1889, Gauguin complains that Sérusier "speaks only of his evolution" but won't show his work).

Despite Gauguin's disquiet with the Académie Julian students at Pont-Aven (*M*LXXXV), he takes Sérusier with him to Le Pouldu on or about October 2 (Chassé, *Pont-Aven*, p. 23). Just before this departure Sérusier tells Denis of his disillusionment with Gauguin (Sérusier, pp. 39-41), but upon his arrival in Le Pouldu (for a two-week stay) he reverses this judgment and writes of his "fever for work" (*ibid.*, p. 41).

About mid-October he again writes Denis (*ibid.*, pp. 42-45) and includes the most essential formulation of his art theory which survives from this period. In this letter he also announces his imminent departure for a visit to his parents in Villerville as antecedent to four weeks of military service and his return to Paris, which therefore could not have occurred much before the end of the year.

1890

In January the twenty-six-year-old Sérusier establishes himself in his first *atelier*, rue de Trevise (Guicheteau, p. 163) and in June meets Redon (*ibid.*).

Sérusier spends summer 1890 in Le Pouldu, except for a *circa* August vacation with his parents in Auvergne (*M*CIX). He possibly returns to Le Pouldu for September, but from Paris some time in October informs Gauguin (see *M*CXIII) of Bernard's plans for a memorial exhibition for Vincent van Gogh.

1891

Sérusier apparently associates closely with Gauguin during winter 1890-91, and is present at the testimonial banquet given Gauguin at the café Voltaire and at his departure for Tahiti. Sérusier continues his leadership of the Nabi movement, acquiring another convert in the person of Jan Verkade, a Dutch painter whom he meets through Meyer de Haan (Verkade, p. 71).

He again passes the summer in Brittany and Auvergne and in November is represented in the exhibition of "Impressionists and Symbolists" at the Gallery of Le Barc de Boutteville. The same month he receives a letter from Gauguin in Tahiti inquiring about events in Paris.

1892-1927

Throughout the 1890s Sérusier participates in group exhibitions organized by Le Barc de Boutteville and Samuel Bing and thereafter exhibits at the galleries of Vollard, Durand-Ruel and Bernheim-Jeune and at the *Indépendants*. His work continues to favour Breton subjects, but also Biblical stories and other esoteric religious legends. His style becomes self-consciously decorative and archaizing. He also does designs for stained-glass windows, produces theatre scenery and acts in several Symbolist plays.

His interest in Theosophy is augmented by contact via his friend Jan (now Dom Willibrord) Verkade with the art theories of Father Pierre Lenz, whose basic text he translates as *L'Esthétique de Beuron* (1905).

In 1909 he teaches at the Académie Ranson, and in 1921 publishes his own art theory as *ABC de la Peinture*, which is weighted toward an analysis of colour and sacred numerology. In 1927 he dies suddenly of a heart attack.

137.
The Talisman: The Bois d'Amour at Pont-Aven
October 1888
oil on panel: 27 x 22 cm
Not signed or dated
Inscribed on the reverse:
Fait en October 1888 sous la Direction de
Paul Gauguin par P. Sérusier Pont-Aven
Lent by the family of Maurice Denis, Alençon,
France

Having already spent some part of summer 1888
at nearby Concarneau, Sérusier arrived *circa* early
fall in Pont-Aven. Here at the Pension Gloanec he
met Gauguin, who agreed to give him a lesson in
his own way of painting.[1] The result was the
famous little painting on wood known primarily as
The Bois d'Amour ("Woods of Love") for its
picturesque riverside setting in Pont-Aven. Upon
his return to Paris Sérusier, according to Maurice
Denis who received this painting as a gift, chris-
tened the panel "The Talisman."[2] Both titles
suggest the mystical and magic powers which
would be attributed to works of art by Sérusier,
Denis and their associates in the Nabi movement.
Sérusier showed this work to his fellow students at
the Académie Julian in Paris, recalling how Gauguin had enjoined him to look for the dominant
tonality of an object depicted and then render it
exclusively with the purest version of that hue at
one's disposal.[3]

Maurice Denis stated that he was the first convert to this approach to painting, but Sérusier
gradually convinced other fellow students to the
point that the co-fraternity of Nabi artists (the
word being Hebrew for prophets) was formed.
This account may oversimplify a more complex
confluence of events and influences, but it is
apparent from a letter by Vincent van Gogh
(*CL* 607) that in Arles Gauguin had given the
Dutch artist a remarkably similar lesson to that
provided Sérusier a month or so earlier in Pont-
Aven. Although the young artists surrounding
their student *atelier* leader Sérusier would have to
wait until the Volpini exhibition of late spring
1889 to see a full display of the work of Gauguin,
Bernard and their associates, Denis also informs us
that by this time the fledgling *Nabiim* already
were assiduous visitors to the art shops of Théo
van Gogh and Père Tanguy.

1 Differing versions giving the circumstances of this
   meeting exist, as outlined in Jaworska, pp.
   123-24.

2 That Sérusier provided the secondary title is
   specified by Denis in his Introduction to the 1942
   edition of Sérusier's *ABC de la Peinture*, p. 42.

3 Denis first recounted the episode in 1903 (L'Influence de Paul Gauguin," *L'Occident*, as reprinted

in Denis, *Théories*, p. 167) with the following
quotation from Gauguin to Sérusier: "How do
you see this tree, is it truly green? Then put on
some green, the most beautiful green of your
palette; and this shadow—rather blue? Don't be
afraid to paint it as blue as possible."

Just how important was the role played by this single painting in the stylistic development of Nabi art remains open to speculation. There is little reason to think that Sérusier's secondary title rested in any way on Gauguin's authority, but it is probable that Sérusier formulated and promulgated an "art as magic and mystery" philosophy with this painting as chief illustration. Denis cited it as the specific source of his own pronouncement that a painting before all else is a "flat surface covered with colours assembled in a determined order," yet implied its mystical significance by calling it a "relic" as well.[4] In his own paintings of *circa* 1889-90 (*see* cat. nos. 142-43) the flat areas of bright colouration all but dissolve the natural imagery into indecipherable shapes, an immediate echo of the style of the *Bois d'Amour*. This echo, in fact, for a brief period is heard more clearly in Denis' art than in contemporary finished paintings by either Gauguin or Sérusier.

It should be noted that *The Talisman* was executed essentially as a *plein air* sketch, without being intended either by the teacher or his pupil as a finished painting for sale or exhibition. A rather good parallel illustration of such a usage in Gauguin's work is provided by the small oil study on wood (*W* 274) for his larger and eminently more naturalistic *Boys Wrestling* (*W* 273) from summer 1888. This does not detract from the historic significance of *The Talisman*, however, since the evolution of artistic style frequently remains impervious to such niceties of art historical analysis. Hence, although this painting was painted from nature rather than memory and contains an identifiable landscape setting, those who wish to interpret it as the first small step leading to the abstract art of the twentieth century will continue to do so, little deterred by a knowledge of its actual circumstances of origin.[5]

Fig. 150
Paul Gauguin:
Harvest in Brittany,
1889,
oil on canvas
(The Home House
Trustees, Courtault
Institute of Art,
London).

4   The link between his "colours in a certain order" dictum occurs both in *ibid.*, and as cited note 2 above, where he recounts receiving *The Talisman* as a "relic."

5   M.A. Stevens, London *P-I*, cat. no. 187, discusses this question of historical relevance for *The Talisman* further and gives additional bibliography on it.

138.
Farmyard at Le Pouldu
early fall 1889 or summer 1890
Not signed or dated
Lent by Mr. and Mrs. Arthur G. Altschul,
New York

The traditionally assigned date of 1890 is probably correct, although this unsigned and undated painting by Sérusier could possibly have been executed the previous year. It is a fall harvest subject at Le Pouldu, which the artist, despite theories to the contrary, first visited during October 1889, spending approximately three weeks at the inn of Marie Henry in the company of Gauguin and Meyer de Haan, and revisited summer 1890.[1] Given the fact that at the time only a handful of farm complexes made up the hamlet of Le Pouldu, it is more than likely that a Gauguin painting dated [18]89 and

now at the Courtauld Art Gallery, London, England (*fig. 150*) represents the same setting with haystacks and log. Whereas Gauguin chose to arrange his composition in vertical tiers of draft animals, road embankment, threshing peasant women, hay mound and roof gables, Sérusier here was more inclined to depict the farmyard itself with only three figures engaged in the less arduous chores of cleaning up after the work-day was over.

Sérusier's achievement in this subtly balanced composition is not the less remarkable for its retention of a conventionally picturesque setting. The equation among the yellow hay, thatched rooves and sun-drenched courtyard is appropriately balanced by the blue of the sky and the several areas of indicated shadow. While retrograde in terms of the incipient abstraction of the previous year's *Talisman*, this essay in the manner of Gauguin was nonetheless a necessary experiment in

assimilating the style of that master before Sérusier could develop his art further in the direction of Nabi quasi-abstraction. He was the first to acknowledge the importance of the contact with and example of Gauguin in this respect, and few instances would serve better than the *Farmyard at Le Pouldu* as witness to this importance.

1   Cf., *P-I*, pp. 254-55, 288 n. 4. Just how much landscape painting Sérusier did summer 1889 is open to question, since no subjects clearly identifiable as Pont-Aven are known and only one of the few Le Pouldu landscapes now attributed to this year (Guicheteau, pp. 196-98) is dated. Moreover, Guicheteau, p. 199, ill. 17, reproduces another Sérusier painting of the same farmyard setting which is dated 1890.

139.

Landscape at Le Pouldu:
Young Breton Girl at a Riverbank
summer 1890
oil on canvas: 74.3 x 92.1 cm
Signed and dated lower right:
P. Sérusier–1890
Lent by the Museum of Fine Arts,
Houston;
Gift of Alice C. Simkins,
in memory of
Alice C. Hanszen.

Whereas at Le Pouldu in 1889 Gauguin painted a considerable number of landscapes and only few the following year, the situation is reversed with Sérusier. Along with the fact that he spent only three weeks there in 1889 and a good part of the summer in 1890, Sérusier concentrated during this period on transforming his style, under the influence of Gauguin, into a personal idiom. In a letter to Maurice Denis in Paris, Sérusier described this new development as comprising a change in his approach to both drawing and colour.[1] Regarding drawing, he stresses avoidance of "mathematical regularity," a principle broadly in evidence in the *Landscape at Le Pouldu*, where irregularly dispersed curvilinearity is the rule. As for colours he explained that he had begun to "calm them down," in part by tonalizing his undercoat with an admixture of white to his formerly pure hues, and in part by using broken or mixed colours alongside the pure hues that remain. Such usages thus attempt a novel combination of style and colour theory. Above all he advises against juxtaposing

colours too distant on the colour wheel (that is, by implication, complementary contrasts) and favours employing gradations of neighbouring hues. These rules also seem to have been followed in this painting with its rich variations of verdant greens and variety of tonal and colouristic nuance. As in most other landscapes dating from summer 1890, he virtually excludes the depiction of the sky, thus heightening the sense of shallow space and overall decorative effect.

The unmistakable debt to Gauguin's landscape iconography and general style should not be taken to imply a direct student-teacher relationship. Those canvases by Gauguin which seem closest in these respects to Sérusier's *Le Pouldu* (*W* 354, 356, 372 and, in lesser degree, cat. no. 64) were all executed in 1889, and there is no exact counterpart in Gauguin to this Sérusier painting, although one finds a certain indebtedness in colouration, uniform brush technique and spatial investigations. The young girl seen in profile and lost in contemplation suggests that this Breton

landscape is symbolic of Brittany as a land of mystery.[2] It is perhaps the instance of this type of painting in his own *oeuvre* which Sérusier had in mind when he echoed Bernard's claim that Cézanne had been one of the founding fathers of the Cloisonist movement.[3]

1   The letter published in Sérusier, pp. 45-47 is there assigned to 1889. My husband, R.P. Welsh, kindly pointed out that it should be summer 1890, since Sérusier refers to the dining room of the inn of Marie Henry as already decorated, which was scarcely complete when he left Le Pouldu in October 1889.

2   Guicheteau, p. 206, no. 29 entitles this work *Young Breton Girl at a Riverbank*. A similarly posed girl near a riverbank was painted in 1891 by Sérusier, see Guicheteau, p. 206, no. 48.

3   Sérusier's explanation of how Cézanne was a Cloisonist before Bernard or Gauguin is related by Chassé, *Pont-Aven*, pp. 72-73.

Maurice Denis (1870-1943)

Biographical Data

SOURCES

Unaccountably no comprehensive and scholarly monographic study has yet been published on this major artist and theoretician of the Nabi movement. Certainly the materials exist on which a scholarly study might be based, even if only the already published documents are taken into account. Unfortunately for the present modest investigation, all too few genuinely informative source references from the years 1888-90 seem to exist. Denis' earliest recorded letter to his Nabi colleague dates from 1891 (Sérusier, pp. 49-52) and those to his friend, the writer and playright A.F. Lugné-Poë, are of greatest significance in the present context for winter 1890-91 (Lugné-Poë, *Le Sot du tremplin I*; Paris: Ballimard, 1931), pp. 243-72.

The diary entries published in his *Journal* I, *1884-1904* (Paris: La Colombe, 1957) are of greater relevance to his inner spiritual life than in documenting his development as an artist. His accounts of the life of Sérusier (especially the Introduction to the 1942 edition of the latter's *ABC de la Peinture*) cast some light on his own activities, but do not give a complete account of the formation of the Nabi community of artists. His collected writings, first published in 1912 as *Théories*, are deserving of a detailed separate analysis.

As for Sérusier, the brief chapter in Jaworska, pp. 149-56, constitutes the best summary account of Denis (also in Eng. trans.), while the exhibition catalogue by H. Adhémar and A. Dayez, *Maurice Denis* (Paris: Orangerie des Tuileries, 1970; here below, "Denis cat.") now serves in lieu of a full monographic survey. The monograph on the Nabi movement by G.L. Mauner (*see* cat. no. 142, n. 1) provides much valuable information and insight regarding Denis.

EARLY LIFE

1880-87

Maurice Denis is born on November 25, 1870, in Granville, to which town his parents had retreated during the Franco-Prussian war, but he lives thereafter throughout his life at Saint-Germain-en-Laye, a short distance from Paris. In 1882 he begins to study classic literature at the Lycée Condorcet, where he wins first honours with his *baccalauréat* examinations in 1887-88. By 1884 he begins to receive drawing lessons from a Professor Zani at Saint-Germain, and beginning the following year he spends his summers working at the Paris *atelier* of a Brazilian painter named Balla. He is a great admirer of traditional painting in the Louvre, particularly, and in keeping with his deeply religious nature, Fra Angelico. Late in 1887 he is impressed by the calm, simplicity and decorative qualities of Puvis de Chavannes at the Durand-Ruel gallery exhibition of this master (*Journal I*, p. 67).

1888

Denis enters the Académie Julian at the beginning of the year and there meets Sérusier. In July he is accepted into the Ecole des Beaux Arts as well.

Some time after Sérusier's return from Pont-Aven to Paris in October 1888, Denis associates with him in founding the Nabi brotherhood.

1889

In January Denis dedicates himself and his colleagues to producing a mystical and Symbolist art in the service of Christianity and in his diary commends to his Lord Jesus Christ the glory and salvation of Paul Sérusier.

Following the strong impression made by Gauguin's contributions at the Volpini exhibition, he begins work on his illustrations for Paul Verlaine's *Sagesse* "in the style of ancient woodcuts."

1890

Due to his residence at Saint-Germain, Denis cannot attend as regularly as other Nabi artists the group meetings held at "the temple" in the residence of Paul Ranson. This year Denis exhibits at the *Salon* for the first time.

At the request of his old school friend Lugné-Poë he publishes under the pseudonym Pierre Louys the essay "Définition du Néo-traditionnisme," *Art et critique*, August 23 and 30 (reprinted in *Théories*, pp. 1-13).

His style displays a varying allegiance to the Pont-Aven group and the late Medieval Italian "primitives."

1891

Denis now shares an *atelier* in Montmartre with Bonnard, Vuillard and Lugné-Poë and, via Sérusier, meets Verkade. He works on the costumes and decor for the play *Antonia* by Edouard Dujardin, and begins to exhibit at the *Indépendants*.

In August-September he participates in what amounts to the first Nabi group exhibition held significantly at the Château, Saint-Germain-en-Laye, and is represented in December at the first exhibition of the "Peintres Impressionnistes et Symbolistes" at the gallery of Le Barc de Boutteville along with Bernard, Anquetin, Lautrec, Gauguin and van Gogh.

This year he begins to receive favourable critical recognition. He is also experimenting with a modified Pointillist style and is on the point of evolving a mature personal style. By winter Denis had made the acquaintance of Gauguin (Lugné-Poë, *Le Sot*, p. 252).

1892-1943

Denis enjoys a long and varied career as a painter, book illustrator, decorator in several contexts and writer on art. He travels widely, is liked and respected in diverse art circles and receives commissions in both sacred and profane contexts.

Between 1908 and 1921 he teaches at the Académie Ranson and, beginning 1918, at the Ateliers d'Art Sacré.

After receiving many honours throughout his life, Denis is killed in an automobile accident.

140.
The Way to Calvary
1889
oil on canvas: 41 x 32.5 cm
Signed and dated lower left: *M.D. Nov.* [18]89
Lent by a private collection

Apart from the first sketch, an annunciation theme dated April 1889 for his *Catholic Mystery*, *The Way to Calvary* is the earliest dated religious paint-ing by Denis. It is also a painting in which he has clearly attempted to combine a generalized feeling for Medieval style and iconography with the pre-cepts of the Pont-Aven or Synthetist style as he had experienced it at the Volpini exhibition, where Bernard had exhibited a ''Marche au Calvaire'' (Volpini cat. no. 18). Although not available at this date to Denis in the original, one or more of Gauguin's *Yellow Christ* (cat. no. 61), *Breton Calvary* (cat. no. 62), *Breton Pardon* (cat. no.

65) or the *Christ in the Garden of Olives* (cat. no. 66) could have been known to him from a sketch or oral description by Sérusier, who recently had been with Gauguin in Brittany.[1] If he merely knew that Gauguin was undertaking a series of such religious paintings, this might have been sufficient reason for Denis to believe that his own experi-ments with sacred art were in keeping with an important preoccupation of the Pont-Aven group.

The style of this canvas is Cloisonist, particu-larly in reference to the figures, but features muted colour tonalities and a retention of atmospheric effect. The general sense of a consciously archa-izing Medieval style is due less to any specific artis-tic model than to the inclusion of the tapestry-like pattern of flower clusters and the silhouetting of the figures against a background of more or less even colouration. The style is perhaps most closely related to his woodcut illustrations for *Sagesse* by the poet Paul Verlaine (see *Japonisme*, cat. no. 146), which he described to the poet as ''homely images in the style of ancient woodcuts'' (Denis cat., p. 90) and which this painting approximates in date of execution. Of course his immediate stimulus for undertaking this woodcut series must have been the stylized series of lithographs by Gauguin and Bernard (cat. no. 58 and 109) at the Volpini exhibition, which ended only the month this painting is dated.

The iconography is somewhat untraditional. Granting that this may be considered one of the Stations of the Cross (itself a tradition little sanctioned by Biblical narrative), the inclusion of a horde of Roman soldiers and six lamenting females (mentioned exclusively in Luke and not including an embrace by one of them) is hardly standard. The background may be the valley of the Seine as overlooked from Saint-Germain, a usage which, if so, Denis was to repeat in a number of subsequent paintings. And whereas the Bible does mention Christ robed in red or purple, as Denis clothes him here, this was appropriate to the Mocking of Christ as a false King of the Jews, but not to the Road to Calvary, where he wore his own clothes. In this instance such minor discrepancies simply point up the synthetic use of iconography by the artist, which so well accords with the Synthetist style he here newly adopts.

1   However, it is not likely that Gauguin would have had more than one or two of these paintings com-pleted before Sérusier's departure from Le Pouldu *circa* the third week of October, nor is it certain that he would have seen Denis back in Paris before *The Way to Calvary* was executed.

141.
The Mass
c. 1890
oil on board: 24 x 10 cm
Signed lower left: *MAUD* (vertical)
Lent by a private collection

Except for the presence of a formal signature, *The Mass*, like other small paintings of *circa* 1889-90 in a Cloisonist-Synthetist style (see cat. nos. 142 and 143), might be thought sketches for larger and more finished compositions. A more likely explanation is that Denis conceived their function—apart from being essays in style—as that of private devotional images. Denis was known to his closest artist-colleagues as the Nabi of the beautiful icons, and in these virtually portable paintings on panel or cardboard that appellation finds its truest justification In *The Mass* the colours are so intense that they recall the art of the Byzantine tradition, an analogy which was drawn as early as 1891.[1] The simplification of figural content also parallels that found in the artist's illustrations to the *Sagesse* of Verlaine, which were much appreciated at the same early date.[2] Whereas the title of this painting might suggest a narrative mode of representation, the general effect despite the asymmetrical composition is that of a hieratic art form in which symbolism and dogma are more important than the story told.

Typically, Denis here leaves uncertain what, if any, moment in the celebration of the Catholic Mass is intended, except that the priest and his assistant are turned toward the altar, the most sacred location in the church and one symbolic of the eternal presence of the Lord. The viewer's attention, like that of the priest, is drawn to the circular medallion suspended in front of the Holy Shrine. This form contains no holy image, but by analogy with the oval found at the centre of the cross embroidered at the back of the priest's robe, evokes a recognition of Christ's perfection in accordance with the age-old associations of this geometric form.[3] The celebrant's raised arm, by framing it, recognizes this sacred presence, which itself implies a magical function for the painting. In leaving the viewer to wonder which religious truth or dogma is being celebrated, Denis enhances the mystery of his beautiful icon and thus treats it in an eminently Symbolist fashion.

[1]   By A. Germain, "Théorie des Déformateurs," *La Plume*, *III* (September 1, 1891), p. 290, which along with a short study on Denis by A. Rette in the same issue (p. 301) signalled the emergence of Denis as a painter deserving of serious critical attention.

[2]   *Ibid.*, where an illustration for *Sagesse* analogous in subject and pictorial structure to *The Mass* was reproduced (p. 289). In his "Les Peintres symbolistes" of 1892 A. Aurier also cites the illustrations for *Sagesse* as among the most significant work by Denis (Aurier, p. 308).

[3]   In Christian tradition the orb of Christ, the Holy Wafer and his representation within a tondo testify to the frequency of this association.

142.
Sunlight on the Terrace
October 1890
oil on cardboard: 20 x 20 cm
Dated lower right: Oct[ober 18]90
Lent by a private collection

Like *The Orange Christ* (cat. no. 143), the
equally small *Sunlight on the Terrace* appears
indebted to Sérusier's *Bois d'Amour* (cat. no.
137) in its use of broad flat areas of bright colour
and vagueness in the imagery. Denis is even
slightly more reductive in his mode of representing
nature than was Sérusier when under instruction
from Gauguin, and it is difficult to be absolutely
sure of the setting although, by analogy with other
paintings by Denis, it is likely the terrace at the
Château of Saint-Germain-en-Laye which was
intended.[1] By extension the iconography remains
that of the Pont-Aven *Bois d'Amour*, which Denis
would have known to be a place of courting for the
local citizenry with a touch of Druid mystery
attached to its legend. The Château at Saint-
Germain, with its thirteenth century *Sainte
Chapelle* and nearby forest, is more specifically
Medieval, an era which the paintings of Denis so
often seek to evoke. Whereas the figure located left
of centre in the *Terrace*, the head framed by a
kind of mandorla, is the only one which hints
directly at a religious meaning, the pair strolling
toward the upper right corner more subtly suggest
the age of the troubadours. The total impression is
that of a sacred grove or enchanted garden, into
which a touch of sunlight penetrates as if an outpouring of some divine radiance.[2]

[1]   Although M.A. Stevens, London *P-I*, cat. no. 66,
      is all but surely correct in identifying the setting as
      Saint-Germain, its generality of reference is under-
      lined by the fact that G.L. Mauner, *The Nabis:
      Their History and Their Art, 1888-96* (New
      York: Garland Publishing, 1978), p. 220, called
      it *Bois de Boulogne*. His discussion of Nabi subject
      matter (pp. 224-70) is quite revealing of the com-
      plex interrelationship between nature and abstrac-
      tion in the art of Denis and other Nabi artists.

[2]   Stevens, *ibid.*, rightly stresses that this painting
      also embodies most purely the dictum by Denis
      that a painting is before all else "a flat surface
      covered with colours...in a certain order."

143.

The Orange Christ

c. 1890

oil on cardboard: 24 x 19 cm

Signed lower left: *MAUD* (vertical)

Lent by the family of Maurice Denis, Alençon

This tiny painting is exceptional in several respects. Smaller even than the *Bois d'Amour* by Sérusier, it is the clearest indication that Denis considered that panel painting (*cf.* cat. no. 141) as the point of departure for his own, as well as the group, Nabi style. The Cloisonist areas of colour, though uncircumscribed by outlines, are similarly irregular in pattern and painted in a related manner. The style of this painted sketch by the younger Denis could be considered his most personal tribute to Gauguin as received via the *Talisman* of Sérusier.

Iconographic considerations intervene. The *Orange Christ* by Denis is not conceivable without the precedent of the *Yellow Christ* (cat. no. 61) by Gauguin, although the problem of which precedent he employed is a difficult one. He could have known the *Yellow Christ* by Gauguin, if only by verbal description, as early as late 1889, and that painting along with Gauguin's *Self-Portrait with the Yellow Christ* (*W* 324) might have been available to him in the original the following year.[1] Whatever the year of its execution, *The Orange Christ* remains the painting by Denis which best, and likely intentionally, reveals his indebtedness to Sérusier's *Bois d'Amour* and to the aesthetic precepts of Gauguin which guided its creation.

For its iconography *The Orange Christ* necessarily goes beyond this model, since it concerns the cardinal event of Christian history. Denis here again transformed Biblical narrative by including a small crowd of shrouded blue-black, female silhouettes seemingly approaching a hovering image of the crucifixion. The red areas at the foot of the cross left and right may also be read as kneeling figures, in contrast to the lone figure at right who stands upright with outstretched arms in a gesture of praise or supplication. Possibly the brown foreground ground plane and turquoise area beyond indicate a seaside setting, which, if true, could reflect a knowledge of Gauguin's *Breton Calvary* (cat. no. 65).[2] This painting is in fact more of a Calvary group than simply a crucifixion, with the artist's recurrent collection of processional figures here as elsewhere suggesting a form of religious pilgrimage.

[1] Now generally dated to fall 1889, these paintings would have been in Paris at the latest by the following fall, when Gauguin himself returned. Moreover, *The Yellow Christ*, with its Pont-Aven setting, is likely to have been finished by early fall 1889 and known to Sérusier, who in that case is likely to have described it to the devoutly religious Denis.

[2] Denis would have seen this painting at the Boussod and Valadon gallery run by Théo van Gogh; he mentions it in his *Définition du Néo-Traditionnisme* of summer 1890 (see *Sources*, above). The "*MAUD*" signature found on this painting seems not to occur before this year.

Index

The index consists of works of art and artists discussed in the catalogue entries, lenders and additional figures. Catalogue numbers are given in square brackets. Page references to illustrations are given in *italics*. Page references to catalogue entries, when different from illustrations, are given in regular type.

Aarau, Aargauer Kunsthaus:
Bernard, *Afternoon at St. Briac*, [93], 280, col. pl. 25

Above the Precipice: Au-dessus du Gouffre (Gauguin), [50], 180

The Actor (Anquetin), [83], 252

Afternoon at St. Briac (Bernard), [93], 280, col. pl. 25

Agostina Segatori In the Café Le Tambourin (van Gogh), [3], 100, *101*

Albi, Musée Toulouse-Lautrec:
Bernard, *Portrait of My Sister*, [102], *297*;
Toulouse-Lautrec, *At the Elysée Montmartre*, [114], 326, *327*; *The Hangover: The Drinker: Gueule de Bois: La Buveuse*, [122], 340

Alençon, Maurice Denis family Collection:
Bernard, *Portrait of Madeleine with Blue Background*, [107], 306;
Denis, *The Orange Christ*, [142], 379;
Serusier, *The Talisman: The Bois d'Amour at Pont-Aven*, [137], 371

Les Alyscamps (van Gogh), [28], 140

Among the Mangoes: Martinique (Gauguin), [46], 175, *176*

Amsterdam, Rijksmuseum Vincent van Gogh:
Bernard, *Brothel Scene*, [100], 293; *Lane in Brittany*, [101], 294, *295*; *Portrait of the Artist's Grandmother*, [95], 284, *285*; *Self Portrait dedicated to Vincent*, [105], 302, *303*;
Gauguin, *Among the Mangoes: Martinique*, [46], 175, *176*; *Breton Girls Dancing a Rondel: Study*, [48], 178; *Self Portrait called Les Misérables*, [52], 184; *Woman in the Hay: Pigs: In Full Heat*, study, [57B], 192, *193*;

Amsterdam, Rijksmuseum Vincent van Gogh:
van Gogh, *Agostina Segatori in the Café Le Tambourin*, [3], 100, *101*; *La Barrière with Horsetram*, [6], 105; *Boats on the Beach at Saintes-Maries*, [16], 124; *A Bugler of the Zouave Regiment*, [15], 122, *123*; *Death's-Head Moth*, [37], 154, *155*; *Flowerbed with Sunflowers*, [20], 130, *131*; *Japonaiserie: The Courtesan (after Kesai Eisen)*, [10], 114;

Amsterdam, Rijksmuseum Vincent van Gogh:
Japonaiserie: The Flowering Plumtree (after Hiroshige), [9], 110, *111*; *The Langlois Bridge with Road alongside the Canal*, [14B], *120*, 121; *The Orchard with View of Arles*, [35], 150, *151*; *Portrait of Camille Roulin*, [31], 145; *Roses and a Beetle*, [40], 160; *Self-Portrait with Straw Hat*, [7], 106, *107*; *The Sower*, [27], 139; *Still Life: Absinthe*, [2], 98, 99; *Still Life: Parisian Novels*, [12], 117; *Still Life: Vase with Fourteen Sunflowers*, [33], 147, col. pl. 18; *Still Life: Vase with Irises against a Yellow Background*, [39], 158, *159*; *Trees, Roots and Branches*, [42], 162; *The Vestibule of*

Saint Paul's Hospital, [36B], 153; *View of Auvers*, [41], 161; *View from Vincent's Room in the Rue Lepic*, [4], 102, *103*; *Vincent's Bedroom at Arles*, [26], 138, col. pl. 15; *Vincent's House at Arles*, [25], 137; *Vincent's House on the Place Lamartine, Arles*, [24], 136, col. pl. 14; *The Walk: Falling Leaves*, [38], 156, *157*; *Window of Vincent's Studio at Saint Paul's Hospital*, [36A], 152;
Laval, *Martinique Panorama*, [132], 361; *Self Portrait dedicated to Vincent*, [136], 367;
Toulouse-Lautrec, *Portrait of Vincent van Gogh*, [117], 332; *Rice Powder: Poudre de Riz*, [118], 333; *Two Prostitutes in a Café*, [112], 323

Amsterdam, Stedelijk Museum:
van Gogh, *La Berceuse: Madame Augustine Roulin*, [34B], 148

The Annunciation (Bernard), fig. 135, *315*

ANQUETIN, Louis
The Actor, [83], 252; *At the Bar*, fig. 83, *231*; *Avenue de Clichy: Five o'clock in the Evening*, [76], 239, col. pl. 2; *Boat at Night*, [77], 242, *243*; *The Bridge of Saints-Pères: Gust of Wind*, [82], 250, col. pl. 27; *The Dance Hall at the Moulin Rouge*, [86], 256, *257*, col. pl. 30; *Equestrian Self-Portrait*, [78], 244; *Female Head in Profile with Blue Hat*, [85], 254; *Frontispiece for Edouard Dujardin's Pour la Vierge du roc ardent*, fig. 82, *321*; *Girl Reading a Newspaper*, fig. 95, *255*; *Horses on the Bridge of Saints-Pères*, fig. 93, *251*; *Illustration for Exhibition List of the Catalogue of "Les Vingt,"* fig. 81, *230*; *The Kiosk: Boulevard de Clichy*, [73], 236; *Lady Wearing a Cape*, fig. 92, *248*; *Landscape with Trees*, [71], 232, *233*; *The Mower at Noon: Summer*, [74], 237, col. pl. 20; *Portrait of Emile Bernard*, fig. 80, *229*; *Portrait of Henri de Toulouse-Lautrec*, [72], 234, *235*; *Portrait of the Artist's Mother*, [79], 245; *Portrait of Toulouse-Lautrec*, fig. 84, *234*; *Profile of Young Boy with Images of Fire*, [75], 238; *Riders*, fig. 89, *244*; *The "Rond Point" of the Champs Elysées*, [80], 246, *247*; *Seated Woman with Umbrella*, fig. 94, *253*; *Walking Old Woman in Profile facing right: The Bigot* (?), [84], 253; *Woman in a Carriage*, [81], 248, *249*; *The Woman in Red*, fig. 37, *56*; *Woman with Umbrella*, fig. 91, *248*

The Apple Harvest (Bernard), [110], 314

Aristide Bruant in his Cabaret (Toulouse-Lautrec), [124], 342

L'Arlésienne: Madame Ginoux with Books (van Gogh), [30], 142, *143*

At the Bar (Anquetin), fig. 83, *231*

At the Café (Toulouse-Lautrec), [116], 330, *331*

At the Circus Fernando: The Horsewomen (Toulouse-Lautrec), [119], 334, *335*, col. pl. 28

At the Elysée Montmartre (Toulouse-Lautrec), [114], 326, *327*

At the Nouveau Cirque: Father Chrysanthemum (Toulouse-Lautrec), [123], 341

At the Nouveau Cirque: Father Chrysanthemum, stained glass (Toulouse-Lautrec), fig. 139, *322*

Au Bord de l'Etang (Gauguin), fig. 14, *29*

Aux Roches noires (Gauguin), fig. 60, *181*

Avenue de Clichy: Five o'clock in the Evening (Anquetin), [76], 239, col. pl. 2

Une Baignade, Asnières (Seurat), fig. 20, 36

Ball at the Moulin de la Galette (Toulouse-Lautrec), [121], 338, *339*, col. pl. 29

Bank of the Seine at Asnières (Bernard), fig. 104, 262

Bar of the Café de la Rue de Rome (Toulouse-Lautrec), [113] 324, *325*

La Barrière with Horsetram (van Gogh), [6], 105

Basel, Kunstmuseum:
Bernard, *Portrait of Père Tanguy*, [97], 288, *289*

The Bathers (Laval), [134], 364, *365*

Bathers in Brittany (Gauguin), [58C], 194, *196*

Be a Symbolist-Portrait of Jean Moreas (Gauguin), fig. 31, 47

Be in Love and You will be Happy (Gauguin), fig. 67, *204*

Be Mysterious (Gauguin), fig. 68, *205*

Beach and Cliffs at Cancale (Bernard), [88], 270, *271*

The Beach at Cancale (Bernard), fig. 112, 270

La Belle Angèle (Portrait of Mme Sartre) (Gauguin), fig. 34, *52*

La Berceuse: Madame Augustine Roulin (van Gogh), [34A], 148, col. pl. 19

La Berceuse: Madame Augustine Roulin (van Gogh), [34B], 148

BERNARD, Emile
Afternoon at St. Briac, [93], 280, col. pl. 25; *The Annunciation*, fig. 135, *315*; *The Apple Harvest*, [110], 314; *Bank of the Seine at Asnières*, fig. 104, 262; *Beach and Cliffs at Cancale*, [88], 270, *271*; *The Beach at Cancale*, fig. 112, 270; *Breton Girl Seated in a Landscape*, [90], 274, *275*; *Breton Interior*, fig. 105, *263*; *Breton Women in the Meadow at Pont-Aven*, [103], 298, 299; *Breton Women in the Meadow: Pardon at Pont-Aven*, [104], 300, *301*, col. pl. 9; *Bretonneries*, [109], 308, *309-313*; *Brothel Scene*, [100], 293; *The Buckwheat Harvesters, Pont-Aven: Moissonneurs de blé noir, Pont-Aven*, [106], 304, *305*, col. pl. 8; *The Buckwheat Harvesters*, study, fig. 133, *304*; *Christ at the Foot of the Cross: Lamentation*, [111], 315; *Christ in the Garden of Olives*, fig. 77, *219*; *Christ in the Garden of Olives*, notes on (Gauguin), fig. 78, *219*; *A Corner of a Chapel*, fig. 129, *295*; *The Courtyard of Sainte-Barbe College*, fig. 101, *261*; *Fireworks on the River*, fig. 109, *265*; *First Torso executed at Cormon's*, fig. 102, *261*; *Five Bretons on Hill Overlooking Pont-Aven*, fig. 131, *298*; *Girl in a Street: Paris*, fig. 107, *265*; *Hour of the Flesh: L'Heure de la Viande*, [87], 268, *269*; *Hour of the Flesh*, pen drawing, fig. 110, *268*; *The House of the Artist's Parents at Asnières*, fig. 122, *287*; *Landscape in Brittany*, fig. 118, *282*; *Landscape with Trees at Ribay*, fig. 116, *278*; *Landscape with Trees, Pont-Aven*, [89], 272, *273*; *Landscape with Villa, St. Briac*, fig. 113, *272*; *Lane in Brittany*, [101], 294, *295*; *Madeleine*, fig. 99, *260*; *Madeleine in the Bois d'Amour*, fig. 33, *50*; *A Nightmare—Portraits of Emile Schuffenecker, Emile Bernard and Paul Gauguin*, fig. 30, 46; *La Place St. Briac*, fig. 16, *30*; *Portrait of Breton Girl*, fig. 15, *30*; *Portrait of Madeleine with Blue Background*, [107], 306; *Portrait of My Sister*, [102], 296, *297*; *Portrait of Père Tanguy*, [97], 288,

289; *Portrait of Père Tanguy*, fig. 124, 288; *Portrait of the Artist's Grandfather*, fig. 103, 262; *Portrait of the Artist's Grandmother*, [95], 284, *285*; *Portrait of the Artist's Grandmother*, drawing, fig. 120, *284*; *Pots de grès et pommes*, fig. 126, *291*; *Promenade in the Bois d'Amour*, [94], 282, 283; *Quai de Clichy on the Seine*, [91], 276, *277*; *The Ragpickers: Iron Bridges at Asnières (Chiffonnières-Clichy)*, [96], 286, col. pl. 26; *Sailing in Brittany*, [109 E], 308, *313*; *The Saltimbanques*, fig. 128, *293*; *The Seaweed Gatherers: Les Goëmons*, [108], 307; *The Seaweed Gatherers*, study, fig. 134, *307*; *Self-Portrait dedicated to Vincent*, [105], 302, *303*; *Still Life with Blue Coffeepot*, [98], 290, col. pl. 6; *Study of the Don Quixote by Gustave Doré*, fig. 100, *260*; *The Tavern*, fig. 111, *268*; *Three Breton Women at the Coast*, [99], 292; *Three Women and a Cow in a Meadow*, [109 A], 308, *309*; *Three Women Hanging Wash*, [109 B], 308, *310*; *View from the Pont d'Asnières*, fig. 115, *276*; *Village Park*, fig. 106, *264*; *Woman Tending Geese: Femme aux Oies*, [92], 278, *279*; *Woman with a Red Umbrella*, fig. 108, *265*; *Woman with High Hat in a Dance Hall*, fig. 141, *326*; *Women Feeding Pigs*, [109 C], 308, *311*; *Women Gathering Grain with Geese*, [109 D], 308, *312*

BERNARD, Emile (attributed to)
Ragpicker Fishing, fig. 123, *287*; *Still Life, Blue Flower Vase and Cup*, fig. 127, *291*

The Blue Trees (Gauguin), fig. 119, *283*

Boat at Night (Anquetin), [77], 242, *243*

Boats: Night and Day (Signac), fig. 88, *242*

Boats on the Beach at Saintes-Maries (van Gogh), [16], 124

Boston, Boston Museum of Fine Arts:
van Gogh, *La Berceuse: Madame Augustine Roulin*, [34A], 148, col. pl. 19

Bremen, Kunsthalle:
Anquetin, *The Bridge of Saints-Pères: Gust of Wind*, [82], 250, col. pl. 27;
Bernard, *Breton Women in the Meadow at Pont-Aven*, [103], 298, 299; *Still Life with Blue Coffeepot*, [98], 290, col. pl. 6;
Laval, *The Bathers*, [134], 364, 365

Breton Boys Bathing: Les Baigneurs (Gauguin), [47], 177

Breton Calvary, notes on (Gauguin), figs. 74 and 75, *212*

Breton Calvary: Pardon in Brittany (Gauguin), [62], 209

The Breton Calvary: The Green Christ (Gauguin), [65], 214, *215*, col. pl. 21

Breton Girl Seated in a Landscape (Bernard), [90], 274, 275

Breton Girls Dancing a Rondel (Gauguin), fig. 57, *172*

Breton Girls Dancing a Rondel: Study (Gauguin), [48], 178

The Breton Goose Boy (Gauguin), [64], 212, *213*

Breton Interior (Bernard), fig. 105, *263*

Breton Peasant Girl Spinning: Joan of Arc (Gauguin), [63], 210, *211*, col. pl. 17

Breton Women at a Fence Gate (Gauguin), [58D], 194, *197*

Breton Women in the Meadow (after Bernard) (van Gogh), [29], 141, col. pl. 10

Breton Women in the Meadow at Pont-Aven (Bernard), [103], 298, *299*

Breton Women in the Meadow: Pardon at Pont-Aven (Bernard), [104], 300, *301*, col. pl. 9

Bretonneries (Bernard), [109], 308, *309-313*

Bridge at Langlois (van Gogh), fig. 49, *121*

The Bridge of Saints-Pères: Gust of Wind (Anquetin), [82], 250, col. pl. 27

The Bridges at Asnières (van Gogh), fig. 29, *45*

Brothel Scene (Bernard), [100], 293

Brussels, Musées Royaux des Beaux-Arts de Belgique:

Gaugin, *The Breton Calvary: The Green Christ*, [65], 214, *215*, col. pl. 21

The Buckwheat Harvesters, Pont-Aven: (Bernard), *Moissonneurs de blé noir, Pont-Aven* [106], 304, *305*, col. pl. 8

The Buckwheat Harvesters, study (Bernard), fig. 133, *304*

Buffalo, Albright-Knox Art Gallery:

Gauguin, *The Yellow Christ*, [61], 206, *207*, col. pl. 22;

Toulouse-Lautrec, *The Divan Japonais*, [125], 343

A Bugler of the Zouave Regiment (van Gogh), [15], 122, *123*

Bust-Portrait of the Matsushimaya Actor (Kunisada), fig. 121, *284*

The Café Terrace on the Place du Forum, Arles at Night (van Gogh), [22], 133, col. pl. 3

Chicago, Art Institute of Chicago:

Gauguin, *Bathers in Brittany*, [58C], 194, *196*; *Breton Women at a Fence Gate*, [58D], 194, *197*; *Design for a Plate*, [58A], 194, *195*; *Dramas of the Sea: Brittany*, [58G], 194, *198*

Christ at the Foot of the Cross: Lamentation (Bernard), [111], 315

Christ in the Garden (Gauguin), fig. 76, *218*

Christ in the Garden of Olives (Bernard), fig. 77, *219*; notes on (Gauguin), fig. 78, *219*

Christ in the Garden of Olives (Gauguin), [66], 216, *217*

Cleveland, Cleveland Museum of Art:

Gauguin, *Undine: In the Waves*, [60], 204, *205*, col. pl. 1;

Toulouse-Lautrec, *The Laundress*, [120], 336, *337*

Cloisonné enamels: fig. 1, *18*; fig. 2, *18*; fig. 6, *20*

Coll-Toc

Le Tambourin, fig. 39, *100*

Copenhagen, Ordrupgaardsamlingen:

Gauguin, *Grape Gathering: Human Miseries: La Vendange: Misères Humaines*, [56], 190, col. pl. 23

A Corner of a Chapel (Bernard), fig. 129, *295*

COURBET, Gustave

The Meeting, or Bonjour, Monsieur Courbet, fig. 8, *22*

The Courtyard of Sainte-Barbe College (Bernard), fig. 101, *261*

The Cove II (Gauguin), fig. 62, *185*

Cows in a Landscape (Gauguin), [67], 220

The Dance at the Moulin Rouge (Toulouse-Lautrec), fig. 98, *257*,

Dance Hall at the Moulin Rouge (Anquetin), [86], 256, *257*, col. pl. 30

Dancer with a Bouquet (Degas), fig. 7, *21*

The Dancers (Toulouse-Lautrec), fig. 28, *40*

Death's-head Moth (van Gogh), [37], 154, *155*

DEGAS, Edgar

Dancer with a Bouquet, fig. 7, *21*; *Interior*, fig. 53, *138*

DELACROIX, Eugène

Tasso in the Hospital of St. Anna, Ferrara, fig. 56, *164*

DENIS, Maurice

The Mass, [141], 378; *The Orange Christ*, [143], 380; *Sunlight on the Terrace*, [142], *379*; *The Way to Calvary*, [140], 377

Design for a Plate (Gauguin), [58A], 194, *195*

The Divan Japonais (Toulouse-Lautrec), [125], 343

Dramas of the Sea: Brittany (Gauguin), [58G], 194, *198*

Dramas of the Sea: Descent into the Maelstrom (Gauguin), [58H], 194, *199*

Elysée Montmartre (Toulouse-Lautrec), fig. 140, *326*

Ephemera:

fig. 43, *108*; fig. 48, *115*; fig. 51, *129*; fig. 54, *144*

Equestrian Self-Portrait (Anquetin), [78], 244

Eve (Gauguin), [59], 202, *203*

Farmhouse with Haystack, Arles (Ferme à Arles) (Gauguin), [54], 186, *187*

Farmyard at Le Pouldu (Serusier), [138], 373

Female Head in Profile with Blue Hat (Anquetin), [85], 254

The Fiancée (Gauguin), [49], 179

The Field of Derout-Lollichon: I: Church at Pont-Aven (Gauguin), [44], 172, *173*

The Fifer (Manet), fig. 10, *23*

Fireworks on the River (Bernard), fig. 109, *265*

First Torso executed at Cormon's (Bernard), fig. 102, *261*

Five Bretons on Hill Overlooking Pont-Aven (Bernard), fig. 131, *298*

Flowerbed with Sunflowers (van Gogh), [20], 130, *131*

Four Breton Women (Gauguin), fig. 24, *38*

Frontispiece for Edouard Dujardin's Pour la Vierge du roc ardent (Anquetin), fig. 82, *231*

Fuji seen from the Outskirts of Koshigaya in Musashi province (Hiroshige), fig. 114, *274*

Gas Tanks at Clichy (Signac), fig. 41, *102*

GAUGUIN, Paul

Above the Precipice: Au-dessus du Gouffre, [50], 180; *Among the Mangoes: Martinique*, [46], 175, *176*; *Au Bord de l'Etang*, fig. 14, *29*; *Aux Roches noires*, fig. 60, *181*; *Bathers in Brittany*, [58 C], 194, *196*; *Be a Symbolist— Portrait of Jean Moreas*, fig. 31, *47*; *Be in Love and You will be Happy*, fig. 67, *204*; *Be Mysterious*, fig. 68, *205*; *La Belle Angèle (Portrait of Mme Sartre)*, fig. 34, *52*; *The Blue Trees*, fig. 119, *283*; *Breton Boys Bathing: Les Baigneurs*, [47], 177; *Breton Calvary*, notes on (Gauguin), figs. 74 and 75, *212*; *Breton Calvary: Pardon in Brittany*, [62], 209; *The Breton Calvary: The Green Christ*, [65], 214, *215*, col. pl. 21; *Breton Girls Dancing a Rondel*, fig. 57, *172*; *Breton Girls Dancing a Rondel: Study*, [48], 178; *The Breton Goose Boy*, [64], 212, *213*; *Breton Peasant Girl Spinning: Joan of Arc*, [63], 210, *211*, col. pl. 17; *Breton Women at a Fence Gate* [58 D], 194, *197*; *Christ in the Garden*, fig. 76, *218*; *Christ in the Garden of Olives*, [66], 216, *217*; *The Cove II*, fig. 62, *185*;

Cows in a Landscape, [67], 220; *Design for a Plate*, [58 A], 194, *195*; *Dramas of the Sea: Brittany*, [58 G], 194, *198*; *Dramas of the Sea: Descent into the Maelstrom*, [58 H], 194, *199*; *Eve*, [59], 202, *203*; *Farmhouse with Haystack, Arles (Ferme à Arles)*, [54], 186, *187*; *The Fiancée*, [49], 179; *The Field of Derout-Lollichon: I: Church at Pont-Aven*, fig. 24, *38*; *Four Breton Women*, fig. 24, *38*; *Grape Gathering: Human Miseries: La Vendange: Misères Humaines*, [56], 190, col. pl. 23; *Grape Gathering*, sketch, fig. 64, *190*; *The Grasshoppers and the Ants*, [58 J], 194, *200*; *Harvest in Brittany*, fig. 150, *372*; *Harvest: Le Pouldu*, [69], 223; *Human Miseries*, [58 E], 194, *197*; *Joys of Brittany*, [58 B], 194, *196*; *The Loss of Virginity: La Perte du Pucelage*, [70], 224, *225*; *Maker of Wooden Shoes*, [53], 185; *Man with Cap—Head of Mimi*, fig. 149, *356*; *Martinique Pastorale*, [58 I], 194, *200*; *Nirvana: Portrait of Meyer de Haan*, [68], 221; *Seaweed Gatherers*, fig. 36, *53*; *Self-Portrait called Les Misérables*, [52], 184; *Still Life Fête Gloanec*, [51], 182, col. pl. 31; *Still Life with Profile of Laval*, [45], 174; *Still Life with Three Puppies*, fig. 61, *183*; *Two Breton Boys Wrestling*, fig. 58, *177*; *Undine: In the Waves*, [60], 204, *205*, col. pl. 1; *Vase with Breton Girls*, fig. 25, *38*; *Vision after the Sermon*, fig. 47, *113*, col. pl. 7; *Washerwomen*, [58 F], 194, *198*; *Window Open on the Sea*, fig. 59, *179*; *Woman in the Hay: Pigs: In Full Heat*, [57 A], 192, *193*; *Woman in the Hay: Pigs: In Full Heat*, study, [57 B], 192, *193*; *Women at Arles*, studies, fig. 63, *189*; *Women of Arles: The Mistral*, [55], 188, *189*, col. pl. 24; *Women of Arles: The Mistral*, lithograph, [58 K], 194, *201*; *The Yellow Christ*, [61], 206, *207*, col. pl. 22

GAUGUIN, Paul: letter to van Gogh, Dec. 1889, fig. 35, *52*; notebook, Three studies of Breton subjects, fig. 72, *212*; notes on the *Breton Calvary*, figs. 74 and 75, *212*; notes on the *Christ in the Garden of Olives* (Bernard), fig. 78, *219*

Geneva, Musée Petit Palais:

Bernard, *Beach and Cliffs at Cancale*, [88], 270, *271*

Girl in a Street: Paris (Bernard), fig. 107, *265*

Girl Reading a Newspaper (Anquetin), fig. 95, *255*

GOGH, Vincent van

Agostina Segatori in the Café Le Tambourin, [3], 100, *101*; *Les Alyscamps*, [28], 140; *L'Arlésienne: Madame Ginoux with Books*, [30], 142, *143*; *La Barrière with Horsetram*, [6], 105; *La Berceuse: Madame Augustine Roulin*, [34 A], 148, col. pl. 19; *La Berceuse: Madame Augustine Roulin*, [34 B], 148; *Boats on the Beach at Saintes-Maries*, [16], 124; *Breton Women in the Meadow* (after Bernard), [29], 141, col. pl. 10; *Bridge at Langlois*, fig. 49, *121*; *The Bridges at Asnières*, fig. 29, *45*; *A Bugler of the Zouave Regiment*, [15], 122, *123*; *The Café Terrace on the Place du Forum, Arles at Night*, [22], 133, col. pl. 3; *Death's-Head Moth*, [37], 154, *155*; *Flowerbed with Sunflowers*, [20], 130, *131*; *Interior of a Restaurant*, [5], 104, col. pl. 13; *Interior of a Restaurant in*

Arles, [23], 134, *135*; *The Italian Woman with Daisies: La Segatori*, [13], 118, col. pl. 12; *Japonaiserie: The Bridge in the Rain*, fig. 21, *37*; *Japonaiserie: The Courtesan (after Kesai Eisen)*, [10], 114; *Japonaiserie: The Flowering Plumtree (after Hiroshige)*, [9], 110, *111*; *The Langlois Bridge with Road alongside the Canal*, [14 B], 120, 121; *The Langlois Bridge with Women Washing*, [14 A], 119, 121; *The Mowers, Arles in the Background*, [19], 128, *129*, col. pl. 5; *The Orchard with View of Arles*, [35], 150, *151*; *Outskirts of Paris near Montmartre*, fig. 23, *37*; *Père Tanguy*, fig. 42, *108*; *Portrait of Camille Roulin*, [31], 145; *Portrait of Dr. Paul Gachet*, [43], 163, *165*; *Portrait of Patience Escalier*, [21], 132; *Portrait of Père Tanguy*, fig. 22, *37*; *Portrait of Père Tanguy*, [8], 108, *109*, col. pl. 11; *A Public Garden in Paris*, fig. 38, *96*; *Roadway in a Paris Park*, [1], 96, *97*; *Roses and a Beetle*, [40], 160; *Self-Portrait*, fig. 32, *49*; *Self-Portrait with Bandaged Ear and Pipe*, [32], 146; *Self-Portrait with Straw Hat*, [7], 106, *107*; *The Sower*, [27], 139; *The Sower with Yellow Sun*, [18], 126, *127*; *Still Life: Absinthe*, [2], 98, *99*; *Still Life: Blue Enamel Coffeepot, Earthenware and Fruit*, fig. 125, *290*; *Still Life: Parisian Novels*, [12], 117; *Still Life: Parisian Novels with a Rose*, fig. 18, *33*; *Still Life: Plaster Statuette and Books*, [11], 116; *Still Life: Vase with Fourteen Sunflowers* (1888), col. pl. 20; *Still Life: Vase with Fourteen Sunflowers* (1889), [33], 147, col. pl. 18; *Still Life: Vase with Irises against a Yellow Background*, [39], 158, *159*; *Tracing of Hiroshige Plum Trees in Flower*, fig. 46, *112*; *Trees, Roots and Branches*, [42], 162; *The Vestibule of Saint Paul's Hospital*, [36 B], 153; *View of Auvers*, [41], 161; *View from Vincent's Room in the Rue Lepic*, [4], 102, *103*; *View of Saintes-Maries*, [17], 125; *Vincent's Bedroom at Arles*, [26], 138, col. pl. 15; *Vincent's House at Arles*, [25], 137; *Vincent's House on the Place Lamartine, Arles*, [24], 136, col. pl. 14; *The Walk: Falling Leaves*, [38], 156, *157*; *Window of Vincent's Studio at Saint Paul's Hospital*, [36 A], 152; *The Zouave: Half Length*, fig. 50, *122*

GOGH, Vincent van: letter from Gauguin, Dec. 1889, fig. 35, *52*

Going to the Market, Brittany (Laval), [135], 366, col. pl. 32

La Goulue at the Moulin Rouge (Toulouse-Lautrec), fig. 138, *321*

Grape Gathering: Human Miseries: La Vendange: Misères Humaines (Gauguin), [56], 190, col. pl. 23

Grape Gathering, sketch (Gauguin), fig. 64, *190*

The Grasshoppers and the Ants (Gauguin), [58], 194, *200*

The Green Wave (Monet), fig. 87, *242*

Haan, Jakob Meyer de

Labo(r): Breton Women Scutching Flax, [126], 350, *351*, col. pl. 16; *Landscape at Le Pouldu*, [131], 358; *Motherhood: Marie Henry and her Child*, [127], 352, *352*; *Portrait of a Girl*, fig. 144, *346*; *Self-Portrait with Japanese Background*, [128], *354*; *Still Life with Profile of Mimi*, [130], 356, *357*; *Still Life with Two Flowers in a Glass*,

[129], 355; *Théo van Gogh*, fig. 146, 348; *Uriel Acosta*, fig. 145, 347; *View from Théo van Gogh's Window, Rue Lepic*, fig. 147, 348
HAAN, Jakob Meyer de (attributed to)
Still Life with Onions and a Pot, fig. 148, 355
HAGBORG, August
Portrait of Agostina Segatori, fig. 40, 100
Hamburg, Kunsthalle:
Gauguin, *Breton Boys Bathing: Les Baigneurs*, [47], 177
The Hangover: The Drinker: Gueule de Bois: La Buveuse (Toulouse-Lautrec), [122], 340
Hartford, Wadsworth Atheneum:
Anquetin, *Avenue de Clichy: Five o'clock in the Evening*,
Gauguin, *Nirvana: Portrait of Meyer de Haan*, [68], 221
Harvest in Brittany (Gauguin), fig. 150, 372
Harvest: Le Pouldu (Gauguin), [69], 223
HIROSHIGE
Fuji seen from the Outskirts of Koshigaya in Musashi province, fig. 114, 274; *The Nihonbashi Bridge at Daybreak*, fig. 4, 20; *The Plumtree Teahouse at Kameido*, fig. 45, 112; *Scene of the Saru Wakacho (Theatre Street) by Night*, fig. 52, 133
HOKUSAI
Irises and a Grasshopper, fig. 55, 158
Horses on the Bridge of Saints-Pères (Anquetin), fig. 93, 251
Hour of the Flesh: L'Heure de la Viande (Bernard), [87], 268, 269
Hour of the Flesh, pen drawing (Bernard), fig. 110, 268
The House of the Artist's Parents at Asnières (Bernard), fig. 122, 287
Houston, Lenoir M. Josey, Inc.:
Bernard, *Quai de Clichy on the Seine*, [91], 276, 277
Houston, Museum of Fine Arts:
Serusier, *Landscape at Le Pouldu: Young Breton Girl at a Riverbank*, [139], 374
Houston, Taylor/Royall/Hrdy Collection:
Gauguin, *The Breton Goose Boy*, [64], 212, 213
Huisen, v.d. Waals-Koenigs Collection:
Toulouse-Lautrec, *At the Café*, [116], 330, 331
Human Miseries (Gauguin), [58E], 194, 197
Illustration for Exhibition List of the Catalogue of "Les Vingt" (Anquetin), fig. 81, 230
Illustration for Exhibition List of the Catalogue of "Les Vingt" (Toulouse-Lautrec), fig. 137, 320
Imagerie populaire: fig. 9, 22; fig. 11, 23; fig. 70, 207; fig. 85, 237
Indianapolis, Indianapolis Museum of Art:
Gauguin, *Farmhouse with Haystack, Arles (Ferme à Arles)*, [54], 186, 187
Interior (Degas), fig. 53, 138
Interior of a Restaurant (van Gogh), [5], 104, col. pl. 13
Interior of a Restaurant in Arles (van Gogh), [23], 134, 135
Irises and a Grasshopper (Hokusai), fig. 55, 158
The Italian Woman with Daisies: La Segatori (van Gogh), [13], 118, col. pl. 12
Jane Avril (Toulouse-Lautrec), fig. 97, 256
Japonaiserie: The Bridge in the Rain (van Gogh), fig. 21, 37
Japonaiserie: The Courtesan (after Kesai

Eisen) (van Gogh), [10], 114
Japonaiserie: The Flowering Plumtree (after Hiroshige) (van Gogh), [9], 110, 111
Joys of Brittany (Gauguin), [58B], 194, 196
A Kabuki Actor (Kuniyoshi), fig. 5, 20
The Kiosk: Boulevard de Clichy (Anquetin), [73], 236
KUNISADA
Bust-Portrait of the Matsushimaya Actor, fig. 121, 284
KUNIYOSHI
A Kabuki Actor, fig. 5, 20; *Shirasuka: The Legend of Onnaya*, fig. 117, 281
Labo(r): Breton Women Scutching Flax (de Haan), [126], 350, 351, col. pl. 16
Lady Wearing a Cape (Anquetin), fig. 92, 248
Landscape at Le Pouldu (de Haan), [131], 358
Landscape at Le Pouldu: Young Breton Girl at a Riverbank (Serusier), [139], 374
Landscape in Brittany (Bernard), fig. 118, 282
Landscape with Trees (Anquetin), [71], 232, 233
Landscape with Trees at Ribay (Bernard), fig. 116, 278
Landscape with Trees, Pont-Aven (Bernard), [89], 272, 273
Landscape with Villa, St. Briac (Bernard), fig. 113, 272
Lane in Brittany (Bernard), [101], 294, 295
The Langlois Bridge with Road alongside the Canal (van Gogh), [14B], 120, 121
The Langlois Bridge with Women Washing (van Gogh), [14A], 119, 121
The Laundress (Toulouse-Lautrec), [120], 336, 337
LAVAL, Charles
The Bathers, [134], 364, 365; *Going to the Market, Brittany*, [135], 366, col. pl. 32; *Martinique Panorama*, [132], 361; *Martinique Women*, [133], 362, 363; *Self Portrait dedicated to Vincent*, [136], 367
London, Tate Gallery:
Gauguin, *Harvest: Le Pouldu*, [69], 223
The Loss of Virginity: La Perte du Pucelage (Gauguin), [70], 224, 225
Madeleine (Bernard), fig. 99, 260
Madeleine in the Bois d'Amour (Bernard), fig. 33, 50
Maker of Wooden Shoes (Gauguin), [53], 185
Man with Cap-Head of Mimi (Gauguin), fig. 149, 356
MANET, Edouard
The Fifer, fig. 10, 23; *Olympia*, fig. 79, 225; *Portrait of Emile Zola*, fig. 132, 302
Maps (Paris): fig. 12, 26; fig. 13, 26
Martinique Panorama (Laval), [132], 361
Martinique Pastorale (Gauguin), [58I], 194, 200
Martinique Women (Laval), [133], 362, 363
The Mass (Denis), [141], 378
The Meeting, or Bonjour, Monsieur Courbet (Courbet), fig. 8, 22
Milan, Galleria Civica d'Arte Moderna:
van Gogh, *Breton Women in the Meadow (after Bernard)*, [29], 141, col. pl. 10
MONET, Claude
The Green Wave, fig. 87, 242
Motherhood: Marie Henry and her Child (de Haan), [127], 352, 352
The Mower at Noon: Summer (Anquetin),

[74], 237, col. pl. 20
The Mowers, Arles in the Background (van Gogh), [19], 128, 129, col. pl. 5
Mummy: fig. 65, 191
Nantes, Musée des Beaux Arts:
Bernard, *The Apple Harvest*, [110], 314
New York, Altschul Collection:
Anquetin, *The Kiosk: Boulevard de Clichy*, [73], 236; *Walking Old Woman in Profile facing right: The Bigot (?)*, [84], 253;
de Haan, *Landscape at Le Pouldu*, [131], 358; *Self-Portrait with Japanese Background*, [128], 354;
Sérusier, *Farmyard at Le Pouldu*, [138], 373
New York, Metropolitan Museum of Art:
van Gogh, *L'Arlésienne: Madame Ginoux with Books*, [30], 142, 143
New York, Museum of Modern Art:
Bernard, *The Ragpickers: Iron Bridges at Asnières (Chiffonnières-Clichy)*, [96], 286, col. pl. 26;
Toulouse-Lautrec, *Aristide Bruant in his Cabaret*, [124], 342
A Nightmare-Portraits of Emile Schuffenecker, Emile Bernard and Paul Gauguin (Bernard), fig. 30, 46
The Nihonbashi Bridge at Daybreak (Hiroshige), fig. 4, 20
Nirvana: Portrait of Meyer de Haan (Gauguin), [68], 221
Norfolk, Chrysler Museum:
Gauguin, *The Loss of Virginity: La Perte du Pucelage*, [70], 224, 225
Olympia (Manet), fig. 79, 225
The Orange Christ (Denis), [143], 380
The Orchard with View of Arles (van Gogh), [35], 150, 151
Orléans, Musée des Beaux-Arts:
Gauguin, *Still Life Fête Gloanec*, [51], 182, col. pl. 31
Otterlo, Rijksmuseum Kröller-Müller:
van Gogh, *The Café Terrace on the Place du Forum, Arles at Night*, [22], 123, col. pl. 3; *Interior of a Restaurant*, [5], 104, col. pl. 13; *The Langlois Bridge with Women Washing*, [14A], 119, 121; *The Sower with Yellow Sun*, [18], 126, 127; *Still Life: Plaster Statuette and Books*, [11], 116; *View of Saintes-Maries*, [17], 125
Outskirts of Paris near Montmartre (van Gogh), fig. 23, 37
La Parade (Seurat), fig. 86, 241
Paris, Altarriba Collection:
Bernard, *Christ at the Foot of the Cross: Lamentation*, [111], 315; *Hour of the Flesh: L'Heure de la Viande*, [87], 268, 269; *Three Breton Women at the Coast*, [99], 292
Paris, Durand-Ruel & Cie.:
Bernard, *Promenade in the Bois d'Amour*, [94], 282, 283
Paris, LeGlouannec Collection:
Bernard, *Landscape with Trees, Pont-Aven*, [89], 272, 273
Paris, Musée des Arts Decoratifs:
Gauguin, *Above the Precipice: Au-dessus du Gouffre*, [50], 180
Paris, Musée d'Orsay:
Anquetin, *Profile of Young Boy with Images of Fire*, [75], 238
Paris, Musée du Jeu de Paume:
van Gogh, *The Italian Woman with Daisies: La Segatori*, [13], 118, col. pl. 12
Paris, Musée Rodin:
van Gogh, *The Mowers, Arles in the Background*, [19], 128, 129, col. pl. 5
Paris, Velluz Collection:

Anquetin, *The Mower at Noon: Summer*, [74], 237, col. pl. 20
Père Tanguy (van Gogh), fig. 42, 108
Philadelphia, Philadelphia Museum of Art:
Toulouse-Lautrec, *At the Nouveau Cirque: Father Chrysanthemum*, [123], 341
Photographs:
frontispiece; fig. 17, 32; fig. 71, 210; fig. 96, 255; fig. 130, 296; fig. 142, 328
PISSARRO, Camille
Portrait of Paul Cezanne, fig. 44, 109
La Place St. Briac (Bernard), fig. 16, 30
The Plumtree Teahouse at Kameido (Hiroshige), fig. 45, 112
Portrait of a Girl (de Haan), fig. 144, 346
Portrait of Agostina Segatori (Hagborg), fig. 40, 100
Portrait of Breton Girl (Bernard), fig. 15, 30
Portrait of Camille Roulin (van Gogh), [31], 145
Portrait of Dr. Paul Gachet (van Gogh), [43], 163, 165
Portrait of Emile Bernard (Anquetin), fig. 80, 229
Portrait of Emile Bernard (Toulouse-Lautrec), fig. 136, 319
Portrait of Emile Zola (Manet), fig. 132, 302
Portrait of Henri de Toulouse-Lautrec (Anquetin), fig. 72, 234, 235
Portrait of Madeleine with Blue Background (Bernard), [107], 306
Portrait of My Sister (Bernard), [102], 296, 297
Portrait of Patience Escalier (van Gogh), [21], 132
Portrait of Paul Cezanne (Pissarro), fig. 44, 109
Portrait of Père Tanguy (Bernard), [97], 288, 289
Portrait of Père Tanguy (Bernard), fig. 124, 288
Portrait of Père Tanguy (van Gogh), fig. 22, 37
Portrait of Père Tanguy (van Gogh), [8], 108, 109, col. pl. 11
Portrait of the Artist's Grandfather (Bernard), fig. 103, 262
Portrait of the Artist's Grandmother (Bernard), [95], 284, 285
Portrait of the Artist's Grandmother, drawing (Bernard), fig. 120, 284
Portrait of the Artist's Mother (Anquetin), [79], 245
Portrait of Toulouse-Lautrec (Anquetin), fig. 84, 234
Portrait of Vincent van Gogh (Toulouse-Lautrec), [117], 332
Pots de grès et pommes (Bernard), fig. 126, 291
Profile of Young Boy with Images of Fire (Anquetin), [75], 238
Promenade in the Bois d'Amour (Bernard), [94], 282, 283
A Public Garden in Paris (van Gogh), fig. 38, 96
The Quadrille of the Louis XIII Chair at the Elysée Montmartre (Toulouse-Lautrec), fig. 26, 39
Quai de Clichy on the Seine (Bernard), [91], 276, 277
Quimper, Musée des Beaux Arts:
Bernard, *Bretonneries*, [109], 308, 309 - 313
Ragpicker Fishing (attributed to Bernard), fig. 123, 287
The Ragpickers: Iron Bridges at Asnières (Chiffonnières-Clichy), (Bernard), [96], 286, col. pl. 26

The Refrain of the Louis XIII Chair at the Cabaret of Aristide Bruant (Toulouse-Lautrec), fig. 27, *39*

Rice Powder: Poudre de Riz (Toulouse-Lautrec), [118], 333

Riders (Anquetin), fig. 89, *244*

Riders Approaching the Bois de Boulogne (Toulouse-Lautrec), fig. 90, *246*

Roadway in a Paris Park (van Gogh), [1], 96, *97*

The "Rond Point" of the Champs Elysées (Anquetin), [80], 246, *247*

Roses and a Beetle (van Gogh), [40], 160

SADAHIDE

Seaweed Gatherer, fig. 66, *199*

Sailing in Brittany (Bernard), [109 E], 308, *313*

The Saltimbanques (Bernard), fig. 128, *293*

San Antonio, Marion Koogler McNay Art Institute:
Gauguin, *Eve*, [59], 202, *203*

Scene of the Saru Wakacho (Theatre Street) by Night (Hiroshige), fig. 52, *133*

Sculpture: fig. 69, *206*; fig. 73, *214*

Seated Woman with Umbrella (Anquetin), fig. 94, *253*

Seaweed Gatherer (Sadahide), fig. 66, *199*

Seaweed Gatherers (Gauguin), fig. 36, *53*

The Seaweed Gatherers: Les Goëmons (Bernard), [108], 307

The Seaweed Gatherers, Study (Bernard), fig. 134, *307*

Self-Portrait (van Gogh), fig. 32, 49

Self-Portrait dedicated to Vincent (Bernard), [105], 302, *303*

Self-Portrait called Les Misérables (Gauguin), [52], 184

Self-Portrait dedicated to Vincent (Laval), [136], 367

Self-Portrait with Bandaged Ear and Pipe (van Gogh), [32], 146

Self-Portrait with Japanese Background (de Haan), [128], 354

Self-Portrait with Straw Hat (van Gogh), [7], 106, *107*

SERUSIER, Paul

Farmyard at Le Pouldu, [138], 373; *Landscape at Le Pouldu: Young Breton Girl at a Riverbank*, [139], 374; *The Talisman: The Bois d'Amour at Pont-Aven*, [137], 371

SEURAT, Georges

Une Baignade, Asnières, fig. 20, *36*; *La Parade*, fig. 86, *241*; *Sunday Afternoon on the Island of the Grande-Jatte*, fig. 19, *34*

Shirasuka: The Legend of Onnaya (Kuniyoshi), fig. 117, *281*

SIGNAC, Paul

Boats; Night and Day, fig. 88, *242*; *Gas Tanks at Clichy*, fig. 41, *102*

The Sower (van Gogh), [27], 139

The Sower with Yellow Sun (van Gogh), [18], 126, *127*

Stained glass: fig. 3, *19*

Still Life: Absinthe (van Gogh), [2], 98, *99*

Still Life: Blue Enamel Coffeepot, Earthenware and Fruit (van Gogh), fig. 125, *290*

Still Life, Blue Flower Vase and Cup (attributed to Bernard), fig. 127, *291*

Still Life Fête Gloanec (Gauguin), [51], 182, col. pl. 31

Still Life; Parisian Novels (van Gogh), [12], 117

Still Life: Parisian Novels with a Rose (van Gogh), fig. 18, *33*

Still Life: Plaster Statuette and Books (van Gogh), [11], 116

Still Life: Vase with Fourteen Sunflowers, 1888 (van Gogh), col. pl. 20

Still Life: Vase with Fourteen Sunflowers, 1889 (van Gogh), [33], 147, col. pl. 18

Still Life: Vase with Irises against a Yellow Background (van Gogh), [39], 158, *159*

Still Life with Blue Coffeepot (Bernard), [98], 290, col. pl. 6

Still Life with Onions and a Pot (attributed to de Haan), fig. 148, *355*

Still Life with Profile of Laval (Gauguin), [45], 174

Still Life with Profile of Mimi (de Haan), [130], 356, *357*

Still Life with Three Puppies (Gauguin), fig. 61, *183*

Still Life with Two Flowers in a Glass (de Haan), [129], 355

Study of the Don Quixote by Gustave Doré (Bernard), fig. 100, *260*

Sunday Afternoon on the Island of the Grande-Jatte (Seurat), fig. 19, *34*

Sunlight on the Terrace (Denis), [142], *379*

The Talisman: The Bois d'Amour at Pont-Aven (Serusier), [137], 371

Le Tambourin (Coll-Toc), fig. 39, *100*

Tasso in the Hospital of St. Anna, Ferrara (Delacroix), fig. 56, *164*

The Tavern (Bernard), fig. 111, *268*

Théo van Gogh (de Haan), fig. 146, *348*

Three Breton Women at the Coast (Bernard), [99], 292

Three Women and a Cow in a Meadow (Bernard), [109A], 308, *309*

Three Women Hanging Wash (Bernard), [109 B], 308, *310*

TOULOUSE-LAUTREC, Henri de

Aristide Bruant in his Cabaret, [124], 342; *At the Café*, [116], 330, *331*; *At the Circus Fernando: The Horsewomen*, [119], 334, *335*, col. pl. 28; *At the Elysée Montmartre*, [114], 326, *327*; *At the Nouveau Cirque: Father Chrysanthemum*, [123], 341; *At the Nouveau Cirque: Father Chrysanthemum*, stained glass, fig. 139, *322*; *Ball at the Moulin de la Galette*, [121], 338, *339*, col. pl. 29; *Bar of the Café de la Rue de Rome*, [113], 324, *325*; *The Dance at the Moulin Rouge*, fig. 98, *257*; *The Dancers*, fig. 28, *40*; *The Divan Japonais*, [125], 343; *Elysée Montmartre*, fig. 140, *326*; *La Goulue at the Moulin Rouge*, fig. 138, *321*; *The Hangover: The Drinker: Gueule de Bois: La Buveuse*, [122], 340; *Illustration for Exhibition List of the Catalogue of "Les Vingt"*, fig. 137, *320*; *Jane Avril*, fig. 97, *256*; *The Laundress*, [120], 336, *337*; *Portrait of Emile Bernard*, fig. 136, *319*; *Portrait of Vincent van Gogh*, [117], 332; *The Quadrille of the Louis XIII Chair at the Elysée Montmartre*, fig. 26, *39*; *The Refrain of the Louis XIII Chair at the Cabaret of Aristide Bruant*, fig. 27, *39*; *Rice Power: Poudre de Riz*, [118], 333; *Riders Approaching the Bois de Boulogne*, fig. 90, *246*; *The Trace Horse of the Bus Company*, fig. 143, *336*; *Two Prostitutes in a Café*, [112], *323*; *Waiting at Grenelle*, [115], 328, *329*

The Trace Horse of the Bus Company (Toulouse-Lautrec), fig. 143, *336*

Tracing of Hiroshige Plum Trees in Flower (van Gogh), fig. 46, *112*

Two Breton Boys Wrestling (Gauguin), fig. 58, *177*

Two Prostitutes in a Café (Toulouse-Lautrec), [112], 323

Trees, Roots and Branches (van Gogh), [42], 162

Undine: In the Waves (Gauguin), [60], 204, *205*, col. pl. 1

Uriel Acosta (de Haan), fig. 145, *347*

Vase with Breton Girls (Gauguin), fig. 25, *38*

The Vestibule of Saint Paul's Hospital (van Gogh), [36B], 153

View from the Pont d'Asnières (Bernard), fig. 115, *276*

View from Théo van Gogh's Window, Rue Lepic (de Haan), fig. 147, *348*

View from Vincent's Room in the Rue Lepic (van Gogh), [4], 102, *103*

View of Auvers (van Gogh), [41], 161

View of Saintes-Maries (van Gogh), [17], 125

Village Park (Bernard), fig. 106, *264*

Vincent's Bedroom at Arles (van Gogh), [26], 138, col. pl. 15

Vincent's House at Arles (van Gogh), [25], 137

Vincent's House on the Place Lamartine, Arles (van Gogh), [24], 136, col. pl. 14

Vision after the Sermon (Gauguin), fig. 47, *113*, col. pl. 7

Waiting at Grenelle (Toulouse-Lautrec), [115], 328, *329*

The Walk: Falling Leaves (van Gogh), [38], 156, *157*

Walking Old Woman in Profile facing right: The Bigot (?) (Anquetin), [84], 253

The Way to Calvary (Denis), [140], 377

West Palm Beach, Norton Gallery and School of Art:
Gauguin, *Christ in the Garden of Olives*, [66], 216, *217*

Williamstown, Sterling and Francine Clark Art Institute:
Toulouse-Lautrec, *Waiting at Grenelle*, [115], 328, *329*

Window of Vincent's Studio at Saint Paul's Hospital (van Gogh), [36A], 152

Window Open on the Sea (Gauguin), fig. 59, *179*

Washerwomen (Gauguin), [58F], 194, *198*

Woman in a Carriage (Anquetin), [81], 248, *249*

The Woman in Red (Anquetin), fig. 37, *56*

Woman in the Hay: Pigs In Full Heat (Gauguin), [57A], 192, *193*

Woman in the Hay: Pigs In Full Heat, study (Gauguin), [57B], 192, *193*

Woman Tending Geese: Femme aux Oies (Bernard), [92], 278, *279*

Woman with a Red Umbrella (Bernard), fig. 108, *265*

Woman with High Hat in a Dance Hall (Bernard), fig. 141, *326*

Woman with Umbrella (Anquetin), fig. 91, *248*

Women at Arles, studies (Gauguin), fig. 63, *189*

Women Feeding Pigs (Bernard), [109 C], 308, *311*

Women Gathering Grain with Geese (Bernard), [109 D], 308, *312*

Women of Arles: The Mistral (Gauguin), [55], 188, *189*, col. pl. 24

Women of Arles: The Mistral, lithograph (Gauguin), [58 K], 194, *201*

The Yellow Christ (Gauguin), [61], 206, *207*, col. pl. 22

The Zouave: Half Length (van Gogh), fig. 50, *122*

Prepared by Karen McKenzie,
Head Librarian,
Art Gallery of Ontario

Graphic design by Frank Newfeld.

Photography, unless otherwise credited, by Photographic Services, Art Gallery of Ontario.

Typeset in Bauer Bodoni by Trigraph, Toronto.

Colour separations by Prolith Inc., Toronto.

Printed by Ashton-Potter Ltd., Toronto.

Bound by The Hunter Rose Company, Ltd., Toronto.